Adobe® Premiere®
Pro Bible

Adobe® Premiere® Pro Bible

Adele Droblas and Seth Greenberg

WILEY

Wiley Publishing, Inc.

Adobe® Premiere® Pro Bible

Published by
Wiley Publishing, Inc.
10475 Crosspoint Boulevard
Indianapolis, IN 46256
www.wiley.com

Copyright © 2004 by Wiley Publishing, Inc., Indianapolis, Indiana

Published by Wiley Publishing, Inc., Indianapolis, Indiana

Published simultaneously in Canada

ISBN: 0-7645-4226-5

Manufactured in the United States of America

10 9 8 7 6 5 4 3 2 1

1O/RS/RS/QT/IN

About the Authors

Adele Droblas is an artist, writer, and computer consultant. She has produced digital video clips that appear on the Web for her clients. For all about Adele, go to www.bonitavida.com.

Seth Greenberg is a computer consultant, programmer, and author. He has worked as a television producer and scriptwriter.

Credits

Acquisitions Editor
Mike Roney

Project Editor
Melba Hopper

Technical Editor
Dennis R. Short

Copy Editor
Paula Lowell

Editorial Manager
Robyn Siesky

Vice President & Executive Group Publisher
Richard Swadley

Vice President and Executive Publisher
Bob Ipsen

Vice President and Publisher
Barry Pruett

Project Coordinator
Ryan Steffen

Graphics and Production Specialists
Jennifer Click
Lauren Goddard
Lynsey Osborn
Heather Ryan
Janet Seib

Quality Control Technicians
Andy Hollandbeck
Carl Pierce
Kathy Simpson

Permissions Editors
Carmen Krikorian and Laura Moss

Media Development Specialist
Kit Malone

Media Development Coordinator
Sarah Cummings

Proofreading and Indexing
TECHBOOKS Production Services

Special Help
Adrienne Porter

To our family and to Angelique and Laurence, the stars of our videos, who make every day and every night shine.

Foreword

As you may be aware, Premiere Pro is a complete rewrite that has taken place over two plus years. What this means to those of us on the development team is that we have finally brought to fruition the results of a vision that we collectively held for what a nonlinear editing application should look like.

One of the advantages of embarking on a rewrite is that you are no longer confined by the legacy technologies that you have carried forward from previous versions. What this meant for Premiere Pro was that we were able to take advantage of all the latest and greatest developments from both Intel and Microsoft. Our overriding vision for this version of Premiere was to be able to accomplish as much in real time as possible in software only. In other words, with a copy of Premiere Pro and an up-to-date PC, you would be able to edit DV in real time and view the output of your work not only on a computer screen, but also on a video monitor attached to the system. This was no small undertaking, as this level of performance has previously been possible only by the addition of dedicated video hardware.

Of course, in addition to the real-time performance, we completely overhauled the user interface, added multiple timelines, integrated DVD production, added three-point color correction, updated the effects engine, and greatly simplified the tool changes and a host of other features that I think make this version of Premiere the best one yet.

The truth is that no software is ever truly finished. We take great pride here on the Premiere team that we really listen to our users. In fact, the truth is that Premiere Pro is largely the result of people like you providing great feedback and innovative ideas for ways in which we could improve our product. With that in mind, I'd like to invite you to participate in that process and join our community. Many Premiere users have discovered that their feature ideas have materialized in Premiere Pro.

If you think of a great idea for how Premiere can be improved, we would love to hear from you. Please include lots of detail and send us an e-mail at premierewishlist@ adobe.com. Our interface designers, product managers, and engineers read all these e-mails, but please do not expect a personal response.

Try the Adobe User to User Forums at www.adobe.com/support/forums/main.html where you can lurk or actively participate in discussions about digital video, creative solutions to problems, special techniques, and so on. Forums are offered for each Adobe application and by platform.

Adobe, of course, is renown for other software apart from Premiere. So, in addition to all the cool editing features that were added to Premiere Pro, we also had a goal to "play well with others." To this end, we greatly enhanced the interaction with well-established Adobe family members — After Effects and Photoshop. In addition, we expanded our integration with Adobe's new kids on the block — Encore DVD and Audition.

If you are using these products together, you will find that moving between the applications becomes very easy. After Effects will import Premiere Projects (complete with effects and key frame data), Markers from Premiere Pro's Timeline will show up in Encore, Photoshop files brought into Premiere Pro will now come in as Timelines with every layer as a separate track, Encore can actually undo edits on PSD files that were performed by Photoshop, editing an audio file in Premiere will load the original session file in Audition, and After Effects and Premiere Pro will load vector artwork from Illustrator.

In the publication you are now holding, Adele Droblas and Seth Greenberg have done a fantastic job of taking you beyond editing with Premiere Pro and explaining how the other powerful software that Adobe produces can enhance the results of your efforts.

I hope that you enjoy the experience of working with Premiere Pro and its siblings. I also hope that the time you spend with these tools is both creatively rewarding and enjoyable.

Richard Townhill

Group Product Manager
Adobe Video Products

Preface

As you read these words, a revolution in desktop video is taking place. One of the main causes of the revolution is the advent of the digital video camera, which digitizes high-quality video directly in the camera. After the signal has been digitized, it can be transferred directly over a cable to a personal computer. After your computer gets hold of the video, you need Adobe Premiere Pro to help you creatively shape it into a compelling desktop video production.

Adobe Premiere Pro combines power and ease of use to provide a complete authoring environment for producing desktop digital video productions. By using Premiere Pro, you can capture video directly from your camcorder into Premiere Pro's capture window. After you've captured or imported video and sound, you can assemble your clips into a production by simply clicking and dragging a video clip from one window to another. Placing clips and reassembling them is almost as easy as snapping together the cars in a child's toy railroad train set. Creating transitions that dissolve one scene into another or wipe one scene away to reveal another is simply a matter of dragging an icon representing the transition between the two clips. To fine-tune your work, Premiere Pro provides numerous digital-editing tools — some similar to those available in professional editing studios, others only possible through digital magic. After you've finished editing, you can output your digital movie with settings for the Web, videotape, or DVD. If you've ever tried creating a video production by using traditional videotape hardware, Adobe Premiere Pro will revolutionize the way that you work.

Who Should Read This Book

The *Adobe Premiere Pro Bible* is for multimedia producers, Web designers, graphic designers, artists, filmmakers, and camcorder users — anyone interested in using his or her computer to create desktop video productions or to output desktop video to videotape, DVDs, or the Web. As you read through the *Adobe Premiere Pro Bible,* you'll soon see that it is more than just a reference to virtually all the features in Adobe Premiere Pro. The book is filled with short tutorial exercises that help you understand concepts and put into practice the key Premiere Pro features covered in a chapter. You'll find this book indispensable as you learn to use Adobe Premiere Pro (and a useful reference book after you've mastered Premiere Pro's key features). So don't wait another moment — start reading and learning what you can do with your creative visions.

How This Book Is Organized

If you read the *Adobe Premiere Pro Bible*'s chapters in order, you'll gradually become an expert at using Adobe Premiere Pro. However, we expect that most readers will jump in and out of chapters as needed or as their interest moves from subject to subject. Throughout the book, we've included numerous step-by-step tutorials to guide you through the process of creating video sequences by using many Adobe Premiere Pro features. As you work, you'll find many clips on the DVD that will aid you in quickly and efficiently creating short examples that illustrate and help explain chapter topics.

Note   For updated information on Adobe Premiere Pro, be sure to visit Adobe's Web site at www.adobe.com.

The *Adobe Premiere Pro Bible* is broken down into seven main parts, each described in the following sections.

Part I: Getting Started with Premiere Pro

Part I provides an introduction to as well as an overview of Adobe Premiere Pro. Chapter 1 includes a getting-started tutorial that introduces you to the basics of creating a desktop video production by using Adobe Premiere Pro. Chapter 2 provides an overview of the Premiere Pro interface, its menus, palettes, and tools. Chapter 3 takes a look at how to customize Premiere Pro so that you can save time when creating projects. Chapter 4 introduces you to Premiere Pro's basic project settings. Chapter 5 shows you how to capture video directly into Premiere Pro from a digital video camcorder or an analog camcorder.

Part II: Editing with Premiere Pro

Part II provides a thorough look at the basics of putting together a digital video production. Chapter 6 shows you how to use Premiere Pro's Timeline and sequences to assemble a video production. Chapter 7 continues editing essentials. Chapters 8 and 9 provide a look at Premiere Pro's audio features. Chapter 10 rounds out this part with a discussion of how to use transitions to smooth changes from one clip to another.

Part III: Working with Type and Graphics

Part III is dedicated to type and graphics. This part shows you how to use the Title Designer window and titling tools. You'll learn how to create titles with styles, templates, and logos; how to create rolling and scrolling credits; and how to create titles with drop shadows. You'll also learn how to create graphics by using the Title Designer window, Adobe Illustrator, and Adobe Photoshop. Chapters 11 and 12 cover creating type and graphic effects.

Part IV: Advanced Techniques and Special Effects

Part IV covers advanced editing techniques and special effects. Chapter 13 covers the sophisticated editing features in Premiere Pro, such as three- and four-point edits. It also provides a discussion of using Premiere Pro's Rolling Edit and Ripple Edit tools as well as using its Slip and Slide editing tools. Chapter 13 also covers precise frame-by-frame editing by using the Trim window. Chapter 14 reviews the video effects in the Effects window, while Chapter 15 covers the program's transparency effects (found in the Keying folder of the Effects window). Chapter 16 provides you with information on how to create color mattes and backgrounds using Adobe Photoshop and Illustrator. If you want to create motion effects in Premiere Pro, check out Chapter 17, which provides a thorough look at Motion effects. Chapter 18 takes you on a guided tour and shows you how to enhance your video using both Adobe Premiere Pro and Adobe Photoshop.

Part V: Outputting Digital Video from Premiere Pro

After you've learned how to create a digital video production in Premiere Pro, your next concern is how to output your work in the best possible manner. This part covers all the bases. Chapter 19 reviews Premiere Pro's settings for exporting QuickTime, AVI, and MPEG movies. Chapters 20 and 21 describe how to obtain the best possible quality when outputting a movie to the Web. Chapter 22 provides a discussion of outputting to videotape, while Chapter 23 covers outputting to CD-ROM as well as using Premiere Pro with Macromedia Director and Flash.

Part VI: Premiere Pro and Beyond

The chapters in this section (Chapters 24–30) provide a look at using Premiere Pro with different software packages, such as Adobe Encore, Adobe Photoshop, Adobe Illustrator, and Adobe After Effects. Chapters 24 and 25 take you on a tour of how to use Adobe Encore to create a DVD. Chapter 26 provides a look at how you can use Adobe After Effects to edit Premiere Pro projects. Chapter 27 shows you how to create alpha channels in Photoshop that can be used in Premiere Pro; it also shows you how to edit Premiere Pro filmstrip files in Photoshop and export them back into Premiere Pro. Chapter 28 shows how to create graphics and text by using Adobe Illustrator. These graphics and texts are then imported and used in Adobe Premiere Pro, many times as masks. Chapters 29 and 30 deal with working with Adobe After Effects. In Chapter 29, you learn how to create masks using After Effects Bézier masks. In Chapter 30, you also learn how to use the After Effects powerful motion paths and how to create composite video clips.

Part VII: Appendixes

The *Adobe Premiere Pro Bible* appendixes provide a hardware overview geared to nontechnical users, a resource guide, and a guide to the *Adobe Premiere Pro* DVD. The appendixes also feature a section on how to license QuickTime from Apple Computer. If you are going to distribute a Premiere Pro movie on a CD-ROM as a QuickTime movie, you'll probably want to include QuickTime; therefore, you'll need to obtain a software license from Apple Computer. The hardware overview appendix provides a look at computer systems and IEEE 1394/FireWire ports, and it also provides a short guide to DV camcorders and audio. The resource appendix provides a Web guide for digital video and sound equipment as well as the Web addresses for magazines and publishers specializing in video, audio, and lighting.

Things to Note

The *Adobe Premiere Pro Bible* runs only on Windows XP Pro and XP Home Edition. The program's target user is the video professional.

Key combinations

Here are some conventions in this book that you should note. To save your file, press Ctrl+ S. When keyboard instructions call for pressing several keys simultaneously, the keys are separated by a plus sign. For example, to deselect all clips in the Timeline, press Ctrl+Shift+A.

Mouse instructions

When the text specifies to click an item, move the mouse pointer over the item and click once. Windows users always click the left mouse button unless otherwise instructed. If the text specifies double-click, click the mouse twice without moving the mouse.

Menu commands

When the text specifies steps for executing a menu command, the menu and the command are separated by an arrow symbol, such as Sequence ⇨ Render Work Area. When submenus are specified, you'll often see an arrow separating each menu command. For instance, to export a project from Premiere Pro, you'll see the instructions written as File ⇨ Export ⇨ Movie.

Acknowledgments

Thanks to Adobe Systems for creating products that allow us to express our creative visions. A special thanks to the entire Adobe Premiere Pro team for doing such a good job in coming out with a great product. Thanks also to Bruce Bowman, Liz McQueen, Jill Devlin, Daniel Brown, Marcus Chang, Matt Douglas, Meredith Yeary, Kristen Chang, Patty Stoop, Wendy Shobloom, Barbara Rice, Eric Lundblade, Michelle Love-Escobar, and Amacker Bullwinkle at Adobe Systems for their help.

Thanks to everyone at Wiley Publishing, Inc., especially Mike Roney who helped get the *Adobe Premiere Pro Bible* off the ground and who always kept us on schedule. Thanks to publishers Richard Swadley, Bob Ispen, and Barry Pruett for believing in us. Thanks to Rev Mengle and Robyn Siesky for managing all the loose ends. Thanks also to editors Melba Hopper and Paula Lowell for doing such a careful and meticulous job. Thanks, too, to Ryan Steffen the production coordinator and Lynsey Osborn and Lauren Goddard in the graphics department for their help with the book. For their help putting the DVD together, we thank Laura Moss and Kit Malone. Thanks especially to Dennis Short for his job in tech editing the *Adobe Premiere Pro Bible*.

Thanks to Thomas Smith from Digital Vision for supplying us with digital stock clips for use on the DVD that accompanies the book.

Thanks to all the people (family; friends, especially our musician and computer friends; the children of today, who are the future; and to all those people we have met who radiate peace and happiness for all) who have touched our lives and inspired us to want to capture those wonderful moments that life has to offer. Hopefully, the *Adobe Premiere Pro Bible* will help capture those special moments in your life and allow you to share them with friends and loved ones.

We hope you enjoy the *Adobe Premiere Pro Bible*.

Contents at a Glance

Contents

Part III: Working with Type and Graphics   205

Part VI: Premiere Pro and Beyond   557

Getting Started with Premiere Pro

Premiere Pro Quickstart

Welcome to the world of Adobe Premiere Pro and digital video. For both experts and beginners alike, Adobe Premiere Pro packs the power you need to create sophisticated digital video productions. You can create digital movies, documentaries, sales presentations, and music videos directly from your desktop computer or laptop. Your digital video production can be output to videotape or the Web, or you can integrate it into projects in other programs, such as Adobe After Effects, Adobe Live Motion, Macromedia Director, and Macromedia Flash.

This chapter introduces you to the basics of Adobe Premiere Pro: understanding what it is and what you can do with it. This chapter also provides a simple Quickstart project to get you acquainted with the Adobe Premiere Production process. You'll see how easy it is to load digital video clips and graphics into an Adobe Premiere Project and edit them into a short presentation. After you've completed the editing process, you'll export the movie as either a QuickTime or Windows Media file for use in other programs.

What You Can Do with Premiere Pro

Whether you need to create a simple video clip for the Web or a sophisticated documentary or presentation, Premiere Pro has the tools you need to create a dynamic video production. In fact, the best way to think about Premiere Pro is to visualize it as a complete production facility. You would need a room full of videotape and special effects equipment to do everything that Premiere Pro can do.

Here's a short list of some of the production tasks that you can accomplish with Premiere Pro:

✦ Edit digital video clips into a complete digital video production.

✦ Capture video from a digital camcorder or videotape recorder.

✦ Capture audio from a microphone or audio recording device.

✦ Load stock digital graphics, video, and audio clips.

✦ Create titles and animated title effects, such as scrolling or rolling titles.

✦ Integrate files from different sources into your production. Premiere Pro loads not only digital video and audio files, but also Adobe Photoshop, Adobe Illustrator, JPEG, and TIFF graphics.

✦ Create special effects, such as distortions, blurring, and pinching.

✦ Create motion effects in which logos or graphics move or bounce across the screen.

✦ Create transparency effects. You can superimpose titles over backgrounds or use color, such as blue or green, to mask the background from one image so that you can superimpose a new background.

✦ Edit sound. Premiere Pro enables you to cut and assemble audio clips as well as create sophisticated audio effects, such as cross fades and pans.

✦ Create transitions. Premiere Pro can create simple dissolves from one scene to another, as well as a host of sophisticated transition effects, such as page curls and curtain wipes.

✦ Output files in a variety of digital formats. Premiere Pro can output QuickTime and Video for Windows files, which can be viewed directly in other programs, as well as streamed over the Web. Premiere Pro also features Web-specific file formats, such as animated GIF.

✦ Output files to videotape.

How Premiere Pro Works

To understand the Premiere Production process, you need a basic understanding of the steps involved in creating a conventional videotape production in which the production footage is *not* digitized. In traditional, or *linear*, video production, all production elements are transferred to videotape. During the editing process, the final production is electronically edited onto one final or *program* videotape. Even though computers are used while editing, the linear or analog nature of videotape makes the process very time-consuming; during the actual editing session, video-tape must be loaded and unloaded from tape or cassette machines. Time is wasted as producers simply wait for videotape machines to reach the correct editing point. The production is usually assembled sequentially. If you want to go back to a previous scene and replace it with one that is shorter or longer, all subsequent scenes must be rerecorded to the program reel.

Nonlinear video-editing programs such as Premiere Pro have revolutionized the entire process of video editing. Digital video and Premiere Pro eliminate many of the time-consuming production chores of traditional editing. When using Premiere Pro, you don't need to hunt for tapes or load and remove them from tape machines. When producers use Premiere Pro, all production elements are digitized to disk. An icon in Premiere Pro's Project window represents each element in a production, whether it is a video clip, a sound clip, or a still image. The final production is represented by icons in a window called the *Timeline*. The focal points of the Timeline are its video and audio tracks, which appear as parallel bars that stretch from left to right across the Timeline. When you need to use a video clip, sound clip, or still image, you simply click it in the Project window and drag it to a track in the Timeline window. You can place the items of your production down sequentially or drag them anywhere to different tracks. As you work, you can access any portion of your production by clicking with the mouse in the desired portion in the Timeline window. You can also use the mouse to click either the beginning or end of a clip and shorten or extend the clip's duration.

To fine-tune your edits, you can view and edit the clips frame by frame in the Timeline window. You can also set in and out points in the Monitor window. Setting an *in point* affects where a clip starts playing, and setting an *out point* affects where a clip stops playing. Because all clips are digitized (and no videotape is involved), Premiere Pro can quickly adjust the final production as you edit.

The following list summarizes some of the digital-editing magic that you can perform in Premiere Pro by simply dragging clips in the Timeline:

✦ **Rolling edit.** As you click and drag to add frames to the clip in the Timeline, Premiere Pro automatically subtracts from the frames in the next clip. As you click and drag to remove frames, Premiere Pro automatically adds back frames from the next clip in the Timeline.

✦ **Ripple edit.** As you add or subtract frames, Premiere Pro automatically adds to or subtracts from the entire program's duration.

✦ **Slip edit.** Dragging a clip to the left or right automatically changes in and out points without changing the program duration.

✦ **Slide edit.** Dragging a clip to the left or right keeps its duration intact but changes the in or out points of the preceding or succeeding clip.

Cross-Reference

Chapters 7 and 13 both provide in-depth discussion of Premiere Pro editing techniques.

As you work, you can easily preview edits, special effects, and transitions. Changing edits and effects is often a simple matter of changing in and out points. There's no hunting down the right videotape or waiting for the production to be reassembled on tape. When all of your editing is completed, you can export the file to videotape or create a new digital file in one of several formats. You can export it as many times as you want, in as many different file formats as you want. Furthermore, if you want to add more special effects to your Premiere Pro projects, you can easily import them into Adobe After Effects. You can also integrate your Premiere Pro movie into a Web page using Adobe GoLive.

Cross-Reference   Adobe After Effects is covered in Chapters 26 and 30. Adobe GoLive is discussed in Chapter 20.

Your First Video Production

The following sections provide a Quickstart tutorial that leads you step by step through the basics of video production in Premiere Pro. As you work through the tutorial, you'll learn how to place clips in the Timeline, edit clips in the Monitor window, apply transitions, and fade video and audio.

In this project, you'll create a simple video sequence called Nite Out. Figure 1-1 shows frames of the production in Premiere Pro's Timeline window. The clips used to create the project are from Digital Vision's Night Moves CD-ROM. The production begins with a title created in Adobe Title Designer, viewed over an opening scene of people walking in the city. After a few seconds, a dissolve transitions to the scene of diners in a restaurant. Soon the dining scene dissolves into one showing kitchen workers preparing food. The project ends with another title superimposed over the last scene.

Starting a Premiere Pro project

A Premiere Pro digital video production is called a *project* instead of a video production. The reason for this is that Premiere Pro not only enables you to create the production, but it also enables you to create and store titles, transitions, and effects. Thus, the file you work in is much more than just a production—it's truly a project.

Your first step in creating a digital video production in Premiere Pro is to create a new project. Here's how:

1. **To load Premiere Pro, double-click the Adobe Premiere Pro icon.** When you load Premiere Pro, the program automatically assumes that you want to create a new project or open one previously created.

2. **To create a new project, click the New Project icon.** If Premiere Pro is already loaded, you can create a new project by choosing File ➪ New Project.

Figure 1-1: Scenes from the Nite Out project.

Note If Premiere Pro is already loaded and you already have a project onscreen, you need to close that project because you can only have one project open at a time.

Specifying project settings

Before you can start importing files and editing, you must specify video and audio settings for the project. The New Project dialog box, shown in Figure 1-2, appears whenever you create a new project. This dialog box enables you to quickly choose predetermined video and audio settings. The most important project settings determine the frame rate (frames per second) and the frame size (viewing area) of your project as well as how the digital video will be compressed.

Cross-Reference   For a detailed description of project settings, see Chapter 4.

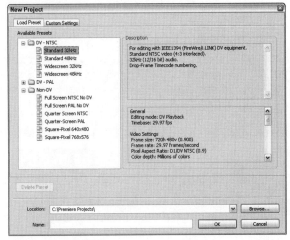

Figure 1-2: Use the New Project dialog box to pick project presets.

As a general rule, choose project settings that match your source footage. The footage used for this tutorial conforms to a video standard called NTSC D1. The frame size is 720 by 486. The audio file is 16-bit 44 kHz.

1. **To work with the tutorial footage, choose the DV NTSC Standard 32 kHz.**
   After you click, Premiere Pro displays information about the project settings.

   Notice that the Frame Size is 720 by 480, the standard DV frame size (which is close enough to our 720 by 480 footage. Also note that under Video Settings, the display reads D1/DV Pixel Aspect Ratio (0.9). This indicates that you are creating a project for footage with non-square pixels. Since the tutorial footage uses non-square pixels, this is the correct choice for the project. However, since the tutorial audio is 44 kHz (better quality than 32 kHz, you need to change one of the audio presets.

2. **To change a preset, click the Custom Settings tab.**

3. **In the Audio section of the dialog box, click the Sample Rate pop-up menu and choose 44 kHz.**

Cross-Reference To learn more about Pixel Aspect Ratio and choosing project settings see Chapter 4. Audio Samples are discussed in Chapter 8.

4. **Select a location to store your file.** If you want to change the default location, click Browse and use the mouse to navigate to the folder where you want to store your file.

5. **Enter a name such as Nite Out in the name field**.

6. **To open your new project, click OK.**

Setting a workspace

Before you start editing, you may want to set your workspace so that you can easily view the most important Premiere Pro windows used in editing. This is easily accomplished by picking an editing workspace. Choose Window ➪ Workspace ➪ Editing. This opens the Project, Monitor, and Timeline windows as well as the Info and History palettes. In this tutorial, you use the Project window as your home for source footage. You'll edit your clips in the Timeline and Monitor window, and you'll view the edited project in the Monitor window.

Note If the Timeline doesn't open, double-click Sequence 01 in the Project window. The sequence will open onscreen in the Timeline window.

Importing production elements

You can place and edit video, audio, and still images in your Premiere Pro projects as long as they are in a digital format. Table 1-1 lists the major file formats that Premiere Pro supports. All media footage, or *clips*, must first be saved to disk. Even if your video is stored on a digital camcorder, it still must be transferred to disk. Premiere Pro can capture the digital video clips and automatically store them in your projects. Analog media such as motion picture film and videotape must first be digitized before Premiere Pro can use it. In this case, Premiere Pro, in conjunction with a capture board, can capture your clips directly into a project.

Cross-Reference For more information about capturing video and audio, see Chapter 5.

Table 1-1
Supported Files in Adobe Premiere Pro

Media	*File Formats*
Video	QuickTime (MOV) and Video for Windows (AVI)
Audio	AIFF WAV, AVI, and MOV
Still images, and Sequence	TIF, JPEG, BMP (Windows only), GIF, Filmstrip, Illustrator, and Photoshop

After the Premiere Pro windows open, you're ready to import the various graphic and sound elements that will comprise your digital video production. All the items that you import are stored in the Project window. An icon represents each item. Next to the icon, Premiere Pro displays whether the item is a video clip, an audio clip, or a graphic.

When importing files into Premiere Pro, you can choose whether to import one file, multiple files (by pressing and holding the Shift key), or an entire folder. If desired, you can even import one project into another, using the File ➪ Import ➪ Project command.

Here's how to load the production elements for the Nite Out project:

1. **Choose File ➪ Import.**

2. **Open the Tutorial Projects folder on the *Adobe Premiere Pro Bible* DVD-ROM.**

3. **If you want to load the files, select the Nite Out folder in the Chapter 1 folder and then click Import Folder.** The Nite Out folder now appears in the Project window.

On the DVD-ROM

The video clips (705008f.mov, 705009f.mov and 705029f.mov) used in the Nite Out project are from Digital Vision's NightMoves CD. The sound clip (705001.aif) used in the Nite Out project is also from Digital Vision's NightMoves CD. The Nite Out folder is in the Chapter 1 folder in the Tutorial Projects folder on the DVD that accompanies this book.

4. **To view the titles, and video and audio clips, double-click the Nite Out folder in the Project window.**

5. **Rename each clip.** Because the names of imported clips may not clearly describe their footage, you can rename them in the Project window. To rename a clip, click on it in the Project window and choose Clip ➪ Rename. (As a shortcut, you can also right-click the clip and then rename it.) Here are the file-names and the new names to use:

   • Name the 705001.aif audio clip: **Background Music.**

   • Name the 705008f clip: **Diners.**

   • Name the 705009f clip: **Chefs.**

   • Name the 705029f clip: **Walkers.**

Figure 1-3 shows the Project window with all the clips needed to create the Nite Out project clip. Notice that the Project window displays the Start and Stop time of each clip as well as its duration.

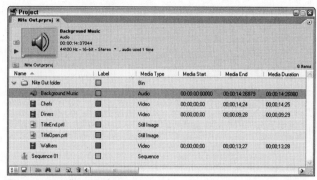

Figure 1-3: The Project window with the items needed to create the Nite Out project.

The Nite Out project requires the following files:

✦ A video clip showing shadows of people walking in the city (Walkers)

✦ A video clip of people out in a restaurant (Diners)

✦ A video clip of chefs working in a restaurant (Chefs)

✦ Two title files created using templates from Adobe Title Designer

✦ A sound clip of background music

Note   The video footage was captured at 30 frames per second. Although not necessary for this tutorial, you could change the footage frame rate to the Project frame rate by selecting the footage in the Project window and choosing File ➪ Interpret Footage. In the Interpret Footage dialog box, you can enter a new frame rate for the footage.

Cross-Reference   Creating titles in Premiere Pro is discussed in Chapter 11.

Viewing clips in the Project window

Before you begin assembling your production, you may want to view a clip or graphic, or listen to an audio track. You can see a thumbnail preview of any of the clips in the Project window by clicking the clip. The preview appears at the upper-left corner of the Project window. If you are previewing a video or audio clip, a small triangle (Play button) appears to the left of the thumbnail preview window. Click the Play button to see a preview of a video clip or to hear an audio clip. If you prefer, you can click and drag the tiny slider below the thumbnail preview to gradually view the clip.

Note Double-clicking the clip in the Project window opens the clip in the Monitor window. You can preview the clip there by clicking the Play button.

Assembling production elements

After you import all of your production elements, you need to place them in a sequence in the Timeline window so that you can start editing your project. A sequence is a graphical preview of the footage that you are editing. Using the mouse, you can place, edit, rearrange, and create transitions in the Timeline window sequence.

Note If you are working on long projects in Premiere Pro, you'll probably want to break your work into multiple sequences. After you've edited the sequences, you can drag them into another Timeline window where they'll appear as nested sequences. Using nested sequences is discussed in Chapter 6.

Placing clips in the Timeline

To move an item from the Project window to the Timeline window, simply click it in the Project window and then drag it to a track in the Timeline window. The item then appears in the Timeline as an icon. The duration of the clip or graphic is represented by the length of the clip in the Timeline.

Note You can place clips directly in the Timeline by opening them in the Monitor window, then clicking the Insert or Overlay button. This technique is discussed in Chapter 7.

Selecting clips in the Timeline

You'll spend a great deal of time positioning clips in the Timeline while editing your production. Premiere Pro's Selection and Range Select tools help you assemble your program's clips in the order you want.

Here's how to select and move clips:

✦ **Single clip.** Click the Selection tool (the arrow icon in the upper-left corner of the Timeline). Next, click in the middle of the clip in the Timeline window. (To quickly activate the Selection tool, press V on your keyboard.) With the clip selected, click and drag it to the desired location.

✦ **Multiple clips.** Click the Range Select tool (the empty dotted-line square icon in the toolbox located to the right of the Selection tool). Next, click and drag over the clips that you want to select. To select the Range Select tool using your keyboard, press M.

Figure 1-4 displays the Timeline window for the Nite Out project. The title appears in the Video 2 track. We put it here because it enables us to create a transparency effect in which we fade in the title text over background video. The Walkers video clip appears in track Video 1, as does the next clip (the Diners clip). Between the two tracks is a transition. In this case, we dragged a dissolve from the Effects window. The project also ends with a transition to a scene of chefs working in a kitchen, before the final title appears and then fades out.

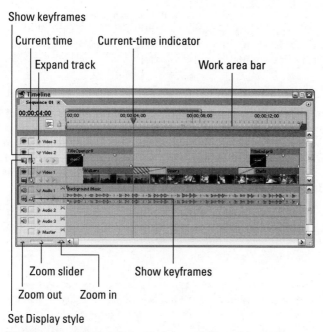

Figure 1-4: The Timeline window with the clips for the Nite Out video project.

Trying out the Timeline window

As mentioned earlier, the Timeline window provides a graphical overview of your project. Before continuing, try changing zoom settings, moving the Timeline indicator, and expanding a video track. Doing so will help familiarize you with the Timeline tools you need as you work in this chapter.

Changing the zoom level

Most Premiere Pro users create their video projects at 29.97 or 30 frames per second. Viewing all of these frames on the Timeline quickly consumes Timeline space. As you work, you'll probably want to zoom in and out between close-up and bird's-eye views of your work. When you zoom in, you'll see fewer frames, which may make fine-tuning your project easier, particularly because the space between time intervals in the Timeline expands. When you want an overview of your entire project, you may want to zoom out.

To zoom in and out, click the Timeline zoom level slider in the lower-left corner of the Timeline. Figure 1-4 shows the Timeline zoom slider as well as the zoom in and zoom out buttons. Clicking and dragging left (zooming out) shows more footage in the Timeline; clicking and dragging to the right (zooming in) shows less footage.

For example, if you zoom out, a one-minute clip will take up less space in the Timeline — which means you'll be able to see many different clips as well as your one-minute clip. If you zoom in a one-minute clip will occupy more space in the Timeline, which means that it may be the only clip visible.

Moving the current-time indicator

The current-time indicator (sometimes referred to as CTI) is the blue triangular icon at the tip of the ruler area in the Timeline. If you click and drag the current current-time indicator, you move the red edit line. The edit line shows you the current editing position in the Monitor window. Try clicking and dragging the current current-time indicator. Notice that as you drag the blue current time readout changes, showing your current position in the Timeline. In Figure 1-4, the edit line is on the 4-second mark on the Timeline, and the current time reads 00;00;04;00. If you want to quickly jump to an area in the Timeline, just click in the ruler area. If you want to slowly move through the Timeline one frame at a time, press the right or left arrow keys.

Expanding tracks

By default, you'll see three video tracks in the Timeline. If you expand a track, you can see video frames in the track and video effects. Later, you'll change the display style to show frames in the video tracks, and volume in audio tracks. The white dots in the audio and video tracks in Figure 1-4 are keyframes, which indicate a change in volume or opacity. By default, Video track 1 and Audio track 1 are expanded. In this project, you will also be using Video track 2. Try expanding it now by clicking the right-pointing triangle to the left of Video track 2.

Adding the title to the Timeline

Start the production process by adding the opening title to the Timeline. The title includes an *alpha channel*, which allows the background video to be seen beneath the title. The title was created from a template in Premiere Pro's Title Designer. In this section, you'll place the title in the Video 2 track because it enables you to easily fade in the text over the video in lower tracks.

 See Chapter 11 to learn more about Adobe Title Designer.

The following steps explain how to add the title to the Timeline window, fading it in and out:

1. **Click the Nite Out title (TitleOpen) in the Project window and drag it into Video track 2.**

2. **If you would like the clip to appear longer in the Timeline, zoom in by clicking and dragging the zoom slider to the right.**

3. **Now view the footage as individual frames in the Timeline. In Video track 2, click the Set Display Style drop-down menu and choose Show Frames. (This drop-down menu is a tiny box directly below the Eye icon in the track.)**

4. **Reduce the length of the title to 4 seconds by clicking and dragging left on the right end of the title.** Use the time readout at the top of the Timeline as a guide.

 Tip   Here's a technique that will allow you to work more precisely in the Timeline. Click and drag the current-time indicator to the 4-second mark. Then use the red edit line as a stopping point when you click and drag on the end of the title clip.

Fading in the title

Next, you'll fade in the titles. In Figure 1-4, the diagonal line immediately in the track represents the fade-in effect. The diagonal line indicates that the title fades in gradually over the first second. In this section, you'll create the fade-in effect by changing the opacity of the title clip in the Effects Control window. Figure 1-5 shows the Effect Controls window and the Opacity slider. The diamonds on the right side of the window are called *keyframes*. Each time you make a change in the Opacity setting, Premiere Pro creates a keyframe; then Premiere Pro adjusts the opacity between the keyframes to gradually change.

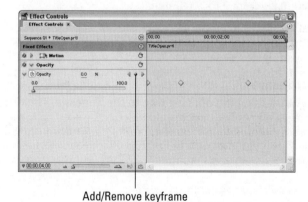

Add/Remove keyframe

Figure 1-5: Use the Opacity slider to create keyframes, which create a gradual fade-in effect.

The following steps show you how to change opacity.

1. **Display the Opacity handles in the track.** Click in the Show Keyframes drop-down menu (the tiny box to the right of the Set Display Style drop-down menu) and choose Show Opacity Handles.

2. **Select the TitleOpen file in the Timeline by clicking it.**

3. **Open the Effect Controls window by choosing Window ⇨ Effect Controls.** Before continuing, note that the Effect Controls window includes a Zoom slider in the lower left and a current-time indicator. Both function exactly as they do in the Timeline window.

4. **Now expand the Opacity control by clicking the right-pointing triangle button (to the left of the word Opacity).** The Opacity control expands. You can easily change opacity by clicking and dragging the Opacity slider. To view the slider, click the right-pointing arrow button to the left of the stopwatch in the Opacity section.

5. **Lower the opacity to 0.** To lower opacity, click and drag left until the display reads 0%, as shown in Figure 1-5.

6. **Now drag the current-time indicator in the Effect Controls window to the 1-second mark.** As you click and drag, you'll see the time display change in the lower-left corner. Stop when you reach 1 second.

7. **Now raise the opacity back to 100 percent. Click and drag the slider to the right.** As you drag, the percentage begins to increase.

8. **The change in opacity created two keyframes, one at the start of the clip and another one second later.** Between the two keyframes, Premiere Pro adjusts opacity to gradually increase from 0 to 100 percent

9. **Now create a fade out at the 3-second mark. Click and drag the current-time indicator to the 3-second mark, then click the Add/Remove Keyframe button.** Then drag the Timeline indicator slider to the 4-second mark. Click and drag the Opacity slider to set it to 0%. After you make the change, Premiere Pro adds another keyframe to the window. When you're done, the Effect Controls window should resemble Figure 1-5.

Note   You can also change video opacity directly in the Timeline with the Pen tool. Control+clicking on the Opacity rubberband in the Timeline creates keyframes. After you create keyframes, you can adjust opacity by clicking and dragging with the Pen tool.

Tip   If you need to delete a keyframe, right-click it and choose Clear.

Trimming clips in the Timeline window

You can edit video and audio clips in several ways. We'll start simply by editing the first clip by clicking and dragging its out point in the Timeline. Before editing a clip, you may want to play it in the Monitor window. To play any clip, double-click the video clip in the Project window. When the Monitor window appears, click the Play button to view the clip. The Play button is shown in Figure 1-6.

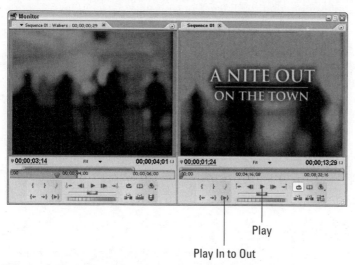

Play

Play In to Out

Figure 1-6: The Monitor window's Play button.

The following steps explain how to add the first video clip, the Walkers clip, to the Timeline window. If you haven't viewed the clip, you can play it by double-clicking it in the Project window, then clicking the Play button in the Monitor window. Alternatively, you can play a thumbnail version of it in the Project window. Click it in the Project window and then click the left arrow button at the top of the Project window. Also note that the clip is 14 seconds long. You only need the first 4 seconds of it.

1. **Drag the Walkers clip from the Project window into the Video 1 track.**
   Position the clip so that it starts where the title fade-in ends — about 1 second on the Timeline. If you want to be precise, drag the Timeline indicator to the 1-second mark and then drag the Walkers clip to the current-time indicator edit line. When the clip touches the edit line, it will snap to it.

2. **Position the mouse pointer at the end of the clip.** The cursor changes to a bracket.

3. **Click and drag to the left to shorten the clip.** Make the clip about 4 seconds long so that it ends on the 5-second mark (00;00;05;00) on the Timeline. Once again, you may want to drag the current-time indicator to the 5-second mark first and then adjust the clip by clicking and dragging the right edge of the clip so it snaps on the edit line.

Tip   If you get lost in the Timeline and inadvertently move out of the edited area, zoom out so that you can see the clips you've placed in the Timeline, move the current-time indicator into the edited area, and then zoom in.

Previewing in the Monitor window

To view the video production so far, you can play the program in the Monitor window. Make sure that the Monitor window is open by choosing Window ➪ Monitor. The right side of the Monitor window displays the program being edited in the current sequence in the Timeline window, as shown in Figure 1-6. The left side shows source clips. To play from the beginning to the end of your project, click the Play In to Out button at the bottom of the right side of the Monitor window.

As soon as you click, the video clip rewinds and begins playing in the window. As it plays you'll see the clip fade in, and you'll see the Walkers clip superimposed beneath the opening title. The Walkers clip appears only in the black area of the Title clip.

Editing in the Monitor window

The Monitor window provides precise controls for editing clips. Using the Monitor window, you can easily navigate to specific frames and then mark in or out points. After you set the in and out points, you can drag the clip directly to the Timeline. Now you'll set the in and out points in the Monitor window. To learn about the different ways to edit a video clip, see Chapters 7 and 13.

Note   You can also click the Insert or Overlay button in the Monitor window to place a clip in the Timeline. This technique is described in Chapter 7.

Note   By default, Premiere Pro automatically snaps two adjacent clips together. You can turn snap on or off by clicking the Magnet icon in the Timeline window.

1. **Double-click the clip in the Project window.** This opens the clip in the left side of the Monitor window, shown in Figure 1-7. The left side of the window shows source clips, and the right side of the window shows the edited sequence in the Timeline window. If the current-time indicator is on the Walkers clip, you'll see it in the Sequence section of the Monitor window.

2. **Play the clip by clicking the Play button in the left side of the Monitor window.** The scene eventually shows a waitress handing out menus. Before you edit the clip's in and out points, you need to go to the precise frame that you want to edit.

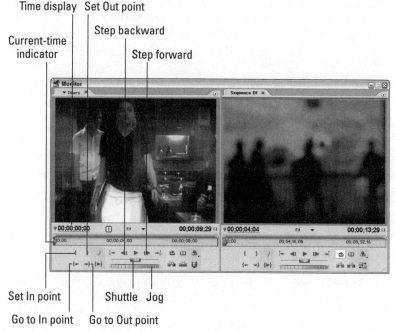

Figure 1-7: You can use the Monitor window to edit clips.

3. **Before editing the clip, you can jump back to its first frame by clicking the Go to In Point button.**

4. **Now you want to be able to slowly move through the clip to set the in point. Here are several options:**

   - Click the current-time indicator in the Monitor window and drag. As you drag, you'll move or scrub through the clip frame by frame.

   - Click and drag in the jog tread at the bottom of the Monitor window. As you click and drag, you'll move through the clip frame by frame.

   - Click and hold down the shuttle control to move in slow or fast motion. Speed is controlled by how far left or right you move the shuttle. Moving right moves forward through the clip. Dragging the shuttle to the left moves backward.

   - Click the Step back or Step forward button to move one frame at a time forward or backward.

5. **Now click and drag the jog icon to the right or drag the current-time indicator in the Monitor window to the right.** After about 6 seconds, the scene switches to a long shot of the waitress handing out menus.

6. **Either by clicking and dragging or by entering the precise location into the Time display using your keyboard, position the current-time indicator at 00;00;06;00.**

7. **Click the Set Out Point button (refer to Figure 1-7).**

Note   To clear an in or out point, press Alt, while clicking the in or out point button.

8. **Now drag the clip to the Timeline so that it snaps to the Walkers clip.**

Note   Although you edited the clip, the original clip on your hard disk is untouched. At any point in time, you can reedit the clip to return the missing parts.

Creating a transition

Now view your production by previewing it in the Monitor window. To start the preview from the beginning of the Timeline, click the Play In to Out button in the Sequence section of the Monitor window. As you watch the preview, notice that the cut from the Walkers clip to the Diners clip is quite abrupt. To smooth the flow of the production, you'll add a *transition* between the two clips.

Cross-
Reference   For more information on using transitions, turn to Chapter 10.

Here's how to add a Cross Dissolve transition to your project:

1. **Open the Effects window by choosing Window ⇨ Show Effects palette, if it is not already open.**

2. **In the Effects palette, open the Video Transitions folder by clicking its triangle icon.**

3. **Open the Dissolve folder by clicking its triangle icon.**

4. **To add the transition to your project, click and drag it to beginning of the Diners clip or between the Walkers and the Diners clip.**

5. **To open the window for the Cross Dissolve, double-click the Cross Dissolve icon in the Timeline.** This opens the transition in the Effect Controls window.

6. **Adjust the position and length of the transition.** You can adjust the position and the duration of the transition by clicking and dragging the mouse on the transition icon in the Effect Controls window. However, the fastest technique is to enter a value in the Duration readout and change settings in the Alignment drop-down menu. Set the Duration to 2 seconds by changing the time readout to 00;00;02;00. Then choose Center at Cut in the Alignment drop-down menu, as shown in Figure 1-8.

Play button

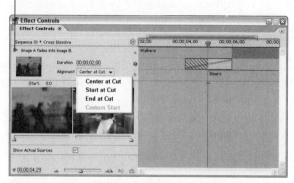

Figure 1-8: The Cross Dissolve transition in the Effect Controls window.

7. **View a thumbnail preview.** Preview the final transition by clicking the play transition button in the Effect Controls window. To see the effect with the footage, select Show Actual Sources.

Previewing the transition

Premiere Pro includes a real-time preview feature that enables you to view transitions and video effects as you work. Press the spacebar to play the project and show transitions.

Editing the Chefs clip

Next, you'll add the Chefs clip to the program and edit it in the Monitor window:

1. **Double-click the Chefs clip in the Project window.** This opens the clip in the source section of the Monitor window.

2. **Set the in point.** Click and drag the current-time indicator in the Monitor window (in the area below the Monitor preview and above the Play button) to choose a frame at about a little more than 3 seconds into the clip. Click the Set In Point button.

3. **Set the out point.** Click and drag the Monitor window's current-time indicator to find a point about 6 and ½ seconds into the clip. Watch the time display at the bottom-right of the window to pick the frame. When you have found the frame you want, click the Set Out Point button.

4. **After you've set the in and out points, you can drag the clip from either the Project window or you can drag it directly from the Timeline.**

Adding another dissolve

Now create another transition—this time between the Diners clip and the Chefs clip:

1. **Open the Dissolve folder in the Effects window.**

2. **Drag the Cross Dissolve transition over the Chefs clip.**

3. **Double-click the transition icon between the Diners and Chefs clips in the Timeline.**

4. **In the Effect Controls window, set the Alignment pop-up menu to Center of Cut.** If you want to change the duration of the transition, edit the Duration time display.

Adding the last title

Your next step is to add the end title to the Video 2 track:

1. **Drag the end title image (Title End) from the Project window to the Video 2 track.** Position the title clip so that it begins where the Chefs clip starts.

2. **Drag the clip's end point to make its duration 3 seconds long or select the title and choose Clip ⇨ Speed/Duration.** In the Clip Speed Duration dialog box, set the display to 00;00;03;00 and click OK.

3. **Create the fade in and fade out as you did for the opening title.** Remember to select the clip in the Timeline, then open the Effect Controls window by choosing Window ⇨ Effect Controls. Use Figure 1-4 as a reference.

4. **Preview your work, by pressing Spacebar.**

Adding and fading in the audio track

Now that the majority of editing is complete, it's time to add the audio track. Fortunately, the Timeline treats audio much the same as it treats video. In this section, you drag the music track to the Timeline, then use the Pen tool to create a keyframe in the audio channel.

1. **Listen to the Background Music clip by double-clicking it in the Project window.** After the clip opens in the Monitor window, click the Play button.

2. **Drag the Background Music clip from the Project window to the Audio 1 track in the Timeline window.** Line up the beginning of the audio track with the beginning of the video track.

3. **Expand the Audio 1 track by clicking the triangle icon at the far left of the track.**

4. **Click the Audio track's Show keyframes drop down menu and choose Show Clip Volume.**

5. **Activate the Pen tool in the tool palette.**

6. **With the Pen tool activated, Ctrl+click at the beginning of the audio to create keyframe.**

7. **Create another keyframe about 2 seconds into the track by Ctrl+clicking again with the Pen tool.**

8. **Use the Pen tool to drag down the start of the volume line.**

9. **Use the Pen tool to create a keyframe at the end of the audio.** About 1 second from the end, use the Pen tool to drag the volume line down to fade out.

10. **Preview your project to see the production and hear the fade out.** If you want to fine-tune the effect, use the Pen tool to adjust the volume line in the audio track.

Note Audio fade-ins can also be created by using the Crossfade audio transition. See Chapter 8 to learn more about audio effects. Also note that Premiere Pro allows you to change the volume of the entire audio track as well as individual clips.

Fine-tuning the project

The project you've worked on is a simple introduction to editing in Premiere Pro. Feel free to enhance, change, and re-edit as you desire. If you want, create a fade up from black or fade out to black. You can create pure black video and place it in a video track. To create black, choose File ⇨ New ⇨ Black Video. This command places the black video clip into the Project window. From there, you can drag it into the Timeline. If you want to fade in or out, place the clip in Video track 2. You might also want to add a fade out to the Chefs clip. You can easily do so by selecting the clip and changing the opacity of the last second of the clip.

Exporting your first movie

When you finish editing your movie, you can export it in a variety of different formats. Premiere Pro enables you to export movies in video formats such as QuickTime, RealVideo, and Advanced Windows Media, as well as formats for DVDs.

Here is a summary of Premiere Pro's export commands:

✦ If you want to export your file in a format for Web or DVD use, you can use Premiere Pro's Adobe Media Encoder. The Media Encoder allows you to create MPEG, Windows Media, Real Video, and QuickTime streaming files.

✦ If you want to export your movie as an AVI, QuickTime, or animated GIF file, choose File ⇨ Export Movie.

✦ If you want to export your movie to videotape, choose File ⇨ Export to Tape.

The following section shows how to export a Windows Media file using the Adobe Media Encoder. A later section shows you how to export your project as a QuickTime movie.

Exporting a Windows Media file

If you are a Windows user, you may want to export your project in Windows Media format. This format can be read by most Windows users, and can be used for projects that appear on the Web. To export your movie in Windows Media format, follow these steps:

1. **Choose File ➪ Export ➪ Adobe Media Encoder.** The Transcode Settings dialog box appears (see Figure 1-9).

2. **In the Format pop-up menu, choose Windows Media.**

3. **Click a preset.** For example, if you want to export your file for multiple Web audiences and want to export your file for users with a high-speed Internet connection, you could choose WMA9 NTSC512. The summary information displays frame height, frame rate, and other exporting details. To continue with the export, click OK.

4. **Select a destination folder in which to store the finished Windows Media file, and enter a filename.** In the Destination section, click the button with three dots on it. This opens the Save As dialog box where you can navigate to the folder area where you want to save your file.

5. **In the Export range drop-down menu, choose Entire Sequence, if it isn't already chosen.**

6. **To start the export, click Save.**

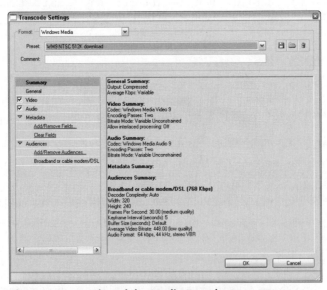

Figure 1-9: Use the Adobe Media Encoder to create a Windows Media file for the Web.

A note about rendering and playback quality

As Premiere Pro plays your program in the Monitor window, it attempts to adjust the output to deliver the highest quality possible. If possible, it tries to play back at the project's full frame rate. If a portion of your program cannot be properly displayed, a red preview bar appears onscreen. This indicates that the area must be rendered to disk. After rendering, Premiere Pro uses the rendered disk file to properly display the effect. If you want to render your entire project, press Enter. If you want to render only a portion of your project, first adjust the work area bar so that it only encompasses the area that you want to render, then press Enter. If you want to lower the processing requirements so that you can see effects at a lower quality setting without rendering, you can change to Draft Quality in the Monitor pop-up menu.

It's also important to note that despite the Quality Setting in the Monitor window, playback quality in the Monitor window will not be as high as that of exported video. When Premiere Pro processes video in the Monitor window, it uses *bilinear pixel resampling*. When Premiere Pro exports, it uses *cubic resampling*, a higher quality method that also produces higher quality sound.

Exporting a QuickTime movie

Both Mac and Windows users can export Premiere Pro projects as QuickTime movies. QuickTime is widely used on the Web and can be imported into other programs such as Macromedia Director and Macromedia Flash. Depending on the final destination of your project, you may want to change the frame size and frame rate of your video before exporting. For example, if you want to export a file composed of DV footage to a multimedia project, you'll probably want to reduce the DV frame size from 720 × 480 to a smaller size that fits comfortably into your production.

Here are the steps for exporting your project as a QuickTime movie:

1. **Select the Timeline window, or select the Sequence 01 in the Project window.**

2. **Choose File ⇨ Export ⇨ Movie.** The Export Movie dialog box appears.

3. **Click the Settings button.** The Export Movie Settings dialog box appears, in which you can view export settings.

4. **Choose QuickTime from the File Type drop-down list, as shown in Figure 1-10.**

5. **To switch frame size and frame rate, choose Video from the list box at the upper-left of the dialog box.** The Video Settings dialog box appears. These settings are covered in detail in Chapter 4.

6. **If you are creating a multimedia project that will play on a computer, select either Sorenson or Cinepak as the compressor.** Optionally, you can change the frame size to 320 × 240 and change the frame rate, if desired. If you will be outputting the file for computers with older CD-ROM drives, you need to lower the data rate to about 250 Kbps. Doing so slows the data rate to prevent frames from being dropped during playback.

7. **After you make your changes, click OK.** Premiere Pro returns you to the Export Movie dialog box.

8. **In the Export Movie dialog box, type a name for your file.**

9. **Click OK.** Premiere Pro builds the export file and soon opens it in the Monitor window for viewing.

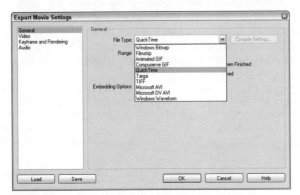

Figure 1-10: Choose QuickTime in the File Type drop-down menu.

Summary

This chapter gave you a chance to experiment with the basic concepts of editing in Premiere Pro. You learned how to do the following:

✦ Create a project.

✦ Add clips to the Timeline.

✦ Edit clips in the Monitor window and in the Timeline.

✦ Change clip opacity.

✦ Create transitions.

✦ Preview your production.

✦ Fade in and out audio.

✦ Export your production.

✦   ✦   ✦

Premiere Pro Basics

✦   ✦   ✦   ✦

In This Chapter

Touring Premiere Pro's windows

Touring palettes

Premiere Pro's menu commands

✦   ✦   ✦   ✦

The Adobe Premiere Pro user interface is a combination of a video-editing studio and an electronic image-editing studio. If you're familiar with film, video editing, or audio editing, you'll feel right at home working within Premiere Pro's Project, Monitor, and Audio windows. If you've worked with such programs as Adobe After Effects, Adobe Live Motion, Macromedia Flash, or Macromedia Director, Premiere Pro's Timeline, digital tools, and palettes will seem familiar. If you're completely new to video editing and computers, don't worry; Premiere Pro palettes, windows, and menus are efficiently designed to get you up and running quickly.

To help get you started, this chapter provides an overview of Premiere Pro windows, menus, and palettes. Consider it a thorough introduction to the program's workspace and a handy reference for planning and producing your own digital video productions.

Premiere Pro's Windows

After you first launch Premiere Pro, several windows automatically appear onscreen, each vying for your attention. Why do you need more than one window open at once? A video production is a multifaceted undertaking. In one production, you may need to capture video, edit video, and create titles, transitions, and special effects. Premiere Pro windows help keep these tasks separated and organized for you.

This section provides an overview of the windows that enable you to create the various elements of your digital video project: the Project, Timeline, and Audio Mixer windows. The History, Video/Audio Effects, and Tools palettes float above all other windows. We discuss them separately in the Premiere Pro's floating palettes section.

Manipulating Premiere Pro windows

Although the Premiere Pro program's primary windows open automatically onscreen from time to time, you may want to close one of them. To close a window, simply click its close window *X* icon. If you try to close the Project window, Premiere Pro assumes that you want to close the entire project and prompts you to save your work before closing. If you want to open the Timeline, Monitor, Audio Mixer, History, Info, or Tools windows, choose the Window menu and then click the desired window name. If you have more than one timeline on the screen, you'll see it listed in the Window ⇨ Timelines submenu.

If you have your windows and palettes set up in specific positions at specific sizes, you can save this configuration by choosing Window ⇨ Workspace ⇨ Save Workspace. After you name your workspace and save it, the name of the workspace appears in the Window ⇨ Workspace submenu. Any time you want to use that workspace, simply click its name.

The Project window

If you've ever worked on a project with many video and audio clips as well as other production elements, you'll soon appreciate the Premiere Pro program's Project window, which is shown in Figure 2-1. The Project window provides a quick bird's-eye view of your production elements and enables you to preview a clip right from the Project window.

Note   In Figure 2-1, the Project window includes two video clips, diners.mov and chefs.mov, which are from the Nite Out project found in Chapter 1. Both clips are from Digital Vision's NightMoves CD (705008f.mov and 705009f.mov). The diners.mov is Digital Vision's clip 705008f.mov, and the chefs.mov is Digital Vision's clip 705009f.mov.

As you work, Premiere Pro automatically loads items into the Project window. When you import a file, the video and audio clips are automatically loaded into a Project window *bin* (a folder in the Project window). If you import a folder of clips, Premiere Pro creates a new bin for the clips, using the folder name as the bin name. When you capture sound or video, you can quickly add the captured media to a Project window bin before closing the clip. Later you can create your own bins by clicking the Bin button, at which point you can drag production elements from one bin to another. The New Item button enables you to quickly create a new title or other production element, such as a color matte (covered in Chapter 13) or bars and tone (used to calibrate color and sound when editing). The Project window also includes a New Item button that allows you to add new sequences, offline files, titles, bars and tone, black video, color mattes, or universal counting leaders. If you click the

Icon button, all production elements appear as icons onscreen rather than in list format. Clicking the List button returns the display of the Project Window to List view. If you want to quickly add Project window elements to the Timeline, you can simply select them and then click the Automate to Sequence button.

If you expand the Project window by clicking and dragging the Window border, you'll see that Premiere Pro lists the Start and Stop time as well as the in and out points and the duration of each clip. In the Project window, production elements are grouped according to the current sort order. You can change the order of production elements so that they are arranged by any of the column headings. To sort by one of the column categories, simply click it. The first time you click, production items are sorted in ascending order. To sort in descending arrow, click again on the column heading. The sort order is represented by a small triangle. When the arrow points up, the sort order is ascending. When it points down, the sort order is descending.

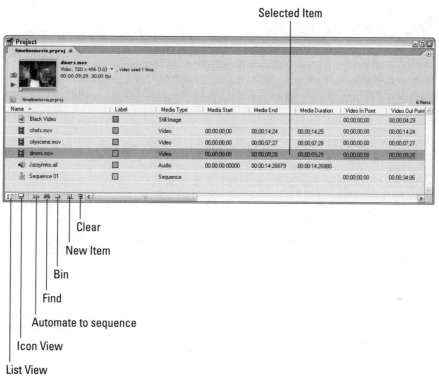

Figure 2-1: Premiere Pro's Project window stores production elements.

To keep your production materials well organized, you can create bins to store similar elements. For example, you may create a bin for all sound elements or a bin for all interview clips. If the bin gets stuffed, you can see more elements at one time by switching from the default thumbnail view to List view, which lists each item but doesn't show a thumbnail image.

If you want to play a clip in the thumbnail monitor in the Project window, click the clip, then click the tiny right arrow next to the thumbnail monitor. If you want to preserve space and hide the Project window's thumbnail monitor, choose View ⇨ Preview Area in the Project window menu. This toggles the monitor display off and on.

Tip

You can change the speed and duration of a clip by right-clicking the clip in the Project window and choosing Speed/Duration. You can also quickly place the clip in the Monitor Source window by right-clicking the clip and choosing Open in Source window.

The Timeline window

The Timeline, shown in Figure 2-2, is the foundation of your video production. It provides a graphic and temporal overview of your entire project. Fortunately, the Timeline is not for viewing only — it's interactive. Using your mouse, you can build your production by dragging video and audio clips, graphics, and titles from the Project window to the Timeline. Using Timeline tools, you can arrange, cut, and extend clips. By clicking and dragging the work area Markers at either end of the work area bar — edges of the light gray bar at the top of the Timeline — you specify the portion of the Timeline that Premiere Pro previews or exports. The thin, colored bar beneath the work area bar indicates whether a preview file for the project exists. A red bar indicates no preview, and a green bar indicates that a video preview has been created. If an audio preview exists, a thinner, light green bar appears. (To create the Preview file, choose Sequence ⇨ Render Work Area, or press Enter to render the work area.)

Tip

Rendering the work area helps ensure that your project is played back at the project frame rate. Also, if you create video and audio effects, the Preview file stores the rendered effects. Thus, the next time you play back the effect, Premiere Pro does not have to process the effect again.

Note

In Figure 2-2, the first video clip in Video 1 track is from Digital Vision's CityMix CD (567005f.mov). It is found in the Chapter 28 folder (which is in the Tutorial Projects folder) on the DVD that accompanies this book. The second clip is from Digital Vision's MightMoves CD (705008f.mov). This clip is in the Chapter 1 folder. The sound clip is Digital Vision's NightMoves CD (705001.aif). This clip is also in Chapter 1.

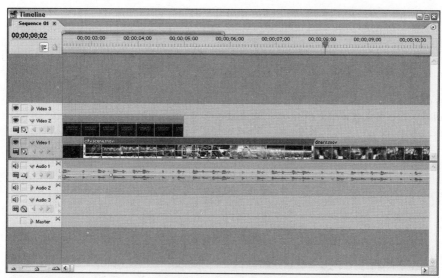

Figure 2-2: The Timeline window provides an overview of your project and enables you to edit clips.

Undoubtedly, the most useful visual metaphor in the Timeline window is its representation of video and audio tracks as parallel bars. Premiere Pro provides multiple, parallel tracks so that you can both preview and conceptualize a production in real time. For instance, parallel video and audio tracks enable you to view video as audio plays. The parallel tracks also enable you to create transparency effects where a portion of one video track can be seen through another. The Timeline also includes icons for hiding or viewing tracks. Clicking the Toggle Track Output button (Eye icon) hides a track while you preview your production; clicking it again makes the track visible. Clicking the audio Toggle Track Output button (Speaker icon) turns audio tracks on and off. Beneath the Eye icon is another icon that sets the display mode for clips in the track. Clicking the Set Display icon allows you to choose whether you want to see frames from the actual clip in the Timeline or only the name of the clip. At the bottom left of the window, the Time Zoom Level slider enables you to change the Timeline's time intervals. For example, zooming out shows your project over less Timeline space, and zooming in shows your work over a greater area of the Timeline. Thus, if you are viewing frames in the Timeline, zooming in reveals more frames. You can also zoom in and out by clicking the edges of gray bar at the top of the Timeline.

The other buttons — Track Options dialog box, Toggle Snap to Edges, Toggle Edge Viewing, Toggle Shift Tracks Options, and Toggle Sync Mode — at the bottom left of the window enable you to change options for syncing tracks and for making edges snap together. These options are discussed in detail in Chapters 6 and 7.

The Monitor window

The Monitor window, shown in Figure 2-3, is primarily used to preview your production as you create it. When previewing your work, click the Play button to play the clips in the Timeline and click the Loop button to start from frame 1. As you work, you can also click and drag in the *tread area* (serrated lines just below the clip) to *jog*, or slowly scroll, through your footage. Below the tread area is a triangular icon called the *shuttle slider*. You can click and drag the shuttle slider to jump to a specific clip area. As you click, the time readout in the Monitor window indicates your position in the clip. The Monitor window can also be used to set the in and out points of clips. As discussed in Chapter 1, the in and out points determine which part of a clip appears in your project.

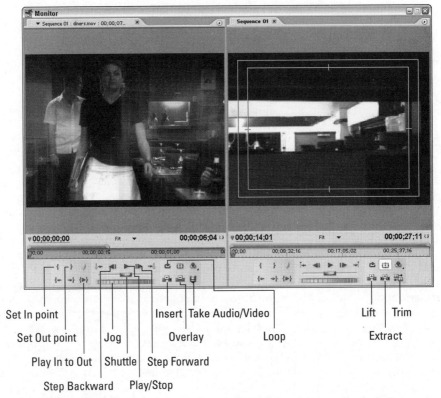

Figure 2-3: The Monitor window can be used to set in and out points of clips while you edit.

Note   In Figure 2-3, the first video clip in the Monitor window is from Digital Vision's NightMoves CD (705009f.mov). The second video clip in the Monitor window is from Digital Vision's NightMoves CD (705008f.mov). Both video clips are found in the Nite Out folder in the Chapter 1 folder (which is in the Tutorial Projects folder) that is on the DVD that accompanies this book.

The Monitor window provides three viewing modes. To switch the mode, choose Dual View, Single View, or Trim View in the Monitor Window menu. (You can also open Trim View by clicking the Trim icon at the bottom of the Monitor window.)

✦ **Dual View.** The Monitor window is set up similarly to a traditional videotape-editing studio. The source clip (footage) appears on one side of the Monitor window, and the program (edited video) appears on the other side of the window. This mode is primarily used when creating three- and four-point edits, which we cover in Chapter 13.

✦ **Single View.** The window displays one monitor as you preview your production. Using this mode is similar to viewing your production on a television monitor.

✦ **Trim View.** This mode allows for precision editing. One clip appears in one Monitor window, and the other clip appears in the second Monitor window. Precision editing of clips is covered in Chapter 13.

All the Monitor window modes provide icons (refer to Figure 2-3) that enable you to quickly set in and out edit points as well as step through the video frames.

The Audio Mixer window

The Audio Mixer window, shown in Figure 2-4, enables you to mix different audio tracks, and to create cross fades and pans. (*Panning* enables you to balance stereo channels or shift sound from the left to the right stereo channels, and vice versa). Users of earlier versions of Premiere Pro can appreciate the Audio Mixer's capability to work in real time, which means that you can mix audio tracks while viewing video tracks.

Using the palette controls, you can raise and lower audio levels for three tracks by clicking and dragging the volume fader controls with the mouse. You can also set levels in decibels by typing a number into the dB level indicator field (at the bottom of the Volume fader area). The round knob-like controls enable you to pan or balance audio. You can change the settings by clicking and dragging the knob icon. The buttons at the top of the Audio Mixer let you play all tracks, pick the tracks that you want to hear, or pick the tracks that you want to mute.

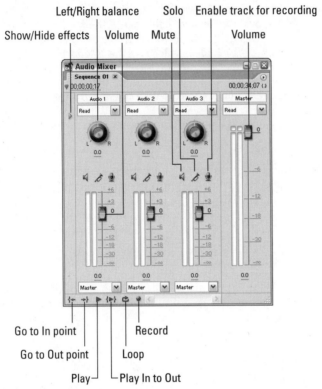

Figure 2-4: Use the Audio Mixer to mix audio and create audio effects.

The familiar controls at the bottom of the Audio Mixer window enable you to start and stop recording changes while the audio runs. Chapter 9 provides an in-depth discussion of how to use the Audio Mixer.

The Effects window

The Effects window allows you to quickly apply audio and video effects and transitions. The Effects window provides a grab bag of useful effects and transitions. For example, the Video Effects folder includes effects that change an image's contrast and distort and blur images. As you can see from Figure 2-5, the effects are organized into folders. For instance, among the many folders in the Effects window is the Distort folder, which features effects that distort clips by bending or pinching them.

Applying an effect is simple—just click and drag the effect from its palette to a clip in the Timeline. Typically, doing this opens a dialog box in which you specify options for the effect.

Tip

The Effect window allows you to create your own folders and move effects into them so that you can quickly access the effects you want to use in each project.

Premiere Pro's Transitions folder, which also appears in the Effects window, features more than 70 transitional effects. Some effects, such as the Dissolve group, can provide a smooth transition from one video clip to another. Other transitions, such as page peel, can be used as a special effect to dramatically jump from one scene to another.

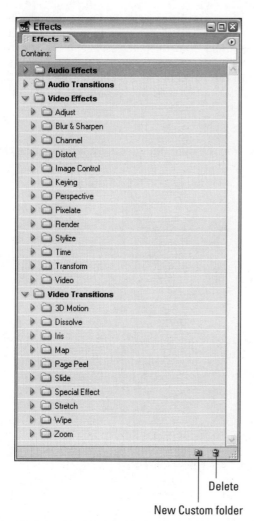

Delete

New Custom folder

Figure 2-5: Use the Effect windows to apply transitions and special effects.

If you'll be using the same transitions throughout a production, you can create a folder, name it, and keep the transitions in the custom folder for quick access.

 Cross-Reference   See Chapter 10 for more information on creating transitions; see Chapter 14 for more information on using video effects.

The Effect Controls window

The Effect Controls window, shown in Figure 2-6, allows you to quickly create and control audio and video effects and transitions. For instance, you can add an effect to a clip by selecting it in the Effect window and then dragging the effect over the clip in the Timeline or directly into the Effect Controls palette. As you can see from Figure 2-6, the Effect Controls palette includes its own version of the Timeline as well as a slider control for zooming into the Timeline. By clicking and dragging the Timeline and changing effect settings, you can change effects over time. As you change settings, you create keyframes (indicated by diamond icons) along the Timeline.

If you create effects for a clip, you can see the different effects by selecting the clip and opening the Effect Controls window.

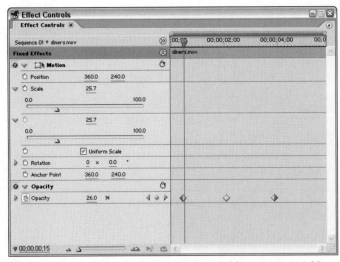

Figure 2-6: The Effect Controls palette enables you to quickly display and edit video and audio effects.

Premiere Pro's Floating Palettes

Premiere Pro's Tools, History, Info, and Effect Control *palettes* function differently than Premiere Pro's other windows. Palettes are actually floating windows that never drop below other windows, which makes them readily accessible. In addition, the tabbed format of these windows enables you to keep them in groups that can be split apart and added to.

To activate any palette, just click it. To separate it from its group, click the palette tab and then drag it away from its palette group. To add one palette to another palette group, click the palette's tab and drag it to another group.

The following sections describe each of the palette windows.

The Tools palette

The tools in Premiere Pro's Tools palette, shown in Figure 2-7, are primarily used to edit clips in the Timeline. Each tool is activated by clicking it in the toolbox. Here's a brief summary of the tools:

✦ The Selection tool is often used for selecting and moving clips on the Timeline.

✦ The Track Select tool selects all items on a track.

✦ The Ripple Edit, Rolling Edit, Slip, and Slide tools, covered in Chapter 13, are used to adjust edits on the Timeline. The Razor tool allows you to cut a clip simply by clicking on it.

✦ The Rate Stretch tool allows you to change the speed of clip by clicking and dragging a clip edge with the tool.

✦ The Pen tool allows you to create keyframes on the Timeline when adjusting video and audio effects. Audio effects are covered in Chapter 8. Video effects are covered in Chapter 14.

✦ The Hand tool enables you to scroll through different parts of the Timeline without changing the Zoom level.

✦ The Zoom tool provides yet another means of zooming in and out in the Timeline. With the Zoom tool activated, click to zoom in, and Ctrl+click to zoom out.

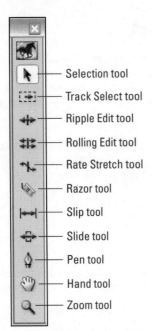

Figure 2-7: Premiere Pro's Tool palette.

- Selection tool
- Track Select tool
- Ripple Edit tool
- Rolling Edit tool
- Rate Stretch tool
- Razor tool
- Slip tool
- Slide tool
- Pen tool
- Hand tool
- Zoom tool

The History palette

Premiere Pro's History palette, shown in Figure 2-8, lets you perform virtually unlimited Undo operations. As you work, the History palette records your production steps. To return to a previous version of your project, just click that history state in the History palette. After you click and begin working again, you rewrite history— all past steps following the state you returned to are removed from the palette as new ones appear. If you want to clear all history from the palette, choose Clear in the History palette's menu (launched by clicking the right triangle). To delete a history state, select it and then click the Delete button (trashcan icon) in the palette.

Caution

If you click a history state in the History palette to undo an action and then begin to work, all steps after the one you clicked are removed from your project.

The Info palette

The Info palette provides important information about clips and transitions, and even about gaps in the Timeline. To see the Info palette in action, click a clip, transition, or empty gap in the Timeline. The Info palette shows the clip's (or gap's) size, duration, and starting and ending points, as shown in Figure 2-9.

Figure 2-8: The History palette provides virtually unlimited Undo operations.

Figure 2-9: The Info palette displays information about clips and transitions.

The Info palette is very handy when doing precise editing, because the palette displays starting and ending points of the clips as you move them in the Timeline.

The Menus

Premiere Pro features seven main menus: File, Edit, Project, Clip, Timeline, Window, and Help. The following sections provide an overview of the different menus and include tables that summarize each menu's commands.

The File menu

The File menu consists of standard Windows commands such as New, Open, Close, Save, Save As, Revert, and Quit. The menu includes commands for loading movie clips and folders full of files. The File New Sequence command can be used to add Timelines to a project. Table 2-1 summarizes the File menu commands.

Table 2-1
File Menu Commands

Command	Shortcut*	Description
New Project	N	Creates new file for new digital video production.
New ⇨ Sequence		Adds a new sequence to the current project.
New ⇨ Bin	/	Creates new bin in Project window.
New ⇨ Offline File	Alt+Shift+N	Creates new disk file that can be used for missing footage.
New ⇨ Title	F9	Opens Title window for creating text and graphic titles.
New ⇨ Bars and Tone		Adds color bar and sound tone to bin in Project window.
New ⇨ Black Video		Adds pure black video clip to bin in Project window.
New ⇨ Color Matte		Creates new color matte in Project window.
New ⇨ Universal Counting Leader		Automatically creates countdown clip.
Open Project	O	Opens Premiere Pro project files.
Open Recent Project		Loads recently used Premiere Pro movie.
Close	W	Closes Project window.
Save	S	Saves file to disk.
Save as	Shift+S	Saves file under new name or saves to different disk location; leaves user in newly created file.
Save a Copy	Alt+Shift	Creates a copy of the project on disk, but user remains in original.
Capture		Captures clips from videotape.
Capture ⇨ Batch Capture		Automatically captures multiple clips from the same tape; requires device control.
Import		Imports video, audio clip, or graphic.
Import Recent File		Imports files that have been recently used into Premiere Pro.

Command	Shortcut*	Description
Export ⇨ Movie		Exports movie to disk according to Export Movie settings dialog box.
Export ⇨ Frame		Exports Frame to be used as still image.
Export ⇨ Audio		Exports Timeline audio to disk according to settings in Audio Settings dialog box.
Export ⇨ Export to Tape		Exports Timeline to videotape.
Export ⇨ Adobe Media Encoder		Allows exporting using settings for QuickTime, Windows Media, MPEG, and Real Media Formats. Exports Timeline to videotape.
Export ⇨ Export to DVD		Burns DVD from Timeline.
Get Properties for ⇨ File		Provides size, resolution, and other digital info about project file.
Get Properties for ⇨ Selection		Provides size, resolution, and other digital info about selection. Provides size, resolution, and other digital info about project file.
Interpret Footage		Can change frame rate and pixel aspect ratio of selected item in Project window. Can also invert and ignore alpha channel.
Timecode		Sets timecode starting point of selected clip in Project window.
Exit	Q	Quits Premiere Pro.

*When using the keys in the Shortcut column, first press and hold Ctrl.

The Edit menu

Premiere Pro's Edit menu consists of standard editing commands, such as Copy, Cut, and Paste, which can be used throughout the program. The Edit menu also provides special paste functions for editing, as well as preferences for Premiere Pro's default settings. Table 2-2 describes the Edit menu commands.

Table 2-2
Edit Menu Commands

Command	Shortcut*	Description
Undo	Z	Undoes last action.
Redo	Shift+Z	Repeats last action.
Cut	X	Cuts selected item from screen, placing it into clipboard.
Copy	C	Copies selected item into clipboard.
Paste	V	Changes out point of pasted clip so it fits in paste area.
Paste Insert	Shift+V	Pastes and inserts clip.
Paste Attributes	Alt+V	Pastes attributes of one clip to another.
Clear		Cuts item from screen without saving it in clipboard.
Ripple Delete	Shift+Delete	Deletes selected clips and without leaving gap in Timeline.
Duplicate	Shift+/	Copies selected element in Project window.
Select All	A	Selects all elements in Project window.
Deselect All	Shift+A	Deselects all elements in Project window.
Find	F	Finds elements in Project window (Project window must be active).
Label		Allows choice of label colors in Project window.
Edit Original	E	Loads selected clip or graphic from disk in its original application.
Keyboard Customization		Assigns keyboard shortcuts.
Preferences		Allows you to access a variety of setup preferences.

*When using the keys in the Shortcut column, first press and hold Ctr.

The Project menu

The Project menu provides commands that change attributes for the entire project. The most important commands enable you to set compression, frame size, and frame rate. Table 2-3 describes the Project menu commands.

Table 2-3
Project Menu Commands

Command	Description
Project Settings ➪ General	Sets video movie, timebase, and time display; displays video and audio settings.
Project Settings ➪ Capture	Provides settings for capturing audio and video.
Project Settings ➪ Video Rendering	Sets options for rendering video.
Project Settings ➪ Default Sequence	Sets Timeline defaults for video and audio tracks.
Automate to Sequence	Sequentially places contents of project window files into Timeline.
Import Batch List	Imports Batch list into Project window.
Export Batch List	Exports Batch list from Project window as text.
Export Project as AAF	Exports Project in Advanced Authoring Format for use in other applications.

The Clip menu

The Clip menu provides options that change a clip's motion and transparency settings. It also includes features that aid in editing clips in the Timeline. Table 2-4 describes the Clip menu commands.

Table 2-4
Clip Menu Commands

Command	Shortcut*	Description
Rename	H	Renames clip.
Capture Settings		Changes settings for capturing audio and video.
Insert		Automatically inserts clip into Timeline at editing point.
Overlay		Drops clip into area at edit line, overlaying any existing footage.
Enable		Allows clips in Timeline to be viewed in Monitor window.

Continued

Table 2-4 *(continued)*

Command	Shortcut*	Description
Unlink Audio Video		Unlinks audio from video clip/links audio to and video.
Group	G	Places Timeline clips in a group so they can be manipulated together.
UnGroup	Shift+G	Ungroups clips.
Video Options ⇨ Frame Hold		Specifies settings for making still frame from clip.
Video Options ⇨ Field Options		Sets interlace options; also can set reverse field Field dominance.
Audio Options ⇨ Audio gain		Allows change of audio level.
Audio Options ⇨ Breakout to mono clips		Separates stereo or 5.1 clips in Project window into multiple mono clips.
Audio Options ⇨ as Stereo		Allows selected mono clip in Project window to Treat be used in stereo track.
Audio Options ⇨ Render and Replace		Renders footage and replaces old preview files.
Speed/Duration	R	Enables changing speed and/or duration.

*When using the keys in the Shortcut column, first press and hold Ctrl.

The Sequence menu

The Sequence menu enables you to preview the clips in the Timeline window and to change the number of video and audio tracks that appear in the Timeline window. Table 2-5 describes the Sequence menu commands.

Table 2-5
Sequence Menu Commands

Command	Shortcut*	Description
Render Work Area	Enter	Creates preview of work area and stores preview file on disk.
Delete Render Files		Removes render files from disk.
Razor at Current Time Indicator	K	Cuts project at current-time indicator in Timeline.

Command	Shortcut*	Description
Lift		Removes frames from in to out point set in Program section of Monitor window and leaves gap in Timeline.
Extract		Removes frames from sequence from in to out point set in Program section of Monitor window, without leaving gap in Timeline.
Apply Video Transition	D	Applies default video transition between two clips at current-time indicator.
Apply Audio Transition	Shift+D	Applies default audio transition between two clips at current-time indicator.
Zoom in	=	Zooms into Timeline.
Zoom out	-	Zooms back from Timeline.
Snap	S	Turns on/off snap to edges for clips.
Add tracks		Adds tracks to Timeline.
Delete tracks		Deletes tracks from Timeline.

*When using the keys in the Shortcut column, first press and hold Ctrl.

The Marker menu

Premiere Pro's Edit menu provides commands for creating and editing clip and sequence markers. Markers are designated by pentagon shapes just below the Timeline ruler or within a clip in a Timeline. You can use Markers to quickly jump to a specific area of the Timeline or to a specific frame in a clip. Table 2-6 summarizes the Marker menu.

Table 2-6
Marker Menu Commands

Command	Description
Set Clip Marker	Sets clip Marker for selected clip at point specified in submenu.
Go to Clip Marker	Goes to clip Marker at point specified in submenu.
Set Sequence Marker	Sets sequence Marker specified in submenu.
Go to Sequence Marker	Goes to sequence Marker specified in submenu.
Clear Sequence Marker	Clears sequence Marker specified in submenu.
Edit Sequence Marker	Edits sequence Marker.

The Title menu

Premiere Pro's Title menu becomes activated when Premiere Pro's Title Designer is open onscreen. The commands in the Title menu alter text and graphics created in the Title Designer. Table 2-7 summarizes the Title menu commands.

<table>
<tr><th colspan="3">Table 2-7
Title Menu Commands</th></tr>
<tr><th>Command</th><th>Shortcut*</th><th>Description</th></tr>
<tr><td>Font</td><td></td><td>Provides choice of fonts.</td></tr>
<tr><td>Size</td><td></td><td>Provides choice of sizes.</td></tr>
<tr><td>Type Alignment</td><td></td><td>Allows left, center, or right alignment.</td></tr>
<tr><td>Word Wrap</td><td></td><td>Turns on and off word wrap.</td></tr>
<tr><td>Orientation</td><td></td><td>Controls Horizontal and Vertical orientation of objects.</td></tr>
<tr><td>Tab Stops</td><td>Shift +T</td><td>Sets tabs in text box.</td></tr>
<tr><td>Templates</td><td>J</td><td>Allows use and creation of templates for titles.</td></tr>
<tr><td>Roll/Crawl Options</td><td></td><td>Allows creation and control of animated titles.</td></tr>
<tr><td>Logo</td><td></td><td>Allows graphics to be imported into title.</td></tr>
<tr><td>Transform</td><td></td><td>Provides visual transformation commands: Position, Scale, Rotation, and Opacity.</td></tr>
<tr><td>Select</td><td></td><td>Provides commands for selecting stacked objects.</td></tr>
<tr><td>Arrange</td><td></td><td>Sends stacked objects forward and backward.</td></tr>
<tr><td>Position</td><td></td><td>Positions selected item onscreen.</td></tr>
<tr><td>Align Objects</td><td></td><td>Aligns deselected objects.</td></tr>
<tr><td>Distribute Objects</td><td></td><td>Distributes or spreads out selected objects onscreen.</td></tr>
<tr><td>View</td><td></td><td>Allows viewing of title and action-safe areas, text baselines, and tab Markers.</td></tr>
</table>

*When using the keys in the Shortcut column, first press and hold Ctrl.

The Window menu

The Window menu enables you to open windows and palettes. Most of the commands work identically to each other. Choose the name of the window or palette that you want to open in the menu, and that window opens. You can open windows specific to different types of editing work by choosing Window ⇨ Workspace ⇨ Editing, Window ⇨ Workspace ⇨ Effects, Window ⇨ Workspace ⇨ Audio, or Window ⇨ Workspace ⇨ Color Correction.

You can also save your viewing setup by choosing Window ⇨ Workspace ⇨ Save Workspace. Later, you can delete the workspace by choosing Window ⇨ Workspace ⇨ Delete.

Cross-Reference   To learn more about workspace settings, refer to Chapter 1.

The Help menu

Premiere Pro's Help menu provides formatted documents that are viewable in a Web browser. Choose Help ⇨ Contents to load the main help screen. From this screen, which is shown in Figure 2-10, you can click a topic to learn about it. If you click Index, the alphabet appears. Clicking a letter loads the index listings for terms that begin with that letter. If you click the Search button, you can search for help by entering a word to search for. For example, if you type the word *edit* and click Search, a long list of topics related to the word edit appears. Clicking one of the edit topics brings you to the Help page for that item.

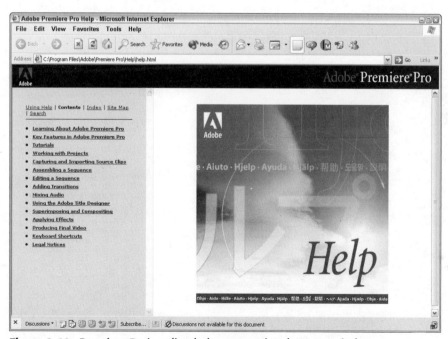

Figure 2-10: Premiere Pro's online help appears in a browser window.

Other Help menu commands access information from the Web. Choose Help ➪ Adobe Online to access Adobe's Web site. Choose Help ➪ Support or Updates to download information from Adobe. To register your version of Premiere Pro online, choose Help ➪ Registration.

Summary

Premiere Pro's windows, menus, and palettes provide you with an efficient interface and powerful tools to create digital video productions.

✦ The Project window displays production elements.

✦ The Timeline window provides a visual display of your project. You can edit audio and video directly in the Timeline.

✦ Use the Effect Controls window to create video and audio effects and audio transitions.

✦ The Monitor window previews your production and allows you to preview edits.

✦ The Audio Mixer enables you to mix audio and create audio effects.

✦   ✦   ✦

Customizing Premiere Pro

✦   ✦   ✦   ✦

In This Chapter

Customizing
keyboard commands

Setting preferences

✦   ✦   ✦   ✦

Once you become familiar with Premiere Pro, you're certain to appreciate its many time-saving features. Nevertheless, as you edit and fine-tune your work, you'll undoubtedly want to save as much time as possible. Fortunately, Premiere Pro provides numerous utilities for keyboard and program customization. This chapter takes a look at how you can create your own keyboard shortcuts to customize Premiere Pro to respond to your every touch. The chapter also provides an overview of Premiere Pro's default settings, which you can customize to your own specifications.

Creating Keyboard Shortcuts

Keyboard shortcuts can help take the drudgery out of repetitive tasks and speed up your production work. Fortunately, Premiere Pro provides keyboard shortcuts for activating its tools, opening all its windows, and accessing most of its menu commands. As you'll soon see, these commands are preset but can easily be altered. If a keyboard command does not exist for a Premiere Pro operation, you can create your own.

To change keyboard shortcuts, open the Keyboard Customization dialog box by choosing Edit ➪ Keyboard Customization. The Keyboard Customization dialog box, shown in Figure 3-1, is divided into three sections: Application, Windows, and Tools.

Changing Application keyboard preferences

To change Application keyboard commands, choose Application in the Set drop-down menu. To change or create a keyboard setting, click the triangle to open up the menu heading that contains the command. For instance, assume that you want to create a keyboard shortcut to use for the Revert command, which allows you to immediately return to the previously saved version of your work. First, click the triangle icon to open the File menu commands. To create the command, next click in the Shortcut column in the Revert line. When the Revert command line is activated, dotted lines appear around it, as shown in Figure 3-2. To create the keyboard command, simply press a function key or a modifier key combination, such as Ctrl+R, Ctrl+Shift+R, or Alt+Shift+R. If you make a mistake or want to cancel the command, simply click Clear.

Changing Premiere Pro Windows keyboard preferences

Premiere Pro's keyboard customization of its Window commands is quite extensive. To access Premiere Pro's Windows Keyboard commands, choose Windows from the drop-down menu in the Keyboard Customization dialog box. The keyboard commands found here provide shortcuts for many commands that would normally require one click or clicking and dragging the mouse. Thus, even if you are not going to create or change the existing keyboard commands, it's worth examining the Windows Keyboard commands to see the many timesaving shortcuts Premiere Pro offers. For instance, Figure 3-3 shows the keyboard shortcuts for Timeline operations. Notice that you can use a few simple keystrokes to nudge a clip left or right one or five frames. If you want to change a keyboard command, follow the same procedures described in the preceding section: Click in the shortcut column of the command line and press the command keys you want to use for the shortcut.

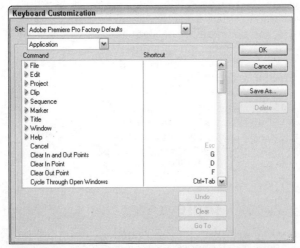

Figure 3-1: The Keyboard Customization dialog box allows you to customize keyboard commands.

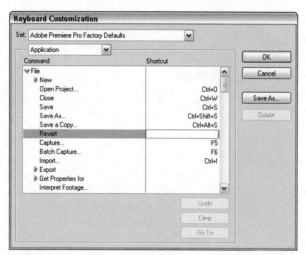

Figure 3-2: Creating a keyboard shortcut for the Revert command.

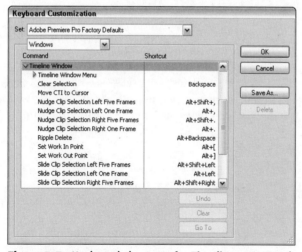

Figure 3-3: Keyboard shortcuts for Timeline commands.

Changing Tools keyboard preferences

Premiere Pro provides keyboard shortcuts for each of its tools. To access the Tools keyboard shortcuts, shown in Figure 3-4, choose Tools from the drop-down menu in the Keyboard Customization dialog box. To change a keyboard command in the Tools section of the dialog box, simply click in the shortcut column in a tool's row and enter your keystroke shortcut on the keyboard.

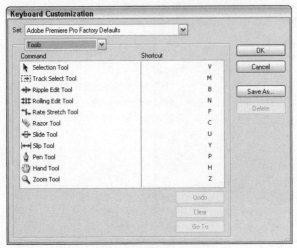

Figure 3-4: Keyboard shortcuts for tools.

Saving and loading custom commands

As you change keyboard commands, Premiere Pro automatically adds a new Custom set to the Set menu. This prevents you from overwriting Premiere Pro's factory default settings. If you want to provide a name for the Custom set or create multiple custom sets, click Save As in the Keyboard Customization window. This opens the Name Key Set dialog box, shown in Figure 3-5, where you can enter a name. After you save the name, it appears in the Set drop-down list, along with Adobe's factory default settings. If you want to delete the custom set, select it from the drop-down list and click Delete.

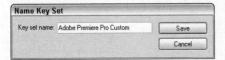

Figure 3-5: Name a custom setting in the Name Key Set dialog box.

Setting Program Preferences

Premiere Pro's Program preferences control a variety of default settings that load each time you open a project. You can change these preference settings in the current project, but the changes aren't activated until you create or open a new one. You can change the defaults for capture devices and the duration of transitions and still images, as well as the label colors in the Project menus. This section provides an overview of the many default settings Premiere Pro offers. You access each of the settings by choosing Edit ⇨ Preferences and then picking a choice from the Preferences submenu. Here is a review of the different sections of Premiere Pro's Preferences dialog box.

General

The General preferences, shown in Figure 3-6, provide settings for a variety of Premiere Pro default preferences. The commands control a few interface and clip settings:

✦ **Show Tool Tips.** Turns on Premiere Pro's "hover help," which displays the names of tools and buttons when you move the mouse over them.

✦ **In/out points, show media offset.** These settings allow you to change the video and audio that appear before and after in and out points. Set the time in seconds in the Preroll field for video and audio you want to appear before in points. Set the time in seconds in the Postroll field for video and audio that you want to appear after the out point.

✦ **Video Transition Default Duration.** Controls the duration of transitions when you first apply them. By default, this field is set to 30 frames — approximately 1 second.

✦ **Audio Transition Default Duration.** Controls the duration of audio transitions when you first apply them. The default setting is 1 second.

✦ **User Interface Brightness.** Controls the brightness of Premiere Pro's windows. Click and drag the slider to the left to create a lighter gray background; click and drag to the right to darken window backgrounds.

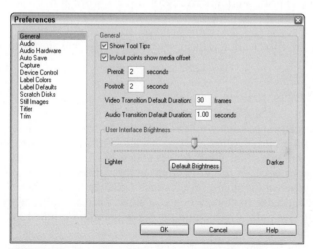

Figure 3-6: The General section in the Preferences dialog box.

Audio

Premiere Pro's Audio preferences, shown in Figure 3-7, control settings for Premiere Pro's Audio mixer:

✦ **Automatch Time.** This setting is used in conjunction with the Touch options in the Audio Mixer. When you choose the Touch option in the Audio Mixer window, Premiere Pro returns to the previous values used before changes were made—but only after a specific number of seconds. The Automatch setting controls the time interval before Premiere Pro returns to the previous values before audio changes were made.

✦ **5.1 Mixdown Type.** These settings control 5.1 surround-sound track mixes. A 5.1 track is composed of these essential channels: left, center, and right channels (the first three of five main channels), with left- and right-rear channels (two more channels make five), plus a low frequency channel (LFE). The 5.1 Mixdown Type drop-down menu allows you change settings for the channels used when mixing, which reduces the number of audio channels.

Cross-
Reference   For more information about using the Audio Mixer, see Chapter 9.

Audio Hardware

The Audio Hardware preferences, shown in Figure 3-8, provide details and options about installed audio hardware. The figure shows two audio channels providing both stereo and 5.1 surround sound. The Audio Hardware section also includes settings for Audio Stream Input/Output cards (ASIO). In the Audio Hardware section, the Latency option controls the size of a memory cache when available audio is processed. Adobe recommends short latency settings for precise work and long latency for special effects processing.

If you click ASIO Settings, the choices that appear are based on the specific hardware installed in your computer.

Auto Save

If you're worried about forgetting to save your projects as you work, don't worry too much. By default, Premiere Pro's Auto Save preference is turned on. When this option is turned on, Premiere Pro saves your project every 20 minutes and creates five different versions of your work. In the Auto Save section, shown in Figure 3-9, you can change the time interval for saving. You can also change the number of different versions that you would like to save. When you enlist Auto Save, Premiere Pro saves your work along this path: MyDocuments/Adobe/Adobe Premiere Pro/1.0 Adobe Premier Pro Auto Save.

Note Don't worry about consuming massive amounts of disk space with Auto Save. When Premiere Pro saves, it only saves references to the media files. It doesn't resave the files each time it creates a new version of your work.

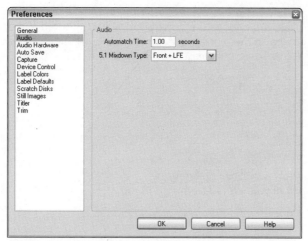

Figure 3-7: The Audio section in the Preferences dialog box provides options relating to Premiere Pro's Audio Mixer.

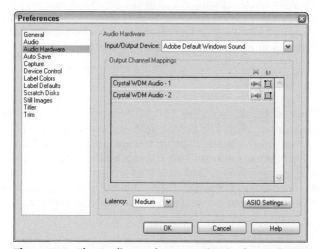

Figure 3-8: The Audio Hardware section in the Preferences dialog box provides settings for Premiere Pro's Audio Mixer.

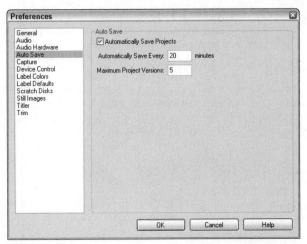

Figure 3-9: Using Premiere Pro's Auto Save preferences, you can have multiple versions of your work saved automatically.

Capture

Premiere Pro's default Capture settings provide options for Video and Audio capture. The Capture preferences are self-explanatory. You can choose to abort the capture when frames are dropped. You can choose to view a report onscreen about the capture process and dropped frames. The Generate batch log file option saves a log file to disk, listing the results of an unsuccessful batch capture.

Device Control

The Device Control preferences, shown in Figure 3-10, let you choose a current capture device such as a camcorder or VCR. The Preroll setting allows you to set the interval between the times the tape rolls and capture begins. This lets the camcorder or VCR get up to speed before capture. The Timecode Offset option allows you to specify an interval in quarter-frames that provides an offset between the timecode of the captured material and the actual tape. This option allows you to attempt to set the timecode of the captured video so that it matches frames on the videotape.

Clicking the Options button in the dialog box opens the DV Device Control options dialog box where you can choose the brand of your capture device, set the timecode format, and check to see whether the device is online or offline.

For more information about capturing video and the DV Device Control Options dialog box, see Chapter 5.

Label Colors and Label Defaults

The Label Colors default setting allows you to change colors of the labels that appear in the Project window. As discussed in Chapter 2, you can assign specific colors to different media types in the Project window. To change colors, click the colored label swatch. This opens Premiere Pro's Color Settings dialog box. Here you can change colors by clicking and dragging the vertical slider and by clicking in the rectangular colored box. You can also change colors by entering numbers into the numeric fields. After you change colors, you can edit the color names in the Label Colors section of the Preferences dialog box.

If you don't like the choices Adobe made when assigning label colors to different media types, you can change color assignments in the Label Defaults section. For instance, to change the Label color of video to red, click the pop-up menu in the Video line and choose Red.

Scratch Disks

The Scratch Disks section allows you to set the default disks for Captured Video, Captured Audio, Video Previews, Audio Preview, and Conformed Audio. To set a specific disk and folder, click the Browse button and navigate to the folder on the storage device that you want to use.

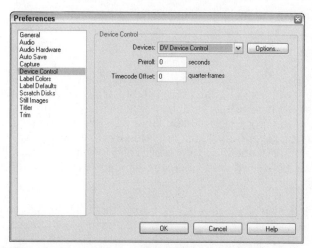

Figure 3-10: Premiere Pro's Device Control preferences allow you to choose a Capture device.

Still Images, Titler, and Trim

The Still Images, Titler, and Trim preferences provide a variety of default settings for still images and clips. The Still Images setting allows you to set the duration of still images that you insert into a production.

The Titler preferences control the display of the style swatches and fonts browser that appear in the Adobe Title Designer (choose File ➪ New ➪ Title to open the Title Designer).

The Trim preferences allow you to change the Large trim offset that appears in the Monitor window when the Monitor window is in Trim view. By default, the Large Trim offset is set to 5 frames. When you click the Trim offset button, five frames are trimmed from the program's in or out point. If you change the value in the Large Trim offset field in the Trim section, the next time you create a project, that value appears as a button in the Monitor window.

Cross-Reference   See Chapter 13 for a discussion on how to edit in Trim view in the Monitor window.

Summary

Premiere Pro provides many options for customizing its commands and features:

✦ Use the Edit ➪ Keyboard Customization command to customize keyboard commands for the tools and other windows.

✦ To edit default settings in Premiere Pro, choose Edit ➪ Preferences.

✦   ✦   ✦

Working with Project Settings

When you first begin creating projects in Premiere Pro, the desktop video terminology and vast number of settings for video, compression, capturing, and exporting can seem overwhelming. If you're just getting started with Premiere Pro and are primarily interested in learning the basics of the program, you needn't worry too much about understanding all the commands in all the program's project-setting dialog boxes. However, if you don't understand such terms as *frame rates*, *frame size*, and *compression* — terms used in Premiere Pro's project-setting dialog boxes — you're likely to be frustrated when you attempt to output your production.

This chapter provides an overview of key desktop video concepts. It also provides a guide to the different dialog boxes in which you designate the startup settings for Premiere Pro projects. For the most part, these are settings that Premiere Pro uses while you are importing and editing in Premiere Pro. Settings for capturing video are covered in Chapter 5. Project settings for exporting video are covered later in Part V of this book.

What Is Digital Video?

In the past few years, the term *digital video* has taken on a variety of new meanings. To the consumer, digital video may simply mean shooting video with the latest video camera from Canon, Sony, or JVC. A digital video camera is named as such because the picture information is stored as a digital signal. The camera translates the picture data into digital signals and saves it on tape in much the same way that your computer saves data to a hard drive.

Older video-recording systems store information in an analog format on tape. In analog format, information is sent in waves rather than as specific individual bits of data.

In Premiere Pro, a digital video *project* usually contains video, still images, and audio that has been *digitized*, or converted from analog to digital format. Video and audio information stored in digital format from digital video cameras can be transferred directly to a computer through an IEEE 1394 port. (Although Apple Computer's trade name for the IEEE port is *FireWire* and Sony's is i.LINK, the specifications are identical.) Because the data is already digitized, the IEEE 1394 port provides a fast means of transferring the data. Using video footage shot on an analog video camera or recorded on an analog video deck, however, requires the additional step of first digitizing the footage. Analog-to-digital capture boards that can be installed in PCs generally handle this process. These boards digitize both audio and video. Other types of visual media, such as photographs and slides, also need to be converted to a digital format before Premiere Pro can use them. Scanners digitize slides and still photos, but you can also digitize slides and photos by photographing them with a digital still camera. Scanning an analog image saves the image to the computer's hard drive, where it can then be loaded directly into Premiere Pro. After the project has been fine-tuned, the last step of the digital video production process is to output it to your hard drive, a DVD, or to videotape.

Note   The abbreviation DV refers to the digital video format used in consumer and "prosumer" camcorders. D1 is a digital format used by many professionals in the broadcasting industry. Both DV and D1 formats utilize specific frame sizes and frame rates, which are discussed in the section "Digital video essentials" later in this chapter.

Digital video provides numerous advantages over traditional analog video. If you use a digital video camera, your video clips are generally superior to analog clips. In digital video, you can freely duplicate video and audio without losing quality. With analog video, on the other hand, you "go down a generation" each time you copy a clip on videotape, thus losing a little quality.

In the context of Premiere Pro, one advantage of digital video is that it enables you to edit video in a *nonlinear* fashion. Traditional video editing requires the editor to assemble a videotape production piece by piece from start to finish in a *linear* manner. In linear editing, each video clip is recorded after the previous clip onto a *program* reel. One problem with a linear system is the time it takes to re-edit a segment or to insert a segment that is not the same duration as the original segment to be replaced. If you need to re-edit a clip in the middle of a production, the entire program needs to be reassembled. The process is similar to creating a necklace with a string of beads. If you want to add beads to the middle of the necklace, you need to pull out all the beads, insert the new ones, and put the old beads back in the necklace, all the while being careful to keep everything in the same order.

In a nonlinear video system, you can freely insert, remove, and rearrange footage. If you reconsider the bead necklace analogy, nonlinear editing enables you to magically pop the beads on the necklace wherever you want, as if the string didn't exist. Because the image is made up of digital pixels that can be transformed and replaced, digital video enables you to create numerous transitions and effects that are not possible on a purely analog system. To return to the necklace analogy, a digital system lets you not only insert and replace beads freely, but also change their color and shape at will.

Digital video essentials

Before you begin creating a digital video project, it's important to understand some basic terminology. Terms such as *frame rate, compression,* and *frame size* abundantly populate Premiere Pro's dialog boxes. Understanding these terms helps you make the right decisions as you create new projects and export them to videotape, to your hard drive, or to DVD.

Video frame rates

If you take a strip of motion picture film in your hand and hold it up to the light, you'll see the individual picture frames that comprise the production. If you look closely, you'll see how motion is created: Each frame of a moving image is slightly different than the previous frame. A change in the visual information in each frame creates the illusion of motion.

If you hold up a piece of videotape to light, you won't see any frames. However, the video camera does electronically store the picture data into individual video frames. The standard DV NTSC (North American and Japanese standard) frame rate in video is 29.97 frames per second; in Europe, the standard frame rate is 25 frames per second. Europe uses the PAL system (Phase Alternate Line). The standard frame rate of film is 24 frames per second.

Frame rate is extremely important in Premiere Pro because it helps determine how smooth the motion will be in your project. Typically, you set the frame rate of your project to match your video footage. For example, if you capture video directly into Premiere Pro using DV equipment, the capture rate is set to 29.97 frames per second, which matches Premiere Pro's DV project setting frame rate. If you need to import footage captured at different frame rates, you can use Premiere Pro's Interpret Footage command to change the frame rate of clips to match that of your project. Although you will want the project frame rate to be the same rate as the source footage, you may want to export at a lower frame rate if you are preparing the project for the Web. By exporting at a lower frame rate, you enable the production to quickly download to a Web browser.

Frame size and square and non-square pixels

The frame size of a digital video production determines the width and height of your production onscreen. In Premiere Pro, frame size is measured in *pixels.* A pixel is the smallest picture element displayed on a computer monitor. The standard shape of a computer pixel is square. If you are working on a project that uses DV (Digital Video) footage, you'll typically be using the DV standard of 720 x 480 pixels. The standard frame size for D1 is 720 x 486. If you're not creating a DV or D1 project, you should still set the frame size of your project to match the frame size of your footage. For instance, if your footage was shot at 640 x 480, you'll typically use these frame dimensions as the frame dimensions of your project. If you're outputting to the Web or to a multimedia project, you can change frame size when exporting your project to your hard disk.

Before the advent of DV, the frame size used in most computer video systems was 640 x 480 pixels. This conformed nicely to the aspect ratio (width to height) of television, which is 4:3 (640/160=4 and 480/160=3). Thus, for every four square horizontal pixels, there are three square vertical pixels.

But when you're working with a frame size of 720 x 480 or 720 x 486, the math isn't so clean. The problem: If you create a 720 x 486 image in a program that uses square pixels, the aspect ratio is 3:2, not the television standard of 4:3. How do you squeeze 720 x 480 pixels into a 4:3 ratio? The answer is to use rectangular pixels, essentially non-square pixels that are taller than they are wide.

Understanding pixel aspect ratio

If the concept of square versus non-square pixels seems a bit confusing, remember that 640 x 480 provides a 4:3 aspect ratio. One way of viewing the problem presented by a 720 x 480 frame size is to ask how you can convert the width of 720 down to 640. Try a little high school math: 720 times what number equals 640? The answer is .90 — 640 is 90% of 720. Thus, if each square pixel would be kind enough to shave its width to $\frac{9}{10}$ of its former self, you could translate 720 x 480 into a 4:3 aspect ratio. If you're working with DV, you'll frequently see the number 0.9. When you create a DV project in Premiere Pro, you'll see that the DV pixel aspect ratio is set to 0.9 (short for 0.9:1) instead of 1 (for square pixels). Furthermore, if you import footage with a frame size of 720 x 480 into Premiere Pro, the pixel aspect ratio is automatically set to 0.9. In PAL DV systems (720 x 576), the pixels are horizontally longer than they are wide, and the pixel aspect ratio is 1.067.

Tip   You can calculate the pixel aspect ratio for an image by using this formula: frame height/frame width x aspect ratio width/aspect ratio height. Thus, for a 4:3 aspect ratio, 480/640 * 4/3=1 and 720/480 x 4/3=.9. For PAL systems, the calculation would be 576/720 x 4/3=1.067.

Fortunately, when you create a DV project in Premiere Pro, the pixel aspect ratio is chosen automatically. Premier also adjusts the computer display so that images created from non-square pixel footages are not distorted when viewed on your square pixel computer display. Nonetheless, it's important to understand the concept of square versus non-square pixels because you may find it necessary to work in a project with source material created from both square and non-square pixels. For instance, if you import footage created with an analog video board (which digitizes using square pixels) and images created in Photoshop (square pixels) into a DV project with DV footage, you'll have two flavors of pixels in your video stew. To prevent distortion, you may need to use Premiere Pro's Interpret Footage command and properly set frame sizes of graphics created in Photoshop and Illustrator. (For more information, see the sidebar "Preventing display distortion" later in this chapter.)

RGB color and bit depth

A color image on the computer screen is created from the combination of red, green, and blue color phosphors. The combination of different amounts of red, green, and blue light enables you to display millions of different colors. In digital imaging programs, such as Premiere Pro and Photoshop, the red, green, and blue color components are often called *channels*. Each channel can provide 256 colors (2^8 — often referred to as 8-bit color because 8 bits are in a byte), and the combination of 256 red colors × 256 green colors × 256 blue colors results in over 17.6 million colors. Thus, when creating projects in Premiere Pro, you'll see most color depth options set to millions of colors. A color depth of millions of colors is often called *24-bit color* (2^{24}).

Note   Although television uses a monitor very much like a computer display to provide color, it does not use RGB color. Instead, television uses a color system called YCC. The Y stands for *luminance*, which essentially controls brightness levels for grayscale or black-and-white images. Both C channels are color channels. YCC was created when television was transitioning between black-and-white and color systems to enable those with black-and-white systems as well as those with color systems to view the TV signal.

Compression

Larger frame sizes provide greater bit depth, and more frames per second produce a better quality Premiere Pro digital video project. Unfortunately, a full-frame, 24-bit color, 30 frames per second video production requires vast amounts of storage space. You can easily calculate how much hard drive space a full-frame production would take up. Start by multiplying the frame dimensions. Assume that you are creating a project at 720 × 480 pixels. Each pixel needs to be capable of displaying red, green, and blue elements of color, so multiply 720 × 480 × 3. Each frame is more than 1MB. Thus, one second of video at 30 frames a second more than 30MB. (This doesn't even include sound.) A five-minute uncompressed production consumes more than 8GB of storage space.

To store more data in less space with a minimum loss of quality, software engineers have created a variety of video compression schemes. The two primary compression schemes are spatial and temporal:

  ✦ **Spatial compression (also known as intra-frame).** In spatial compression, computer software analyzes the pixels in an image and then saves a pattern that simulates the entire image. DV camcorders primarily use intra-frame compression.

  ✦ **Temporal compression.** Temporal compression works by analyzing the pixels in video frames for screen areas that don't change. Without temporal compression, different frames are saved to disk for each second of video, whether the image onscreen changes or not. Rather than creating many frames with the same image, temporal compression works by creating one keyframe for image areas that don't change. The system calculates the differences between frames to create the compression. For example, for a video that consists of frames of a flower that sometimes blows in the wind, the computer needs to store only one frame for the flower and record more frames only when the flower moves.

When you work with compression in Premiere Pro, you don't choose spatial or temporal compression. Instead, depending upon your project settings, you choose compression settings by specifying a *CODEC*. CODEC stands for compression and decompression. Software manufacturers create codecs. For example, when exporting from Premiere Pro, you can use a CODEC called Cinepak, which provides temporal compression. When you export your project, you can specify how many keyframes you want to output per second.

A DV camera compresses the video even before it is transferred to your computer. The standard compression ratio used is 5:1, which makes the transferred video signal five times smaller than the original video signal. The DV video data rate is 25 Mbytes a second, which means that every second of video consumes approximately 3.5MB of disk space. DV camcorders primarily use *intra-frame*. For a very technical discussion on how a DV camera compresses video, see the Video Signal Processing section of the DVCAM1 Overview brochure at `www.sony.ca/dvcam`. Click the Reference menu and choose brochures.

QuickTime, Video for Windows, and MPEG

In order for your computer to use a video compression system, software and sometimes hardware must be installed. Both Macs and PCs usually come with video compression software built into their operating systems. QuickTime is the digital video compression system automatically installed with the Macintosh operating system; Video for Windows is the digital video compression system automatically installed in the Windows operating system. QuickTime can also be installed on PCs. Because QuickTime is cross-platform, it is one of the most popular digital video systems for CD-ROM and Web digital video. When you export a movie from Premiere Pro, you can access the QuickTime or AVI compression settings, enabling you to choose from a list of QuickTime or AVI codecs. If you have a capture board installed in your computer, the capture board typically provides a set of codecs from which to choose.

It's also important to understand that the QuickTime and AVI video clips can be edited in Premiere Pro and integrated into a Premiere Pro project. Other compression systems, such as MPEG (named after the Motion Picture Engineering Group, which oversees the creation of different MPEG file formats), require Premiere Pro to do too much processing to maintain high quality and compressed video—without added hardware. Although you can import an MPEG file into Premiere Pro, the program is not designed to render video in this format without a video board that handles MPEG. The best indicator of this limitation is the fact that no MPEG listings appear in the New Project dialog box when you create a project (see Figure 4-1 in the upcoming section "Understanding Project Settings").

Although Premiere Pro provides no MPEG project settings, it enables you to output in MPEG-1 or MPEG-2 format. Outputting in MPEG formats is covered in Chapter 19. MPEG-2 compression is used to create DVDs, which can provide up to two hours of video with eight tracks of audio. MPEG-1 compression, which can be used on the Web or on CD-ROMs, provides VHS-quality video. The newest MPEG standard, MPEG-4 (available in QuickTime 6), provides even better compression than MPEG-2. Because MPEG-4 is an international standard, it will undoubtedly be one of the chief file formats used to deliver audio and video over the Web.

Digital format overview

If you haven't dealt extensively with the concepts of video formats, frame sizes and aspect ratios, you might find it helpful to see these formats organized in tabular format. Table 4-1 provides an overview of DV formats for NTSC and PAL. As you work in Premiere Pro, you'll find that the items listed in this table are in project settings and export settings dialog boxes.

Table 4-1
Digital Video Specs

Format	Frame Size	Aspect Ratio/ Pixel Aspect Ratio	Frames per Second
D1/DV NTSC NTSC	720 x 486/720 x 480	4:3/0.9	29.97
DV NTSC (WideScreen)	720 x 480	16:9/1.2	29.97
D1/DV (PAL)	720 x 576	4:3/1.067	25
DV Widescreen (PAL)	720 x 576	16:9/1.422	25

Understanding Project Settings

After you gain a basic understanding of frame rate, frame size, and compression, you can better choose settings when you create a project in Premiere Pro. If you choose your project settings carefully, you'll produce the best quality video. Figure 4-1 shows Premiere Pro's New Project dialog box, which appears when you create a new project in Premiere Pro.

The New Project dialog box appears when you click New Project after starting Premiere Pro or when you choose File ➪ New Project. The creators of Premiere Pro have streamlined the process of choosing project settings. To get started, you simply need to click one of the available presets. Notice that Premiere Pro provides DV (Digital Video format) presets for NTSC television and the PAL standards. Premiere Pro also provides non-DV presets for NTSC, PAL, and other projects based on square pixel footage.

How do you decide which preset to choose? If you are working on a DV project and your video is not going to be in a widescreen format (16:9 aspect ratio), you could choose the Standard 32 Khz option. The 32 Khz indicates the sound quality, which should match the sound quality of your source footage. If your footage was digitized using an analog to digital capture board, your footage undoubtedly uses square pixels. If this is the case, use one of the Non-DV presets. If your source footage is composed of graphics created in a computer animation program or a computer application such as Photoshop (which uses square pixels), you should also choose one of the non-DV presets. When choosing a non-DV preset, choose a preset that matches the frame size of your footage. If you have a third-party video capture board, you may see other presets specifically created to work with your capture board.

Clicking one of the presets displays the preselected settings for Compression, Frame Size, Pixel Aspect Ratio (discussed later in this chapter), Frame Rate, and Bit Depth, as well as for audio settings. If you are working with DV footage, you probably will not need to change the default settings. If you need to alter the presets, click the Custom Settings tab. This opens up the General section of the New Project dialog box.

Tip If you create a custom preset in the Custom Tab of the New Project dialog box, you can save it for use in other projects by clicking Save Preset. Saved presets can be loaded from a folder called Custom that appears in the Load Preset tab in the New Project dialog box.

When you export a movie, a Settings button also lets you change settings.

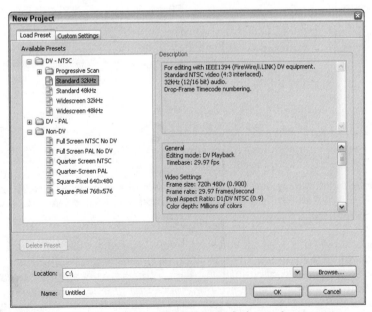

Figure 4-1: The New Project dialog box includes project presets.

Preventing display distortion

When non-square pixels that haven't been altered are viewed on a computer monitor (which displays square pixels), images may appear distorted. The distortion does not appear when the footage is viewed on a video monitor instead of on a computer display. Fortunately, Premiere Pro adjusts non-square pixel footage on a computer display and, thus, does not distort non-square footage when imported into a DV project. However, if you create a graphic at 720 × 480 (or 720 × 486) in a square pixel program such as Photoshop 7 and then import it into an NTSC DV project, the graphic may appear distorted in Premiere Pro. The graphic is distorted because Premiere Pro automatically converts it to a non-square 0.9 pixel aspect ratio. If you create a graphic at 720 × 576 in a square pixel program and import it into a PAL DV project, Premiere Pro also converts it to a non-square pixel aspect ratio. Distortion can occur because Premiere Pro interprets any digital source file created at a DV frame size as non-square pixel data. (This file import rule is specified in a text file called "Interpretation Rules.txt." The file is found in Premiere Pro's Plug-in folder and can be edited so that Premiere Pro interprets graphic and video files differently.)

Fortunately, if you are creating graphics in Photoshop CS, you're in luck. Photoshop CS features a 720 × 480 DV preset that sets the pixel aspect ratio in a file to 0.9. If you use this preset, you should be able to import Photoshop files seamlessly into Premiere Pro DV projects without any distortion. However, If you are *not* using Photoshop CS, you should create full-screen graphics for DV projects at 720 × 534 or 720 × 540 (768 × 576, PAL). After creating your graphics, import them into Premiere Pro with the General Project Settings option "Scale clip to project dimensions when adding to sequence" selected. This will squeeze graphics to fit into your DV project without distortion.

If you do create a graphic file at 720 × 480 in a square pixel program such as Photoshop 7 and import it into a Premiere Pro DV project, you may notice distortion because Premiere Pro displays the file as thought it was created with non-square pixels. Fortunately, you can "fix" the image in Premiere Pro using its Interpret Footage command. Note that, if you use this technique, Premiere Pro must interpolate (adding about 10% more pixels to the image), which might make it appear less sharp.

Here's how to convert your graphics back to square pixels using Premiere Pro's Interpret Footage command:

1. **Select the graphic image in the Project window. Note that the Project window indicates that the pixel aspect ratio is not set to 1.0.**

2. **To change the Pixel Aspect ratio back to square pixels, choose File⇨Interpret Footage.**

3. **In the Pixel Aspect Ratio section of the Interpret Footage dialog box, click Conform to.** Then choose Square Pixels (1.0) in the pop-up menu. Click OK.

   After you click OK, the listing in the Project window indicates that the image has been converted to square pixels.

Video and audio project settings are divided into four categories: General, Capture, Video Rendering, and Default Sequence. The sections that follow describe the General, Video Rendering, and Default Sequences settings. All of these sections of the New Project dialog box are accessible when you first create a project. If you want to view project settings after creating a project, choose, Project ➪ Project Settings ➪ General Settings. Note, however, that after you create a project, most settings cannot be changed.

Cross-Reference   You can find out more about audio settings in Chapter 8 and capture settings in Chapter 5. See Chapter 19 for more information about exporting Premiere Pro projects.

General settings

The General settings section of the New Project dialog box, shown in Figure 4-2, provides a summary of the individual project settings.

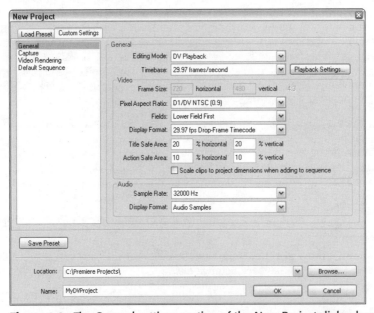

Figure 4-2: The General settings section of the New Project dialog box.

You can access this dialog box by choosing File ➪ New Project (or by clicking the New Project button) and then clicking the Custom Settings tab. To access this dialog box after creating a project, choose Project ➪ Project Settings ➪ General.

The following list describes the choices.

✦ **Editing mode.** The editing mode is determined by the chosen preset in the Load Preset tab of the New Project dialog box. The editing mode choice sets the Timeline playback method as well as compression settings. When you choose a DV preset, the Editing mode is automatically set to DV Playback. If you are working with analog video that uses non-square pixels, you can change the Editing mode to Video for Windows, which allows you to access frame size options and which can be changed to match the footage you will be using.

If you are wording with a DV preset, you can click the Playback Settings button, which opens the DV Playback Settings dialog box shown in Figure 4-3. There you can select Playback on DV Hardware and Desktop. This option allows you to view the playback on a monitor connected to a VCR or your DV camcorder. If you will be exporting your project to videotape, outputting to a video monitor or to your camcorder monitor (rather than to your computer display) will provide the best preview of your project. The window also allows you to choose where you prefer to have effects rendered. If you're not outputting to video, choose Desktop Only. The last choice allows you to choose where you want the audio played if you are exporting to videotape.

Note Third party software plug-ins may also allow different playback options.

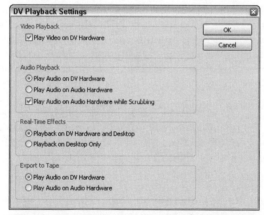

Figure 4-3: Use the DV Playback Settings dialog box to select playback options for DV camcorders and VCRs.

✦ **Timebase.** Timebase determines how Premiere Pro divides video frames each second when calculating editing precision. In most projects, the Timebase should match the frame rate of captured footage. For DV projects, the Timebase is set to 29.97 and cannot be changed. Timebase for PAL projects should be set to 25; film projects should be set to 24. The Timebase setting also determines which choices are available in the Display Format field. Both the Timebase and the Display Format field) determine the positions of the ruler tick marks in the Timeline window.

✦ **Frame size.** The frame size of your project is its width and height in pixels. The first number represents the frame width, and the second number represents the frame height. If you choose a DV preset, the frame size is set to the DV defaults (720×480). If you are using the DV editing mode, you cannot change the project frame size. However, frame size can be changed if you switch to the Video for Windows editing mode. If you do need to change the frame size, use a frame size that matches you video footage. If creating a project for the Web or CD-ROM, you can reduce its frame size when exporting your project (discussed in Part V later in the book).

✦ **Pixel aspect ratio.** This setting determines the shape of the image pixels — the width to height of one pixel in your image. For analog video and images created in graphics programs or scanned, choose square pixels. The default setting for D1/DV project is 0.9. The pop-up menu allows you to choose different settings. If your footage and project will be D1/DV Widescreen (16:9 aspect ratio), choose 1.2; for D1/DV PAL, use 1.0666; for D1/DV PAL Widescreen, use 1.4222. Choose the Anamorphic 2:1 choice if the video was shot on film with an anamorphic lens. These lenses squeeze the images during shooting, but when projected, an anamorphic projection lens reverses the compression to create a widescreen effect.

Tip   If you need to change the frame rate of an imported clip or the pixel aspect ratio (because either one doesn't match your Project settings), select the clip in the Project window and choose File ➪ Interpret Footage. To change frame rate, in the Interpret Footage dialog box, click Assume this frame rate. Then enter the new frame rate in the field. To change pixel aspect ratio, click Conform to. Then choose from a list of pixel aspect ratios. After you click OK, the Project window indicates the changes.

Tip   If you need to import widescreen footage (16:9) aspect ratio into a project that uses a 4:3 aspect ratio, you can scale or manipulate widescreen footage using the Position and Scale options of the Motion video effect. See Chapter 17 for more information about using the Motion video effect.

✦ **Fields.** Fields are relevant only when working on a project that will be exported to videotape. Each video frame is divided into two fields that appear for one-sixtieth of a second. In the PAL standard, each field is displayed every one-fiftieth of a second. Choose either the Upper or Lower setting in the fields section depending upon which field your system expects. (See Chapter 22 for more information.) If you are creating a project for the Web or that's to be viewed on a computer, choose the No fields option.

✦ **Display format.** This setting determines the number of frames Premiere Pro uses when it plays back from the Timeline and whether drop frame or non-drop frame timecode is used. In Premiere Pro time for video projects is displayed in the Timeline and other windows using SMPTE (Society of Motion Picture Television Engineers) video time readouts called *timecode*. In non-drop frame timecode, colons are used to separate hours, minutes, seconds, and frames. At 29.97 or 30 frames per second in non drop frame time code, the frame following 1:01:59:29 is 1:02:00:00.

In drop-frame Timecode, semi-colons are used to separate hours, minutes, seconds, and frames. For instance, the frame after 1;01;59;29 is 01;02;00;02. (The visual frame display drops numbers each minute to compensate for the fact that the NTSC video frame rate is 29.97, not 30 frames a second. Note that video frames are not dropped, only numbers in the timecode display are dropped.

The difference between drop frame and non-drop frame time code is discussed in more detail in Chapter 5.

✦ **Title safe area.** These two settings are important if your project will be viewed on a video monitor. The settings help you compensate for monitor *overscan*, which can cause a TV monitor to cut off the edges of the pictures. The settings provide a warning border, showing the limits where titles and actions can safely be viewed. You can change the percentages for the title and action safe zones. To view the safe areas in the Monitor window, choose Safe Margins from the Monitor window menu. When the safe areas, shown in Figure 4-4, appear, make sure that all titles appear within the first boundary and all actions appear within the second boundary. The clip in Figure 4-4 is 705008f from Digital Vision's NightMoves CD.

✦ **Scale clip to project dimensions when adding to sequence.** As you import clips into your project, you need to understand how Premiere Pro deals with clips that don't match the project frame size. If you select this option, Premiere Pro reduces or enlarges imported images to match the frame size of the current project. Be warned that if this option is turned on, imported images and clips may appear distorted. For instance, if you create a graphic in Photoshop with different pixel dimensions than those of your project, the image will appear distorted when it is imported into Premiere Pro. By default, this setting is turned off.

✦ **Sample rate.** The audio sample rate determines audio quality. Higher rates provide better quality audio. It's best to keep this setting at the rate your audio was recorded. If you change this setting to another rate, more processing is required, and quality may be adversely affected.

✦ **Display format.** When working with audio clips, you can change the Timeline or Monitor window display to show Audio units instead of video frames. The audio display format allows you to set audio units to be in milliseconds or audio samples. (Like a frame in video, an audio sample is the smallest increment that can be used in editing.)

For more information about Audio sample rates and audio display formats, see Chapter 8.

Since DV projects use industry standard settings, you should not change settings for pixel aspect ratio, time base, frame size, or fields.

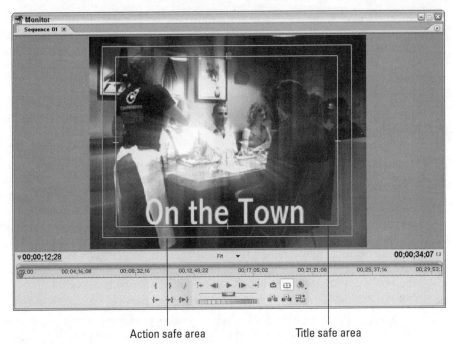

Action safe area   Title safe area

Figure 4-4: Title (inner rectangle) and action safe areas (outer rectangle) viewed in the monitor window.

Video rendering

The Video Rendering section of the New Project dialog box, shown in Figure 4-5, specifies settings for playing back video. You can access the Video Rendering Section by choosing File ⇨ New Project (or by clicking the New Project button), clicking the Custom Settings tab, and clicking Video Rendering. To access this dialog box after creating a project, choose Project ⇨ Project Settings ⇨ Video Rendering.

✦ **Compressor.** As mentioned earlier, compression is used to store as much data as possible in as little space as possible with a minimum loss of quality. The compressor setting describes the CODEC Premiere Pro uses during Timeline playback. If you capture video into Premiere Pro, you will typically use the same compressor setting as you did when capturing video (such as DV-NTSC or DV-QuickTime). If you are exporting to videotape, you'll typically use the same CODEC again. (The CODECs are set automatically when you choose a preset.) If you pick a DV setting, the Compressor field is set to DV (NTSC) or DV (PAL).

✦ **Color Depth.** Specifies how many colors your project displays when playing back video. For the best quality video, leave the color depth set to millions. You can switch to 256 colors if allowed by the current CODEC chosen in the Compressor field.

✦ **Optimize Stills.** Choosing this option instructs Premiere Pro to use fewer frames when rendering still images. For instance, instead of creating 30 frames of video to render a one-second still image, Premiere Pro can optimize output by creating one frame that is one second long. If still images are not cleanly displayed with this option selected, deselect it and export your video again.

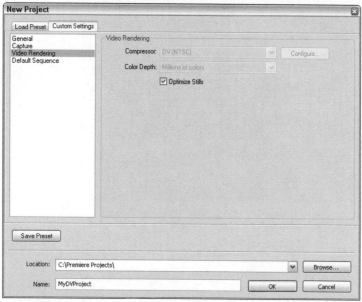

Figure 4-5: The Video Rendering section of the New Project dialog box provides settings for outputting video.

Default Sequence

The Default Sequence section of the New Project dialog box, shown in Figure 4-6, provides options for setting up Timeline defaults for new projects, including the number of video and audio tracks in the Timeline window. You can access Default Sequence settings when you create a new project by choosing File ➪ New Project (or click the New Project button). Next, click the Custom Settings tab and then click Default Sequence. To access this dialog box after creating a project, choose Project ➪ Project Settings ➪ Default Sequence.

Changing settings in this dialog box section does not alter the current Timeline. However, if you create a new project or a new sequence (by choosing File ➪ New Sequence), the next Timeline added to the project displays the new settings. Options in the dialog box allow you change the number of video and audio tracks. You can also choose whether to create submix tracks and Dolby Digital tracks. The audio submix and Dolby 5.1 choices are covered in Chapters 8 and 9.

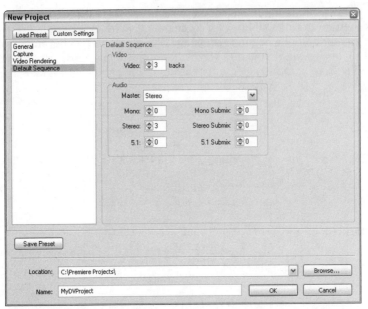

Figure 4-6: Use the Default Sequence section of the New Project dialog box to set timeline defaults.

Summary

Premiere Pro provides a nonlinear system of creating desktop video projects. A nonlinear system lets you edit video quickly and efficiently. You can easily edit and insert clips without reassembling your entire project. When you create a new project, you need to specify project settings. In this chapter, you learned the following:

✦ When creating a new project, the easiest way to pick project settings is to choose a preset from the New Project dialog box.

✦ If you are creating a DV project, you shouldn't need to change most DV presets.

✦ To change project settings in a new project, click the Custom Settings tab in the New Project dialog box.

✦ Use the Default Sequence section of the New Project or Project Settings dialog box to change the number of video and audio tracks in new projects.

✦   ✦   ✦

Capturing Video and Audio

The quality of video clips in a Premiere Pro project can often mean the difference between a production that attracts viewers and firmly holds their attention or one that sends them looking for other sources of information or entertainment. Undoubtedly, one of the primary factors in determining the quality of source material is how the video is captured. Fortunately, Premiere Pro provides extremely efficient and reliable capture options.

If you have a capture board or peripheral card that digitizes analog video, you may be able to access the capture board directly from Premiere Pro to digitize video. If you have an IEEE 1394 port, you may also be able to use Premiere Pro's Capture window to transfer clips directly from your DV camera. Depending upon the sophistication of your equipment and the quality requirements of your production, you may be able to capture all of your video source material by using Premiere Pro.

This chapter focuses on the process of capturing video and audio using Premiere Pro. It leads you step-by-step through the process of using Premiere Pro's Capture window to capture videotape to your computer's hard disk. If your equipment enables device control, you'll be able to start and stop a camcorder or tape deck directly from Premiere Pro. You may also be able to set up a batch capture session in which Premiere Pro automatically uses list clip in and out points to capture multiple clips during one session.

Getting Started

Before you start capturing video for a production, you should first realize that the quality of the final captured footage depends on the sophistication of your digitizing equipment and the speed of the hard drive that you are using to capture the material. Much of the equipment sold today can provide quality suitable for the Web or in-house corporate video. However, if your goal is to create very high-quality video productions and transfer them to videotape, you should analyze your production needs and carefully assess exactly what hardware and software configuration best suits your needs.

Fortunately, Premiere Pro can capture audio and video using low-end and high-end hardware. Capture hardware, whether high- or low-end, usually falls into two categories:

✦ **FireWire/IEEE1394.** Apple Computer created the IEEE 1394 port primarily as a means of quickly sending digitized video from video devices to a computer. In Apple computers, the IEEE 1394 board is called a FireWire port. Several PC manufacturers, including Sony (Sony calls its IEEE 1394 port an i.LINK port) and Dell, sell computers with IEEE pre-installed. If you are shopping for an IEEE1394, hardware should be OHCI (Open Host Controller Interface) compliant. OHCI is a standard interface that allows Windows to work with and recognize the card. If Windows has no problems recognizing the card, most DV software applications will be able to utilize the card without problems.

If your computer has an IEEE 1394 port, you can transfer digitized data directly from a DV camcorder to your computer. As mentioned in Chapter 4, DV camcorders actually digitize and compress the signal as you shoot. Thus, the IEEE 1394 port is a conduit between the already digitized data and Premiere Pro. If your equipment is Premiere Pro-compatible, you'll be able to use Premiere Pro's Capture window to start, stop, and preview the capture process. If you have an IEEE 1394 board in your computer, you may be able to start and stop a camcorder or tape deck from within Premiere Pro; this is called *device control*. With device control, everything is controlled from Premiere Pro. You can cue up the video source material to specific tape locations, record timecode, and set up batch sessions, which enable you to record different sections of videotape automatically in one session.

Note   To ensure high-quality capture, your hard disk should be able to sustain a 3.6 data rate—the DV data rate.

✦ **Analog to digital capture cards.** These cards take an analog video signal and digitize it. Some computer manufacturers have sold models with these boards built directly into the computer. On the PC, most analog-to-digital capture boards are add-ins that must be installed in the computer. More expensive analog-to-digital capture boards permit device control, enabling you to start and stop a camcorder or tape deck as well as cue it up to the tape location that you want to record. If you are using an analog to digital capture card, it's important to realize that not all cards are designed with the same standards, and some may not be compatible with Premiere Pro. To check video card compatibility, see www.adobe.com/products/premiere/dvhdwrdb.html.

Making the right connection

Before you begin the process of capturing video or audio, make sure that you've read all relevant documentation supplied with the hardware. Many boards include plug-ins so that you can capture directly into Premiere Pro (rather than first capturing in another software application and then importing it into Premiere). Here's a brief description of the connection requirements for analog to digital boards and IEEE 1394 ports:

✦ **Analog to digital.** Most analog-to-digital capture boards use Composite Video or S-Video systems. Some boards provide both Composite and S-Video. Hooking up a Composite system usually entails connecting a cable with three RCA jacks from the video and sound output jacks of your camcorder or tape deck to the video and sound input jacks of your computer's capture board. The S-Video connection provides video output from your camcorder to the capture board. Typically, this means simply connecting one cable from the camcorder or tape deck's S-Video output jack to the computer's S-Video input jack. Some S-Video cables have an extra jack for sound as well.

✦ **The IEEE/FireWire connection.** Making the connection to your computer's IEEE 1394 port is easy. Simply plug the IEEE 1394 cable into the DV In/Out jack of your camcorder, and plug the other end into the IEEE 1394 jack of your computer. Despite the simplicity, be sure to read all documentation. The connection may not work unless you supply external power to your DV cameras. The transfer may not work on the DV camera's batteries alone.

IEEE 1394 cables for desktop and laptop computers are usually different, and not interchangeable. Furthermore, an IEEE 1394 cable that connects an external FireWire hard drive to a computer may be different from an IEEE 1394 cable that connects a computer to a camcorder. Before purchasing an IEEE 1394 cable, make sure you have the right cable for your computer.

Starting the Capture Process

It's important to understand that many settings in Premiere Pro depend upon the actual equipment you have installed in your computer. It's also important to understand that the dialog boxes that appear when capturing change depending upon the hardware and software installed in your computer. The dialog boxes that appear in this chapter may vary from what you see on your computer, but the general steps for capturing video and audio are pretty much the same. However, if you have a capture board that digitizes analog video, the setup process is different than if you have an IEEE 1394 port installed in your computer. The following sections describe how to set up Premiere Pro for both systems.

To ensure that your capture session is successful, be sure to read all manufacturers, read-me files and documentation. Know exactly what is installed in your computer.

Reviewing default capture settings

Before you begin the capture process, it's a good idea to review Premiere Pro's project and default settings, which affect the capture process. After the defaults are set, they remain saved when you reload the program. Defaults that affect capture include scratch disk settings and device control settings.

Setting scratch disk default settings

Whether you are capturing digital video or digitizing analog video, one of your first steps should be to ensure that Premiere Pro's *scratch disk* is set up properly. The scratch disk(s) is the disk used to actually perform the capture. Make sure that the scratch disk is the fastest one connected to your computer and that the hard drive is the one with the most free space. In Premiere, you can set different scratch disk locations for video and audio. To check scratch disk settings, choose Edit ➪ Preferences ➪ Scratch Disks. If you want to change settings for captured video or audio, click the appropriate Browse button and set a new capture path by navigating to a specified drive and folder with your mouse.

In the Capture Locations section, click the Browse button to choose the hard disk or disks that you want to use for capturing video and audio

> **Note**   During the capture process, Premiere Pro also creates a conformed high-quality audio file that Premiere Pro uses to quickly access audio. The Scratch Disk section of the Preferences dialog box (Edit ➪ Preferences) also allows you to set a scratch disk location for conformed audio.

Device control default settings

If your system allows device control, you'll be able to start and stop recording and set in and out points using onscreen buttons in Premiere. You'll also be able to perform batch capture operations in which Premiere captures multiple clips automatically. To access the default settings for device control, choose Edit ➪ Preferences ➪ Device Control. As discussed in Chapter 3, the Device Control section of the Preferences dialog box, shown in Figure 5-1, allows you to set Preroll and Timecode settings as well as choose your video/audio source device.

The Device Control section contains the following options:

✦ **Devices.** If you are using device control, set this drop-down menu to DV Device Control or a device control choice provided by your board manufacturer. If you are not using device control, you can set this option to None.

✦ **Preroll.** Set a preroll time to enable your playback device to back up and get up to speed before the capture starts. Refer to camcorder and tape deck instructions for specifics.

✦ **Timecode Offset.** This setting allows you to alter the timecode recorded on the captured video so that it accurately matches the right frame on the source videotape.

✦ **Options.** Clicking the Options button opens up the DV Device Control Options dialog box, as shown in Figure 5-2. Here you can set your preferred video standard (NTSC or PAL), the Device Brand, Device Type, and Timecode Format (Drop-Frame or Non-Drop-Frame). If your device is properly connected to your computer, is turned on, and is in VCR mode, the status readout should be "Online." If you can't get your device Online and you have an Internet connection, try clicking Go Online for Device Info. You'll be taken to an Adobe Web page with compatibility information.

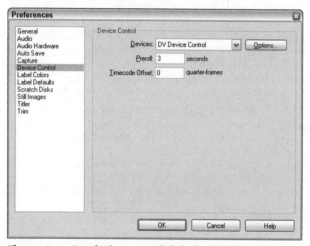

Figure 5-1: Set device control defaults in the Device Control section of the Preferences dialog box.

Figure 5-2: Choose your video source and check its status in the DV Device Control Options dialog box.

Drop frame versus non-drop frame timecode

SMPTE (Society of Motion Picture and Television Engineers) timecode is "striped" (recorded) on tape on a track separate from the video track. Video producers use the timecode as a means of specifying exact in and out points during edit sessions. When previewing footage, producers often create a "window dub "of the timecode so that the timecode appears in a window. This enables the producers to view the tape and the timecode at the same time. By default, Premiere Pro uses the SMPTE timecode to display times in this format: hour: minute: second: frame.

If you're new to video or Premiere, this can take some getting used to. For example, the next readout after 01:01:59:29 is 01:02:00:00. This timecode format code is called *non-drop frame*. However, professional video producers typically use a timecode format called *drop frame*.

Drop frame timecode is necessary because the NTSC professional video frame rate is 29.97 (not 30 frames a second). Over a long duration, the .03 time difference between 30 frames and 29.97 frames begins to add up, resulting in inaccurate program times. To solve the problem, professional video producers created a timecode system that would actually visually drop frames in the code without dropping frames in the video. When SMPTE non-drop frame is striped, two frames of every minute are skipped—except for the tenth minute. In drop frame timecode, the frame after 01;01;59;29 is 01;02;00;02. Notice that semicolons are used to designate drop frame from non-drop frame.

If you are not creating video where exact time duration is important, you do not need to use drop-frame timecode. You can capture and use 30 frames per second instead of the 29.97 project setting. Furthermore, non-drop frame was created for NTSC video. Do not use it for PAL or SECAM, which use 25 frames per second.

Capture Project settings

The capture settings for a project determine how video and audio are captured. The capture settings are determined by project presets. If you want to capture video from a DV camera or DV tape deck, the capture process is straightforward. Because DV cameras compress and digitize, there are very few settings to change. However, to ensure the best quality capture, you must create a DV project before the capture session.

Here are some general project setup steps to review before capturing:

1. **Create a new project, by choosing File ➪ New Project.** If you are capturing from a DV source, choose a DV project preset. If you are capturing from an analog card, you will probably need to pick a non-DV preset provided or recommended by your manufacturer.

2. **Check Capture Settings.** To open the Capture Settings window, choose Project ⇨ Project Settings ⇨ Capture. Looking at the Capture section of the Project Settings dialog box, shown in Figure 5-3, you might wonder where all the settings went. If you are capturing using DV equipment, Premiere Pro uses the IEEE 1394 capture standard. (Many of these settings are visible in the General section of the Project Settings dialog box. If you are using a third-party board, you may see settings for frame rate, frame size, compressor, format [or bit depth], and number of audio channels.)

3. **Check connections.** Check all connections from video equipment to your computer. Turn on your video/audio source. If you're using a camcorder, set it to VCR mode.

Note   To prevent dropped frames during a DV capture session, your hard drive should be able to sustain a 3.6MB per second data rate.

4. **If your equipment supports device control, check settings by choosing Edit ⇨ Preferences Device Control.** In the Device Control section, the Devices drop-down menu should be set to DV Device Control. To set device control for your playback device, click Options. In the DV Device Control Options dialog box, choose your brand and Device Type. If your camcorder is already attached to your computer and is turned to VCR mode, it should appear online (you can also check this later in the Capture window).

5. **Choose Project ⇨ Project Settings ⇨ Capture.** If you are capturing DV using an IEEE 1394 connection, you should see DV/IEEE 1394 Capture. Those with third-party boards may be able to change frame size and frame rate and audio settings.

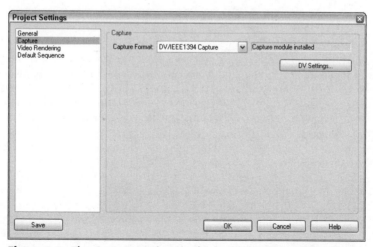

Figure 5-3: The Capture settings in the Project Settings dialog box.

Timecode troubles

If you are using device control and are capturing a videotape with recorded timecode, it's very important that the timecode is continuous — that no time code is repeated. If you start and stop recording timecode while shooting, two or more frames on one tape may have the same timecode. For instance, two different frames on the tape may have 01;02;00;02 as their recorded code. This creates a problem for Premiere Pro. When Premiere Pro captures video using device control and batch processing, it seeks out a specific frame of recorded timecode for the in point and captures until a frame of timecode is designated as the out point. If the same timecode appears on the tape at different points, Premiere Pro will get confused and will not capture the correct sequence.

One solution to this problem is to stripe all tape with continuous timecode before shooting. Simply record black while you record timecode on the entire tape. Alternatively, you can try a sort of rhythm method of shooting that prevents timecode numbers from being re-recorded. To do so, shoot an extra 5 to 10 seconds of video after the scene that you want recorded ends. When you start recording again, first rewind the tape so it begins at a location that already has timecode recorded on it. If you see the timecode starting again at 00;00;00, rewind until you reach a section of previously recorded timecode.

Tip   Before beginning a capture session, make sure that no other programs besides Premiere Pro are running. Also, it's a good idea to be sure that your hard disk is not fragmented. Windows XP Pro users can defragment and test for hard drive errors by right-clicking their hard drives and then clicking Properties. Next, click the Tools tab to access hard drive maintenance utilities.

Capture window settings

Before you start capturing, becoming familiar with the Capture Window settings is a good idea. The settings determine whether video and audio are captured together or separately. The window also allows you to change scratch disk and device control settings.

To open the Capture window, shown in Figure 5-4, choose File ⇨ Capture. To view capture settings, click the Settings tab. If the Settings tab isn't visible, click the Capture window menu, and choose Expand Window (which changes to Collapse window once the window is expanded) as shown in Figure 5-4. The following sections describe different areas of the Capture window: the Capture window menu and the Capture Settings, Capture Locations, and Device Control sections.

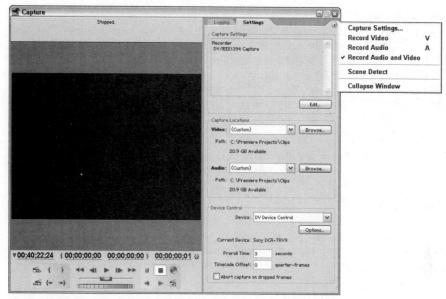

Figure 5-4: The Capture window with the Settings tab selected.

Capture window menu

The following sections describe the key areas of the Capture Settings menu shown at the upper-right corner in Figure 5-4.

✦ **Capture Settings.** Clicking this menu item opens up the Project Settings Capture dialog box, where you can check or change capture settings.

✦ **Record Audio and Record Video.** Here you can choose whether to capture Audio only or Video only. The default setting is Audio and Video.

✦ **Scene Detect.** Turns on Premiere's automatic scene detection available with device control. When Scene Detect is on, Premiere Pro automatically breaks up the capture into different clips when Premiere Pro detects a change in the video time stamp, which occurs when the Pause button is pressed on a camcorder.

✦ **Collapse Window.** This command removes the Setting and Logging tabs from the Window. When the window is collapsed, the menu command changes to Expand Window.

Capture Settings

This section of the Capture window displays the selected capture settings from the Project Settings dialog box. Clicking the Settings button opens the Capture Settings dialog box. As mentioned earlier, if you are capturing DV, you will not be able to change frame size or change audio options because all capture settings conform to the IEEE standard. Those Premiere Pro users with a third-party board may see settings that allow them to change frame size, frame rate, and audio sample rates.

Capture Locations

The Capture Locations section displays the default settings for Video and Audio. You can change locations for Video and Audio by clicking either of the Browse buttons.

Device Control

The Device Control section displays defaults from the Device Control Preferences dialog box. You can change the defaults here as well, and click the Options button to set your playback device and see whether it is online. In this section, you can also choose to abort the session if any frames are dropped during capture.

Capturing Video in the Capture Window

If your system does not allow device control, you can capture video by turning on your tape deck or camera and viewing the footage in the Capture window. By manually starting and stopping the camera or tape deck, you can preview the source material. Here are the steps to follow:

1. **Make sure that all cables are properly connected.**

2. **Choose File ⇨ Capture ⇨ Capture.** You can change the window size by clicking and dragging the lower-right edge of the window.

3. **If you want to capture only video or only audio, change settings in the Capture window menu.** (You can also change settings by clicking the Logging tab and choosing Video [only] or Audio [only] from the drop-down list.)

4. **Set the camera or tape deck to Play mode.** You should see and hear the source clip in the Capture window as the tape plays.

5. **Five to Seven seconds before the section that should be recorded appears, click the Record button in the Movie Capture window.** At the top of the capture screen, you'll see a display of the capture progress, including whether any frames were dropped during the recording.

6. **To stop recording, press Esc.** When the recording is paused, the File Name dialog box appears.

7. **Type a filename for the clip.** Optionally, you may type additional comments in the Comments box.

8. **Click OK to save the file.** The captured clip appears in the Project window.

9. **Press the Stop button on your playback device.**

Tip

To view clip information about dropped frames, data rate, and file location, right-click the clip in the Project window and choose Properties from the drop-down menu that appears. Alternatively, select the clip and choose File ⇨ Properties ⇨ Selection.

Capturing with device control

During the capture session, device control enables you to start and stop a camera or tape deck directly from Premiere. If you have an IEEE 1394 connection and are capturing from a camcorder, chances are you'll be able to use device control. Otherwise, to work with device control, you need a capture board that supports device control as well as a frame-accurate tape deck (that is controlled by the board). If you do not have a DV board, you will probably need a Premiere Pro-compatible plug-in to use device control. If device control is supported by your system, you may also be able to import the timecode and automatically generate a batch list to batch capture clips automatically.

The device control buttons provided at the bottom of the Capture window magically control your camcorder or VCR. The buttons and callouts for them are shown in Figure 5-5. Using these buttons, you can start and stop and set in and out points for the video.

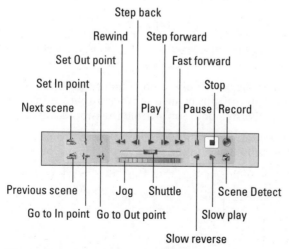

Figure 5-5: The Capture window Device Control buttons.

Tip   Clicking the Fast Forward button when the tape is either playing or paused allows you to fast forward while previewing the video; clicking the Rewind button when the tape is either playing or paused, allows you to rewind while previewing the video.

You might also want to review the default keyboard commands for the Capture window:

Eject	E
Fast forward	F
Go to In point	Q
Go to Out point	W
Record	G
Rewind	R
Set Out point	O
Set In point	I

When you are ready to capture with device control, follow these steps:

1. **Choose File ➪ Capture ➪ Movie Capture.**

2. **Check Capture Settings by clicking the Settings tab.** In the Device Control area, make sure that the Device drop-down menu is set to Device Control. If you need to check the status of your playback device, click Options.

   If you want to change settings, you can change project settings by clicking the Edit button in the Capture Settings area. If you want to change the location of video or audio scratch disks, click the Browse button(s) in the Capture Locations area.

3. **Click the Logging tab.** The Logging section of the Capture window includes buttons for automatically capturing from a clip's in point to its out point. It also includes a Scene Detect check box, another method of turning on Premiere Pro's Scene Detect option.

4. **Click the controls onscreen to move to the point from which you want to start capturing video.**

Tip   Click and drag the jog control area to the left to rewind one frame; click and drag to the right to advance one frame. Drag the shuttle control to change speed as you view the footage.

5. **Click either the Set In point icon or the Set In button in the Timecode section of the Logging tab (see Figure 5-6).**

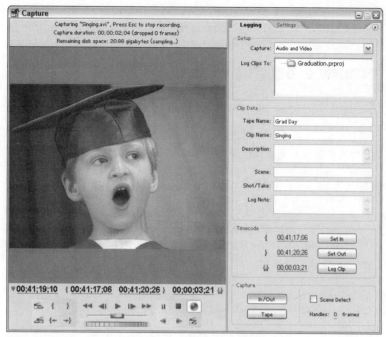

Figure 5-6: Video captured in the Capture window.

6. **Click the controls onscreen to move to the point at which you want to stop capturing video.**

7. **Click either the Set Out point icon or the Set Out button in the Timecode section of the Logging tab.** At this point, you can review your in and out points by clicking the Go to In point button or Go to Out point button.

8. **To begin capturing, click the In/Out button in the Capture section of the Logging tab.** Premiere Pro starts the preroll. After the preroll, your video appears in the Capture window, as shown in Figure 5-6. Premiere Pro starts the capture session at the in point and ends it at the out point.

9. **When the Filename dialog box appears, type a name for the clip.** If a project is open onscreen, the clip automatically appears in the Project window.

> **Note**
> If Scene Detection is on, Premiere Pro might break a clip into many clips whether or not the in and out points are set.

> **Note**
> If you don't want to set in and out points for recording, you can just click the Play button and then click Record to capture the sequence that appears in the Capture window.

Tip   To capture an entire tape, rewind the tape and click the Tape button at the bottom of the Capture section in the Logging tab of the Capture window.

Performing a batch capture

If your capture board supports device control, you can set up a *batch capture list* that appears in the Project window, as shown in Figure 5-7. The checks in the Capture Settings column indicate which offline clips will be captured. Note that the icon for the offline clips is different than the normal online icon in the Project window. Other columns in the Project window indicate the in and out points for the clips that will be captured. After creating the list, you can have Premiere Pro capture each of the clips automatically while you go off and take a coffee break. You can create a batch capture list manually or by using device control. If you create a batch list manually, you will need to type the timecode in and out points for all clips. If you use device control, Premiere Pro enters the start and stop times, after you click the Set In and Set Out buttons in the Timecode section of the Logging tab in the Capture window.

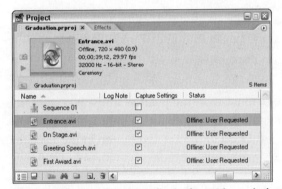

Figure 5-7: A batch capture list in the Project window.

Creating a batch capture list manually

To create a batch capture list of clips that you specify manually, follow these steps:

1. **If you want the batch list in a bin in the Project window, open the bin or create one by clicking the Folder button at the bottom of the window.**

2. **To create the batch file listing, choose File ⇨ New Offline File (or click the New Item and choose New Offline file).** The Offline File dialog box, shown in Figure 5-8, opens.

3. **Type an in point, an out point, and a filename for the clip. Add other descriptive notes such as a real name.**

4. **Click OK.** The clip's information is added to the Project window.

Figure 5-8: Use the Offline File dialog box to manually log clips.

5. **For each clip that you want captured, repeat steps 2–4.**

Note

You can edit the in and out points of offline files by clicking in the video in and out point column for the specific clip and changing the timecode readouts.

6. **If you want to save the batch list to disk so that you can capture the clips at another time, or so that you can load the list into another computer application, choose Project ➪ Export Batch list.** You can reload the list later when you want to begin the capture session by choosing Project ➪ Import Batch list.

Creating a batch capture list with device control

If you want to create a batch capture list but do not want to type the in and out points of all clips, you can use Premiere Pro's Capture window to do the job for you. Here are the steps:

1. **Open the Movie Capture window by choosing File ➪ Capture ➪ Capture.**

2. **Click the Logging tab. In the Clip Data section, enter a Tape Name and the Clip Name that you want to see in the Project window. Add other comments as desired.**

3. **Use the capture control icons to locate the portion of the tape that includes the section you want to capture.**

4. **Click the Set In button.** The in point appears in the Logging tab's In field.

5. **Use the capture control icons to locate the clip's out point.**

6. **Click the Set Out button.** The out point appears in the Out field.

7. **Click the Log Clip button and enter a filename for the clip (unless you want to use the default name provided).** If desired, type comments in the dialog box and then click OK.

8. **For every clip you want to capture, repeat Steps 4–8.**

9. **If you want to save the batch list to disk, so that you can capture the clips at another time, or so that you can load the list into another computer application, choose Project ⇨ Export Batch list.** You can reload the list later when you want to begin the capture session by choosing Project ⇨ Import Batch list.

10. **Close the Movie Capture window.**

Capturing using a batch list

After you've created a batch list of clips that you want to capture, you can have Premiere Pro capture the clips automatically from a list in the Project window. In order to complete the following steps, you need to create a batch list as described in the previous section.

Note Batch lists can be automatically captured only by systems that support device control.

1. **If your batch list of offline files is saved and not loaded into the Project window, load the list by choosing Project ⇨ Import Batch list.** This loads the list of files into the Project window.

2. **To specify which clips you want captured, select the offline clips in the Project window and then choose File ⇨ Batch Capture.** This opens the Batch Capture dialog box where you can change capture settings by clicking override clip settings, if desired; otherwise, click OK.

3. **When the Insert Tape dialog box appears, make sure the correct tape is in your camcorder/playback device and then click OK.** The Capture window opens, and the capture process begins.

4. **Check to see capture status.** When the batch process is over, an alert will appear, indicating that the clips have been captured. In the Project window, Premiere Pro changes the icons of the filenames to indicate that they are now linked to files on disk. To see the status of the captured clips, scroll right in the Project window. You'll see check marks for captured clips in the Capture Settings column. The status for the clips should be "Online," another indication that the clips are linked to disk files.

Where's my audio?

If you've captured video and audio and don't hear the audio, you may need to wait until Premiere Pro finishes creating an audio conforming file for the captured segment. When an AVI video file is created, the audio is interleaved with the video. By creating a separate high-quality conforming audio file, Premiere Pro can access and process audio faster as you edit. The downside of a conforming file is that you must wait for it to be created, and it takes up extra hard disk space. However, the advantages of faster audio processing outweigh the disadvantages.

Note   If you have offline files in the Project window and you want to link them to files that have already been captured, right-click the clip in the Project window, then choose Link Media. You will then need to navigate with the mouse to the actual clip on your hard disk.

Adding Timecode to a Clip

High-end video cameras and mid-range DV cameras can record timecode to videotape (often called SMPTE timecode, for the Society of Motion Picture and Television Engineers). The timecode provides a frame-accurate readout of each videotape frame in Hour:Minute:Second:Frame format. Timecode is used by video producers to move to specific locations on tape and also to set in and out points. During an edit session, broadcast equipment uses the timecode to create frame-accurate edits of the source material onto the final program tape.

When capturing with device control, Premiere Pro captures the timecode along with the video. When capturing video or importing video, you may want to use a clip that doesn't have timecode striped on the tape, yet does have the timecode visible onscreen (called a *window dub*). In these cases, you can't actually capture timecode from the clip. However, you can use Premiere Pro to set timecode on the tape. To add timecode to a clip, follow these steps:

1. **Select the clip in the Project window and double-click on it to open it in the Monitor window.** If you don't want the timecode to start at the beginning of the clip, move to the frame at which you want to begin recording.

2. **Choose File ⇨ Timecode.**

3. **In the Timecode dialog box, shown in Figure 5-9, enter the timecode that you want to use.**

4. **If you moved to a specific frame and want to start the timecode at that point, click Set at Current Frame.**

5. **Enter a Tape Name.**

6. **Click OK.**

Figure 5-9: Use the clip Timecode dialog box to set the timecode for a clip.

Capturing Audio

Premiere Pro enables you to capture audio independently of video using its Audio Mixer window. When you capture audio, quality is based on the sample rate and bit depth. The sample rate is the number of samples taken each second. The bit depth is the number of bits (eight bits are in a byte of data) per each sample of the actual digitized audio (the minimum bit depth of most audio CODECs is 16). Premiere's audio settings options enable you to specify sample rates and bit depth as well as choose between Mono and Stereo. As you capture, remember that higher bit rates and sample rates create larger files. Remember also that Stereo capturing requires more hard drive space than mono files.

If you are using a PC and have a video or soundboard installed in your computer, you can review or change capture settings for capturing analog audio by choosing File ➪ Project Settings Capture. If you have analog capture equipment, these settings control how audio will be captured. Remember that the higher the sample and bit rates, the better the audio. However, these files will consume more disk space than files recorded at lower quality settings.

To record using the audio mixer, follow these steps:

1. **Connect the tape recorder, microphone, or other audio source to the sound port or sound card of your computer.**

Note

If you want to create a new audio track for your audio capture, choose Sequence ⇨ Add Track. In the Audio track section, enter **1** in the Add Audio Track field. If you are using a monophonic microphone, choose Mono in the Track Type drop-down menu and enter **0** in the Add Video Track and Add Submix tracks fields.

2. **Open the Audio Mixer window, shown in Figure 5-10, by choosing Window ⇨ Audio Mixer.**

3. **If you have video on the Timeline and want to record narration for the video, move the Timeline about 5 seconds before you want the audio to begin.**

4. **To prepare for recording, click the Record Enable button (Microphone) in the Audio Mixer window in the track section for the track you are recording. The Record button is at the bottom of the Audio Mixer window.**

5. **Test audio levels. In the Audio Mixer window choose Meter Input(s) Only.** This displays hardware inputs in the VU meter displays for tracks being recorded. Note that when Meter Input(s) Only is activated, you can still view track levels for those tracks that you aren't recording.

Record button

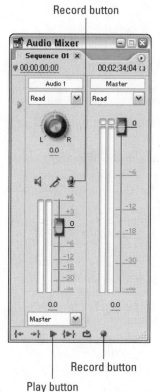

Figure 5-10: Use the Audio Mixer to record analog audio directly into Premiere Pro.

Record button

Play button

6. **Speak into the microphone. Adjust levels for the track if necessary.** As you speak, sound levels should be near 0 db without entering the red zone. If desired, you can turn off Meter Input(s) Only.

7. **To actually start recording, click the Play button at the bottom of the Audio Mixer window.**

8. **Play the tape recorder or begin recording the narration.** As you record, watch the levels in the Audio Mixer, and adjust as the faders as needed.

9. **When the narration or audio is complete, click the Record button to stop recording in the Audio Mixer window.**

Summary

Premiere Pro enables you to capture video and audio directly from a video camera or videotape recorder. You can also capture audio from a camcorder or other sound device.

✦ Before starting a capture session, read all documentation related to your capture hardware.

✦ Be sure to set up cables properly before the capture session.

✦ If you are digitizing analog video, specify capture settings in the Capture Settings dialog box (File ➪ Capture ➪ Capture Movie).

✦ If you are capturing digital video, create a project before the capture session. Use settings recommended by your computer or board manufacturer.

✦ If your equipment allows device control, you can set up a batch capture session.

✦ To capture analog audio, use Premiere Pro's Audio Mixer.

✦   ✦   ✦

Editing with Premiere Pro

Using the Timeline and Sequences

CHAPTER

In This Chapter

Touring the Timeline

Ruler options

Video track options

Creating sequences

Nesting sequences

Undoubtedly, Premiere Pro's Timeline is its most versatile and elaborate window. Not only does the Timeline provide a graphical overview of clips, transitions, and effects, but it also abounds with buttons, icons, drop-down menus, and sliders that control how footage is viewed and exported. Using the Timeline, you can edit and assemble digital footage, and you can also fine-tune video transparency and audio volume, as well as the placement of keyframes for both audio and video effects. With all of this power jam-packed in one window, you'll want to take full advantage of all the Timeline has to offer. If you do, you're sure to be working as efficiently as possible in Premiere Pro.

To get you started, this chapter provides a thorough review of the Timeline window features and options. It shows you how to move through footage in the Timeline, add tracks, lock tracks, and change viewing modes. The chapter also includes a section on how to use *sequences.* In Premiere Pro, a sequence is the assembled footage that is placed in the Timeline window. As you'll soon see, Premiere Pro allows you to create multiple sequences in a Timeline window, separate sequences into different Timeline windows, and drag one sequence into another to create a "nested" sequence.

Touring the Timeline

At first glance, trying to decipher all the Timeline buttons, icons, sliders, and controls may seem like an overwhelming task. But you'll find that after you start using the Timeline, you'll gradually learn what each feature does and how to use it. To make the process of exploring the Timeline easier, this section is organized according to three specific Timeline locales: the ruler area and icons that control the ruler, the Video tracks, and the Audio tracks. Before you get started, you may want to place a video and audio clip from the Chapter 1 or Chapter 6 folder of the *Adobe Premiere Pro Bible* DVD into the Timeline window. This will allow you to experiment with the different viewing options discussed in this section. To load the video and audio clip from the Chapter 1 or Chapter 6 folder of the *Adobe Premiere Pro Bible* DVD, choose File ⇨ Import. After the clip appears in the Project window, click and drag the video footage to Video track 1. Click and drag the audio file into Audio track 1. (The video clip in Chapter 1 is 705008f; the audio clip is 705001.aif; both are from Digital Vision's NightMoves CD. The clip in the Chapter 6 folder is 65005f.mov from Digital Vision's SkyRider CD.)

Tip　If the Timeline window is not visible onscreen, you can open it by double-clicking Sequence listing in the Project window.

Timeline ruler options

The Timeline ruler icons and controls determine how footage is viewed and what areas are rendered and exported by Premiere Pro. Figure 6-1 provides a look at the Timeline ruler icons and controls.

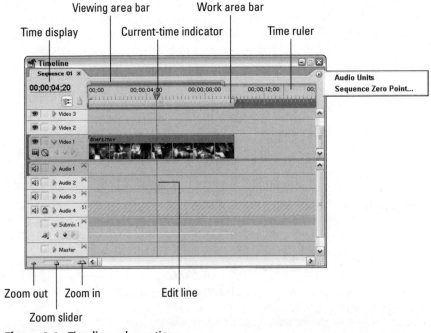

Figure 6-1: Timeline ruler options.

Here is a description of the Timeline ruler controls:

✦ **Time ruler.** The Time ruler is a visual display of time intervals divided into frames per second, which corresponds to your project frame rate. The actual number of tick marks between numbers that appear on the ruler are controlled by the current zoom level (which you can adjust by dragging the viewing area bar or zoom slider).

Tip
By default, the Timeline ruler displays timer intervals in frames per second. If you are editing audio, you can change the ruler to display audio units in milliseconds or audio samples. To switch to audio units, choose Audio units in the Timeline menu (shown in Figure 6-1). Choose either milliseconds or audio samples in the Audio section of the Project Settings dialog box (Project ➪ Project Settings ➪ General).

✦ **Current-time indicator.** The current-time indicator (CTI) is the blue triangular icon that appears in the ruler. You can click and drag the CTI to gradually move through your footage. You can click in the Ruler area to move the CTI to a specific frame, and you can type a time in the Time display and press Enter to move to that position. You can also click and drag left or right in the Time display to move the current-time indicator left or right along the ruler.

✦ **Time display.** As you move the current-time indicator through the Timeline, the Time display indicates the position of the current frame. You can quickly jump to a specific frame by clicking the Time display and entering a time. When you type, you do not need to enter semicolons or colons. For instance, you can move to frame 02:15:00 by clicking in the Frame readout area, typing **215**, and pressing Enter. If you set a project's Display Format to be drop frame, time is displayed with semi-colons. If you set a project's Display Format to be non-drop frame, time is displayed with colons. To view or change the Display Format for a project, choose Project ➪ Project Settings ➪ General.

✦ **Viewing area bar.** Clicking and dragging the viewing area bar changes the zoom level in the Timeline. The zoom level determines ruler increments and how much footage appears in the Timeline window. You can click and drag on either end of the viewing bar to change the zoom level. Clicking and dragging the right viewing endpoint of the Viewing area bar to the left displays fewer frames on the Timeline. Consequently, this increases the distance on the ruler between tick marks as shorter time intervals are displayed. Dragging right shows more footage and decreases the time intervals on the Timeline. To summarize: To zoom in, click and drag left on the viewing area bar; to zoom out, click and drag right. As you click and drag, notice that the zoom slider in the lower-left corner changes accordingly. Figure 6-2 shows the Timeline footage zoomed in. Note the difference between the zoomed-out view in Figure 6-1 and the zoomed-in view in Figure 6-2.

Figure 6-2: Timeline zoomed-in view.

✦ **Work area bar.** Beneath the Timeline ruler is Premiere Pro's work area bar, which can be used to designate a work area for exporting or rendering. You can click and drag either end point of the work area bar or drag the entire bar from left to right. Why would you change the work area bar? When you render your project, Premiere Pro only renders the area defined by the work area bar. Furthermore, when you export your file you can choose to only export the work area section of the selected sequence in the Timeline.

Tip   You can quickly adjust the width and position of the work area bar by resetting its in and outpoints with keyboard shortcuts. To set an in point, move the current-time indicator to a specific frame and press Alt+[; to set an out point, move the current-time indicator to a specific frame and press Alt+]. You can also expand or contract the work area bar to encompass the footage in the current sequence or the width of the Timeline window (whichever is shorter) by double-clicking the work area bar.

✦ **Preview indicator.** The preview indicator displays which portion of your program has been rendered. Once footage is rendered, transitions and effects appear at their highest quality (if Highest Quality or Automatic Quality is set as the display choice in the Monitor menu). As a sequence is rendered, Premiere Pro saves the rendered work file to disk. Green areas in the Preview indicator area indicate footage that has been rendered. Red indicates non-rendered footage. To render the work area, press Enter or choose Sequence ➪ Render Work Area.

✦ **Zoom slider.** Clicking and dragging the zoom slider serves the same purpose as clicking and dragging the viewing area bar. Clicking and dragging left zooms in (you can also click the zoom in button). As you zoom in, more tickmarks are displayed on the Timeline, allowing you to see more of your footage within the boundaries of the Timeline window. Clicking and dragging to zoom out increases the distance between tick marks and shows less of your footage.

✦ **Set Unnumbered Marker button.** Sequence markers allow you to set points on the Timeline to which you can quickly jump. Sequence markers can also help you divide up your work in the Timeline as you edit. Markers can also be used as chapter headings when you export Premiere Pro projects to DVD. To set an unnumbered marker, drag the current-time indicator to the frame where you want the marker to appear and then click the Set Unnumbered Marker button (pentagon icon to the right of magnet icon).

Timeline track icons and options

Undoubtedly, the most important areas of the Timeline are its video and audio tracks, which provide a visual representation of your video and audio footage, transitions, and effects. Using the Timeline track options, you add and delete tracks and control how tracks are displayed. You can also control whether specific tracks are output when you export your project. You can also lock tracks and specify whether to view video frames in video tracks.

The following is a review of the icons and track options shown in Figure 6-3:

✦ **Snap.** The Snap icon toggles Premiere's Snap to Edges command. When Snap is on, frames from one sequence snap to touch frames from the next sequence. This electronic magnetic effect helps ensure that no gaps appear in your production. To enable Snap, you can simply click the Snap icon or choose Sequence ⇨ Snap. When Snap is on, the magnet in the upper-left corner of the Timeline appears as though it is pressed down.

✦ **Target.** When you edit footage using the Monitor window, Premiere Pro places the footage in the current target track in the Timeline. To specify a target track, simply click in the far-left area of the track. The target track changes to display rounded edges, as shown in track 1 in Figure 6-3.

✦ **Collapse/Expand.** To view all the options available for a track, click the Collapse/Expand track button. If you are not using a track, you might as well leave the track in its unexpanded mode so that it doesn't consume too much screen space. If you've expanded a track and want to collapse it, simply click the Collapse/Expand icon again.

✦ **Toggle Track Output.** Clicking the Eye icon toggles on and off track output, which prevents the track from being viewed either in the Monitor window during playing or when exporting. To turn output on again, click the button again, and the Eye icon returns, indicating that the track will be viewed in the Monitor window and output when exporting.

✦ **Toggle Track Lock.** Clicking the Toggle Track Lock track icon locks the track. When a track is locked, no changes can be made to the track. When you click on the Lock track icon, a lock appears indicating that the track is locked. To unlock the track, click again on the icon.

✦ **Set Display Style.** Clicking on this pop-up menu allows you to choose how and whether thumbnail images appear in the Timeline tracks. The choices are Head and Tail, Show Head Only, Show Frames, and Show Name only. To view footage in the frames throughout a clip, choose Show Frames.

✦ **Show keyframes/Opacity handles.** Clicking this pop-up menu allows you to view keyframes or opacity handles in the Timeline. Keyframes denote control points for special effects set in the Effects window. Opacity indicates transparency in frames. After you've created effects with keyframes, you can alter them by clicking and dragging the keyframes in the Timeline or dragging the opacity handles up or down. Dragging down lowers opacity, and dragging up raises opacity.

✦ **Add/Remove keyframe.** Clicking this button allows you to add or remove a keyframe from a track's effects graph line. To add a keyframe, move the current-time indicator to where you want the keyframe to appear and click the Add/ Remove keyframe button. To remove the keyframe, move the current-time indicator to the keyframe and then click the Add/Remove keyframe button.

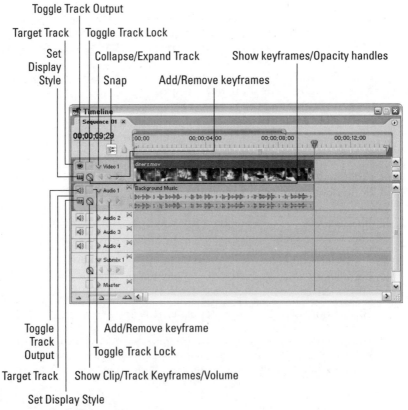

Figure 6-3: Timeline track options.

Tip You can also create and remove keyframes by Ctrl+clicking with the Pen tool.

Audio track icons and options

Audio track Timeline controls are similar to video track controls. Using the audio track Timeline options, you can adjust audio volume, choose which tracks are exported, and show and hide keyframes. Premiere Pro provides a variety of different audio tracks: standard audio, Submix tracks, Master tracks, and 5.1 tracks. Use the standard audio track for .wav and .aif clips. The Master track is used for a mix of all tracks. Submix tracks allow you to create effects with a subset of your tracks rather than all of them. Audio is placed in the Master and Submix tracks using Premiere Pro's Audio Mixers. The 5.1 tracks are special tracks only used for surround sound audio. Figure 6-3 shows the audio section of the Timeline with a Master, Submix, and 5.1 track.

 Cross-Reference Chapter 8 covers using audio in the Timeline and creating audio effects. Chapter 9 covers the Audio Mixer, Master, and Submix tracks.

 Note If you drag a video clip that contains audio to a video track, the audio automatically is placed in the corresponding audio track. Otherwise, you can simply drag music audio to an audio track; as the Timeline plays, the video and corresponding audio will play.

The following describes many of the audio icons and options see in Figure 6-3:

✦ **Target.** As you edit, Premiere Pro outputs to the target track. The target track in Figure 6-3 is Audio 1. Note that audio has rounded corners. To select a target track, click it.

✦ **Enable Track Output.** Clicking this icon turns off and on audio output for the track. When output is off, audio is not output when played in the Monitor window or when the project is output.

✦ **Toggle Lock.** Locks the track so it cannot be altered. Clicking the Toggle Lock track icon toggles track locking on or off. When a track is locked, a lock icon appears.

✦ **Set Display Style.** Click this drop-down menu to choose whether audio clips are displayed by name or as a waveform.

✦ **Show Clip/Track keyframe/Volume.** This drop-down menu allows you to choose to view keyframes or volume settings for audio clips or for the entire track. Keyframes in the audio track indicate changes in audio effects. If you choose to show volume settings for clips or the entire track, you can adjust the volume in the Timeline using the Pen tool.

✦ **Add/Remove keyframe.** Clicking this button allows you to add or remove a keyframe from a track's volume or audio effect's graph line. To add a keyframe, move the current-time indicator to where you want the keyframe to appear and click the Add/Remove keyframe button. To remove the keyframe, move the current-time indicator to the keyframe and click the Add/Remove keyframe button.

Clicking this button allows you to add or remove a keyframe from a track's Effects graph line. To add a keyframe, move the current-time indicator to where you want the keyframe to appear and click the Add/Remove keyframe button. To remove the keyframe, move the current-time indicator to the keyframe and then click the Add/Remove keyframe button.

✦ **Show Track Keyframes/Volume.** This drop-down menu allows you to choose whether audio keyframe and volume for an audio track are displayed. If you display keyframes and volume, you can click and drag to move keyframes and change volume settings.

✦ **Master track.** The Master track is used in conjunction with the Audio Mixer (see Chapter 9). Like other audio tracks, the Master track can be expanded; you can show keyframes and volume. and you can set or remove keyframes.

Track Commands

As you work with the Timeline, you may want to add or remove or rename audio and video tracks. This section reviews the commands for renaming, adding, and removing tracks, as well as for changing the Snap options and the starting point of a sequence, the sequence zero point. Some of the commands described next are activated by right-clicking in the Timeline window; others are activated through menu commands.

✦ **Rename Track.** To rename an audio or video track, right-click its name. After you release the mouse, you will be able edit the track's name.

✦ **Add Track.** To add a track, choose Sequence ➪ Add Track (or right-click on a track name and choose Add Track). This opens the Add Tracks dialog box, shown in Figure 6-4. Here you can choose what type of track to create and where to place it.

✦ **Delete Track.** Before deleting a track, decide whether you want to delete a target track or empty tracks. If you want to delete a target track, click at the left side of the track to select it and choose Sequence ➪ Delete Track (or right-click the track name and choose Delete Track). This opens the Delete Tracks dialog box where you can choose to delete empty tracks, the target tracks, or Submix tracks.

✦ **Snap.** The Snap icon (magnet) toggles Premiere Pro's Snap Edges command. When activated, clips snap together automatically when you click and drag one near the other. This prevents Timeline gaps between edits. To enable Snap, you can also choose Sequence ⇨ Snap.

✦ **Sequence Zero Point.** You can change the zero point of a sequence by moving the Timeline to the position you want the sequence timecode to start and choosing Sequence Zero Point from the Timeline window menu. Why change the sequence zero point? You may start your production with a countdown, or other sequence, but not want the duration of this opening sequence to be added to Timeline frame count.

✦ **Display Audio Units.** By default, Premiere Pro shows Timeline intervals in frames. You can change the Timeline interval to display audio samples, by choosing Audio Units in the Timeline Window menu. If you choose Audio Units, the display shows audio samples in milliseconds.

Figure 6-4: Use the Add Tracks dialog box to specify options for new tracks.

Using Multiple Sequences

An assembled production in a Timeline is called a *sequence*. Why differentiate between the Timeline and the sequence within it? The answer is that you can have multiple sequences within a Timeline, each sequence featuring different footage. Furthermore, each sequence has a name and can be renamed. You may want to use multiple sequences to divide your project into smaller elements. After you've completed editing in the smaller sequences, you can then combine them into one sequence before exporting. You may also want to copy and paste footage from one sequence into another to simply experiment with different edits, effects, or transitions. Figure 6-5 shows a Timeline window with two sequences within it.

Creating a new sequence

When you create a new sequence, it is automatically added to the active Timeline window as a new tab in the window, as shown in Figure 6-5. Creating a sequence is easy; simply choose File ➪ New ➪ Sequence. This opens the New Sequence dialog box, shown in Figure 6-6. Here you can rename the sequence and choose how many tracks to add. Clicking OK creates a new sequence and adds it to the currently selected Timeline. If you want to view the sequence in a separate window, click its tab and drag it off the Timeline window. After you have two sequences onscreen, you can cut and paste from one to the other or edit a sequence and nest it into another sequence.

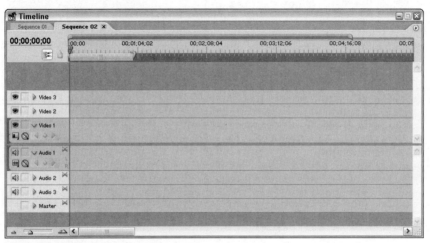

Figure 6-5: The Timeline window with two sequences.

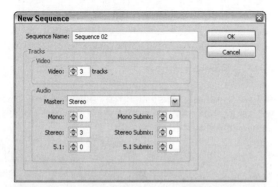

Figure 6-6: The New Sequence dialog box controls how tracks are created in new sequences.

To move from sequence to another in the Timeline window, you click the sequence's tab. If you want to separate a sequence into another Timeline window, drag its tab out of the Timeline window. When you release the mouse, Premiere Pro creates a new Timeline window with the sequence within it. If you have multiple Timeline windows open onscreen, you can activate a Timeline window with a sequence in it by choosing Window ⇨ Timelines and then choosing the sequence name in the submenu.

Nesting sequences

After you create a new sequence in a project, you can place footage in it and create effects and transitions. Later, if desired, you can embed or nest it into another sequence. You can use this feature to gradually create a project in separate short sequences and later assemble them all into one sequence.

One advantage of nesting is that you can reuse an edited sequence again and again, by simply nesting it several times in another Timeline. Each time you nest one sequence in another, you can trim it or change the transitions surrounding it on the Timeline. When you add an effect to a nested sequence, Premiere Pro applies the effect to all the clips in the sequence, saving you from having to apply the same effect to multiple clips.

If you are going to nest sequences, it's important to note that nested sequences always refer to their original source clips. If you change the original source clips, the change will be reflected in the sequences in which it is nested.

Figure 6-7 shows how a nested sequence appears in the Timeline window. In this figure, Sequence 02 was nested within Sequence 01, and audio and video transitions were added between the two sequences.

On the DVD-ROM

The nested sequence in Figure 6-7 includes an mage is from the Skyrider folder from Digital Vision's SkyRider CD-ROM. The clip, 652005f.mov, is included in the Chapter 6 folder of the *Adobe Premiere Pro Bible* DVD. Figure 6-7 also includes two video clips called diners.mov and chefs.mov. These clips are from the Nite Out project in Chapter 1. The clips are Digital Vision's NightMoves 705008f.mov and 705009f.mov.

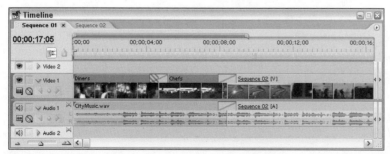

Figure 6-7: Sequence 02 nested within Sequence 01.

Here's how to nest one sequence within another:

1. **Create a new sequence by choosing File ➪ New ➪ Sequence.**

2. **In the new sequence, create edits, transitions, and effects as needed.**

3. **To nest one sequence in another sequence, click and drag a sequence from the Project window or from the Source section of the Monitor window into the track of another sequence.**

Tip   To open a sequence in the Source section of the Monitor window, Ctrl+double-click it in the Project window or in the Timeline window.

Tip   To quickly return to the original sequence of a nested sequence, double-click the nested sequence in the Timeline window.

Summary

Premiere Pro provides numerous features in the Timeline window to control how clips are viewed and exported. In the Timeline window you can create more than sequence, or you can create a new sequence and view it in another window.

✦ Use Timeline ruler options to change zoom levels.

✦ Select a track by clicking at the head of the track to make it the target track.

✦ Tracks can be locked and hidden.

✦ You can view keyframe and opacity settings in video tracks.

✦ To create a new sequence, choose File ➪ New ➪ Sequence.

✦ To nest one sequence in another, click and drag the sequence from the Project window into a track in the Timeline window of another sequence.

✦   ✦   ✦

Basic Editing with the Timeline and Monitor Windows

Editing drives a video program. The careful assembly of sound and video clips can control excitement, tension, and interest. Fortunately, Premiere Pro makes this crucial element of digital video production a logical, creative, and rewarding process rather than a tedious and frustrating one. Premiere Pro's interface—which features its Timeline and Monitor windows—combines with its track selection and editing tools to provide a fully integrated and powerful working environment.

This chapter introduces you to the basic techniques of editing in Premiere Pro. It begins with an overview of the editing process and proceeds to basic Timeline editing tasks, such as selecting and moving clips from one part of the Timeline to another. The chapter concludes with a discussion of creating insert and overlay edits by using the Source and Program views in the Monitor window. Premiere Pro's advanced editing techniques are discussed in Chapter 13.

The clips used in the figures in this chapter are from 705008f.mov from Digital Vision's Night Moves CD-ROM. This clip and others can be found in the Chapter 1 folder on the Adobe Premiere Pro Bible DVD-ROM.

Basic Editing Concepts and Tools

Before you begin editing video in Premiere Pro, you need a basic idea of different techniques that you can use to edit a digital video production. Premiere Pro provides two main areas for editing clips and assembling them—the Timeline window and the Monitor window. As discussed earlier in this book, the Timeline provides a visual overview of your project. You can begin creating a rough edit by simply dragging clips from the Project window over the Timeline. Using the selection tools in the Timeline, you begin arranging the clips in a logical order.

As you work, you can fine-tune your production by performing edits in the Monitor window. When you edit in the Monitor window, you can set up the Source view to show you a clip that isn't in the Timeline, while the Program view shows you clips already edited the Timeline. Using controls in the Monitor window, you can insert the source clip into the clip that's already in the Timeline, or overlay the source clip so that it replaces a portion of the clip that is in the Timeline. The steps and examples in this chapter lead you to the point where you can create, insert, and overlay edits.

To further fine-tune your editing work, you can use Premiere Pro Pro's editing tools to perform ripple, slide, and slip edits. These, along with more sophisticated editing techniques that can be performed in the Monitor window—such as three- and four-point editing, lifts, and extracts—are discussed in Chapter 13.

As you work, you undoubtedly develop habits that suit the types of productions you are creating. For example, many editing commands feature keyboard shortcuts. You may find it more efficient to set the in and out points of clips by using keyboard shortcut keys.

Note   When you are performing edits, you may find that using keyboard shortcuts saves time. To display the keyboard commands, choose Edit ⇨ Keyboard Customization. Choose Windows in the pop-up menu and then open the section for Monitor and Trim Windows.

The workspace

An important consideration before actually editing a project is to plan how you want your workspace set up. To pick a predefined workspace, choose Window ⇨ Workspace and then choose from the four choices presented: Editing, Audio, Effects, and Color Correction.

In the Editing workspace, shown in Figure 7-1, the Timeline, Monitor, and Project windows consume the entire screen. These are the most important windows you'll be using as you assemble a project. You can drag clips from the Project window into the Source section of the Monitor window, or you can drag them directly from the Timeline. As you'll see later in this chapter, you can edit the clips in either the Timeline or Monitor window.

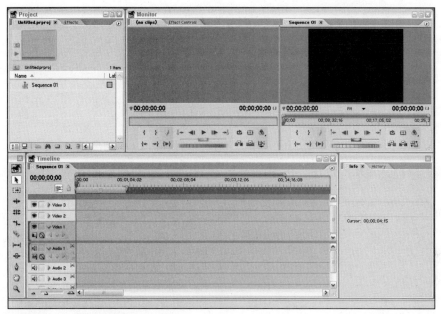

Figure 7-1: The Editing workspace.

At any point in time, you can change the arrangement of palettes onscreen and save your workspace by choosing Window ⇨ Workspace ⇨ Save Workspace. This command adds your workspace to the options in the Windows ⇨ Workspace submenu. When you want to reload your workspace, simply choose Window ⇨ Workspace and select your workspace from the menu.

Getting Started

After you've imported your video, audio, and still footage into the Project window, you may be tempted to immediately start dragging clips to the Timeline to begin the process of editing your production. If you're working on a long project with many production elements, you'll undoubtedly want to plan your production on paper beforehand. If you work from a script that describes the video elements and includes all narration, you'll save yourself hours of time when you begin to edit your production. To help you visualize your production or various parts of it, you may also want to create a storyboard, which contains drawings or printouts of the video. After you've loaded the various production elements into bins in the Timeline, you may find it helpful also to double-click each clip in the Project window, and click the play button in the Monitor window to view each clip before editing.

For beginners who are working on new projects, it may also be a good idea to practice editing short video and audio sequences so that you become familiar with the basic techniques of creating a production. In Premiere Pro, you can edit clips either in the Monitor or Timelime window. Beginners may be tempted to drag all clips into the Timeline and click and drag to edit them there. But for precision editing, the Monitor window provides better controls for fine-tuning your work. After you've edited a clip's in and out points in the Monitor window, you can then drag the clip to the Timeline, or have Premiere Pro place it there for you.

Working with the Monitor Window

The Monitor window is not only used for previewing your production as you work, but it can also be used for precise editing and trimming. You can use the Monitor window to trim clips before placing them on the Timeline, for dropping edited clips in the Timeline. You can also use it to fine-tune edits of clips already assembled in the Timeline. When editing using the Monitor window, you can choose to set in and out points in Single View (see Figure 7-2), Dual View (see Figure 7-3), or Trim View (see Figure 7-4). In Single View mode, the Monitor displays just the edited program (clips on the Timeline). Dual View mode displays a source clip (a clip not yet added to the Timeline) in the left side of the window and the program material (clips on the Timeline) on the right side of the window. In Trim View mode, the frame to the right and the frame to the left of the edit line are represented in a separate section to provide greater precision for setting in and out points. To select a view mode for the Monitor window, click one of the mode buttons near the top of the Monitor window or choose Single View, Dual View, or Trim from the Monitor window's menu.

Figure 7-2: The Monitor window in Single View.

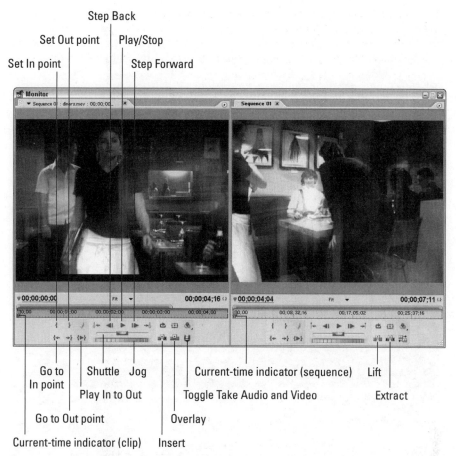

Figure 7-3: The Monitor window in Dual View.

Monitor-safe margins enable you to show the video-safe zones for movement and for titles. By clicking the Monitor menu and choosing Safe Margins, you can activate safe-zone markers in the Monitor window that indicate the image area that is safely within the monitor viewing area, as well as the image area that might be over-scanned. A safe zone is needed because television monitors overscan an image, thus expanding portions of it beyond the screen. To view the safe-zone markers in the Monitor window, choose Safe Margins from the Monitor window menu. When the safe-zone margins appear in the Monitor window, the inner safe zone is the title-safe area, and the outer is the action-safe area.

In most editing situations, you want to view the Monitor window in Dual View mode. This enables you to view a source clip (clips to be used in the program) and the program material (the clips already placed in sequence in the Timeline window) at the same time. Before you use more sophisticated editing techniques, you should become familiar with the two sections of the Monitor window in Dual View mode. Beneath the source clip monitor (left side) is the source controller, which enables you to play source clips that haven't been added to the Timeline. The In and Out point icons enable you to set in and out points of source clips.

Beneath the program or sequence side (right side) is the program controller, which enables you to play the program that exists on the Timeline. Clicking the In and Out point icons in the Program View changes the in and out points of the sequence already on the Timeline. You use the sequence In and Out point icons when performing lift and extract edits, which remove footage from the current sequence, and when you create three-point edits (covered in Chapter 13).

Figure 7-4: The Monitor window in Trim View.

Trimming clips in the Monitor window

Before placing clips in the Timeline, you may want to first trim them (set the in and out points) in the Monitor window, since captured clips invariably contain more footage than needed. If you trim a clip before placing it in the Timeline, you'll probably find that you save time that would otherwise be spent clicking and dragging clip edges in the Timeline. Here are the steps for setting the in and out points of a clip in the Monitor window:

1. **To display the Monitor window, double-click a clip in the Project window.** Double-clicking video footage in the Project window displays the clip so that both video and audio can be edited. If you double-click the clip's video track in the Timeline window, only the video portion appears in the Clip window. If you double-click the audio track of the clip, Premiere Pro displays only the audio part, allowing you to edit only audio.

When the Clip window appears in the Monitor window, you can use the controls shown in Figure 7-1 to view the clip. It's a good idea to view the clip before you edit it.

2. **Click the Play button to play the entire clip (play the clip continuously by clicking the Loop button).** When you find a section you want to edit, you can stop it by clicking the Stop button. When you stop the clip, look at the time readout to see at which frame you have stopped. This can help you when setting in and out points and when setting markers.

3. **To precisely access the frame that you want to set as your in point, start by clicking and dragging the blue triangle current-time indicator (CTI) over the ruler area in the Monitor window.** If you don't stop at the correct frame, you can use the Step forward and Step backward buttons to slowly move one frame at a time forward or backwards. You can also click and drag the shuttle (refer to Figure 7-3) or the jog tread area to move back and forth through your clip.

Note   You can jump to a specific frame in a clip by double-clicking over the Location Time display in the bottom-left corner of the monitor display and typing a specific timecode position. You do not need to type colons or semi-colons.

4. **When you reach the in point, click the Set In point button. A left brace appears in the ruler area.**

5. **Now locate the frame that you want to set as the out point and click the Set Out button.** A right brace now appears in the ruler area. After you set the in and out points, you can easily edit their positions by simply clicking and dragging on one of the brace icons. After you've set the in and out points, note the Time display with the delta symbol in front of it. This number indicates the duration from the in point to the out point.

After you've edited a clip in the Monitor window, you can drag it to the Timeline from the Project window. Later in the chapter, you'll see how to use the Monitor window to add the clip to the Timeline.

Note   If you edit a clip in the Monitor window that is already on the Timeline, you'll see the sequence shrink or grow, depending whether you've shaved frames or added frames to the in and out points.

Choosing clips in the Monitor window

Once you start working with clips in the Monitor window, you can easily return to previously used clips. When you first work with a clip in the Monitor window, the clip's name appears at the top of the source section of the window. If you want to return to a clip that you previously used in the Monitor window, simply click the clip's name in the Monitor window. This opens a drop-down menu in which you can pick previously used clips. After you choose the clip in the drop-down menu, it appears in the source section of the Monitor window.

"Taking" audio and/or video

When working with clips in the source section of the Monitor window, you can easily instruct Premiere Pro to use both the clip's audio and video when editing audio only or video only. If the clip that you are editing in the Monitor window includes both video and audio, you can use the Take Audio and Video button to take audio only or video only. If you want to edit using only a clip's video, click the Toggle Take Audio and Video icon in the Monitor window (refer to Figure 7-3) until it changes to the Take Video icon. If you want to edit using only audio from the clip, click the Toggle Take Audio and Video icon until the take Audio icon appears. When you perform an insert or overlay edit, Premiere Pro will create the edit using the audio and video, the video only, or the audio only option, depending on the setting of the Toggle Audio and Video icons.

Editing in the Timeline

As discussed in Chapter 3, Premiere Pro's Timeline provides a graphical representation of your project. By simply analyzing the clip's effects and transitions in the Timeline, you can get a visual sense of how it is edited without actually viewing the footage. Premiere provides a variety of ways of placing clips into the Timeline:

✦ Click and drag the clip or image from the Project window into the Timeline.

✦ Select the clip in the Project window, then choose Clip ➪ Insert or Clip ➪ Overlay. The clip is inserted into the target track at the current Timeline location.

✦ Double-click the clip in the Project window to open it in the Monitor window, then click the Insert or Overlay buttons in the Monitor window.

✦ If you want to place multiple clips in the Timeline to create a rough cut of your work, you can use the Automate to Sequence command described in the next section.

Note   To make a track the target track, click in the track's header area.

Automate to Sequence

Premiere Pro's Automate to Sequence command provides a fast way to assemble a project on the Timeline. You might view this command as an efficient means of creating a quick rough cut. Automate to Sequence not only places clips in the Timeline, but it also can add a default transition between clips as well. If the clips in the Project window contain a lot of footage that you will not need, your best bet is to trim the clips in the Monitor window by executing Automate to Sequence. Here are the steps for using Automate to Sequence:

1. **Select the clips in the Project window that you want to place in the Timeline.**
   To select a group of adjacent clips, click on the first clip you want to have in
   the sequence, then press Shift. While holding Shift, click on the last clip you
   want in the sequence.

   Tip To select non-adjacent clips, Ctrl+click on different clips in the Project window.

2. **To add the selected clips to the Timeline, choose Project ⇨ Automate to
   Sequence, or click the Automate to Sequence button in the Project window.**
   This opens the Automate to Sequence dialog box, shown in Figure 7-5.

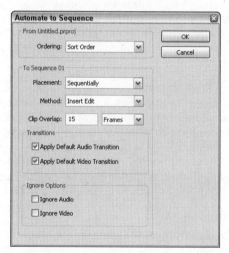

Figure 7-5: Use Automate to Sequence
to create a rough edit.

3. **In the Automate to Sequence dialog box, choose the options to control how
   the clips are placed on the Timeline.** Here is a review of the choices:

   • **Ordering.** Allows you to choose to have the clips placed in their sorted
     order in the Project window or according to how they were selected in
     the Project window.

   • **Placement.** Choose to have the clips ordered in their project sequence
     or at each unnumbered Marker in the Timeline. If you choose the
     Unnumbered Marker option, Premiere Pro disables the Transitions
     option in the dialog box.

   • **Method.** Allows you to choose Insert or Overlay edit. If you choose
     Insert, clips are added to the Timelime; if you choose Overlay, clips from
     the Project window replace clips in the Timeline.

   • **Clip Overlap.** Allows you to specify how many seconds or frames are
     used as overlapping frames for the default transition.

- **Apply Default Audio/VideoTransition.** Applies the currently set default transition between clips.

- **Ignore Audio.** If this option is selected, Premiere Pro doesn't place the audio linked to clips.

- **Ignore Video.** If this option is selected, Premiere Pro doesn't place the video in the Timeline.

4. **To execute the Automate to Sequence command, click OK.**

Selecting and moving clips in the Timeline

After you've placed clips in the Timeline, you'll often need to reposition them as part of the editing process. You can choose to move one clip at a time, or you can move several clips at the same time. (You can also move either the video or audio of a clip independently. To do this you need to temporarily unlink the clip.)

Using the Selection tool

The simplest way to move a single clip is to click it with the Selection tool and move it within the Timeline window. If you want the clip you move to snap to the edge of another clip, make sure the Snap to Edges command is selected. Choose either Sequence ⇨ Snap or click the Snap icon (a magnet) in the upper-left corner of the Timeline window. Here is a description of how to select clips, tracks, and multiple clips using Premiere Pro's Selection tool. After a clip or clips are selected, you can move them by clicking and dragging or delete them from the Timeline by pressing Delete.

- ✦ To select a clip, activate the Selection tool, and click on the clip.

- ✦ To select more than one clip, press Shift and then click on the clips that you want to select. Alternatively, you can also click and drag to create a marquee selection around the clips that you want to select. After you release the mouse, the clips within the marquee are selected. You can also use this technique to select clips that are on different tracks.

- ✦ If you want to select the video without the audio portion of a clip, or the audio without the video, Alt+click the video or audio track.

- ✦ To add or subtract a clip or a selection of clips to or from a selection, press Shift and then click and drag a marquee selection around the clip or clips.

Using the Track Select tool

If you want to quickly select several clips on a track or to delete clips on a track, use the Track Select tool. The Track Select tool does not select all clips on the track. It selects all clips from the point at which you click. Thus, if you've placed four clips on the Timeline and want to select the last two, click on the third clip. Figure 7-6 shows clips selected with the Track Select tool.

Figure 7-6: Clips selected with the Track Select tool.

If you want to quickly select multiple clips on different Timeline tracks, press Shift while you click in a track with the Track select tool. This selects all clips on all tracks starting at the point you first click.

Grouping clips

If you know you'll need to select and reselect the same clips again and again, you should place them in a group. After you've created a group of clips, you can select every member of the group by clicking on any group member. You can also delete all clips in a group by selecting any member of the group and pressing Delete.

To create a group of clips, start by selecting the clips and then choose Clip ➪ Group. To ungroup the clips, choose Clip ➪ Ungroup.

If you move a clip on the Timeline that is linked to another clip — such as a video clip that is linked to its audio clip — the linked clips move together.

Setting In and Out Points in the Timeline Window

Once you're familiar with the how to select clips in the Timeline, you can easily perform edits. You can edit by either using the Selection tool or setting in and out points using Markers.

Using the Selection tool to set in and out points

One of the simplest ways to edit in the Timeline window is to set in and out points using the Selection tool. To edit an in or out point with the Selection tool, follow these steps:

1. **Select the Selection tool in the Tools palette.**

2. **To set a clip's in point, move the Selection tool over the left edge of the clip in the Timeline.** The Selection tool changes to an Edge icon.

3. **Click and drag the edge of the clip to where you want the clip to start.**

4. **To set a clip's out point, move the Selection tool over the right edge of the clip in the Timeline.** The Selection tool changes to an Edge icon.

5. **Click and drag the edge of the clip to where you want the clip to end.**

Creating insert and overlay edits by clicking and dragging

After you learn how to edit clips with the Selection tool, you can begin assembling a project into a production. As you work, you can use a few simple procedures to streamline the editing process as you add clips to the Timeline. For instance, you can overlay or insert one clip between the frames of other clips by simply clicking and dragging. When you create an overlay edit, you replace old footage with new footage; when you insert, the new footage is added to the Timeline, but no footage is removed.

For example, assume that you have a clip of a galloping horse in the Timeline. You want to place a three-second close-up of the jockey on the horse into the clip. If you perform an insert edit, the clip is split at the Timeline edit location, and the jockey is inserted into the clip. The entire Timeline sequence is three seconds longer. If you perform an overlay edit, on the other hand, the three-second-jockey footage replaces three seconds of horse footage. An overlay enables you to continue using the audio track that is linked to the galloping horse clip, providing more consistent continuity in the final video.

Adding Sequence Markers

You can add numerical markers to a clip and use them as visual landmarks on the Timeline that you want to quickly return to later. These are especially useful with longer projects.

To add a marker, move the Sequence Marker icon in the Timeline window to where you want to add a marker and then choose Marker ➪ Set Sequence Marker ➪ Next Available Numbered.

You can jump to a marker by choosing Marker ➪ Go To Sequence Marker ➪ Next or Marker ➪ Go To Sequence Marker ➪ Numbered.

To create an overlay edit on the Timeline, click and drag a clip from the Project window over a clip in the Timeline. As you move one clip over the other, the mouse pointer changes to an Overlay icon. When you release the mouse, Premiere Pro places one clip over the other and removes the underlying video. Figure 7-7 shows the Timeline before and after an overlay edit.

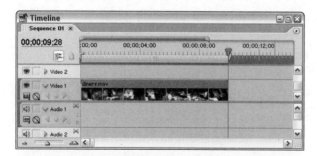

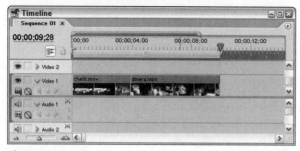

Figure 7-7: Sequence in Timeline window before and after an overlay edit.

To create an insert edit, press and hold Ctrl and then click and drag a clip from the Project window over a clip in the Timeline. As you move one clip over the other, the mouse pointer changes to an Insert icon. When you release the mouse (make sure Ctrl is still pressed), Premiere Pro inserts the new clip in the Timeline and pushes the footage at the insert point to the right. Figure 7-8 shows the Timeline before and after an insert edit.

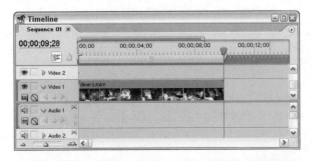

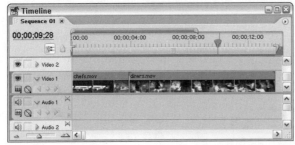

Figure 7-8: Sequence in Timeline window before and after an insert edit.

Inserting and overlaying using the Monitor window

Although you can create insert and overlay edits while dragging clips to the Timeline, performing these edits in the Monitor window ensures better precision. When you perform an insert edit, the source clip is inserted into the Timeline at the current-time indicator. If you perform an overlay edit, the source clip replaces a section of the sequence at the current-time indicator. When you perform the edit in the Monitor window, Premiere Pro adds the new edited section to the current sequence in the Timeline.

The following steps show you how to set the target track for the edit, add a clip to the source section (left side) of the Monitor window and then perform an insert or overlay edit:

1. **Select the target track in the Timeline window by clicking in the header area (far left) of the track.**

Note If a track is locked, you cannot set it as the target track.

2. **Click Dual View from the Monitor window pop-up menu.**

3. **If you don't have program material in the current sequence in the Timeline window, click and drag a clip into the Timeline.** This clip appears in the Program section of the Timeline. Assume that this is part of the program you are editing and you now want to insert a clip two seconds into it.

4. **Use the controls on the program (right side) of the Monitor window to move to the frame where you want the source clip inserted.** You can click the Frame Forward and Frame Back buttons, or you can use the shuttle or jog controls.

5. **To place a clip in the Source section of the Monitor window, double-click it in the Project window, or drag a clip from the Project window to the Source section of the Monitor window.** If multiple clips appear in the Source section of the Monitor window, choose the clip in the drop-down menu in the tab at the top of the Source section.

   To view the clip, click the Play button. To use both the video and audio for the clip, there should not be a diagonal line through the Take Video and Take Audio icons. By default, no diagonal line exists. A diagonal line appears only if you click these icons. If the line is present, simply click the icon to toggle the Take Audio or Take Video icon off.

   If your source clip contains audio and you want to insert or overlay video only, click the Toggle Take Audio and Video icon until the Take Video icon appears.

6. **In the Source clip section of the Monitor window, click the Frame Forward and Frame Back buttons to move to the frames that you want to set as the in and out points.**

7. **When you reach the in point, click the Set In point button.**

8. **Move to the desired out point.**

9. **Set the out point by clicking the Set Out point button.** Now you can perform an insert or an overlay edit.

10. **Perform the insert or overlay edit.** To insert the clip at the current-time indicator, choose Clip ⇨ Insert at Edit line, or click the Insert button in the Monitor window. After you click, the clip in the Timeline is cut at the frame that you set in the Monitor window. Inserted into the clip is the source clip whose in and out points you set in the Source window. If you want to overlay the clip instead of inserting it, choose Clip ⇨ Overlay at Timeline or click the Overlay button. After you click, the source clip replaces a section of the Timeline.

11. **To view the final edit, click the Play button in the Monitor window.**

Editing with Sequence Markers

You also can perform basic editing in the currently selected sequence by setting
in and out points using the Marker ➪ Set Sequence Marker ➪ In and Marker ➪
Set Sequence Marker ➪ Out commands. These commands set in and out points
for the beginning and end of the Timeline sequence. After you create Sequence
Markers, you can use them as in and out points for lift and extract edits (described
in the next section).

Setting in and out points

Here's how to set in and out points on the Timeline using menu commands:

1. **Click and drag the current-time indicator to where you want to set the
   Timeline in point.**

2. **Choose Marker ➪ Set Sequence Marker ➪ In.** An In point icon appears at the
   ruler line on the Timeline at the position of the current-time indicator.

3. **Click and drag the current-time indicator to where you want to set the out
   point.**

4. **Choose Marker ➪ Set Sequence Marker ➪ Out.** An Out point icon appears on
   the Timeline at the current-time indicator position.

Note   After you create the in and out points, you can easily move them by clicking and
dragging them in the Timeline window.

Tip   You can also set in and out points for the current sequence by clicking the Set In
point and Set Out point icons in the Sequence side of the Monitor window.

Clearing in and out points

After creating Sequence Markers, you can easily clear them with the following menu
commands:

✦ To clear both the in and out points and to start all over again, choose
Marker ➪ Clear Sequence Marker ➪ In and Out.

✦ To clear just the in point, choose Marker ➪ Clear Sequence Marker ➪ In.

✦ To clear just the out point, choose Marker ➪ Clear Sequence Marker ➪ Out.

Performing lift and extract edits at Sequence Markers

You can use Sequence Markers to easily remove clip segments from the Timeline by
executing the Sequence Lift command or the Sequence Extract command. When you
perform a lift edit, Premiere Pro lifts a segment off the Timeline and leaves a blank

space where the deleted clip existed. When you perform an extract edit, Premiere Pro removes a section of the clip and then joins the frames of remaining clip sections together so no blank area exists.

To perform a lift edit using Sequence Markers, follow these steps:

1. **Set in and out Sequence Markers at the section that you want to delete.** The top of Figure 7-9 shows in and out points created with Sequence Markers in the Timeline window. See the earlier section "Setting in and out points" for information on creating sequenced in and out points.

2. **To perform a lift edit, choose Sequence ➪ Lift.** Premiere Pro removes the section bordered by the in and out markers and leaves a blank area in the Timeline, as shown at the bottom of Figure 7-9.

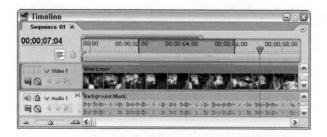

Figure 7-9: Sequence in Timeline window before and after a lift edit.

To perform an extract edit using Sequence Markers, follow these steps:

1. **Set in and out Sequence Markers at the section that you want to delete.** See the earlier section "Setting in and out points" for steps on creating sequenced in and out points.

2. **To perform an extract edit, choose Sequence ➪ Extract.** Premiere Pro removes the section bordered by the in and out markers and joins the edited sections together.

Summary

Premiere Pro provides graphical tools to aid in editing a digital video production. The Timeline, the Selection tools, and the Monitor window all come into play when you begin to assemble and fine-tune your production. When you edit in Premiere Pro, you can do the following:

✦ Drag clips to the Timeline from the Project window.

✦ Use the Selection tools to select and move clips in the Timeline.

✦ Set in and out points in the Timeline.

✦ Set in and out points in the Monitor window.

✦ Perform insert and overlay edits using controls in the Monitor window.

✦ Perform lift and extract edits using the menu commands or the controls in the Monitor window.

✦   ✦   ✦

Editing Audio

Just as a picture is worth a thousand words, sound can create a mood that could take a thousand words to describe. Sound can be used to capture your audience's attention. The right background music can create a feeling of intrigue, comedy, or mystery. Sound effects can add realism and suspense to the visual elements that you present. Undoubtedly, the success of many of the best video productions and movies is related to the sound underlying the video.

Fortunately, Premiere Pro provides a wealth of features that enable you to integrate sound into your video projects. When you place a clip in the Timeline, Premiere Pro automatically takes the sound along with it. If you want to fade in or fade out background music or narration, Premiere Pro's Effect Controls window provides the tools. If you want to add an audio effect that enhances an audio clip or add a special effect, you can simply drag it from the Effects window to the clip. If you want to mix audio into a master track, Premiere Pro's Audio Mixer will do the job.

This chapter focuses on audio track basics. It provides a look at how to use Premiere Pro's audio tracks and how to create effects in the Timeline window. The chapter also includes an overview of Premiere Pro's many audio effects and concludes with a look at how to export audio.

Cross-Reference
Chapter 9 covers creating audio effects and mixing tracks with the Audio Mixer.

What Is Sound?

Before you begin to use Premiere Pro's audio features, it's helpful to have a fundamental idea of what sound is and the terms used to describe it. It will help you to understand exactly what type of sound you're working with and its quality. Terms such as sample rate of 32,000 Hz and bit rate of 16 appear in the custom settings dialog boxes, Export dialog boxes, and in the Project window, as shown in Figure 8-1.

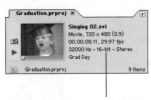

Figure 8-1: Audio information shown in Project window.

Audio sample rate and bit rate

To understand digital sound, it's best to start in the real world where a sound such as someone beating on a drum or playing a musical instrument in a concert hall travels to us through waves. We hear sounds because of the vibrations the waves create. The speed of the vibration, or *sound frequency*, is measured in hertz (Hz). Humans can generally hear within a range from 20 Hz to about 20,000 Hz (20 kHz).

The size of sound wave curve or its amplitude is measured in *decibels*. The greater the curve, the greater its amplitude and the louder the sound.

When sound is digitized, thousands of numbers represent *amplitude*, or height and depth of waves. In digital sound, the frequency of the digital waves is called the *sample rate*. When you load Premiere Pro, you'll see the sample rate of 32 kHz. Thus, every second, 32,000 samples are created to make a sound. When a sample is digitized, it is created by a series of 1s and 0s, or *bits*. Higher quality digital recording uses more bits. CD-quality stereo uses 16 bits. Thus, one sample of CD quality sound could be digitized into a series of 1s and 0s to look like this:

1011011011101010

Older digital video software typically used 8-bit sound rates, which provided poorer quality sound, yet produced smaller digital sound files.

Timeline Audio Tracks

Premiere Pro's Timeline window audio tracks provide a bird's eye view of the sound that accompanies your video. As you can see from Figure 8-2, the audio tracks are grouped together beneath the video tracks. You can drag separate tracks to the audio tracks, click and drag to move them, and use the Razor tool to slice audio.

When you place a video clip into the Timeline that includes an audio track, Premiere Pro places it into the corresponding track automatically. Thus, if you place a video clip with audio in Video track 1, the audio is automatically placed in Audio track 1. If you slice a video clip with the Razor tool, the audio is sliced along with it.

As discussed in Chapter 6, you can expand and compress audio tracks by clicking the Collapse/Expand icon. Once the track is expanded, you can choose from the following display options:

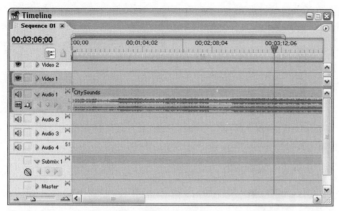

Figure 8-2: Audio tracks with 5.1, Submix, and Master tracks.

✦ You can choose to view the audio by name or by waveform by choosing from the Set Display Style pop-up menu in the Timeline window.

✦ You can view the volume and changes in audio levels for the clip or the entire track by choosing Show Clip Volume or Show Track Volume in the Show Keyframes pop-up menu, as shown in Figure 8-3.

✦ You can view audio effect keyframes by choosing Show Clip Keyframes or Show Track Keyframes.

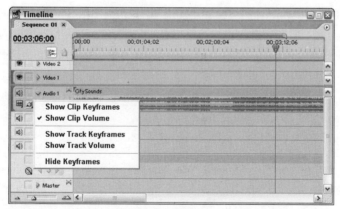

Figure 8-3: Choices from the Keyframes pop-up menu.

As you work with audio in Premiere Pro, you'll encounter different types of audio tracks. The Standard audio track allows for either Mono or Stereo (two-channel sound). The other tracks available include the following:

✦ **Master track.** Displays keyframes and volume for the Master track. You can mix sound from other tracks onto the Master track using Premiere Pro's Audio Mixer.

✦ **Submix tracks.** These are mixed tracks used by the Audio Mixer to mix a subset of all audio tracks.

✦ **5.1 track.** 5.1 tracks are used in Dolby's Surround Sound. 5.1 tracks are used often for DVD movies in surround sound. In 5.1 sound, the left, right, and center channels are in front of the audience, with ambient sounds produced from two speakers behind. This is a total of five channels; the extra .1 channel is a subwoofer that produces sudden explosive-type sounds.

Playing a Sound Clip

After you import a sound clip using Premiere Pro's standard Import command, you can play it in the Project window or Monitor window.

On the DVD-ROM The DVD-ROM includes practice sound clips from Digital Vision's royalty-free CD *Acoustic Chillout.* The filename of the sound clip used in this chapter is 730009aw.wav. We renamed it citysounds to keep our files organized. You can locate the sound clip in the Chapter 8 folder on the *Adobe Premiere Pro Bible* DVD-ROM. You can also use the audio clip used in Chapter 1 (705001.aif from Digital Visions NightMoves CD).

Here are the steps:

1. **Choose File ⇨ Import ⇨ File to import a sound file into your new project.**

2. **At this point, you can play the clip in the Project window by clicking the Play button, as shown in Figure 8-4.** Alternatively, you can double-click the sound file in the Project window. The clip opens in the clip (source) section of the Monitor window,

3. **If you opened the clip in the Monitor window, click the Play button in the clip (source) section of the Monitor window.**

Play button

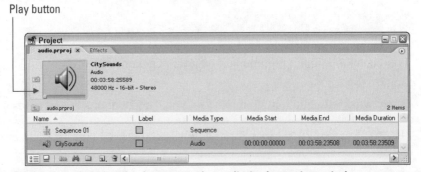

Figure 8-4: Click the Play button to play a clip in the Project window.

Using Audio Units

As you edit in the Monitor window, the standard unit of measurement is the video frame. This is perfect for editing video where you can precisely set the in or out point on a frame-by-frame basis. However, with audio, you may need more precision. For example you may want to edit out an extraneous sound that is less than a frame long. Fortunately, Premiere Pro can display audio time in audio "units" as opposed to frames. You can view audio units in milliseconds or the smallest possible increment — the audio sample. To view audio units and an audio clip's waveform, place a video clip with audio or an audio clip in the Timeline and follow these step:

1. **Click the Collapse/Expand button (the triangle in front of the phrase Audio 1) to expand the audio track.**

2. **Click the Set Display Style icon and choose Show Waveform.**

3. **Change units to audio samples by choosing Audio Units in the Timeline menu.** This changes the Timeline ruler display to audio units as either audio samples or milliseconds. (The default setting is audio samples; however, this can be changed by choosing Project ⇨ Project Settings and choosing Milliseconds in the Audio Section Display Format drop-down menu.)

To edit the audio, follow these steps:

1. **Zoom in by clicking and dragging toward the right on the Timeline zoom slider.** Figure 8-5 shows the ruler with audio units in view. Note that the time readout is shown in audio samples, and notice in the audio track how much audio exists between two adjacent video frames.

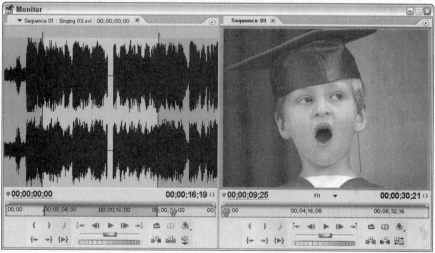

Figure 8-5: Audio units shown in Timeline and in Time display.

2. **Click and drag either clip edge to change in and out points. Or you can edit by activating the Razor tool in the Tool palette and clicking to slice the audio at a specific point.**

Unlinking audio and editing it in the Monitor window

If you place a clip with audio in the Timeline, you can edit its audio separately from the video. To do this, you first need to unlink the audio from the video; then you can edit audio in and out points separate from the video. You can even view the audio waveform in the Monitor window and edit it there. Here are the steps:

1. **Select the clip in the Timeline.**

2. **Unlink the clip by choosing Clip ⇨ Unlink Audio and Video.**

3. **Deselect the audio and video tracks by clicking in an empty Timeline track.**

4. **Double-click the audio portion of the clip.** The audio opens in the left section of the Monitor window. Here you can view an enlarged image of the waveform, as shown in Figure 8-6.

5. **Change the time display from frames to audio units by choosing Audio Units in the menu of the left section of the Monitor window.** (Open this menu by clicking the small triangle in the upper-right corner of the left section of the Monitor window.)

Set Out point button

Set In point button

Figure 8-6: Audio in and out points set in the Monitor window.

6. **To set in and out points, move the current-time indicator to in the left side of the Monitor window to the in point.** As you drag the current-time indicator, you'll hear the audio. Click the Set In point button. Move the current-time indicator to the out point and click the Set Out point button. The audio in the current sequence in the Timeline window now reflects the new in and out points for the audio. Figure 8-6 shows an audio clip in the left section of the Monitor window with its in and out points changed.

 Tip If the display in the left side of the Monitor window is set to Audio Units, use the Step Back or Step Forward button (or press the left or right arrow key) to step through the audio one audio unit at a time.

7. **To avoid confusion, you may want to rename the unlinked audio clip.** To do this, select it, choose Clip ➪ Rename and enter a new name in the Rename Clip dialog box.

Gaining, Fading, and Balancing

One of the most common sound effects is to slowly fade in sound at the beginning of a clip and fade out the sound at the end. You can do this by setting keyframes on the keyframe line that appears when you choose Show Clip Volume the audio tracks show display pop-up menu. You can also change the balance of a sound in a stereo channel. When you balance, you remove a percentage of the sound information from one channel and add it to the other. This is called *panning*. You can change the entire volume of a sound clip by using Premiere Pro's Gain command. The following sections show you how to adjust audio gain, fade audio in and out, and balance stereo channels.

Adjusting sound volume using the Gain command

The Gain command enables you to change the sound level of the entire clip by raising or lowering audio gain in decibels. Generally in audio recording, engineers raise or lower gain during recording. If sound levels dip, the engineer "riding the gain" raises the gain; if the levels go too high, he or she can lower the gain. Here's how to use the Premiere Pro Gain command, which adjusts the uniform volume of the clip:

1. **Choose File ➪ Import to import a sound clip or a video clip with sound.**

2. **Click the clip in the Project window or drag the sound clip from the Project window to an audio track in the Timeline window.**

3. **If the clip is in the Timeline, click the sound clip in the audio track in the Timeline window.**

4. **Choose Clip ➪ Audio Options ➪ Audio Gain.** The Clip Gain dialog box appears (see Figure 8-7).

Figure 8-7: Use the Clip Gain dialog box to adjust audio gain for an entire clip.

5. **Type a value in the field in the Clip Gain dialog box.** The 0 setting is the original clip volume in decibels. A number greater than 0 increases the sound volume of the clip. A number less than 0 decreases the sound volume. If you click Normalize, Premiere Pro sets the maximum gain possible without audio clipping. Clipping occurs when an audio signal is too high, and it can result in distortion.

Tip   Click and drag the mouse over the dB value in the Clip Gain dialog box to increase or decrease audio gain. Clicking and dragging right increases the dB value; clicking and dragging left decreases it.

Fading track sound

Premiere Pro provides a variety of options for fading in or out a clip's volume. You can fade a clip in or out and change its volume using the Volume audio effect in the Effect Controls window, or you can fade a clip in or out by applying a crossfade transition from the Effects window to the in or out point of a clip. As shown in the following steps, you can also change volume using the Pen tool to create keyframes in the Timeline. After the keyframes are set, you can adjust volume by clicking and dragging on the keyframe graph line.

When you fade sound in a track, you can choose to fade the entire track or a clip's volume. In this section, you'll fade track volume:

1. **Choose File ➪ Import ➪ File to import a sound clip or a video clip with sound.**

2. **Drag the sound clip from the Project window to an audio track in the Timeline window.**

3. **Expand the audio track and choose Show Track Volume from the Show Keyframes drop-down menu (refer Figure 8-3).** A yellow graph line now appears in the middle of the audio track.

Note   You can also choose Show Clip Keyframes or Show Volume Keyframes from the Show Keyframes drop-down menu. This causes a Volume drop-down menu to appear in the Track. If you are changing Clip Volume, click the Volume drop-down menu and choose Level.

4. **If the Tool palette is not open, open it by choosing Window ➪ Show Tools.**

5. **Select the Pen tool.**

6. **Set the current-time indicator to the Timeline location where you want the fade to end.**

7. **Move the Pen tool the point where you want the fade to end; then press Ctrl+click in the graph line to create a keyframe.** This keyframe icon serves as a placeholder for the sound to stay at 100 percent of its volume at the middle of the sound clip.

8. **Move the Pen tool to the beginning of the clip, and create another handle there by Ctrl+clicking.**

9. **Drag the handle at the beginning of the graph line downward.** This makes the audio clip fade in. Dragging it upward increases the sound. As you click and drag, a tiny readout shows the current Timeline position and the change in decibels. Figure 8-8 shows the Timeline with the adjusted volume keyframes.

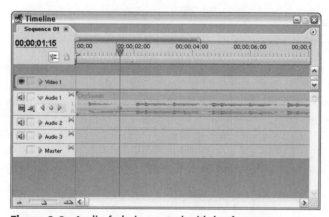

Figure 8-8: Audio fade is created with keyframes.

10. **To create a fade out, repeat the preceding steps to create a keyframe at the end of the clip and a few seconds before the end of the clip. Drag the keyframe at the end of the graph line downward to make the audio clip fade out.**

    If desired, you can use the Pen tool to add more keyframes to the graph lines. Adding more keyframes to the graph line enables you to fade a sound clip in different sections within the clip.

11. **To play the sound clip, press the spacebar on your keyboard.**

Note   You can adjust overall volume for a clip or a track by clicking and dragging a track's volume graph line up or down with the Pen tool.

Removing keyframes

As you edit audio in the Timeline, you may want to remove keyframes. The easiest way to do so is to have Premiere Pro jump to the specific keyframe and then click the Add/Remove Keyframe button in the Timeline. Here's how to remove a keyframe from an audio track in a sequence:

1. **Move the current-timeline indicator in front of the keyframe that you want to remove.**

2. **Click the Go to Next Keyframe button.**

3. **Click the Add/Remove keyframe button.** The keyframe is removed.

Balancing stereo in the Timeline

Premiere Pro enables you to adjust stereo channel balance in a stereo track. When you balance a stereo track, you redistribute the sound from one track to another. Although balancing is also covered in Chapter 9, we include it here because you can accomplish it simply in the Timeline window.

Here's how to balance a stereo track:

1. **Expand the audio track if it isn't already expanded.**

2. **Choose Show Track Keyframes from the Show Keyframes drop-down menu at the head of the track.** The Keyframe graph line appears as does an L and R, indicating the left and right tracks. A Volume drop-down menu also appears in the track.

3. **In the Volume drop-down menu, choose Panner.** In the Panner drop-down menu, choose Balance, as shown in Figure 8-9.

4. **Select the Pen tool in the Tool palette.**

Figure 8-9: Choosing the Balance audio effect in the Timeline window.

5. **To adjust stereo levels, click and drag with the Pen tool on the track keyframe graph line.** If you want to set keyframes, Ctrl+click and drag with the Pen tool to adjust the balance.

Creating Transitions Using Audio Effects

Premiere Pro's Audio Effects folder in the Effects window provides audio effects and audio transitions that enable you to enhance and correct audio. The effects provided in the Audio Effects folder are similar to many found in professional audio studios.

To display the Effects window, as shown in Figure 8-10, choose Window ➪ Effects. When the Effects window opens, note that it includes folders for Mono, Stereo, and 5.1 tracks. In addition, note that the Audio Effects folder also includes audio transitions.

Figure 8-10: The Effects window includes audio transitions and audio effects.

Creating bins in the Effects window

To view the effects in each folder, click the triangle in front of the folder.

In a project, you may need to use a few effects that are in different folders again and again. If so, you may want to place the effects into one folder. To create a new folder, choose New Custom Bin from the Audio palette pop-up menu. You can also click the New Custom Bin folder icon at the bottom of the Effects window. When the New Folder dialog box appears, Premiere Pro conveniently names it "Favorites" for you. If you want to rename it, simply click on Favorites and change the folder's name. To populate the folder with effects, simply click and drag your favorite effects into the folder. Premiere Pro puts a copy of the effect into the new folder.

If you want to delete the folder or an effect within the folder, simply click it and then click the Trash icon at the bottom of the folder.

Applying audio transitions

The Effects window's Audio Transitions folder provides two crossfade effects that allow you to fade in and fade out audio. Premiere Pro provides two varieties of transitions: Constant Gain and Constant Power. Constant Power, the default audio transition, produces an effect that should sound like a gradual fading in and out to the human ear. Constant Gain produces a mathematical fade in and fade out.

Typically, crossfades are applied to create a smooth transition between two audio clips. However, when using Premiere Pro, you can place a crossfade transition at the front of an audio clip to create a fade in, or at the tail end of the audio clip to create a fade out.

Here are the steps for creating an audio transition:

1. **Place two audio clips so that they are next to each other on the Timeline.**

2. **Open the Effects palette by choosing Window ⇨ Effects.**

3. **Open the Transitions folder by clicking the small triangle to the left of the folder.**

4. **Open the Crossfade folder by clicking small triangle to the left of the folder.**

5. **Drag the crossfade and drop it between the two clips in the audio track.** Don't worry if the transition does not drop directly over the middle of the two clips. You'll see the transition icon in the Timeline.

6. **Open the Effect Controls window by choosing Window ⇨ Effect Controls.**

7. **To center the transition between the two clips, choose Center at Cut from the Alignment drop-down menu, as shown in Figure 8-11.**

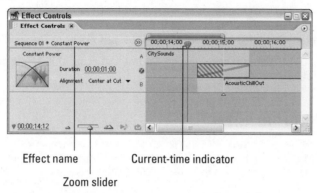

Effect name   Current-time indicator

Zoom slider

Figure 8-11: The Crossfade transition with Alignment set to Center at Cut.

8. **To change the duration of the transition, click and drag either end of the transition icon or edit the time display in the Effect Controls window.**

Note   The default audio transition duration can be set by altering the Default Audio Transition Duration setting found in the General Preferences dialog box. Choose Edit ➪ Preferences ➪ General.

9. **To play the transition, in the Effect Controls window set the current-time indicator before the transition and press the spacebar.**

Tip   You can quickly open the Effect Controls window by double-clicking a transition in the Timeline.

Using the default audio transition

If you know that you will be using the same audio transition again and again, you can easily apply it using Premiere Pro's Apply Audio Transition command. Here's how:

1. **Place two audio clips so that they are next to each other on the Timeline.**

2. **Choose Sequence ➪ Apply Audio Transition.**

Fading in and out using a crossfade transition

Earlier in this chapter, you saw how to manually create a fade in and fade out effect using keyframes in the Timeline. You can also create a fade in or fade out by using a crossfade transition. Here's how to create a fade-in using a crossfade transition:

1. **Drag a Crossfade transition to the front of the in point of the audio clip.**

2. **In the Effect Controls window, choose Start at Cut from the Alignment pop-up menu.**

Here's how to create a fade out using a crossover transition:

1. **Drag a Crossfade transition to the back of the out point of the audio clip.**

2. **In the Effect Controls window, choose End at Cut from the Alignment drop-down menu.**

Applying an audio effect

Like transitions, you access audio effects from the Effects palette, and they are controlled by the Effect Controls window. To display the Effect Controls window, shown in Figure 8-12, choose Window ➪ Show Effect Controls.

To apply an audio effect to audio clip, follow these steps:

1. **Select the clip in the Timeline window. If the clip is linked to video, unlink it by choosing Clip ➪ Unlink Audio Video.**

2. **Select the effect in the Effects palette and either drag it into the Effects Control palette or drag it over the audio track in the Timeline and let go of the mouse.**

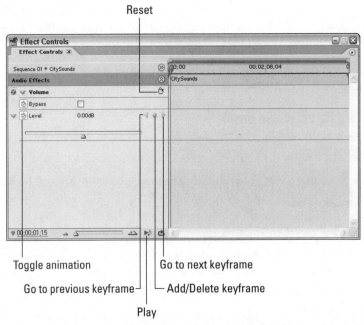

Figure 8-12: You can adjust audio effects in the Effect Controls window.

Most audio effects provide settings that allow you to adjust the effect. If an audio effect provides settings that can be adjusted, the settings appear in the Effect Controls window when the effect is expanded. To expand/collapse the effect, click the triangle in front of the effect's name.

You can adjust the effect in the Effect Controls window either by moving the sliders in the palette or by entering a value into a control's field. In Figure 8-12, the slider allows you to change the decibel level for the Volume effect. The palette also features a Play button, enabling you to play the sound.

You delete an effect from the Effects palette by right-clicking its name and choosing Clear from the pop-up menu. You can also click the effect in the Effect Controls window and then click the Trash icon at the bottom of the palette. If you want to prevent an effect from playing, essentially turning it off, then click the *f* button next to the effect's name. To turn the effect back on, click the *f* again.

Audio effects can also be applied to audio tracks from Premiere Pro's Audio Mixer window. See Chapter 9 for details.

Applying an audio effect over time

If you want to change the settings of an effect as an audio clip plays, you need to apply an effect over time and set keyframes where you want to make a change. A *keyframe* stores the effect at a specific point on a line in the Timeline in the Effect Controls window. To apply an audio effect over time, you should have a project open containing an audio clip in an audio track. Then follow these steps:

1. **Choose Window ⇨ Show Effect Controls to display the Effect Controls window.**

By default, Volume always appears as an effect in the Effect Controls window. It cannot be removed from the palette.

2. **Select the clip in the Timeline to which you want to apply the effect.**

3. **Drag an audio effect from the folder corresponding to the selected video track to the Effect Controls window or drop the effect over the clip.**

4. **Turn on keyframe mode by clicking the Stopwatch icon.** The Add/Delete Keyframe button appears in the Effect Controls window.

5. **Now click and drag the current-time indicator in the Effect Controls window to a new position.**

6. **Adjust a setting for the effect in the Effect Controls window.** This creates a keyframe.

7. **If needed, repeat the previous step to create new keyframes.** Figure 8-13 shows the Timeline in the Effect Controls window with various keyframes.

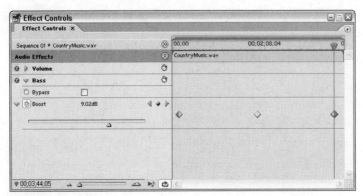

Figure 8-13: Effect Controls window keyframes created in Audio Effects.

8. To delete a keyframe, move the current-time indicator over the keyframe that you want to delete or click the Next or Previous Keyframe button and then click the Add/Delete Keyframes button. (You can also press Backspace on your keyboard.)

9. To play the effect, click the Play button in the Effect Controls window.

Note   If you want to delete all keyframes for one of an effect's controls, click the Stopwatch icon for that control.

Premiere Pro's audio effects

The following sections provide a review of Premiere Pro's audio effects. Since many effects from the Stereo folder also reside in the Mono and 5.1 folders, our audio effects overview is based on the contents of the Stereo folder. As you read through the overview of each effect, try them out. Remember, after you apply an audio effect, you can listen to it by clicking the Play button n the Effect Controls window.

Note   Premiere Pro's audio effects conform to the Steinberg VST (Virtual Studio Technology) plug-in standard. This means that third-party VST audio effects can be applied from within Premiere Pro. They will also appear in the Effects window with other plug-ins.

Balance

Balance changes the volume of the left and right stereo channels in a stereo clip. A positive number adds to the right channel and subtracts from the left. Negative values subtract from the right channel and add volume to the left. The controls for Balance are shown in Figure 8-14.

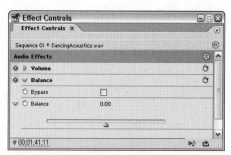

Figure 8-14: Balance audio effect options.

Bandpass

Use the Bandpass filter to remove frequencies beyond a frequency band. The Center field indicates the center of the frequency band to keep. The Q settings indicate the frequency band range you want to preserve. To create a wide range of frequencies to preserve, use a low setting; to preserve a narrow band of frequencies, use a high setting.

Bass

Use the Bass filter to adjust lower frequencies (200 Hz and below). Use the Boost option to raise or lower decibels.

Channel Volume

Use the Channel Volume effect to adjust channel volume in stereo or 5.1 clips or tracks. Unlike Balance, Channel Volume adjusts channels independently of other channels.

DeNoiser

Use the DeNoiser effect to automatically remove noise from analog audio. Figure 8-15 shows the DeNoiser audio effect controls. In the Custom Setup area, you can click and drag on the knob icons to adjust the effect. To set keyframes, use the Individual Parameters section.

✦ **Noisefloor.** This setting indicates the noise floor in decibels when the clip plays.

✦ **Freeze.** Click Freeze to halt the Noisefloor readout at its current decibel level.

✦ **Reduction.** Click and drag to indicate how much noise to remove. The range is –20 to 0 dB.

✦ **Offset.** This control sets an offset value or range for denoising between the Noisefloor and the values from –10 and +10 dB.

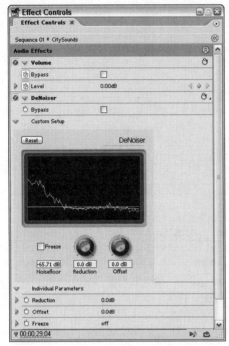

Figure 8-15: The DeNoiser audio effect controls.

Delay

Use Delay to create an echo effect that occurs after the time entered in the Delay field. Feedback is a percentage of the audio that is popped back into the delay. Use the Feedback option to create a series of delaying echoes. Use the Mix option to specify how much echo occurs in the effect.

Dynamics

The Dynamics effect provides a diverse set of options that can be used to adjust audio (see Figure 8-16).

✦ **Gate.** Shuts the gate on unwanted audio signals. This control removes the unwanted signal when its level drops below the dB setting for the Threshold control. When the signal goes beyond the Threshold, the Attack option determines the time interval for the gate to open. If the signal goes beyond the Threshold, the Release option determines the time interval for the gate to close. When the signal drops below the Threshold, the Hold time determines how long the gate stays open.

✦ **Compressor.** Attempts to balance the clip's dynamic range by boosting soft sound levels and decreasing loud sound levels (*dynamic range* is the range from the highest level to the lowest level).

✦ **Expander.** Produces a subtle Gate effect by dropping signals that are below the Threshold setting to the Ratio setting. A ratio setting of 2:1 would expand the decrease from 1 dB to 2 dB.

✦ **Limiter.** Allows you to level out audio peaks to reduce clipping. Use the Threshold option to adjust the maximum signal level. Use the Release Time to set the time necessary for gain to drop to its normal level after clipping.

✦ **SoftClip.** Like Limiter, SoftClip also reduces clipping when signals peak.

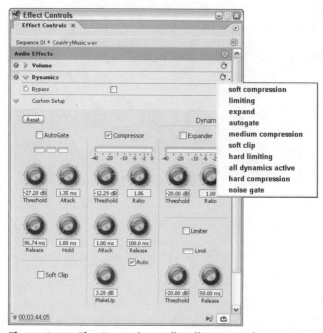

Figure 8-16: The Dynamics audio effect controls.

EQ

EQ effects cut or boost specific frequency ranges. The EQ effect serves as a *parametric equalizer*. Thus, it controls frequency, bandwidth, and level using three bands: low, middle, and high. Figure 8-17 shows the EQ audio effect controls. Here is a summary of the controls:

✦ **Frequency.** Use to increase or decrease frequency between 20 and 2000 Hz.

✦ **Gain.** Adjusts the gain between –20 and 20 dB.

✦ **Cut.** Switches the low and high bands from a shelving filter that can boost or lower part of a signal to a cutoff filter, which excludes or cuts offs the signal at specified frequencies.

✦ **Q.** Use to specify filter width between 0.05 and 5.0 octaves.

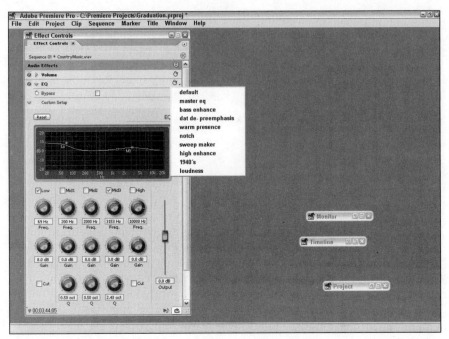

Figure 8-17: EQ effect controls.

Fill Left

Fill Left copies the audio in the right stereo channel and fills the left channel with it — replacing the previous audio in the channel.

Fill Right

The Fill Right effect copies the audio in the left channel and fills the right channel with it — replacing the previous audio in the channel.

Highpass

Use Highpass to remove frequencies above the Cutoff frequency.

Invert

Use Invert to invert the audio phase of each channel.

Lowpass

Use Lowpass to remove frequencies below the Cutoff frequency.

MultibandCompressor

Use the MultibandCompressor (see Figure 8-18) for compressing sounds according to three bands that correspond to low-mid-high frequencies. Adjust the handles for controlling gain and frequency range. Use Band Select to select a band and Crossover Frequency to change the frequency range for the selected band. MultibandCompressor produces a softer effect than the Dynamics audio effect.

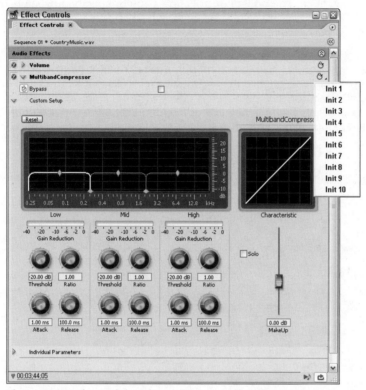

Figure 8-18: The MultibandCompressor audio effect controls.

Multitap Delay

The Multitap Delay Settings dialog box enables you to use four delays or taps (a *tap* is a delay effect) to control the overall delay effect. Use Delay 1 through Delay 4 controls to set the time of the delay. To create multiple delaying effects, use the Feedback 1 through Feedback 4 controls. The feedback controls add a percentage of the delayed signal back into the delay. Use the mix field to control the percentage of delayed to non-delayed echo.

Notch

Use the Notch command to remove hum and other extraneous "noises." Use the Center control to set the frequency that you want to exclude. Use the Q setting to control the width of the frequency.

Parametric EQ

Parametric EQ allows you to boost or lower frequency near a specified Center frequency. Use the Center control to set the frequency. Use the Q control to set the range of frequency that you want to affect. A high setting affects a wide range; a low setting affects a low range. The Boost control allows you to specify how many decibels you want to boost or lower the frequency range — between –20 and 20 dB.

PitchShifter

As its name suggests, you can use the PitchShifter effect to alter pitch, particularly when you want to produce a change in voices (see Figure 8-19). Use the Pitch control to alter pitch in semitones. Fine-tune the effect with the Finetune control. FormantPreserve prevents high-pitched voices from sounding like cartoon characters by preventing PitchShifter from altering formants (a *formant* is a resonant frequency).

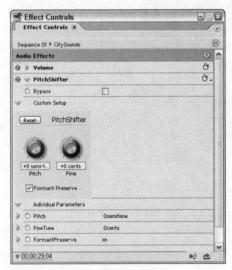

Figure 8-19: The PitchShifter Compressor audio effect controls.

Reverb

Reverberation refers to sound waves bouncing off an interior space. Reverb effects are commonly applied to simulate the sound or acoustics of a room. Thus, you can use Reverb to add ambience and a sense of humanity to dry electronic sound. Figure 8-20 shows the Reverb controls. Notice that a pop-up menu allows you to automatically generate settings for specific environments. Note that you can also control the effect by clicking and dragging the figures in the room area of the effect display.

✦ **PreDelay.** Use this control to simulate the time it takes for sound to hit a wall and bounce back to the audience.

✦ **Absorption.** Use to set sound absorption.

✦ **Size.** Use to set room size in percentage—thus, the larger the percentage, the larger the room.

✦ **Density.** Sets the size or density of the "tail" of the reverberation.

✦ **Lo Damp.** Sets low-frequency dampening.

✦ **Hi Damp.** Sets high-frequency dampening.

✦ **Mix.** Sets how much reverb effect is added to the sound.

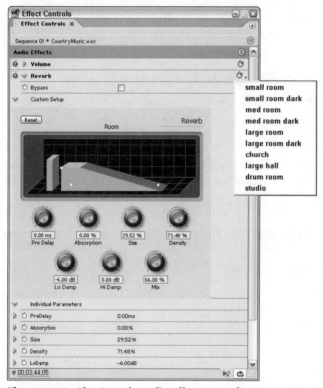

Figure 8-20: The Reverb audio effect controls.

Swap Channels

This effect swaps or exchanges left and right channels in stereo tracks.

Treble

Use the Treble effect to adjust higher frequencies (4000 Hz and above). Use the Boost slider to adjust the effect. Dragging right increases the amount in decibels, dragging left decreases it.

Volume

Use the Volume effect for clips only when you want to have volume rendered first. The Volume effect prevents distortion by preventing clipping when you increase volume. Increase volume with positive values, and decrease volume with negative values.

Exporting Sound Files

After you've edited and refined your audio tracks, you may want to export them as separate sound files so that they can be used in other software or other Premiere Pro projects. When you export a sound clip, you can export it in a variety of formats, such as .Windows Waveform (.wav), QuickTime (.mov), Microsoft AVI (.avi), and Microsoft DV AVI (.avi). Here are the steps for exporting an audio file from Premiere Pro:

1. **Select the audio track with the audio clip you want to export.**

2. **Choose File ➪ Export ➪ Audio.** The Export Audio dialog box appears.

3. **Type a name for your audio file.**

4. **Click the Settings button.**

5. **In the Export Audio Settings dialog box, set the File Type drop-down menu to Windows Waveform, QuickTime, or one of the AVI choices.** You can set the Range drop-down menu to be either the entire sequence or to only the work area.

6. **Click the General drop-down list and choose Audio.** In the Audio section, you can set the Rate (in Hz) and the Format (8-bit or 16-bit, Mono or Stereo).

7. **Click OK to close the dialog box.**

8. **Click Save to save audio file.**

Summary

Premiere Pro provides numerous features for adjusting and editing audio. You can control fade ins and fade outs in the Timeline window. You can adjust and create professional audio effects using Premiere Pro's audio effects and transitions.

✦ Using keyframes, you can fade in and fade out and adjust the volume of audio clips.

✦ You can adjust audio gain by choosing Clip ➪ Audio Options ➪ Gain.

✦ Use Premiere Pro's audio transitions to create crossfades.

✦ Use the effects in the Premiere Pro Effects window to enhance and correct audio.

✦   ✦   ✦

Mixing and Creating Effects with the Audio Mixer

Creating the perfect blend of music, narration, and effects is certainly an audio art. The audio engineer who blends or mixes various tracks together into a master track must have a deft touch and sensitive ear. Music and narration can't be overpowering; sound effects must sound real. Mixing these together at the perfect sound levels produces audio that truly enhances the accompanying video.

In a recording studio, engineers use a mixing console to control the mixing of music tracks. In Premiere Pro, you can create a mix using its Audio Mixer. Using the Premiere Pro Audio Mixer, you can mix sound from a maximum of five tracks into a master track, or you can apply effects to several tracks at once using a submix track, which can also be routed into the master track. Like a professional mixer, Premiere Pro allows you to adjust audio levels, fade in and fade out, balance stereo, control effects, and create effects "sends." Premiere Pro's Audio Mixer also allows you to record audio and isolate and listen to one "solo" track even while others play. You can even use it to add and adjust audio effects found in the Effects palette.

This chapter provides a thorough look at the Audio Mixer and how to use it. After touring the Audio Mixer palette, this chapter covers the Audio Mixer's Automation settings, which allow you to adjust audio while it plays. After you learn how to create a mix, you'll see how to balance and pan audio, add effects, and create submixes.

Audio Mixer Tour

Premiere Pro's Audio Mixer is undoubtedly one of its most complex and versatile utilities. To use it efficiently, you should become familiar with all of its controls and its functionality. If the Audio Mixer isn't open onscreen, open it by choosing Window ➪ Audio Mixer. If you would like to open the Audio Mixer in Premiere Pro's Audio Workspace, choose Window ➪ Workspace ➪ Audio. When the Audio Mixer, shown in Figure 9-1, opens onscreen, it automatically shows at least two tracks and the master track for the current active sequence. If you have more than two audio tracks in the sequence, click and drag on the lower-right corner of the Audio Mixer palette to extend the palette. Although the sight of so many knobs and levels probably wouldn't intimidate an audio engineer, it's important to understand and slowly examine the buttons and features. Note that the Audio Mixer offers two major views: the collapsed view (shown in Figure 9-1), which does not show the effects area, and the expanded view, which shows effects for the different tracks. To switch from one view to another, click the small triangle to the left of Audio track 1.

Note   The Audio Mixer only shows the current active sequence's audio tracks. If you want to show tracks from different sequences in the Audio Mixer window simultaneously, you must nest the sequences in the current active sequence. Chapter 6 covers how to nest one sequence into another.

To become familiar with the Audio Mixer, start by examining the track area of the Audio Mixer. The vertical areas headed by Audio 1, Audio 2, and so on correspond to the tracks on the active sequence. When you are mixing, you can see audio levels in the displays in each track column and make adjustments using the controls in each column. As you make adjustments, the audio is mixed or blended together into a master track or submix track. Note that the drop-down menu at the bottom of each track indicates whether the current track signal is being sent to a submix track or the master track. By default, all tracks are output to the master track as shown in Figure 9-1.

Note   You can set the master track to be either mono, stereo, or 5.1 by choosing Master track settings in the Default Sequence Section of the New Project dialog box (you must first click the Custom Settings tab after creating a new project) or in the New Sequence dialog box (File ➪ New Sequence).

Below the track names are the track Automation options. In Figure 9-1, automation is set to Read. When the Automation options are set to Read, track adjustment written to the tracks with keyframes are read by the track. If you change Read to Write, keyframes are created in the current sequences audio tracks reflecting adjustments made in the Audio Mixer.

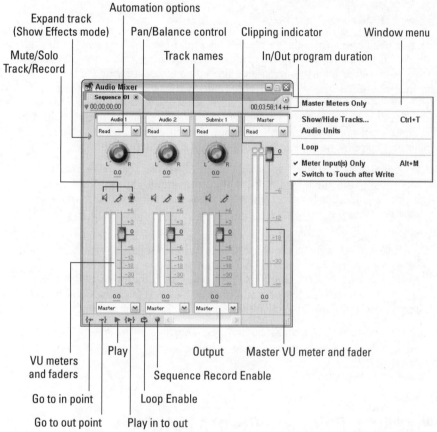

Automation options

Expand track
(Show Effects mode)   Pan/Balance control   Clipping indicator   Window menu

Mute/Solo
Track/Record   Track names   In/Out program duration

VU meters
and faders   Play   Output   Master VU meter and fader

Sequence Record Enable

Go to in point   Loop Enable

Go to out point   Play in to out

Figure 9-1: Audio Mixer collapsed view.

The following sections discuss the major controls and areas of the Audio Mixer, including the controls for Automation, Mute/Solo/Record, Pan/Balance, Volume, and Playback, as well as the Audio Effects menu and the Audio Sends area that appear in the expanded view (see Figure 9-2, later in this chapter).

Automation

The Automation options (Off, Read, Latch, Touch, and Write) determine whether Premiere Pro reads or saves the adjustments you make in the Audio Mixer as keyframes in the Timeline window. A detailed description of each option is provided later in this chapter in the section "Mixing Audio."

Tracks versus clips

Before you begin working with Premiere Pro's Audio Mixer, it's important to understand that the Audio Mixer affects the audio in an entire track. When you work in the Audio Mixer, you make audio track adjustments, not audio clip adjustments. When you create and alter effects in the Audio Mixer, you apply audio effects to tracks, not to specific clips. As discussed in Chapter 8, when you apply effects in the Effects Control window, you apply them to clips. The current sequence's Timeline window can provide an overview of your work, and it's important not to lose track (no pun intended) of whether clip or track keyframes are being displayed in the Timeline window. Here's a review of audio track display options:

✦ To view audio adjustments for clips, choose Show Clip Volume or Show Clip keyframes in the audio track's Show Keyframes pop-up menu. Note that the keyframe graph line for a clip extends from the in to the out point of the clip, not to the entire track.

✦ To view audio adjustments for the entire track, choose Show Track Volume or Show Track Keyframes in the audio track's Show Keyframes pop-up menu. The graph line for keyframes in a track extends throughout the entire track. When you apply audio effects using the Audio Mixer, these Effects appear by name in a Track pop-up menu in the Audio track's graphline. If you choose the effect from the pop-up menu in the audio track graph line, the keyframes for the effect appear on the graphline.

For both clip and track graph lines, you can create keyframes by Ctrl+clicking with the Pen tool and make adjustments to keyframe placement by clicking and dragging with the Pen tool.

The Mute, Solo, and Record buttons

The Mute and Solo buttons below the Automation options enable you to choose which audio tracks you want to work with and which ones you don't. The Record button allows you to record Analog sound (which could be from a microphone attached to a computer audio input).

✦ Click the Mute button to mute or silence tracks that you don't want to affect during Audio Mixer playback. When you click Mute, no audio levels are shown in the Audio Mixer VU (audio level) meter for the track. Using Mute, you can set levels for multiple tracks without hearing others. For instance, assume your audio includes music and sound effects of footsteps nearing a pond of croaking frogs. You could adjust levels of footsteps and frog croaking only as the video shows the pond coming into view.

✦ Click the Solo button to isolate or work with one specific track in the Audio Mixer window (though you will still be able to hear the other tracks). When you click Solo, Premiere Pro mutes all other tracks, except the Master track.

✦ Click the Record button to record and set levels using the Audio Mixer. Using the Audio Mixer to capture sound is covered in Chapter 5.

Note To completely turn off output for an audio track, click the Toggle Track Output button (speaker icon). After you click, the Speaker icon disappears. Click again on the Toggle Track Output button to turn audio output back on.

The Pan and Balance controls

Panning allows you to control levels of mono tracks when outputting to stereo or 5.1 tracks. Thus, by panning you could increase a sound effect like birds chirping in the right channel as trees come into view in the right side of your video monitor.

Balancing allows you redistribute output in Stereo and 5.1 tracks. So, as you add to the sound level in one channel, you subtract from another, or vice versa. Depending upon the type of track that you are working with, you control either balance or panning by using the Pan/Balance knob.

As you pan or balance, you can click and drag over the Pan/Balance knob or click and drag over the numeric readout below the knob. You can also click the numeric readout and type a value using your keyboard.

Volume

Dragging the Volume Fader control up or down adjusts track volume. Volume is recorded in decibels. The decibel volume is displayed in the field below the Volume Fader control. When the volume of an audio track is changed over time by clicking and dragging the Volume Fader control, Audio Mixer Automation settings can place keyframes in the track's audio graph line in the Timeline window. If you want, you can further adjust the volume by dragging the keyframes on the graph line in the track with the Pen tool. Note that when the VU meter (to the left of the Volume Fader) turns red, it is a warning that clipping or sound distortion may be occurring.

Playback

Six icons appear at the lower-left side of the Audio Mixer window. These icons are Stop, Play, Loop, Go to In point, Go to Out point, Play In to Out. Click the Play button to play an audio clip. To work with only a portion of the sequence in the Timeline window, set in and out points and then jump to the in points by clicking the Go to In point button. Next, click the Play In to Out button to mix only the audio between your in and out points. If you click the Loop button, playback is repeated so that you can continue to fine-tune the audio between the in and out points without starting and stopping playback.

Tip You can set in and out points in a sequence by clicking the Set In and Set Out point buttons in the Program section of the Monitor window or by moving the current-time indicator and choosing Marker ➪ Set Sequence Marker ➪ In, or Marker ➪ Set Sequence Marker ➪ Out. You can also select a clip in the sequence and choose Marker ➪ Set Sequence Marker ➪ In and Out around Selection.

Audio Mixer menu

Because the Audio Mixer contains so many icons and controls, you may want to customize it to display just the controls and features you want to use. Here is a list of custom settings available in the Audio Mixer menu shown in Figure 9-1.

✦ **Show/Hide Tracks.** Shows or hides individual tracks.

✦ **Master Meters Only.** Displays only master track meters.

✦ **Meter Input(s) Only.** Displays hardware (not track) input levels. To display hardware input levels on the VU meters (not track levels in Adobe Premiere Pro), choose Meter Input(s) Only. When this option is on, you can still monitor audio in Adobe Premiere Pro for all tracks that aren't being recorded.

✦ **Audio Units.** Sets the display to audio units. If you want to display units in Milliseconds rather than Audio Samples, change this setting in the General tab of the Project Settings window (Project ➪ Project Settings). The Audio setting changes the time display in the Timeline and Monitor windows as well.

✦ **Switch to Touch after Write.** Automatically switches the Automation mode from Write to Touch mode after using Write Automation mode.

Effects and Sends options

The following Effects and Sends options appear in the expanded view of the Audio Mixer, shown in Figure 9-2. To display the effects and sends, click the triangle to the left of the Automation options drop-down menus. To add an effect or send, click any of the triangles on the right side of the effects and sends lists. Figure 9-2 shows several of these triangles, which appear vertically down the effects and sends portion of each track.

Choosing Audio Effects

Clicking a triangle in the Audio Effects area allows you to choose an audio effect. You can place up to five effects in each track's Effects area. When an effect is loaded, you can adjust settings for the effect at the bottom of the Effects area. Figure 9-2 shows the Notch and Reverb effects loaded in the Audio Effects window. The PreDelay adjustment for the Reverb effect is shown at the bottom of the Effects area.

Effects Sends area

Below the Effects area is the Effects Sends region. Figure 9-2 shows the pop-up menu that creates sends, which send a percentage of track volume to a submix track.

Sends or effects option

Sends

Effects

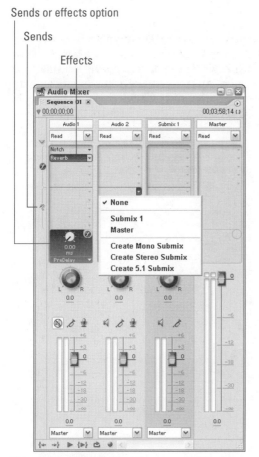

Figure 9-2: The Audio Mixer expanded view.

Mixing Audio

When you use the Audio Mixer to mix audio, Premiere Pro can add keyframes in the Timeline window for the currently selected sequence. As you add effects, these are also displayed in a track's pop-up menu. After you've placed all of your audio clips in Premiere Pros' tracks, you're almost ready to start a trial mix. However, before you begin, you should understand the Audio Mixer's Automation settings, because these control whether changes are made in the sequence or not.

On the DVD-ROM If you would like to practice using the Audio Mixer, you can use the audio clips in the Chapter 11 and Chapter 8 folders of the *Adobe Premiere Pro Bible* DVD.

Automation settings

You will not be able to successfully mix audio with the automation unless settings at the top of each track in the Audio Mixer are properly set. For example, in order to record your track adjustments with keyframes, you'll need the automation drop-down menu set to Write, Touch, or Latch. After you make adjustments and stop audio playback, your adjustments are represented by keyframes in the Timeline window (in the track graphline). Figure 9-3 shows the master track with the Automation pop-up menu exposed.

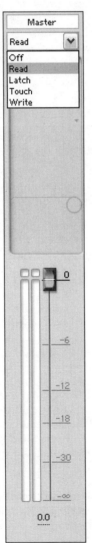

Figure 9-3: Automation pop-up menu choices.

Here is a brief description of each automation setting:

✦ **Write.** Immediately saves adjustments made for the track and creates keyframes in the Timeline window that represent the audio adjustments. Write, unlike Latch and Touch, starts writing as soon as playback starts, even if changes are not made in the Audio Mixer.

> **Note** You can right-click on a setting and choose Safe During Write to prevent changes to the setting while adjustments are made. You can also have Write mode switch to Touch mode automatically when playback is finished by choosing Switch to Touch After Write in the Audio Mixer menu.

✦ **Latch.** Like Write, this mode saves adjustments and creates keyframes in the Timeline. But automation does not start until you begin to make adjustments. However, if you change settings (such as volume) when playing back a track that already has recorded automation, the settings do not return to their previous levels after current adjustments are made.

✦ **Touch.** Like Latch, Touch creates keyframes in the Timeline and does not make adjustments until you change control values. However, if you change settings (such as volume) when playing back a track that already has recorded automation, the settings return to their previous levels after current adjustments are made.

> **Note** The rate of return for values when Touch is the automation setting is controlled by the Automatch Time audio preference. This preference can be changed by choosing Edit ⇨ Preferences ⇨ Audio. The default time is 1 second.

✦ **Read.** Plays each track's automation setting during playback. If you adjust a setting, such as volume, during play back, you hear the change and see the change in the track's VU meters, and the entire track remains at that level.

If you previously made adjustments using an animation mode such as Write to record changes to a track and then play back in Read mode, settings return to the recorded values after you stop making adjustments in Read mode.

Like Touch, the rate of return is based on the Automatch Time preference.

✦ **Off.** Disregards the stored automation settings during playback. Thus, if you adjust levels using an automation setting such as Write and play back the track with the Automation mode set to Off, you will not hear the original adjustments.

Creating a mix

After you've reviewed the automation settings and have become familiar with Audio Mixer controls, you're ready to try out a mix. The following steps outline how to do so. Before you begin, place audio in a minimum of two tracks in the current sequence in the Timeline window.

Tip   As you experiment with the Audio Mixer, you can quickly undo your changes by clicking on previous history states in the History palette.

1. **In the Audio Mixer window or Timeline window, set the current-time indicator to the position where you want to start the mix.**

2. **At the top of the tracks that you want to set automation, choose an automation setting, such as Write.** Note that the drop-down menu at the bottom of the track indicates where the signal is being sent. By default, track output is routed to the master track, although it can be changed to a submix track (which can output to the master track).

Note   If you don't want a control such as the Volume Fader to affect the track, right-click on it and choose Safe During Write.

3. **Click the Play button in the Audio Mixer window.** If you want to play from the sequence in point to out point, click the Play In to Out Point button.

4. **While the tracks play, make adjustments to the controls in the Audio Mixer.** If you work with the Fader controls, you'll see the changes in the meters for the different tracks.

5. **When you have completed making adjustments, click the Stop button in the Audio Mixer.** If the Timeline window is open and the Show Keyframe pop-up menu set to Track Keyframes, you can click the Track pop-up menu to show Volume, Balance, or Panning keyframes.

6. **To play back the adjustments, return the current Time indicator to the beginning of the audio, and click the Play button.**

Panning and Balancing

As you work a mix in the Audio Mixer, you can Pan or Balance. *Panning* allows you to adjust a mono track to emphasize it in a multitrack output. For example, as mentioned before, you could create a panning effect to increase the level of a sound effect in the right channel of a Stereo track as an object appears in the right side of the video monitor. You can do this by panning as you output mono tracks to a stereo or 5.1 master track.

Balancing redistributes sound in multichannel tracks. For example, in a stereo track, you could subtract audio from one channel and add to the other. As you work, it's important to realize that the ability to pan or to balance depends upon the tracks you are playing back and outputting to. For instance, you can pan a mono track if you are outputting to a stereo or 5.1 surround track. You can balance a stereo track if you are outputting to a stereo or 5.1 track. If you output a stereo track or 5.1 surround track to mono, Premiere Pro *downmixes*, or puts the sound tracks into fewer channels.

Note   You can set the Master track to be either mono, stereo, or 5.1 by choosing master track settings in the Default Sequence Section of the New Project dialog box (you must first click the Custom Settings tab after creating a new project) or in the New Sequence dialog box (File ⇨ New Sequence).

If you are panning or balancing a mono or stereo track, simply set up the Audio Mixer to output to a submix or master track and use the round knob shown in Figure 9-4 to adjust the effect. If you are panning a 5.1 track, the Audio Mixer replaces the knob with a "tray" icon. To pan using the tray, slide the puck icon within the tray area. The "pockets" along the edges of the tray represent the five surround sound speakers. You can adjust the center channel by clicking and dragging the Center percentage knob (upper-right of the tray). You can adjust the sub-woofer channel by clicking and dragging the knob above the Bass Clef Icon.

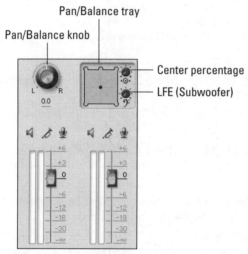

Figure 9-4: Panning/Balance controls for Stereo and 5.1 surround track.

After you complete a panning or balancing session using the Audio mixer, you can see recorded automation adjustments in the keyframe graphline for the adjusted audio tracks in the Timeline window. To see the keyframes in the graphline, the Show Keyframe pop-up menu in the adjusted tracks should be set to Show Track Keyframes. In the Track pop-up menu that appears in the keyframe graphline, choose either Panner or Balance.

Tip   You can copy a stereo track into two mono tracks by selecting it in the Project window and choosing Audio Options ⇨ Breakout to Mono Clips. You can convert a Mono audio clip to Stereo by selecting it in the Project window and choosing Treat as Stereo.

Note You can pan or balance in the Timeline without using the Audio mixer. To do this, set the Show Keyframes pop-up menu to Show Track Keyframes. In the Track pop-up menu, choose Panner ⇨ Pan or Panner ⇨ Balance. Use the Pen tool to adjust the graph line. If you want to create keyframes, Ctr+click with the Pen tool.

Creating Effects Using the Audio Mixer

After you become familiar with the Audio Mixer's powers of adjusting audio on the fly, you'll probably want to start using it to create and adjust audio effects for audio tracks. Adding effects to the Audio Mixer is quite easy: You load the effects into the effects area and then adjust individual controls for the effect (a control appears as a knob). If you intend to apply many effects to a track, be aware that the Audio Mixer allows you to add only five audio effects. The following steps show you how to load an effect and adjust it:

1. **Place an audio clip in an audio track or place a video clip that contains audio in a video track.**

2. **If the Effects section of the Audio Mixer is not open, open it by clicking the small expand/collapse triangle icon (refer to Figure 9-1).**

3. **In the track to which you want to apply the effect, click the down triangle in the effects area.** This opens a list of audio effects, as shown in Figure 9-5.

4. **Choose the effect that you want to apply from the list of effects.** After you select the effect, its name is displayed in the effects section of the Audio Mixer window.

5. **If you want to switch to another control for the effect, click the down arrow to the right of the control name and choose another control.**

6. **Proceed to set Automation for the track.**

7. **Click the Play button in the Audio Mixer window and adjust effect controls as desired.**

Removing effects

If you want to remove an effect from an Audio Mixer track, select the triangle for the effect and choose None in the drop-down list.

Bypassing an effect

You can turn off or bypass an effect by clicking the *f* (Bypass icon) that appears to the right of the effects control knob. After you click, a slash appears in the icon. To turn the effect back on, simply click the Bypass icon again.

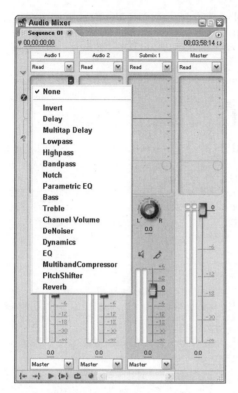

Figure 9-5: Choosing effects in the Audio Mixer window.

Creating a Submix

Premiere Pro's Audio Mixer not only allows you to mix audio into a master track, but it also allows you to combine audio from different tracks into a submix track. Why use a submix track? Assume that you have four audio tracks and you want to apply the same effects to two of the tracks simultaneously. Using the Audio Mixer, you can route the two tracks to the submix track and apply the effect to this track, which could in turn output it to the master track.

When using submix tracks, it's important to understand that you don't manually drag clips into them. Their input is solely created from submixing. Here are the general steps for setting up a submix track:

1. **Create a submix by choosing Sequence ➪ Add track.** In the Add Tracks dialog box, shown in Figure 9-6, type **1** in the Add Audio Submix Track(s) field. In the Track Type drop-down menu, choose whether you want the submix track to be mono, stereo, or 5.1. You will probably want to type 0 in other fields so that you do not add other audio or video tracks.

Figure 9-6: Creating a submix track.

2. **In the Audio Mixer window, set the output for the submix track if necessary (you could output a submix track to another submix track, depending upon your track setup).**

3. **Set the output for individual tracks that you want routed to the submix track in the output drop-down menu at the bottom of the track.**

4. **Choose effects for the submix track by clicking one of the effects triangles icons and selecting an effect.** Figure 9-7 shows one possible submix setup.

Creating sends

Premiere Pro's Audio Mixer allows you to create *sends*, which can be used to send a portion of a track's signal to a submix track. When a send is created, a control knob appears at the bottom of the track's area, as shown in Figure 9-8. (In Figure 9-8, the control knob is set to Volume. However by clicking the word Volume, you may be able to set the knob to Balance or Pan, depending upon whether you are working with mono or multichannel tracks.) This control knob allows you to adjust how much of a track's signal is duplicated to the submix track. In audio terminology, this is akin to the track portion of the signal being referred to as "dry," and the submix portion referred to as "wet."

When you create a send, you can choose to set the send to be Pre-Fader or Post-Fader (the default choice). This allows you to control whether the signal is sent from the track before or after its fader control is adjusted. If you choose Pre-Fader, raising or lowering the send track's fader does not affect the send output. Choosing Post-Fader utilizes the control knob setting as you change volume in the send track. You can choose between Pre- and Post-Fader settings by right-clicking the listed send in the Audio Mixer window. In Figure 9-8, right-clicking Submix 1 will open the Pre/Post-Fader pop-up menu.

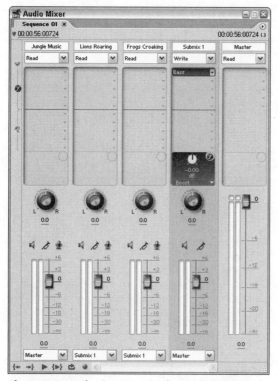

Figure 9-7: Submix set up in the Audio Mixer.

Here are the steps for creating a submix track in the Audio Mixer and then creating the effects send:

1. **If the effects/send area of the Audio Mixer is not open, expand it by clicking the expand/collapse triangle icon (refer to Figure 9-1).**

2. **Click one of the triangles in a track's Send area to open the send area pop-up menu.** Figure 9-8 shows the pop-up menu in Audio track 2.

3. **If you haven't created a submix track, you can create it by choosing one of the create submix choices in the pop-up menu.** After you make the choice, a send is automatically created for the submix track. You can see the send in Audio track 1 of Figure 9-8. If the submix track already exists in the Audio Mixer, choose it from the Send pop-up menu.

4. **When the send is created, a volume knob appears, allowing you to control the ratio of volume from the track that is sent to the submix track when you mix the tracks.**

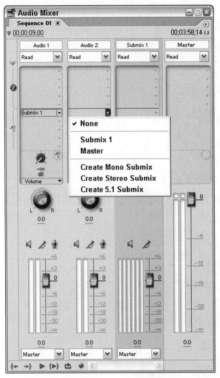

Figure 9-8: Effects send created for Submix.

Audio Processing Order

With all of the controls available for audio, you might wonder what order Premiere Pro uses to process audio. For instance, are clip effects processed before track effects or vice versa? Here's an overview: First, Premiere processes audio according the audio settings you set in the New Project dialog box. When audio is output, Premiere follows this general order:

1. **Clips adjusted with Premiere's Audio Gain command.**

2. **Clip effects.**

3. **Track effect settings such as pre-fader effects, fader effects, post-fader effects, then pan/balance.**

4. **Track volume from left to right in the Audio Mixer with output routed through any submix tracks to the master track.**

You certainly don't need to memorize this, but having a general idea of the order audio is processed may prove helpful as you work on complex projects.

Summary

The Premiere Pro Audio Mixer provides a variety of utilities for mixing audio. After you've set the automation mode in the automation pop-up menu, you can mix to a master or submix track during playback.

✦ Use the Audio Mixer automation controls to write changes to tracks when mixing.

✦ Use the Audio Mixer to pan and balance.

✦ Use a submix track to apply one effect to multiple tracks.

✦ You can add effects and adjust them in the Audio Mixer during playback.

✦ You can create effects sends in the Audio Mixer.

✦   ✦   ✦

Creating Transitions

Acut from one scene in your video production to another
provides an excellent transition for action clips or for
clips that move the viewer from one locale to another. However,
when you want to convey the passage of time or create an
effect in which a scene gradually transforms into the next, a
simple cut just won't do. To artistically show passage of time,
you may want to use a *cross dissolve* — which gradually fades
one clip in over another. For a more dramatic and abrupt
effect, you can use a *clock wipe,* in which one scene is rotated
onscreen, as if it were swept into the frames by the hands of
a clock.

Whether you're trying to turn night into day, day into night,
youth into age — or simply wake up your audience with a
startling special effect that bridges one scene to another —
you should find what you're looking with Adobe Premiere
Pro's Video Transitions. This chapter takes you on a tour of
Premiere Pro's video transitions.

Touring the Video Transitions Folder

The Video Transitions folder in the Effects window stores
over 70 different transitional effects. To view the Video
Transitions folder, choose Window ➪ Effects. To see a list of
the transition categories, click the triangle icon in front of the
Video Transitions folder. As shown in Figure 10-1, the Effects
window keeps all the video transitions organized into subfold-
ers. To view the contents of a transition folder, click the triangle
icon to the left of the folder. When the folder opens, the triangle icon points down. Click the downward-pointing triangle
icon to close the folder.

Figure 10-1: The Effects window contains more than 70 different video transitions.

Navigating within the Video Transitions folder

The Effects window can help you locate transitions and keep them organized. To find a video transition, click in the Contains field in the Effects window, and then start typing the name of the transition. You needn't type in the full name. For example, type the word *cross*, and Premiere Pro opens all the folders that have the name *cross* in the effects. Type the word *invert*, and Premiere Pro opens all the folders that have the name *invert* in the effects.

To organize your folder, you can create new custom folders to keep the transitions that you most often use grouped together. To create a new custom folder, click either the New Custom Folder at the bottom of the Effects window or the triangle icon at the upper-right of the window and choose New Custom Bin. To rename a custom folder, first select the custom folder, and then click the name of the folder. When the name is highlighted, begin typing the new name. To delete a custom folder, either click it to select it and click the Delete Custom Items icon, or choose Delete Custom Item from the window pop-up menu. When the Delete Item dialog box appears, click OK to delete the folder.

The Effects window also allows you to set the default transition and a transition to be the default transition. By default, the video transition default duration is set to 30 frames. To change the default transition duration, click the Default Transition Duration command, found in the Effects window pop-up menu. In the Preferences dialog box, you can change the default video transition by entering a new number in the appropriate field. To select a new transition as the default, first select a video transition and then click the Set Default Transition from the Effects window pop-up menu.

Applying a transition in Single-Track editing mode

In Premiere Pro, there is no A/B editing, only Single-Track editing. Single-Track editing is similar to traditional video editing: The transition is placed between two clips in the track. The transition uses the extra frames at the out point of the first clip and the extra clips at the in point of the second clip as the transitional area. When you use Single-Track editing, extra frames beyond the out point of one clip and the extra frames before the in point of the next clip are used as the transitional area (if no extra frames are available, Premiere Pro enables you to repeat ending or beginning frames).

In Figure 10-2, you will find a sample transition project with its windows and palettes. In the Timeline window, you can see video clips with transitions using Single-Track editing. The Info palette shows information on the selected transition. The Effect Controls window displays the options for the selected transition. In the Monitor window, you can see a preview of the selected transition.

Tip   The Effects workspace helps organize all the windows and palettes you'll need onscreen when working with transitions. To set your workspace to Effects, choose Window ➪ Workspace ➪ Effects.

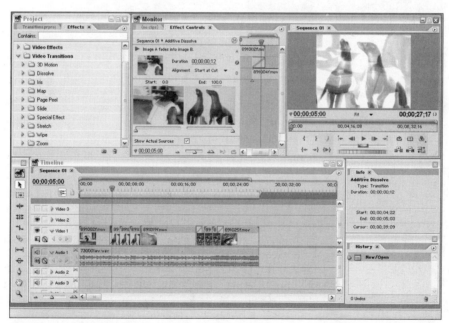

Figure 10-2: Premiere Pro's Effects workspace was used when applying transitions using Single-Track editing.

Figures 10-3, 10-4, 10-5, and 10-6 show frames from the transition project that we cre-ated using Premiere Pro's new Single-Track editing features. We applied the Additive Dissolve, Cross Dissolve, Dither Dissolve, and Iris Points transitions. The clips we used to create the transition project are from Digital Vision. We used five video clips from Digital Vision's ComicCuts CD (891002f.mov, 891004f.mov, 891019f.mov, 891025f.mov, and 891033f.mov) and Digital Vision's Acoustic Chillout sound clip, 730001aw.wav. These clips are on the DVD that accompanies this book.

Figure 10-3: Frames from a transition project showing an Additive Dissolve. The clips used are Digital Vision's ComicCuts CD 891002f.mov and 891004f.mov.

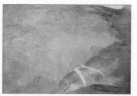

Figure 10-4: Frames from a transition project showing a Cross Dissolve. The clips used are Digital Vision's ComicCuts CD 891004f.mov and 891019f.mov.

Figure 10-5: Frames from a transition project showing a Dither Dissolve. The clips used are Digital Vision's ComicCuts CD 891019f.mov and 891033f.mov.

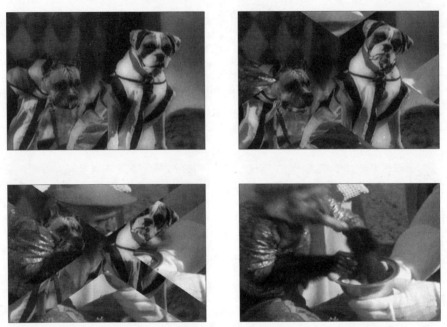

Figure 10-6: Frames from a transition project showing an Iris Points transition. The clips used are Digital Vision's ComicCuts CD 891033f.mov and 891025f.mov.

Here are the steps for creating a transition in Single-Track editing:

1. **Create a new project by choosing File ➪ New ➪ Project.** In the New Project dialog box, pick a preset or create a custom setting. Name your new project, and then click OK to create a new project.

2. **Choose Window ➪ Workspace ➪ Editing to set Premiere Pro's workspace to Editing mode.** In Editing mode, all the necessary windows and palettes needed to apply and edit transitions are onscreen.

3. **Choose File ➪ Import to import video clips.** In the Import dialog box, select the clips you want to import. If you want to import a folder, click the Import Folder button in the Import dialog box, then select a folder. Click Open to import a video clip into the Project window.

On the DVD-ROM

The five video clips shown in Figures 10-2 through 10-6, from Digital Vision's ComicCuts CD (891002f.mov, 891004f.mov, 891019f.mov, 891025f.mov, and 891033f.mov) and Digital Vision's Acoustic Chillout sound clip, 730001aw.wav, are found on the Digital Vision folder in the Chapter 10 folder that is in the Tutorial Projects folder on the DVD that accompanies this book.

4. **Drag one video clip from the Project window into Video track 1 of the Timeline. Then drag another clip next to it.** Set the out point of the first clip and the in point of the second clip. The first clip should have extra frames that extend beyond the out point. The second clip should have extra frames that extend beyond the in point. These extra frames are used by Premiere Pro to determine the length of the transition. When you set the in and out points, each clip should have an equal number of extra frames. The extra frames determine the length of the transition. For example, to create a 30-frame dissolve, each clip should have 15 extra frames in each clip. You can set in and out points by using either the Selection tool, Timeline markers, the Source window, or the Monitor window. For more information on setting in and out points, refer to Chapter 7.

5. **Another way to overlap two clips in the Timeline is to use the Snap option and the current-time marker.** To do so, drag a clip to the Timeline window and then move the current-time marker toward the end of the first clip. Now drag the second clip to the current-time marker. As you drag, notice that the second clip snaps to align at the left, right, or center of the current-time marker.

6. **Now pick a transition from the Effects window and place it over the area where the two clips meet.** Premiere Pro highlights the area where the transition occurs and then places the transition within the track. If the number of extra frames for each clip is not sufficient to create the transition, Premiere Pro opens the Fix Transition dialog box. In the Fix Transition dialog box, you can change the duration of the transition or click a radio button to have Premiere Pro repeat the last and first frames of the clips to accommodate the transition.

7. **You can edit a transition in the Timeline window either by moving the clip to the right or left or by changing its duration by moving one of the transitions edges.**

 Tip If you move a transition edge, you may also move the edge of a clip. To move a transition edge without affecting any clips, press Ctrl while you click and drag the Transition edge.

8. **To see the overlapping areas and the transition displayed below the first clip and above the next clip (shown in Figure 10-7), double-click the transition in the Timeline window.** Display the Effect Controls window. To see the clips and transition in the Timeline of the Effect Controls window, select the Show/Hide Keyframes option. You can edit the transition using either the Timeline features or the Duration and Alignment option in the Effect Controls window. How to use these features is discussed in the next section.

9. **To preview a transition in the Effect Controls window (shown in Figure 10-7), click the Play the Transition button or select the Show Actual Sources check box and move the sliders below the Start and End previews.**

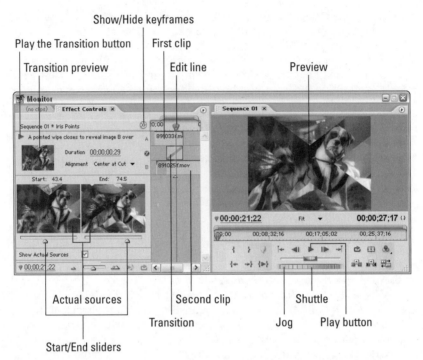

Show/Hide keyframes

Play the Transition button   First clip

Transition preview   Edit line   Preview

Actual sources   Second clip   Shuttle

Transition   Jog   Play button

Start/End sliders

Figure 10-7: The Effect Controls window and Monitor window with a preview of a transition.

10. **To preview a transition in the Monitor window (shown in Figure 10-7), either use the shuttle or jog slider or click the Play button.** You can also view the transition in the Monitor window when you move the current-time marker in the Timeline window. By default, the Monitor window displays the preview in Automatic Quality. To change the preview quality, click the Monitor pop-up menu and choose either Highest Quality or Draft Quality.

If you want, import a sound clip and place it in Audio track 1.

11. **To render the work area, choose Sequence ➪ Render Work Area.**

12. **Save your work by choosing File ➪ Save.**

13. **To make a movie from your Premiere Pro project, choose File ➪ Export ➪ Movie.**

Proceed to the next section to learn how to edit transitions.

Editing transitions

After you apply a transition, you can either edit it in the Timeline window or you can use the Effect Controls window. To edit a transition, you first need to select it in the Timeline window. Then you can either move the transition's alignment or change its duration.

Changing a transition's alignment

To change a transition's alignment using the Timeline window, click the transition then drag it either left or right or center it. When you drag left, you align the transition to the end of the edit point. When you drag right, you align the transition at the beginning or the edit point. When you center the transition, you align the transition so that it is centered within the edit point.

The Effect Controls window allows you to make more editing changes. To change a transition's alignment using the Effect Controls window, first double-click the transition in the Timeline window. To view the clips and transition in the Timeline of the Effect Controls window, the Show/Hide Keyframes option must be selected. Then choose an option from the Alignment pop-up menu to change the transition's alignment. To create a custom alignment, manually move the transition in the Timeline of the Effect Controls window.

Changing a transition's duration

In the Timeline window, you can either increase or decrease the number of frames the transition is applied to by dragging on one of its edges. For accuracy, be sure to use the Info palette when making adjustments on the Timeline.

To change a transition's duration using the Effect Controls window, first double-click the transition in the Timeline window. To view the clips and transition in the Timeline of the Effect Controls window, the Show/Hide keyframes option must be selected. Then click and drag on the Duration value to change the duration.

The alignment and duration of a transition work together. Changing the transition's duration is affected by its alignment. When the alignment setting is set to Center at Cut or Custom Start, changing the Duration value affects both the in and out points. When alignment is set to Start at Cut, changing the Duration value affects the out point. When alignment is set to End at Cut, changing the Duration value affects the in point. Besides using the Duration value to change duration of a transition, you can also manually adjust the duration of the transition by clicking either the right or left edge of the transition edge and dragging either outward or inward.

Changing a transition's settings

Many of the transitions include setting options that enable you to change how a transition appears onscreen. After a transition is applied to a clip, you can find the settings for that transition at the bottom of the Effect Controls window. To preview the settings for a transition, you need to lengthen the Effect Controls window, as shown in Figure 10-8.

After you apply a transition, you can edit the transition direction by clicking the Reverse check box in the Effect Controls window (shown in Figure 10-8). By default, a clip transitions from the first clip to the second (A to B). Occasionally, you might want to create a transition in which scene B transitions to scene A—even though scene B appears after scene A. To see a preview of the transition effect, click and drag the A or B slider. To see the actual clips previewed in the window, select the Show Actual Sources check box and then click and drag the sliders (shown in Figure 10-7). To preview the transition, you can also click the Play the Transition button.

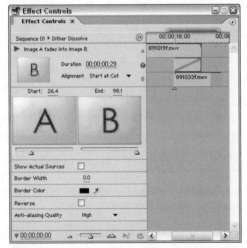

Figure 10-8: The Effect Controls window with the Dither Dissolve settings.

Many transitions enable you to reverse the effect. For example, the Curtain Transition in the 3D Motion folder normally applies the transition with Clip A onscreen; the curtain opens to display clip B. However, by clicking the Reverse check box at the bottom of the Effect Controls window, you can make the curtain close to reveal Clip B. The Doors Transition is quite similar. Normally the Doors open to reveal Clip B. If you click the Reverse check box, the doors close to reveal Clip A.

Several transitions also enable you to smooth the effect or create a soft-edge effect by applying anti-aliasing to the transitions. To smooth the effect, click the Anti-aliasing Quality pop-up menu (shown in Figure 10-8) and choose Anti-aliasing Quality. Some transitions also allow you to add a border. To do so, click and drag on the Border Width value to set the width of the border, then pick a border color. To pick a border color, use either the Eyedropper or the swatch next to Border Color.

Creating a default transition

If you are applying the same transition many times throughout a project, you can set a default transition. After you've specified a default transition, you can easily apply it without having to drag it to the Timeline from the Effects window.

Here are the steps for creating a default transition:

1. **If the Effects window is not open, open it by choosing Window ⇨ Effects.**

2. **In the Effects window, click the transition that you want to set as the default.** By default, Premiere Pro sets the Cross Dissolve transition to be the default transition.

3. **In the Effects window menu, choose Set Default Transition.**

Note   The default transition remains the default transition for all Premiere projects until you choose another default transition.

Applying a default transition

To use a default transition, organize the clips in Video track 1 as you would for a normal transition. For Single-Track editing, you must position the clips so that the in and out points meet in the single track. To apply the transition, do the following:

1. **Move the current-time indicator to the extra frames between the two clips.**

2. **Choose Sequence ⇨ Apply Video Transition.** Alternatively, you can apply the default transition by pressing Ctrl+D.

Tip   You can create a keyboard shortcut for applying a default transition.

Replacing and deleting transitions

After you've created a transition, you may decide that it doesn't quite provide the effect you originally intended. Fortunately, replacing or deleting transitions is easy:

✦ To replace one transition with another, simply click and drag one transition from the Effects window over the transition that you want to replace in the Timeline. The new transition replaces the old transition.

✦ To delete a transition, simply select it with the mouse and then press the Delete or Backspace key.

Creating interesting animated graphic backgrounds using video transitions

You can create a simple graphic file in Photoshop using filters, then import it into Premiere Pro and apply video effects and video transitions to it to make a really interesting animated background. You can also take that simple graphic file and animate it using Photoshop filters and Adobe ImageReady (for more information on using Adobe ImageReady, turn to Chapter 12). An animated background can be used in any project as the backdrop of a title, or it can be superimposed onto another clip.

In Figure 10-9, we started with an animated graphic clip (Digital Vision's Ambient Space 434004f.mov). We used the same clip five different times. Each time we dragged the clip to the Timeline window, we made it overlap the previous clip. The overlapping area is where we applied a transition. We applied these transitions: Paint Splatter (shown in Figure 10-10), Multi-Spin (shown in Figure 10-11), Center Peel (shown in Figure 10-12), and Iris Star (shown in Figure 10-13). For the clip to look like a different clip, four different times, we applied the Color Balance video effect to change the clip's colors.

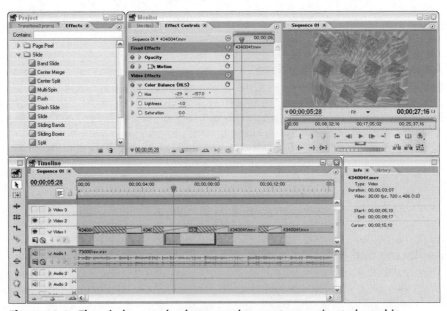

Figure 10-9: The windows and palettes used to create an animated graphic background project.

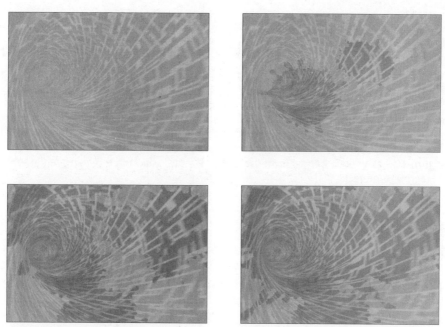

Figure 10-10: Various frames from the Paint Splatter transition in the animated graphic background project.

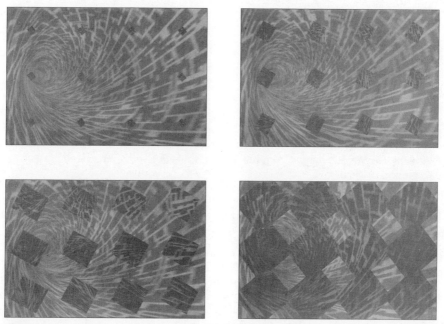

Figure 10-11: Various frames from the Multi-Spin transition in the animated graphic background project.

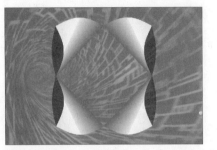

Figure 10-12: Various frames from the Center Peel transition in the animated graphic background project.

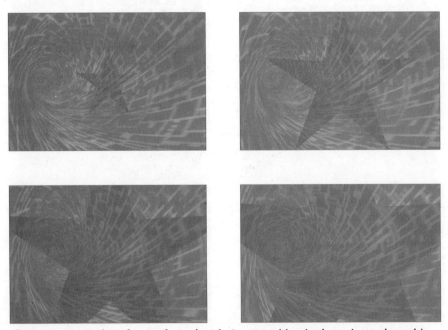

Figure 10-13: Various frames from the Iris Star transition in the animated graphic background project.

Here's how to use video transitions to animate a graphic background:

1. **Create a new project.**

2. **Import a still image or clip into the Premiere project.** Import a file that you created in Photoshop using filters or import a generic-looking video clip, to which you can apply various Premiere Pro Video Effects to make it more interesting. We imported an animated graphic clip from Digital Vision's Ambient Space CD-ROM (434004f.mov).

On the DVD-ROM The video clip shown in Figure 10-9 is from Digital Vision's Ambient Space CD (434004f.mov) and is found in the Digital Vision folder in the Chapter 10 folder that is in the Tutorial Projects folder on the DVD that accompanies this book. For this project, we also used Digital Vision's Acoustic Chillout sound clip, 730001aw.wav.

3. **Drag the imported clip from the Project window to Video track 1 of the Timeline window.** If you want apply a video effect to it, click and drag a video effect over the clip in the Timeline window. For more information on using video effects, turn to Chapter 14.

4. **Drag the same imported clip from the Project window so that it overlaps the clip already in Video track 1.**

5. **Apply a video effect to the second clip so that it is not exactly the same as the first clip.** We used the Color Balance video effect to change the color of the clip. The Color Balance video effect is in the Image Control folder.

6. **Click and drag a video transition on the overlapping area of two clips in the Timeline window.** For a more animated feel, you might want to try a transition from either the Wipe, Slide, Page Peel, or Iris folder.

7. **Repeat Steps 5 to 7 as many times as you want.**

8. **Click the Play button in the Monitor window to preview the project.**

9. **If you want, import a sound and place it in Audio track 1.**

10. **Remember to save your work.**

Transitions Review

Premiere Pro's Video Transitions folder provides ten different transition folders: 3D Motion, Dissolve, Iris, Map, Page Peel, Slide, Special Effect, Stretch, Wipe, and Zoom. Each folder features its own set of eye-catching transitions. This section features a tour of virtually every transition in each folder, along with examples of some of the transitions. The examples shown in the figures use clips from Digital Vision's Ambient Space CD (434004f.mov). It is on the DVD that accompanies this book. To view the transitions in the Video Transitions folder choose Window ➪ Effects. In the Effects folder, click the triangle in front of the Video Transitions folder to display the video transition folders.

Note To aid in describing the transitions, we call the clip in Video track A, *Clip A*; the clip in Video track B is called *Clip B*. In the following sections, we describe how Clip A transitions to Clip B. However, note that many transitions can be reversed so that Clip B transitions to Clip A.

3D Motion

The 3D Motion folder features ten transitions: Cube Spin, Curtain, Doors, Flip Over, Fold Up, Spin, Spin Away, Swing In, Swing Out, and Tumble Away. Each one of the transitions includes motion as the transition occurs.

Cube Spin

The Cube Spin transition uses a spinning 3D cube to create the transition from Clip A to Clip B. In the Cube Spin settings, you can set the transition to be from left to right, right to left, top to bottom, or bottom to top. Drag the Border slider to the right to increase the border color between the two video tracks. Click the color swatch if you want to change the border color.

Curtain

The Curtain transition simulates a curtain that opens to reveal Clip B replacing Clip A. You can see the Curtain settings in Figure 10-14.

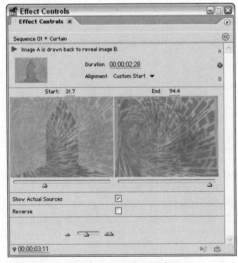

Figure 10-14: The Curtain settings.

The Doors transition simulates opening a door. What's behind the door? Clip B, (replacing Clip A). You can have the transition move from left to right, right to left, top to bottom, or bottom to top. The Doors settings, shown in Figure 10-15, include a Border slider. Drag the Border slider to the right to increase the border color between the two video tracks. Click the color swatch if you want to change the border color.

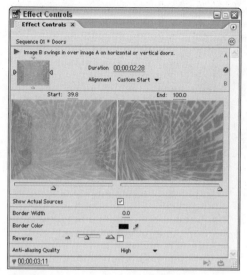

Figure 10-15: The Doors settings.

Flip Over

The Flip Over transition flips Clip A along its vertical axis to reveal Clip B. Click the Custom Settings button in the Flip Over Settings to set the number of bands and cell color.

Fold Up

The Fold Up transition folds up Clip A (as if it were a piece of paper) to reveal Clip B.

Spin

Spin is very similar to the Flip Over transition, except that Clip B spins onto the screen, rather than flipping, to replace Clip A. Figure 10-16 shows the Spin settings.

Spin Away

In the Spin Away transition, Clip B spins onscreen similarly to the Spin transition. However, in Spin Away, Clip B consumes more of the frame than the Spin transition. The Spin Away settings are shown in Figure 10-17.

Swing In

In the Swing In transition, Clip B swings onto the screen from screen left, like a gate that is open and is being shut.

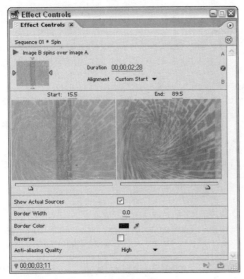

Figure 10-16: The Spin settings.

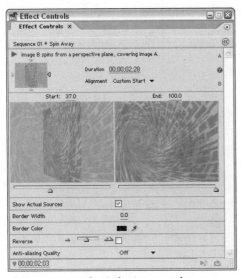

Figure 10-17: The Spin Away settings.

Swing Out

In the Swing Out transition, Clip B swings onto the screen from screen left, like a gate that is closed and is being opened.

Tumble Away

In the Tumble Away transition, Clip A spins and gradually becomes smaller as it is replaced by Clip B. The Tumble Away settings are shown in Figure 10-18.

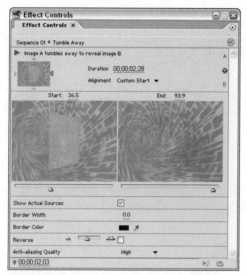

Figure 10-18: The Tumble Away settings.

Dissolve

The Dissolve transition gradually fades in one video clip over another. Five dissolve transitions exist: Additive Dissolve, Cross Dissolve, Dither Dissolve, Non-Additive Dissolve, and Random Invert.

Additive Dissolve

The Additive Dissolve transition creates a fade from one clip to the next.

Cross Dissolve

In this transition, Clip B fades in before Clip A fades out.

Dither Dissolve

In the Dither Dissolve transition, Clip A dissolves to Clip B, as tiny dots appear onscreen.

Non-Additive Dissolve

In this transition, Clip B gradually appears in colored areas of Clip A.

Random Invert

In the Random Invert transition, random dot patterns appear as Clip B gradually replaces Clip A.

Iris

The Iris transitions all begin or end at the center point of the screen. The Iris transitions are Iris Cross, Iris Diamond, Iris Points, Iris Round, Iris Shapes, Iris Square, and Iris Star.

Iris Cross

In this transition, Clip B gradually appears in a cross that grows bigger and bigger until it takes over the full frame.

Iris Diamond

In this transition, Clip B gradually appears in a diamond that gradually takes over the full frame. The Iris Diamond settings are shown in Figure 10-19.

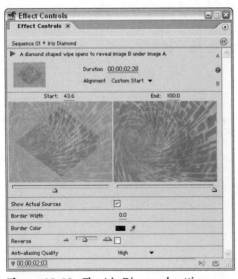

Figure 10-19: The Iris Diamond settings.

Iris Points

In this transition, Clip B appears in the outer edges of a large cross, with Clip A in the cross. As the cross becomes smaller, Clip B gradually comes full screen.

Iris Round

In the Iris Round transition, Clip B gradually appears in an ever-growing circle that gradually consumes the full frame.

Iris Shapes

In this transition, Clip B gradually appears inside either diamonds, ovals, or rectangles that gradually grow and consume the frame. When you choose this transition, the Iris Shapes Settings dialog box appears, allowing you to pick the number of shapes and the shape type. The Iris Shapes Settings dialog box is shown in Figure 10-20. The Iris Shapes settings are shown in Figure 10-21.

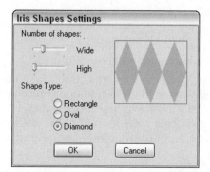

Figure 10-20: The Iris Shapes Settings dialog box allows you to choose a shape type.

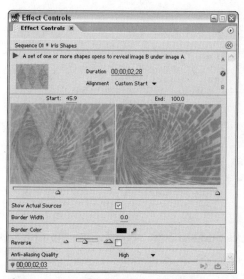

Figure 10-21: The Iris Shapes settings.

Iris Square

In this transition, Clip B gradually appears in an ever-growing square that gradually consumes the full frame.

Iris Star

In this transition, Clip B gradually appears in an ever-growing star that gradually consumes the full frame.

Map transitions

The Map transitions remap colors during the transition. The available Map transitions are Channel Map and Luminance.

Channel Map

The Channel Map transition enables you to create unusual color effects by mapping image channels to other image channels. When you use this transition, the Channel Map Settings dialog box appears, as shown in Figure 10-22. In this dialog box, select the channel from the pop-up menu and choose whether to invert the colors. Click OK and then preview the effect in the Effect Controls window or Monitor window. Click the Custom button at the bottom of the Effect Controls window to change the Channel Map settings.

Figure 10-22: The Channel Map Settings dialog box.

Luminance Map

The Luminance Map transition replaces the brightness levels of one clip with another.

Page Peel

The transitions in the Page Peel folder simulate one page of a book turning to reveal the next page. On the first page is Clip A, and on the second page is Clip B.

This transition can be quite striking, as Premiere Pro renders the image in Clip A curled onto the back of the turning page.

Center Peel

Center Peel creates four separate page curls that rip out of the center of Clip A to reveal Clip B.

Page Peel

This transition is a standard peel where the page curls from the upper-left of the screen to the lower-right to reveal the next page. Figure 10-23 shows the Page Peel settings.

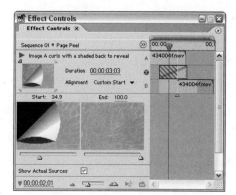

Figure 10-23: The Page Peel settings.

Page Turn

With the Page Turn transition, the page turns, but doesn't curl. As it turns to reveal Clip B, you see Clip A reversed on the back of the page.

Peel Back

In this transition, the page is peeled back from the middle to the upper-left, then to the upper-right, then the lower-right, and then the lower-left.

Roll Away

In this transition, Clip A rolls from left to right off the page (with no curl) to reveal Clip B.

Slide

The Slide transitions enable you to slide clips in and out of the frame to provide transitional effects.

Band Slide

In this transition, rectangular bands appear from screen right and screen left, gradually replacing Clip A with Clip B. When you use this transition, the Band Slide Settings dialog box appears. In this dialog box, type the number of bands you want. Click the Custom button at the bottom of the Effect Controls window to change how many band slides you want. The Band Slide settings are shown in Figure 10-24.

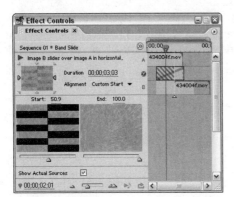

Figure 10-24: The Band Slide settings.

Center Merge

In this transition, Clip A gradually shrinks and squeezes into the center of the frame as it is replaced by Clip B. Figure 10-25 shows the Center Merge settings.

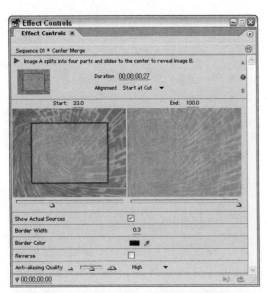

Figure 10-25: The Center Merge settings.

Center Split

In the Center Split transition, Clip A is split into four quadrants and gradually moves from the center out as it is replaced by Clip B.

Multi-Spin

In the Multi-Spin transition, Clip B gradually appears in tiny spinning boxes that grow to reveal the entire clip. Click the Custom Settings button in the Multi-Spin Settings dialog box to set the horizontal and vertical values.

Push

In this transition, Clip B pushes Clip A to one side. You can set the transition to push from either West to East, East to West, North to South, or South to North.

Slash Slide

In this transition, diagonal slashes filled with pieces of Clip B gradually replace Clip, as seen in Figure 10-26. You can set the slashes to move from Northwest to Southwest, Southeast to Northwest, Northeast to Southwest, Southwest to Northeast, West to East, North to South, East to West, or South to North. When you use this transition, the Slash Slide Settings dialog box appears. In the dialog box, set the number of slashes you want. Click the Custom button at the bottom of the Effect Controls window to change the number of slashes.

Slide

In the Slide transition, Clip B gradually slides over Clip A. You can set how the transition slides. The transition can slide from either Northwest to Southwest, Southeast to Northwest, Northeast to Southwest, Southwest to Northeast, West to East, North to South, East to West or South to North.

Sliding Bands

In this transition, Clip B begins in a compressed state and then gradually stretches across the frame to replace Clip A. The sliding bands can be set to move from either North to South, South to North, West to East or East to West.

Sliding Boxes

In the Sliding Boxes transition, vertical bands composed of Clip B gradually move across the screen to replace Clip A. When you use this transition, the Sliding Boxes Settings dialog box appears. In the dialog box, set the number bands you want. Click the Custom button at the bottom of the Effect Controls window to change the number of slashes.

Split

In this transition, Clip A splits apart from the middle to reveal Clip B behind it. The effect is like opening two sliding doors to reveal the contents of a room.

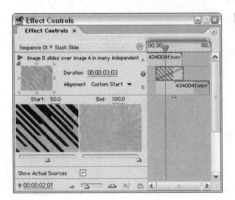

Figure 10-26: The Slash Slide settings.

Swap

In the Swap transition, Clip B swaps places with Clip A. The effect almost looks as if one clip moves left or right then behind the previous clip.

Swirl

In the Swirl transition, seen in Figure 10-27, Clip B swirls onto the screen to replace Clip A. When you use this transition, the Swirl Settings dialog box appears. In this dialog box, set the horizontal, vertical, and rate amount. Click the Custom button that is at the bottom of the Effect Controls window to change the Swirl settings.

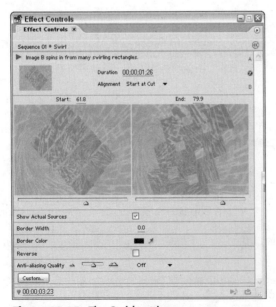

Figure 10-27: The Swirl settings.

Special Effects

The transitions in the Special Effects folder are a grab bag of transitions that create special effects, many of which change colors or distort images. The Special Effects transitions are Direct, Displace, Image Mask, Take, Texturizer, and Three-D.

Direct

The Direct transition is actually a cut. Place the transition between two overlapping clips, and the scene cuts from A to B with audio from track A. By clicking and dragging on the transition edge, you can control the in and out points of Clip B without actually editing Clip B. The transition is most useful when you need to drop in a short piece of video. In other words, you can have Clip A play and use the Direct transition to create a short insert edit to Clip B before the program returns to Clip A.

Displace

In the Displace transition, the colors in Clip B create an image distortion in Clip A. When you use this transition, the Displace Settings dialog box appears. This dialog box allows you to change the Scale settings. The lower the Scale, the larger the displacement. If the displacement would cause the image to stretch beyond the frame, the Wrap Around option tells Premiere Pro to wrap the pixels to the other side of the frame. The Repeat Pixels option repeats the pixels along the image edges instead of wrapping them on the other side of the frame. Clicking the Custom button at the bottom of the Effect Controls window enables you to change Displace Settings.

Image Mask

The Image Mask transition uses a black-and-white mask image to determine how the transition appears. When you apply this transition, the Image Mask Settings dialog box immediately appears. Click the Select Image button to select a black-and-white image to use as a mask. You can see Clip B through white areas of the mask. You can see Clip A through black areas of the mask.

 If you select a grayscale image to use as a mask, the transition converts all pixels below 50% black to white and all pixels above 50% black to black. This can result in a very aliased (jaggy) transition if the mask image is not carefully chosen.

Take

The Take transition is similar to Direct, providing a cut from Clip A to B. If you click and drag the end of the transition beyond Clip B, Premiere Pro inserts black rather than returning to Clip A.

Texturizer

The Texturizer transition maps color values from Clip B into Clip A. The blending of the two clips can create a textured effect.

Three-D

The Three-D transition distorts the colors in Clips A and B creating a composite between the two images. The brightness values of Clip A applied to Clip B can create a three-dimensional effect.

Stretch transitions

The Stretch transitions provide a variety of effects that usually stretch at least one of the clips during the effect.

Cross Stretch

This transition is more like a 3D cube transition than a stretch. When the transition occurs, the clips appear as if on a cube that turns. As the cube turns, Clip B replaces Clip A.

Funnel

In this transition, Clip A is gradually transformed into a triangular shape and then sucked out the point of the triangle to be replaced by Clip B. The Funnel settings are shown in Figure 10-28.

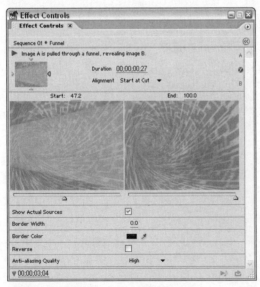

Figure 10-28: The Funnel settings.

Stretch

In the Stretch transition, Clip B starts compressed and then gradually stretches across the frame to replace Clip A.

Stretch In

Clip B appears over Clip A stretched but then gradually unstretches. When you use this transition, the Stretch In Settings dialog box appears. In this dialog box, choose the number of bands you want. Click the Custom button at the bottom of the Effect Controls window to change the number of bands.

Stretch Over

In this transition, Clip B appears over Clip A in a thin, elongated stretch but then gradually unstretches. Figure 10-29 shows the Stretch Over settings.

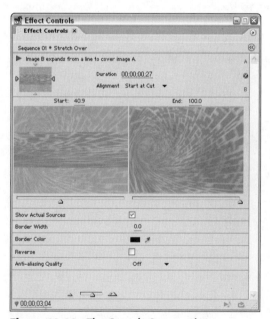

Figure 10-29: The Stretch Over settings.

Wipe transitions

The Wipe transitions wipe away different parts of Clip A to reveal Clip B. Many of the transitions provide a very modern-looking digital effect.

Band Wipe

In the Band Wipe transition, rectangular bands from screen left and screen right gradually replace Clip A with Clip B. When you use this transition, the Band Wipe Settings dialog box appears. In the dialog box, type the number of bands you want.

Barn Doors

In this transition, Clip A opens to reveal Clip B. The effect is more like sliding doors than barn doors that swing open.

Checker Wipe

In the Checker Wipe transition, a checkerboard pattern of square slices across the screen with Clip B in it. When you use this transition, the Checker Wipe Settings dialog box appears, allowing you to choose the number of horizontal and vertical slices. To change the number of slices, click the Custom button that is at the bottom of the Effect Controls window. Figure 10-30 shows the Checker Wipe settings.

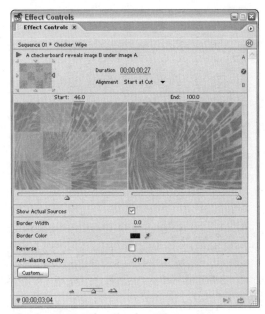

Figure 10-30: The Checker Wipe settings.

CheckerBoard

In the CheckerBoard transition, a checkerboard pattern with Clip B in the pattern gradually replaces Clip A. This effect provides more squares than the Checker Wipe transition. When you use this transition, the CheckerBoard Settings dialog box appears, allowing you to choose the number of horizontal and vertical slices. To change the number of slices, click the Custom button that is at the bottom of the Effect Controls window. The CheckerBoard settings are shown in Figure 10-31.

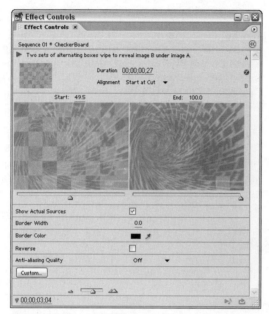

Figure 10-31: The CheckerBoard settings.

Clock Wipe

In this transition, Clip B appears onscreen gradually revealed in a circular motion. It's as if the rotating hand of a clock is sweeping the clip onscreen.

Gradient Wipe

In this transition, Clip B gradually wipes across the screen using the brightness values of a user-selected grayscale image to determine which image areas in Clip A to replace. When you use this wipe, the Gradient Wipe Settings dialog box appears. In this dialog box, you can load a grayscale image by clicking the Select Image button. When the wipe appears, image areas of Clip B corresponding to the black areas and dark areas of Clip A show through first. In the Gradient Wipe Settings dialog box, you can also click and drag the softness slider to soften the effect. Click OK to apply the settings. To return to these settings, click the Custom button at the bottom of the Effect Controls window.

Inset

In this transition, Clip B appears in a small rectangular box in the upper-left corner of the frame. As the wipe progresses, the box grows diagonally until Clip B replaces Clip A.

Paint Splatter

In the Paint Splatter transition, Clip B gradually appears in splashes that look like splattered paint.

Pinwheel

In this transition Clip B gradually appears in a growing star that gradually consumes the full frame. When you use this transition the Pinwheel Settings dialog box appears. In the dialog box, choose the number of wedges you want. Figure 10-32 shows the Pinwheel settings. Notice the Custom button at the bottom of the Effect Controls window. Clicking the Custom button displays the Pinwheel Settings dialog box.

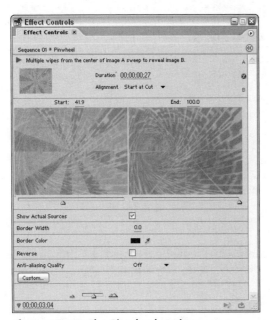

Figure 10-32: The Pinwheel settings.

Radial Wipe

In the Radial Wipe transition, Clip B is revealed by a wipe that begins horizontally across the top of the frame and sweeps through an arc clockwise, gradually covering Clip A.

Random Blocks

In this transition, Clip B gradually appears in tiny boxes that appear randomly onscreen. When you use this transition, the Random Blocks Settings dialog box appears. In the dialog box you can set the value for how wide and how high you want the boxes.

Random Wipe

In this transition, Clip B gradually appears in small blocks that gradually drop down the screen.

Spiral Boxes

In the Spiral Boxes transition, a rectangular border moves around the frame gradually replacing Clip A with Clip B. When you use this transition, the Spiral Boxes Settings dialog box appears. In the dialog box, set the horizontal and vertical value.

Venetian Blinds

In this transition, Clip B appears as if seen through Venetian blinds that open gradually and reveal Clip B's full frame. When you use this transition, the Venetian Blinds Settings dialog box appears. In the dialog box choose the number of bands you want. Figure 10-33 shows the Venetian Blinds settings in the Effect Controls window. Notice that at the bottom there is a Custom button. Clicking the Custom button displays the Venetian Blinds Settings dialog box allowing you to change the number of blinds that will appear.

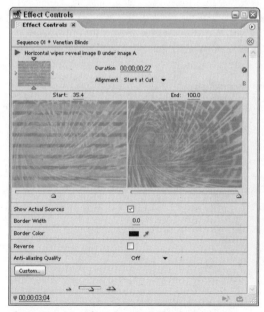

Figure 10-33: The Venetian Blinds settings.

Wedge Wipe

In the Wedge Wipe transition, Clip B appears in a pie wedge that becomes larger, gradually replacing Clip A with Clip B.

Wipe

In this simple transition, Clip B slides in from left to right replacing Clip A.

Zig-Zag Blocks

In this transition, Clip B gradually appears in horizontal bands that move from left to right and right to left down the screen When you use this transition the Zig-Zag Blocks Settings dialog box appears. In the dialog box choose the number of horizontal and vertical bands you want.

Zoom transitions

The Zoom transitions provide effects in which the entire clip zooms in or out, or boxes zoom in and out to replace one clip with another.

Cross Zoom

The Cross Zoom transition zooms into Clip B, which gradually grows to consume the full frame.

Zoom

In this transition, Clip B appears as a tiny dot and then gradually enlarges to replace Clip A. Figure 10-34 shows the Zoom settings.

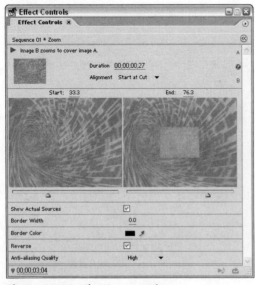

Figure 10-34: The Zoom settings.

Zoom Boxes

In this transition, tiny boxes filled with Clip B gradually enlarge to replace Clip A. When you use this transition, the Zoom Boxes Settings dialog box appears. In the dialog box, choose the number of shapes you want.

Zoom Trails

In the Zoom Trails transition, Clip A gradually shrinks (a zoom-out effect), leaving trails as it is replaced by Clip B. When you use this transition, the Zoom Trails settings dialog box appears. In the dialog box, choose the number of trails you want. Figure 10-35 shows the Zoom Trails settings.

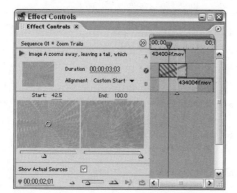

Figure 10-35: The Zoom Trails settings.

Summary

Premiere Pro's video transitions provide a variety of transitions that you can use to smooth the flow from one clip to another.

✦ To add a transition between two clips in Single-Track editing mode, drag the transition from the Effects window and place it between two overlapping video clips.

✦ To edit a transition, use the Effect Controls window or click the transition in the Timeline window.

✦ To replace one transition with another, click and drag the new transition over the old transition.

✦ To specify a default transition, select the transition in the Effects window and then choose Set Default Transition from the Effects window pop-up menu.

✦   ✦   ✦

Working with Type and Graphics

◆　◆　◆　◆

◆　◆　◆　◆

Creating Titles and Graphics with Adobe Title Designer

Titles can help turn day into night, night into day, summer into fall, and fall into winter. Used effectively, titles at the beginning of a production can help build expectations, introduce a subject, establish a mood, and, of course, provide the title of the production. Throughout a video production, titles can provide transitions between one segment and another; they can help introduce speakers and locales, or reveal their names. Titles used with graphics can help convey statistical, geographical, and other technical information. At the end of the production, you can use titles to give yourself and your production crew the credit you so richly deserve for your creative efforts.

Although titles can be created in graphics programs, such as Adobe Photoshop and Adobe Illustrator, you may find that Premiere Pro's Adobe Title Designer window offers all the titling capabilities you need for many productions without your ever leaving the Premiere Pro environment. As you'll soon see, Adobe Title Designer not only enables you to create text and graphics, but it also enables you to create drop shadows and animation effects with crawling and scrolling text.

This chapter provides a step-by-step look at how to create production titles using Adobe Title Designer. We then show you how to integrate your titles into your digital video productions.

Exploring the Adobe Title Designer Window

The Adobe Title Designer window provides a simple and efficient means of creating text and graphics that can be used for video titles in Premiere Pro projects.

To display the Adobe Title Designer window, you first need to load Premiere Pro and create a new project. When creating a new project, make sure to use the aspect ratio and frame size you want your title drawing area to have. The title drawing area takes on the aspect ratio and frame size of the existing project. The *aspect ratio* is the ratio of screen width to screen height. By having the title and the output dimensions the same, you ensure that your titles appear exactly where you want them to be in your final production.

The standard aspect ratio for digital video is 4:3. For example, the Standard 32 kHz DV-NTSC preset uses 720 × 480 pixels with an aspect ratio of 4:3. The Non-DV Square Pixel preset uses 640 × 480 pixels and also has an aspect ratio of 4:3. A Non-DV Square Pixel uses 640 × 480 pixels and also has an aspect ratio of 4:3. If you plan to create a quarter screen project (320 × 240 pixels), you may want to use the Non-DV Quarter Screen NTSC preset. Use a different aspect ratio only if you are outputting your production using nonstandard dimensions. For example, you can create a digital video production at 240 × 320, rather than 320 × 240. If so, your production's aspect ratio would be 3:4. To create a project using nonstandard dimensions, choose File ➪ New ➪ Project. In the New Project dialog box, you can choose to load a preset or create a custom preset. To create a custom preset, type in the appropriate Frame Size in the Custom Settings section of the New Project dialog box. Then name the file project and click OK.

Creating a simple title

To familiarize you with the core tools and features of Adobe Title Designer, use the following steps as a guide through the process of creating and saving a simple title clip for use in a Premiere Pro project:

1. **Choose File ➪ New ➪ Project to create a new project.** The New Project dialog box appears. Name your project, pick a preset, and click OK to create a new project. For more information on Premiere Pro digital video project settings, refer to Chapter 4.

2. **Choose File ➪ New ➪ Title to create a new title.** The Adobe Title Designer window appears, as shown in Figure 11-1. The drawing area of the title is the same size as the project frame size. If you plan on outputting your titles to film or videotape, you should display the safe title margin and safe action margin areas. By default, these options are already displayed. To view and hide these options, choose Title ➪ View ➪ Safe Title Margins and Title ➪ View ➪ Safe Action Margin.

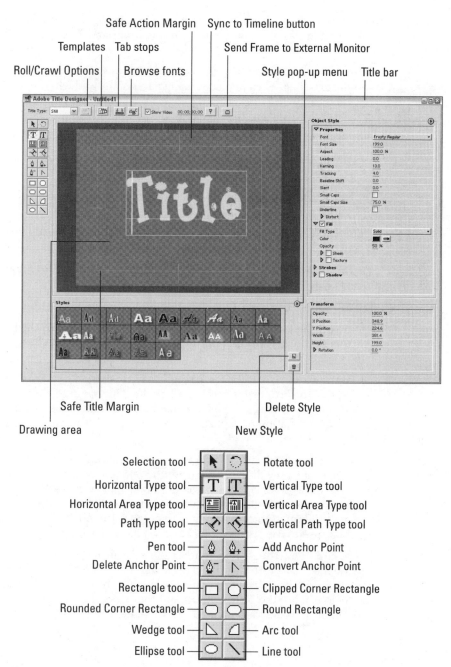

Figure 11-1: Use Adobe Title Designer to create text and graphics for production titles.

The tools and drawing area in the Adobe Title Designer window resemble those found in simple drawing and painting programs. The window is divided into the following sections:

- **Main toolbar.** Edit these options to specify whether you are creating still, crawling, or rolling text, using a template, and whether to show a video clip in the background.
- **Toolbox.** The graphic and text tools are grouped vertically here, along the left side of the window.
- **Object Style.** The settings in this area enable you to stylize text and graphic objects.
- **Transform.** The settings in this area enable you to transform text and graphic objects.
- **Styles.** The icons in this area enable you to apply preset custom styles to text and graphic objects.

3. **Click the Horizontal Title tool (the "T" below the arrow) and move the mouse to the center of the drawing area.**

4. **Click the mouse and type** Title.

5. **Format your text in the Object Style area.** This area contains the Properties, Fill, Strokes, and Shadow text options. For example, you can change the following parameters:

- **Font or font size.** Click the triangle in front of the word Properties to expand the Properties section. Click the Font menu to change the font, and click and drag on the Font Size value to change the font size. For more information on stylizing type, turn to the "Creating and Stylizing Type" section.
- **Font color.** Click the triangle before the word Fill to expand the Fill section. Leave the Fill Type menu set to Solid and click the Color Swatch next to the Color option. When the Color Picker dialog box appears, click a color and then click OK. The new color is applied to the title text. For more information on working with color in the Adobe Title Designer window, turn to the "Using Color" section later in this chapter.

6. **To save and name the Adobe Title Designer window, choose File ➪ Save.** The Title file is saved to your hard drive and placed in the current project's Project window. If you want to place the title file into your project, all you need to do is close the Title window and then drag the title file from the Project window to a video track in the Timeline window.

Touring the Adobe Title Designer window tools

The Toolbox in the Adobe Title Designer window enables you to create graphics and text. Table 11-1 reviews the tools and other graphic controls.

Table 11-1
Adobe Title Designer Window Toolbox Items

Shortcut Key	Name	Description
V	Selection tool	Selects objects so that they can be moved or resized (stretched or shrunk); can also be used to select text before changing text attributes.
O	Rotation tool	Allows you to rotate text.
T	Horizontal Type tool	Creates type horizontally.
C	Vertical Type tool	Creates type vertically.
	Horizontal Area Type tool	Creates wrapped text horizontally.
	Vertical Area Type tool	Creates wrapped text vertically.
	Path Type tools	Creates text along a path.
P	Pen tool	Creates curved shapes using Bézier curves.
	Add Anchor Point tool	Adds anchor points to path.
	Delete Anchor Point tool	Deletes anchor points from path.
	Convert Anchor Point	Converts curved point to corner point and vice versa.
R	Rectangle tool	Creates rectangles.
	Clipped Corner Rectangle tool	Creates rectangles with dog-eared corner.
	Rounded Corner Rectangle tool	Creates rectangles with round corners.
W	Wedge tool	Creates triangular shapes.
A	Arc tool	Creates curved shapes.
E	Ellipse tool	Creates ellipses.
L	Line tool	Creates lines.

Using the Title menu

Premiere Pro's Title menu enables you to change the settings of many of the tools in the Title window and to change the visual attributes of text and graphic objects. For example, you can use the Title menu to set the font, size, and style of the text that you create in the Adobe Title Designer window. You can also use it to set the speed and direction of rolling title text. Table 11-2 summarizes the Title menu commands. The Title menu appears only when the Adobe Title Designer window is open onscreen.

Table 11-2 The Title Menu Commands	
Menu Command	**Description**
Font	Changes typeface.
Size	Changes size of text.
Type Alignment	Sets text to flush left, flush right, or centered.
Orientation	Sets text to be horizontal or vertical.
Word Wrap	Sets text to wrap, when it reaches the safe title margin.
Tab Stops	Enables you to create tabs within a text box.
Templates	Enables you to apply, create, and edit templates.
Roll/Crawl Options	Provides options for setting direction and speed of rolling and crawling text.
Logo	Enables you to insert logos in the entire Adobe Title Designer drawing area as a background, in a portion of the drawing area or within a text box.
Transform	Enables you to change the position, scale, rotation, and opacity of an object or text.
Select	Enables you to select from a stack of objects, the first object above, next object above, next object below, last object below.
Arrange	Enables you to bring selected objects to the front, back, forward, or backward of a stack of objects.
Position	Moves object so that it is either horizontally or vertically centered, or to the lower third part of the Adobe Title Designer drawing area. The lower third position is frequently used for text that must be read without covering up the onscreen image.

Menu Command	Description
Align Objects	Enables you to align selected objects horizontally, left, right, or centered and vertically, top, bottom, or centered.
Distribute Objects	Enables you to distribute selected objects horizontally, left, right, centered, or even spacing and vertically top, bottom, centered, or even spacing.
View	Enables you to view safe title margin, safe action margin, text baselines, and tab markers.

Saving, Closing, and Opening a Title File

After you've created some stunning text and graphics in the Adobe Title Designer window, make sure to save it so that you can use it in one of your Premiere Pro projects. If you save your title, you can always load the title into any project. You can even create one title as a template and then load it, edit the text and graphics, and save it under a new name.

Caution You can place one title in multiple projects, but editing the title contents causes Premiere Pro to replace every instance of the title in your projects with the newly edited version.

To save your title, choose File ➪ Save. In the Save File As dialog box, type a name for your title and choose the location where you want to save it. To close the Title window, choose File ➪ Close or click the close box icon.

Note When you save a title, the title is placed in the Project window of the current project onscreen.

When you want to load your title file back into the Adobe Title Designer window, choose File ➪ Import. Choose the title file from the correct folder and then click Open to load the file. The file is imported into the Project window. From here, you can drag the title into a video track in the Timeline window of an existing Premiere Pro project. To edit the title file, double-click the title file. When the title appears in the Adobe Title Designer window, make the changes. Then either choose File ➪ Save to save the file and replace it with the changes or choose File ➪ Save As to create a copy of the file and save the file under a new name.

Tip Double-clicking a title clip in the Project window opens that title in the Adobe Title Designer window.

Creating and Stylizing Type

Premiere Pro's horizontal and vertical Type tool works very much like Type tools in graphic programs. Creating text, selecting and moving it, and stylizing fonts works very much the same as most other Type tools. Changing type color and adding shadows is somewhat different but very simple when you get the hang of it. The Path Type tools even enable you to create text along a Bézier path.

Cross-Reference

Creating text along a path with the Path type tools, along with creating Bézier paths and shapes with the Pen tool, is covered later in this chapter in the section "Working with the Bézier Tools."

Using the Horizontal and Vertical Type tools

Text in video productions should be clear and easy to read. If viewers need to strain their eyes to read your titles, they'll either stop trying to read them or they'll ignore the video and audio as they try to decipher the text onscreen.

Premiere Pro's Type tools provide the versatility that you need to create clear and interesting text. Not only can you change size, font, and color, but by using the Object Style options in the Adobe Title Designer window, you can also create drop shadows and emboss effects.

Premiere Pro's Type tools enable you to place type anywhere in the Adobe Title Designer window drawing area. As you work, Premiere Pro places each block of text within a text *bounding box* that you can easily move, resize, or delete.

Here's how to create horizontal and vertical text:

1. **Choose File ➪ New ➪ Project to create a new project.** Set the preset to the size of your Title and production.

2. **Choose File ➪ New ➪ Title to create a new title.** The Adobe Title Designer window appears. Set the Title Type pop-up menu to Still because you are creating still text rather than rolling or crawling text.

Cross-Reference

To learn how to create rolling and crawling text, turn to the section "Rolling and Crawling Titles" later in this chapter.

3. **Click either the Horizontal Type or Vertical Type tool in the Toolbox.** The Horizontal Type tool creates text horizontally from left to right, and the Vertical Type tool creates text vertically.

4. **Drag the I-beam cursor to where you want your text to appear and then click the mouse.** A blinking cursor appears.

Note Select the Horizontal Paragraph and Vertical Type Paragraph tool to create horizontal and vertical text that wraps.

5. **Type your title text.** If you make a mistake and want to delete the last character you typed, press Backspace. Figure 11-2 shows text being entered in a bounding box.

Note You can choose Edit ➪ Undo to undo your last entry.

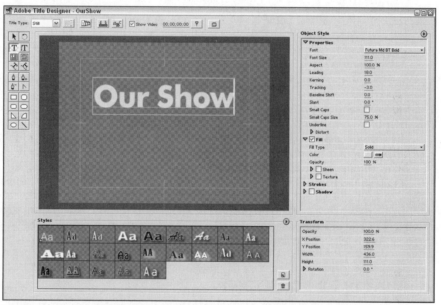

Figure 11-2: Text created with Premiere Pro's Horizontal Type tools.

Editing with the Type tools

If you want to edit text after you finish using the Type tool, you must reselect the text with the Type tool. Move the I-beam cursor over the characters that you want to edit and then click. The blinking cursor appears where you clicked; you can then edit your text. To select all the text within a text box, choose Edit ➪ Select All.

If you are using the Horizontal or Vertical Type tool and you want to create a new line, press Enter and then begin typing. Before you press Return/Enter, make sure that the I-beam cursor is set to where you want the new line to begin.

Wrapping text

The Horizontal and Vertical Type tools do not automatically wrap text to the next line. If you want to have Premiere Pro automatically wrap text created with the Horizontal and/or Vertical tool, choose Title ➪ Word Wrap. The Horizontal and Vertical Paragraph Type tools automatically wrap text to the next line. To use the Horizontal and Vertical Paragraph Type tools, select the tool from the Toolbox. Move the tool to the drawing area, click and drag to create a text box, and begin typing. Notice that as you type, the text automatically wraps to the next line.

Using tabs

You can add spacing between words and align them left, center, or right using tabs. Tabs can help make your titles (or rolling and crawling text) more readable. To apply tabs to your text, you need to use the tab ruler in the Tab Stops dialog box. Before you display the tab ruler, you may want to display the tab markers. By displaying tab markers, Premiere Pro has lines appear where you set your tabs. By displaying the tab markers as lines, you can better visualize how your tabs will appear within your text. To display tab markers, choose Title ➪ View ➪ Tab Markers. To display the tab ruler, choose Title ➪ Tab Stops or click on the Tab Stops icon that is at the top of the Adobe Title Designer dialog box. To create a tab, just click the ruler with the either the left, center, or right tab selected. To move a tab, click and drag on it. To apply the tab, click OK to close the Tab Stops dialog box. Then move the text beam in front of where you want to apply a tab and then press the Tab key on your keyboard. If you want to change the tabs after you've closed the Tab Stops dialog box, just reopen the Tab Stops dialog box and then click and drag the tab on the ruler to the desired location. The text is automatically updated. To delete tab markers, just click the tab and drag it off to either side of the ruler.

Moving text onscreen

You can move a text box by using the Selection tool, choosing Title ➪ Transform ➪ Position or by changing the X and Y Position in the Transform section of the Adobe Title Designer window. You can also move text by pressing and holding the left button on the mouse while you drag left or right on the X and Y position values in the Transform section. The Selection tool, the Title menu, and the Transform options can also be used to rotate the text box onscreen.

Manipulating text with the Selection tool

You can quickly move the type's bounding box. Here's how:

1. **In the Adobe Title Designer window, click inside the bounding box with the Selection tool.**

2. **Drag the text to a new location.** The X and Y Position values change in the Transform area.

Adobe Title Designer enables you to resize the bounding box. To do so, follow these steps:

1. **Using the Selection tool, move the Selection tool over one of the bounding box handles.** The cursor changes to a small, straight line with two arrows at either end of it.

2. **Click and drag to increase or decrease the bounding box and font size.** Notice in the Transform section that the Width, Height, X Position, and Y Position values change.

Adobe Title Designer enables you to rotate a bounding box using the Selection tool. To do so, follow these steps:

1. **Move the Selection tool over one of the bounding box handles.**

2. **When the cursor icon changes to a small, curved line with two arrows at either end of it, click and drag to rotate the bounding box and text size.** Notice that the Rotation value in the Transform section changes.

Note

To rotate a bounding box, you can use the Rotate tool in the Toolbox. To use the Rotate tool, click on it in the Toolbox. Then move it to the bounding box and click and drag in the direction you want to rotate the text box.

Manipulating text with the Transform values

You can use the Transform values to move, resize, and rotate a bounding box. Before you can move, resize, or rotate a bounding box, you must select the bounding box by clicking inside it with the Type tool or the Selection tool.

✦ **Opacity of a bounding box.** Click and drag to the right or left on the Opacity value to change it. Values less than 100% make the items in the bounding box translucent.

✦ **Moving a bounding box.** Click and drag to the right or left on the X and Y Position values to change them. To move the text box in increments of ten, press and hold the Shift key as you drag to the right or left on the X and Y Position values.

✦ **Resizing a bounding box.** In the Transform section, click and drag to the right or left on the Width and Height values to change them. Pressing the Shift key as you drag left or right increases the values in increments of ten.

✦ **Rotating a bounding box.** Click the Rotation value and drag to the right or left to change it. Dragging left rotates the box counterclockwise, and dragging right rotates the box clockwise.

Manipulating text with the Title menu

Before you can move, resize, or rotate a bounding box, you must select it. If it is not already selected, click inside the text box with either the Type tool or the Selection tool.

✦ **Moving the bounding box.** Choose Title ⇨ Transform ⇨ Position. In the Position dialog box, type a value for the X and Y Position and then click OK. The Title ⇨ Position command enables you to move the box horizontally center, vertically center, and to the lower third area.

✦ **Resizing the bounding box.** Choose Title ⇨ Transform ⇨ Scale. In the Scale dialog box, type a scale percentage. You can choose to scale uniformly or nonuniformly. Finally, click OK.

✦ **Rotating the bounding box.** Choose Title ⇨ Transform ⇨ Rotation. In the Rotation dialog box, type the degrees you want to rotate the text box and then click OK.

As you move, resize, and rotate the text box, notice that the options in the Transform section in the Adobe Title Designer dialog box are updated to reflect the changes.

Changing text attributes

When you first type with the Type tool, Premiere Pro places the type onscreen in its default font and size. You can change type attributes by changing the Properties in the Object Style section of the Adobe Title Designer window or using the menu commands found in the Title menu. The Properties section allows you not only to change font and font size, but it also allows you to set the aspect ratio, kerning, tracking, leading, baseline shift, slant, and small caps and to add an underline. You can use the Type menu to change font and size, and you can also change the type orientation from horizontal to vertical, and vice versa.

Changing font and size attributes

You can use both the Title menu and the Properties options in the Adobe Title Designer window to change the font and size of your type. Adobe Title Designer offers three basic techniques for editing font and size attributes.

To change the font and size text attributes before typing, follow these steps:

1. **Click a Type tool.**

2. **Click where you want the text to appear.**

3. **Change the settings for font and size by using the Title ⇨ Font command and the Title ⇨ Size command.** You can also change the font and size from the

Font pop-up menu in the Properties section in the Type Designer window or by clicking on the Browse icon (which is next to the Show Video check box). As you type, the new text you type features the attributes of the current font and size settings.

To change individual characters or words, try this:

1. **Select the text with the Type tool by clicking and dragging over the character.**

2. **Change type attributes using either the Title menu commands or the Properties options in the Object Style area of the Adobe Title Designer window.**

Tip

To browse through the fonts available, choose Title ➪ Font ➪ Browse. In the Font Browser dialog box, click the down arrow to see a preview of the fonts. The character display in the Font Browser dialog box can be changed. To do so, choose Edit ➪ Preferences ➪ Titler. In the dialog box that appears, change the letters in the Font Browser field.

If you want to change all text in a text block, click the text with the Selection tool. Then change the font and size text attributes.

Changing spacing attributes

Typically, a typeface's default *leading* (space between lines), *kerning* (space between two letters), and *tracking* (space between various letters) provides sharp, readable type onscreen. If you begin using large type sizes, however, white space between lines and letters may look awkward. If this happens, you can use Premiere Pro's leading, kerning, and tracking controls to change spacing attributes.

Here's how to change leading:

1. **Use either the Horizontal Paragraph or Vertical Paragraph Type tool to create more than one line of text in the drawing area of the Adobe Title Designer window.**

2. **Click and drag left or right on the Leading value.** Increase the leading value to add space between each line. Decrease the leading value to remove space between each line. If you want to reset spacing to its original leading, type **0** in the Leading field. The Leading field is in the Properties section of the Adobe Title Designer window.

You can also change the spacing between lines by using Baseline Shift. Changing the Baseline Shift moves text up or down. Here's how to change the spacing between lines using Baseline Shift:

1. **Use the Horizontal or Vertical Type tool to create more than one line of text.**

2. **Click the triangle in front of the Properties section to display the Properties.** The Baseline Shift property is located below the Tracking property.

3. **Click and drag on the Baseline Shift value to change it.** Increasing the Baseline Shift moves the baseline of the text up. Decreasing the Baseline Shift moves the baseline of the text down.

Here's how to change kerning:

1. **Use a Type tool to create a word in the Adobe Title Designer window.**

2. **Click between the two letters whose spacing you want to change.**

3. **Increase or decrease the kerning values in the Properties section of the Adobe Title Designer window.** As you increase kerning value, the space between letters increases. If you decrease kerning value, the space between the letters decreases.

Here's how to change tracking:

1. **Use a Type tool to create a word or two in the Adobe Title Designer window.**

2. **Click and drag over the text with the Type tool.**

3. **Increase or decrease the tracking value in the Properties section of the Adobe Title Designer window.** Increasing the tracking value increases the spacing between the letters. Decreasing the tracking value decreases the spacing between the letters.

Changing other text attributes

Some of the other text attributes allow you to change the look and feel of the text. These are the Aspect, Slant, Distort, Small Caps, and Underline attributes. Figure 11-3 shows text before and after changing the Aspect, Slant, and Distort attributes.

Figure 11-3: Text before and after changing the Aspect, Slant, and Distortion attributes.

Here's how to change the look and feel of your text using some of the text attributes in the Properties section of the Type Designer window:

1. **Select a font and font size.**

2. **Type a word using the Horizontal Type tool.**

3. **Click and drag to the right and left on the Aspect value to increase or decrease the horizontal scale of the text.**

4. **To slant the text to the right, click and drag on the Slant value to the right. To slant the text to the left, click and drag on the Slant value to the left.**

5. **To distort the text, click the X and Y values in the Distort section.**

6. **If you want to underline or convert the text to small caps, click the option's check box.** Doing so selects the option.

Using Color

The colors you choose for text and graphics can add to the mood and sophistication of your video project. Using the Premiere Pro color tools, you can pick colors as well as create gradients from one color to another. You can even add transparency effects that show background video frames through text and graphics.

How do you know what colors to pick when creating titles? The best guide is to use colors that stand out from background images. When watching broadcast television, pay special attention to titles. You'll often notice that many television producers simply use white text against a dark background, or they'll use bright text with drop shadows to prevent the titles from looking flat. If you are creating a production that includes many titles — such as *lower thirds* (graphics at the bottom of the screen, often providing information such as the names of speakers), keep the text the same color throughout the production to avoid distracting the viewer.

Choosing color with the Color Picker

Any time you select a color in Premiere Pro, you are using Premiere Pro's Color Picker. Picking colors in Premiere Pro can be as simple as clicking the mouse. To see how easy it is to pick a color in Premiere Pro, open the Color Picker, shown in Figure 11-4, by clicking on the Solid Fill Color swatch. Click the Fill triangle to expand the Fill section and display the Color Swatch. (The Fill section is found in the Object Style section of the Adobe Title Designer window.) For the Solid Fill Color Swatch to appear, the Fill Type pop-up menu should be set to Solid.

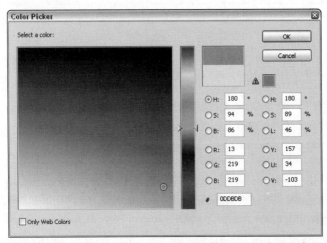

Figure 11-4: Use Premiere Pro's Color Picker to select colors.

You can pick colors for text and graphic objects in the Color Picker window by clicking in the main color area of the dialog box, or you can enter specific RGB values. As you work in the Color Picker, the color that you are creating is previewed in the bottom swatch in the upper-right of the Color Picker dialog box. The top swatch displays the original color. If you want to return to the original color, simply click the top color swatch.

If you pick a color that falls beyond the NTSC video color gamut, Premiere Pro displays a gamut warning signal that looks like a gray triangle with an exclamation mark in it (shown in Figure 11-4). To drop the color back to the nearest NTSC color, simply click the gamut warning signal. If you want to work with colors that are specifically for the Web, click on the Only Web Colors option that is at the bottom left of the Color Picker dialog box.

Note PAL and SECAM video feature larger color gamuts than NTSC video does. You can ignore the gamut warning if you are not using NTSC video.

Understanding RGB colors

Computer displays and television video monitors create colors by using the red, green, and blue color model. In this model, adding different values of red, green, and blue light creates millions of colors.

Premiere Pro's Color Picker simulates adding light by enabling you to enter values into its Red, Green, and Blue fields. The concept is illustrated in Table 11-3.

The largest number that can be entered into one of the color fields is 255, and the smallest is zero. Thus, Premiere Pro enables you to create over 16 million colors ($256 \times 256 \times 256$). When each RGB value equals zero, no light is added to create colors; the resulting color is black. If you enter 255 in each of the RGB fields, you create white.

To create different shades of gray, make all field values equal. R 50, G 50, B 50 creates a dark gray; R 250, G 250, B 250 creates a light gray.

Table 11-3 The Color Values for RGB Colors			
Color	**Red Value**	**Green Value**	**Blue Value**
Black	0	0	0
Red	255	0	0
Green	0	255	0
Blue	0	0	255
Cyan	0	255	255
Magenta	255	0	255
Yellow	255	255	0
White	255	255	255

Choosing color using the Eyedropper tool

Apart from the Color Picker, the most efficient way of picking colors is to click a color with the Eyedropper tool. The Eyedropper tool automatically copies the color you click into the Color swatch. Therefore, you can recreate a color with one click of the mouse, rather than wasting time experimenting with RGB values in the Color Picker.

You can use the Eyedropper tool to do the following:

✦ Select a color from a type or graphic object in the drawing area.

✦ Select a specific color from a logo, style, or template.

✦ Copy a specific color from a video clip in the background of the Adobe Title Designer window.

The Eyedropper tool can be very handy for selecting colors from a video clip, logo, style, or template. Here's how to use the Eyedropper tool:

1. **Create a New Project using the presets you want your title to have.**

   If you want to use the Eyedropper tool to select a color from a video frame (shown in Figure 11-5), you need to import a video clip into your project by choosing File ⇨ Import.

   The video clip that appears in Figure 11-5 is in the Digital Vision folder in the Chapter 11 folder, in the Tutorial Projects folder that is on the DVD that accompanies this book. The video clip is from Digital Vision's NightMoves (705018f.mov).

2. **Drag the video clip from the Project window to the Timeline window.**

3. **Choose File ⇨ New ⇨ Title to create a new title.**

4. **To display the video clip in the Adobe Title Designer window, click the Show Video check box to display the video clip.**

5. **Click and drag in the Timeline location area to display the frame you want to appear in the background of the Adobe Title Designer drawing area.**

   Notice that the Fill, Strokes, and Shadow sections all have Eyedropper tools. Using the Fill Eyedropper tool changes the Fill Color Swatch. Using the Strokes Eyedropper tool changes the Strokes Color Swatch. Using the Shadow Eyedropper tool changes the Shadow Color Swatch. Click the Eyedropper tool you want to use.

   To import a graphic file as the background or as a logo into the Adobe Title Designer window drawing area, choose Title ⇨ Logo ⇨ Insert Logo. To import a template into the drawing area of the Adobe Title Designer window, use the Template button.

6. **Move the Eyedropper tool over the color you want to select and click the mouse.** The Color Swatch changes to the new color.

Figure 11-5: Use the Eyedropper tool to select colors from a frame of a video clip.

Applying solid colors to text and graphics

After you've created a graphic object or some text, applying a solid fill color using Premiere Pro's Color Picker is quite simple. Here's how:

1. **Use a Type tool to create a text object or use a Graphic tool to create a graphic object onscreen.** You can use the Selection tool to select a text or graphic object already onscreen.

2. **Verify that a check mark appears in front of the Fill option in the Properties section in the Title Designer dialog box.** Deselecting the Fill check box option removes the fill. Keep the Fill option selected.

3. **Click the triangle in front of the Fill option to display the options.**

4. **Set the Fill Type pop-up menu to Solid.**

5. **Click on the Color Swatch.** Doing so opens the Color Picker.

6. **Pick your new color and close the Color Picker.** You can also use the Eyedropper tool to pick a color from an object in the drawing area or from a video clip in the background (see the preceding section).

7. **To make the color translucent so that you can see through it, reduce the Opacity percentage.** The lower the opacity, the more translucent the object. You can change the opacity percentage by using either the Opacity field in the Object Style section or in the Transform section. You can also use the

Title ➪ Transform ➪ Opacity command. By lowering the opacity in an object, you can create interesting graphic effects where portions of objects below show through the object above.

Applying highlights and textures with text and graphic objects

You can also add a highlight and/or a texture to the fill and stroke of text or a graphic object. To add a highlight, use the Sheen option. To view the Sheen option, click the triangle in front of Properties to display all the properties. Then click the triangle in front of Fill to display the Fill options. The Sheen option is located with in the Fill section.

Adding a highlight

Follow these steps to create a sense of light and shadow in your text or graphic:

1. **In the Adobe Title Designer window, with an object selected, click the triangle in front of the Fill property to display the Sheen option.** Then click the Sheen check box.

2. **Click the triangle in front of the Sheen check box to display the Sheen options.**

3. **Double-click the Color Swatch to pick a color.** You can also use the Eyedropper tool to pick a color from an object onscreen or from a background video clip.

4. **Click and drag on the Size value to change the size of the highlight.** Drag to the right to increase the size. Drag to the left to decrease the size.

5. **Click and drag on the Angle value to change the value of the highlight.**

6. **Click and drag on the Offset value to move the highlight up or down.** Increasing the offset value moves the highlight up and decreasing the offset value moves the offset down.

7. **Change the Opacity value to make the highlight translucent.** Reducing the Opacity value makes the highlight more translucent.

Adding a texture to text or graphics

You can easily make text and graphics more realistic by applying a texture. Figure 11-6 shows the selected objects and text with a texture applied to it.

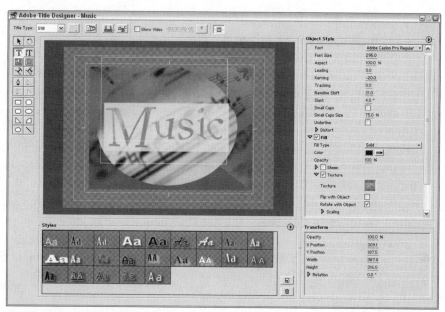

Figure 11-6: In the Adobe Title Designer dialog box, you can see textures applied to text and graphics.

Follow these steps to learn how to apply textures:

1. **With an object selected in the Adobe Title Designer window, click the triangle in front of the Fill property to display the Texture option.** Then click the Texture check box.

2. **Click the triangle in front of the Texture check box to display the Texture options.**

3. **Click the Texture Swatch to display the Choose a Texture Image dialog box.**

4. **In the Choose a Texture Image dialog box, pick a texture from the Premiere Pro Textures folder.**

5. **Click Open to apply the texture to the selected object.**

Note

You can create your own textures. You can use Photoshop to save any bitmap file and save it in psd, jpeg, Targa, or Tiff format. Or you can use Premiere Pro to output a frame from a video clip.

6. Specify optional settings:

- **Flip With Object or Rotate With Object.** Premiere Pro flips and/or rotates a texture with the object.

- **Scaling.** Premiere Pro scales the texture. First, click the triangle in front of the option and then click and drag on the Horizontal and Vertical values.

  The Scaling section also contains the Tile X and Tile Y option, which you use to specify whether you want the texture to be tiled to an object.

  You use the Object X and Object Y pop-up menu in the Scaling section to determine how the texture is stretched along the X and Y axes. The four choices from the pop-up menu are Clipped Face, Arbitrary, Face, and Extended Character. The choice you pick determines how the texture is stretched. By default the Clipped Face option is selected.

- **Alignment.** Use the Object X and Object Y pop-up menu in the section to determine how the texture aligns with the object. The four choices from the pop-up menu are Clipped Face, Arbitrary, Face, and Extended Character. The choice you pick determines how the texture is aligned. By default the Clipped Face option is selected.

  You use the Rule X and Rule Y check boxes in the Alignment section to determine how the texture is aligned. Choose Top Left, Center, or Bottom Right.

  You use the X Offset and Y Offset values to move the texture within the selected object.

- **Blending.** Use the Mix value in the Blending section to blend the texture with the fill color. Decreasing the Mix value increases the fill color and decreases the texture.

  The Fill Key and Texture Key check boxes in the Blending section allow for transparency of the object to be considered.

  Lowering the Alpha Scale value in the Blending section makes the object more translucent. The Composite Rule pop-up menu allows you to pick which channel is going to be used in determining the transparency. Clicking the Invert Composite check box inverts the alpha values.

Creating and applying gradients to text and graphics

Premiere Pro's color controls enable you to apply gradients to text and graphic objects created in the Adobe Title Designer window. A *gradient*, which is a gradual blend from one color to another, can help add interest and depth to otherwise flat color. Used effectively, gradients can also help simulate lighting effects in graphics. The three types of gradients you can create in the Type Designer window are Linear Gradient, Radial Gradient, and 4 Color Gradient. Linear and Radial Gradients are created from two colors. The 4 Color Gradient is created from four colors.

Figure 11-7 shows a graphic created using gradients. To create the kite object shown in Figure 11-7, we used the 4 Color Gradient. To learn how to create a diamond shape using the Graphic tools in the Adobe Title Designer window, turn to the "Working with the Bézier tools" section. The highlight area in the middle of the kite was created using the Sheen option. To the text inside the kite object, we applied a linear gradient.

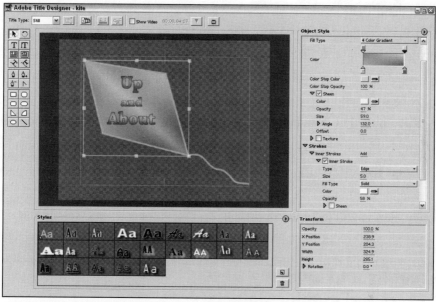

Figure 11-7: Graphic object and text created using gradients.

Here's how to create a linear and radial gradient:

1. **In the Adobe Title Designer window, select or create text or a graphic object with the Selection tool.**

Note

If you want to apply a gradient to specific letters in a text block, select the text by clicking and dragging over it with the Type tool.

If you are outputting to video, gradients created in small text may make the text unreadable on a television monitor.

2. **The Fill check box should be selected and the triangle in front of the check box should be facing downward.** Do so, if it isn't. The Fill option is found in the Object Style section of the dialog box. In the Object Style section of the dialog box, click the triangle that is in front of the word Properties to display the Fill option.

Moving the Gradient Start and End Color Swatches

You can move the Gradient Start Color Swatch and the Gradient End Color Swatch. Moving the swatches changes how much color of each swatch is applied to the gradient.

The Color Stop Color Swatch allows you to change the color of the selected color swatch. The Color Stop Opacity allows you to change the opacity of the selected color swatch. The selected color swatch is the color swatch with a black triangle above it.

To change the angle in a linear gradient, click and drag on the Angle value.

To increase the number of repeats in the linear or radial blend, click and drag on the Repeat value.

3. **From the Fill Type pop-up menu, choose either Linear Gradient or Radial Gradient.**

4. **To set the start and ending colors of the gradients, use the Gradient Start and End Color Swatches.** They are the two tiny rectangles below the gradient bar. Pick the starting gradient color by double-clicking the Gradient Start Color Swatch. When the Color Picker opens, pick a color. Double-click the Gradient End Color Swatch. When the Color Picker opens, pick an ending gradient color.

Creating and applying bevels to text and graphic objects

Premiere Pro enables you to create some really cool bevels in the Adobe Title Designer window. You can add a three-dimensional effect to your text and graphic objects by beveling them, as shown in Figure 11-8.

Here's how to bevel an object:

1. **In the Adobe Title Designer window, select or create text or a graphic with the Selection tool.**

2. **The Fill check box should be selected and the triangle in front of the check box should be facing downwards.** Do so, if it isn't.

3. **From the Fill Type pop-up menu, choose Bevel.**

4. **Click the Highlight Color Swatch or use the Eyedropper tool to pick a highlight color.** Then click the Shadow Color Swatch or the Eyedropper tool to pick a shadow color.

5. **Click and drag the Size slider to the right to increase the bevel size.**

6. **To increase or decrease the highlight color, click and drag on the Balance value.** Increasing the highlight color decreases shadow color, and vice versa.

7. **To make your bevel look more decorative, click the Tube check box.** Notice that a tubular border appears between the highlight and shadow area.

8. **Click the Lit check box to increase the bevel effect and make the object more three-dimensional.** Click and drag on the Light Angle value to change the angle of the light. Click and drag on the Light Magnitude value to increase or decrease the amount of light.

9. **If you want to make the bevel translucent, click and drag to the left on either the Highlight Opacity or Shadow Opacity value.**

Figure 11-8: Text objects with a bevel.

Applying shadows to text and graphics

To add a finishing touch to your text or graphic object, you may want to add a shadow to it. You can add either an inner or outer stroke to an object. Here's how:

1. **In the Adobe Title Designer window, select text or a graphic with the Selection tool.**

Note

If you want the selected object to fill but with a shadow, set the object's Fill Type to Ghost Fill.

2. **Click the Shadow check box to select it.**

3. **To see all the Shadow options, click the triangle in front of the Shadow option, so that it is facing downward.**

4. Click and drag on the Size value to set the size of the shadow.

5. Click and drag on the Distance and Angle values to move the shadow to the desired location.

6. Click and drag on the Spread value to soften the edges of the shadow.

7. **Double-click the Color Swatch to change the color for the drop shadow.** You can also use the Eyedropper tool to pick a color from a background video clip or template.

8. Reduce the Opacity value if you want to make the shadow translucent.

Note   Don't let a shadow fool you. If you are changing the opacity of an object that has a solid shadow, the opacity effect you desire may not be possible until you remove the shadow or make the shadow transparent.

Applying strokes to text and graphics

To separate the fill color from the shadow color, you may want to add a stroke to it. You can add either an inner or outer stroke to an object. Here's how:

1. **In the Adobe Title Designer window, select text or a graphic with the Selection tool.**

Note   If you want the selected object to have a stroke, but no fill or shadow, set the object's Fill Type to Eliminate Fill. This way you can use the selected object as a frame.

2. Click the triangle in front of the Strokes option so that it is facing downward.

3. Click Add next to either the Inner Strokes and/or Outer Strokes option to add either inner and/or outer strokes to the selected object.

Note   You can click the Object Style menu — the tiny circle with an arrow surrounding it — to add, delete, or move a stroke.

4. Click the Stroke Type pop-up menu to pick a stroke type.

5. Click and drag the Size value to change the stroke size.

6. Click and drag in the Angle value to change the angle of the Depth and Drop Face stroke type.

7. Click the Fill Type pop-up menu to pick a fill type.

8. **Double-click the Color Swatch to pick a color for the drop shadow.** You can also use the Eyedropper tool to pick a color from a background video clip or template, and so on.

9. Reduce the Opacity value if you want to make the stroke translucent.

Using Styles

Although setting text attributes is quite simple, sometimes finding the right combination of font, size, style, kerning, and leading can be time-consuming. After you've
spent the better part of an hour fine-tuning text attributes to one text block, you
may want to apply the same attributes to other text in the Adobe Title Designer
window or to other text that you've previously saved. You can save attributes and
color using styles.

The Premiere Pro Adobe Title Designer enables you to save and load preset styles
for text and graphics. Thus, instead of picking font, size, and color each time you
create a title, you can apply a style name to the text and have all the attributes
applied at once. Using one or two styles throughout your project helps ensure con-
sistency. If you don't want to create your own styles, you can use the preset styles
appearing at the bottom of the Adobe Title Designer. All you need to do to apply a
style is select the text and click the style swatch that suits your needs.

The styles section introduces you to a new interface feature of Adobe Premiere Pro.
The choices for styles are hidden from the screen but are accessible by clicking the
Styles menu—the tiny circle with an arrow surrounding it. The Styles menu is
shown in Figure 11-9. Clicking the Styles menu arrow opens up commands that
allow you to create styles, save them to disk, and change the way styles appear
onscreen.

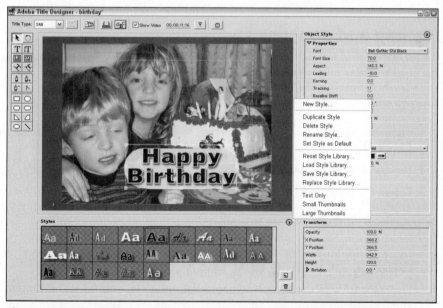

Figure 11-9: The Styles menu displays styles and available style library options.

Here's how to create a style:

1. **Create the text using attributes that you have in the style.**

2. **Choose New Style from the Styles pop-up menu, or you can click the New Style button (above the Delete Style button).**

3. **Enter a name for the style and then click OK.** You'll see either a swatch of the new style or the style name will appear in the Styles area.

Styles only remain during the current Premiere Pro project session. If you want to use a style again, you must save the styles into a style file. Here's how to save a style file:

1. **Select the name of the style you want to save or select its thumbnail.**

Note You can also start by selecting each object containing the style that you want to save.

2. **Choose Save Style Library from the Styles menu.**

3. **Enter a name for the style and designate its location on your hard drive.**

4. **Click Save.** Premiere Pro saves the file using a .prtl file extension.

Note You can replace a preexisting style name with a new style by choosing Replace Styles rather than save styles.

Loading and applying styles

If you want to load a style from the hard drive to use in a new Premiere Pro session, you must load the style library before you can apply it.

Here's how to load styles from the hard drive:

1. **Click the triangle in the Styles section to display the Styles pop-up menu. Choose Load Style Library from the Styles pop-up menu.**

2. **Use the mouse to navigate to the hard drive location containing your style.**

3. **Select the style and then click Open.** After styles are loaded, you can easily apply a style by clicking the text or object and then simply clicking the swatch for the style that you want to apply.

Renaming, deleting, and changing style swatch

You can duplicate styles and rename them. You can delete saved styles that you don't need to use anymore. You can also change the way the style swatches appear in the Adobe Title Designer window.

Here's how to duplicate, rename, and delete styles:

1. **With a style selected, choose Duplicate Style from the Styles menu.**

2. **To rename a style, first select it and then choose Rename Style from the Styles menu.**

3. **In the dialog box that appears, type a new name.**

4. **To delete a style, select it from the Styles section.**

5. **With a style selected, choose Delete Style from the Styles pop-up menu. In the dialog box that appears, click OK to delete the selected style.**

If you feel the style swatches consume too much screen space, you can change the display of styles so that they appear as text or as small icons. To change the display, simply click the Styles menu and then choose either Text only, Large Thumbnails, or Small Thumbnails.

Note   To change the two characters that appear in the style swatch, choose Edit ⇨ Preferences ⇨ Titler. In the dialog box that appears, type the two characters that you want in the Style Swatches field.

Placing a Title in a Project

To use the titles you create in the Adobe Title Designer window, you need to add them to a Premiere Pro project. When you save a title, Premiere Pro automatically adds the title to the Project window of the current project. After the title is in the Project window, you add titles to the Timeline window much the same way as you add video clips and other graphics — by dragging and dropping them from the Project window to the Timeline window. Titles can either be placed in a Video track above a video clip or in the same track as a video clip. Typically, you could add a title to the Video 2 track so that the title or title sequence appears over the video clips in the Video 1 track. If you want to have a Title file gradually transition into a video clip, you can place the Title file in the same Video track, so that the title either overlaps the video clip at the beginning or at the end. The transition is applied to the overlapping section. For more information on working with video transitions, refer to Chapter 10.

You can add a preexisting title to a project onscreen by importing it into a project. Here's how to add a title to the Project window by using the Import command:

1. **Choose File ⇨ Open to open the project file that you want to work with.**

2. **Choose File ⇨ Import to import the title file that you want to use.**

   You should have the title file in the Project window of the project file.

3. **Drag the title file from the Project window to the Timeline window.** If the Timeline window is not open, you can open it by choosing Window ⇨ Timelines or by double-clicking on Sequence 01 in the Project window.

4. **After you add your title to a video track in the Timeline window, you'll probably want to preview your project.** In the Timeline window, move the Current-time indicator over the area you want to preview. Then open the Monitor window (choose Window ⇨ Program Monitors ⇨ Monitor). Press the Play button to have Premiere Pro play the video clip in the Monitor window. (For more information about previewing Premiere Pro projects, see Chapter 4.)

Tip   After you place a title file into a project, you can edit the title file by double-clicking it. When you double-click, the Adobe Title Designer window appears.

5. **Choose File ⇨ Save to save your work.**

Adding a Background to a Title Clip

In this section, you'll create a new project. In the project, you'll import a video clip to use behind the title you create using the Premiere Pro Adobe Title Designer window. Then you'll save the title and place it in your production. Figure 11-10 shows the Premiere Pro layout of a production created using a title superimposed over a video clip. In the Monitor window, you can see the Title file superimposed over the video clip. In the Timeline window, the Title file is selected. Premiere Pro creates titles files with transparent backgrounds, allowing you to see a video clip below the Title file. Notice that in the Timeline window the Title file appears in the Video 2 track, the video clip appears in the Video 1 track (Digital Vision's CityMix 567023f.mov), and a sound clip (Digital Vision's Sounds from the Chill CD-ROM (665002aw.wav) appears in the Audio 1 track.

Here are the steps to create a title and to overlay it onto a video clip:

1. **Choose File ⇨ New ⇨ Project to create a project.** Make sure that you use the proper preset.

2. **Choose File ⇨ Import to import the video clip you want to appear behind the title.**

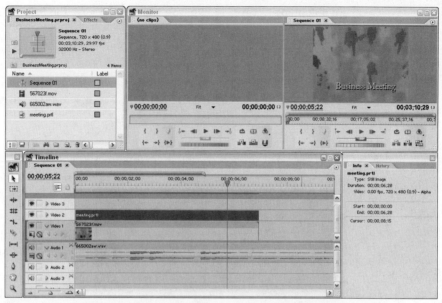

Figure 11-10: The production layout of a Premiere Pro project with a title superimposed over a video clip.

If you want, you can use the video clip that appears in Figure 11-10. It is found in the Digital Vision folder, inside the Chapter 11 folder, in the Tutorial Projects folder that is on the DVD that accompanies this book. The video clip is from Digital Vision's CityMix CD-ROM (567023f.mov), and the sound clip is from Digital Vision's Sounds from the Chill CD-ROM (665002aw.wav).

3. **Drag the video clip from the Project window to the Video 1 track in the Timeline window.**

4. **Choose File ⇨ New ⇨ Title to create a new title.**

5. **Make sure to select the Show Video check box to display the video clip in the drawing area of the Adobe Title Designer window.** Premiere Pro places the frame in the background where the current-time indicator is located. To use a different frame in the video clip, move the current-time indicator in the Timeline window and then click the Sync to Timeline button, or you can click and drag the Timeline values to the right of the Show Video check box.

Note   If you are outputting to video or film, you will want to have the Safe Title Margin and Safe Action Margin displayed. If they are not displayed, choose Type ➪ View ➪ Safe Title Margins and Type ➪ View ➪ Safe Action Margins. If you are outputting to the Web, you don't need to select these options.

6. **Click the Type tool and move the I-beam cursor to the drawing area and type Business Meeting (as shown in Figure 11-11) or whatever else you prefer.**

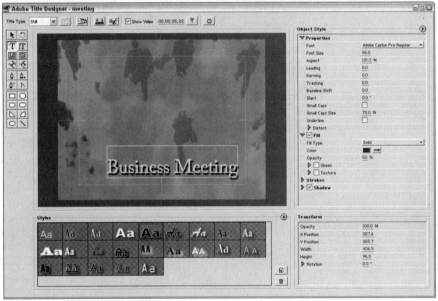

Figure 11-11: The Adobe Title Designer window for the production shown in Figure 11-10.

7. **Choose a style.** You can change the text attributes, color, and shadow as desired.

8. **Save the title and name it by choosing File ➪ Save.** The title is saved to your hard drive and in the Project window of the project.

9. **Drag the title you just saved from the Project window to the Video 2 track of the Timeline window.** Move the title into position. We moved the title shown in Figure 11-10 so that it lines up with the video clip in the Video 1 track.

10. **If you need to extend the title so that it matches the length of the video clip, click the right side of the title in the Timeline window and drag to the right.**

Note You can change the duration of a title by clicking the title in the Timeline window and choosing Clip ⇨ Speed/Duration. In the Clip Speed/Duration dialog box, click the chain to unlink the speed and duration. Then type the new duration. Click OK to activate the changes.

11. **Display the Monitor window, if it is not already open by choosing Window ⇨ Program Monitors ⇨ Monitor.** Click the Play button to play the project.

Note You can animate your title, by using either Perspective, the Basic 3D Video Effect, or by using the Motion options in the Effect Controls window. Click the triangle in front of Motion in the Effect Controls window to display the Motion options. The Motion options are Position, Scale, Rotation, and Anchor Point. For more information on using the Motion options, turn to Chapter 17.

12. **To add sound to your clip, choose File ⇨ Import.** Locate the sound you want to import. When the sound clip is in the Project window, click and drag it to Audio Track 1 of the Timeline window. If the sound clip is too long, you can cut it using the Razor tool. For more information on editing sound, refer to Chapter 8.

13. **Choose File ⇨ Save to save the project.**

Working with Logos

Logos can be imported into the Adobe Title Designer window and used either in a portion or in the entire area of the drawing area. A logo can be either a graphic or a photograph. In Figure 11-12, we created the title by inserting two logos: a photograph of a sky into the background and a graphic of a sun into the center of the drawing area. The photograph is a Photoshop file, and the sun is an Illustrator file. To create the text, we used three different styles in from the Styles section.

Here's how to import a logo into a title:

1. **Choose File ⇨ New ⇨ Project to create a new project.** In the New Project dialog box, choose the Non-DV Square-Pixel 640 x 480 preset. Name your project and click OK.

2. **Choose File ⇨ New ⇨ Title to create a new title.**

3. **In the Adobe Title Designer window, choose Title ⇨ Logo ⇨ Insert Logo.** In the Import Image as Logo dialog box, pick a file to import into the Adobe Title Designer drawing area. You can either use one of the logos in the Logo or Texture folder that comes with Premiere Pro or make your own by using Adobe Illustrator and/or Adobe Photoshop.

**On the
DVD-ROM**

If you want, you can use the images that appear in Figure 11-12. They are found in the logo folder, inside the Chapter 11 folder, in the Tutorial Projects folder that is on the DVD that accompanies this book.

Note

To insert a logo in a text box, double-click the text box with the Selection tool. Then choose Title ➪ Logo ➪ Insert Logo into Text.

4. **To change the logo in the drawing area to a different graphic, click the box to the right of Logo Bitmap in the Properties section.** When the dialog box appears, pick a file.

5. **After the logo is in the drawing area, you can move, resize, and rotate it with the Selection tool.** You can also use the Transform commands in the dialog box or the Title menu.

6. **To restore the logo to its original settings, choose Title ➪ Logo ➪ Restore Logo Size or Title ➪ Logo ➪ Restore Logo Aspect Ratio.**

Figure 11-12: A title created by inserting two logos: a photograph of a sky into the background and a graphic of a sun in the center of the drawing area.

Using Templates

Creating titles using preexisting styles and templates can help speed up the time it takes to create a Premiere Pro project. Creating a title using a template is easy.

Here is how to use a template:

1. **Choose File ➪ New ➪ Project to create a new project.**

2. **Choose File ➪ New ➪ Title to create a new title.**

3. **In the Adobe Title Designer window, click the Templates icon or choose Title ➪ Templates.** In the Templates dialog box that appears, pick a template from one of the folders. Then click Apply to apply the template to the drawing area.

You can use the Templates pop-up menu in the Templates dialog box to save a title as a template, rename a template, delete a template, plus other options. Here's how:

1. **Create a new title or open an existing title.**

2. **Click the Templates icon in the Adobe Title Designer window.**

3. **Click the triangle in the Templates dialog box to display the Templates menu, shown in Figure 11-13.**

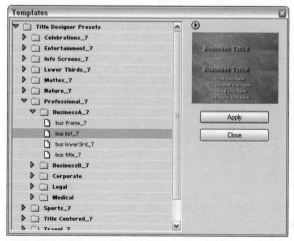

Figure 11-13: The Templates menu enables you to save a title onscreen as a template.

4. **To save the title onscreen as a template, choose Save as Template.**

5. **To rename or delete a template, click the template you want to change and then pick Rename Template or Delete Template from the Templates menu.**

6. **To import a file as a template, select a file and then choose Import File as Template.**

After the template is in the Adobe Title Designer window, you can change it how you want. Click and drag over the text in the template with the Type tool to edit the text. If you want, you can also change the style of the text. You can select items in the template with the Selection tool and move them to a new position. You can also change the fill style and color.

Using a Title Created from a Template

In this section, you create a project using two different titles using templates. One title will go at the beginning of the project in the Video 1 track; the other title will be at the end of the project, in Video 1 track. The first title template will be used as an opening screen, which will gradually fade out to the first video clip that is in the Video 1 track, and the second title template will be used as a closing screen. The second template fades in and out over the video clip that is in Video 2 track. Figure 11-14 shows the Premiere Pro Timeline window for the project.

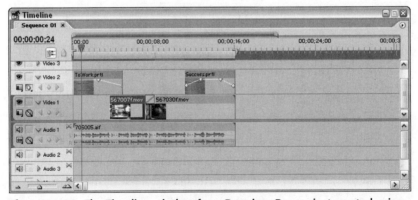

Figure 11-14: The Timeline window for a Premiere Pro project created using two titles that were created using templates.

Here's how to create a project using two titles created from templates:

1. **Choose File ⇨ New ⇨ Project to create a project.** Make sure that you use the proper preset.

2. **Choose File ⇨ New ⇨ Title to create a new title.**

3. **In the Adobe Title Designer window, click the Templates button or choose Title ➪ Templates.** In the Templates dialog box that appears, pick a template from one of the folders. For the project, you need to create two titles. The first template will be used at the beginning of the project, and the second template will be used at the end of the project. Start by creating the first title. The first title in the project has a title at the top and a subtitle and at the bottom. Click the bus title_7 file that is located in the BusinessA_7 folder, within the Professional_7 folder. The Professional_7 folder is within the Title Designer Presets folder. A preview of the bus title_7 file appears in the Templates dialog box. Click Apply to for the bus list template to appear in the drawing area of the Adobe Title Designer dialog box, as shown in Figure 11-15.

Figure 11-15: The bus title_7 template appears in the Adobe Title Designer dialog box.

4. **Click and drag over the Business Title text with the Horizontal Type tool and type** GOING TO WORK. Use the Horizontal Type tool to click and drag over the Subtitle Goes Here text and type **Make success your target**, as shown in Figure 11-16. In order to have the text fit within the drawing area, you may need to reduce the font size of the subtitle text. When you are done, choose File ➪ Save to save the title to your hard drive and have Premiere Pro place it in the Project window of the project.

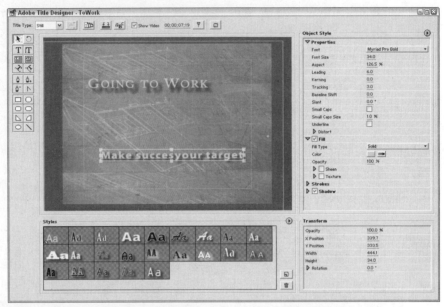

Figure 11-16: The template from Figure 11-15 after editing the text.

5. **Now that you've created the first title of your project (shown in the Video 2 track in Figure 11-14), create the second title (shown in the Video 2 track in Figure 11-14) by choosing File ➪ New ➪ Title.** In the Adobe Title Designer window, click the Templates button. In the Templates dialog box, click the bus list_7 file that is located in the BusinessA_7 folder within the Professional_7 folder. The Professional_7 folder is within the Title Designer Presets folder. A preview of the bus list_7 file appears in the Templates dialog box. Click Apply to for the bus list_7 template to appear in the drawing area of the Adobe Title Designer dialog box, as shown in Figure 11-17. Click and drag over the Business Title text with the Horizontal Type tool and type **AFTER A SUCCESSFUL DAY**, as shown in Figure 11-18. You may need to reduce the size of the font of the Title text. Use the Horizontal Type tool to click and drag over the first bullet and type **Going to a Meeting**, as shown in Figure 11-18. Then click and drag over the second bullet and type **Going out to Dinner**. Then click and drag over the third bullet and type **Going to the Movies**. Then click and drag over the fourth bullet and type **Going to a Show**. Then click and drag over the fifth bullet and type **Going Home**. When you are done, choose File ➪ Save to save the title to your hard drive and have Premiere Pro place it onscreen in the Project window of the project.

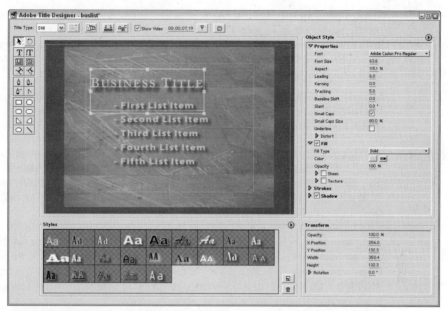

Figure 11-17: Editing the bus list_7 template in Adobe Title Designer.

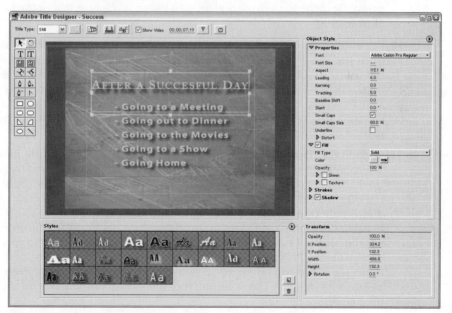

Figure 11-18: The template from Figure 11-17 with edited text.

6. **Click and drag the first title you created at the beginning of the Video 2 track, as shown in Figure 11-14.** Then click and drag the second title to Video 2, as shown in Figure 11-14. The end of the second title will line up with the end of the last video clip in the Video 1 track. To extend the title duration, click and drag the end of the title left.

7. **Choose File ⇨ Import to import the video clip that you want to appear at the beginning of the project.** Then import the video clip that you want to appear at the end of the project.

On the DVD-ROM

The video clips and sound clip that appear in Figure 11-14 are found in the Digital Vision folder, inside the Chapter 11 folder, in the Tutorial Projects folder that is on the DVD that accompanies this book. The video clips (567007f.mov and 567030f.mov) are from Digital Vision's CityMix. The sound clip (705005.aif) is from Digital Vision's NightMoves CD-ROM.

8. **Drag one video clip to the beginning of the Video 1 track and another video clip so that it overlaps the first video clip in the Video 1 track, as shown in Figure 11-14.** We put Digital Vision's video clip 567007f.mov at the beginning of Video 1 track and Digital Vision's video clip 567030f.mov in the Video 1 track so that it overlaps video clip 567007f.mov.

9. **In the Effects window, click the triangle in front of the Video Transitions folder.** Click the triangle in front of the Iris folder, and click the Iris Cross transition. Drag the Iris Cross transition to Video track 1, to where the two video clips overlap.

10. **For a quick preview of the transition, use the Effect Controls window.** To open the Effect Controls window, choose Window ⇨ Effect Controls. Next, click the transition in the Video 1 track. To preview the transition with the video clips, click the Show Actual Sources check boxes, then click the Play the Transition button. You can also use the settings and the Timeline in the Effect Controls window (shown in Figure 11-19) to edit the transition. For more information on using transitions, turn to Chapter 10.

11. **To fade the first title into the first video clip, click the first title to select it.** Then click the triangle in front of the words "Video 2" to expand the Video track. Next click on the Show Keyframes icon and choose Show Opacity Handles. To fade the title into the first video clip, you have to create two handles on the Opacity line, then drag the last handle downward. To create the first handle (shown in Figure 11-14), move the current-time indicator at the middle of the title. Then click the Add/Remove Keyframe button to add a handle. To create the last handle (shown in Figure 11-14), move the current-time indicator at the end of the title. Then click the Add/Remove Keyframe button to add a handle. Use the Selection tool to click and drag down on the last handle on the Opacity line.

Figure 11-19: The Effect Controls window with the Transition settings.

12. **To preview the fade from the first title to the first video clip, click and drag the current-time indicator in the Timeline over the areas.**

13. **To gradually fade the last title into the last video clip you have to add two handles to the second title's Opacity line.** First, select the last title in the Timeline window. Move the current-time indicator at the beginning of the second title and then click the Add/Remove Keyframe button to add the first handle. Move the current-time indicator toward the middle of the second title, then click the Add/Remove Keyframe button to create a second handle. Use the Selection tool to click and drag down on the first handle on the Opacity line. To gradually fade the last title out, you need to create two more handles. Move the current-time indicator to the right of the second handle, then click the Add/Remove Keyframe button to add a third handle (as shown in Figure 11-14). Move the current-time indicator to the end of the last title, then click the Add/Remove Keyframe button to add a fourth handle. Use the Selection tool to click and drag down on the last handle on the Opacity line. For more information on fading video clips, turn to Chapter 15.

14. **To preview your project, click the Play button in the Monitor window.**

15. **To add sound to your project, click and drag the sound clip from the Project window to Audio 1 of the Timeline window.** For more information on working with sound clips, refer to Chapter 8.

16. **Choose File ⇨ Save to save your project.**

Rolling and Crawling Titles

If you'll be creating production credits or a long sequence of text, you'll probably want to animate the text so that it scrolls up or down or crawls left or right across the screen. Premiere Pro's Adobe Title Designer provides just what you need — it enables you to create smooth attractive titles that stream across the screen.

Here are the steps for creating scrolling or crawling text:

1. **Create a new project or load a project.**

2. **Create a new title by choosing File ➪ New ➪ Title.**

Note   If you want to place a graphic in the background of the scrolling titles, you can choose Title ➪ Logo ➪ Insert Logo or Title ➪ Logo ➪ Insert Logo into Text.

3. **To roll text vertically up or down, choose Roll from the Title Type pop-up menu. To make the text crawl across the screen, choose Crawl.**

4. **Select a Type tool.** Position the cursor in the area where you want the titles to appear and then click. Start typing the text that you want to scroll across the screen. For scrolling text, press Enter to add new lines. Figure 11-20 shows scrolling text. Notice that a scroll bar appears to the right of the drawing area in the Adobe Title Designer window.

Figure 11-20: When you create scrolling text in the Adobe Title Designer window, a scrolling bar appears to the right of the drawing area.

5. **Use the techniques described earlier in this chapter to stylize the text that you want to Roll or Crawl.** If you want to reposition or resize the bounding box, click outside the box. The Text window disappears and is replaced by a bounding box with four handles. To move the box, click in the middle and drag it to reposition it onscreen. To resize the box, click one of the four handles and drag with the mouse. Enter the text that you want to scroll across the screen.

6. **Set the Rolling and Crawling options by choosing Title ⇨ Roll/Crawl Options or by clicking the Roll/Crawl Options icon at the top of the Title Designer dialog box.** In the Roll/Crawl Options dialog box (shown in Figure 11-21), the options provide choices to customize the roll or crawl.

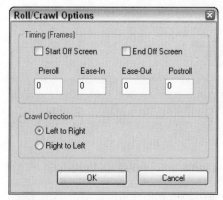

Figure 11-21: The Roll/Crawl Options dialog box.

The options provide the following effects:

- **Start Off Screen.** Choose this option to have the roll/crawl effect begin with the text offscreen.

- **End Off Screen.** Choose this option to have the roll/crawl effect end with the text offscreen.

- **Preroll.** If you want the text to appear motionless before the animation begins, enter the number of static frames in this field.

- **Ease-In.** Enter the number of frames that you want to ramp up, or gradually accelerate, until normal playing speed.

- **Ease-Out.** Enter the number of frames that you want the titles to ramp down, or gradually slow down, to a complete stop.

- **Postroll.** If you want the text to appear motionless after the animation ends, enter the number of static frames in this field.

7. **Choose a Rolling and Crawling option from the Roll/Crawl Options dialog box.** Then click OK to close the dialog box. After you've created your titles, a vertical scroll bar appears indicating rolling titles; a horizontal bar appears if you have created horizontal titles.

Note

You can create templates from your rolling and scrawling text. To save the rolling or scrawling title onscreen as a template, click the Templates button. In the Templates dialog box, click the triangle to display the Templates pop-up menu. Choose Save as Template and then click Apply to save the title onscreen as a template.

8. **Choose File ➪ Save to save the title.** After you create the title, drag the icon from the Project window on to the Timeline window to see the scrolling or rolling type put to action.

Creating Basic Graphics

Premiere Pro's graphics tools enable you to create simple shapes such as lines, squares, ovals, rectangles, and polygons. You can find these basic graphic tools in the lower portion of the Toolbox (the last four rows). They are the Rectangle, Clipped Corner Rectangle, Rounded Corner Rectangle, Wedge, Arc, Ellipse, and Line tools.

Here are the steps for creating a rectangle, a rounded rectangle, an ellipse, or a line:

1. **Select one of Premiere Pro's basic graphic tools, such as the Rectangle, Rounded Rectangle, Ellipse, or Line tool.**

2. **Move the pointer into the Adobe Title Designer window area where you want to have the shape appear and then click and drag onscreen to create the shape.** To create a perfect square, rounded square, or circle, press the Shift key as you click and drag. To create a line at 45-degree increments, press the Shift key while dragging with the Line tool. Press and hold the Alt key to create an object from its center out.

3. **As you drag, the shape appears onscreen.** Release the mouse after you finish drawing the shape.

4. **To change a graphic from one shape to another, click the Graphic Type pop-up menu and make a selection.** The Graphic Type pop-up menu is located inside the Properties section within the Object Style area of the Type Designer window.

5. **To distort a graphic shape, change the X and Y values in the Distort section.** The Distort section is located below the Graphic Type section.

6. **Click the Graphic Type pop-up menu to transform an object into another.**

Transforming Graphics

After you create a graphic shape in Premiere Pro, you may want to resize or move it. The following sections provide step-by-step instructions on how to move and resize graphic shapes.

Moving graphic objects

To move a graphic object, follow these steps:

1. **Click the Selection tool and click a graphic shape to select it.**

If you have various shapes onscreen overlapping each other and are having diffi-culty selecting a specific shape, you may want to use one of the Title ⇨ Select com-mands and/or the Title ⇨ Arrange commands.

2. **With the Selection tool activated, click and drag the shape to move it.** As you move the graphic, notice that the X and Y position in the Transform sec-tion of the Type Designer window changes.

3. **If you want, you can change the position of a graphic shape by changing either the X position or the Y position in the Transform section of the Designer Type window or by using the Title ⇨ Transform ⇨ Position command.**

4. **To center a graphic horizontally, vertically, or in the lower-third section of the Adobe Title Designer area, choose one of the Title ⇨ Position com-mands.**

If you have various shapes selected onscreen and are having difficulty distributing or aligning them horizontally or vertically, you may want to use one of the Title ⇨ Align Objects commands or the Title ⇨ Distribute Objects commands.

Resizing graphic objects

Follow these steps to resize and rotate an object:

1. **Click the Selection tool.**

2. **Resize the shape by moving the mouse pointer to one of the shape's han-dles.** When the icon changes to a line with arrows at either end of it, click and drag on the shape's handle to enlarge or to reduce the graphic shape. As you resize the graphic, notice that the X and Y position and the Width and Height values in the Transform section of the Type Designer window change.

Note   Pressing and holding the Shift key while resizing a shape with the Selection tool keeps the shape's proportions. Press and hold Alt as you resize with the Selection tool to create an object from its center out.

3. **If you want, you can change the size of a graphic shape by changing the Width or Height in the Transform section of the Type Designer window or by using the Title ➪ Transform ➪ Scale command.**

4. **Rotate the shape by moving the mouse pointer to one of the shape's handles.** When the icon changes to a curved line with arrows at either end of it, click and drag on the shape's handle to rotate the graphic shape. As you rotate the graphic, notice that the Rotation value, in the Transform section of the Type Designer window, changes.

5. **If you want, you can change the rotation of a graphic shape by changing the Rotation in the Transform section of the Type Designer window, by using the Title ➪ Transform ➪ Rotation command, or by using the Rotate tool in the Toolbox.**

Stylizing Graphic Objects

After you've created a graphic object, you may want to change the attributes and stylize it. You change the fill color, fill style, opacity, stroke, and size and apply a shadow to it. You can also change the shape of a graphic. All these effects can be changed using the options in the Object Style section of the Type Designer dialog box.

Changing the fill color

Here's how to change the fill color of an object:

1. **Use the Select tool to select the graphic shape you want to change.**

2. **Click the Fill Type pop-up menu and pick a fill style.**

Note   For more information on picking a color and fill style, turn to the section on using colors in the section "Using Color."

3. **Double-click the Color Swatch and pick a color from Premiere Pro's Color Picker.**

4. **If desired, you can change the opacity to make your object translucent.** Decreasing the Opacity value makes your object more translucent.

5. **You can also add a sheen (a highlight) or texture to your object.** You can add sheen by clicking the Sheen check box. You can add texture by clicking the Texture check box. Then click the triangle before the Sheen and/or Texture section to display the options.

Adding a shadow

Here's how to add a shadow to your object:

1. **Use the Select tool to select the graphic shape you want to change.**

2. **Click the Shadow box to add a check box.** Then click the triangle in front of the check box to expand the Shadow section.

3. **By default, the shadow color is black. If you want to change the shadow color, double-click the Shadow Color Swatch to change the color.** If you have either a video clip or a graphic in the background of the Adobe Title Designer window, you can use the Eyedropper tool to change the shadow color to one of the colors in the background. Just click the Eyedropper tool and click the color to which you want to change the Shadow Color Swatch.

4. **Use the Size, Distance, and Angle options to customize the magnitude and direction of the shadow.** To soften the edges of the shadow, use the Spread and Opacity options.

5. **To remove the shadow, click the Shadow check box.**

Applying a stroke

Here's how to add a stroke to your object:

1. **Select the filled object with the Selection tool.**

2. **Click the triangle before Strokes to expand the Strokes section.**

3. **To add a stroke using the default settings, click Add after the words Inner Strokes and/or Outer Strokes.**

4. **To customize the inner stroke or outer stroke, click the triangle before Inner Stroke and Outer Stroke.**

5. **Pick a stroke type and size.** Then pick a fill type and fill color. If you want, you can add a sheen and pattern.

6. **To remove a stroke, click the Inner Stroke and/or Outer Stroke check box.**

Working with the Bézier Tools

Premiere Pro features a Pen tool (as found in Adobe Illustrator), a curve-drawing tool that enables you to create freeform shapes with round and/or corner edges. These freeform polygon shapes are created from anchor points, lines, and curves. You can edit these Bézier shapes by using the Selection tool to move anchor points or by using the Add Anchor Point or Delete Anchor point tools to add or delete anchor points. You can also use the Convert Anchor Point tool for rounding the corners of polygons or for making rounded corners into pointed corners. For example, you can transform large triangles into mountains or many small triangles into waves.

Here's how to use the Pen tool to create a line (before continuing, you should have the Adobe Title Designer window open):

1. **Select the Pen tool.**

2. **Move the Pen tool to the left side of the Adobe Title Designer work area and then click the mouse to establish an anchor point.**

3. **To create a straight line, move the Pen tool to the right side of Adobe Title Designer work area and then press and hold the Shift key as you click the mouse.** Now you have two anchor points connected by a straight line.

4. **If you click again, the Pen tool will keep creating anchor points and lines.** To have the Pen tool stop creating anchors, click the Select tool. If you accidentally created an extra anchor point, you can delete it by selecting it with the Delete Anchor Point tool.

Here's how to convert a rectangle into a diamond:

1. **Select the Rectangle tool.**

2. **Move the Rectangle to the Adobe Title Designer drawing area. Then click and drag to create a rectangle.**

3. **Notice that the Graphic Type pop-up menu is set to Rectangle; change it to Closed Bézier.** The rectangle now has four anchor points at each corner.

4. **Use the Pen tool to click the anchor points and drag them so that you are slowly converting the rectangle into a diamond, as shown in Figure 11-22.**

5. **To fill the diamond, click the Graphic Type pop-up menu and choose Filled Bézier.** Then use the Fill options to customize the fill. You can also add a shadow and strokes to the diamond using the Shadow and Stroke options.

6. **When you are done creating and filling the diamond, you can use the Rotate tool to rotate it or use the Title ➪ Transform commands to transform it.**

To convert a pointed corner to a rounded corner, follow these steps:

1. **Use the Pen tool to create four joining, small mountains (downward-pointing triangles), as shown in Figure 11-23. If you need to, you can use the Pen tool to edit the points so that the points at the top and bottom line up.**

2. **Select the Convert Anchor Point tool from the Toolbox.**

3. **Click and drag the anchor points with the Convert Anchor Point tool to convert a pointed corner to a rounded corner, as shown in Figure 11-23.** Any time you want to move a point, use the Pen tool.

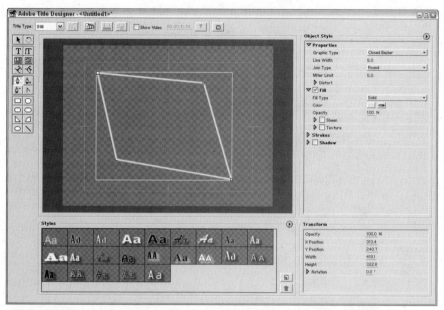

Figure 11-22: A rectangle converted to a diamond shape using the Pen tool.

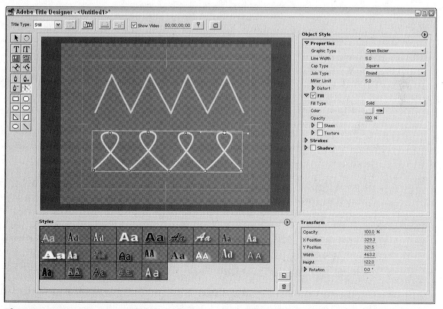

Figure 11-23: We created this path from pointed anchor points using the Pen tool and then converted to rounded anchor points using the Convert Anchor Point tool.

You can use the Add Anchor Point, Delete Anchor Point, and Pen tools to transform objects, as shown in Figure 11-24.

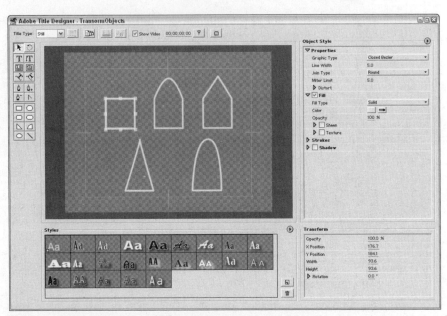

Figure 11-24: We converted a square into a house shape and a triangle into a triangle with a rounded point using the Add and Delete Anchor Point tools.

Follow these steps to learn how to transform an object:

1. **Start by creating a square using the Rectangle tool.** As you use the Rectangle tool, press and hold the Shift to constrain the aspect ratios.

2. **To edit the object, choose Closed Bézier from the Graphic Type pop-up menu.**

3. **To turn the square into a house shape, you need to use the Add Anchor Point tool to add an anchor point in the middle of the top two anchor points.**

4. **Then use the Pen tool to drag the anchor point up, as shown in Figure 11-24.**

5. **Now use the Convert Anchor Point tool to click the new anchor point to convert it from a curve anchor point to a corner anchor point.**

6. **To convert the house shape into a triangle (shown in Figure 11-24), use the Delete Anchor Point tool to delete the two anchor points below the newly added anchor point.**

7. **To convert the triangle into a dome shape (shown in Figure 11-24), use the Convert Anchor Point tool to click and drag on the point of the triangle to convert it into a rounded anchor point.**

8. **To fill the shape, set the Graphic Type pop-up menu to Filled Bézier.** Then use the Fill, Shadow, and Stroke options to customize the fill.

To create curves with the Pen tool, follow these steps:

1. **Select the Pen tool from the Toolbox.**

2. **Move the mouse to the left side of the Adobe Title Designer window and click to establish an anchor point.** Don't release the mouse. Instead, drag straight up about half an inch (shown in Figure 11-25). Then release the mouse. The line that appears above and below the anchor point is called a *directional line.* The angle and direction at which the direction line is created determines the angle and direction of the curve being created. By extending the anchor point up rather than down, the first part of the curve bump will point up rather than down.

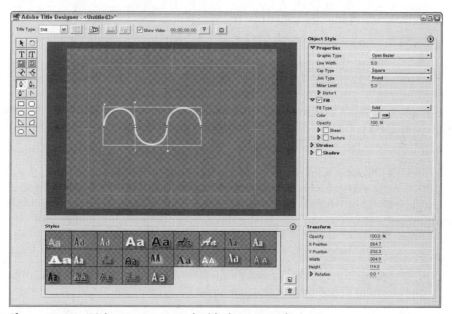

Figure 11-25: Bézier curves created with the Pen tool.

3. **Move the mouse about half an inch to the right of the anchor you created in Step 2. Then click and drag straight down about half an inch.** As you drag down, notice that a new directional line appears. Release the mouse to create a curve that has the first part of the curve bump pointing up and the last part of the curve bump pointing down. Congratulations, you've just created your first curve.

4. **If you want, you can edit the curve. Use the Pen tool to move the curve's directional lines.** As you move the directional lines, the curve's shape alters.

5. **To continue drawing curves, move the mouse about half an inch to the right from the anchor point you created in Step 3.** Click and drag straight up about half an inch to create a curve pointing down.

6. **To draw another curve, pointing up, move the mouse about half an inch to the right from the anchor point you created in Step 5.** Then click and drag straight down about half an inch.

7. **To continue creating curves going down and up, repeat Steps 3 and 5.**

To create curves that connect to line segments, follow these steps:

1. **Select the Pen tool from the Toolbox.**

2. **Now create a curve using the Pen tool.**

   Move the mouse to the left side of the Adobe Title Designer window, click and drag straight up about half an inch. Move the mouse about an inch to the right of the anchor you just created. Then click and drag straight down about half an inch to create a curve. If you want your curve to point down instead of up, you need to reverse the dragging part of this step. Instead of starting by clicking and dragging up, you start by clicking and dragging down, and you finish by clicking and dragging up, instead of clicking and dragging down.

3. **Connect a line to the curve, as shown in Figure 11-26.** Move the mouse cursor over to the last anchor point you created in Step 2. Press and hold the Alt key, and notice that a tiny diagonal line appears at the bottom of the Pen tool icon. Click the anchor point to create a corner point. After you convert the point to a corner point, the shape of the curve might change. To adjust the shape of the curve, click the directional line above the corner point and move it to adjust the curve. To create the line segment, move the mouse pointer about an inch to the right and click the mouse. If you need to adjust the position of the line, use the Pen tool.

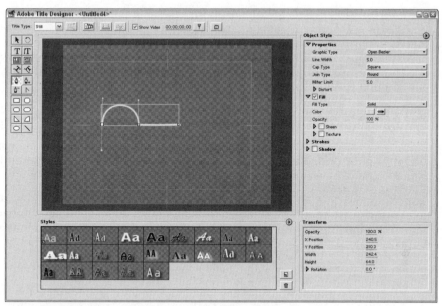

Figure 11-26: A curve connected to a line segment.

To create lines that connect to curve segments, follow these steps:

1. **If you have the curve and line segment onscreen from the preceding section, click the Selection tool to deselect the curve and line segment.**

2. **Select the Pen tool so that you can create a line Bézier outline.**

3. **Use the Pen tool to create a line. To create a line, click in the middle of the screen, then move the mouse over about an inch to the right and click again.** Then press and hold the Alt key as you click the anchor point and drag up and to the right to establish a directional line.

4. **To connect a curve to the line you just created (shown in Figure 11-27), move the mouse straight to the right about an inch and then click and drag down about half an inch.** The curve you created is pointing up. If you want the curve to point down, make the directional line point down, rather than up; and then click and drag up with the mouse, rather than down.

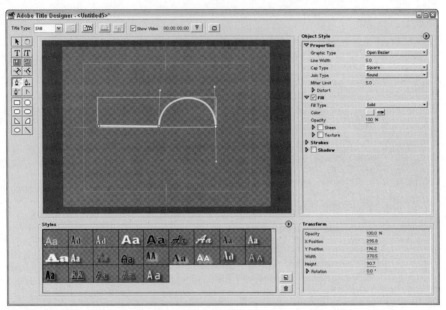

Figure 11-27: A line connected to a curve.

Creating Text on a Bézier Path

To create text on a path, use the Path Type tools. To use the Path Type tool, you first need to create a path and then you can begin typing alongside it. Figure 11-28 shows text along a curve path.

Here's how to use the Path Type tool:

1. **In the Adobe Title Designer window, select the Path Type tool from the Toolbox.**

2. **Use the Path Type tool to create a path.** The Path Type tool creates paths the same way as the Pen tool. To review how to use the Pen tool, go to the previous section.

3. **If you want to create a curved path and still don't feel confident in creating curves, create a path using the Path Type tool to create corner anchor points.** Then use the Convert Anchor Point tool to convert the corner anchor points to curve anchor points.

4. **Use the Pen tools to make the desired path.**

5. **Switch back to the Path Type tool and start typing.**

6. **Use a Style to stylize your text. Use the Object Style options to edit the style.**

7. **If you want, use the Pen tools to create a shape below the text, as shown in Figure 11-28.** After you have finished creating the shape, choose Filled Bézier from the Graphic Type pop-up menu so that you can fill the shape with a color or gradient. Then use the Fill options to fill the shape.

If you want, you can edit the text or stylize it. As you edit the text and stylize it, you may find that you need to edit the path.

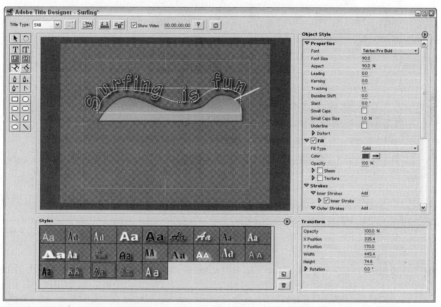

Figure 11-28: Text created along a curved path by using the Path Type tool.

Creating a Logo

Logos may appear either at the beginning of a video clip, at the end of a video clip, or throughout a video clip. You can either import a logo created from another program or create logos using the Premiere Pro Adobe Title Designer window. Figure 11-29 shows a sample logo for a sailing school. The logo was created by using Premiere Pro's graphic tools and by using the Type tools in the Adobe Title Designer window. The background video clip is from Digital Vision's Drifting Skies CD-ROM (386027f.mov).

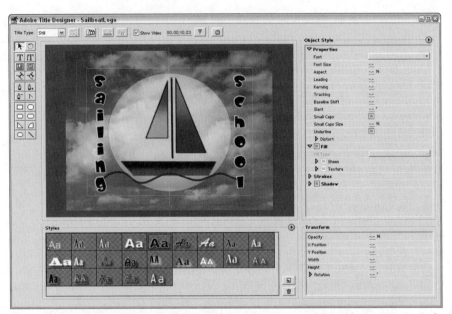

Figure 11-29: Sailboat logo created using the tools in the Adobe Title Designer window.

Here's how to create the Sailboat logo shown in Figure 11-29:

1. **Choose File ➪ New ➪ Project to create a new project.** Then choose File ➪ New ➪ Title to create a new title.

2. **Use the Ellipse tool to create the circle surrounding the boat. Press Shift while clicking and dragging to create a perfect circle. Press the Alt key while clicking and dragging to create a circle from the center out.**

3. **Use the Rectangle tool to create the mast.**

4. **To create the sailboat shown in Figure 11-29, use the Wedge tool to create the sails.**

5. **Use the Pen tool to create the sailboat's hull.**

6. **Use the Pen tool to create small mountains (downward-pointing triangles). Use the Convert Anchor Point tool to turn the mountains into waves.**

Note   Use the Title ➪ Arrange commands to shift different shapes forward or backwards as needed. Use the Title ➪ Position commands to horizontally and vertically center the geometric pieces.

7. **Color the objects with gradients and shadows.**

8. **To give the logo a layered look, use the Opacity field to reduce the opacity of the different shapes.**

9. **Use the Vertical Type tool to create the text. Set the attributes and color.**

10. **Save your title by choosing File ⇨ Save. Close the Adobe Title Designer dialog box.**

11. **Drag and drop the logo from the Project window to the Video 2 track in the Timeline window of the Sailboat project.** Move the sailboat logo to the beginning if you want it to appear there. If not, drag it to the location where you want it. To stretch the logo over time, click and drag on the edge of the clip and drag outward.

12. **Choose File ⇨ Import to import a video clip.** If you want, you can load a video clip from the DVD that accompanies this book. Drag the video clip to the Video 1 track. We imported a video clip of a sky background from Digital Vision's Drifting Skies CD-ROM (386027f.mov).

Digital Vision's Drifting Skies CD-ROM (386027f.mov) is in the Digital Vision folder that is in the Chapter 11 folder that is in the Tutorial Projects folder that is on the DVD that accompanies the book.

13. **To preview the sailboat logo in the Sailboat project, display the Monitor window (Window ⇨ Monitor) and click the Play button to view the preview.**

14. **Choose File ⇨ Import to import a sound clip.** Then drag the sound clip from the Project window to Audio track 1. We imported a sound clip from Digital Vision's Sounds from the Chill CD-ROM (665011aw.wav).

Digital Vision's Sounds from the Chill CD-ROM (665011aw.wav) is in the Digital Vision folder that is in the Chapter 11 folder that is in the Tutorial Projects folder that is on the DVD that accompanies the book.

15. **Choose File ⇨ Save to save the changes to the Sailboat project to your hard drive.**

Summary

Premiere Pro's Adobe Title Designer window provides an easy-to-use interface for creating digital video titles. By using the Adobe Title Designer window, you can quickly create text and graphics to introduce video segments or to roll your final credits. In this chapter, you learned to do the following:

✦ Use the tools in the Adobe Title Designer window to create text and graphics.

✦ Edit object attributes by using the Title menu or the options in Object Style section.

✦ Drag titles from the Project window to the Timeline window.

✦ Create titles using styles, templates, and logos.

✦ Create rolling and scrolling text by using the Rolling and Crawling options.

✦   ✦   ✦

Creating Type and Graphic Effects

✦ ✦ ✦ ✦

In This Chapter

Using Photoshop to
create text and
graphics

Using Photoshop
layers and
ImageReady to
create a QuickTime
video clip

Creating
Transparency
text effects

Creating Illustrator
text and graphic
effects for
Premiere Pro

Animating titles
over graphics

✦ ✦ ✦ ✦

Adobe Premiere Pro packs enormous power as a digital video production tool. However, if you're creating a sophisticated project, designed to appeal to and impress viewers, you need to turn to other applications to create your text and graphics. During the course of production, many Premiere Pro producers turn to such graphics applications as Adobe Photoshop and Adobe Illustrator to create eye-catching text and graphics.

This chapter provides several tutorials to teach you how to create text and graphic effects in Adobe Photoshop and Adobe Illustrator. After you see how to create the graphics effects, you integrate them into Premiere Pro projects. After your graphics are loaded into Premiere Pro, you use Premiere Pro's effects to create some digital magic. Soon your Adobe Photoshop and Adobe Illustrator artwork appears with digital video in the background.

Creating and Importing Graphics from Adobe Photoshop

Adobe Photoshop is one of the most powerful digital imaging programs available for both PCs and Macs. Photoshop easily surpasses Premiere Pro in its capability to create and manipulate graphics. For example, by using Adobe Photoshop, you can quickly create three-dimensional text or grab a piece of text or graphics and bend, twist, or skew it. Because both Adobe Premiere Pro and Adobe Photoshop are friendly cousins in the Adobe family of graphics products, it's not surprising that you can create graphics, text, or photomontages in Photoshop and then import them to use as titles in Premiere Pro.

You can even use Adobe Photoshop's Web-application partner, Adobe ImageReady (free with Adobe Photoshop), to create animation for a Premiere Pro project. For example, you can import Photoshop layers into ImageReady, create animation from the individual layers, and then export the animation as a QuickTime movie. After you've created a QuickTime movie, you can import the file into Premiere Pro to make a slideshow presentation.

Creating a digital movie of warped text using Photoshop, ImageReady, and Premiere Pro

You can use Adobe Photoshop to create a layered file and then import the Photoshop layered file into Adobe ImageReady to create a QuickTime animation. The QuickTime animation can be imported into a Premiere Pro project to create a slideshow effect. Figure 12-1 shows a Photoshop file with a Background layer and four layers with warped text. The following steps show you how to create a QuickTime movie of a Photoshop layer file.

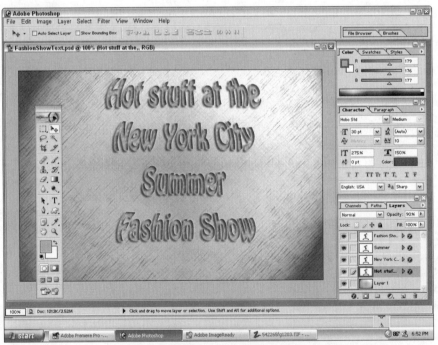

Figure 12-1: A Photoshop layer file can be made into a QuickTime movie.

1. **Load Adobe Photoshop and choose File ⇨ New.**

2. **In the New dialog box, name your file, TypeLayers.** Because you will probably import the animation of this file into a Premiere project, pick a frame size that will match your Premiere project. As mentioned in Chapter 4, if you are creating full-screen graphics for an NTSC DV project (which uses nonsquare pixels), create your Photoshop CS file at 720 × 480 or 720 × 486 (DI). If you are using Photoshop 7, create your file at 720 × 534 or 720 × 540. When you import the file, Premiere Pro will need to scale down the image (see Chapter 4 for more details).

   When creating the file, set the Background mode to RGB Color and set the Contents to Background Color. Click OK to create the file.

   Note If you create a graphic at 720 × 480 (or 720 × 486) in a square pixel program such as Adobe Photoshop 7 and then import it into a Premiere Pro NTSC DV project, the graphic may appear distorted in Premiere Pro. The graphic is distorted because Premiere Pro automatically converts it to a non-square 0.9 pixel aspect ratio. To convert the imported Photoshop graphic file back to square pixels, first select the graphic image in the Project window. Then choose File ⇨ Interpret Footage. In the Pixel Aspect Ratio section of the Interpret Footage dialog box, click Conform to and choose Square Pixels (1.0). Then choose Square Pixels (1.0) in the pop-up menu and click OK.

3. **Create your own background graphic, using Photoshop's tools, colors and filters to create an image onscreen.** To create the background in Figure 12-1, we started by first creating a white and gray gradient with the Gradient tool. Then we applied the Add Noise filter with the amount set to 17.95 and Distribution set to Uniform. Next we applied the Artistic Colored Pencil filter. In the Colored Pencil dialog box, we set the Pencil width to 4, the Stroke Pressure to 8, and the Paper Brightness to 25. Lastly, we applied the Render Lighting Effects filter. In the Lighting Effects dialog box, we set the Style pop-up menu to 2 O'clock Spotlight.

   Note Instead of creating your own graphic in Photoshop, you can use a photograph or create a photo collage as the background image. Open the file or files you want to use, then drag and drop the digital image into the new file you created in step 2. Photoshop automatically places the digital image in a new layer. If the image is too big for the file, you can scale it down by choosing Edit ⇨ Transform ⇨ Scale. Press Shift as you click and drag on one of the handles. By pressing Shift, the image retains its proportions.

4. **Now you're ready to create some text.** Select the Horizontal Type tool from the Toolbox.

5. **Use the Horizontal Type tool to create some text and then choose a font and size (we used the font Hobo with a font size of 30) either by using the Character palette or by using the options on the Type tab.** You can also change the color by using either the Colors palette or Swatches palette.

6. **To move the text onscreen, use the Move tool.**

7. **Choose Layer ⇨ Layer Style ⇨ Blending Options to stylize your text.** In the Layer Style dialog box, click on the style you want and then customize it. Figure 12-2 shows the Layer Style dialog box with the settings we used to create the text shown in Figure 12-1. In Figure 12-1, we applied a drop shadow, an inner shadow, an outer glow, a white color overlay with a 42% opacity, and a pattern overlay.

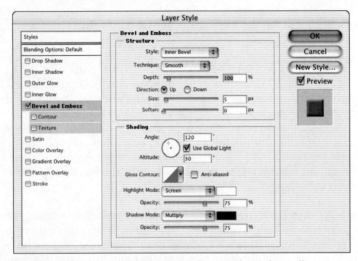

Figure 12-2: The Layer Style dialog box in Photoshop allows you to stylize text.

8. **Click the Warp button in the Type palette.** In the Warp Text dialog box, shown in Figure 12-3, pick a warp option to warp the text. Then click OK to close the dialog box and apply the effect.

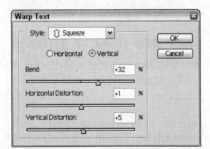

Figure 12-3: Photoshop's Warp Text dialog box allows you to warp type.

9. **If Photoshop's Layer palette is not onscreen, open it by choosing Window ⇨ Show Layers.** The text layer should be selected and at the top of the palette.

10. **Choose Duplicate Layer from the Layer pop-up menu to duplicate the text layer.** In the Duplicate Layer dialog box, name the layer and keep the Destination set to the document you are working on. Then click OK. When the layer is duplicated, the text appears on top of the previous one.

11. **Use the Move tool to move the text down.** Then use the Type tool to select the text and edit it.

12. **Repeat Steps 10 and 11 as many times as you need.**

13. **You may want to rearrange the layers in the Layers palette so that the bottom layer is the background, the second layer is the text first layer of your presentation, and the third layer is the second text layer of your presentation.** To move a layer in the Layers palette, click and drag on it and move it either up or down.

14. **Choose File ⇨ Save to save the file in Photoshop format.** Photoshop format saves a file with all of its layers.

Note

The Photoshop TypeLayers file, seen in Figure 12-1, is found in the Chapter 12 folder of the DVD that accompanies this book.

Now you're ready to transform your Photoshop layers into a digital movie:

1. **After you've saved your Photoshop file, choose File ⇨ Jump to Adobe ImageReady.** ImageReady opens and automatically loads the Photoshop file.

Note

You may not have enough memory to have both Photoshop and ImageReady open at the same time. If not, first save your work and quit Photoshop. Next, load ImageReady and choose File ⇨ Open to load the TypeLayers file.

2. **Open the Animation palette by choosing Window ⇨ Show Animation.** Now you are ready to make frames from layers.

3. **To create frames from each layer and keep adding the background to each frame, you first need to hide all the layers except the text layers.** To do so, click the Eye icon next to the text layer in the Layers palette. Next click the New Frame command from the Animation palette. A second frame will be created with the background. To add a text layer, click the Eye icon next to the text layer you want to display. To create a third frame, click the New Frame command. A third frame is created with both the background and the text from frame 2. To add another text layer, click another Eye icon to display the text layer in the frame. Continue creating new frames and displaying text layers until you have converted all the layers into frames. Figure 12-4 shows Photoshop layers converted to animation frames.

Note To create a frame from each layer, you can choose Make Frames from Layers from the Animation palette window. After you execute the command, ImageReady creates a frame with each Photoshop layer in it. This command will create frames for each layer, but it will not duplicate the background into each layer. Note that when you create frames using this command, ImageReady uses the bottom layer for the first frame and the top layer for the last frame.

Note The Photoshop TypeLayers QuickTime movie file seen in Figure 12-4 is found in the Chapter 12 folder of the DVD that accompanies this book.

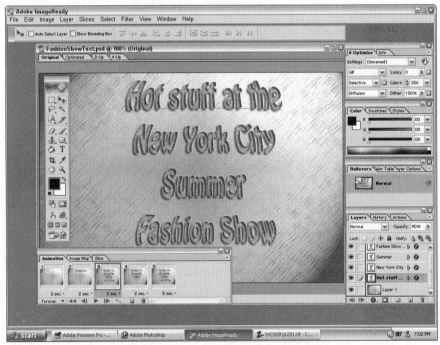

Figure 12-4: Adobe ImageReady converts the Adobe Photoshop layers into animation frames.

4. **To set a delay between frames, click Sec. at the bottom of the frame you want to change, then choose a frame delay.** We set the delay to 2 seconds, except for the last frame, which we set to 5 seconds.

5. **Click the Play button in the Animation palette to preview the animation.**

6. **In ImageReady, choose File ➪ Export Original to export the file as a digital movie.** In the Export Original dialog box, choose QuickTime movie from the Save as Type pop-up menu. Name your file TypeEffect. Locate a place to save your file, and then click Save.

7. **In the Compression Settings dialog box that appears (shown in Figure 12-5), choose a type of compression.** To save each frame with no compression, choose the Animation setting and then set the slider to Best. If you're working with digital video, you may also want to choose Apple DV-NTSC so that the compression setting matches that of your project. Click OK to make a QuickTime movie.

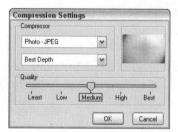

Figure 12-5: ImageReady's Compression Settings dialog box allows you to choose a compression setting.

After you've created a movie using Photoshop and ImageReady, you can import it into Premiere Pro.

1. **Create a new Premiere project.** Make sure to use the same settings as the Photoshop and ImageReady files created in the previous sections.

2. **Choose File ➪ Import.** In the Import dialog box, locate the ImageReady movie (TypeEffect) and click Open.

3. **Drag the movie from the Project window to a video track in the Timeline window.**

4. **To preview the movie, click the Play button in the Monitor window.**

To have your presentation slowly fade into the first keyframe of the TypeEffect movie, follow these steps:

1. **In the Timeline window, click the Expand/Collapse Track icon, and then click the Show Keyframes icon and choose Show Opacity Handles.**

2. **Move the current-time indicator to the beginning of the clip and then click the Add/Remove Keyframe option to add a keyframe.**

3. **Move the current-time indicator to the right of the keyframe and click the Add/Remove Keyframe option to add another keyframe.**

4. **Use the Selection tool to drag the first keyframe down, as shown in Figure 12-6.**

Cross-Reference

For more information on fading in and out, turn to Chapter 15.

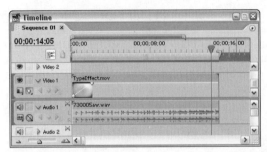

Figure 12-6: Using Premiere Pro to fade a video clip.

5. **To preview the fade, click and drag on the current-time indicator in the Timeline window.**

To add sound to your movie, follow these steps:

1. **Choose File ➪ Import. In the Import dialog box, locate a sound clip and click Open to import the clip into the Project window.** We used Digital Vision's 730005aw.wav Acoustic Chillout sound clip.

2. **Drag the sound clip from the Project window to Audio 1 of the Timeline window.**

   If the sound clip is too long for the TypeEffect clip, click the end of the sound clip and drag left.

For more information on working with sound clips, refer to Chapters 8 and 9.

Digital Vision's 730005aw.wav Acoustic Chillout sound clip is in the Chapter 12 folder on the DVD that accompanies the book.

3. **Choose File ➪ Save to save your work.**

Creating a digital movie using Adobe Photoshop and ImageReady

Many users consider Adobe Photoshop to be one of the most powerful digital imaging programs available for personal computers. Its ability to manipulate images, colors, and text far surpasses Premiere Pro's. Therefore, you may want to use Adobe Photoshop to create or enhance graphics for eventual loading into Premiere Pro. The following project, called TimeFlies, leads you through the steps in manipulating and enhancing an Adobe Photoshop layer file. After you create it, you can animate the Adobe Photoshop file using Adobe ImageReady.

Here's how to create a Photoshop layered file using two photographs:

1. **Open the file with the photograph that you want to animate.** We used a clock image, shown in Figure 12-7. The clock image is in the Chapter 12 folder on the DVD that accompanies this book.

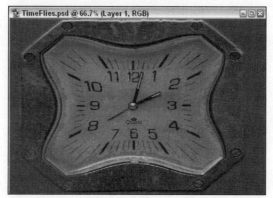

Figure 12-7: The clock image used to create the TimeFlies project.

2. **Duplicate the layer with the photograph in it by choosing Duplicate Layer from the Layers palette drop-down menu or by clicking the digital image layer and dragging it over the Create a New Layer icon in the Layers palette.** (The Create a New Layer icon is to the left of the Trash icon.)

Caution

Remember that the more layers in an image, the larger the file. Make sure that your computer has enough RAM and hard drive space to handle all the layers you create.

3. **Choose Filter ⇨ Distort ⇨ Pinch. In the Pinch dialog box (shown in Figure 12-8), move the Amount slider to the right.** Click OK to apply the changes.

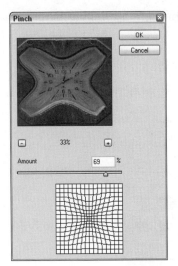

Figure 12-8: The Pinch filter dialog box.

4. **Duplicate the Pinched layer, shown in Figure 12-9.**

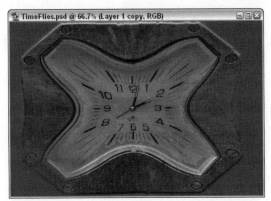

Figure 12-9: The clock image after applying the Pinch filter.

Note

You may want to isolate (mask) part of your digital image from its background. This way, only the masked object is affected and not the background. You can use one of Photoshop's eraser tools to isolate the object from the background. If you are a Photoshop expert, you may want to use some of Photoshop's more advanced techniques.

5. **Use the Polygonal Lasso tool to select only the inner part of the clock (the x shape).**

6. **Choose Select ➪ Save Selection.** Leave the default settings in the Save Selection dialog box, shown in Figure 12-10. By saving the selection, you can return to the same selection at any time.

Figure 12-10: The Save Selection dialog box allows you to save a selection.

7. **Choose Select ➪ Inverse to inverse the selection.**

8. **Set the Foreground color to blue and the Background color to white.** Then choose Filter ➪ Render ➪ Clouds. For a more interesting affect, apply another filter. We applied the Filter ➪ Artistic ➪ Film Grain command. Figure 12-11 shows the image after applying the Clouds and Film Grain command.

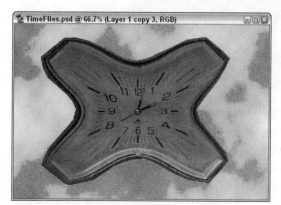

Figure 12-11: The clock image from Figure 12-7 after applying the Clouds and Film Grain command.

9. **Duplicate the layer you are working on.**

10. **Choose Filter ➪ Artistic ➪ Colored Pencil.** The Colored Pencil dialog box is shown in Figure 12-12. The background of the clock image should now look similar to the one in Figure 12-13.

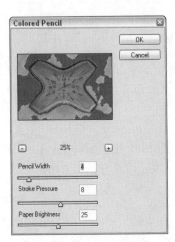

Figure 12-12: The Colored Pencil dialog box.

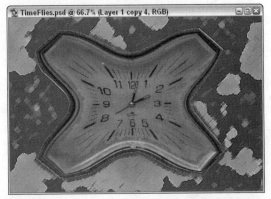

Figure 12-13: The clock image from Figure 12-11 after applying the Colored Pencil filter.

11. **Duplicate the Colored Pencil layer.**

12. **Choose Select ➪ Deselect to deselect the selection.**

13. **Choose Filter ⇨ Render ⇨ Lighting Effects.** In the Lighting Effects dialog box (shown in Figure 12-14), click on the Style drop-down menu and choose Soft Direct Lights. Then click OK to apply the effect.

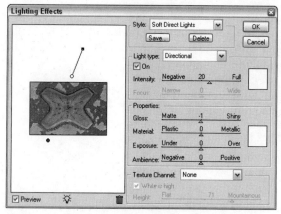

Figure 12-14: The Lighting Effects dialog box.

14. **Choose Filter ⇨ Distort ⇨ Spherize.** In the Spherize dialog box (shown in Figure 12-15), set the Amount to 100 and the Mode drop-down menu to Vertical. Click OK to apply the effect. Figure 12-16 shows the clock image after applying the Spherize command.

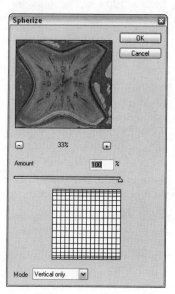

Figure 12-15: The Spherize dialog box.

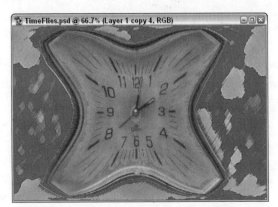

Figure 12-16: The clock image from Figure 12-13 after applying the Lighting Effects filter and the Spherize filter.

15. **Choose File ➪ Save to save your file.** Now you are ready to animate your Photoshop layer file.

16. **Choose File ➪ Jump To ➪ ImageReady.**

17. **Open the Animation palette by choosing Window ➪ Show Animation.** Now you are ready to make frames from layers.

18. **To create a frame from each layer, you can choose Make Frames from Layers from the Animation palette window.** After you execute the command, ImageReady creates a frame with each Photoshop layer in it, as shown in Figure 12-17.

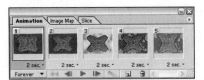

Figure 12-17: The Animation palette.

19. **To set a delay between frames, click Sec. at the bottom of the frame you want to change, then choose a frame delay.** We set the delay to 2 seconds.

20. **Click the Play button in the Animation palette to preview the animation.**

21. **In ImageReady, choose File ⇨ Export Original to export the file as a digital movie.** In the Export Original dialog box, choose QuickTime movie from the Save as Type drop-down menu. Name your file TypeEffect. Locate a place to save your file, and then click Save.

22. **Now choose a compression setting in the Compression dialog box.** To save each frame with no compression, choose the Animation setting and then set the slider to Best or leave the default settings and click OK.

Creating Semitransparent Text

In Chapter 11, you created different title effects using Premiere's Title Designer window. Although the Adobe Title Designer window provides many features for creating text effects, it can't compare with the text manipulation tools and filters that are available in Adobe Photoshop. In this section, you use Photoshop's Layer Styles to create a beveled text effect. You create an alpha channel out of the beveled text. When the text is loaded into Photoshop, the type appears semitransparent, allowing part of the background image to show through the highlighted areas of the text. To create color for the text in Premiere Pro, you use Premiere Pro's Color matte command.

Creating beveled text in Photoshop

Here are the steps to create the beveled text effect shown in Figure 12-18. If you're an experienced Photoshop user, feel free to vary any of the Photoshop effects.

Figure 12-18: Beveled text created in Adobe Photoshop.

1. **In Photoshop, create a new file that matches the pixel dimensions of your Premiere project.**

2. **Using Photoshop's Type tool, create your title text.** We typed the word *Zoo* at 100 points. If you want to enlarge or stretch the text, choose Edit ⇨ Free Transform and manually scale the text.

3. **Apply a beveled look to the text by choosing Layer ⇨ Layer Style ⇨ Bevel and Emboss.**

4. **In the Layer Style dialog box, choose the Inner Bevel from the Style menu and then use the dialog box controls to fine-tune the effect.** In the Technique pop-up menu, choose Chisel Soft and then edit the Gloss Contour.

5. **After you've finished the effect, flatten the file by choosing Layer ⇨ Flatten Image.**

6. **Now you need to create an alpha channel from the text (Premiere Pro uses the alpha channel to create the transparency effect).** To quickly create an alpha channel, convert the image to Lab color mode and then duplicate the lightness channel. To convert to Lab mode, choose Image ⇨ Mode ⇨ Lab. The Lightness channel is essentially a grayscale version of the RGB color image. To turn it into an alpha channel, simply drag the Lightness channel over the New Channel icon in the Layers palette. After the alpha channel appears, convert the image back to RGB by choosing Image Mode ⇨ RGB Color (if you don't do this, Premiere Pro is not able to read the file).

7. **Save your file in Photoshop format.**

Creating the Zoo project

Now that you've created the text in Photoshop, you're ready to import the text into Premiere Pro and create the Zoo project. Figure 12-19 shows a frame from the Zoo project.

Figure 12-19: A frame from the Zoo project.

1. **Choose File ➪ New ➪ Project to create a new project in Adobe Premiere Pro.**

2. **In Premiere Pro, choose File ➪ New ➪ Color Matte to create a color matte that will later be used for the color of the text.** After the Color Picker dialog box opens, select a color. Click OK to close the Color Picker. Then name the color matte in the Color Matte dialog box.

3. **Drag the color matte from the Project window to Video track 3.** Click and drag to extend the length of the graphic in the Timeline to your desired duration.

4. **Choose File ➪ Import to import a video clip that you want to use behind the Photoshop text graphic file.** We used Digital Vision's ComicCuts 891004f.mov.

5. **Choose File ➪ Import to import the Photoshop text graphic file you want to use.**

On the DVD-ROM

The Digital Vision's ComicCuts 891004f.mov (shown in Figure 12-19) and the Zoo text file (shown in Figure 12-19) are in the Chapter 12 folder, inside the Tutorial Projects folder that is on the DVD that accompanies this book.

6. **Drag the background video clip from the Project window to Video track 3.**

7. **Drag the text clip from the Project window to Video track 2.** Figure 12-20 shows the Timeline window for the Zoo project.

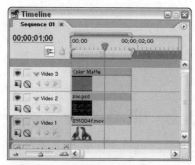

Figure 12-20: The Timeline window for the Zoo project.

8. **Choose Window ➪ Effect.** Then drag the Screen Key effect onto the color matte in Video track 3.

9. **Click the Play button in the Monitor window.**

10. **If you want to add motion to the text, use the Motion settings in the Effect Controls window.** For more information about using the Motion Settings dialog box, see Chapter 17.

Using Video Effects to Animate Adobe Illustrator Type and Graphics

Adobe Illustrator is known as a powerful digital drawing tool. By using Adobe Illustrator, you can create precision drawings and type effects. After creating graphics in Illustrator, you can apply Effects and Filters. You can also import them into Premiere Pro. (You can also import the graphics into Photoshop first, to apply more filters, and from there into Premiere Pro.) This project (Hurricane Season) shows you how to create text on a curve in Adobe Illustrator and then use the text in a Premiere Pro project with video effects. The Timeline window for the Hurricane Season is shown in Figure 12-21. The Illustrator text is in Video track 3, the Illustrator graphic is in Video track 2, and a white matte is in Video track 1.

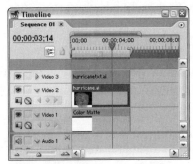

Figure 12-21: Hurricane Season Timeline window.

Creating curved text in Adobe Illustrator

Figure 12-22 shows type created on a curved path in Adobe Illustrator. We imported this illustration, along with a graphic created in Illustrator (shown in Figure 12-22), into Adobe Premiere Pro to create the Hurricane Season project. We created the distorted spiral graphic (shown in Figure 12-23) by applying filters to a spiral. This graphic was used as the background video track in the Hurricane Season project.

Figure 12-22: Curved text created in Adobe Illustrator.

Here's how to create text on a curve by using Adobe Illustrator:

1. **Create a new file in Adobe Illustrator by choosing File ➪ New.**

2. **In Adobe Illustrator, use the Pen tool or the Freeform tool to create a curved path.**

3. **Use the Path Type tool to type on the curved path.**

4. **Click the Path Type tool in the Toolbox.**

5. **Drag the Path Type tool to the far-left side of the curved path that you created and then click.**

6. **When the blinking cursor appears, start typing.**

7. **After you've finished typing, select the text by clicking and dragging over it with the mouse and then choose a font and size from the Font menu.**

8. **Choose File ➪ Save to save the file.**

Figure 12-23: Graphic created in Adobe Illustrator.

Creating a graphic in Adobe Illustrator

Here's how to create the distorted spiral in Illustrator used as the background to create the Hurricane Season project:

1. **Pick a Foreground and Background color.**

2. **Click the Star tool in the Toolbox.**

3. **Create a star using the Star tool (Alt+click).** In the Star dialog box, increase the number of sides that the star has. Click OK to close the dialog box and to make a star. Feel free to experiment using various numbers of sides on your star.

4. **Distort the star by using the ZigZag and Twirl filters in the Distort sub-menu.** Experiment with the settings in the dialog box for the desired effect.

5. **Save the file in Illustrator format.**

Creating the Hurricane Season project

In creating this project, we used the Effects window to apply the Bend video effect to the background and the Strobe effect to the text. Figure 12-24 shows a frame from the Hurricane Season project.

Figure 12-24: A frame from the Hurricane Season project.

You can create still images in other programs and then import them and animate them using Premiere Pro's Video Effects.

Here's how to animate Adobe Illustrator text and graphics using Adobe Premiere Pro:

1. **Choose File ➪ New Project to create a new project.**

2. **Choose File ➪ Import to import the text and graphic (created previously).** If you don't have Adobe Illustrator, you can import these two graphics from the *Premiere Pro Bible* DVD. They are located in the Hurricane folder, found in the Chapter 12 folder.

To load the Hurricane text and graphic file (shown in Figure 12-21), choose File ➪ Import. Click Import Folder. Then locate the Hurricane folder and click on the Import Folder button. This folder is in the Chapter 12 folder in the Tutorial Projects folder on the DVD that accompanies this book.

3. **Drag the (Hurricane) text to Video track 3 and the (hurricane) graphic to Video track 2.**

4. **Choose File ⇨ New ⇨ Color Matte.** Select a white background and click OK. Choose a name for your matte and click OK. The color matte appears in the Project window.

5. **Drag the color matte to Video track 1.**

6. **Display the Effects window by choosing Window ⇨ Show Effects.** Open the Video Effects folder. Inside each folder are many effects. For more information on using the video effects in the Effects window, turn to Chapter 14.

7. **Open the Stylize folder in the Effects window.**

8. **Click a Strobe Light video effect and drag it over the icon representation of the text in Video track 3.**

9. **Click the background graphic icon in Video track 2 to select it.** In our example, we used the distorted spiral.

10. **Open the Distort folder in the Effects window.**

11. **Click a Bend video effect and drag it over the icon representation of the graphic in Video track 2.** In the Bend Settings dialog box (shown in Figure 12-25), select the options you want from the pop-up menus and sliders.

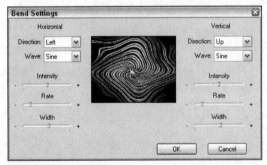

Figure 12-25: A preview of the Bend effect (in the Bend Settings dialog box) on the distorted graphic.

12. **Choose File ⇨ Save to save the project.**

13. **Click the Play button in the Monitor window to preview the effect.**

Animating Titles over Graphics by Using Motion and the Alpha Adjust Invert Option

You can manipulate text within a video track in order to make a background (that is in a video track below the text video track) appear within the text. You can then make the text move over the same background graphic.

This effect is shown in the frames from the Mosaic project in Figure 12-26. To create the moving text, we applied motion and the Alpha Adjust Reverse option to the word Mosaic. We created the mosaic text (shown in Figure 12-27) in Adobe Illustrator. The mosaic background (shown in Figure 12-28) was created using Corel Painter.

Figure 12-26: Frames from the Mosaic project.

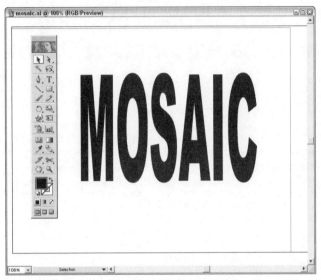

Figure 12-27: Mosaic text created using Adobe Illustrator.

Figure 12-28: Mosaic background created using Corel Painter.

Here's how to animate using motion and a reverse alpha channel:

1. **In Premiere Pro, choose File ➪ New ➪ Project to create a new project.** In the New Project dialog box, click the Non-DV Square-Pixel 640x480 preset. Name your file and click OK.

2. **Choose File ➪ Import to import a text graphic and background video clip.** You can create text using Premiere Pro's Adobe Title Designer window or Adobe Illustrator, Adobe Photoshop, or Corel Painter. To create a background, use either Adobe Photoshop or Corel Painter.

To load the mosaic text (mosaic.ai) and mosaic background (stainedglass.psd) files seen in Figure 12-20, choose File ⇨ Import. Then locate the Mosaic folder and click the Import Folder button. The folder is in the Chapter 12 folder inside the Tutorial Projects folder on the DVD that accompanies this book.

3. **When the text and background files have been imported, they appear in the Project window.** Click the text file from the Project window and drag it to Video track 2 in the Timeline window.

4. **Click the background file in the Project window and drag it to Video track 1 of the Timeline window.** The background file should extend over the entire text area. To increase the duration of either clip, click on the end of the clip and drag to the right.

5. **Move the Timeline indicator over the text clip in Video track 2.** Notice that a preview of the text and the background clips appears in the Monitor window. The text clip should be the same size as the background clip.

6. **To increase the size of the text clip, click the clip (in Video track 2) in the Timeline window. To scale the clip, use the Motion Scale option.** Click the triangle in front of the word Motion in the Effect Controls window to display the Scale option. Click and drag to the right on the Motion Scale field to increase the scale.

7. **Click the Alpha Adjust Keying effect in the Keying folder (which is in the Video Effects folder in the Effects window) and drag it over the text clip in Video track 2.** When the Alpha Adjust effect appears in the Effect Controls window, click the triangle in front of the word Alpha. Adjust to view the options. Click the Invert Alpha to invert the alpha channel. Then reduce the Opacity to 70% so that you can see the background in Video track 1.

8. **Apply Motion to the text in Video track 2 by creating keyframes.** Start by moving the Timeline indicator (in either the Timeline window or Effect Controls window) to the beginning of the text clip in Video track 2. Then click on the stopwatch in front of the word Position. A keyframe is created.

   To create a second keyframe, move the Timeline indicator to the right and click on the word Motion in the Effect Controls window. Now move the text in the Monitor window to the left as seen in Figure 12-26. Notice that a second keyframe is created.

   To create a third keyframe, move the Timeline indicator to the right. Now move the text in the Monitor window to the right so that the text is centered as seen in Figure 12-26. Notice that a third keyframe is created.

   To create a fourth keyframe, again move the Timeline indicator to the right. Now move the text in the Monitor window farther to the right, as seen in Figure 12-26. A fourth keyframe is created.

To create a fifth keyframe, again move the Timeline indicator to the right. Now move the text in the Monitor window back to the center. Notice that a fifth keyframe is created.

To create a sixth keyframe, again move the Timeline indicator to the right. Now move the text in the Monitor window up, as seen in Figure 12-26. Notice that a sixth keyframe is created. For more information on using the Motion Effect, turn to Chapter 17.

9. **Click the Play button in the Monitor window to preview the project.**
   When the preview rolls, you should see the background graphic within the typed letters.

10. **Choose File ➪ Save to save your work.**

Summary

To create the most attractive and elaborate text and graphics effects, you may need to use the digital power of such programs as Adobe Photoshop, Adobe Illustrator, or Corel Painter in conjunction with Premiere Pro.

✦ Both Photoshop and Illustrator provide excellent text features that can be used in conjunction with Premiere Pro.

✦ Premiere Pro successfully interprets Photoshop transparency and alpha channels.

✦ Background transparent areas in Illustrator are automatically read as alpha channel masks in Premiere Pro.

✦ You can create a variety of different transparency effects using Premiere Pro and Photoshop or Illustrator.

✦   ✦   ✦

Advanced Techniques and Special Effects

Advanced Editing Techniques

Premiere Pro is so versatile that you could create and edit an entire project using little more than Premiere Pro's Selection tool. However, if you need to make precise edits, you want to explore Premiere Pro's advanced editing functions.

For example, Premiere Pro's Trim window enables you to shave one frame at a time from the in or out point of a clip by simply clicking the mouse. As you click, you see the last frame of one out point in one side of the window, and the first frame of the adjacent in point in another side of the window. Premiere Pro also enables you to create sophisticated three-point edits where you specify an in or out point to maintain in a source clip, and an in and out point for placement in your program. When you perform the edit, Premiere Pro calculates the precise section of the source clip to overlay into your program material.

This chapter provides a guide to Premiere Pro's intermediate and advanced editing features. It starts with a look at some basic editing utilities, such as the Razor and Multiple Razor tools, and then proceeds to discuss Premiere Pro's toolbox editing tools — the Ripple Edit, Rolling Edit, Slip, and Slide tools. The chapter continues with a look at three- and four-point editing and how to trim using the Trim window. The chapter has been designed to enable you to quickly move from subject to subject so that you can learn or review editing features and immediately put them to use.

Editing Utilities

From time to time, you may want to edit by simply copying clips from one section and pasting them in another. To aid in editing, you may want to unlink audio from video. This section covers several different commands that can aid you as you edit your production. It starts with a discussion of the History palette, which enables you to quickly undo different stages of your work.

Undoing edits with the History palette

Even the best editors change their minds and make mistakes. Professional editing systems enable you to preview edits before actually recording the source material onto the program tape. However, professional editing systems can't provide as many levels of undo as Premiere Pro's History palette, shown in Figure 13-1.

Figure 13-1: The History palette.

As discussed in Chapter 2, the History palette can record your editing steps made while using Premiere Pro. Each step appears as a separate entry in the History palette. If you want to return to a previous step, simply click it in the History palette, and you return to it. When you go forward with your work, the previously recorded steps after the step you returned to disappear.

If you haven't already tried the History palette, open it by choosing Window ➪ Show History. In a new or existing project, drag several clips to the Timeline. As you drag, watch how the states are recorded in the History palette. Now select one of the clips in the Timeline and delete it by pressing Delete. Then delete another clip. Again, note how each state is recorded in the palette.

Now assume that you want to return the project to the state it was in before you deleted any clips. Just click in the History palette to the left of the first Delete state in the palette. The project returns to its state before any of the deletions. Now move one of the clips in the Timeline with the Selection tool. As soon as you move the clip, a new state is recorded in the History palette, erasing the second Delete state in the History palette. After you return to one state in the History palette and begin to work, you can't go forward again.

Cutting and pasting clips

If you've ever used a word processor to edit text, you know that one of the easiest ways to rearrange your work is to copy and paste from one part of the text to another. In Premiere Pro, you can easily copy and paste, or cut and paste, a clip from one part of the Timeline window to another. In fact, Premiere Pro has three paste commands — Paste, Paste to Fit, and Paste Attributes.

Splitting a clip with the Razor and Multiple Razor tools

Before copying and pasting or moving a clip, you may want to slice it into two pieces and only paste or move a portion of the clip. An easy way to slice a clip is to use Premiere Pro's Razor tool, shown in Figure 13-2. One click of the Razor tool splits a clip into two pieces. Here's how to use the Razor and Multiple Razor tool:

1. **If you want to split one clip in one unlocked track into two pieces, select the Razor tool.** If you want to split all unlocked tracks into two separate pieces, you first need to press Shift to activate the Multiple Razor tool.

 Figure 13-2: The Razor tool.

 Tip   Press C on the keyboard to activate the Razor tool.

2. **Move the current-time indicator to the frame that you want to split.**

3. **In the sequence that you want to edit, click the clip to cut it with either the Razor tool or Multiple Razor tool, as shown in Figure 13-3.** (Or you can choose Sequence ⇨ Razor at Current Time Indicator.) After you click with either the Razor or Multiple Razor tool, you can move the cut portion of the clip independently of the rest of the clip.

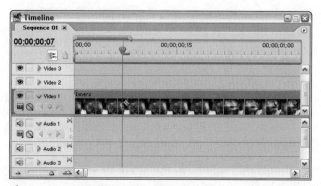

Figure 13-3: Cutting with either the Razor or Multiple Razor tool splits the clip into two clips.

Pasting clips

After you've split a clip, you may want to copy and paste it or cut and paste it to another location in the Timeline.

If the area into which you want to paste the clip already has clips within it, you can use Premiere Pro's Paste, Paste Insert, or Paste Attributes commands. Premiere Pro's Paste command pastes a clip over any clip at the current-time indicator position, its Paste Insert command inserts the pasted clip in a Timeline gap, and its Paste Attributes command copies motion, opacity, volume, and color settings of one clip into another clip.

Using Paste to overlay clips

Premiere Pro's Paste command enables you to paste clips into gaps in the Timeline. It also provides options for how you want the inserted clips to fit within your production. Here's how to paste a clip so that it overlays or replaces clips in the current sequence in the Timeline.

1. **Select the clip or clips that you want to copy or paste.**

2. **Choose Edit ⇨ Cut or Edit ⇨ Copy.**

3. **Move the current-time indicator to where you want to overlay the clip.**

4. **Choose Edit ⇨ Paste.** Premiere Pro drops the new material over any clip at the current-time indicator.

Using Paste Insert to insert clips

Premiere Pro's Paste Insert command enables you to paste clips into gaps in the Timeline. It also provides options for inserting clips to fit within your production. Here's how to use Paste to Fit to insert a clip:

1. **Select the clip or clips that you want to copy or paste.**

2. **Choose Edit ⇨ Cut or Edit ⇨ Copy.**

3. **Move the current-time indicator to where you want to insert the clip.**

4. **Choose Edit ⇨ Paste Insert.** Premiere Pro drops the clip at the current-time indicator and pushes all subsequent clips to the right.

Using Paste Attributes

Premiere Pro's Paste Attributes command allows you to copy one clip's attributes and apply them to another clip's. For example, using Paste Attributes, you can copy the color settings, opacity, volume, and effects of one clip and apply them to another. To use the Paste Attributes command, follow these steps:

1. **Select the clip or clips that that have the attributes that you want to copy.**

2. **Choose Edit ⇨ Cut or Edit ⇨ Copy.**

3. **Select one or more clips.**

4. **Choose Edit ⇨ Paste Attributes.**

Removing sequence gaps

During the course of editing, you may purposely or inadvertently leave gaps in the Timeline. Sometimes the gaps aren't even visible because of the zoom level in the Timeline window. Here's how to automatically remove a gap in the Timeline:

1. **Right-click the mouse in the gap in the Timeline.** (You might need to zoom in to see small gaps.)

2. **Choose Ripple Delete from the drop-down menu that appears in the sequence, as shown in Figure 13-4.** Premiere Pro removes the gap.

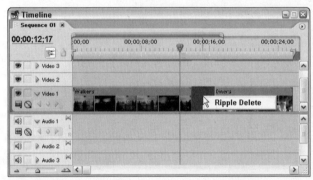

Figure 13-4: Right-click and choose Ripple Delete to remove gaps.

Unlinking and linking audio and video

While performing video edits, you may decide that you would like to create audio effects where the audio from one clip fades into another video clip (called a *split edit*). Although editing the video is a simple chore, you may find that you need to *unlink* the audio from the video to create the effect you want.

When you capture video using the Premiere Pro Capture command, Premiere Pro links the video information to the audio. This marriage is evident as you work. When you drag a clip to the Timeline, its audio automatically appears in an audio track. When you move the video, the audio moves with it. If you delete the video from the track, the audio is deleted. However, during editing, you may want to separate the video from its audio to create effects or to replace the audio altogether.

> **Tip**
>
> If you are trying to sync audio to video, it's helpful to view the audio's waveform in the audio track. To view the waveform, expand the audio track by clicking the triangle at the front of the track. Next choose Show Waveform from the Set Display Style drop-down menu.

To unlink video from audio, follow these steps:

1. **Select the audio track that you want to unlink.** Note that the names of linked clips are underlined.

2. **Choose Clip ⇨ Unlink Audio and Video.** You can also right-click the clip and choose Unlink Audio and Video from the pop-up menu, as shown in Figure 13-5. Note that the clips are no longer underlined. If you want, you can also delete either the video or audio portion.

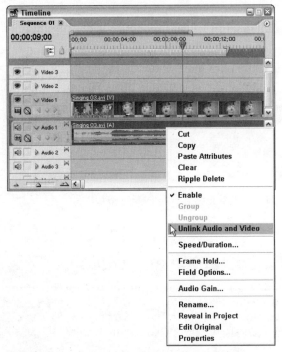

Figure 13-5: Right-click a linked clip and choose Unlink Audio and Video to unlink it.

Editing Clips with the Tool Palette Tools

After you've edited two clips together in a sequence Timeline, you may want to fine-tune the edit by changing the out point of the first clip. Although you can use the Monitor window to precisely change the edit point, you may prefer to use sequence-editing tools, such as the Rolling Edit tool and the Ripple Edit tool. Both tools enable you to quickly edit the out point of adjacent clips.

If you have three clips edited together, the Slip and Slide tools provide a quick means for editing the in or out point of the middle clip. The following sections describe how to use the Rolling Edit and Ripple Edit tools to edit adjacent clips and how to use the Slip and Slide tools to edit a clip between two other clips. As you try out these tools, keep the Monitor window open. It provides an enlarged view of the clips. When using the Slip and Slide tools, the Monitor window also shows how many frames have been edited.

Figure 13-6 shows the Rolling Edit, Ripple Edit, Slip, and Slide tools.

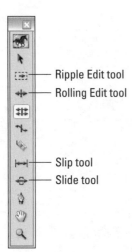

Figure 13-6: The Rolling Edit, Ripple Edit, Slip, and Slide tools.

— Ripple Edit tool
— Rolling Edit tool

— Slip tool
— Slide tool

On the DVD-ROM

The clips shown in this chapter use video footage from the Chapter 1 folder of the *Adobe Premiere Pro Bible* DVD. The clips are 705008f and 705009f from Digital Vision's Night Moves CD.

Creating a rolling edit

The Rolling Edit tool enables you to click and drag the edit line of one clip and simultaneously change the in or out point of the next clip on the edit line. When you click and drag the edit line, the duration of the next clip is automatically edited to compensate for the change in the previous clip. For example, if you add five frames to the first clip, five frames are subtracted from the next. Thus, a rolling edit enables you to edit one clip without changing the duration of your edited program. Here's how to create a rolling edit:

1. **Onscreen you should have a project with at least two adjacent clips in a video track in the Timeline window.** As a further aid, open the Monitor window, which previews the edit for you.

2. **Click the Rolling Edit tool to select it or press N on the keyboard.**

3. **Move the Rolling Edit tool to the edit line between two adjacent clips.**

4. **Click and drag either left or right to trim the clips.** If you drag right, you extend the out point of the first clip and reduce the in point of the adjacent clip. If you click to the left, you reduce the out point of the first clip and extend the in point of the next clip. Figure 13-7 shows a rolling edit. In the figure, dragging the Rolling Edit tool right simultaneously changes the in point of the clip on the right and the out point of the clip on the left. The figure also shows how the Monitor window previews the edit.

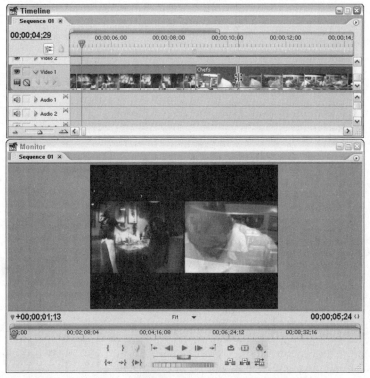

Figure 13-7: Simultaneously changing in and out points of two different clips with a rolling edit.

Creating a ripple edit

The Ripple Edit tool enables you to edit a clip without affecting the adjacent clip. Performing a ripple edit is the opposite of performing a rolling edit. As you click and drag to extend the out point of a clip, Premiere Pro pushes the next clip to the right to avoid changing its in point — thus, creating a ripple effect throughout the production, changing its duration. If you click and drag to the left to reduce the out point, Premiere Pro doesn't change the in points of the next clips. To compensate for the change, Premiere Pro shortens the duration of the sequence. Here's how to perform a ripple edit with the Ripple Edit tool:

1. **Onscreen you should have a project with at least two clips touching side by side in a video track in the Timeline window.** As a further aid, open the Monitor window, which previews the edit for you.

2. **Click the Ripple Edit tool to select it or press B on the keyboard.**

3. **Move the Ripple Edit tool to the out point of the clip you are going to trim.**

4. **Click and drag right to increase the clip's length or left to decrease the clip's length.** The duration of the next clip remains unchanged, but the duration of the sequence is changed. Figure 13-8 shows a ripple edit. In the figure, the in point of the Chefs clip remains unchanged, as the out point of the Diners clip (on the left) is extended.

Figure 13-8: The in point of the Chefs clip remains unchanged as a ripple edit is performed.

Tip   If you want to perform a ripple edit without affecting audio, press Alt while clicking and dragging the Ripple Edit tool.

Tip   To edit only the audio or video of a linked clip, Alt+drag with the Ripple or Rolling
Edit tool.

Creating a slip edit

A slip edit enables you to change the in and out points of a clip sandwiched between
two other clips while maintaining the middle clip's original duration. As you click
and drag the clip, the clip's neighbors to the left and right do not change, so neither
does the sequence duration. Here's how to perform a slip edit with the Slip tool:

1. **Onscreen you should have a project with at least three clips side by side in
   a video track in the Timeline window.** If you want to preview the edit as you
   work, open the Monitor window as well.

2. **Click the Slip tool to select it, or press Y on the keyboard.**

3. **With the Slip tool selected, click the clip that is in the middle of two
   other clips.**

4. **To change the in and out points without changing the duration of the
   sequence, click and drag left or right.** Figure 13-9 shows a slip edit. In the
   figure, the middle clip is dragged to the right, which changes its in and out
   points.

Tip   Although the Slip tool is generally used to edit one clip between two others, you
can edit the in and out points of a clip with the Slip tool even if it is not between
other clips.

Creating a slide edit

Like the slip edit, the slide edit is performed on one clip placed between two others
in sequence. A slide edit maintains the in and out points of the clip that you are
dragging while changing the duration of clips abutting it. When performing a slide
edit, dragging right extends the out point of the previous clip as well as the in point
of the next clip (making it occur later). Dragging left on a clip reduces the out point
of the previous clip, as well as the in point of the following clip (causing it to occur
earlier). As a result, the duration of the edited clip and the entire edited program do
not change. Here's how to perform a slide edit with the Slide Edit tool:

Figure 13-9: A slip edit changes the in and out points of the edited clip, but not the duration of the sequence.

1. **Onscreen you should have a project with at least three clips side by side in a video track in the Timeline window.** If you open the Monitor window, you can preview the edit as you work.

2. **Click the Slide tool to select it, or press U on the keyboard.**

3. **Click and drag on the clip that is in the middle of two other clips to move it.** Dragging left shortens the previous clip and lengthens the following clip. Dragging right lengthens the previous clip and shortens the following clip. Figure 13-10 shows a slide edit. In the figure, the Monitor window shows the effect on all clips. As the Diners clip is dragged left, the out point of the Walkers clip (on the left) is extended and causes the in point of the Chefs clip to occur later.

Figure 13-10: Dragging right to create a slide edit that changes the out point of the clip on the left and the in point of the clip on the right.

Creating a Three- or Four-Point Edit

Three- and four-point edits are commonly performed in professional video editing studios, using a monitor set up that is similar to Premiere Pro's Dual View in the Monitor window. In Dual View, the Source section of the Monitor window typically shows a clip that hasn't been added to the Timeline, while the Program section shows a section of the program that has already been placed on the Timeline.

Performing a three-point edit

Typically, a three-point edit is used to overlay or replace a portion of the program with a portion of the source clip. Before the edit is performed, three crucial points are specified. Usually the three points are as follows:

✦ **The in point of the source clip.** The frame where you want the inserted clip to first appear.

✦ **An in point of the program clip.** The frame where you want the source clip to first appear in the current sequence in the Timeline.

✦ **An out point in the program clip.** The frame where you want the source replacement to end.

When the edit is performed, Premiere Pro automatically calculates the exact section of the source clip needed to replace the section designated by the in and out points of the program.

You could use a three-point edit in the following situation. Assume that you have a clip of a sailboat in the Timeline and you want to replace two seconds of it with a clip of waves crashing. To set this up, you place the Waves clip in the Source section of the Monitor window and set the in point for the Waves clip in the Source section. Then you set the in and out points in the Sailboat clip in the Monitor section of the Monitor window. When you perform the three-point edit, the Waves clip appears in the section in the Timeline designated by the area you set as the in and out points of the Sailboat clip.

Follow these steps to perform a three-point edit. Before creating a three-point edit, you need a project onscreen containing at least one clip in the Timeline.

If you want to practice using one of the tutorial files, start by importing the file 705008f.mov from the Chapter 1 folder of the *Adobe Premiere Pro Bible* DVD-ROM. This clip shows a waitress leading diners to a table in a restaurant. After the file is imported, drag it into track 1 in the Timeline. This clip will appear in the Program section of the Monitor window. Next, import clip 705009f.mov from the Chapter 1 folder of the DVD-ROM. This clip shows chefs working in the kitchen of a restaurant. Don't place this on the Timeline; Premiere Pro will do it for you when you create the three-point edit. The three-point edit will create a cut-away from the restaurant diners to the chefs in the kitchen for a few seconds, before returning to the diners clip.

1. **Select the target track in the Timeline by clicking at the far the left of the track.** (You should already have a clip in this track.)

2. **If the Monitor window is not open, open it by choosing Window ⇨ Show Monitor.** Set the monitor to Dual View by clicking the Dual View button or by choosing Dual View in the Monitor window menu. If you click the Play button in the Monitor window, you'll see that the clip in the Timeline appears in the Program section.

3. **Place a clip in the Source section (left side) of the Monitor window.** If you are using this book's DVD-ROM tutorial files, double-click clip 705009f.mov in the Project window. The clip should appear in the Source section, and its name should appear in the Source section tab. Note that you may be able to choose another clip from the Clip pop-up menu (in the left side of the Monitor window) if you've already been working with clips in the source section.

4. **In the Source section, set the in point for the source clip.** This is the first frame that you want overlaid into the program. If you are using the tutorial files, set the in point about 3 seconds, or 25 frames, from the beginning of clip 705009b.mov. To move to the frame, click and drag in the jog tread control or the current-time indicator in the Source section and then use the Step Forward or Step Back buttons to navigate to the precise frame.

5. **Click the Set In point button.**

6. **In the Program view of the Monitor window, move to the first frame that you want to replace with the source clip.** If you are using the tutorial files, move to about 2 seconds from the beginning of clip 7005008f.mov. To move to the frame, click and drag in the job tread or current-time indicator in the Program view and then use the Step Forward or Step Back buttons to navigate to the precise frame. Alternatively, you can click and drag the edit line in the Timeline window.

7. **Set the in point by clicking the In Point button in the Program or Sequence section of the Monitor window.**

8. **In the Program section of the Monitor window, move to the last frame that you want replaced by the source clip.** If you are using the tutorial files, move about 4 seconds, or 18 frames, into clip 705008f. mov.

9. **Click the Set Out point button.**

10. **To perform the edit, click the Overlay button (in the Source section of the Monitor window, to the left of the Toggle Take Audio and Video button).** Figure 13-11 shows a three-point edit.

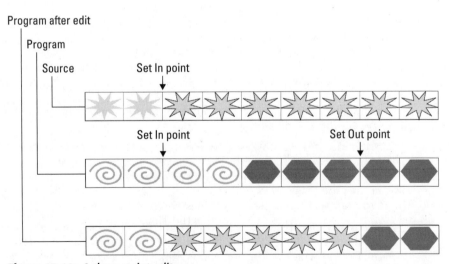

Figure 13-11: A three-point edit.

Performing a four-point edit

Three-point edits are performed more frequently than four-point edits because you only need to specify three points. In a four-point edit, you specify the in and out points of the source clip as well as the in and out points of the program clip.

Before performing the edit, make sure that the target track is set. If not, choose the track that you want to have the clip dropped into on the Timeline by clicking at the far left of track.

Otherwise, performing a four-point edit (see Figure 13-12) is identical to performing a three-point edit, except that you must set an out point as well as an in point in the Source side of the Monitor window. What happens if the source duration (the duration between in and out source points) does not match the duration between the program's in and out points? Premiere Pro opens an alert enabling you to choose whether you want to trim the source clip or change the speed of the source clip.

Figure 13-12: A four-point edit.

Performing Lift and Extract Edits

Premiere Pro's Monitor window provides two buttons that enable you to quickly remove sections of program material in the Timeline:

✦ **Lift button.** Removes frames from the Timeline but does not close the gap created by the deleted frames.

✦ **Extract button.** Removes frames from the Timeline but closes the gap that is created. This changes the duration of the project.

Before performing a Lift edit, you need to have a project onscreen with at least one clip in the Timeline window. The Monitor window should be open. The Monitor window can be in Single or Dual View. Here's how to perform a Lift edit:

1. **In the Program (right) side of the Monitor window, move to the first frame that you want removed from the program in the Timeline.**

2. **Click the In Point button.**

3. **Move to the last frame that you want to remove from the program.**

4. **Click the Set Out point button.**

5. **Click the Lift button in the Program side or choose Sequence ⇨ Lift.** Premiere Pro removes the frames from the Timeline, leaving a gap where the removed frames used to be.

Before performing an Extract edit, you need to have a project onscreen with at least one clip in the Timeline. The Monitor window should be open. Here's how to perform an Extract edit:

1. **In the Program (right) side of the Monitor window, move to the first frame that you want moved from the program in the Timeline.**

2. **Click the Set In point button.**

3. **Move to the last frame that you want to remove from the program.**

4. **Click the Set Out point button.**

5. **Click the Extract button in the Program side.** After you click, Premiere Pro removes the frames from the Timeline. Any adjacent clips in the Timeline move to close the gap that the deletion caused.

Fine-Tuning Edits Using Trim Window

The Trim window enables you to precisely change the edit points of clips on the Timeline. When you work in the Trim window, shown in Figure 13-13, you can click to move from edit point to edit point and then remove or add frames on either side of the edit line. The Trim window enables you to create ripple edits and rolling edits. When you create a ripple edit, the project duration increases or decreases depending on whether frames are added to or subtracted from the edit. If you create a rolling edit, the project duration remains the same. Premiere Pro accomplishes this by adding frames from one side of the edit as it subtracts from the other and by subtracting from one side of the edit while it adds to the other.

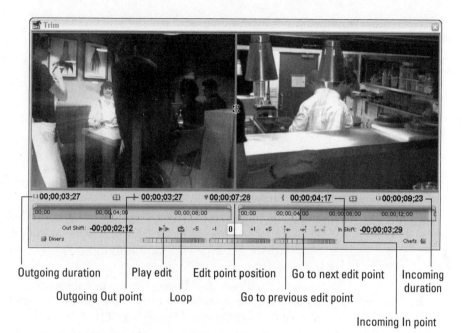

Figure 13-13: The Monitor window in Trim mode.

Here's how to use the Trim mode to trim an edit. Before beginning, you should have at least two separate clips on the Timeline that are adjacent to each other. The Monitor window should be open onscreen. If you keep the Timeline window open, you'll see the effects of the edit in the Timeline as you work.

1. **Select the target track by clicking at the far left side of the track.**

2. **Move the current-time indicator close to the area that you want to fine-tune or use the controls in the Monitor window to move close to the area that you want to edit.**

3. **Open the Trim window.** Click the Trim button in the Monitor window (lower-right corner) or choose Trim in the Monitor window menu.

4. **Click the Go to Next Edit Point or Go to Previous Edit Point button to move to the edit that you want to adjust.** The Out Shift section of the window shows the left side of the edit; the In Shift section of the window shows the right side of the edit (as if you were standing in the Timeline in the middle of a cut). Note that onscreen, the Trim window shows you the outgoing out point, the current edit point position, and the incoming in point.

5. **Edit the clip.**

6. **To create a ripple edit, follow these steps:**

   a. **Click and drag on either clip in the monitor displays.** For instance, if you click and drag left on the clip in the left window, you make this clip's duration shorter (changing its out point), without affecting the change the duration of the clip on the right. If you click and drag right on the clip in the right window, you delay its in point in (causing it to be further into the clip), thereby shortening this clip, but not changing the duration of clip on the left.

   b. **After you start the process of creating a ripple edit, add or remove frames by clicking in the bordered frame and entering a positive or negative number.** Enter a positive number of frames if you want to add frames to the last selected clip, enter a negative number to subtract from the selected clip.

   Clicking the –5 or –1 button removes five frames or one frame from the last selected clip. Clicking the +5 or +1 button adds five frames or one frame to the last selected clip.

   You can also create a ripple edit by clicking the Jog in point or Jog out point treads, clicking and dragging the in or out point icons, or clicking and dragging the Time code display of the incoming, outgoing, and current edit position.

7. **To create a rolling edit, follow these steps:**

   a. **Click and drag in the middle of the two clips.** If you click and drag right, you simultaneously change the in point of the clip on the right, (making it later in the clip) and the out point of the clip on the left (making it later as well). Clicking and dragging left produces the opposite effect.

   You can also create a rolling edit by clicking the Jog In and Out point treads.

   b. **After you start the process of creating a rolling edit, you can add or remove frames by clicking in the bordered frame and entering a positive or negative number.** Enter a positive number to specify the number of frames that you want to add to both clips or a negative number to specify the number of frames to delete from both clips.

   Clicking the –5 or –1 button removes five frames or one frame from both clips. Clicking the +5 or +1 button adds five frames or one frame to both clips.

8. **To play back the edit, click the Play button.** If you want to cancel the edit, click the Cancel edit button.

Note

If you need to cancel an edit, press Ctrl+Z or click in the History palette on the previous state.

Tip

To set the default trim to a large trim amount (by default, set at 5), choose Edit ⇨ Preferences ⇨ Trim.

Creating Duplicate Clips

As Premiere Pro users edit a production, most simply drag clips from the Project menu and place them into the Timeline. Doing this works well on short projects. However, if you are working on a long production with complicated edits, you may want to use Premiere Pro clip options that enable you to duplicate clips in the Project window. To understand duplicate clips, it's important to review how Premiere Pro categorizes the clips that you use:

✦ **Source clip.** When you import a file into Premiere Pro, the source clip of the file appears in the Project window. The source clip is a screen representation of the digitized material on disk.

✦ **Instance.** When you drag a clip to the Timeline, you create an *instance* of the master clip. Premiere Pro enables you to create multiple instances of the master clip in the Timeline. If you delete the master clip from the Project window, all instances are removed as well.

✦ **Duplicate clip.** Although using clip instances can be very efficient, there's one major drawback: Keeping track of all instances of the master clip in sequences in the Timeline can be difficult. The solution is to create a duplicate with a new name (you can even trim the clip before duplicating it). Each time you want to use the clip in the Timeline, you create another duplicate and drag it to the Timeline. Each duplicate remains listed separately in the Project window.

Instead of capturing many short clips and adding them to the Project window, capturing one long sequence and then creating duplicate clips from the original or master clip can be more efficient. If you create a duplicate clip, it's important to understand that a duplicate clip is a copy of the master clip, which never loses its link to the original source file on disk. Thus, if you delete the master clip in the Project window, any duplicate clips created from it remain in the project.

Here are the steps for creating a duplicate clip:

1. **Select the clip in the Project window.**

2. **Choose Edit ⇨ Duplicate.** A duplicate of the clip appears in the Project window with the word *copy* following the original clip name.

3. **Rename the clip by choosing Edit ⇨ Rename.**

Tip

You duplicate a clip by Ctrl+dragging it into another location in the Project window or by clicking and dragging a clip from the Source section of the Monitor window into the Project window.

Editing a Clip Using Clip Commands

When editing a production, you may find that you need to adjust a clip to maintain continuity in a project. For example, you may want to slow the speed of a clip to fill a gap in your production or to freeze a frame for a moment or two.

Various commands in the Clip menu enable you to edit a clip. Premiere Pro enables you to change the duration and/or the speed of a clip using the Clip ➪ Speed/Duration command. You can change the frame rate of a clip using the Clip ➪ Video Options ➪ Frame Hold command. Or you can use the Clip ➪ Video Options ➪ Frame Hold command to freeze a video frame. Using the Clip ➪ Video Options ➪ Field Options command, you can have Premiere Pro adjust interlaced clips.

Using the Duration and Speed commands

You can use the Clip ➪ Speed/Duration commands to change the length of a clip or to speed up, slow down, or play a clip in reverse.

Here's how to change the duration of a clip:

1. **Click the clip in a video track or in the Project window to select it.**

2. **Choose Clip ➪ Speed/Duration.** The Clip Duration dialog box appears (see Figure 13-14).

Figure 13-14: Use the Clip Speed/Duration dialog box to change a clip's speed or duration.

3. **Click the Link button to Unlink Speed and Duration.**

4. **Type a duration.** You can't expand the clip to extend past its original out point.

5. **Click OK to close the dialog box and set the new duration.**

Note   You can also change the duration of a clip by extending its edge with the Selection tool in the Timeline.

Here's how to change the speed of a clip (onscreen you should have a project with a clip in a video track in the Timeline window):

1. **Click the clip in the video track or select it in the Timeline.**

2. **Choose Clip ⇨ Speed.** The Clip Speed/Duration dialog box appears.

3. **Type a value in the Speed field.** Type a value greater than 100 percent to speed up the clip or type a value between 0 percent and 99 percent to slow down the clip. If you want to reverse speed, click the Reverse Speed checkbox.

4. **Click OK to close the Clip Speed/Duration dialog box and to apply the new speed.**

Note   You can change a clip's speed in the Timeline window by clicking and dragging on either edge of the clip with the Rate Stretch tool.

Using the Frame Hold command

Premiere Pro's Frame Hold command allows you to freeze one frame of a clip so that the frame appears from the in point to the out point of the clip. You can create a freeze frame from the in point, the out point, or at Marker point 0:

1. **Click the clip in the video track to select it.**

2. **If you want to freeze at a specific frame other than the in or out point, set an unnumbered marker for the clip in the Source section of the Monitor window.**

3. **Choose Clip ⇨ Video Options ⇨ Frame Hold.** This opens the Frame Hold Options dialog box, shown in Figure 13-15.

4. **In the pop-up menu, choose whether to create the freeze frame on the In Point, Out Point, or at Marker 0.**

5. **Click the Hold On check box.**

6. **If you want to prevent keyframe effects from being viewed, click the Hold Filters check box.**

7. **To remove the effects of video interlacing, click the Deinterlace check box.** This deletes one of the fields and replaces it with a duplicate of the other field.

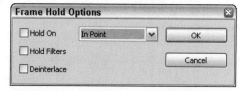

Figure 13-15: Use the Frame Hold Options dialog box to create a freeze frame.

Summary

Premiere Pro provides numerous tools and commands that enable you to quickly and precisely edit a digital video production. Premiere Pro's editing tools can be found in the Timeline toolbox. Most other editing utilities reside in the Monitor window.

✦ Use the Razor and Multiple Razor tools to snip a clip into two pieces.

✦ Use the Ripple Edit and Rolling Edit tools to change the in and out points of clips in the Timeline. A ripple edit changes the project duration; a rolling edit does not.

✦ You can click and drag with the Slip or Slide tools to edit the in and out points of a clip in between two other clips. The Slip tool does not change project duration; the Slide tool does.

✦ Use the Monitor window to create three- and four-point edits.

✦ Use the Trim window to precisely shave frames from clips.

✦ Use the Clip commands to change clip speed and duration.

✦ Create duplicate clips to use the same clip with different names in the Timeline.

✦   ✦   ✦

Using Video Effects

Adobe Premiere Pro's special effects can wake up even the dullest video production. Using the video effects in Premiere Pro's Effects window, for example, you can blur or skew images and add bevels, drop shadows, and painterly effects. Some effects can correct and enhance video; others can make it seem as though the video is out of control. By changing controls for the effects, you can also create startling motion effects, such as making it appear as if an earthquake or tornado has struck your clip.

As this chapter illustrates, Premiere Pro's video effects work in sync with the keyframe track, enabling you to change effect settings at specific points on the Timeline. All you need to do is specify the settings for the start of an effect, move to another keyframe, and set the ending effect. When you create a preview, Premiere Pro does the rest: It interpolates the video effect, editing all the in-between frames to create a fluid effect over time.

If you haven't been adding effects to your video, this chapter provides everything you need to get up and running. You'll explore every video effect in the Effects window and see how the Effect Controls window enables you to change effect settings. You'll also have a chance to practice creating effects with keyframes and image mattes with sample clips from the DVD-ROM that accompanies this book.

If you've already started working with Premiere Pro effects, this chapter shows how to use Premiere Pro's keyframe track and provides a reference for every effect in the Effects window.

Exploring the Video Effects

Premiere Pro's Effects window is a storehouse of video effects. However, before you begin to use the effects, you should become familiar with the window interface. To display the Effects window, choose Window ➪ Effects. The Effects window, shown in Figure 14-1, not only contains the Video Effects, but also the Audio Effects, the Audio Transitions, and Video Transitions. To view the Video Effects, click the triangle to the left of the Video Effects folder that is the Effects window. Within the Video Effects folder are 14 folders that contain different video effects.

Figure 14-1: Premiere Pro's Effects window provides access to Premiere's video effects.

Open a folder within the Video Effects folder to view a video effect. After the folder is open, a list of effects appears. An icon to the left of the video effect's name represents each effect. After you've opened a folder, you can apply a video effect to a video track by clicking and dragging it over a clip in the Timeline window. To close a folder, click the triangle to the left of the folder.

Navigating within the video effects

The Effects window features options that can help you keep organized while using Premiere Pro's many video effects. The following is a brief description of these options:

✦ **Find.** The Contains field at the top of the Effects window helps locate effects. In the Contains field, type the name of the effect that you want to find. Premiere Pro automatically starts the search.

✦ **New Custom Folder.** When you create custom folders, you can use them to organize effects. To create a custom folder, either click the folder icon at the bottom of the Effects window or click the Effects pop-up menu and choose New Custom Bin. After you create a folder, drag the effects into it. With all of your chosen effects in one folder, you'll find that they are easier to use and locate.

✦ **Rename.** You can change a name of a custom folder at any time by selecting the folder and then clicking on the name. When the name of the folder is highlighted, type the name that you want in the Name field.

✦ **Delete.** If you have finished using a custom folder, you can delete it by selecting it and then choosing the Delete Custom Item from the Effects pop-up menu or by clicking on the Delete icon at the bottom of the window. A prompt appears asking whether you want to delete the item. If you do, click Yes.

The Effect Controls window

When you apply a video effect to an image, the effect appears in the Effect Controls window, as shown in Figure 14-2.

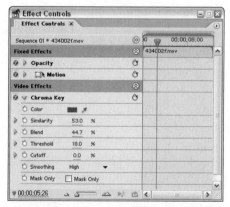

Figure 14-2: The settings for a video effect appear in the Effect Controls window after a video effect is applied to a clip.

At the top of the window, the name of the selected clip appears. To the right of the clip name is a button that enables you to create and/or show or hide keyframes over a Timeline. At the bottom left of the Effect Controls window is a time display showing you where the clip appears in the Timeline. To the right of the time display are options allowing you to zoom out or in.

Below the name of the selected sequence and clip name appears the Fixed Effects heading. Below the Fixed Effects heading appears the Fixed Effects options — Motion and Opacity. If a video effect has been applied to the selected clip, the Video Effects heading is displayed below the Opacity option. All the video effects that have been applied to the selected clip are displayed below the Video Effects heading. The video effects appear in the order in which the video effect has been applied. To the left of the Fixed Effects (Motion and Opacity) and a Video Effects name appears a box with an *f* in it. The *f* means that this effect is enabled. You can disable the effect by clicking the *f* or deselecting Effect Enabled in the Effect Controls pop-up menu. Also next to the effect name is a small triangle. If you click the triangle, the settings for that effect appear.

Many clips also feature a dialog box that includes a preview area. If the effect provides a dialog box, you will see a little dialog box icon to the right of the name of the video effect in the Effect Controls window. Click the icon to access the Setup dialog box. Many effects can be applied with Premiere Pro's keyframe option. If so, a small stopwatch will be shown in front of the name of the effect. To enable keyframing, click the small stopwatch icon. After you click, a small blue frame appears around the stopwatch icon. (Keyframing is explained later in this chapter.)

The Effect Controls menu

The Effect Controls pop-up menu provides control over all the clips in the window. The menu enables you to turn previewing on and off and to select preview quality as well as to enable and disable effects. The following is a brief description of the Effect Controls menu commands:

✦ **Effect Enabled.** Click this command to disable or enable effects. By default, Effect Enabled is selected.

✦ **Delete Selected Effect.** This command removes the selected effect from the clip.

You can remove an effect from the window by selecting it in the Effect Controls window, then pressing Delete.

✦ **Delete All Effects from Clip.** This command removes all effects from the clip.

The Audio commands in the Effect Controls menu are covered in Chapters 8 and 9.

Applying a Video Effect

You can apply one video effect or multiple video effects to an entire video clip by dragging the effect from the Effects window to the Timeline. The video effects allow you to change the color of a clip, blur it, or even distort it.

Here's how to apply a video effect to a clip in the Timeline:

1. **Create a New Project and call it VideoEffects.**

Note Refer to Chapter 4 for information on choosing a project preset.

2. **Choose Window ⇨ Workspace ⇨ Effects to display all the palettes and windows you will need.**

3. **Choose File ⇨ Import to import a video clip to use as the background.** If you want, you can use Digital Vision's Drifting Skies (386022f.mov) video clip as the background. It is located on the DVD that accompanies this book.

On the DVD-ROM Digital Vision's Drifting Skies 386022f.mov is in the Digital Vision folder in the Chapter 14 folder that is in the Tutorial Projects folder on the DVD that accompanies this book.

4. **Drag the background video clip from the Project window to Video track 1 of the Timeline window.**

5. **To apply an effect to the background, you first need to select it in the Timeline window.** Click the background clip in Video track 1.

6. **Choose an effect by clicking on it.** For a simple effect, try the Directional Blur found in the Blur & Sharpen folder. We used the Lens Flare effect, which is found in the Render folder. Figure 14-3 shows the Lens Flare effect in the Monitor window and the effects options in the Effect Controls window.

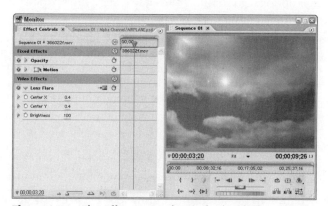

Figure 14-3: The Effect Controls window with the Lens Flare settings and a preview of the effect in the Monitor window.

Note If you didn't choose the Directional Blur effect, the effect you chose may provide more settings in a dialog box. If a dialog box is provided for the effect, a Setup icon appears to the right of the effect in the Effect Controls window. Click the Setup icon to open the dialog box and change the settings. Figure 14-4 shows the Lens Flare Settings dialog box.

Figure 14-4: The Lens Flare Settings dialog box.

7. **To apply the effect, drag the effect from the Effects window directly onto the clip in Video track 1 or into the Effect Controls window.** To adjust the settings of the effect, use the options found beneath the effect's name in the Effect Controls window. To set an effect to its default settings, click the Reset button to the right of the effect's name. For a full discussion on the video effects and their options, go to the "Touring Premiere Pro's Video Effects" section at the end of this chapter.

8. **Try different effects, such as those found in the Adjust, Distort, Image Control, Pixelate, Render, Stylize, Time, and Transform folder.** To turn the effect on or off, click the small *f* in front of the effect's name in the Effect Controls window. To delete an effect, click the effect in the Effect Controls window and press Delete or click the pop-up menu and choose Delete Selected Effect. To remove all the effects from a clip, click the Effect Controls pop-up menu and choose Delete All Effects from Clip.

Note You can add multiple effects to an image. You can also add the same effect with different effect settings to the same image.

9. **Click the Play button in the Monitor window to see a preview of the effects.** As you work, watch the preview in the Monitor window.

10. **Choose File ➪ Import to import a sound clip and drag the sound clip to Audio track 1.** We used Digital Vision's The Acoustic Chillout clip

(730007aw.wav). This sound clip is located on the DVD that accompanies this book.

Digital Vision's The Acoustic Chillout clip (730007aw.wav) is in the Digital Vision folder in the Chapter 14 folder that is in the Tutorial Projects folder on the DVD that accompanies this book.

11. **Choose File ➪ Save to save your project so that you can use it in the next section.**

Applying a video effect to a clip with an alpha channel

Not only can you apply an effect to a video clip, but you can also apply an effect to a still image that has an alpha channel. To apply an effect to just an image and not its background, it must have an alpha channel. You can use Adobe Photoshop to mask an image and save the mask either as an alpha channel or a layer. For more information on creating alpha channels using Photoshop, turn to Chapter 27.

Here's how to apply a video effect to a Photoshop file with an alpha channel:

If you want to apply an effect to an image with an alpha channel, you can apply video effects to the Airplane.psd image (shown in Figure 14-3) and use Digital Vision's Drifting Skies 386022f.mov as the background. They are found in the Chapter 14 folder that is in the Tutorial Projects folder on the DVD that accompanies this book.

Before you start, either load the video effects project from the previous section or create a new project and import a video clip and drag it into Video track 1. We used Digital Vision's Drifting Skies 386022f.mov as the background. It is found in the Chapter 14 folder that is in the Tutorial Projects folder on the DVD that accompanies this book.

1. **Choose Window ➪ Workspace ➪ Effects to display all the palettes and windows you will need.**

2. **Choose File ➪ Import to load a Photoshop file with an alpha channel.**

3. **In the Import dialog box, locate a Photoshop file that has an alpha channel so that only the image and not the background are imported.** We used the Airplane.psd image (found on the DVD that accompanies this book). After you've located the file, click Open. In the Import Layered File dialog box, make sure Footage is selected in the Import As pop-up menu and select the Choose Layer option. In the Choose Layer pop-up menu, choose Alpha Channel or the appropriate channel.

4. **Click OK.** The Photoshop file and its alpha channel appear in the Project window.

5. Drag the still image with an alpha channel (the airplane image) from the Project window to Video track 2. Place it directly above the background clip in Video track 1. The Timeline Marker should be over both clips.

6. Double-click the airplane image in the Timeline window to display it in the Monitor window. On one side of the Monitor window the Photoshop file (airplane image) appears on a black background. On the other side of the image, the Photoshop file (airplane image) appears over the selected background from Video track 1, as shown in Figure 14-5. The Photoshop file (airplane image) from Video track 2 takes on the background of the clip from Video track 1 because it has an alpha channel.

Figure 14-5: The Monitor window on one side displays the Photoshop file with an alpha channel. On the other side, you can see the Photoshop file over a sky background. The background clip is in Video track 1 of the Timeline window, and the Photoshop file is in Video track 2.

7. To see the Photoshop alpha channel, click the Monitor window pop-up menu and choose Alpha. Figure 14-6 shows the Photoshop alpha channel. To return to standard view, click Composite from the pop-up menu.

Figure 14-6: The Photoshop alpha channel.

8. **Select the Photoshop file (airplane image) in Video track 2.**

9. **Drag the desired video effect from the Effects window onto the Photoshop file (airplane image) in Video track 2 or into the Effect Controls window.** In our example, we applied the Emboss effect, which is found in the Stylize folder. We also applied the Drop Shadow and Bevel Edges effects found in the Perspective folder. In the next section, we apply the Basic 3D effect, found in the Perspective folder, by setting keyframes. By setting keyframes, you can change the effect over time. Proceed to the next section if you want to learn how to use video effects with keyframes.

10. **To preview your work, either click and drag on the shuttle or jog slider in the Monitor window.** You can also move the Timeline Marker in the Timeline. To preview your entire clip, click the Play button in the Monitor window.

11. **Choose File ➪ Import to import a sound clip and then drag the sound clip to Audio track 1.** We used Digital Vision's The Acoustic Chillout clip (730007aw.wav). This sound clip is located on the DVD that accompanies this book.

Digital Vision's The Acoustic Chillout clip (730007aw.wav) is found in the Digital Vision folder in the Chapter 14 folder that is in the Tutorial Projects folder on the DVD that accompanies this book.

12. **Choose File ➪ Save to save your work so that you can use it in the next section.**

Using Video Effects with Keyframes

Premiere Pro's keyframe feature enables you to change video effects at specific points in the Timeline. With keyframes, you can have Premiere Pro use the settings of an effect at one point on the Timeline, gradually changing to the settings at another point on the Timeline. When Premiere Pro creates the preview, it interpolates the effect over time, rendering all the frames that change in between the set points. Keyframing can be used to make video clips or stills more interesting. You can also import a still image of your logo and animate it using keyframes. If you want, you can use Adobe Premiere Pro's Title Designer window to create a logo. To learn how to create a logo using Premiere Pro, refer to Chapter 11.

Figure 14-7 shows frames of the airplane image from the previous sections, animated over a sky background video clip. The airplane image is animated using the Basic 3D effect found in the Perspective folder. To make the airplane swivel and tilt to its original state, we set keyframes.

The keyframe track

Premiere Pro's keyframe track makes creating, editing, and manipulating keyframes quick, logical, and precise. The keyframe track is found in both the Timeline window and the Effect Controls window. Figure 14-8 shows the Timeline window with the keyframe track. Figure 14-9 shows the Effect Controls window with the keyframe track. To view the keyframe track in the Timeline window, expand the track by clicking the track's Expand button. To view the keyframe track in the Effect Controls window, make sure the Show/Hide Keyframes button is activated.

Note   The keyframe track does not appear if you do not have a clip in the track.

Figure 14-7: Frames from the airplane clip with the Basic 3D effect applied using keyframes.

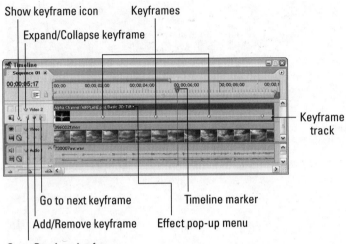

Show keyframe icon   Keyframes

Expand/Collapse keyframe

Keyframe track

Go to next keyframe   Timeline marker

Add/Remove keyframe   Effect pop-up menu

Go to Previous keyframe

Figure 14-8: The Timeline window with Video track 2 expanded with keyframes.

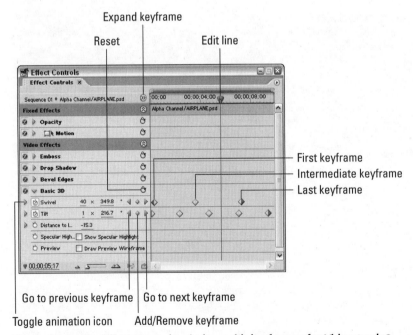

Expand keyframe

Reset   Edit line

First keyframe

Intermediate keyframe

Last keyframe

Go to previous keyframe   Go to next keyframe

Toggle animation icon   Add/Remove keyframe

Figure 14-9: The Effect Controls window with keyframes for Video track 2 displayed.

To enable keyframing, click a tiny stopwatch next to one of the settings for an effect in the Effect Controls window. You can also turn keyframing on and off by clicking the Show Keyframes icon in the Timeline window and choosing an effect setting from the video clip's pop-up menu. In the keyframe track, a circle or diamond indicates a keyframe exists at the current Timeline frame. Clicking the right arrow icon (Go to Previous Keyframe) jumps the Timeline Marker from one keyframe to the next. Clicking the left arrow (Go to Next Keyframe) moves the Timeline Marker backward from one keyframe to the next.

Here's how to apply an effect to a clip using keyframes:

1. **Before you start, load the Video Effects project from the previous section or create a new project and import a background video clip for Video track 1 and import a still image or logo (that has an alpha channel) for Video track 2.** We used Digital Vision's Drifting Skies 386022f.mov as the background and the Airplane.psd for Video track 2. They are found in the Chapter 14 folder that is in the Tutorial Projects folder on the DVD that accompanies this book.

If you want, you can use the Airplane.psd image in Video track 2 and use Digital Vision's Drifting Skies 386022f.mov as the background (Video track 1). They are found in the Chapter 14 folder that is in the Tutorial Projects folder on the DVD that accompanies this book.

2. **Choose Window ➪ Workspace ➪ Effects to display all the palettes and windows you will need.**

Using an image in Video track 2 that has an alpha channel will allow a background clip that is in Video track 1 to show through when previewed in the Monitor window. To see a preview in the Monitor window, click the Play button. To superimpose two video clips without alpha channels you need to used the Keying Effects. The Keying Effects are briefly discussed in the next section. For a full description on these effects, turn to Chapter 15.

3. **Add an effect to the image in Video track 2 by clicking on an effect in the Effects window and then dragging it to the clip in the Timeline window.** If you are animating a logo, for an unusual effect, you might want to try the Twirl effect. The Twirl effect is found in the Distort folder, in the Video Effects folder that is in the Effects window. In Figures 14-7, 14-8, and 14-9, we used the Basic 3D effect.

4. **To create a keyframe for the effect you applied in Step 3 using the Timeline window, move the Timeline Marker (edit line) over the first frame of the image in Video track 2.**

5. **In the Timeline window, click the Expand/Collapse Track icon (a triangle icon that appears before the track name) to expand the track.** Then click the Shows keyframes icon to show the keyframe track.

6. **Click the clip's title bar pop-up menu and choose an effects control.**

7. **Click the Add/Delete Keyframe icon to add a keyframe.** A circle appears on the keyframe track.

8. **To add another keyframe, move the Timeline Marker (edit line) to a new position. Then click the Add Keyframe icon.** Change the settings for the effect by clicking the keyframe in the Timeline window and moving it up or down.

9. **To add more keyframes using the Timeline window, repeat Step 8 as many times as desired.** Figure 14-8 shows the Timeline window with keyframes.

Note To delete a keyframe, click it and press Delete. You can move a keyframe by clicking and dragging it to a new location.

The keyframes that you created using the Timeline window appear in the Effect Controls window.

10. **You can also use the Effect Controls window to adjust the settings for a keyframe.** In the Effect Controls window, click the triangle in front of the effect to display the controls. Then move the Timeline Marker (edit line) over the keyframe you want to edit. Then make the necessary changes.

11. **To create a keyframe for the effect you applied in Step 3 using the Effect Controls window, move the edit line in the Timeline of the Effect Controls window to the beginning of the clip.** Then click the Toggle Animation icon in front of the Effects control that you want to work with. A keyframe is added, and keyframing is enabled.

12. **Move the edit line in the Timeline of the Effect Controls window to a new position and adjust the control's setting.** As you adjust the control's setting, a keyframe is added.

13. **To add more keyframes using the Effect Controls window, repeat Step 12 as many times as desired.** Figure 14-9 shows the Effect Controls window with keyframes.

Note When keyframing is enabled for an effects control, you can click the Toggle Animation icon to delete all the existing keyframes for that effects control.

14. **To preview the video effect, choose Play from the Monitor window.** You can also drag the Timeline Marker as you view the preview in the Monitor window.

15. **Choose File ⇨ Import to import a sound clip.** Then drag the sound clip to Audio track 1. We used Digital Vision's The Acoustic Chillout clip 730007aw.wav. This sound clip is located on the DVD that accompanies this book.

On the DVD-ROM Digital Vision's The Acoustic Chillout clip 730007aw.wav is found in the Digital Vision folder that is in the Chapter 14 folder that is in the Tutorial Projects folder on the DVD that accompanies this book.

16. **Choose File ➪ Save to save your project.**

Superimposing Video Clips Using the Keying Video Effects

To superimpose two video clips that don't have alpha channels, you'll need to use the Keying video effects. Figure 14-10 shows the windows and palettes we used to create a project using the Chroma Key effect. To create the project, we superimposed two video clips: a graphic video clip in Video track 2 and a sky background in Video track 1. In Video track 3, we used an Adobe Photoshop file with an alpha channel so that you could see the backgrounds from the clips in Video tracks 1 and 2. Figure 14-10 shows the Monitor window with a frame of the final result of the three clips from the three video tracks superimposed onto one another.

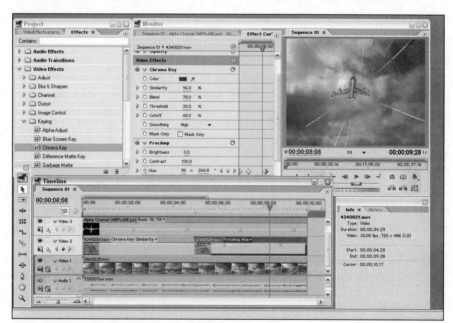

Figure 14-10: The windows and palettes used to create a project using the Chroma Key effect.

In the project in Figure 14-10, we used the sky background and an Adobe Photoshop file with an alpha channel from the previous section. The sky background that we used is from Digital Vision's Drifting Skies 386022f.mov. To superimpose a video clip over the sky background, we moved the Adobe Photoshop file (Airplane.mov) from Video track 2 to Video track 3. Then we imported a new video clip (Digital Vision's Ambient Space clip 434002f.mov) and dragged it into Video track 2, as shown in Figure 14-10. To jazz up our project, we added sound. The sound file we used is Digital Vision's The Acoustic Chillout 730007aw.wav.

On the DVD-ROM

The video clips used to create the project shown in Figure 14-10 are found in the Chapter 14 folder in the Tutorial Projects folder that is located on the DVD that accompanies this book. The clips are Airplane.mov, Digital Vision's Drifting Skies 386022f.mov, Digital Vision's Ambient Space clip 434002f.mov, and Digital Vision's The Acoustic Chillout clip 730007aw.wav.

Here's how to superimpose two video clips using the Chroma Key video effects:

1. **Choose File ⇨ Open Project to open the project from the previous section or Choose File ⇨ New ⇨ Project to create a new project.**

2. **Your project onscreen should have two video clips and a third image with an alpha channel. Choose File ⇨ Import to import the necessary clips.** If you are using a new project, you will need to import three files. If you are using the project from the previous section, you'll need to import one new video clip. We used Digital Vision's Ambient Space clip 434002f.mov. This video clip is located on the DVD that accompanies this book.

3. **Now you are ready to drag the clips from the Project window to the Timeline window.** If you are using a new project, you'll need to drag a background video clip from the Project window to Video track 1. Then drag another video clip into Video track 2 and the clip with an alpha channel into Video track 3. This clip should have an alpha channel so that the background shows through. If you are using the project from the previous section, move the Airplane file with the alpha channel from Video track 2 to Video track 3. Note that all the effects remain with the video clip as you move it. Then drag the new video clip into Video track 2. The video clip in Video track 2 should be directly above the video clip in Video track 1. If the video clip in Video track 2 is not as long as the one in Video track 1, you may want to copy the video clip in Video track 2 and paste a copy next to it.

4. **To superimpose the clips in Video Tracks 1 and 2, we used the Chroma Key effect from the Keying folder and reduced the opacity.** To apply the Chroma Key effect to clip in Video track 2, select the Chroma Key effect from the Effects window and drag it over the clip in Video track 2.

5. **Use the Effect Controls window to adjust the settings of the effect.** As you work, you can preview the effect in the Monitor window. Start by clicking on the color swatch and pick a color that is similar to the color of the background clip in Video track 1. Then increase the Similarity value and Blend value. If you need to, increase also the Threshold and Cutoff values.

Note

For more information on superimposing clips using the Video Keying effects and the Opacity option, turn to Chapter 15.

6. **To see more of the clip in Video track 1, reduce the opacity of the clip in Video track 2 by using either the Opacity option in the Effect Controls window or the Timeline window.** To access the Opacity option in the Timeline window, you need to expand the track then click the title bar of the track and choose Opacity. A white line appears below the track's title bar. Drag this bar down to reduce the opacity.

7. **We made further adjustments to the colors of the clip in Video track 2 by applying the ProcAmp video effect from the Adjust folder.** To use the ProAmp video effect, drag it over the clip in Video track 2.

8. **To have the colors of the clip in Video track 2 change over time, you need to create keyframes for the ProcAmp Hue control.** Move the edit line to the beginning of the clip. Then click the Toggle Animation icon in front of the Hue control to enable keyframing and create your first keyframe. Then move the edit line to a new position and adjust the Hue control to create another keyframe.

9. **To jazz up your project, you can add a sound clip.** Choose File ⇨ Import to import a sound clip. In the Import dialog box, locate a sound clip and click Open. We used Digital Vision's The Acoustic Chillout clip 730007aw.wav. This sound clip is located on the DVD that accompanies this book.

10. **Drag the sound clip from the Project window to Audio track 1.** If the sound clip is too long, click the left side of the clip and drag it inward. For more information on working with sound clips, turn to Chapter 8.

11. **Be sure to save your work.**

12. **Click the Play button in the Monitor window to preview your work.**

13. **If you want, you can export your project as a movie.** Choose File ⇨ Export ⇨ Movie. In the Export Movie dialog box, name your movie. To change the settings, click the Settings button. Click Save to save the project as a movie.

Applying Effects to Different Image Areas Using the Image Matte Keying Effect

You can use an image matte to show an effect only in specific areas of a clip. When you apply a matte, Premiere Pro masks out the areas that you don't want shown.

An *image matte* is either a black-and-white image or a grayscale image. By default, Adobe Premiere Pro applies effects to the clip areas corresponding to white portions of the matte. (The effect does not appear in clip regions corresponding to black areas.) In the gray areas, the effect is applied with some degree of transparency—

which means that the areas where the effect is applied appear to be see-through to some extent.

You can use Adobe Photoshop, Adobe Illustrator, Procreate Painter, or even Adobe Premiere Pro's Title Designer window to create an image matte. After you've created an image matte, you need two clips, one for Video track 1 and one for Video track 2. If you don't have an image matte or video clips, you can use any of the sample files found on the DVD that accompanies this book. Figure 14-11 shows the windows and palettes used to create an Image Matte project. The clips used in Figure 14-11 are from Digital Vision's Electro clip 579020f.mov and Digital Vision's CityMix clip 567017f.mov.

Figure 14-11: Frames from the sample image matte project using the emboss effect only on a certain area of the clip (outside the arrow).

Here's how to apply an effect using an image matte:

1. Open or create a new project.

> **Note** Refer to Chapter 4 for information on choosing a project preset.

2. Choose Window ➪ Workspace ➪ Effects to display all the windows and palettes you'll need.

3. Import two video clips into the Project window.

On the DVD-ROM The clips used to create the project in Figure 14-11 are in the Digital Vision folder in the Chapter 14 folder that is in the Tutorial Projects folder located on the DVD that accompanies this book. The images are from Digital Vision's Electro clip 579020f.mov and Digital Vision's CityMix clip 567017f.mov. The matte image used in the project is called arrow.psd and is in the Chapter 14 folder.

4. **Click and drag one of the video clips from the Project window to Video track 1 of the Timeline window.** The video clip in Video track 1 will be the clip that appears inside the matte. We used Digital Vision's CityMix clip 567017f.mov in Video track 1.

5. **Click and drag the other video clip to Video track 2.** The video clip in Video track 2 will be the clip that appears in the background of the matte. We used Digital Vision's Electro clip 579020f.mov in Video track 2.

6. **Apply an effect to Video track 2 by dragging an effect from the Effects window to the clip.** If you want, you can apply a different effect to the video clip in Video track 1. If you apply the effect to Video track 2, however, the effect can only be seen outside the matte image. If you apply the effect to Video track 1, the effect is only seen in the inside of the matte image. We applied the Alpha Glow effect (found in the Stylize folder) to Video track 2 and the Crystallize effect (found in the Pixelate folder) to Video track 1.

7. **To superimpose Video track 2 over Video track 1, select Video track 2.**

8. **Choose Image Matte from the Keying folder in the Effects window.** Then click and drag it over Video track 2.

9. **In the Effect Controls window, click the Setup icon.** When the Select a Matte Image dialog box appears, browse to and load the matte image. (We used a file called arrow.psd for our matte image. The file can be found in the Chapter 14 folder on the DVD that accompanies the book.) Click OK to apply the image matte.

10. **Click the Play button in the Monitor window to preview the effect.**

11. **Choose File ➪ Save to save your work.**

Touring Premiere Pro's Video Effects

Premiere Pro boasts 78 video effects that are divided into 14 folders. The folders are Adjust, Blur & Sharpen, Channel, Distort, Image Control, Keying, Perspective, Pixelate, Render, Sample Plug-ins, Stylize, Time, Transform, and Video. That's a lot of video effects to choose from. To help you deal with this overwhelming wealth of video effects, we've assembled a description of each effect according to its category folder.

Note The Keying effects will be discussed in detailed in Chapter 15.

Note

Before undertaking a tour of the effects, remember that many effects provide previews in dialog boxes. If an effect provides a dialog box, click the Setup dialog box icon in the Effect Controls window to see a preview.

Tip

Although most effects can be controlled by sliders that you click and drag, you can also click underlined values at the center of the slider to set effects. When you click the underlined value, a dialog box appears showing the largest and smallest values allowed in the slider setting.

On the DVD-ROM

If you want, you can experiment with the different video effects by applying them to one of the video clips in the Tutorial Projects folder located on the DVD that accompanies the book. In the figures within this section, we used the Plane&Background.psd image. It is located in the Chapter 14 folder.

The Adjust folder

The Adjust folder enables you to adjust the color attributes of selected clips, such as the brightness and contrast of an image. If you are familiar with Adobe Photoshop, you'll find that several Premiere Pro video effects, such as Channel Mixer, Levels, and Posterize, are quite similar to filters found in Adobe Photoshop.

Brightness and Contrast

Using the Brightness and Contrast effects is an easy way to adjust brightness and contrast in your image. Brightness controls how light or dark your image is. Contrast controls the difference between the brightest and darkest pixels in an image. In the Effect Controls window, click and drag the Brightness slider to increase or reduce an image's brightness, and click and drag the Contrast slider to add or subtract contrast from an image.

Channel Mixer

The Channel Mixer effect enables you to create special effects by mixing colors from a clip's channels. With the Channel Mixer you create color effects, as well as turn a color image into a grayscale image or into an image with a sepia tone or tint effect.

To use the Channel Mixer, click and drag any Source Channel slider in the Effect Controls window to the left to decrease the amount of color supplied to the image. Click and drag to the right to increase it.

To convert an image to grayscale, click the Monochrome button and then adjust the sliders.

Convolution Kernel

The Convolution Kernel effect uses mathematical *convolution* to change brightness values of clip. This effect can be used to increase sharpness or enhance image edges. The matrix of numbers in the Convolution Kernel Settings dialog box, shown in Figure 14-12, represents the pixels in the image. The center pixel text field is the pixel being analyzed. In the center box, enter the number that you want to use as the brightness multiplier. In other words, if you enter 2, the pixel's brightness values are doubled. The same concept applies for neighboring text fields. You can enter a brightness multiplier in the surrounding boxes — you can also enter 0 to have no increase in the brightness value.

Figure 14-12: The Convolution Kernel Settings dialog box.

Values entered in the Scale box are used to divide the sum of the brightness values. If desired, enter a value in the Offset field, which is the same as the value added to the Scale field.

When using the Convolution Kernel filter, you can save settings by clicking the Save button; you can reload saved settings by clicking the Load button.

Extract

The Extract filter removes the color from a clip to create a black-and-white effect. The Input and Output sliders in the Extract Settings dialog box, shown in Figure 14-13, enables you to control which image areas are affected. The Softness slider softens the effect. The preview area provides a good idea of the result of the effect.

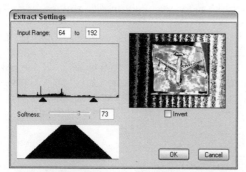

Figure 14-13: The Extract Settings dialog box.

Levels

The Levels effect enables you to correct highlights, midtones, and shadows in an image. To apply the same levels to all color channels, leave the pop-up menu in the Levels Settings dialog box, shown in Figure 14-14, set to RGB. Otherwise, click to choose a red, green, or blue channel to apply the effect to.

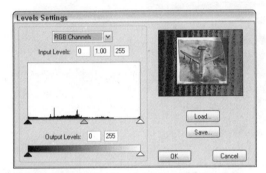

Figure 14-14: The Levels Settings dialog box.

To complete your image correction, use the input slider to increase contrast. Drag the middle slider to raise or lower midtone values. Drag the output slider to decrease contrast.

Posterize

Posterize creates special color effects by reducing the tonal level in the red, green, and blue color channels. Click and drag the Levels amount in the Effect Controls window to set how many levels of color are in an image.

ProcAmp

The Brightness and Contrast options for the ProAmp effect allow for an easy way to adjust brightness and contrast in your image. Brightness controls how light or dark your image is. Contrast controls the difference between the brightest and darkest pixels in an image. In the Effect Controls window, click and drag the Brightness option to the right to increase the image's brightness and drag to the left to reduce an image's brightness. Click and drag the Contrast option right or the left to add or subtract contrast from an image. Click and drag on the Hue values to change the color of your image. Click and drag the Saturation option to the right to make the colors more vibrant. Drag the Saturation option to the left to 0 to take all the colors out of your image and make it a grayscale image. The Split Screen option allows you to apply the effect to only a portion of the image. The Split Percent value determines how much of the image is affected.

The Blur & Sharpen folder

The Blur effects contain options that allow you to blur images. Using blur effects, you can create motion effects or blur out a video track as a background to emphasize the foreground. The Sharpen effects enable you to sharpen images. Sharpening helps bring out image edges when digitized images or graphics appear too soft.

Anti-alias

The Anti-alias effect reduces jagged lines by blending image edges of contrasting colors to create a smooth edge.

Camera Blur

By using this effect with keyframes, you can simulate an image going in or out of focus. You can also simulate a "camera bump" effect. Use the Blur slider in the Camera Blur Settings dialog box, shown in Figure 14-15, to control the effect.

Figure 14-15: The Camera Blur Settings dialog box.

Channel Blur

The Channel Blur effect enables you to blur an image using the Red, Green, Blue Channel, or Alpha channel. By default, the Blur Dimension pop-up is set to Horizontal and Vertical. At the default setting, any blurring you do affects the image horizontally and vertically. If you want to blur only one dimension, set the pop-up menu to either Horizontal or Vertical. When the Edge Behavior/Repeat Edge Pixels option is deselected, the edges around the clip are blurred. When it is selected, they are not.

Directional Blur

The Directional Blur effect creates a motion effect by blurring an image in a specific direction. The sliders in the Effect Controls window control the direction and the length of the blur.

Fast Blur

Use the Fast Blur effect to quickly blur a clip. Use the Blur Dimension pop-up menu in the Effect Controls window to specify whether the blur should be vertical, horizontal, or both.

Gaussian Blur

The Gaussian Blur effect blurs video and reduces video signal noise. Similarly to the Fast Blur effect, you can specify whether the blur should be vertical, horizontal, or both. The word "gaussian" is used because the filter uses a gaussian (bell-shaped) curve when removing contrast to create the blur effect.

Gaussian Sharpen

Apply the Gaussian Sharpen effect to create strong, overall sharpening. You can obtain similar results by applying the Sharpen filter several times. This effect provides no controls.

Ghosting

The Ghosting effect layers image areas from previous frames over one frame. Use this to show the path of a moving object — such as a speeding bullet or a pie thrown in the air.

Radial Blur

This effect creates a circular blurring effect. The Radial Blur dialog box, shown in Figure 14-16, lets you control the degree of blurring. To do so, increase the value in the Amount field by dragging the Amount slider to the right. In the Blur Method area, choose Spin to create a spinning blur; choose Zoom to create an outward blur. In the Quality section, choose Draft, Good, or Best. However, remember that the better the quality, the more processing time needed to create the effect.

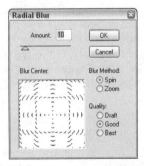

Figure 14-16: The Radial Blur dialog box.

Sharpen

The Sharpen effect includes a value that enables you to control sharpening within your clip. Click and drag the Sharpen Amount value in the Effect Controls window to the right to increase sharpening. The slider permits values from 0 to 100; however, if you click the underlined sharpen amount onscreen, you can enter values up to 4000 into the Value field.

Sharpen Edges

The Sharpen Edges effect applies sharpening effects on image edges.

The Channel folder

The Channel folder contains two effects—Blend and Invert. Use Blend to blend video clips based on color modes. Use Invert to invert the color values within a clip.

Blend

The Blend effect allows you to blend video tracks using different modes: Crossfade, Color Only, Tint Only, Darken Only, and Lighten Only. The Blend with Original option is used to specify which clip you want to blend with. For example, if you apply the Blend effect to a clip in Video track 1A and want to blend it with a clip in Video track 1B, set the Blend with Layer pop-up menu to V1B. For both clips to appear translucent, set the Blend with Original value to 50%. In order to see both clips in the Monitor window, they must be selected with the Timeline Marker. If you apply the Blend effect to a clip in Video track 1A and want to blend it with a clip in Video track 2, set the Blend with Layer pop-up menu to V2. Then hide Video track 2 by clicking on the Eye icon in the Timeline window. In order to see both clips in the Monitor window, they must be selected with the Timeline Marker and the Blend with Original value should be set to less than 90%.

Invert

The Invert effect inverts color values. You can turn black into white, white into black, and colors into their complements.

The Channel pop-up menu in the Effect Controls window enables you to choose a color model: RGB, HLS, or YIQ. YIQ is the NTSC color space. Y refers to luminance; I refers to inphase chrominance; Q refers to quadrature chrominance. The alpha choice enables you to invert the gray levels in an alpha channel. Use the Blend with Original slider if you want to blend the channel effect with the original image.

The Distort folder

The Distort commands, found in the Distort folder, enable you to distort an image either by twirling, pinching, or spherizing it. Many of these commands are similar to the distort filters found in Adobe Photoshop.

Bend

The Bend effect can bend your image in various directions. In the Bend Settings dialog box, which is shown in Figure 14-17, use the Intensity, Rate, and Width sliders to control effects for Horizontal and Vertical Bending. Intensity is the wave height; Rate is the frequency; Width is the width of the wave. The Direction pop-up menu controls the direction of the effect. The Wave pop-up menu specifies the type of wave: sine, circle, triangle, or square.

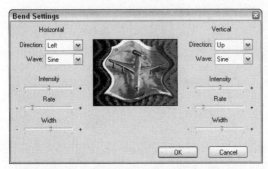

Figure 14-17: The Bend Settings dialog box.

Corner Pin

The Corner Pin effect allows you to distort an image by adjusting the Upper Left, Upper Right, Lower Left, and Lower Right values. Figure 14-18 shows an image after applying this effect.

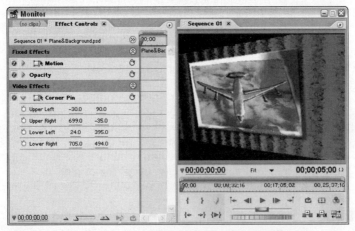

Figure 14-18: Image after applying the Corner Pin effect.

Lens Distortion

Use the Lens Distortion effect to simulate video being viewed through a distorted lens.

Use the Curvature slider in the Lens Distortion Settings dialog box, shown in Figure 14-19, to change the lens curve. Negative values make the curvature more concave (inward); positive values make the curvature more convex (outward). Vertical and Horizontal Decentering sliders change the focal point of the lens.

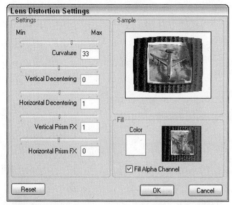

Figure 14-19: The Lens Distortion Settings dialog box.

Vertical and Horizontal Prism FX creates effects similar to changing Vertical and Horizontal Decentering. Use the Fill color swatch to change the background color. Click the Fill Alpha Channel check box to make background areas transparent based on the clip's alpha channel.

Mirror

Mirror creates a mirrored effect. In the Effect Controls window, click the Reflection center values to open the Edit Reflection Center dialog box to designate the X and Y coordinates of the reflection line. The reflection angle option enables you to choose where the reflection appears. The following degree settings should help orient you to how dragging the slider distorts the image:

◆ **0.** Left onto right side

◆ **90.** Right onto left side

◆ **180.** Top onto bottom

◆ **270.** Bottom onto top

Pinch

Pinch provides an effect similar to pinching and pulling the video image as if it were clay. In the Pinch Settings dialog box, shown in Figure 14-20, click and drag the amount slider to the right to pinch the image in; click and drag to the left to expand the image out. Figure 14-19 shows a frame after the Pinch effect is applied.

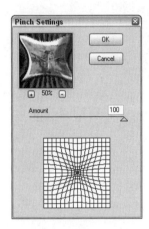

Figure 14-20: The Pinch Settings dialog box.

Polar Coordinates

Polar Coordinates can create a variety of unusual effects by changing the clip's X and Y coordinates to polar coordinates. In the polar coordinate system, the X and Y coordinates are distances radiating out of a focal point. By using this effect, you can transform a line into a half circle or horseshoe shape.

In the Effect Controls window, the Interpolation value controls the amount of the distortion — 0% provides no distortion; 100 % provides the most. In the Type of Conversion pop-up menu, Rect to Polar converts horizontal coordinates to Polar; Polar to Rect converts polar coordinates to rectangular ones. Figure 14-21 shows the Polar Coordinates effect with the Rect to Polar options selected.

Ripple

The Ripple effect turns a clip into rippled patterns. The Ripple Settings dialog box, shown in Figure 14-22, enables you to adjust the ripples on a horizontal and vertical plane and control the intensity and frequency of the ripples.

Figure 14-21: The Polar Coordinates settings and a preview.

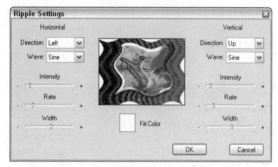

Figure 14-22: The Ripple Settings dialog box.

Shear

The Shear effect bends an image according to the curve specified in the Shear Settings dialog box, which is shown in Figure 14-23. If you shear the clip off screen, you can choose whether to have the image wrap so that it leaves one side of the frame and returns on the opposite side. To do this, choose the Wrap Around option. Otherwise, choose Repeat Edge Pixels. This option applies extra pixels to the image edges.

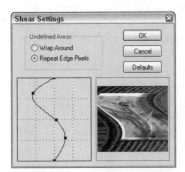

Figure 14-23: The Shear Settings dialog box.

Spherize

The Spherize effect turns a flat image into a spherical one. Use the Amount slider in the Spherize Settings dialog box (shown in Figure 14-24) to control the spherizing effect. Dragging the slider to the right increases the Amount value, providing a larger sphere. In the Mode pop-up menu, choose Normal for a standard sphere effect; choose Horizontal Only or Vertical Only to change directions.

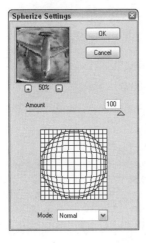

Figure 14-24: The Spherize Settings dialog box.

Transform

The Transform effect allows you to move an image's position, scale its height and weight, skew or rotate, and change its opacity, as shown in Figure 14-25. You can also use the Transform effect to change the position of a clip. To change the position of a clip, click the box next to the word *Position* in the Effect Controls window.

Then click in the Monitor window where you want the clip to move to. Use the Anchor Point option to move a clip based on its anchor point.

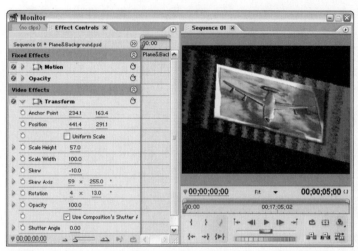

Figure 14- 25: A preview of the Transform effect in the Monitor window with the Transform options in the Effect Controls window.

Twirl

The Twirl effect can turn an image into twirling digital soup. Use the Angle values to control the degree of twirling. Larger angle settings create more twirling. Figure 14-26 shows a preview of the Twirl effect.

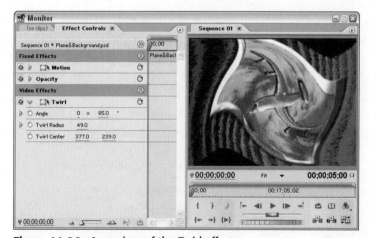

Figure 14-26: A preview of the Twirl effect.

Wave

The Wave effect creates wave-like effects that can make your clip look as if it were hit by a tidal wave. To control the effect, view the Preview window in the Wave Settings dialog box, shown in Figure 14-27, as you click and drag the sliders.

Figure 14-27: The Wave Settings dialog box.

Following is a brief description of the slider controls found in the Wave Settings dialog box:

- ✦ **Number of Generators.** Controls the amount of continuous waves.
- ✦ **Wavelength.** Changes the distance between wave crests.
- ✦ **Amplitude.** Changes the wave height.
- ✦ **Scale.** Controls the amount of horizontal and vertical distortion.
- ✦ **Undefined Areas.** If the Wave effect spills portions of your image off screen, choose Wrap Around to make the image wrap so that it comes out one side of the frame and returns on the opposite side. Otherwise, choose Repeat Edge Pixels to apply extra pixels to the image edges.
- ✦ **Type.** Controls the type of wave crests: Sine (waving), Triangle, or Square.
- ✦ **Randomize.** Randomizes the wavelength and amplitude.

ZigZag

The ZigZag effect distorts a clip outward from a center point. Use this effect to create great looking pond ripple effects The Amount field in the ZigZag Settings dialog box, shown in Figure 14-28, controls the degree of distortion. The Ridges field controls the number of zigzags from the middle to the edge of the clip.

In the Style pop-up menu, choose Pond Ripples to create ripples from the center of an image, as if a rock were dropped in a pond. Choose Out from Center to create zigzags that push outward from the center of the image. Choose Around Center to create zigzags that appear around the center.

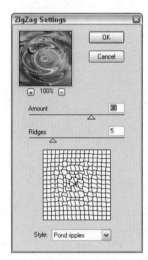

Figure 14-28: The ZigZag Settings dialog box.

The Image Control folder

The Image Control folder contains a variety of color special effects.

Black & White

The Black & White effect produces a grayscale version of a selected clip.

Color Balance (HLS)

The Color Balance HLS effect enables you to change and adjust colors using Hue, Lightness, and Saturation sliders in the Effect Controls window. Hue controls the color; Lightness controls how light and dark the color is; Saturation controls the intensity of the color.

Color Balance (RGB)

The Color Balance effect adds or subtracts red, green, or blue color values in a clip. Color values are easily added and subtracted by clicking the Red, Green, or Blue color sliders (see Figure 14-29). In the Effect Controls window, dragging the sliders to the left reduces the amount of color; dragging the sliders to the right adds color.

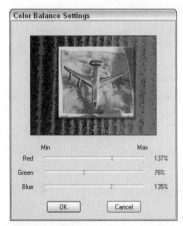

Figure 14-29: The Color Balance Settings dialog box.

Color Corrector

The Color Corrector effect has many controls that allow you to adjust black, white, and gray levels and color correct the color values of a clip for broadcast. For a full description on how to use this effect, turn to Chapter 18.

Color Match

The Color Match effect allows you to match the colors of one clip to another. For a full description on how to use this effect, turn to Chapter 18.

Color Offset

The Color Offset effect enables you to create 3D images out of 2D artwork by enabling you to shift the red, green, and blue color channels up, down, left, and right. Use the Offset slider in the Color Offset Settings dialog box, shown in Figure 14-30, to control the distance between each color channel. Using this effect, you can set up the image for viewing with 3D glasses.

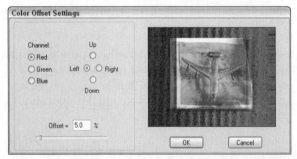

Figure 14-30: The Color Offset Settings dialog box.

Color Pass

The Color Pass effect converts all but one color in a clip to grayscale — or it can convert just one color in a clip to grayscale. Use this effect to draw interest to specific items in a clip. For example, you may want to show a grayscale party scene in which a grayscale man or woman is wearing a colored hat on his or her head, or holding a colored balloon.

Here's how to set the Color Pass color and use the filter:

1. **In the Color Pass Settings dialog box clip area (shown in Figure 14-31), click the color that you want to preserve.** Alternatively, you can click the swatch area and then choose a color in the Color Picker window.

2. **To increase or decrease the color range, drag the Similarity slider to the right or left.**

3. **To reverse the color effect (in other words, make all colors normal and gray except the selected color), click Reverse.**

Figure 14-31: The Color Pass Settings dialog box.

Color Replace

The Color Replace effect replaces one color or a range of colors with another color.

To choose a color or colors to replace, follow these steps:

1. **In the Color Replace Settings dialog box, shown in Figure 14-32, click the Target Color swatch area and then choose a color in the Color Picker window.**

2. **To choose the replacement color, click the Replace Color swatch.** Choose a color in the Color Picker window.

3. To increase or decrease the color range of the replacement color, drag the Similarity slider right or left.

4. Choose Solid Colors to replace the color with a solid color.

Figure 14-32: The Color Replace Settings dialog box.

Gamma Correction

The Gamma Correction effect enables you to adjust the midtone color levels of a clip. In the Gamma Correction Settings dialog box, shown in Figure 14-33, click and drag the Gamma slider to make the adjustment. Dragging to the left lightens midtones; dragging to the right darkens them.

Figure 14-33: The Gamma Correction Settings dialog box.

Median

The Median effect can be used for reducing noise. It creates the effect by taking the median pixel value of neighboring pixels and applying this value to pixels within the radius pixel area specified in the Effect Controls window. If you enter large values for the radius, your image begins to look as if it were painted. Click the Operate on Alpha option to apply the effect to the image's alpha channel as well as to the image.

Tint

Use the Tint effect to apply a color tint to your image. If desired, you can reassign the black-and-white portions of your clip with different colors by clicking the color swatch and choosing a color in the Color Picker window. Choose color intensity by clicking and dragging the slider in the Color Picker window.

 Note The Keying effects are discussed in detailed in Chapter 15.

The Perspective folder

You can use the effects in the Perspective folder to add depth to images, to create drop shadows, and to bevel image edges.

Basic 3D

The Basic 3D effect creates nice flipping and tilting effects. The Swivel slider in the Effect Controls window controls rotation. The Tilt slider adjusts the tilt of the image. Dragging the Distance to Image slider creates an illusion of distance by reducing or enlarging the image. Click the Show Specular Highlight to add a tiny flare of light to your image (indicated by a red + sign). Draw Preview enables you to view a wireframe simulation of the effect, which provides a good idea of how the effect will look without waiting for Premiere Pro to render it.

Bevel Alpha

The Bevel Alpha effect can add a three-dimensional effect to a two-dimensional image by beveling the image's alpha channel. This filter is especially handy for creating beveled effects with text. Sliders in the Effect Controls window enable you to fine-tune the effect by changing bevel edge thickness, light angle, and light intensity. Change the light color by clicking the color swatch and choosing a color in Premiere Pro's Color Picker window.

Bevel Edges

The Bevel Edges effect bevels an image and adds lighting to give a clip a three-dimensional appearance. Image edges created with this effect are sharper than those created with the Bevel Alpha effect. To determine image edges, this filter also uses the clip's alpha channel. Similar to Bevel Alpha, sliders in the Effect Controls window enable you to fine-tune the effect by changing bevel edge thickness, light angle, and light intensity. Change light color by clicking the color swatch and choosing a color in the Color Picker window.

Drop Shadow

The Drop Shadow effect applies a drop shadow to a clip, using the clip's alpha channel to determine image edges. Sliders enable you to control the shadow's opacity, direction, and distance from the original clip. You can change the light color by clicking the color swatch in the window and choosing a color from Premiere Pro's Color Picker window.

The Pixelate folder

The effects found in the Pixelate folder create special effects by shifting, moving, and remapping pixels and their color values. These effects can create dramatic color distortions in your image.

Crystallize

The Crystallize effect can create a crystal-like effect in your image by shifting colors that are similar together into a grid. The size of the grid is controlled by the Cell Size slider in the Crystallize Setting dialog box, as shown in Figure 14-34.

Figure 14-34: The Crystallize Settings dialog box.

Facet

The Facet effect creates a painterly effect by grouping similarly colored pixels together within a clip.

Pointillize

The Pointillize effect simulates a pointillist painting by making your clip appear as if it were created with tiny dots. You can make the dots bigger or smaller by changing the value in the Cell Size field in the Pointillize Settings dialog box, which is shown in Figure 14-35.

Figure 14-35: The Pointillize Settings dialog box.

The Render folder

The Render folder features the Lens Flare effect, which is similar to Adobe Photoshop's Lens Flare filter.

Lens Flare

The Lens Flare effect creates a flaring light effect in your image. In the Lens Flare Settings dialog box, use the mouse to pick the image position of the flare in the Preview area. Click and drag the slider to adjust flare brightness and then pick a lens: Zoom, 35 mm, or 105 mm. Figure 14-36 shows the Lens Flare Settings dialog box.

Figure 14-36: The Lens Flare Settings dialog box.

Lightning

The Lightning effect enables you to add lightning to a clip. With the Lightning setting, you can choose starting and ending points for the lightning. Moving the Segment slider to the right increases the amount of segments the lightning has. Moving the Segment slider to the left decreases the amount of segments.

Conversely, moving the other Lightning effect sliders to the right increases the effect; moving the slider to the left decreases it. You can stylize your lightning bolt by adjusting the Segments, Amplitude, Branching, Speed, Stability, Width, Force, and Blending Mode options. Figure 14-37 shows a lightning bolt created using the Lightning effect.

Figure 14-37: Image after applying the Lightning effect and Lighting options shown in the Effect Controls window.

Ramp

The Ramp effect allows you to create linear or radial blurs. Click the Ramp Shape pop-up menu to choose either Radial Ramp or Linear Ramp. You can set the start and end colors of the blur by clicking a color in your image and using the Eyedropper tool or by clicking the color swatch and using the Color Picker dialog box. Moving the Ramp Scale slider to the left creates a smoother blend. When the Blend Witness slider is set to 50, both the blend and image clip you are applying the effect to are set to 50% translucency. Moving the slider to the right makes the image clip more opaque. Moving the slider to the left makes the blend less opaque.

The Stylize folder

The effects found in the Stylize folder create a variety of effects that change images without creating major distortions. For example, the Emboss effect adds depth throughout your image, whereas the Tiles effect divides your image into mosaic tiles.

Alpha Glow

The Alpha Glow effect adds a glowing effect around alpha channel edges. In the Alpha Glow Settings dialog box, shown in Figure 14-38, use the Glow slider to control how far the glow extends from the alpha channel. Use the Brightness slider to increase and decrease brightness.

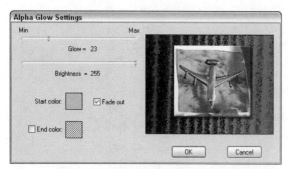

Figure 14-38: The Alpha Glow Settings dialog box.

In the dialog box, the Start color swatch represents the glow color. If you want to change the color, click the color swatch and choose a color from Premiere Pro's Color Picker window.

If you choose an end color, Premiere Pro adds an extra color at the edge of the glow. To create an end color, select the End color check box and click the color swatch to pick the color in the Color Picker window. To fade out the start color, click the Fade Out check box.

Color Emboss

The Color Emboss effect creates the same effect as Emboss (described next), except that it doesn't remove color.

Emboss

The Emboss effect creates a raised 3D effect from image edge areas in a clip. In the Effect Controls window, use the Direction slider to control the angle of the embossing. Drag the Relief slider to raise the emboss level to create a greater emboss effect. To create a more pronounced effect, add more contrast by dragging the Contrast slider to the right. Use the Blend with Original slider to blend shading of the embossing with the clip's original image.

Find Edges

Find Edges can make the image in a clip look as if it is a black-and-white sketch. The effect seeks out image areas of high contrast and turns them into black lines that appear against a white background, or as colored lines with a black background. In the Effect Controls window, use the Blend with Original slider to blend the lines with the original image. Figure 14-39 shows a preview of the Find Edges effect.

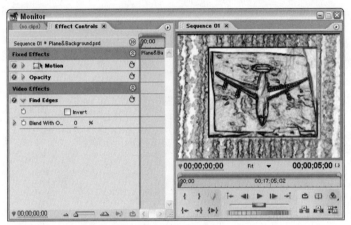

Figure 14-39: A preview of the Find Edges effect.

Mosaic

The Mosaic effect turns your image areas into rectangular tiles. In the Effect Controls window, enter the number of mosaic blocks in the Horizontal/Vertical blocks field. This effect can be animated for use as a transition, where normally the average of the colors in the other video track is used to pick tile color. However, if you choose the Sharp color option, Premiere Pro uses the pixel color in the center of the corresponding region in the other video track. Figure 14-40 shows a preview of the Mosaic effect.

Noise

The Noise effect randomly changes colors in a video clip to give your clip a grainy appearance. In the Effect Controls window, use the Amount of Noise slider to designate how much "noise," or graininess, you want added to the clip. The more noise you add, the more your image disappears into the noise you create.

If you choose the Color Noise option, the effect randomly changes the pixels in the image. If Color Noise is turned off, the same amount of noise is added to each red, green, and blue channel in the image.

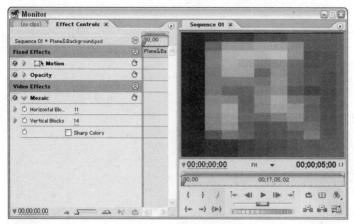

Figure 14-40: A preview of the Mosaic effect.

Clipping is a mathematical stopgap that prevents noise from becoming larger than a set value. When the Clipping option is not selected, noise values start at lower values after reaching a certain point. If you turn Clipping off, you may find that your image completely disappears into the noise.

Replicate

The Replicate effect creates multiple versions of the clip within the frame. The effect produces this replication effect by creating tiles and placing multiple versions of the clip into the tiles. Dragging the Replicate Settings Count slider in the Replicate Settings dialog box (shown in Figure 14-41) to the right increases the number of tiles on-screen.

Figure 14-41: The Replicate Settings dialog box.

Solarize

The Solarize effect creates a positive and negative version of your image and then blends them together to create the solarizing effect. This can produce a lightened version of your image with darkened edges. In the Solarize Settings dialog box, shown in Figure 14-42, click and drag the Threshold slider to control the brightness level at which the Solarizing effect begins.

Figure 14-42: The Solarize Settings dialog box.

Strobe Light

The Strobe Light effect creates the illusion of a strobe light flashing at regular or random intervals in your clip. In the Effect Controls window, click the color swatch to choose a color for the strobe effect. Enter the duration of the strobe flash in the Duration field. In the Strobe Period field, enter the duration between strobe effects. (Duration is measured from the time the last strobe flashed — not when the flash ends.) If you want to create a random strobe effect, drag the Random Strobe Probability slider to the right. (The greater the probability setting, the more random the effect.)

In the Strobe area of the Effect Controls window, choose Operates on Color only if you want the strobe effect to be applied to all color channels. Choose Make Layer Transparent to make the track transparent when the strobe goes off. If you choose Operates on Color, you can select an arithmetic operator from the Strobe Operator pop-up menu that can further alter the strobe effect.

Note   If you set the strobe period longer than the strobe duration, the strobe will be constant — not flashing.

Texturize

The Texturize effect can create texture in a clip by applying texture, such as sand or rocks, found in one track to another track. To choose the video track supplying the texture, click in the Texture Layer pop-up menu in the Effect Controls window and choose the track. Click and drag the Light Direction and Contrast slider to create the best effect. In the Texture Placement pop-up menu, choose Tile Texture to repeat the texture over the clip. Choose Center Texture to place the texture in the clip's center, and then choose Stretch Texture to stretch the text over the entire frame area.

Tiles

The Tiles effect turns your image into tiles. In the Tiles Settings dialog box, shown in Figure 14-43, choose how many tiles you want to see and offset the tiles by entering a percentage in the Tiles Offset field. In the Fill Empty Areas With field, choose the color you want to appear between the tiles. Background and Foreground colors fills the space between the tiles with white; Inverse Image uses a negative version of the clip to fill the space; Unaltered Image simply uses the clip. Figure 14-44 shows a frame with the Tiles effect applied.

Figure 14-43: The Tiles Settings dialog box.

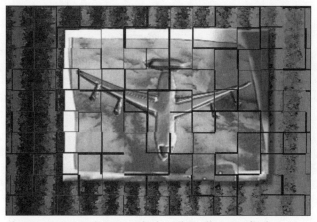

Figure 14-44: A frame with the Tiles effect applied.

Wind

As you probably guessed, the Wind effect applies a windswept look to your clip. To create a simple wind effect, choose Wind in the Method area of the Wind Settings dialog box, shown in Figure 14-45. For a tornado-like blast, choose Blast. The Stagger choice creates a bit less wind. In the Direction section, choose either From the Left or From the Right.

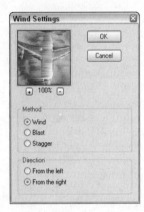

Figure 14-45: The Wind Settings dialog box.

The Time folder

The Time folder contains effects that specifically relate to different frames in the selected clip.

Echo

The Echo effect creates the visual version of an echo, as shown in Figure 14-46. In other words, frames from the selected clip are repeated again and again. The effect is only effective in clips that display motion. Depending on the clip, Echo can produce a repeated visual effect or possibly a streaking type of special effect. In the Effect Controls window, use the Echo Time slider to control the time between the repetitions. Drag the Number of Echoes to designate how many frames to combine for the effect.

Use the Starting Intensity slider to control intensity of the first frame. A setting of 1 provides full intensity; .25 provides quarter intensity. The Decay slider controls how quickly the echo dissipates. If the Decay slider is set to .25, the first echo will be .25 of the starting intensity, the next echo will be .25 of the previous echo, and so on.

The Echo operator pop-up menu creates effects by combining the pixel values of the echoes. Following is a review of the pop-up menu choices:

✦ **Add.** Adds pixel values.

✦ **Maximum.** Uses maximum pixels value of echoes.

✦ **Minimum.** Uses minimum pixel value of echoes.

✦ **Screen.** Similar to Add, but less likely to produce white streaks.

✦ **Composite in Back.** Uses the clip's alpha channels and composites them starting at the back.

✦ **Composite in Front.** Uses the clip's alpha channels and composites them starting at the front.

Note To combine an Echo effect with a Motion Settings effect, create a virtual clip and apply the effect to the virtual clip.

Figure 14-46: A preview of the Echo effect and its settings.

Posterize Time

The Posterize Time effect grabs control of a clip's frame rate settings and substitutes the frame rate specified in the Effect Controls frame rate slider.

The Transform folder

The Transform folder is filled with Transformation effects from Adobe After Effects that enable you to flip, crop, and roll a video clip, and change the camera view.

Camera View

The Camera View effect simulates viewing the clip at a different camera angle. In the Camera View Settings dialog box, shown in Figure 14-47, use the sliders to control the effect. Click and drag the Latitude slider to flip the clip vertically. Use the Longitude slider to flip horizontally. The Roll slider simulates rolling the camera, thus rotating the clip. Click and drag the Focal Length slider to make the view wider or narrower. The Distance slider enables you to change the distance between the imaginary camera and the clip. Use the Zoom slider to zoom in and out. To create a fill color to use as a background, click the color swatch and choose a color in Premiere Pro's Color Picker window. If you want the background area to be transparent, choose Fill Alpha Channel. (The clip must include an alpha channel to use this option.)

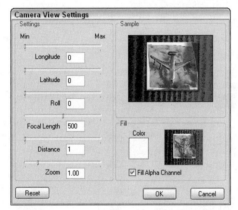

Figure 14-47: The Camera View Settings dialog box.

Clip

The Clip effect hides the frame boundaries — similar to a Crop effect, except that the clip is not resized. The effect can be used to hide noise at image edges.

To use the Clip effect, drag the sliders in the Clipping Settings dialog box, shown in Figure 14-48, to clip the top, left, bottom, and/or right sides of the clip. Choose whether you want to clip according to pixels or percent. Click the Fill Color swatch to open Premiere Pro's Color Picker and choose a background color.

Crop

The Crop effect provides the same settings as the Clip effect except that with the Crop effect Premiere Pro resizes the clip according to the dialog box settings.

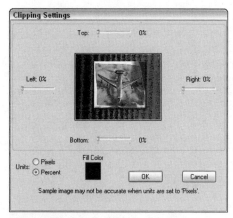

Figure 14-48: The Clipping Settings dialog box.

The Edge Feather

The Edge Feather effect allows you to create a 3D feathered effect around the edge of the image clip you are working with. To apply a feathered edge, click Setup in the Effect Controls window to display the Edge Feather Settings dialog box, shown in Figure 14-49. In the dialog box, move the Feather Value slider to the right to increase the size of the edge of the feather.

Figure 14-49: The Edge Feather Settings dialog box.

Horizontal Flip

The Horizontal Flip effect flips the frame left to right.

Horizontal Hold

The Horizontal Hold effect is named after the horizontal hold knob found on a television set. As you might guess, the effect simulates turning the horizontal hold knob. In the Horizontal Hold Settings dialog box, shown in Figure 14-50, click and drag the slider to create the skewing effect.

Figure 14-50: The Horizontal Hold Settings dialog box.

Roll

The Roll effect provides a rotating effect. The Roll Settings dialog box, shown in Figure 14-51, enables you to roll the image left, right, up, or down.

Figure 14-51: The Roll Settings dialog box.

Vertical Flip

The Vertical Flip effect flips your clip vertically. The result is an upside-down version of the original clip.

Vertical Hold

The Vertical Hold effect simulates turning the vertical hold knob found on a television set. Use the slider in the Vertical Hold Settings dialog box to create the effect you want.

The Video folder

The effects found in the Video folder simulate electronic changes to a video signal. These effects need only be applied if you are outputting your production to videotape.

Broadcast Colors

If you are outputting your production to videotape, you may want to run the Broadcast Colors effect to improve color output quality. As we discuss in Chapters 11 and 18, the gamut, or range of video colors, is smaller than the color gamut of a computer monitor. To use the Broadcast Color effect, choose either NTSC for American television or PAL for European television in the Broadcast Locale pop-up menu. Then choose a method in the How to Make Colors Safe pop-up menu. Following is an explanation of the choices available in this pop-up menu:

- ✦ **Reduce Luminance.** Reduces pixels' brightness values, moving the pixel values toward black.

- ✦ **Reduce Saturation.** Brings pixel values closer to gray. (This makes the colors less intense.)

- ✦ **Key out Unsafe.** Colors that fall beyond the TV gamut become transparent.

- ✦ **Key in Safe.** Colors that are within the TV gamut are transparent.

In the Maximum Signal Field, enter the IRE breakpoint value. (IRE measures image luminance.) Any levels above this value are altered. If you are unsure of what value to use, leave the default setting of 110.

Field Interpolate

The Field Interpolate effect creates missing scan lines from the average of other lines.

Reduce Interlace Flicker

The Reduce Interlace Flicker effect softens horizontal lines in an attempt to reduce interlace flicker (an odd or even interlace line that appears during video capture).

Note Choosing the wrong field settings in the Project Settings dialog box can increase flicker. To access the Project Settings dialog box, choose Project ➪ Project Settings ➪ General. These settings are covered in more detail in Chapter 5.

Summary

Premiere Pro's Video Effects provide dozens of special effects that can add interest to or correct video.

✦ To add an effect to a clip, drag the effect from the Effects window to the clip in the Timeline.

✦ Use the Effect Controls window to specify settings for effects, to turn on and off preview, and to enable and disable keyframing.

✦ Set keyframes where effect settings change in the Timeline.

✦   ✦   ✦

Superimposing

By telling a story or providing information using innovative effects, you can ensure that you get your message across. One of the best techniques for doing so creatively is to use superimposition options. Adobe Premiere Pro helps you create sophisticated transparency effects by enabling you to overlay two or more video clips and then blend the two together. For more sophisticated effects, the Premiere Pro Video Effects Keying options provide a host of different effects that enable you to *key* out (hide) different parts of the image area in one track and fill them with the underlying video in the track beneath it.

This chapter provides a look at two powerful methods of creating transparency: the Premiere Pro Opacity option and the Premiere Pro keying options found in the Video Effects folder of the Effects window. The Opacity option enables you to create blending effects by changing the opacity of one video track. The Keying folder in the Effects window is home to 14 different keying options that enable you to create transparency based on color, alpha channels, or brightness levels. As you read through this chapter, think about all the different ways that you can apply the effects in your current or next project. Using transparency creatively will undoubtedly add to its success.

If you put a video clip or still in Video track 2 and another in Video track 1, you will only see the image that is in the top video track onscreen — in this case, Video track 2. To see both images, you need to either fade Video track 2 or apply a keying effect to it.

Any video track higher than Video track 1 can be faded using Premiere Pro's Opacity option or superimposed using the keying options. Throughout this book, you find various examples of transparency effects. To review some of these examples, see Chapter 11, Chapter 17, and Chapter 28.

Fading Video Tracks

You can fade an entire video clip or still image over a video clip or another still image. The top video clip or still image is faded over the bottom one. When you fade a video clip or still image, you are changing the opacity of the clip or image. Any video track, except for Video track 1, can be used as a superimposed track and can be faded. Premiere Pro's fade option appears when you expand a video track. When a video track is expanded, you can display the Opacity by clicking on the Show Keyframes icon and choosing Show Opacity Handles. The Opacity rubberband line is found underneath a clip when the track is expanded.

Cross-Reference Fading video tracks works similarly to fading sound tracks. For more information on fading sound tracks, see Chapter 8.

Here's how to fade a track:

1. **Choose File ➪ New ➪ Project to create a new project.** Make sure that you use the proper preset. If you are creating a high-resolution project, you may want to use a DV preset. If not, use a Non-DV preset.

2. **Choose File ➪ Import to import two files.** Locate either two video clips or a video clip and a still image. Press and hold the Ctrl key to select more than one file. Click Open to import the files.

On the DVD-ROM If you want, you can use the two video clips that we used in our fade example, shown in Figures 15-1 to 15-5. In the DVD that accompanies this book in the Digital Vision folder that is in the Chapter 15 folder, you will find two Digital Vision video clips that you can use, Electro 579018F.mov and Electro 579023F.mov, and a sound clip, City Life/Urban Moods 672015aw.wav.

3. **When the files appear in the Project window, drag and drop one file to Video track 2 and the other to Video track 1 in the Timeline window.** You will change the opacity of the clip in Video track 2. Make sure that the files in the video tracks overlap each other. Select the clip in Video track 2.

4. **To zoom into the Timeline, click and drag the time Zoom level slider to the right.** The time Zoom level slider is at the bottom of the Timeline window. You can also click the Zoom In button or press the equal sign on your keyboard.

5. **To expand Video track 2, click the Collapse/Expand Track icon to the left of the word Video.**

6. **Click the Show Keyframes icon and choose Show Opacity Handles to reveal the Opacity rubberband line, shown in Figure 15-1.** Notice that a white line beneath the video clip is displayed.

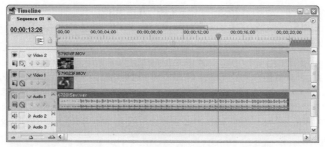

Figure 15-1: The Opacity rubberband line enables you to change the opacity of a video clip.

7. **To decrease the opacity of the file in Video track 2, use the Pen in the Tools palette) to click and drag the white Opacity rubberband line down.** As you drag, the Opacity percent value is displayed. The Opacity percent value is also displayed in the Effect Controls window. To see the Opacity value, click the Collapse/Expand Track icon to display the Opacity percent value.

To slowly fade a video clip, you need to set the left side of the Opacity rubberband line so that it is at the top-left position and drag the far-right side down, as shown in Figure 15-2. To do so, you need to set two points (handles) on the Opacity rubberband line: one at the beginning of the clip and one at the end of the clip.

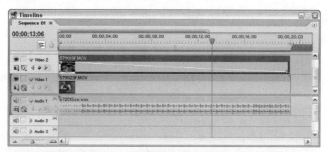

Figure 15-2: The Opacity rubberband line in the Timeline window displays a gradual fade.

8. **To set the first point (handle), move the current-time indicator (Edit line) in the Timeline window to the beginning of the clip and then click the Add/Remove Keyframes button.**

9. **To set the second point, move the current-time indicator (Edit line) in the Timeline window to the end of the clip and click the Add/Remove Keyframes button.**

10. **Use the Selection or Pen tool to drag the last handle down.** The first handle should be at 100%. If it isn't, click the Go to Previous Keyframe button, then click and drag the handle up.

   The fade in Figure 15-2 is gradual because the fade line gradually steps down. The top of the fade line indicates that the video clip is 100 percent opaque. When the fade line follows a long, slow, diagonal path from the top of the fade bar (100 percent opaque) to the bottom (100 percent transparent), the clip gradually fades out.

11. **Choose Window ⇨ Effect Controls to display the Effect Controls window.** To view the Opacity percent in the Effect Controls window (as shown in Figure 15-3), click the Collapse/Expand Track icon in front of Opacity. Then click the Previous Keyframe or Next Keyframe button to move the current-time indicator (Edit line) to the Opacity keyframes on the Timeline. You can also drag the current-time indicator (Edit line) along the Effect Controls Timeline to see the percent values of the gradual fade.

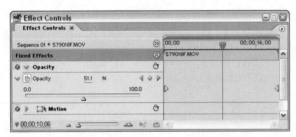

Figure 15-3: The Effect Controls window shows the Opacity percentage value for the selected clip.

12. **To preview the fade effect, click the Play button in the Monitor window.**

You can also fade clips into one another using transitions. For more information on working with transitions, see Chapter 10.

13. **Before you save you work, you may want to import a sound clip into your project.** If the imported sound clip is too long, use the Razor tool to edit it. For more information on working with sound, turn to Chapter 8.

Adding opacity handles with the Pen tool

To create more sophisticated fades, you can add more handles to the Opacity rubberband line using the Pen tool. After you have handles, you can then drag different segments of the Opacity rubberband line. Here's how:

1. **With the Pen tool selected, move the cursor over the Opacity rubberband line (fade line).** Move over to the area where you want to add a handle, then press and hold Ctrl as you click to create a handle. A handle appears as a yellow diamond on the Opacity rubberband line (fade line).

2. **To create a few handles, press and hold Ctrl as you click the Opacity rubberband line a few times.**

3. **Now that you have a few handles on the Opacity rubberband line, you can move them, as shown in Figure 15-4.**

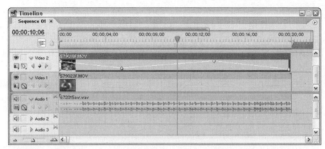

Figure 15-4: You can create handles on the Opacity rubberband line to create a fade.

4. **If you've created too many handles and want to delete one, just click a handle in the Timeline window, then press Delete.** You can also click a keyframe in the Effect Controls window and press Delete.

Tip

To delete all the opacity keyframes from a timeline, click the Toggle Animation icon in the Effect Controls window. When the Warning prompt appears, click OK to delete all existing keyframes.

5. **Click and drag the handle to move up and/or down as shown in Figure 15-4.** When you click the handle, at the bottom of the Pen icon, there should be a yellow diamond. A plus sign indicates that you are going to add a handle when you click the Opacity rubberband line. Make sure you see the yellow diamond, and reposition the mouse more accurately over the handle you want to move.

Tip

Use the Go to Previous Keyframe and the Go to Next Keyframe buttons in the Timeline window to move quickly from one keyframe to another.

6. **Use the Effect Controls window to display the fade level percentage, as shown in Figure 15-5.** To display the Effect Controls window, choose Window ⇨ Effect Controls. Notice all the Opacity keyframes. Either click a keyframe to view its percentage or click and drag on the Timeline to scroll through the different percentages.

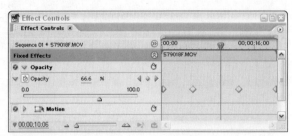

Figure 15-5: The Effect Controls window displays the Opacity effect for the selected video clip.

For a quick preview, click and drag the Edit line through the Timeline (of either the Timeline or Effect Controls window) to preview the fade effect in the Monitor window. To display the Monitor window, choose Window ➪ Monitor. You can also preview an effect by clicking the Play button in the Monitor.

7. **Choose File ➪ Save to save your work.**

Note

If desired, you can fade more video tracks. Just import more video clips and/or still images into the Project window. Create new video tracks and drag the video clips and/or images into the new video tracks. Then use the Opacity rubberband line to fade the video tracks.

Adjusting the Opacity rubberband line using the Pen tool

The Pen tool enables you to move either an entire Opacity rubberband line as a unit or move two handles simultaneously. Follow these steps to use the Pen tool to move two handles simultaneously.

Note

Before you proceed to Step 1, you should have a Premiere Pro project with a clip in Video track 2. Video track 2 should be selected and expanded, and the Opacity rubberband line should be displayed. These steps are covered in the "Fading Video Tracks" section earlier in this chapter.

1. **Use the Pen tool to create two handles on the Opacity rubberband line.** Make the handles so that they appear at the beginning and end of the Opacity rubberband line. Select the Pen tool.

2. **Use the Pen tool to click the Opacity rubberband line to add two more handles.** Place the handles in the middle of the clip. Try to spread all the handles equally apart from each other.

3. **Move the Pen tool between the two middle handles.** When an up and down arrow icon appears next to the Pen tool, click the Opacity rubberband line and drag down. When you click and drag between the two handles, the handles and the Opacity rubberband line between the two handles move as a unit. The Opacity rubberband line outside the handles gradually moves, as shown in Figure 15-6.

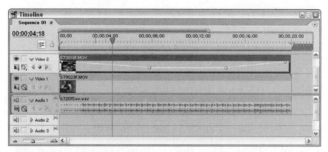

Figure 15-6: The Opacity rubberband line after being adjusted with the Pen tool.

The Pen tool also enables you to move just a section of the Opacity rubberband line completely separate from the rest. Here's how:

Note

Before you proceed to Step 1, you should have a Premiere Pro project with a clip in Video track 2. Video track 2 should be selected and expanded, and the Opacity rubberband line should be displayed. These steps are covered in the "Fading Video Tracks" section earlier in this chapter.

1. **Start with an Opacity rubberband line that has only a beginning and ending handle.**

2. **Create two handles side by side in the middle of the Opacity rubberband line.**

3. **Select the Pen tool, if it is not selected.**

4. **Use the Pen tool to select the first handle.** Then press and hold the Shift key as you select the second handle.

5. **Now click and drag the Opacity rubberband line down.** Notice that only the line between the start of the Opacity rubberband line and second handle moves, as shown in Figure 15-7. The line moves at a constant percentage.

6. **Use the Pen tool to select the third handle.** Press and hold the Shift key as you select the last handle.

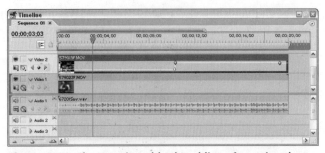

Figure 15-7: The Opacity rubberband line after using the Pen tool to move separate sections independently.

7. **Now, click and drag the Opacity rubberband line down.** Notice that only the Opacity rubberband line between the third and last handle moves, as shown in Figure 15-7. The line moves at a constant percentage.

8. **Move the Pen tool to the right of the third handle and to the left of the last handle.** Then press Ctrl as you click the Opacity rubberband line. As you click, notice that you create a handle. With this handle selected, click and drag the Opacity rubberband line down in the shape of a V, as shown in Figure 15-8.

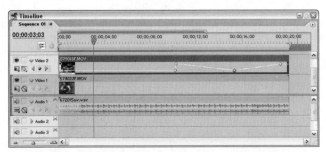

Figure 15-8: The Opacity rubberband line after using the Pen tool to create a V shape.

Setting opacity keyframes using the Effect Controls window and the Timeline window

You can set opacity keyframes by using either the Effect Controls window or the Timeline window. Here's how to set keyframes using the Timeline window.

Note   Before you proceed to Step 1, you should have a Premiere Pro project with a clip in Video track 2, and the track should be selected.

1. **Click the Collapse/Expand Track icon to expand Video track 2.**

2. **Click the Show Keyframes icon and choose Show Keyframes.**

3. **Click in the pop-up menu from the title bar of the clip in Video track 2 and choose Opacity.**

4. **Move the current-time indicator (Edit line) to where you want to set a keyframe and click the Add/Remove Keyframe icon to add a keyframe.**

5. **Repeat Step 4 as many times as you need.**

6. **Use the Selection tool to set the opacity for each keyframe.** With the Selection tool selected, click a keyframe and drag it either up or down on the Opacity rubberband line to where you want the opacity value to be.

Notice that the keyframes that you created using the Timeline window now appear in the Effect Controls window. You can continue editing the keyframes in either the Timeline window or the Effect Controls window. You can also preview the effect of the opacity keyframes by moving the current-time indicator on the Timeline of either the Timeline window or the Effect Controls window.

Here's how to add keyframes using the Effect Controls window.

Note

Before you proceed to Step 1, you should have a Premiere Pro project with a clip in Video track 2, and the track should be expanded.

1. **Click the Collapse/Expand Opacity icon to display the Opacity options.**

2. **Move the current-time indicator (Edit line) in the Effect Controls window to where you want to set a keyframe.**

3. **Adjust the Opacity percent value.**

4. **Click the Toggle Animation icon to set a keyframe.** The keyframe is set with the current Opacity value at the location of the current-time indicator.

5. **To set another keyframe, move the current-time indicator to the desired location.**

6. **Click the Toggle Keyframe button to create a keyframe at the position of the current-time indicator (Edit line).** Then adjust the Opacity value.

7. **Another way to create a keyframe on the Timeline in the Effect Controls window is to move the current-time indicator (Edit line) to where you want to set a keyframe.** Then adjust the Opacity value. Notice that as you adjust the Opacity value that a keyframe is created. As long as the Toggle Animation icon is on, Premiere Pro continues to record your actions. Every time you move the current-time indicator (Edit line) and adjust the Opacity value, Premiere Pro adds a Keyframe to the opacity Timeline.

8. **If you decide you want to delete all the keyframes and start all over again, just click the Toggle Animation icon.** When the warning prompt appears, click OK.

Superimposing Tracks Using the Keying Effects

You can superimpose a video clip and/or still image over another one using the Keying options, which are found in the Keying folder, which is in the Video Effects folder in the Effects window. In the Keying folder, you have 14 key types to pick from. Using the Key options is called *keying*. Keying makes part of the image transparent. The following sections cover how to use the different key options.

Displaying the Keying effects

To display and experiment with the Keying options, shown in Figure 15-9, you first need to have a Premiere Pro project onscreen. Either load an existing Premiere Pro project or create a new one by choosing File ➪ New ➪ Project. Import two video clips into the new project.

Figure 15-9: The Keying effects are in the Keying folder, which is in the Video Effects folder in the Effects window.

If you want, you can use one of the video clips found in the Chapter 15 folder that is located in the Tutorial Projects folder on the DVD that accompanies this book. Most of the images shown in this chapter are located on the DVD.

To display the Keying folder, follow these steps:

1. **Drag a clip from the Project window to Video track 1.**

2. **Drag a clip from the Project window to Video track 2.**

3. **Click and drag the clip in Video track 2 so that it overlaps the clip in Video track 1.**

4. **Select the clip in Video track 2.** This is the clip that you apply a key effect to.

5. **Choose Window ➪ Effects.** In the Effects window, click the Collapse/Expand triangle in front of the Video Effects folder. To display the Keying options, click the Collapse/Expand triangle in front of the Keying folder.

   In the Keying folder, you have 14 key types to choose from: Alpha Adjust, Blue Screen Key, Chroma Key, Difference Matte Key, Garbage Matte, Green Screen Key, Image Matte Key, Luma Key, Multiply Key, Non Red Key, RGB Difference Key, Remove Matte, Screen Key, and Track Matte Key.

6. **To apply a key effect, click and drag it onto the clip in Video track 2 or into the Effect Controls window.**

   Each Keying effect has it own set of controls that you can adjust. The controls that are displayed are based on the key effect that you choose. To learn more about the Key type effects and their controls, proceed to the following sections.

7. **To preview the Keying effect, you can move either the current-time indicator in the Timeline window or the Effect Controls window.** You can also click the Play button in the Monitor window. By default, the preview quality is set to Automatic Quality. To change the preview quality, click the Monitor pop-up menu and choose Highest Quality or Draft Quality. To render the work area, choose Sequence ➪ Render Work Area.

8. **To preview the clip without the Keying effect, you can choose Effect Enabled from the Effect Controls window pop-up menu, or you can click the Toggle the Effect On or Off button in front of the Keying effect.**

Applying Keying effects using keyframes

Premiere Pro allows you to animate a Keying effect control over time using keyframes. You can either add keyframes using the Effect Controls window or the Timeline window.

Here's how to animate a Keying effects control using the Effect Controls window:

 Note
Before you proceed to Step 1, you should have a Premiere Pro project with a clip in Video track 2 and another in Video track 1.

1. Click and drag a Keying effect to the clip in Video track 2.

2. Select the clip in Video track 2 if it is not already selected.

3. Next click the Collapse/Expand triangle in front of the Keying effect to display its controls.

4. To animate a Keying effect control over time, move the current-time indicator (Edit line) to where you want to add your first keyframe.

5. Click the Toggle Animation icon in front of the control to add a keyframe.

6. Make the desired adjustments to the control.

7. **To create a second keyframe, move the current-time indicator (Edit line) to a new location, then adjust the control.** As you adjust the control, a keyframe is added to the control's Timeline. While the Toggle Animation icon is turned on, every time you move the current-time indicator and adjust the control, a keyframe is added to the control's Timeline.

Note

In the Effect Controls window, you can click the Toggle Keyframe button to add keyframes. You can also move to and from keyframes by clicking on the Next Keyframe and Previous Keyframe buttons.

8. To move a keyframe, click and drag it to its new location.

9. To edit a keyframe, move the current-time indicator (Edit line) over the Keyframe and adjust the control.

10. To delete a keyframe, click the keyframe and press Delete.

11. **To delete all the keyframes for a control and start all over again, click the Toggle Animation icon.** When the warning prompt appears, click OK.

Here's how to animate a Keying effects control using the Timeline window.

Note

Before you proceed to Step 1, you should have a Premiere Pro project with a clip in Video track 2 and another in Video track 1. The clip in Video track 2 should have a Keying effect applied to it, and the track should be selected in the Timeline window.

1. Click the Collapse/Expand triangle in front of Video track 2 to expand the track.

2. Click the Show Keyframes icon and choose Show Keyframes.

3. Click the video clip's pop-up menu in the title bar and pick a Keying effect control.

4. Move the current-time indicator (Edit line) to where you want to add a keyframe and click the Add/Remove Keyframe button to add a keyframe.

5. In the Effect Controls window, make the adjustments to the control.

6. **To add a second keyframe, move the current-time indicator (Edit line) to a new location.** Then adjust the control. As you adjust the control, a second keyframe is applied.

7. **To edit keyframes, select the desired keyframe you want to edit by clicking on either the Go to Next Keyframe or the Go to Previous Keyframe button.** Then edit the Keyframe.

Chrome Key

The Chrome Key option in the Keying folder enables you to key out a specific color or a range of colors. This key is often planned during preproduction so that the video is shot against one colored background. To select the color to key out, use the Eyedropper tool to click the background area of the image thumbnail. Alternatively, you can click in the color swatch (under the word *Color*) and choose a key color from the Premiere Pro color picker.

To fine-tune the key, click and drag the sliders and make adjustments to the following options:

✦ **Similarity.** Click and drag to the left or right to increase or decrease the range of colors that will be made transparent.

✦ **Blend.** Click and drag to the right to create more of a blend between the two clips. Dragging to the left produces the opposite effect.

✦ **Threshold.** Clicking and dragging to the right keeps more shadow areas in the clip. Dragging to the left produces the opposite effect.

✦ **Cutoff.** Clicking and dragging to the right darkens shadow areas. Dragging to the right lightens shadow areas. Note that if you drag beyond the level set in the Threshold slider, gray and transparent areas become inverted.

✦ **Smoothing.** This control sets anti-aliasing, which blends pixel colors to create smoother edges. Choose High for most smoothing, Low for some smoothing, or None for no smoothing. Choosing None is often the best choice when keying titles.

✦ **Mask Only.** Selecting the Mask Only option causes only the alpha channel of the clip to be displayed.

Figure 15-10 shows a few frames from a project using the Chroma Key type. The frames show an athlete jumping through a yellow-to-pink gradient. To create the project, we imported a video clip of the athlete into Video track 1 and imported a still image of a yellow-to-pink gradient into Video track 2. The Timeline window for the project is shown in Figure 15-11. In Audio track 1, we placed Digital Vision's Acoustic Chillout 730006aw.wav. To apply the Key effect, we selected the still image in Video track 2 and dragged the Chroma Key effect over it. In the Chroma Key settings, we set the Color to yellow and adjusted the Similarity, Blend, Threshold, and Cutoff values so that we could see the Athlete jumping through the gradient. The controls used to create the project (in Figure 15-10) are shown in Figure 15-12.

On the DVD-ROM   If you want, you can use the files we used to create the Chroma Key project. The athlete clip is Digital Vision's Triangle Sports TRB05005.mov, Digital Vision's Acoustic Chillout 730006aw.wav, and the yellow-and-pink gradient is a Photoshop file (GRADIENT.psd). The clips are found in the Chapter 15 folder that is located in the Tutorial Projects folder on the DVD that accompanies this book.

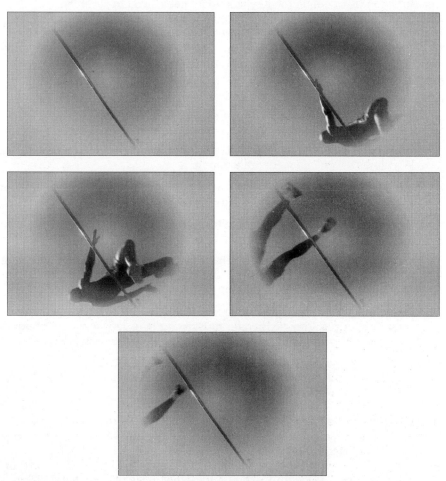

Figure 15-10: An athlete seen through a gradient, in a project using the Chroma key type.

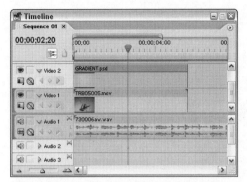

Figure 15-11: The Timeline used to create a project using the Chroma Key type.

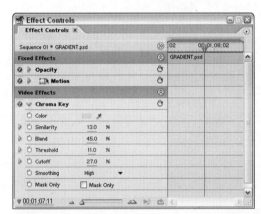

Figure 15-12: The Effect Controls window with Chroma Key settings used to create the project shown in Figure 15-10.

RGB Difference Key

The RGB Difference Key is an easy-to-use version of the Chroma Key option. Use this key when precise keying is not required or when the image being keyed appears in front of a bright background. As with the Chroma Key, RGB Difference Key provides Similarity and Smoothing options but does not provide Blend, Threshold, or Cutoff controls.

Figure 15-13 shows a frame from the clip from the previous section with the RGB Difference Key type applied instead of the Chroma Key type (as was shown in Figure 15-10). Notice that the edges of the gradient do not slowly fade out into soft edges but rather end abruptly. Figure 15-14 shows the Effect Controls window with the RGB Difference Key settings used in Figure 15-13.

Figure 15-13: A frame with the RGB Difference Key type applied to the clip from the project in the previous section.

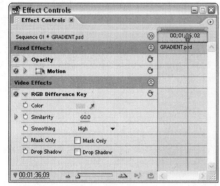

Figure 15-14 The Effect Controls window with the RGB Difference Key type options.

Blue Screen and Green Screen keys

Blue and green are traditional keys used in broadcast television where announcers are often shown in front of a blue or green background. The Blue Screen keys out well lit blue backgrounds. The Green Screen keys out well lit green areas. These keys have the following options:

✦ **Threshold.** Start by dragging to the left to key out more green and blue areas.

✦ **Cutoff.** Click and drag to the right to fine-tune the key effect.

✦ **Smoothing.** This control sets anti-aliasing, which blends pixel colors to create smoother edges. Choose High for most smoothing, Low for some smoothing, or None for no smoothing. Choosing None is often the best choice when keying titles.

✦ **Mask Only.** Allows you to choose whether to display the clip's alpha channel.

Normally when using the Blue or Green Screen Key type, you would videotape a person or object against either a properly lit blue or green background. This way you can import the video clip into Premiere Pro and use either the Blue Screen or Green Screen Key types to remove the background and replace it with any image your heart desires. In our example of a Green Screen Key type, we used two Digital Vision video clips: Working Numbers 577010f.mov and NightMoves 705014f.mov. The Working Numbers clip is pool balls falling onto a green pool top. Frames from this clip are shown in Figure 15-15. The NightMoves clip is of people playing pool on a red pool top. Frames from this clip are shown in Figure 15-16. Figure 15-17 shows a few frames from the Green Screen Key type project.

In Video track 1, we placed the NightMoves 705014f.mov clip. We placed the Working Numbers 577010f.mov clip in Video track 2 and applied the Green Screen Key type. In order to see more of the clip in Video track 1, we reduced the Green Screen Key type Threshold option to 44%. Figure 15-18 shows the Effect Controls window with the Green Screen Key type options. In the Effect Controls window, you can see that we applied the Brightness & Contrast Video Effect. The final project was a little too dark, so we used a Video Effect to lighten it. In Audio track 1, we placed Digital Vision's Acoustic Chillout 730006aw.wav. Figure 15-19 shows the Timeline window that we used to create the project. In Audio track 1, we placed Digital Vision's Acoustic Chillout 730006aw.wav.

Figure 15-15: Shows a few frames from the video clip in Video track 2 of the Green Screen Key type project.

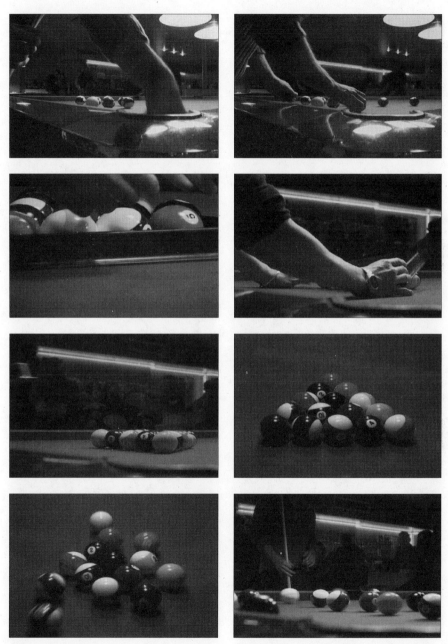

Figure 15-16: Shows a few frames from the video clip in Video track 1 of the Green Screen Key type project.

Figure 15-17: Shows a few frames from a project created using the Green Screen Key effect to superimpose the video clips in Video tracks 1 and 2 (seen in Figures 15-15 and 15-16).

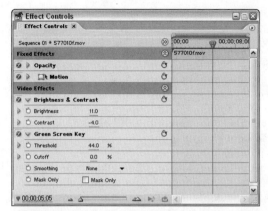

Figure 15-18: Shows the Effect Controls window with the Green Screen Key type options.

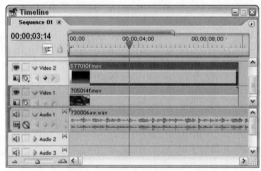

Figure 15-19: Shows the Timeline window used to create the Green Screen Key type project.

On the DVD-ROM

If you want, you can load the clips used to create the Green Screen Key type project from the Chapter 15 folder that is in the Tutorial Projects folder on the DVD that accompanies this book.

Non Red Key

As with the blue and green screens, the Non Red Key is used to key out blue and green backgrounds, but it does both at once. This key also includes a blending slider that enables you to blend two clips together.

Luma Key

The Luma Key type keys out darker image areas in a clip. Use the Threshold and Cutoff sliders to fine-tune the effect, as follows:

✦ **Threshold.** Click and drag to the right to increase the range of darker values that will be keyed out.

✦ **Cutoff.** Controls the opacity of the Threshold range. Click and drag to the right to produce more transparency.

Figure 15-20 shows a few frames from a project using a Luma key type. The frames show numbers counting down, superimposed over a video clip of two boxers fighting. Both clips are from Digital Vision. The numbers counting down clip is Working Numbers 577023f.mov, and the boxers fighting clip is Triangle Sports TRB05013.mov.

To create the Luma project, we imported the numbers counting down video clip into Video track 1 and imported the boxers fighting video clip into Video track 2. We selected the video clip in Video track 2 and applied the Luma Key type option. We adjusted the Threshold and Cutoff values so that we could see both the numbers and boxers fighting. To fine-tune the effect, we reduced the opacity in the middle of the clip in Video track 2. Figure 15-21 shows the Timeline used to create the project shown in Figure 15-20. In Audio track 1, we placed Digital Vision's Acoustic Chillout 730006aw.wav. The Luma Key settings to create the project appear in Figure 15-22. (For another Image Matte example, turn to Chapter 28.)

On the DVD-ROM   If you want, you can load the clips used to create the Luma Key type project from the Chapter 15 folder that is in the Tutorial Projects folder on the DVD that accompanies this book.

Alpha Adjust

Use the Alpha Adjust Key to create transparency from imported images that contain an alpha channel (an image layer that represents a mask with shades of gray, including black and white, to indicate transparency levels). Premiere Pro reads alpha channels from such programs as Adobe Photoshop and three-dimensional software programs and also translates nontransparent areas of Illustrator files as alpha channels.

Figure 15-20: Shows a few frames from the Luma Key type project.

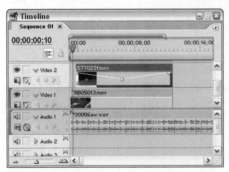

Figure 15-21: Shows the Timeline window
used to create the Luma Key type project.

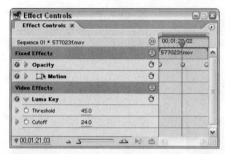

Figure 15-22: Shows the Effect Controls window with the Luma Key type settings used to create the project.

 Note   Click on a file with an alpha channel in the Project window. Then choose File ➪ Interpret Footage. In the Interpret Footage dialog box, you can select the Ignore Alpha Channel to have Premiere Pro ignore the alpha channel of that file, or you can select the Invert Alpha Channel option to have Premiere Pro invert that files alpha channel.

Figure 15-23 shows a few frames of an Alpha Adjust project. The project gives you the feeling that the guy is moving, when in reality the guy is not moving. The background clip is moving. To create the project, we imported a clip of a three-dimensional man that we created in Curious Labs' Poser and saved it in Photoshop format with an alpha channel. The man is on a white background. To mask out the white background, we created an alpha channel of the man. The image of the 3D man was placed into Video track 2. Then we applied the Alpha Adjust Key effect to the clip in Video track 2. Video track 1 has a clip from Digital Vision's Working Numbers (577001f.mov). Figure 15-24 shows the Timeline used to create the project. Figure 15-25 shows the Alpha Adjust effect settings in the Effect Controls window. The settings allow you to adjust how the alpha channel appears. Reducing the Opacity makes the image in the alpha channel more transparent. By selecting Ignore Alpha, Premiere Pro ignores the alpha channel. Selecting Invert Alpha, Premiere Pro inverts the alpha channel, and choosing Mask Only displays only the mask of the alpha channel without the image.

 On the DVD-ROM   If you want, you can load the 3D man image (3Dguy.psd), the Digital Vision Working Numbers video clip 577001f.mov, and Digital Vision's Acoustic Chillout 730006aw.wav audio clip from the Chapter 15 folder that is in the Tutorial Projects folder on the DVD that accompanies this book.

Figure 15-23: Frames from an Alpha Adjust project.

Figure 15-24: The Timeline window from the Alpha Adjust project.

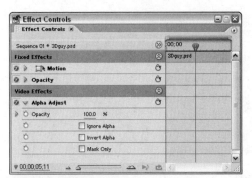

Figure 15-25: The Keying effects settings used in the Alpha Adjust project.

Image Matte Key

The Image Matte Key is used to create transparency in still images, typically graphics. Image areas that correspond to black portions of the matte are transparent; areas corresponding to white areas are opaque. Gray areas create blending effects.

When using the Image Matte Key, click the Setup button (next to the Reset button in the Effect Controls window) to choose an image. The final result depends upon the image you choose. You can create a composite using the alpha channel or the luminance of the clip. If you want to reverse the key effect, making areas that correspond to white transparent, areas corresponding to black areas will be opaque. The controls for the Image Matte Key effect is shown in Figure 15-26.

Figure 15-26 shows a project created using an Image Matte Key effect. To create the project (you can see a preview in the Monitor window in Figure 15-26), we imported Digital Vision's SkyRide 652024f.mov video clip to Video track 1. We selected Video track 1 and dragged the Image Matte Key effect over the clip. Next we clicked the Setup icon in the Effect Controls window. In the Select a Matte Image dialog box, we selected an Adobe Illustrator file. To create the Illustrator file, we used the Brush tool to brush anchors. The anchor was selected from the Object Sample Brushes palette. The Timeline window is shown in Figure 15-26. In Audio track 1, we placed Digital Vision's Acoustic Chillout 730006aw.wav.

On the DVD-ROM   If you want, you can load the files used to create the project in Figure 15-26 from the Chapter 15 folder that is in the Tutorial folder of the DVD that accompanies the book. The files used are Digital Vision's SkyRide 652024f.mov, Digital Vision's Acoustic Chillout 730006aw.wav, and anchors.ai.

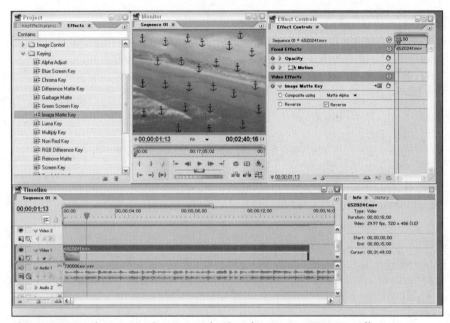

Figure 15-26: Shows a project created using the Image Matte Key effect.

Difference Matte Key

The Difference Matte Key enables you to key out image areas in one clip that match image areas in another clip. Whether you use the Difference Matte Key option will depend upon the clips you use in your project. If in your project you have a background without motion over a clip that does, you might want to use the Difference Matte Key to key out image areas from the static clip.

Track Matte Key

The Track Matte Key enables you to create a moving or traveling matte effect. Often the matte is a black-and-white image that is set in motion onscreen. Image areas corresponding to black in the matte are transparent; image areas corresponding to white are opaque. Gray areas create blending effects.

Cross-Reference

For another example of the Track Matte Key effect, turn to Chapter 17.

Multiply and Screen Key

The Multiply and Screen Key effects are transparency effects in which the lower video track image exhibits a high degree of contrast. Use Multiply Key to create transparency in areas corresponding to bright image areas in the lower video track. Use Screen Key to create transparency in areas corresponding to dark image areas in the lower video track. For both key effects, adjust the Opacity and Cutoff percent values to fine-tune the effect.

Figure 15-27 shows a few frames from a Screen Key type project. To create the Screen Key project, we placed Digital Vision's Working Numbers 577025f.mov clip in Video track 1 and SkyRide 652022f.mov clip in Video track 2. Figure 15-28 shows the Monitor window with a frame from the clip in Video track 1 and a frame from the clip in Video track 2.

We applied the Screen Key to Video track 1. The Screen Key controls are shown in Figure 15-29. Because the video clip in Video track 1 was longer than the clip in Video track 2, we used the Opacity option to slowly fade the clip in Video track 1. In Audio track 1, we placed Digital Vision's Acoustic Chillout 730006aw.wav. Figure 15-29 Shows the Timeline window used to create the Screen Key project.

On the DVD-ROM If you want, you can load the clips used to create the Screen Key type project from the Chapter 15 folder that is in the Tutorial Projects folder on the DVD that accompanies this book.

Garbage Matte

A video clip may contain an object that you don't want to appear in your project. When this happens, you can create a Garbage Matte to eliminate (mask out) the unwanted object. Usually the video clip in which you want to mask out an item will go on Video track 2 in the Timeline window. Another clip that you want to use as a composite will go in Video track 1.

Note Sometimes you may need to create a more sophisticated mask. When this happens, you may want to use Adobe After Effects. For more information on how to create a mask using Adobe After Effects, turn to Chapter 29.

You can also use the Garbage Matte Key to create a split-screen effect that splits the screen between a clip in one track and a clip in another track, as shown in Figure 15-30. Notice that the video clip from Video track 1 is displayed on the left side of the preview and the video clip from Video track 2 is displayed on the right side. The clip in Video track 1 is Digital Vision's Working Numbers 577004f.mov, and the clip in Video track 2 is Working Numbers 577008f.mov. The Timeline used to create the split screen effect is shown in Figure 15-30. In Audio track 1, we placed Digital Vision's Acoustic Chillout 730006aw.wav.

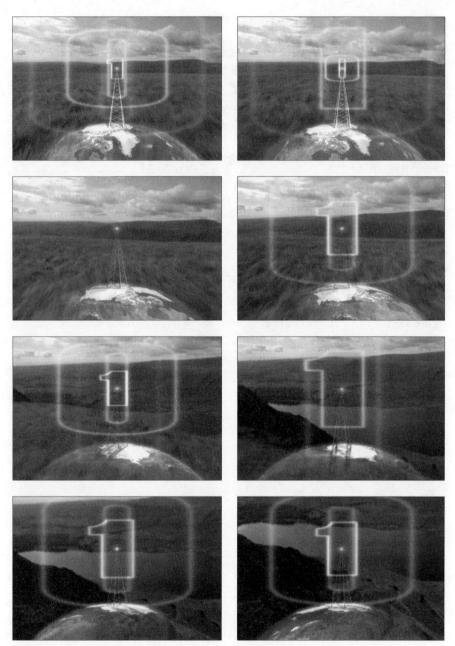

Figure 15-27: A few frames from a project using the Screen Key type.

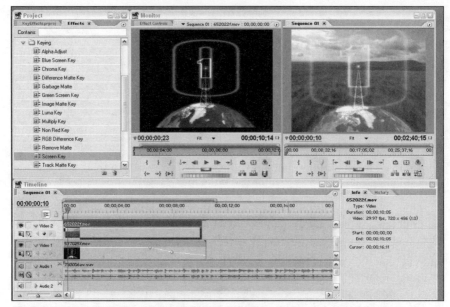

Figure 15-28: The Screen Key effect controls in the Effect Controls window.

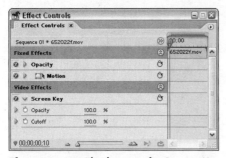

Figure 15-29: The layout of a Screen Key effect project.

To create a split screen, follow these steps:

1. **Choose File ➪ New ➪ Project to create a new project.**

2. **Choose File ➪ Import to import two video clips.** Import a video clip in which you want to mask out an item and import another one in which you want to use to composite (or a still image).

On the DVD-ROM

If you want, you can load the clips used to create the split screen project from the Chapter 15 folder that is in the Tutorial Projects folder on the DVD that accompanies this book.

3. **Drag the video clip that you want to split out from the Project window and into Video track 2 of the Timeline window.**

4. **Drag the video clip that you want to use to composite from the Project window into Video track 1 of the Timeline window.**

5. **Select the video clip in Video track 2.** Then click and drag the Garbage Matte Key from the Effects window to the video clip in the Timeline window or to the Effect Controls window.

6. **Click the Expand/Collapse triangle to display the Garbage Matte controls.** You can either enter numbers in the fields to adjust the matte (by entering numbers in the top left and right fields and the bottom right and left fields) or you can click the words *Garbage Matte* in the Effect Controls window to display an outline around the clip, which is shown in the Monitor window. Click one of the four points on the outline to adjust the matte. In Figure 15-30 we dragged the left corners to the middle of the clip's preview.

7. **Click the Play button in the Monitor window to preview the effect.**

8. **Choose File ➪ Save to save your project.**

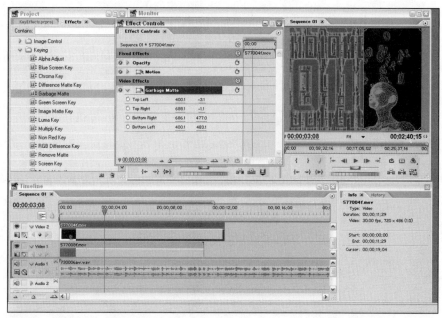

Figure 15-30: The Effect Controls window with the Garbage Matte settings used to create the split screen project and the Monitor window with an example of a split screen.

Remove Matte

The Keying effects create transparency from alpha channels created from red, green and blue channels as well as the alpha channel. Normally the Remove Matte key is used to key out the black or white backgrounds. This is useful for graphics with solid white or black backgrounds.

Summary

Premiere Pro's superimposition options create interesting and attractive effects that blend video tracks together or make various areas of one track transparent.

✦ Use the Premiere Pro Opacity options to blend a higher video track with the one beneath it.

✦ Click and drag on the Opacity handles in the Opacity rubberband line to adjust the fading effect.

✦ To create key effects that make portions of a video track transparent, open Premiere Pro's Effects folder by choosing Window ➪ Effects. Then open the Video Effects folder so that you can open the Keying folder.

✦ Premiere Pro provides 14 different keying effects: Alpha Adjust, Blue Screen Key, Chroma Key, Difference Matte Key, Garbage Matte, Green Screen Key, Image Matte Key, Luma Key, Multiply Key, Non Red Key, RGB Difference Key, Remove Matte, Screen Key, and Track Matte Key.

✦ Use the Blue Screen and Green Screen Key types to key out background image areas based on color.

✦ Use the Alpha Adjust Key to key out images based on an imported image's alpha channel.

✦ Use the Track Matte Key command to create traveling matte effects.

✦   ✦   ✦

Using Color Mattes and Backdrops

During the course of a video production, you may need to create a simple, colored background video track. You may need the track to be a solid color background for text, or you may need to create a background for transparency effects. This chapter looks at how to use colored background mattes and still-frame background images in Adobe Premiere Pro. You learn to create a color background in Premiere Pro and to export still frames from a clip to use as a backdrop. This chapter concludes with tutorials on creating backdrops in three popular digital imaging programs — Adobe Photoshop, Adobe Illustrator, and Corel Painter.

Creating a Color Matte

If you need to create a colored background for text or graphics, use a Premiere Pro *color matte*. Unlike many of the Premiere Pro video mattes, a color matte is a solid matte that comprises the entire video frame. A color matte can be used as a background or as a temporary track placeholder, until you've shot or created the final track.

Note   You may want to use a black video as a background matte. To create a black video, choose File ➪ New ➪ Black Video.

An advantage of using a colored background is its versatility. After you create the color matte, you can easily change its color with a few clicks of the mouse.

Here's how to create a color matte in Premiere Pro:

1. **With a project onscreen, choose File ⇨ New ⇨ Color Matte.** The Color Picker dialog box appears.

2. **Select a matte color.** If an exclamation mark appears next to the color swatches in the upper-right corner of the dialog box (see Figure 16-1), you've chosen a color that is out of the NTSC color gamut. This color cannot be reproduced correctly in NTSC video. Click the exclamation mark to have Premiere Pro choose the next closest color.

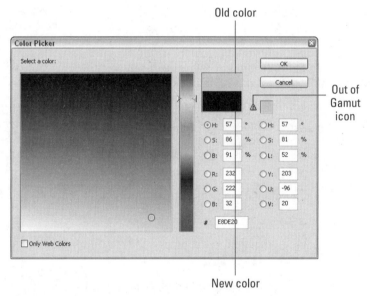

Figure 16-1: The Premiere Pro Color Picker dialog box.

 Cross-Reference   For more information on color gamuts, see Chapter 18.

3. **Click OK to close the Color Picker dialog box.**

4. **In the Choose Name dialog box that appears, type a name for the color matte in the name field (see Figure 16-2).**

5. **Click OK to place the matte in the Project window.**

6. **To use the color matte, simply drag it from the Project window into a video track.**

Note The default duration of a color matte is determined by the Still Frame setting in the General & Still Image Preferences dialog box. To change the default setting, choose File ➪ General & Still Image. In the Still Image area, enter the number of frames that you want to use as the still image default.

Figure 16-2: The Choose Name dialog box.

Creating a color matte from the Project window

Here's how to use the Project window to create a background matte.

 Note Before you begin, you must have a project on the screen.

1. **In the Project window, click the New Item icon, which is located between the New Folder icon and the Trash icon, and choose Color Matte.**

2. **When the Color Picker dialog box appears, pick a color matte.**

3. **Click OK to close the Color Picker dialog box.** The Choose Name dialog box appears.

4. **Type a name for the color matte.**

5. **Click OK.** Instantly, the color matte appears in the Project window, as shown in Figure 16-3, ready for you to drag it to the Timeline window.

New Item icon

Figure 16-3: The Project window with a color matte.

Note To change the duration of a matte, click it in the Project window and choose Clip ➪ Speed/Duration. In the Clip Speed/Duration dialog box, click the Duration values to change them. Then click OK.

Editing a color matte

The Premiere Pro color mattes have a distinct advantage over simply creating a colored background in the Title window or creating titles in another program with a colored background. If you are using a Premiere Pro color matte, you can quickly change colors if the original matte color proves unsuitable or unattractive.

To change the colors of a color matte after you've placed it into the Timeline, simply double-click the matte clip in the Timeline. When Premiere Pro's Color Picker appears, pick a new color and then click OK. After you click OK, the color changes, not only in the selected clip but also in all the clips in the tracks that use that color matte.

Note You can create a color matte in Premiere Pro and then animate and incorporate it into a project. Chapter 16 provides two examples of creating color mattes and incorporating them into projects.

Creating a Backdrop from a Still Frame

As you work in Premiere Pro, you may want to export a still frame from a video clip and save it in a graphic format so that you can use it in another program as part of a background. Figure 16-4 shows a collage we created using four frames from a Digital Vision, CityMix royalty-free video clip collection (clip 567001f).

On the DVD-ROM Digital Vision's CityMix 567001f.mov clip is in the Digital Vision folder that is in the Chapter 16 folder on the DVD that accompanies the book.

To create the collage in Figure 16-4, we found four frames we liked from video clip 567001f. We then exported these frames from Premiere Pro as PICT files. Then we imported the four still frames into Photoshop. Using layers, we composited the collage. We added text and lines. The final collage (shown in Figure 16-4) can be used as promotional material, such as a poster for the actual video clip. The final collage can also be re-imported into Premiere Pro and used as a backdrop of the opening title of a video production.

Figure 16-4: A backdrop created by exporting a frame from a video clip in Premiere Pro into Photoshop.

Following are the steps on how to export and save a portion of a video clip and use the still frame as a backdrop:

Note

Before we begin, open or create a project containing a video clip in one of the Timeline window's video tracks.

1. **Double-click the clip from which you want to create a backdrop in the Project window.** The clip opens in the Clip window.

2. **Use the Scrubbing tool and/or Frame Advance icon to move to the frame that you want to export.**

Cross-Reference

For more information on using the Monitor window, turn to Chapter 7.

3. **Choose File ⇨ Export ⇨ Frame.** The Export Frame dialog box appears.

4. **Click the Settings button.** The Export Still Frame Settings dialog box appears.

5. **Choose TIF, Targa, Windows Bitmap, or CompuServe GIF from the File format pop-up menu.** If you choose GIF, your image can contain a maximum of 256 colors. If you want, you can have the frame imported into the Project window onscreen by selecting the Add to Project When Finished option. Click OK to apply the settings.

6. Click Save to save the file. You can now import the image into Photoshop by loading the program, then choosing File ➪ Open. Photoshop enables you to enhance or manipulate your image. If you want, you can create a collage, as shown in Figure 16-4, by dragging and dropping all the files into one file. You may also want to import the final Photoshop image into Premiere Pro. To import the final Photoshop file into a Premiere project, choose File ➪ Import. Locate and select the file. Then click Open.

Creating Background Mattes in Photoshop

Adobe Photoshop 7 is an extremely versatile program for creating full-screen background mattes, or backdrops. Not only can you edit and manipulate photographs in Photoshop, but you can also create black-and-white or grayscale images to be used as background mattes. In this section, you create two different Photoshop projects. The first is a simple backdrop, showing you how to create a textured backdrop to use as a backdrop when superimposing titles and graphics. The second example is more complicated, but it illustrates more of Photoshop 7's digital imaging power.

Creating simple backgrounds with the Gradient tool

In this section, you create a non-DV project called Orchid Flower Shop. You'll use Photoshop 7's Gradient tool and several filters to create a background. Figure 16-5 shows the final background image created in Photoshop 7.

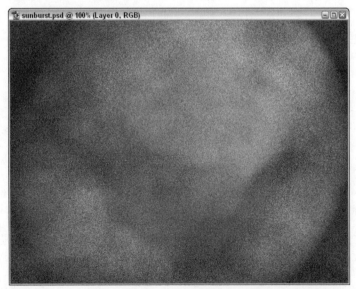

Figure 16-5: Simple background image created in Photoshop.

After you create the background file (seen in Figure 16-5) for the Orchid Flower Shop project, you'll mask a flower from its background by using a transparent background, as shown in Figure 16-6. When this flower file is loaded into Premiere Pro, it reads the Photoshop file with a transparent background. Text appears on top of the two Photoshop images, created by using the Adobe Title Designer window as shown in Figure 16-7.

Figure 16-6: Flower image with transparent background.

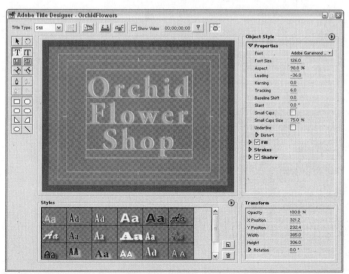

Figure 16-7: Orchid Flower Shop text created using the Adobe Title Designer.

Here's how to create a simple background in Photoshop (shown previously in Figure 16-5):

1. **Choose File ⇨ New to create a new file.**

2. **In the New dialog box, click the Preset Sizes pop-up menu and choose 640 x 480 to set the width to 640 pixels, the height to 480 pixels, and the resolution to 72 pixels per inch.** The mode should be set to RGB. Set the Contents to Background Color.

3. **Click OK to close the dialog box.**

4. **Set the foreground color to a light color and set the background color to a darker shade of the same color.** To change the foreground and background colors, click the foreground and background swatches in the Toolbox. In the Color Picker dialog box that appears, pick a color.

5. **Click the Gradient tool in the Toolbox.** Set the Gradient tool to use a Radial Gradient. The mode should be Normal, and the Opacity set to 100%.

6. **With the Gradient tool selected, click and drag outward from the center of your image to create a gradient.**

7. **With a radial gradient onscreen, choose Filter ⇨ Noise ⇨ Add Noise to add color to the gradient.**

8. **Choose Filter ⇨ Render ⇨ Lighting Effects to add more depth and lighting variations.** Figure 16-8 shows the Lighting Effects dialog box.

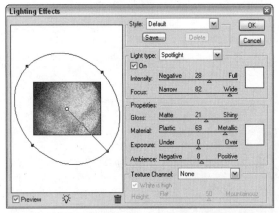

Figure 16-8: Use Photoshop's Lighting Effects filter to create a background.

9. **Choose File ⇨ Save to save your file.** Save your file in Photoshop format. Then close the file.

Now that you've created a background, you need to mask a flower from the background so that you can import it into Premiere Pro with a transparent background. Follow these steps to isolate the orchid flower from its background:

1. **Choose File ⇨ Open to open a file with flowers.** If you don't have a picture of flowers, you can load the orchid.psd file from the DVD that accompanies this book.

2. **Double-click the Background layer in the Layers palette.**

3. **In the New Layer dialog box that appears, rename the layer flower.** Click OK to close the dialog box.

4. **Now mask the flower using one of Photoshop's masking tools.** You can use one of the Selection tools or the Select ⇨ Color Range command to select the background. (For more information on using Photoshop's Color Range command, turn to Chapter 18.) When the background is selected, press Delete to have the flower appear on a transparent background. (By default, Photoshop represents a transparent background with a checkerboard.) You should now have a file with just a flower on a transparent background. Premiere Pro views an image on a transparent background the same way it does if the image had an alpha channel saved in the Channels palette.

 Tip   If you are not familiar with Photoshop's masking features, you can use the Eraser tool to erase the background. If you make a mistake, either choose Edit ⇨ Undo or File ⇨ Revert. If you are familiar with Photoshop's tools, you may want to use the Pen tool to outline the flower and select it. If you use the Pen tool, you need to convert the path into a selection by choosing Make Selection from the Path pop-up menu. Next, reverse the selection by choosing Select ⇨ Inverse and press Delete on your keyboard to erase the background and isolate the flower.

5. **Choose File ⇨ Save As to rename and save your file.** In the Save As dialog box, name your file **OrchidLayer**. Then save your file in Photoshop format and have the Layers option selected. This will keep the flower isolated from the background. Then click Save and close the file.

Orchid Flower Shop project

Now that you have created a background and isolated an image, you're ready to create the Orchid Flower Shop project. Figure 16-9 shows a few frames from the Orchid Flower Shop project. In the frames, you can see that the orchid flower moves across the screen over the background.

Figure 16-9: Frames from the Orchid Flower Shop project.

Follow these steps to create the Orchid Flower Shop project:

1. **Choose File ⇨ New Project to create a new project.**

2. **In the New Project dialog box, set the preset to Non-DV Square-Pixel 640 x 480 to match the size of the Photoshop files to that of the previous section.**

3. **Name your project and click OK to create a new project.**

4. **Choose File ⇨ Import to import the Photoshop gradient background file (sunburst.psd). In the Import dialog box, find the file you want to import. When you've selected your file, click Open to import the file into the Project window.**

5. **Choose File ⇨ Import to import the Photoshop layer file (OrchidLayer.psd).** When you import a Photoshop file with a layer, the Import Layered File dialog box appears. In the Import Layered File dialog box, set the Import As pop-up menu to Footage. Then click Choose Layer from the Layer Options. In the Choose Layer pop-up menu, pick the layer you want. For the OrchidLayer.psd file, choose flower. Click OK to import the file.

If you want, you can load the images in Figures 16-4 (sunburst.psd) and 16-5 (orchid.psd) from the Chapter 16 folder, which is in the Tutorial Projects folder.

6. **Drag and drop the background image from the Project window to Video track 1 in the Timeline window.**

7. **Drag the image with the masked (flower) in Video track 2.**

To extend the duration of either of the Photoshop clips that are in the Timeline window, click the end of the clip and drag to the left.

8. **Select the image in Video track 2 if it's not already selected.**

9. **Choose Window ⇨ Effect Controls.** The Motion Settings appear in the Effect Controls window (see Figure 16-10).

10. **To apply motion that moves from left to right, you first need to click the word Motion in the Effect Controls window.** Using the Monitor window, drag the flower to the left, as shown in Figure 16-10.

Figure 16-10: The Motion settings in the Effect Controls window allow you to add motion to a flower image that was created in Adobe Illustrator.

11. **Now you need to create two keyframes.** First, click the Expand/Collapse icon to display the motion settings. Then move the edit line to the beginning of the clip and click the Position Toggle Animation icon to create the first keyframe. To create the last keyframe, move the flower all the way to the left of the Monitor window. Then move the edit line to the end of the clip and click the Add/Remove Keyframe button.

12. **Click the Play button in the Monitor window to preview the motion.**

13. **Choose File ⇨ New ⇨ Title.** The Adobe Title Designer window opens.

14. **Create some text with the Type tool.** The Adobe Title Designer window is shown in Figure 16-11.

15. **Save the title to make it appear in the Project window.**

16. **Drag and drop the title clip from the Project window to Video track 3 in the Timeline window (see Figure 16-12).**

17. **Choose File ⇨ Save to save the project.**

18. **Preview the file by clicking on the Play button in the Monitor window.**
When the preview plays, you should see the text and flower visible over the background you created in Photoshop. To change the quality of the preview, click the Monitor pop-up menu and choose either Highest Quality, Draft Quality, or Automatic Quality. By default, Premiere Pro sets the preview to Automatic Quality. To render the work area, choose Sequence ➪ Render Work Area.

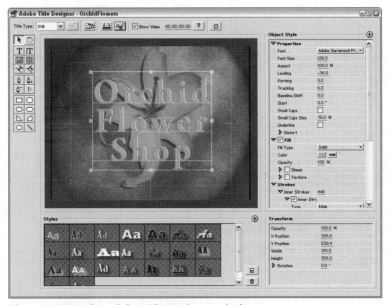

Figure 16-11: The Adobe Title Designer window.

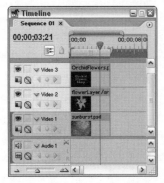

Figure 16-12: The Timeline window for the Orchid Flower Shop project.

Creating background patterns with the Pattern command

This example shows you how to create a background pattern matte (shown in Figure 16-13) using the Pattern command in Photoshop 6.0 or greater. Using the Pattern command, you can quickly choose preset patterns and add 3D effects. The Pattern command creates a pattern on a new layer. After you save the pattern background in Photoshop, you can load it directly into Premiere Pro.

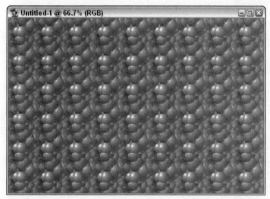

Figure 16-13: Background pattern matte created using Photoshop's Pattern command.

Follow these steps to create a background pattern in Photoshop using the Pattern command:

1. **Create a new file in Photoshop (File ⇨ New) with the same pixel dimensions as you are using in your Premiere project.** When you create the project, set the mode to RGB color and the background contents to Transparent.

2. **To create the pattern in a layer, choose Layer ⇨ New Fill Layer ⇨ Pattern.** The New Layer dialog box appears.

3. **In the New Layer dialog box, click OK.** The Pattern Fill dialog box opens (see Figure 16-14). In the Pattern Fill dialog box, you can choose a pattern by clicking the pattern preview. When the pop-up menu of pattern thumbnails appears, make a selection. If you want, you can use the Scale option to scale the pattern.

4. **Click OK to create the pattern.**

Figure 16-14: Photoshop's Pattern Fill dialog box.

5. **To add 3D or additional special effects to your pattern, choose Layer ⇨ Layer Style ⇨ Bevel and Emboss.** The Layer Style dialog box appears (see Figure 16-15). To add more variation to the pattern, click the Contour pop-up menu and experiment with the contours. Notice that the Layer Style changes, as shown in Figure 16-16, when you click Contour. You can also click the Texture pop-up menu to add a texture to your image. Pick a pattern and experiment with the Scale and Depth sliders, which are shown in Figure 16-17. Use the Depth, Size, and Soften sliders to fine-tune the effect.

   The pattern is created with a mask. The layer mask thumbnail can be seen in the Layers palette.

6. **Choose Window ⇨ Layers to display the Layers palette.** The layer mask thumbnail appears next to the word, Pattern.

7. **To use the pattern's mask to create special effects, select the Brush tool and then pick a brush size. Set the painting color to black and reduce the Opacity to 40%.** Then start drawing in the pattern. To erase your brushstrokes and start over, choose Edit ⇨ Fill. In the Fill dialog box, set the Use pop-up menu to White, the Mode to Normal, and the Opacity to 100%. Click OK.

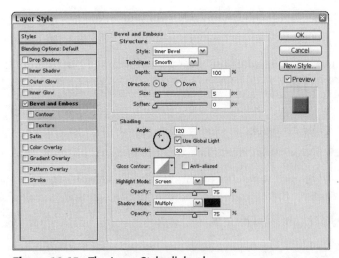

Figure 16-15: The Layer Style dialog box.

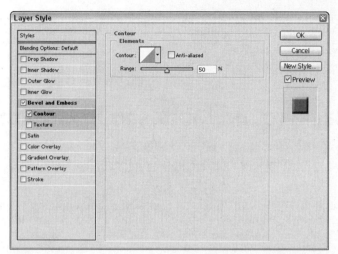

Figure 16-16: The Contour option settings in the Layer Style dialog box.

Figure 16-17: The Texture option settings in the Layer Style dialog box.

Note To remove the mask, choose Layer ➪ Remove Layer Mask ➪ Discard. Removing the mask, removes the mask and discards any changes you might of made on the mask.

8. **When you've completed your background pattern, choose Layer ⇨ Flatten Image.**

9. **Save the file in Photoshop format.** The file can then be imported into any Premiere project.

Creating Background Mattes in Illustrator

In this section, you learn to create a project called Flowers Everywhere. To create this project, you use Adobe Illustrator to create a background matte, as shown in Figure 16-18.

Then you take one of the elements from the background and copy it into another file. This image, shown in Figure 16-19, appears against a background video track in Premiere Pro. Finally, you use Premiere Pro's Adobe Title Designer window to create text (shown in Figure 16-20), which appears over the background and image.

Figure 16-18: Background matte created in Adobe Illustrator.

Figure 16-19: Image created from one of the images from the background.

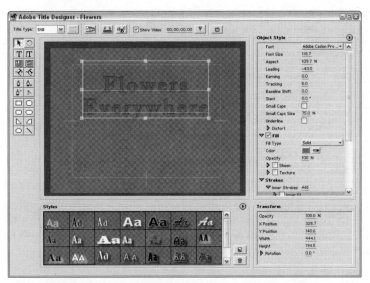

Figure 16-20: Text created in Premiere Pro's Adobe Title Designer window.

Here's how to create a background matte in Adobe Illustrator:

1. **Load Adobe Illustrator.**

2. **Choose File ➪ New to create a new file.** Make sure that the Color Mode is set to RGB Color and not to CMYK Color. (CMYK color is for print work.)

3. **To create the flowers shown in Figures 16-18 and 16-19, click the Polygon tool in the Toolbox.**

4. **With the Polygon tool selected, move to the center of the screen.**

5. **Alt+click to display the Polygon dialog box.**

6. **In the Polygon dialog box, set the Sides to 8.**

7. **Click OK to create a polygon.**

8. **Choose Filter ➪ Distort ➪ Punk & Bloat.** Illustrator converts the polygon into a flower shape.

9. **In the Punk & Bloat dialog box, drag the slider toward Bloat to about 100%.** To preview the effect before applying it, make sure that the Preview option is selected.

10. **Click OK to apply the effect.**

11. **Click the Ellipse tool in the Toolbox.**

12. **Create a circle in the middle of the flower shape.** To create a perfect circle, press and hold the Shift key.

13. **Click the Select tool in the Toolbox.**

14. **Click and drag over the flower and circle to select them.**

15. **Choose Edit ⇨ Copy and Edit ⇨ Paste to duplicate the flower.** Do this a few times, until you have a few flowers on the screen.

16. **Using the Color palette, pick colors for the flowers you created.**

17. **Use the Scale tool to scale some of the flowers.** Double-click the Scale tool in the Toolbox. In the Scale dialog box, make sure that the Uniform option is selected. (Doing this prevents the flowers from being distorted when they are scaled.)

18. **Choose File ⇨ Save to save the file in Illustrator format.** Now that you've created a background using Illustrator, you can easily pick one of the items from the background to use as a separate image in Premiere Pro.

19. **Before you close this file, select a portion of your image and choose Edit ⇨ Copy.**

20. **While still in Illustrator, choose File ⇨ New.**

21. **Paste the flower into the file and save the file.** In Figure 16-18, shown previously, we isolated a flower from the background and copied it into a new file to create the image shown in Figure 16-19.

Flowers Everywhere project

A great feature of using Adobe Illustrator with Premiere Pro is that Premiere Pro translates the blank areas of the Illustrator file as an alpha channel mask. You can now import the flower files that you just created into Premiere Pro and create the Flowers Everywhere project. In this project, the Bend video effect was applied to the background and the Bevel Alpha video effect was applied to the text in the top video track shown in Figure 16-21 (Video track 3). Figure 16-22 shows frames from the Flowers Everywhere project.

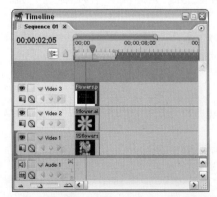

Figure 16-21: The Timeline window used to create the Flowers Everywhere project.

Figure 16-22: Frames from the Flowers Everywhere project.

Here's how to create the Flowers Everywhere project:

1. **Open Adobe Premiere Pro.**

2. **Choose File ➪ New ➪ Project to create a new project.**

3. **In the New Project dialog box, choose a preset.**

4. **Click OK to apply the settings to the new project.** The new project opens.

5. **Choose Window ➪ Workspace ➪ Effects.** The Effects and Effect Controls are displayed.

6. **Choose File ➪ Import.**

On the DVD-ROM

If you want, you can load the images in Figures 16-18 (15flowers.ai) and 16-19 (1flower.ai) from the Chapter 16 folder, which is in the Tutorial Projects folder on the DVD that accompanies this book.

7. **In the Import dialog box, locate and select the 15flowers.ai and 1flower.ai files.** Press and hold the Ctrl key to select more than one file.

8. **Click Open.** Premiere Pro imports the files into the Project window.

9. **Drag the 15flowers.ai (background file) and 1flower.ai files to Video tracks 1 and 2, respectively.**

10. **Choose File ➪ New ➪ Title.** The Adobe Title Designer window opens.

11. **Create some text with the Type tool.**

12. **Save the title to add it to the Project window.** To see the graphic and background below the text, make sure the background is transparent. To verify this, click the Background button in the Adobe Title Designer window. Then, in the Title background window, make sure the Background option is off. Figure 16-20 shows the Adobe Title Designer window with the text for Flowers Everywhere.

13. **Drag and drop the title to Video track 3.**

14. **Click Video track 2 to reduce the opacity of the graphic.** Click the Expand/Collapse icon next to the Opacity option in the Effect Controls window. Then drag the Opacity value to the left.

See Chapter 15 to learn about fading clips and working with transparency.

15. **In the Effects window, open the Video Effects folder to display the effects, then open the Distort folder.**

16. **Drag the Bend filter from the window and drop it on the clip in Video track 1.** Then click the Setup icon in the Effect Controls window to display the Bend Settings dialog box. Figure 16-23 shows the Bend Settings dialog box.

17. **Save the file.**

18. **Click the Play button to preview the file to view the flowers and Bend effect.**

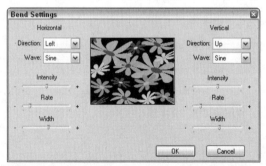

Figure 16-23: The Bend Settings dialog box with flower background file created in Illustrator.

Creating Backgrounds with Corel Painter

You can use Corel Painter to create background mattes and QuickTime movies from graphics. Figure 16-24 displays the Timeline window for a project called Summer Fun. Video track 1 shows a background created in Painter. Video track 2 features an animated horse created in Painter and imported in Premiere Pro as a QuickTime movie. Video track 3 displays the text Summer Sun, which was created by using Adobe Premiere's Title Designer window.

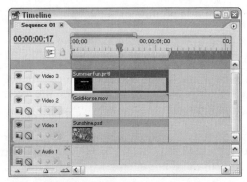

Figure 16-24: The Summer Fun project
Timeline window.

Here's how we created the project. To create the landscape background, we used
Painter's shape tools and layers. To create the animated horse, we first created a
new movie instead of a new canvas. Next, we made a horse as a layer at the far right
of the screen. We filled the horse with a gold color. Then we slowly moved the horse
to the left in different frames. We saved the movie in QuickTime movie format.

In Figure 16-25, you can see the frames for the Summer Fun project. In the frames,
you can see a horse moving over a superimposed background. To add some interest
to the text, we applied motion to it.

Figure 16-25: Frames from the Summer Fun project.

Here's how to assemble the graphic elements in Premiere Pro to create the Summer Fun project:

1. **Create a new project.**

2. **Choose File ➪ Import.** Locate the Summer Folder and click the Import Folder button. The Summer folder appears in the Project window. Open the folder to view the clips (GoldHorse.mov, SummerFun.prtl, and Sunshine.psd).

On the DVD-ROM

You can find the files used to create the Summer Fun project in the Summer project folder that is in the Chapter 16 folder, which is located in the Tutorial Projects folder that is on the DVD that accompanies this book.

3. **Drag the GoldHorse.mov clip to Video track 1.**

4. **Drag sunshine.psd (the background file) to Video track 2.**

5. **Choose Window ➪ Workspace ➪ Effects to display both the Effects and Effect Controls.**

6. **To superimpose both clips, use the Luma Key effect.** In the Effects window, click the Expand/Collapse icon to display all the effects. Open the Keying folder to display the Keying effects. Click and drag the Luma Key effect to Video track 2.

7. **In the Effect Controls window, click the Expand/Collapse icon to display the Luma Key settings.** Click and drag on the settings until the background from the video clip in Video track 2 is removed. As you work, view the effects in the Monitor window.

8. **Now you are ready to add some text to your project.** Choose File ➪ New ➪ Title. In the Adobe Title Designer window, use the Type tool to create some text, as shown in Figure 16-26. When you are done creating and stylizing your title, save it so that it appears in the Project window.

9. **Drag the title file to Video track 3.**

10. **Click the Title file icon in Video track 3.**

11. **To apply motion to the Title file, create two keyframes:**

    a. **Click the Expand/Collapse icon to display the Motion settings and then click the word Motion.**

    b. **Move the text to where you want your motion to begin and move the edit line to the beginning of the Timeline.**

    c. **Click the Toggle Animation icon in front of the Position option.** A keyframe is created.

d. To create a second keyframe, move the edit line to the end of the Timeline and move the text in the Monitor window to where you want the motion to end.

e. Click the Add/Remove Keyframe to add the second keyframe.
Figure 16-27 shows the Effect Controls window with the Motion settings.

12. **Click the Play button in the Monitor window to preview the project.**

13. **Save your file and preview your project.**

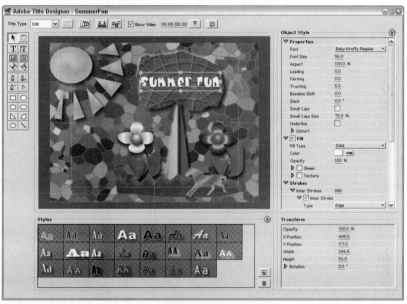

Figure 16-26: The Summer Fun Title Designer window.

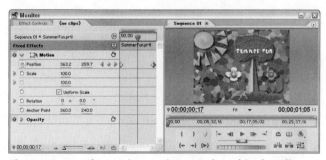

Figure 16-27: The Motion settings are found in the Effect Controls window.

Summary

You can use Premiere Pro's color matte command to easily create solid-color backgrounds for text and graphics.

✦ You can use Adobe Photoshop, Adobe Illustrator, or Corel's Painter to create your own backgrounds to use as background mattes.

✦ Photoshop and Illustrator files can be imported directly into Premiere Pro. All you need to do is save the Photoshop files in Photoshop format and the Illustrator files in Illustrator format.

✦   ✦   ✦

Creating Motion Effects in Premiere Pro

Motion creates interest and adds to the power of just about any presentation. In Adobe Premiere Pro, you can send a title or logo spinning across the screen or bounce a clip off the borders of the frame area. Using a graphic with an alpha channel, you can superimpose one moving object over another. You can also create traveling matte effects, in which one image within a shape moves across the screen over another image. This chapter not only shows you how to create traveling mattes, but also how to set graphics in motion, including how to make them bend and rotate onscreen.

To create these motion effects, you'll use Premiere Pro's new Motion options, found in the Effect Controls window.

Touring the Motion Effects Options in the Effect Controls window

Premiere Pro's new Motion options allow you to scale, rotate, and move a clip. By animating the motion options you can wake up an otherwise boring image by setting it in motion over time using keyframes. You can make any clip move and jiggle or make a still frame move across the screen. (See Chapter 12 to learn how to use Premiere Pro's Motion effects options to add motion to your titles.) The Motion effects are found in the Effect Controls window, which is shown in Figure 17-1.

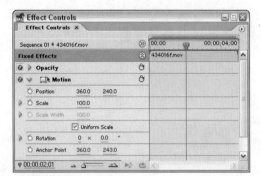

Figure 17-1: The Effect Controls window and the Motion effects options.

To use Premiere Pro's Motion options, you need to have a project onscreen with a video clip selected in the Timeline window. Follow these steps to create a new project, import two video clips, and display the Motion effect options:

1. **Choose File ➪ New ➪ Project to create a new project. In the New Project dialog box, choose a preset and name the project and click OK.**

2. **Load two video clips by choosing File ➪ Import.** You can either use your own video or you can use Digital Vision's Ambient Space 434016f.mov and 434011f.mov files found on the DVD that accompanies this book. After you import the file into your project, it appears in the Project window.

3. **If you want, load a sound clip by choosing File ➪ Import. Locate a sound and click Open.** We used Digital Vision's Cool Lounge 666005aw.wav file. Then drag the sound clip from the Project window to Audio track 1 in the Timeline window.

Digital Vision's Ambient Space 434016f.mov and 434011f.mov video clips and Digital Vision's Cool Lounge 666005aw.wav are found in the Digital Vision folder, in the Chapter 17 folder, which is in the Tutorial Projects folder on the DVD that accompanies this book.

4. **Next, click one of the video clips in the Project window and drag it to Video track 1 in the Timeline window. Then drag the other video clip to Video track 2 in the Timeline window.** We dragged Digital Vision's Ambient Space 434011f.mov to Video track 1 and Digital Vision's Ambient Space 434016f.mov to Video track 2. The Timeline window should now have two video clips, as shown in Figure 17-2.

You can choose how a clip is displayed on the Timeline by clicking on the Set Display Style icon and clicking on one of the options. To view the Set Display Style icon, you need to expand a video track by clicking on the triangle that is in front of the word Video.

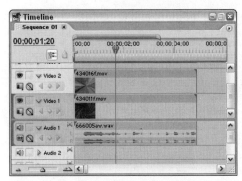

Figure 17-2: The Timeline window with two video clips and a sound clip.

5. **With the clip in Video track 2 selected, choose Window ➪ Effect Controls.** To display the Motion settings, click the triangle in front of the word Motion.

6. **To scale a clip's height and width in unison, make sure the Uniform Scale option is selected. Then click and drag over the value in the Scale section or click on the value and type a value and press Enter.** Acceptable ranges are from 0 to 700. Enter 0 to make the clip invisible; enter 600 to enlarge the clip 7 times its normal size. We scaled our clip down to 42%, as shown in Figure 17-3.

Note

To scale the height of a clip separately from the width, the Uniform Scale option in the Effect Controls window should not be selected.

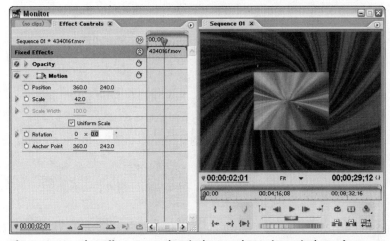

Figure 17-3: The Effect Controls window and Monitor window after adjusting the Motion effects Scale option.

7. **Use the Rotate option to rotate a clip around its center point.** To rotate, click and drag on the Rotate degree value or enter a value in the Rotation degree field. To create one complete rotation, enter 360 degrees. We rotated the clip 90 degrees.

8. **To see a preview of how the Motion effects Scale and Rotation settings have changed the clip in Video track 2, first open the Monitor window by choosing Window ⇨ Monitor. Then either click the Play button in the Monitor window or click and drag on the shuttle or jog slider.** You can also see a preview by moving the current Timeline indicator in the Effect Controls window or the Timeline window. Notice that the clip has been scaled and rotated and that it remains scaled and rotated throughout the duration of the clip.

Tip

To go back to the default motion settings, click the Reset icon that is to the left of the word Motion in the Effect Controls window.

9. **To move the position of a clip, click and drag on the Position values to change the values and move the clip on its X and Y axis.** To move the clip from its center point, click and drag on the Anchor Point values.

10. **To move a clip manually, click the word Motion in the Effect Controls window.** Notice that in the Monitor window, a wireframe appears around the clip, as shown in Figure 17-4. Click inside the wireframe and move the clip. As you move the clip, the Position values change. You can also manually rotate and scale a clip. To scale a clip, move the cursor on either a corner or side handle. To keep the clip's proportions, press and hold the Shift key as you scale. To rotate a clip manually, move the cursor just outside of either a corner or side handle, and then drag in the direction you want to rotate.

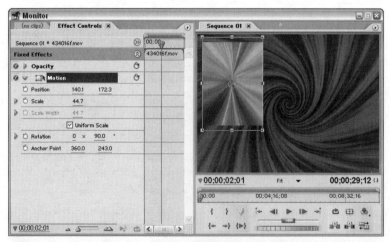

Figure 17-4: To manually adjust a clip, click the word Motion in the Effect Controls window. Notice that in the Monitor window a wireframe appears around the active clip.

11. **Click the Play button in the Monitor window to preview the effects of the Position settings.** To render a work area, choose Sequence ⇨ Render Work Area. Notice that the clip starts at the new position and remains there throughout the duration of the clip. To move the clip's position to different places throughout the duration of the clip, you need to set keyframes. Turn to the next section to learn more about working with keyframes.

By default, Premiere Pro displays a preview in Automatic Quality. To change the preview display, click the Monitor window pop-up menu and choose Highest Quality or Draft Quality.

The following section describes how to use keyframes to animate a clip over time.

Setting keyframes to create motion effects using the Effect Controls window

To create motion that moves in more than one direction or changes size or rotation throughout the duration of a clip, you need to add keyframes. You can use keyframes to create effects at specific points in time — for example, to create an effect using a graphic or video clip in motion simultaneously with another video clip. Using keyframes, the effect can occur at a specific point in your narration, and you can also add music to the effect. The motion path is displayed when the word *Motion* is selected in the Effect Controls window. When the motion path is displayed, keyframes appear as points in the motion path and designate a change in position.

You can also add keyframes to the motion path at specific points by clicking on the Timeline. (The Timeline is described in the next section.)

Here's how to add keyframes to a motion path to create the effect of a clip moving diagonally from top left to bottom right:

1. **Choose File ⇨ New ⇨ Project to create a new project. In the New Project dialog box, choose a preset. Then name the project and click OK.**

2. **Choose File ⇨ Import. In the Import dialog box, locate and select a clip. Then choose Open to import a clip into the Project window.** We used Digital Vision's Ambient Space 434006f.mov file.

If you want, you can use Digital Vision's Ambient Space 434006f.mov, which is found in the Digital Vision folder, in the Chapter 17 folder that is in the Tutorial Projects folder on the DVD that accompanies this book.

3. **Drag the clip from the Project window to Video track 2 of the Timeline.** This is the clip you will be applying motion effects to.

At any time you can import another clip into this project and use it as the background. After you import the clip, drag it into Video track 1 of the Timeline. You can also import a sound clip. After you've imported a sound, drag it into Audio track 1.

4. **Click the clip that is in Video track 2 to select it.**

5. **Choose Window ⇨ Workspace ⇨ Effects to display both the Effect Controls window and the Monitor window. Then click the Effect Controls tab to display it.**

6. **In the Effect Controls window, click the triangle in front of the word Motion to display the motion effects options.**

7. **Move the current Timeline indicator in the Timeline of the Effect Controls window to the beginning of the clip.**

Note Set the Timeline to show clips in one-second intervals by clicking and dragging on the Time Zoom Level slider at the bottom of the window.

8. **Reduce the size of the clip to 39 percent by using the Motion effects Scale option.** The clip will be scaled 39 percent throughout its duration.

9. **Click the word Motion to be able to see the motion path as it is created.** Notice that the clip is selected with an outline around it.

10. **To create a starting point, move the clip in the Monitor window to the top-left corner of the window.**

11. **To set a keyframe, click the Toggle Animation icon in front of the word Position in the Effect Controls window.**

12. **To set a second keyframe, move the current Timeline indicator in the Effect Controls window to the right. Then click in the middle of the clip and move it to the center of the Monitor window.** Notice that a second keyframe is automatically created and that a motion path is displayed from keyframe one to keyframe two, shown in Figure 17-5.

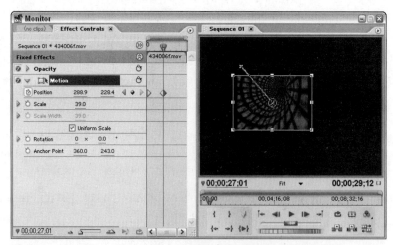

Figure 17-5: The motion path is between keyframes one and two.

13. **To set a third keyframe (the ending point), move the current Timeline indicator in the Effect Controls window to the right (toward the end of the clip). Then click in the middle of the clip and move it to the bottom-right side of the Monitor window.** Notice that a third keyframe is automatically created and that the motion path is showing a specific point for each keyframe, as shown in Figure 17-6.

14. **Move the current Timeline indicator to the beginning of the clip and then click the Play button in the Monitor window to preview the motion effect.** To preview specific segments of the motion effect, click and drag the current-time indicator in the Timeline of the Effect Controls window.

For more motion path options, you may want to try using Adobe After Effects. For more information on using After Effects, turn to Chapters 26, 29, and 30.

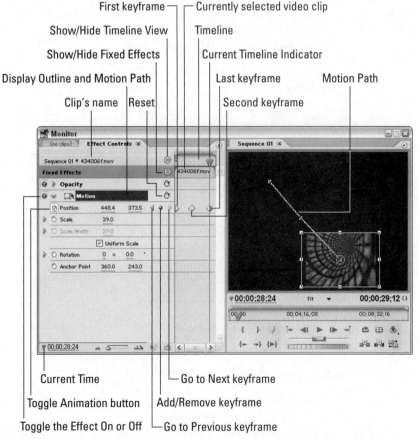

Figure 17-6: The motion path is between keyframes two and three.

Using the Timeline Window to Preview and Add Keyframes

The Timeline window allows you to view, add, and edit motion keyframes very much as you do using the Effect Controls window.

Here's how to preview keyframes in the Timeline window:

1. **Onscreen you should have a project with a video clip in the Timeline window.**

2. **Click the Collapse/Expand Track triangle that is next to the name of the video track with the video clip. Then click the Show Keyframes icon and click Show Keyframes.** Notice that a line appears in the area below the clip's name. If the video clip has any motion effect keyframes applied to it, you will see white diamonds representing the keyframes on the line, as shown in Figure 17-7. To the right of where the clip's name appears is a pop-up menu displaying the Motion Effect options.

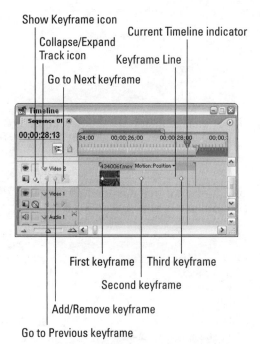

Figure 17-7: A preview of motion keyframes in the Timeline window.

3. **Click and drag on the current Timeline indicator in the Timeline window to see the preview of the motion in the Monitor window.** To see a preview of the motion path, make sure that the word Motion is selected in the Effect Controls window.

Adding keyframes using the Timeline window is the same as adding keyframes using the Timeline in the Effect Controls window. Here's how to add keyframes in the Timeline window:

1. **Move the current Timeline indicator in the Timeline window to where you want to add a keyframe.**

2. **Click the Motion pop-up menu and choose the setting you want to affect.**

3. **Either numerically make the Motion effect change to one of the Motion effect settings you choose or manually adjust the clip in the Monitor window.**

4. **Click the Add/Remove Keyframe icon in the Timeline window to add a keyframe.**

For more information on editing keyframes, move on to the next section.

Editing Motion Paths

To edit motion paths, you can move, delete, or add keyframes, or even copy and paste them. Sometimes, by adding keyframes you can create smoother motion paths. Here's how to add a keyframe:

1. **Select the clip you want to animate.**

2. **Move the current Timeline indicator to where you want to add a keyframe.**

3. **To add a keyframe, use the Effect Controls window or the Timeline window.**

4. **To add a keyframe using the Effect Controls window, turn on the Toggle Animation stopwatch.** If the Toggle Animation stopwatch is already activated, click the Add/Remove Keyframe icon to add a keyframe.

5. **To add a keyframe using the Timeline window, click the Add/Remove Keyframe icon or press and hold the Ctrl key as you use the Pen tool to add a keyframe to the motion line.**

Moving a keyframe point

After you add a motion keyframe, you can return to it at any time to move it. You can either move a motion keyframe point using the Effect Controls window or the

Timeline window. You can also move a keyframe point using the motion path that is displayed in the Monitor window. When you move the keyframe point in the Effect Controls and/or Timeline window, you change when the motion effect will occur on the Timeline. When you move the keyframe point in the motion path, you affect the shape of the motion path.

Here's how to move a keyframe point using the Effect Controls and Timeline window:

1. **Move the current Timeline indicator to where you want to move the keyframe.** As you move the current Timeline indicator, use the Info palette to find the correct location.

2. **Select the keyframe point that you want to move by clicking it with the mouse.** When you click a keyframe point in the Timeline window, the cursor displays its position on the Timeline.

To select more than one keyframe at a time, press and hold the Shift key as you select the keyframe point.

3. **Click and drag on the selected keyframe point to the new location.**

Here's how to move a keyframe point using the motion path displayed in the Monitor window:

1. **To display the motion path in the Monitor window, select the word Motion from the Effect Controls window.**

2. **Select the keyframe point that you want to move by clicking it with the mouse.**

3. **Click and drag the selected keyframe point to the new location.**

Following are tips for making intricate edits on the motion path:

✦ To move a keyframe on the motion path one pixel at a time, press one of the directional arrow keys on your keyboard.

✦ To move the motion path five pixels at a time, press Shift and press a directional arrow key on your keyboard.

✦ Click in the Info box below the Timeline and enter a specific coordinate for the point on the path. When you select a point, the point number appears in the Info box. For example, if you want to center the clip in the middle of the screen, enter 0,0 in the box. If you enter a positive number in the first box, the clip moves to the right. If you enter a negative number, the clip moves to the left. If you enter a positive number in the right box, the clip moves down; entering a negative number makes the clip move up. For example, if you enter –10,10, the clip moves ten pixels to the left and ten pixels down from the middle of the screen.

What's an alpha channel?

Essentially, an alpha channel is an extra grayscale image layer that Premiere Pro translates into different levels of transparency.

Alpha channels are typically used to define the transparent areas of a graphic or title. They enable you to combine a logo or text in one video track with a background video track in another. The background track surrounds the logo or text and is seen through the letters in the text. If you viewed an alpha channel of text, it might appear as pure white text on a black background. When Premiere Pro uses the alpha channel to create transparency, it can place colored text in the white area of the alpha channel and a background video track in the black area.

Alpha channels can be created in image-editing programs, such as Adobe Photoshop and Corel Painter. Most 3D programs create alpha channels as well. When you create titles in the Title Designer window, Premiere Pro automatically creates an alpha channel for the text. (For more information about alpha channels, see Chapter 16. Chapter 27 provides detailed instructions for creating alpha channels in Photoshop.)

Deleting keyframe points

As you edit, you may want to delete a keyframe point. To do this, simply select the point or points and press the Delete key. If you want to delete all the keyframe points for a Motion effect option, click the Toggle Animation icon in the Effect Controls window. A warning prompt will appear, asking you whether you want to delete all existing keyframes; if so click OK.

Copying and pasting keyframe points

You can copy a keyframe point and paste it in another place in the Timeline. Here's how:

1. **To copy a keyframe point, you first need to select it by clicking it.**
2. **Choose Edit ⇨ Copy.**
3. **Move the current Timeline indicator to the new location.**
4. **Choose Edit ⇨ Paste.**

Changing a motion path's speed

Premiere determines motion speed by the distance between keyframes. To increase the speed of motion, create keyframes that are closer together. To slow the speed of motion, set keyframes farther apart.

Here's how to change the speed of motion:

1. **If you don't already have keyframes, create keyframes on the Timeline by using either the Effect Controls window or Timeline window (see the steps earlier in this chapter).**

2. **To increase motion speed, drag keyframes closer together. To decrease motion speed, drag keyframes further apart. To move a keyframe, click the keyframe to select it and then click and drag the keyframe point and move it on the Timeline.**

Note   You can also use the Clip ➪ Speed/Duration command to change the speed and/or duration of a clip.

Changing opacity

In the Fixed Effects section of the Effect Controls window are the Motion Effect options and the Opacity option. By reducing the opacity of a clip, you make the clip more translucent. To change the opacity of a clip throughout its duration, click and drag to the left on the Opacity percent value. You can also change the Opacity percent field by clicking in the field and then typing a number and pressing Enter. Alternatively, you can expand the Opacity option by clicking on the triangle in front of the Opacity name and clicking and dragging on the Opacity slider.

To set keyframes for the Opacity using the Effect Controls window, follow these steps:

1. **Activate the Toggle Animation icon.**

2. **Change the Opacity field and click the Toggle Keyframe icon to set a keyframe.**

To set keyframes for the Opacity using the Timeline window, follow these steps:

1. **Click the Show Keyframes icon.**

2. **Choose Opacity from the clip's title pop-up menu and then click the Add/Remove Keyframe icon to add a keyframe.**

To change the Opacity field, use the white line below the clip's name. Click and drag down on the white line to reduce the opacity of the clip. For more information on using the Opacity option, refer to Chapter 15.

Applying special effects

After you've animated a clip using the Fixed Effects options in the Effect Control window, you may find that you want to add a few more effects to your clip. You can find various effects in the Video Effects folder of the Effects window. To adjust an image's color, try using one of the Image Control video effects. If you want to distort a clip, try using one of the Distort video effects. For more information on using the video effects, refer to Chapter 14. Here's how to add effects to a clip:

1. **Start by moving the current Timeline indicator on either the Timeline in the Effect Controls window or the Timeline window to the place where you want to add an effect.**

2. **Pick an effect from the Effects window and drag it either to the Effect Controls window or Timeline window.**

3. **Adjust the settings for the effect and then click the Toggle Animation icon to create a keyframe.** If you want the effect to change over time, you'll need to create various keyframes.

Using a Clip with an Alpha Channel

If you create motion effects with text or logos, you may want the text or logo to appear as though it were on a sheet of clear acetate to enable a background video track to show through in the background. The standard digital method of creating this effect is to use an alpha channel.

If the image you set in motion includes an alpha channel, Premiere Pro can mask out the background and substitute the background area with visuals from another video track.

The following steps explain how to apply the Motion settings to a clip with an alpha channel. Figure 17-8 shows a 3D still image over a sky background. The 3D image was created using Strata StudioPro. The image was saved with an alpha channel in Photoshop format. The sky background is from Digital Vision's Drifting Skies 386009f.mov file.

Figure 17-8: An image with an alpha channel over a background in the Monitor window.

Follow these steps to apply motion settings to a clip with an alpha channel:

1. **Choose File ➪ New ➪ Project to create a new project. In the New Project dialog box, choose a preset, name the project, and click OK to create a new project.**

2. **Choose File ➪ Import to import two clips into the Project window.** To see the transparency effects of an alpha channel, you need two images in two different video tracks, one on top of the other. One image should be a file that has an alpha channel; the other clip will be used as the background. If you want, you can use the images from Figure 17-8, or you can use the text tools in the Adobe Premiere Title Designer dialog box to create a title with an alpha channel. You can also use the graphic tools in the Adobe Premiere Title Designer dialog box to create a background.

The 3D image (StillLife.psd) and background file (Digital Vision's Drifting Skies 386009f.mov), shown in Figure 17-8, are found in the Digital Vision folder, Chapter 17 folder, which is in the Tutorial Projects folder on the DVD accompanying this book.

To review how to create titles and graphics using the Adobe Premiere Title Designer, see Chapter 11.

3. **Drag the background image to Video track 1 in the Timeline window.**

4. **Drag the file with the alpha channel (either the title clip or graphic file) from the Project window to Video track 2 in the Timeline window.**

5. **Change the duration of the image in Video track 2 to match the background clip in Video track 1.** The clip in Video track 2 should be selected. If it isn't, select it now.

6. **To apply motion effects to the clip in Video track 2, use either the Effect Controls window or the Timeline window to apply motion effect settings.**

7. **To preview the motion effects in the Monitor window, click the Play button.**

8. **To add a sound clip, choose File ➪ Import. In the Import dialog box, select a sound clip and click Open.** We used Digital Vision's CityMix 576009s.mov. It is in the Digital Vision folder, in the Chapter 17 folder, which is in the Tutorial Projects folder on the DVD.

9. **Choose File ➪ Save to save the project.**

Creating Traveling Mattes

A traveling matte (or mask) is a special effect that combines motion and masking. Typically, the matte is a shape that moves across the screen. Within the matte is one image; outside the mask is a background image.

Figure 17-9 shows a frame of the traveling matte effect. Notice that one image is seen through a star-shaped graphic pattern, which is the mask. The matte is simply a star-shaped white graphic created against a black background.

Figure 17-9: A frame for a traveling matte effect.

To create a traveling matte effect, you will need two video clips: one for the background and another one that will travel within the matte. You will also need a graphic image for the matte itself. Figure 17-10 shows the clips in the Timeline used to create the traveling matte effect shown in Figure 17-9. In Video track 3 is a star image. In Video track 2 is a landscape video clip, and in Video track 1 is a video clip of a sky.

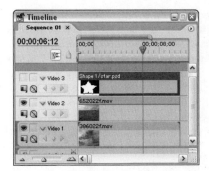

Figure 17-10: Timeline tracks used to create the traveling matte effect in Figure 17-9.

Here are the steps for creating a traveling matte effect:

1. **Choose File ➪ New ➪ Project to create a new project. In the New Project dialog box choose a preset.** If you are using the images from the DVD, choose the DV-NTSC Standard 32 kHz preset. Name the project. Click OK to create a new project.

2. **Choose File ➪ Import to import a clip to use in the background and import a file to use as the element to appear in the mask.** In Figure 17-9, we used a sky video clip as the background and a landscape clip to appear in the mask. Both clips shown in Figure 17-9 are from Digital Vision. The landscape clip is file 65022f.mov from the Sky Ride CD, and the sky clip is file 386022f.mov from the Drifting Skies CD.

The Digital Vision clip Sky Ride 65022f.mov clip and Drifting Skies 386022f.mov clip, shown in Figure 17-9, are found in the Digital Vision folder, in the Chapter 17 folder, which is in the Tutorial Projects folder on this book's companion DVD. If you prefer, you can use any two video clips located in the DVD's Tutorial Projects folder.

3. **Drag the image that you want to use as your background to Video track 1.**

4. **Drag the image that you want to appear within the matte into Video track 2.**

5. **Choose File ➪ Import to import a graphic image to use as a matte.** We used the star.psd image (found on this book's DVD). In the Import Layered File dialog box, leave the Import As pop-up menu set to Footage and select the Choose Layer option. In the Choose Layer pop-up menu, choose the appropriate layer (we chose Shape 1). Click OK to import the star shape into the Project window.

The star.psd image used in Figure 17-9 is found in the Chapter 17 folder, which is in the Tutorial Projects folder on the DVD that accompanies this book.

Note

If you want, you can create a white image against a black background to use as a matte. (We used Photoshop's Shape tool to create the star. When creating the file, set the pixel dimensions to be the same as those you want to use for your project. For more information on using Adobe Photoshop, turn to Chapter 27. For more information on using Adobe Illustrator, turn to Chapter 28.) You can also use the tools in the Title Designer window to create a matte shape. To use the Title Designer window, choose File ➪ New ➪ Title. (For more information on creating shapes in the Title Designer window, refer to Chapter 11.) Remember that after the traveling matte is complete, one clip appears within the white area. A background image appears in the black area.

6. **Drag the graphic image you want to use as a matte from the Project window into Video track 3.** In Figure 17-9, we used the star graphic as the matte graphic.

7. Extend the duration of the image in Video track 3 by clicking and dragging on the left side of the clip. Extend the duration so that it is the same as the clip in Video track 1 and 2.

8. Select the matte in Video track 3 by clicking it with the Selection tool.

9. To apply motion to the matte graphic, use the Motion options in the Effect Controls window or Timeline window.

10. Select Video track 2, which is the track sandwiched between the matte and the background image.

11. Choose Window ⇨ Effects to display the Effects window.

12. Click the triangle in front of the Video Effects folder to display the video effects. Then click the triangle in front of the Keying folder. Select the Track Matte key option and drag it over the clip in Video track 2. The Track Matte Key options are displayed in the Effect Controls window. The Matte pop-up menu should be set to Video 3. (For a detailed discussion of the Keying options, turn to Chapter 15.)

13. Hide Video track 3 by clicking on the eye icon in the Timeline window.

14. Preview the effect in the Monitor window by clicking the Play button.

15. Save your file by choosing File ⇨ Save.

Creating Motion Settings Projects

The following projects provide the steps for integrating graphics with alpha channels to create motion effects. In the first example, a coffee cup and text move across a chart of coffee bean sales. The second example is an animated book cover — an idea that booksellers might start using on their Web sites.

Creating a presentation

You can use the Motion Settings dialog box to create an animated presentation. Figure 17-11 shows the frames used to create a sample Coffee Bean Sales presentation. As you view the frames, notice the motion applied to the coffee cup and text clips.

We created the sample chart shown in Figure 17-12 using Adobe Illustrator and then saved it in Illustrator format. The coffee cup, shown in Figure 17-13, was scanned and manipulated using Adobe Photoshop. We used the Paintbrush and Eyedropper tools to fine-tune the edges and insides of the coffee cup. Then a selection of the coffee cup was created using the Polygonal Lasso tool. To soften the edges of the selection, a two-pixel feather was applied to the selection (Select ⇨ Feather). The selection was saved as an alpha channel (Select ⇨ Save Selection). To save the coffee cup and alpha channel, we saved the file in PICT format (you can also save in Photoshop or TIFF formats). We created the text using Premiere Pro's Title Designer window. All the images were imported into a new project. To make the coffee cup and text overlap, we placed them into different video tracks. We set the coffee cup and text into motion, using the Motion settings.

On the DVD-ROM   All the graphics used in this example can be found in the Chapter 17 Coffee folder, in the Tutorial Projects folder on the DVD that accompanies this book.

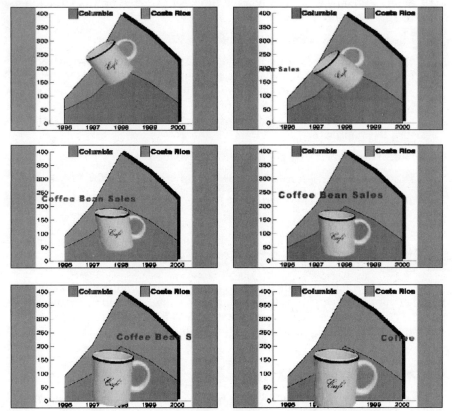

Figure 17-11: Frames from the sample Coffee Bean Sales presentation.

If you want to create your own graphics for a presentation, you'll need to create the following three production elements:

✦ **A background image.**

✦ **A title.** You can create a title in the Adobe Premiere Title Designer window, which is covered extensively in Chapter 11.

✦ **A graphic with an alpha channel.** Create this in a program that enables you to create alpha channels, or save masks, such as Adobe Photoshop, Corel Painter, or a 3D program.

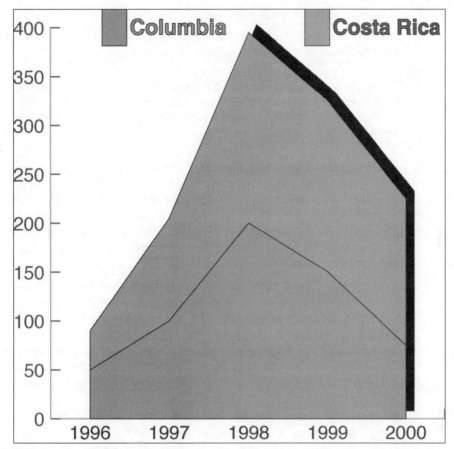

Figure 17-12: Coffee bean chart.

Figure 17-13: Coffee cup.

Follow these steps to create an animated presentation:

1. **Create a new project by choosing File ➪ New ➪ Project.**

2. **In the New Project dialog box, choose your project settings. Pick the Non-DV Square-Pixel 640 x 480 preset.** Name your file. Click OK to create your new project.

3. **To import the sample graphic files from the DVD that accompanies this book, choose File ➪ Import. In the Import dialog box, locate the Coffee folder from the Chapter 17 folder on the DVD and click the Import Folder button.** After you've imported the files, they appear in the Project window, as shown in Figure 17-14.

4. **If you are importing your own files, choose File ➪ Import.** To import more than one file at a time, press and hold the Control key, select the files that you want to import, and then import them. After you've imported the files, they appear in the Project window.

5. **Drag the background file from the Project window to Video track 1 in the Timeline window. Drag the chart file for the Coffee Bean Sales presentation to Video track 1.**

6. **Drag the image with the alpha channel from the Project window to Video track 2 in the Timeline window. Drag the coffee cup image to Video track 2 for the Coffee Bean Sales presentation.**

7. **Drag and drop the title (Coffee Bean Sales) that you imported from the DVD that accompanies this book to Video track 3.** If you want to create your own title, proceed to Step 8; otherwise, skip to the next set of steps in this section to apply motion to your images. The Timeline used to create the Coffee Bean Sales project is shown in Figure 17-15.

8. **To create your own title, choose File ➪ New ➪ Title.** In the Title Designer window, make sure that the Show Video option is selected if you want to see the image in Video track 2. Then use the Text tool to type some text. Stylize the text using the commands in the Title menu or the options in the Object Style section of the dialog box.

9. **Save your title by choosing File ➪ Save.** The title is saved to your hard disk and placed in the Project window. Drag the title to Video track 3.

Figure 17-14: The Project window with the files needed for the Coffee Bean Sales presentation.

Figure 17-15: The Timeline window with the files used for the Coffee Bean Sales presentation.

Now you're ready to apply motion to the images in Video track 2 and Video track 3:

1. **Click the clip in Video track 3 in the Timeline window and then use the Motion settings in either the Effect Controls window or the Timeline window to edit the motion using the techniques described in this chapter.** We set three points on the Motion Timeline: a starting point, a middle point, and a finish point. The text moves from the left to the right. At the middle point, we created a delay so that the text would stop moving long enough for the viewer to read it. The size of the text was decreased at the Start and Finish points, and the text size was increased in the middle point.

2. **To preview the Motion settings, click the Play button in the Monitor window.**

3. **Apply your own Motion settings to the image in Video track 2 by clicking the clip in Video track 2 and then using the Motion settings options in the Effect Controls window.** We made the cup move from the top down. The cup drops to the middle of the chart and then spills into the text. We added left rotations to points on the Motion Timeline. On the points in the middle of the Motion Timeline, we also added a delay for both the coffee cup and text. We also decreased and increased the coffee cup size. We used the clip's alpha channel option so that the white background would be removed from the image.

4. **Preview the motion settings by clicking the Play button in the Monitor window.**

Next, you need to add the audio clip to your presentation:

1. **Choose File ➪ Import. Locate Digital Vision's Cool Lounge 666001aw. wav audio file from the Digital Vision folder in the Chapter 17 folder that is on the DVD that accompanies this book.** When the audio file appears in the Project window, drag it to the Audio 1 track in the Timeline window. (For more information on working with audio, refer to Chapter 8.)

2. **Export the current video settings by choosing File ➪ Export ➪ Movie. If you want to change the export settings, click the Settings button. Otherwise, enter a filename and click Save.**

Animating a book cover

In the following steps, you'll create an animated book cover. You can see a frame from the book cover project in Figure 17-16. Here an angel image moves from the top left of the screen down to the bottom center of the screen. The angel starts on her side and as she moves, slowly rotates to the right, then to the left, and eventually ends in an upright position. When the angel reaches the bottom of screen, she halts for a moment while the text (Angel Stories) appears over a sky background in the middle of the screen. To create the motion for the angel, we used the Motion Settings dialog box. To create the background, we scanned a sky image and saved it in JPEG format. We used Premiere Pro's Adobe Title Designer window to create the text. We used both Adobe Illustrator and Adobe Photoshop to create the angel image.

All the graphics for this example can be loaded from the Angel folder in the Chapter 17 folder, which is in the Tutorial Projects folder on the DVD that accompanies this book.

Figure 17-16: A frame of the book cover project.

If you want to create your own graphics for an animated book cover, you need to create these three production elements:

✦ **A background image.**

✦ **A title.** You can create this in Premiere Pro's Adobe Title Designer window, which is discussed earlier in this chapter and covered extensively in Chapter 11.

✦ **A graphic with an alpha channel.** Create this in a program that enables you to create alpha channels or save masks, such as Adobe Photoshop or MetaCreations Painter. Most 3D programs also create alpha channels.

Following are the steps for creating the angel with an alpha channel:

1. **Create a pencil sketch of an angel image.**

2. **Scan it into Photoshop, or using your scanning software, save it in TIFF format.**

3. **Next, load the pencil sketch into Adobe Illustrator and use the Pen tool to outline the object and fill it with color.**

4. **Open the angel image in Photoshop.** When the image of the angel opens in Photoshop, it opens against a transparent background, called Layer 1. The transparent background enables you to easily create the alpha channel.

5. **To add depth to the angel, either apply a filter such as Texture (Filter ⇨ Texture) or use the Layer ⇨ Layer Style ⇨ Bevel and Emboss command.**

6. **To begin creating the alpha channel, you need to select only the angel onscreen. To do this, press and hold Ctrl as you click in the middle of Layer 1 in the Layers palette.** A selection appears around the angel image.

7. **With the selection onscreen, choose Select ⇨ Save Selection. In the Save Selection dialog box, enter a name for the selection and then click OK.** You should now have an alpha channel in the Channels palette.

8. **To save the file with the alpha channel, choose File ⇨ Save As. In the Save As dialog box, save in TIFF, PICT, or Photoshop format, making sure that the Save Alpha Channels option is selected.**

The steps to create the animated book cover are as follows:

1. **Create a new project by choosing File ⇨ New ⇨ Project. Pick the Non- DV Square-Pixel 640 x 480 preset.** Name your file. Click OK to create your new project.

2. **Choose File ⇨ Import. Locate and select the Angel folder that is located in the Chapter 17 folder on the DVD that accompanies this book. Then choose Import folder.** To import your own images, choose File ⇨ Import to import files needed for the project. In the Import dialog box, press and hold the Ctrl key to select more than one item at a time. Click Open to import the files into the Project window.

3. **Drag and drop the background image (the sky image) from the Project window to Video track 1.**

4. **Drag and drop the graphic image with the alpha channel (Angel) from the Project window to Video track 2.**

5. **Drag and drop the title (Angel Stories) to Video track 3.** To create your own title, choose File ⇨ New ⇨ Title. In the Adobe Title Designer window (shown in Figure 17-17), create the desired type effect.

6. **With the graphic alpha channel image (the angel image) in Video track 2 selected, use the Motion settings to apply motion to the angel image.** We made the angel move from the top-left side to the middle, then downwards.

7. **Use the Selection tool to select the title (Angel Stories) in the Timeline.**

8. Use the Motion settings to make the text move from the top left to the top right.

9. Preview your project by clicking Play in the Monitor window.

10. To export your project according to your project presets, choose File ➪ Export ➪ Movie. Name your file and then click Save.

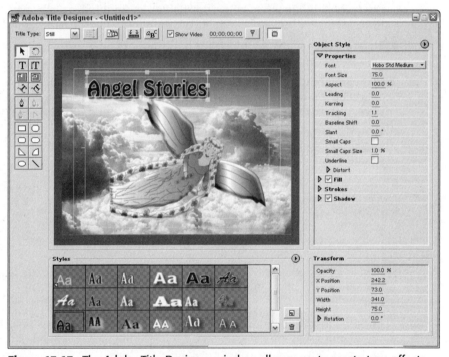

Figure 17-17: The Adobe Title Designer window allows you to create type effects.

Summary

Premiere Pro's Motion settings enable you to create motion effects from graphics and video clips. You can do the following:

✦ Change motion speed and direction with the Motion settings.

✦ Rotate and scale images with the Motion settings.

✦ Use the Motion settings with clips that have alpha channels to create motion effects where image backgrounds are transparent.

✦ Use the track matte Key Type to create a traveling matte effect.

✦   ✦   ✦

Enhancing Video

When shooting video, you will eventually have little control over the locale or lighting conditions. This often results in video clips that are too dark or too bright or that display a colorcast onscreen. Fortunately, Premiere Pro's Video Effects window includes a number of effects specifically designed to change image brightness, contrast, and colors. Many of these effects can be previewed onscreen while you fine-tune the options in the Video Effects window. Although there is no substitute for high-quality video shot with well-planned lighting, Premiere Pro's Video Effects window may be able to boost the overall tonal and color quality of your production.

However, if you find that the Premiere Pro tools aren't powerful enough, you can import your video clip as a Filmstrip file into Adobe Photoshop. You can then use Photoshop's powerful masking and color-correcting tools to enhance your clip frame by frame. You can then import the corrected file back into Premiere Pro.

This chapter looks at the Premiere filters that can be used to enhance colors. It starts with an overview of the RGB color model and then goes into the video enhancement options that Premiere Pro provides. It concludes with a look at how to import a file into Photoshop, correct the video, and then export it back to Premiere Pro.

The RGB Color Model

Before you begin to correct color, lightness, brightness, and contrast in Premiere Pro, you should review a few important concepts about computer color theory. As you'll soon see, Premiere Pro's image-enhancement commands are not based on the basics of television engineering. Instead, they're based on the fundamentals of how a computer creates color.

When you view images on a computer display, colors are created from different combinations of red, green, and blue light. When you need to choose or edit colors, many computer programs, such as Premiere Pro and Photoshop, enable you to choose from 256 levels of red, 256 levels of green, and 256 levels of blue. This results in over 17.6 million color possibilities ($256 \times 256 \times 256$). In both Premiere Pro and Photoshop, each red, green, and blue color component of an image is called a *channel*.

Premiere Pro's Color Picker provides an example of how red, green, and blue channels create color. Using the Color Picker, you can choose colors by specifying red, green, and blue values. To open Premiere Pro's Color Picker, you must first have a project onscreen and then choose File ➪ New ➪ Color Matte. In the Color Picker dialog box, shown in Figure 18-1, notice the Red, Green, and Blue entry fields. If you click a color on the left, the numbers in the entry fields change to show how many levels of red, green, and blue are used to create that color. To change colors, you can also enter a value from 0 to 255 into each of the Red, Green, and Blue fields.

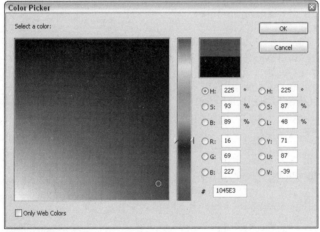

Figure 18-1: Premiere Pro's Color Picker enables you to choose colors by specifying red, green, and blue color values.

Note As you work in Premiere Pro, consider your production's final export destination. If you are exporting to videotape, realize that the color gamut (the range of colors that make up an image) displayed on a computer screen is greater than the color gamut of a television screen. Your computer monitor creates colors using red, green, and blue phosphors. American Broadcast television uses the YCC standard, which uses one luminance, or brightness, channel and two color channels to create an image. The luminance channel was and still is based on the luminance value used for black-and-white television. This value was kept so those viewers with black-and-white television could still view the television signal when color was adapted.

If you will be using Premiere Pro to do color correcting, you need to have a basic understanding of how the red, green, and blue color channels interact to create red, green, and blue color, and their complements (or opposites), cyan, magenta, and yellow. The following list of color combinations can help you understand how different channels create colors. Note that the lower numbers are darker, and the higher numbers are brighter. The combination 0 red, 0 green, 0 blue creates black—the absence of light. If red, green, and blue values are set to 255, white is created—the most amount of light.

> 255 red + 255 green + 255 blue = white
>
> 0 red + 0 green + 0 blue = black
>
> 255 red + 255 green = yellow
>
> 255 red + 255 blue = magenta
>
> 255 green + 255 blue = cyan

Notice that adding two of the RGB color components produces cyan, magenta, or yellow. These are the complements of red, green, and blue. Understanding this relationship is helpful, because it can help provide some direction as you work. From the preceding color calculations, you can see that adding more red and more green to an image produces more yellow; adding more red and blue produces more magenta; adding more green and blue produces more cyan.

The preceding calculations also provide a basis for the results of adding or subtracting one of the Red, Green, or Blue channels from an image:

> Add red = less cyan
>
> Reduce red = more cyan
>
> Increase green = less magenta
>
> Reduce green = more magenta
>
> Add blue = less yellow
>
> Reduce blue = more yellow

As you can see from the examples in this chapter, most of Premiere Pro's image-enhancement commands use red, green, and blue sliders or red, green, and blue channels when called upon to correct color.

Using the Premiere Pro video effects to color correct. In Premiere Pro's Video Effects window, the Adjust and Image Control folders contain color-correcting video effects. (You may also want to use the effects in the Sharpen folder to sharpen the video after you've adjusted its color.) To display the Effects window that contains the Video Effects folder, choose Window ➪ Effects. (For detailed descriptions on using all the video effects, see Chapter 14.)

The Adjust effects

The video effects in the Adjust folder are Brightness & Contrast, Channel Mixer, Convolution Kernel, Extract, Levels, Posterize, and ProAmp.

On the DVD-ROM Before you begin exploring Premiere Pro's color-enhancement commands, start by creating a new project. Import a color clip into Premiere Pro and drag it into Video track 1. If you don't have a video clip to use, you can use one of the clips found in the Chapter 18 folder, which is in the Tutorial Projects folder that is on the DVD that accompanies this book. In the following sections, we used Digital Vision's 567004f.mov from the CityMix CD.

Changing brightness and contrast

The Brightness and Contrast effect is one of the easiest image effects to correct. Brightness controls the light levels in your image, while contrast is the difference between the brightest and darkest levels. To use the Brightness & Contrast effect, click and drag it over the clip in Video track 1. (The Brightness & Contrast effect is found in the Adjust folder that is in the Effect window.) After you drag the effect, the controls for the effect appear in the Effect Controls window. Take a moment to try out each of the Brightness & Contrast Settings:

✦ **Brightness.** To increase overall brightness in your clip, click and drag the Brightness slider to the right. As you drag, the entire image lightens. To decrease Brightness, click and drag to the left. As you drag, the entire clip gets darker.

✦ **Contrast.** To see the effect of the Contrast slider, first click and drag the slider to the right. As you drag, you add contrast, increasing the difference between the lightest and darkest areas of your image. This also tends to create a sharper image. To decrease sharpness, click and drag to the left. As you drag, the entire clip begins to fade out.

Continue to experiment with the Brightness & Contrast Video effect. After you finish, you can remove the effect by clicking on it in the Effect Controls window, then pressing Delete.

Changing levels

The Levels filter is one of the most sophisticated color-correcting controls offered by Premiere Pro. Levels can be used for fine-tuning shadows (dark image areas), mid-tones (mid-level image areas), and highlights (light image areas). If you've worked with Photoshop, you might recognize this command. Premiere Pro's Levels control is virtually identical to Photoshop's. To try out the Levels effect, click and drag the Levels effect over a clip in one of your video tracks. To see the Levels Settings dialog box, as shown in Figure 18-2, click the Setup button in the Effect Controls window.

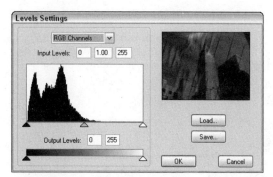

Figure 18-2: Premiere Pro's Levels Settings dialog box enables you to adjust shadows, midtones, and highlights.

In the Levels Settings dialog box, Premiere Pro provides a histogram of the image. The histogram is a chart that provides a graphical representation of the brightness levels of the pixels in your image. If the darker pixel levels are shown at the left end of the histogram, brighter levels are shown to the right of the histogram. The higher the line, the larger the number of pixels there are that occur at that brightness level. The lower the line, the fewer the pixels there are that occur at that brightness level.

The Levels dialog box is confusing, because it provides two different sliders with five different slider controls.

The top slider is called the Input slider. The bottom slider is the Output slider. The best way to summarize the two sliders is this: Use the top slider to add contrast in an image; use the bottom slider to decrease contrast in an image.

Increasing contrast

Here's how to increase contrast in an image. Suppose that the histogram of your image shows that the darkest area of your image appears at the 10 mark on the input slider. You can increase contrast in the darkest areas of your image by clicking and dragging the black input slider to the right. When you click and drag, Premiere Pro begins to remap the brightness levels in the image by taking all pixels that start at 10 and remapping them to 0 and then remapping all corresponding pixels. The result is a darker image with more contrast. Click and drag the white slider to achieve the same effect with the brightest pixels. In other words, you can increase contrast in the lightest areas of your image.

To correct your image, you may want to move the midtone slider to the left to lighten the midtones and drag the midtone slider to the right to darken the midtones, without greatly changing the lightest and darkest parts of an image.

Decreasing contrast

If you have too much contrast in an image, you can lighten an image and reduce contrast by clicking and dragging the left black (or input) slider. When you reduce black levels, you are reducing the number of dark pixels in the image. For example, if you drag the bottom slider from 0 to 10, any pixels that were at 0 are removed from the image and remapped to 10, and the rest of the pixels in the image are adjusted accordingly.

To summarize, click and drag the left input slider to 10. Pixels that were 10 are remapped to 0. Click and drag the bottom slider to 10. Pixels that were 0 are remapped to 10.

Changing channel levels

The Levels Settings dialog box also enables you to change levels for individual Red, Green, and Blue channels. For example, to add contrast to the Red channel, choose red from the pop-up menu in the Levels Settings dialog box. When you pick a channel, the histogram displays changes to show you the pixel distribution of colors for only that channel. As you click and drag the highlight slider, you can increase contrast in the Red channel. By clicking and dragging the output slider, you can reduce contrast in the Red channel.

Note   If you frequently use the same levels settings, you can save them to disk by clicking the Save button. You can reload your settings by clicking the Load button.

Continue to experiment with the Color Balance video effect. When you're done, you can remove the effect by clicking the filter in the Effect Controls window and pressing Delete.

Using other Adjust filters

The other commands in the Adjust folder that affect a video clip's color are summarized here. (For more information about these filters, see Chapter 14.)

- ✦ **Channel Mixer.** Use the Channel Mixer video effect to create special effects, such as sepia or tinted effects.

- ✦ **Posterize.** The Posterize effect enables you to reduce the number of gray levels in your image.

- ✦ **Convolution Kernel.** Use Convolution Kernel to change the brightness and sharpness of your image.

- ✦ **Extract.** The Extract video effect enables you to convert your color clip to black and white.

- ✦ **ProAmp.** The ProAmp video effect enables you to adjust the hue, saturation, and luminance of a clip.

The Image Control effects

Adobe Premiere Pro provides even more color effects in the Image Control folder. The effects in the Image Control folder are Black & White, Color Balance (HLS), Color Balance (RGB), Color Corrector, Color Match, Color Offset, Color Pass, Color Replace, and Tint. (For more information on these effects, see Chapter 14.)

Balancing colors

The Color Balance (RGB) effect enables you to change the balance of a clip's red, green, and blue color channels. To use this color-enhancement effect, click and drag it from the Adjust section of the Video Effects folder in the Effects window and drag it over your clip in the video track.

The Effect Controls window shows you the color slides. To see a preview of the image in the Color Balance dialog box, click Setup in the Effect Controls window, as shown in Figure 18-3. Try experimenting with each slider. As you work, you'll put into practice the RGB color theory.

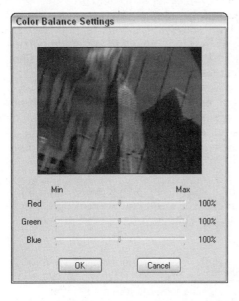

Figure 18-3: Premiere Pro's Color Balance effect enables you to change an image's color balance by adjusting red, green, and blue color components.

✦ Click and drag the red slider to the right. As you drag, you gradually pump red into your image. Drag the slider to the left to decrease red. Note that as you reduce red, you increase cyan. Cyan is added because you now have more green and blue in your image. To increase cyan, click and drag both the green and blue sliders to the right.

✦ Click and drag the green slider to the right. As you drag, you increase green in your image. Drag to the left to decrease green. As you reduce green, you add magenta. Magenta is added because you have more red and blue in your image than green. To add more magenta, click and drag both the red and blue sliders to the right.

✦ Click and drag the blue slider to the right. As you drag, you increase blue in your image. Drag to the left to decrease blue. As you reduce blue, you add yellow. Yellow is added because you have more red and green in your image. You add even more yellow by clicking and dragging both the red and green sliders to the right.

Continue to experiment with the Color Balance (RGB) effect. When you're done, you can remove the effect by clicking on the filter in the Effect Controls window, then pressing Delete.

Using HSL Color Balance

Although the RGB color model is used by computer displays to create colors, it's not very intuitive. For example, if you want to create a bright orange color or a light brown color, what RGB combination would you choose? To help provide more intuitive colors, the Hue Saturation Lightness (HSL) color model was created. In this color model, colors are created in much the same way as color is perceived. *Hue* is the color, *Lightness* is the brightness or darkness of the color, and *Saturation* is the color intensity. If you don't want to use Premiere Pro's RGB Color Balance effect, you can use its HSL Color Balance effect instead.

To try out the HSL Color Balance effect, open the Image Control folder that is in the Video Effects folder, inside the Effects window. Then click and drag the HSL Color Balance effect over a clip in a video track. Because there is no preview in the dialog box, make sure that the Monitor window is open. You can see the preview of this effect in the Monitor window.

Try experimenting with the sliders in the Effect Controls window, which is shown in Figure 18-4. As you drag the slider to the right, it's as if you are moving around a circular color wheel. As you click and drag the slider, you see at what degree of the circle you are.

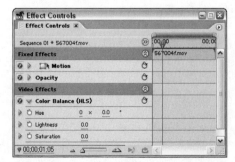

Figure 18-4: The HSL Color Balance effect enables you to adjust color balance using Hue, Saturation, and Lightness controls.

Note If you want to enter a precise number for a slider, click any numeric value above the slider. Doing so opens a dialog box in which you can enter a specific value.

The best way to see the effect of the changing hues is to add saturation to your image. Click and drag the Saturation slider to the right. To see the effect of the lightness slider, click and drag first to the right to add more light to the image, and then to the left to reduce the amount of light.

When you've finished experimenting with this filter, click the filter icon in the Effect Controls window and press Delete.

Gamma Correction

The Gamma Correction filter changes midtones without affecting shadows and highlights. This is an easy filter to use if you just want to make sure that the dark and light areas of your image are in good shape. To use this filter, click and drag the Gamma Correction filter from the Image Control folder in the Effects window over a clip. To see a preview of the effect, click the word Setup in the Effect Controls window. In the Gamma Correction Settings dialog box (shown in Figure 18-5), simply click and drag the slider. As you click and drag to the right, you increase gamma, thereby darkening your image. By clicking and dragging to the left, you lighten midtones as you decrease gamma.

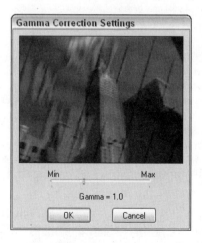

Figure 18-5: Premiere Pro's Gamma Correction effect enables you to change midtones without affecting shadows and highlights.

Color Corrector

The Color Corrector filter is new to Premiere Pro. It allows you to make several color correction adjustments. Click and drag the Color Corrector filter from the Image Control folder in the Effects window over a clip. Click the triangle in front of Color Corrector to display the options for this filter (shown in Figure 18-6). Then click the triangle in front of Settings Key. Notice a folder and a disk icon, shown in Figure 18-6. You can save the color correction adjustments by clicking on the disk icon and load them into any project by clicking on the folder icon.

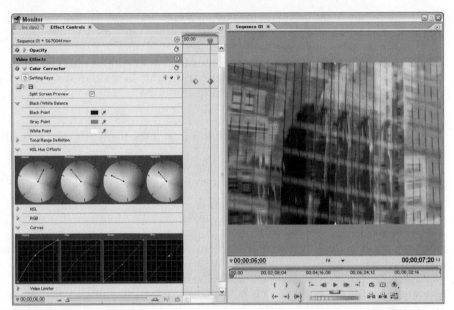

Figure 18-6: Premiere Pro's Color Corrector effect enables you to make several color correction adjustments.

Before you start using the Color Corrector filter, click the Split Screen Preview check box. In the Monitor window, Premiere Pro divides the video clip. The left side of the clip reveals the clip without any color correction. The right side of the clip reveals the adjustments being made (shown in Figure 18-6).

Next, move the current-time indicator to the frame where you want to color correct. If you don't want the color correction to affect the entire clip, click the stopwatch icon that is next to Settings Keys to create a keyframe. Make the adjustments needed for that frame and then move the current-time indicator to another frame and click the Add/Remove Keyframe button to add another keyframe. Any color corrections that you make will affect that frame and all the frames between that one and the next keyframe.

Note   When using the Color Corrector filter, you should color correct using the settings from top to bottom. The order in which you color correct is very important.

Here is the way to color correct using the Color Corrector filter:

1. **Use the Black/White Balance settings to set black, gray, and white points using the eyedroppers.** Use the Black Point eyedropper to click an area in the clip that should represent black. Use the White Point eyedropper to click an area in the clip that should represent white. Use the Gray Point eyedropper to click an area in the clip that should represent gray. The Gray Point eyedropper tool helps remove color cast from an image.

2. **Use the Tonal Range Definition to adjust the shadows, highlights, and midtones.** Adjusting the shadows, highlights, and midtones is sometimes called the *three-point color corrector*. When using the Tonal Range Definition option, try switching the Monitor view to Waveform. In the Waveform Monitor (WFM), shown in Figure 18-7, the black values appear at the bottom and the white values appear at the top.

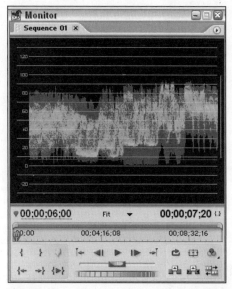

Figure 18-7: The Waveform Monitor displays video signals.

3. **Use Hue Offsets to adjust the Hue and Saturation.** Click the black square in the middle of the wheels to adjust the hue and saturation. As you work with the Hue Offsets settings, try switching the Monitor view to Vectorscope. The Vectorscope view, shown in Figure 18-8, displays hue and saturation.

4. **Use the HSL setting to adjust the hue, saturation, and luminance.** The Tonal Range pop-up menu allows you to choose whether you are going to adjust the Master, the Highlights, Midtones, or Shadows. As you work with the HSL settings, try switching the Monitor view to YcbCr Parade. The YcbCr Parade view, shown in Figure 18-9, displays luma values and chroma saturation.

5. **Use the RGB setting to adjust the gamma, pedestal, and gain for the red, green, and blue colors.** The Tonal Range pop-up menu allows you to choose whether you are going to adjust the Master, the Highlights, Midtones, or Shadows. As you work with the RGB settings, try switching the Monitor view to RGB Parade. The RGB Parade view, shown in Figure 18-10, displays the values of red, green, and blue colors.

Figure 18-8: The Vectorscope view displays hue and saturation.

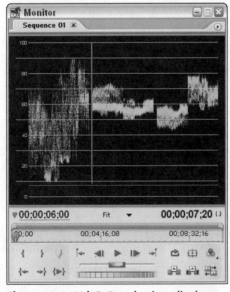

Figure 18-9: YcbCr Parade view displays luma values and chroma saturation.

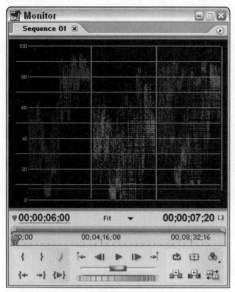

Figure 18-10: RGB Parade view displays the levels of red, green, and blue colors.

6. **Adjust the curves. There are four curves: Master, Red, Green, and Blue.** The master curve adjusts all the colors in the clip. The other curves adjust the separate color channels. Click and drag either up or down on the curve to adjust the colors.

7. **Use the Video Limiter to set the video system to the system to which you will be outputting.**

8. **When you are finished color correcting, be sure to deselect the Split Screen preview from the Setting Keys section.**

9. **If you want to save the color correcting settings, click the disk icon in the Setting Keys section.**

Color Match

The Color Match filter is new to Premiere Pro. The Color Match filter, shown in Figure 18-11, allows you to match colors from one footage to another. When using this filter, you may want to use the Reference monitor view. This way, you can see one footage in the Monitor view and the other in the Reference view.

To use the Color Match filter, use the eyedropper to choose a target color and a sample color. The target color is the color that you want to match. The sample color is the color that you want to adjust so that it matches the target color. After you have set the target and sample color, click the Match button located in the Match section.

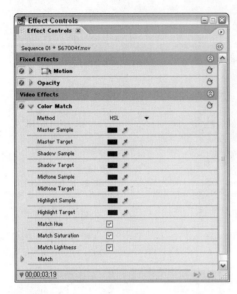

Figure 18-11: Premiere Pro's Color Match allows you to match the colors in one footage with the colors in another.

The Video folder effects

The effects in the Video folder are designed to improve clips that will be exported to videotape. The effects in the Video folder are Broadcast colors, Field Interpolate, and Reduce Interlace Flicker. For more information on video effects, refer to Chapter 14.

Broadcast colors

To use the Broadcast Color effect, click and drag the effect from the Video Effects folder from the Effects window over a clip in a video track in the Timeline window.

Note   If you are exporting your Premiere production to videotape, you can add color bars to the beginning of your production. Color bars enable a video production facility to calibrate colors when duplicating or broadcasting video. Adding color bars is discussed in Chapter 2.

The sliders and controls for the effect appear in the Effect Controls window. To use the effect, choose either NTSC for American television or PAL for European television in the Broadcast locale pop-up menu. Then choose a method in the How to Make Colors Safe pop-up menu. Here is an explanation of the choices:

✦ **Reduce Luminance.** Reduces pixel brightness values. As the values are reduced, colors become darker.

✦ **Reduce Saturation.** Brings pixel values closer to gray. This makes the colors less intense.

✦ **Key out Unsafe.** Colors that fall beyond the TV gamut become transparent.

✦ **Key in Safe.** Colors that are within the TV gamut are transparent.

In the Maximum Signal Field, use the slider to enter the maximum IRE (or image luminance) breakpoint value. Any levels above this value are altered. If you are unsure of what value to use, use the default setting of 110.

In some video cameras, black and white stripes appear in the viewfinder when an image's brightness surpasses 100 IRE. This indicates that the image luminance is too bright.

Field Interpolate and Reduce Interlace Flicker

Two other image-enhancing effects appear in the Video folder: Field Interpolate and Reduce Interlace Flicker.

✦ **Field Interpolate.** This effect creates missing scan lines from the average of other lines.

✦ **Reduce Interlace Flicker.** This effect softens horizontal lines in an attempt to reduce interlace flicker.

Adobe After Effects uses many of the same color-correcting techniques as Adobe Premiere Pro. However, After Effects has a powerful advantage: It enables you to mask or isolate areas onscreen. After you mask an area, you can choose to color correct the masked area only.

To color correct a Premiere project in After Effects, load the Premiere project into After Effects by choosing File ➪ Import. (For more information on working with masks in After Effects, turn to Chapter 29.) After you've completed color correcting in After Effects, you can export your file as a QuickTime or AVI movie and load it into Premiere Pro.

Retouching and Color Correcting with Photoshop

Although Premiere Pro provides a variety of controls for correcting colors, you may need to make a specific adjustment to an image area and may want to use Adobe Photoshop. You can export a Premiere clip to Adobe Photoshop in Filmstrip format or TIFF, PICT, or Targa Sequence format. Adobe specifically designed Filmstrip format to act as a bridge between Adobe Premiere Pro and Adobe Photoshop. When a Premiere Pro clip is loaded into Photoshop, you can see each individual frame and use Photoshop's extensive color-correcting toolset to correct the image.

You can also use Photoshop's powerful masking utilities to isolate areas and then manipulate the shade and colors. Once in Photoshop, you can copy and paste images from one frame to another, or you can select and copy a person from a photograph, for example, and paste it into your video clip. You can also omit a person from a video clip by cloning surrounding areas or by painting over it with the Paintbrush. Figure 18-12 shows a frame from a video clip before masking and color correcting. Figure 18-13 shows the same frame after masking and color correcting.

Figure 18-12: Frame from a video clip before masking and color correcting.

Figure 18-13: Frame from a video clip after masking and color correcting.

Note   Before you take a person out of a video clip or add a person to a video clip, check whether you need permission to do so. This is especially so if you are going to publish or distribute the video you are creating. Make sure that you have permission from the people who appear in the video.

Loading a video clip into Photoshop

Before you can manipulate your video clip in Photoshop, you need to convert the video clip to Filmstrip format. Here's how to export a Premiere clip to Photoshop in Filmstrip format:

1. **Load or create a Premiere project.** If you are in a new Premiere project, open a clip by choosing File ⇨ Open, or import a clip by choosing File ⇨ Import ⇨ File.

You can use the Gondola video clip found in Chapter 18, which is in the Tutorial Projects on the DVD that accompanies this book.

2. **If you used File ⇨ Open to open a clip, choose File ⇨ Export Clip ⇨ Movie. If you used File ⇨ Import to import a file into the Timeline window, choose File ⇨ Export Timeline ⇨ Movie.**

3. **In the Export Movie dialog box, name your movie.**

4. **Click the Settings button to display the Export Movie Settings dialog box.** The Export Movie Settings dialog box appears.

5. **Click the File Type option and choose Filmstrip.** Note that you can also choose to use the TIFF, PICT, or Targa Sequence formats.

6. **Click the Range pop-up menu.** If you have opened a clip, choose Entire Clip to export the entire clip. Choose In to Out to export a clip whose in and out points have been edited. If you have imported a clip to the Timeline window, choose Entire Project to export the entire project. Choose Work Area to export only the area where the preview bar is located.

7. **Click OK.** Premiere Pro exports your project into a Filmstrip file, which you can then import into Photoshop.

Premiere Pro's Export Movie Settings determine the frame size, frame rate, and other features of the exported file. The export settings are covered in detail in Chapter 19.

Use the following steps to import a Premiere Filmstrip file into Photoshop:

1. **In Photoshop, choose File ⇨ Open.** The Open dialog box opens.

2. **Locate the Filmstrip file.** Before you open the file, click on the file. Notice that in the Open dialog box, next to the Filmstrip format, the size of your file appears. The file size may surprise you. Remember that when you open a Filmstrip file in Photoshop, you are opening a video clip that contains various frames at the width and height of your clip. Therefore, the Photoshop file may be very large. Make sure that your system can handle the file. If the file is too big, you may need to go back to Premiere Pro and use the in and out points to cut some frames out of the video clip. Then re-export the file in Filmstrip format, and reopen in Photoshop.

3. **Click Open.** The Filmstrip file loads with the file reduced in size so that you can see all the frames in the file (see Figure 18-14). The more frames in your document, the smaller the frame preview.

Note Filmstrip files may be large and sometimes slow to work on.

4. Choose View ⇨ Zoom In a few times to enlarge the size of the frame preview. When the Filmstrip window is enlarged, you can see the frame preview for only a few frames, as shown in Figure 18-15. Scroll down to see the rest of the frames in the video clip. Notice that below each frame appears the Timeline number. Also notice that the document size appears at the bottom left of the document.

Tip Press Ctrl++ a few times to zoom.

Figure 18-14: When the Filmstrip file opens in Photoshop, all the Premiere frames are loaded.

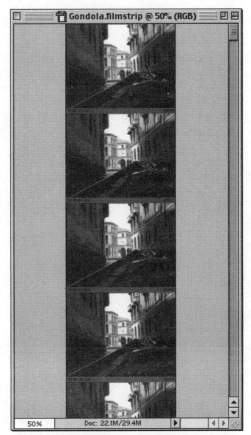

Figure 18-15: Frames from the video clip.

The following sections provide an overview of several of Photoshop's image-enhancing commands. For full details on these commands, consult the Photoshop manual.

Using Selections in Photoshop

One of the best reasons for using Photoshop to make color and tonal adjustments is its masking capabilities. In Photoshop, you can select an image area with a selection tool, such as the Magic Wand or Lasso tool, and then execute an image adjustment command. When the command is applied, Photoshop only applies it to the selected area.

Selecting a color range

If you are selecting image areas in a Filmstrip file or sequence files, it is handy to quickly create a selection that spans multiple frames. You can easily create a selection throughout many frames using Photoshop's Color Range command. Follow these steps to select a color range:

1. **To open the Color Range dialog box, shown in Figure 18-16, choose Select ⇨ Color Range.**

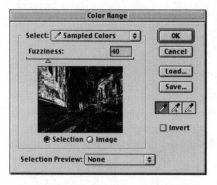

Figure 18-16: Photoshop's Color Range command enables you to select parts of an image by color.

2. **To select a color range, set the Select menu to Sampled Colors.**

3. **Click the Image radio button.**

4. **Choose Grayscale in the Selection Preview menu.** The image appears onscreen in the dialog box's preview area with the selected area in black and white.

5. **With the Eyedropper tool selected, click in the image area of the dialog box that you want to select.** As soon as you click, all colors that match the color you clicked turn white onscreen.

6. **Click and drag the Fuzziness slider to fine-tune the selection.**

7. **Use the Eyedropper + tool to click on the image area you want to add to the selection.** To subtract from the selection, click in the preview image area in the dialog box with the Eyedropper – tool.

8. **Click OK.** The final selection appears onscreen.

Saving selections to alpha channels

Photoshop enables you to save selections and edit them as grayscale mask images in its Channels palette. This provides a sophisticated method of creating an intricate selection. A detailed description of editing masks is beyond the scope of this book. However, the following is a quick review of the steps needed to save a selection as a mask, and to edit the mask:

1. **Create a rough selection onscreen using one of Photoshop's selection tools, such as one of the Lasso tools or the Magic Wand.**

Tip   While using one of the selection tools, press and hold the Shift key to add to a selection. Press and hold the Alt key to subtract from a selection.

2. **To create a mask out of the selection in an alpha channel, choose Select ⇨ Save Selection.** In the Save Selection dialog box, name the selection and then click Save. You can edit it using Photoshop's painting tools.

3. **Activate the mask channel so that you can still see your image onscreen.** To do this, select the channel in the Channels palette to activate the channel for editing and display the mask's eye icon. A red overlay indicates the mask edges.

4. **Select a painting tool, such as the Paintbrush or Pencil.**

5. **Choose a brush size.** Make sure that the painting tool is in normal mode, with opacity set to 100%. Try painting over your image. Try painting with white; try painting with black. If Photoshop's default settings are in effect, painting with white enlarges the mask; painting with black reduces the size of the mask. To fine-tune the mask, choose a small brush size and zoom into your image to edit it.

6. **After you finish editing the mask, reselect the RGB channel in the Channels palette.**

7. **Choose Select ⇨ Load Selection.** Photoshop converts the mask into a blinking selection onscreen and is ready for use in image correction.

Note   To save a file with saved selections in channels, you must save your file in Photoshop format. When you are finished with the saved selections, you can delete the channels by dragging the channel in the Channels palette to the trash. If you don't want to delete the saved selections, you may want to make a copy of the file. Remember, you can't import a Photoshop file into Premiere Pro as a Filmstrip; instead, Premiere will import the Photoshop file as a still image. Thus, to save a Photoshop file in Filmstrip format, which can be imported into Premiere Pro, choose File ⇨ Save As. In the Save As dialog box, choose the Filmstrip format.

Using Photoshop's Image Adjust Commands

This section reviews several Photoshop image-correcting commands that can be useful if you are making color or tonal adjustments to Filmstrip files. Our goal here is to introduce you to these commands, not to make you Photoshop color-correcting experts. If you find that your video clip requires hours and hours of enhancement work in Photoshop, you should consider whether your time might be better spent reshooting or restructuring your Premiere production so that you can use clips that don't need a lot of color correction.

Tip   To quickly retouch and/or color correct various frames in a clip, you can use Photoshop's Actions palette to process through TIFF, PICT, or TARGA sequence files to open a file, apply an Image Adjust command, save, and close a file.

Using the Info palette

Before you start color-correcting a clip, you should display the Info palettes that you can see the values of the colors that you are affecting. Choose Window ➪ Show Info to display the Info palette. The Info palette, shown in Figure 18-17, displays the individual RGB colors as you move the Eyedropper tool over an image. (If the RGB colors don't appear, click the Info palette pop-up menu and choose Palette Options. In the Info Options dialog box, choose Actual Color from the Mode pop-up menu.)

To see the values of your image, move the mouse over your image. As you move the mouse, notice the color values in the Info palette. As soon as you start color correcting, these values change. You can check the values while you are using a dialog box to color correct. In the Info palette, a before and after value appears.

At this point, you should decide whether your image needs simple tonal adjustments or more advanced tonal and color corrections.

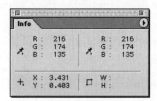

Figure 18-17: Photoshop's Info palette displays a reading of the colors in your image.

Brightness/Contrast

If your image needs minor color adjustments, use the Image ➪ Adjust ➪ Brightness/Contrast command. This command works identically to Premiere Pro's Brightness & Contrast video effect. However, in Photoshop, you can select a portion of your image and then apply the command to adjust the image.

Tip   As you are working with Photoshop's color-correcting commands, you can reset the dialog box options back to their original settings by pressing Alt and then clicking the Cancel button.

Levels

If your image needs more sophisticated tonal adjustments or if you need to make overall adjustments to a red, green, or blue image channel, use Photoshop's Levels command. To open the Levels dialog box, shown in Figure 18-18, choose Image ➪ Adjust ➪ Levels.

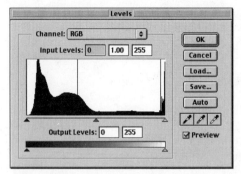

Figure 18-18: The Levels command is used to lighten the first frame of the Gondola video clip.

Photoshop's Levels dialog box works similarly to Premiere Pro's Levels dialog box. However, in Photoshop, if you select an area onscreen, the histogram that appears charts the pixel distribution in the selected area.

In the Levels dialog box, click Save to save the settings in the Levels dialog box. In the dialog box that appears next, name the setting and then click Save. After you save the Levels settings, close the dialog box by clicking OK. Now that you've saved the Levels settings, you can add them to other clips.

Curves

Photoshop's Curves command is considered one of its most powerful tools for adjusting image tones. Unlike the Levels command, which focuses on highlights, midtones, and shadow areas, the Curves command enables you to make tonal adjustments throughout an image's brightness range. And as you make adjustments, you can lock in up to 15 points on the curve.

To open Photoshop's Curves dialog box, choose Image ⇨ Adjust ⇨ Curves. In the Curves dialog box, shown in Figure 18-19, the x-axis of the dialog box represents the original image values, and the y-axis represents the values that are changed. Because all points are equal when you begin, the Curves dialog box opens by displaying a straight diagonal line.

To make adjustments using the curve, start by examining the horizontal axis. The left-end of the horizontal axis represents darker areas of the original image; brighter areas are represented on the right side of the horizontal axis. (This is the default setting. If the default setting has been changed, to appear in percentages rather than in a range from 0 to 255, click the middle of the curve to change the horizontal axis to its default setting.) A quick way to pinpoint where image areas are represented on the curve is to simply click in your image. As you click, a dot appears in the corresponding area on the curve.

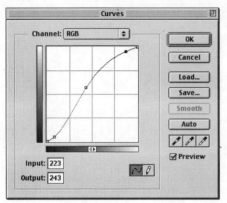

Figure 18-19: Photoshop's Curves dialog box.

To lighten an image area, click and drag up on the curve; to darken an area, click and drag down. As you drag, the curve shows how the rest of the pixels in the image change. To prevent part of the curve from changing, you can click the curve to establish fixed points. As you click and drag, the fixed points lock down the curve.

As with Photoshop's Levels command, Curves also enables you to change the tonal range of individual color channels. To select a channel, choose Red, Green, or Blue from the Channels pop-up menu. If you click and drag a curve representing a channel, dragging upward increases that channel's color in the image, whereas dragging downward reduces it and adds that color's complements. For example, if you select the Green channel, dragging up adds more green and dragging down on the curve adds more magenta.

Variations

If you want to perform a simple correction of shadows, midtones, highlights, and colors in an image and are not a Photoshop expert, try the Variations command. This enables you to color correct visually. To open the Variations dialog box, choose Image ➪ Adjust ➪ Variations.

In the Variations dialog box, shown in Figure 18-20, move the slider at the top toward Finer so that the changes occur gradually. Then choose whether you want to adjust Shadows, Midtones, or Highlights. To lighten the frames, click the Lighter thumbnail. Notice that as the image in the current pick area changes, the original image remains the same. As you make adjustments, the current pick always shows the last change that you made. If you want to return the image to its original state, click the Original image frame.

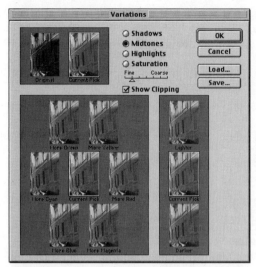

Figure 18-20: Photoshop's Variations dialog box enables you to adjust the shadows, midtones, highlights, and colors in an image.

Sometimes after lightening an image, the image may look washed out. To add color to the image, click the color thumbnails. For example, to increase Red values in an image, click the More Red button. Keep clicking More Red until you've added the correct amount. But what if there's too much red in an image? Notice that there isn't a Less Red button. To remove red, you must add more of red's complement, which is cyan. Therefore, to remove red, click Add Cyan.

Hue/Saturation

To adjust the lightness and intensity of a color, use Photoshop's Hue/Saturation command. This command is far more sophisticated than Premiere Pro's HSL Color Balance command. Using Photoshop's Hue/Saturation command, you can focus on specific colors to change as well as set a hue range that you want to change.

To display the Hue/Saturation dialog box, shown in Figure 18-21, choose Image ➪ Adjust ➪ Hue/Saturation. The easiest way to use the Hue/Saturation command is to leave the Edit mode set to Master. In this mode, the Hue/Saturation is somewhat akin to Premiere Pro's HSL Color Balance. For example, you can change image color values in the frames by clicking and dragging the Hue slider. To change the intensity of a color, move the Saturation slider. To change the lightness of the frames, move the Lightness slider.

Photoshop surpasses Premiere Pro by providing before and after color bars at the bottom of the Color palette. The top color bar represents how colors appear before the adjustment; the bottom shows how those colors will change as you click and drag the slider.

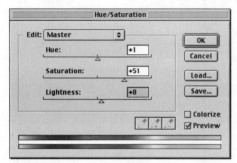

Figure 18-21: The Hue/Saturation dialog box enables you to change the lightness and intensity of colors.

Note You can also use the Hue/Saturation command to colorize a grayscale filmstrip. To do this, click the Colorize button and drag the Hue slider to the desired color.

The Hue/Saturation command also provides a more advanced mode, if you want to adjust a specific color range. To do this, choose Reds, Yellows, Greens, Cyans, Blues, or Magentas in the Edit pop-up menu. When you do this, the bottom color bar enables you to specify a more exact range of colors to adjust.

Note Photoshop also features a Replace Colors command (Image ➪ Adjust ➪ Replace Colors). This command is a combination of the Color Range command and the Hue/Saturation command. You can use the Replace Colors command to isolate a range of colors and replace the colors with a new color chosen from the Replace Colors Hue ➪ Saturation ➪ Lightness sliders.

Color Balance

Photoshop's Color Balance command provides a method of changing the overall balance of colors in an image. Although Photoshop's Color Balance command is similar to Premiere Pro's Color Balance command, Photoshop's command enables you to focus your attention on shadows, midtones, or highlights.

Note Use Adobe Photoshop CS's new Shadow/Highlight correction to maintain an image's overall color balance, while adjusting the shadow and highlight areas of the image.

To open the Color Balance dialog box, which is shown in Figure 18-22, choose Image ➪ Adjust ➪ Color Balance. The dialog box is easy to use. Decide whether you want to focus on shadows, midtones, or highlights. Then click and drag to adjust the sliders. The dialog box clearly shows how RGB colors relate to their complements. As discussed earlier in this chapter, reducing red adds cyan; reducing green adds magenta; reducing blue adds yellow.

 Note The Preserve Luminosity check box helps ensure that the brightness levels of the image are maintained as you edit the color balance.

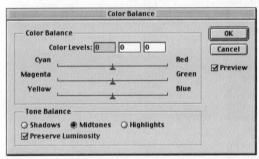

Figure 18-22: The Color Balance dialog box adjusts the RGB and CMY colors.

Using Photoshop to add and delete people from video clips

You can use Photoshop to copy a person into a video clip or to remove a person from a video clip. (However, the practicality of performing such an operation may be limited in many video clips involving action or motion.) You can use the techniques described in this section for still images, or to create interesting special effects. For example, you may want to create or paint an object from scratch in Photoshop and then place it in a video frame. The combination of the realistic and the artistic may be quite interesting.

Figure 18-23 shows a video clip before a person was added. Figure 18-24 shows the video clip from Figure 18-23, after the person was added.

Figure 18-23: Filmstrip video clip in Photoshop before person is added.

Figure 18-24: Filmstrip video clip in Photoshop after person is added.

Here's how to add a person or an object into a video clip:

1. **Load Photoshop.**

2. **Choose File ⇨ Open to open a file of an image that has the person or object that you want to add to the clip.** Note that the person or object you want to add to the video clip may not be in a photograph — the person or object may be in another video clip. In that case, you need to save that video clip in Filmstrip format and open it in Photoshop.

On the DVD-ROM   You can use the Mamina.psd file found in the Chapter 18 folder, in the Tutorial Projects folder, on the DVD that accompanies this book.

3. **Use one of Photoshop's selection tools to select the person or object.** For intricate selection, you should create a selection with a selection tool and then use Photoshop's masking tools to edit the mask with a painting tool.

4. **After you've completed the masking process, reload the selection by choosing File ⇨ Load Selection.**

5. **Choose Edit ⇨ Copy.**

6. **Now choose File ⇨ Open to open the Filmstrip video clip to which you want to add the object or person.** In Figure 18-23, we used the waterscene.mov video clip. The waterscene.mov video is in Chapter 18 folder, in the Tutorial Projects folder, on the DVD that accompanies this book.

7. **Choose Edit ⇨ Paste to paste the person into the Filmstrip video clip.** You may need to reduce the size of the person. If so, choose Edit ⇨ Transform ⇨ Scale to scale the image. (When you paste the object or person into the file, you are pasting that person into a new layer. Choose Window ⇨ Show Layers to open the Layers palette. Notice the new layer with the person in it.)

8. **Use the Move tool to move the person into the frame in which the person is to appear.** To add the person to more than one frame, you must copy the layer that the person is in. Click and drag over the New Layer icon in the Layers palette with the person to make a copy. Then use the Move tool to move it into place. When you copy and paste in Photoshop, a new layer is created. Remember to flatten the image so that you can resave the file in Filmstrip format and open it in Premiere Pro.

Note You may want to use the grid and/or rulers (View ⇨ Show Rulers or View ⇨ Show Grid) to place the person/object in the same position in every frame.

Here's how to omit or remove a person or an object from a video clip:

1. **Choose File ⇨ Open to open the Filmstrip clip that contains the person or object that you want to remove.**

2. **Locate the frame with the person or object.**

3. **Remove the person or object with one of these techniques:**

   • Use the Rubber Stamp tool to clone surrounding areas over the area that you want to remove. After you clone the object from one frame, you may be able to copy and paste that area into other frames.

   • Use the Airbrush, Paintbrush, and/or Pencil tools to paint over the area.

4. **Resave the file in Filmstrip format.** If you executed a copy and paste command, Photoshop automatically creates a new layer. Remember to remove the layers by flattening the image so that you can resave the file in Filmstrip or use the Save As command to save in Filmstrip. After the file is saved in Filmstrip format, it can be reloaded into Premiere Pro.

Summary

If your video clips need color correction or if they need brightness or contrast enhanced, you can use Adobe Premiere Pro's Video Effects. The Adjust, Image Control, and Video folders all contain effects that can enhance video.

✦ Use the Brightness and Contrast effect to quickly correct clips that don't need sophisticated adjustments.

✦ Use the Levels effect to add or reduce contrast and to enhance midtone areas.

✦ Use the Color Balance effect to adjust the Red, Green, and Blue channels in an image.

✦ Use Premiere Pro's new Color Corrector to make various corrections with one filter.

✦ If Premiere Pro's image-enhancement commands aren't sufficient, you can export your Premiere file as a Filmstrip file and correct it in Adobe Photoshop.

✦ Apart from correcting colors and tonal values in Photoshop, you can also add or remove image areas from video clips.

✦   ✦   ✦

Outputting Digital Video from Premiere Pro

Exporting AVI, QuickTime, and MPEG Movies

After you've completed the finishing touches on your Adobe Premiere Pro project, you're ready to export the production as a digital movie. When you export the file, you can output it to videotape, or you can export it to disk for viewing on another computer system. If you export your Premiere Pro project as a QuickTime, Video for Windows, or MPEG file, you can easily view it on most Macs and PCs by simply double-clicking the exported video movie. Movies saved in QuickTime or Video for Windows can be integrated into other multimedia programs, such as Adobe After Effects, Macromedia Director, or Macromedia Flash. MPEG files can be used on the Web, but they're most valuable to Premiere Pro users who want to output their projects to DVD. The Hollywood movies and music videos you see on DVDs are encoded in MPEG format before the DVD is burned.

This chapter explains how to export Premiere Pro projects into QuickTime, Video for Windows, or MPEG files. It covers the simple steps you need to execute to begin the export process and then focuses on key export settings, such as choosing a compressor, keyframes, and data rates.

Note   In this book, we divide the exporting procedure into different chapters — this chapter, which covers exporting QuickTime, Video for Windows, and MPEG movies, and Chapter 20, which covers exporting to the Web. Later, Chapter 21 discusses how to export your Premiere Pro project using the Advanced Windows Media and RealVideo Export plug-ins. Chapter 22 covers exporting to videotape.

Beginning the Export Process

After you edit your work and preview your production, you can export your project by activating the sequence you want to export and then choosing File ⇨ Export ⇨ Movie. Doing so opens the Export Movie dialog box, shown in Figure 19-1. At the bottom-left of the screen, Premiere Pro displays the current video and audio settings. If you want to export using these settings, simply name the file and click Save. The length of time Premiere Pro takes to render the final movie depends on the size of your production, its frame rate, frame size, and compression settings.

Figure 19-1: The Export Movie dialog box displays the current video and audio settings for your Premiere Pro project.

> **Note**   You can export a frame by moving the Timeline indicator to it and then choosing File ⇨ Export ⇨ Frame.

If you exported the movie in Video for Windows (called Microsoft AVI in the Export Movie Settings dialog box) format, your movie can be viewed on systems running Microsoft Windows. Mac users can also view AVI movies by importing them into the latest version of Apple's QuickTime Movie player. On the Web, most Windows have switched from AVI format to Microsoft's Advanced Windows Media format (covered in Chapter 21). However, AVI format is still accepted as a format that can be imported into many multimedia software programs.

Note Video for Windows files are saved with an AVI (audio video interleave) file extension. Video for Windows files are often referred to as *AVI files*.

Changing Export Settings

Although the video and audio settings used during the creation of a Premiere Pro project may be perfect during editing, they may not produce the best quality for specific viewing environments. For example, a digital movie with a large frame size and high frame rate may not play well at slow Web connection speeds. Thus, you may want to change several export settings before saving your export file to disk, if you expect your project to be viewed on the Web. To change export settings, click the Settings button in the Export Movie dialog box. (If the Export Movie dialog box is not onscreen, you can display it by choosing File ➪ Export ➪ Movie.)

After you click Settings, the Export Movie Settings dialog box, shown in Figure 19-2, appears. When this dialog box opens, the pop-up menu at the top of the screen is automatically set to the General setting.

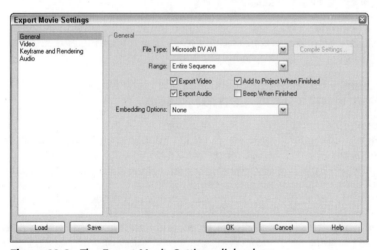

Figure 19-2: The Export Movie Settings dialog box.

Following is a description of the choices available in the Export Movie Settings dialog box:

✦ **File Type.** If you want to switch file types, you can use this menu. Apart from picking a QuickTime or AVI format, you can also choose to save your digital movie as a series of still frames in different file formats, such as GIF, TIF, Windows Bitmap, or QuickTime.

✦ **Range.** Choose to export the Entire Sequence or the Work Area specified in the Timeline.

✦ **Export Video.** Deselect if you do not want to export the video.

✦ **Export Audio.** Deselect if you do not want to export the audio.

✦ **Add to Project When Finished.** Adds the exported movie to the Project window.

✦ **Beep When Finished.** Causes your computer to beep when the project is finished.

✦ **Embedding Options.** Allows you to create a link between the original project and the exported movie. To create the link, choose Project in the Embedding Options drop-down menu. Once the link is created, you can open the original project by selecting the exported movie in the Project window of another project and then choosing Edit ➪ Edit Original. Note that this option isn't available for all export choices.

Changing Video Settings

To review or change Video settings, choose Video in the pop-up menu at the top of the Export Movie Settings screen. The video settings reflect the currently used project settings.

Choosing a QuickTime compressor

When creating a project, capturing video, or exporting a Premiere Pro project, one of the most important decisions you can make is to choose the correct compression settings. A compressor or *CODEC* (COmpression/DECompression) determines exactly how the computer restructures or removes data to make the digital video file smaller. Although most compression settings are designed to compress files, not all of these settings are suitable for all types of projects. The trick is to choose the best CODEC for your Premiere Pro project to produce the best quality with the smallest file size. One CODEC may be better for Web digital video, and another might be best suited to a project that contains animation created in a painting program.

The settings that appear in the Compressor pop-up menu are based upon the file type chosen in the Export Movie Settings dialog box. The QuickTime CODECs, shown in Figure 19-3, are different from the Video for Windows CODECs. Furthermore, depending on the compressor, the options in the Video section of the Export Movie Settings dialog box change.

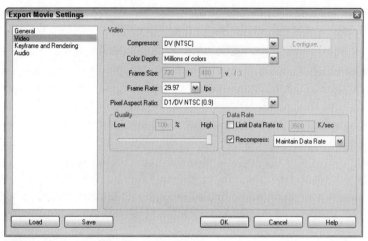

Figure 19-3: The QuickTime CODECs.

Following is a brief review of many of the QuickTime CODEC choices available in the Export Movie Settings dialog box:

✦ **Animation.** Used for creating high-quality output. This setting is particularly useful for animation created in graphics painting programs. Using this compressor, you can set the bit depth to Millions+ (of colors), which enables exporting an alpha channel with the movie. If you choose the 100% option, Animation provides *lossless* compression. This results in smaller file sizes than simply choosing None in the Compression box. Choose this setting for storing high-quality animated titles.

✦ **Cinepak.** This format is one of the most popular for Web and multimedia work. Working with Cinepak can be time-consuming because the compression time is sometimes long; you'll have to wait longer for previews and for final video. However, the recompression time or playback is not slow. When exporting, you can also set the data rate using Cinepak, but be aware that setting the data rate below 30K per second can lower the quality of the video.

✦ **MJPEG-A, MJPEG-B.** Used for editing and capturing video. These CODECs can provide very good results when quality is set to 100%. Both CODECs use spatial compression, so no keyframe control is available. Also, MJPEG usually requires a hardware board for playback.

✦ **Sorenson.** Used for high-quality desktop video for the Web and for CD-ROM. This CODEC provides better compression than Cinepak. Sorenson can reduce file sizes by three to four times as much as Cinepak does. Compression can be time-consuming, so use this setting for exporting but not for editing.

Note   Sorenson also sells a high-end version of the Sorenson CODEC that provides better quality and more features.

✦ **Planar RGB.** A lossless CODEC good for animation created in painting and 3-D programs, and an alternative to the Animation CODEC.

✦ **Video.** Can be used for video editing, but not for exporting.

✦ **Component Video.** Generally used for capturing analog video. Not used when creating or exporting a project. When you capture video, this may be your only choice, depending on the video capture board installed in your computer.

✦ **Graphics.** Used for graphics with 256 colors or less; generally not used in desktop video.

✦ **Photo-JPEG.** Although this CODEC can create good image quality, slow decompression makes this CODEC unsuitable for desktop video.

✦ **H.263.** Used for video conferencing and provides better quality than the H.261 CODEC. This CODEC is not recommended for video editing.

✦ **PNG.** Generally not used for motion graphics. This CODEC is included in QuickTime as a means of saving still graphics in PNG Web format.

✦ **TIF.** Tagged Information File Format. A printing format for still images.

✦ **BMP.** A Windows-compatible graphics format for still images.

✦ **DV-PAL and DV-NTSC.** Digital video format for NTSC and PAL (choose the format that applies to the geographic region for your intended audience), used for transferring digitized data from DV camcorders or from camcorders into Premiere Pro. Useful format for capturing video that is transferred to another video-editing system.

✦ **None.** No compression is used. Premiere Pro creates preview files faster at this setting, but file sizes are very large.

The QuickTime CODECs list may contain hardware-specific CODECs supplied by computer and board manufacturers. For instance, Sony Vaio computer owners see a Sony DV format in the QuickTime CODEC list. Follow the instructions provided with your capture board or computer when choosing one of these CODECs.

Choosing a Video for Windows compressor

If you are exporting a Video for Windows file, the compressor choices are different from the QuickTime choices. Following is a brief review of frequently used AVI CODECs:

✦ **Cinepak.** Originally created by Radius, provides the same features as QuickTime's Cinepak. This CODEC is primarily used for multimedia output. Compression can be time-consuming, but image quality is generally good.

✦ **Indeo Video 5.10.** Created by Intel (makers of the Pentium computer chip), this CODEC provides good image quality. Often used for capturing raw data. Quality is similar to desktop video produced using the Cinepak CODEC.

✦ **Microsoft RLE (Run Length Encoding).** The bit depth for this CODEC is limited to 256 colors, making it only suitable for animation created in painting programs with 256 colors, or images that have been reduced to 256 colors. When the Quality slider is set to High, this CODEC produces lossless compression.

Changing bit depth

After you choose a CODEC, the dialog box changes to show the different options provided by that CODEC. If your CODEC enables you to change bit depth, you can choose another setting in the Bit Depth pop-up menu. For instance, the Sorenson CODEC does not enable you to switch bit depths. However, the Cinepak CODEC enables you to choose 256 colors. Because the Cinepak CODEC allows 256 colors, clicking the Palette button enables you to either load a palette or have Premiere Pro create a 256-color palette from the clips in the movie. However, be aware that reducing the palette to 256 colors could result in poor picture quality. Unless you are working with animation created in a painting program, you probably will not want to reduce the colors in your video project to 256.

Choosing quality

The next option controlled by the selected CODEC is the Quality slider. Most CODECs enable you to click and drag to choose a quality setting. The higher the quality, the larger the file size of the exported movie.

Choosing a data rate

Many CODECs enable you to specify an output data rate. The *data rate* is the amount of data per second that must be processed during playback of the exported video file. The data rate changes, depending on which system plays your production. For instance, the data rate of CD-ROM playback on a slow computer is far less than the data rate of a hard disk. If the data rate of the video file is too high, the system will not be able to handle the playback. If this is the case, playback may be garbled as frames are dropped. Following are a few suggestions for different playback scenarios:

✦ **World Wide Web.** Choose a data rate that accounts for Web connection speeds. Remember, even though a modem may be capable of 56 Kbps (kilobits per second), the actual connection speed is probably slower. Also remember that the data rate field accepts data in kilobits per second, rather than bits per second. For Sorenson and Cinepak CODECs, try a data rate of 50. Adobe recommends trying a data rate of 150K per second for movies with a frame size of 240 × 180. Note that when uploading to the Web, smaller file size is more important than data rate.

✦ **Videotape editing.** If you are exporting video files for further editing, the data rate should be set so that the computer editing system can handle it. To export for further editing, use a CODEC that does not reduce video quality, such as a DV CODEC, or the Animation CODEC.

✦ **CD-ROM.** For CD-ROM playback, specify a data rate consistent with the data rate of the CD-ROM drive. The data rate setting is especially important for older CD-ROM drives. For example, a double-speed CD-ROM has a data rate at 300K per second. Adobe recommends setting the data rate in this case from 150–200. For 12-speed CD-ROMs, the recommended data rate is 1.8MB per second; for 24-speed CD-ROMs, the recommended data rate is 3–3.6MB per second.

✦ **Intranets.** The data rate speed depends upon the actual speed of the network. Because most intranets use high-speed connections, you can generally set the playback to 100K or more.

✦ **Hard disk.** If you are creating a production for playback on a computer system, try to ascertain the data rate of the audience's hard disk. The data rates for most modern hard disks are in excess of 33 million bits per second.

Note   Adobe's Support Knowledgebase document "Applying Data Rate Limits in Premiere Pro" is available online at www.adobe.com/support/techdocs/a60a.htm.

Setting recompression

If you specify a data rate, select the Recompress check box. Doing this helps guarantee that Premiere Pro keeps the data rate beneath the one specified in the data rate field. If you want Premiere Pro to recompress every frame, whether or not it is below the data rate, choose Always in the Recompress pop-up menu. Better quality is produced, however, if you choose the Maintain Data Rate setting. This only recompresses frames that are higher than the specified data rate.

Changing frame rates and frame size

Before exporting video, you may want to reduce the frame rate or reduce the frame size to reduce the file size of your production. The frame rate is the number of frames Premiere Pro exports per second. If you change frame size, be sure to specify the horizontal and vertical dimensions in pixels. If your video was captured at a 4:3 aspect ratio, be sure to maintain this ratio to avoid distorting clips.

Specifying keyframes

Another video export setting that can control export file size is the Keyframe setting in the Export Movie Settings dialog box's Keyframe and Rendering section (see Figure 19-4).

Keyframe settings can be changed when choosing CODECs, such as Cinepak and Sorenson video, with temporal compression. The keyframe setting specifies how many times to save the complete video frame. If the keyframe setting is set at 15, a keyframe is created every 15 frames. As the CODEC compresses, it compares each subsequent frame and only saves the information that changes in each frame. Thus, using keyframes can significantly reduce the file size of your video.

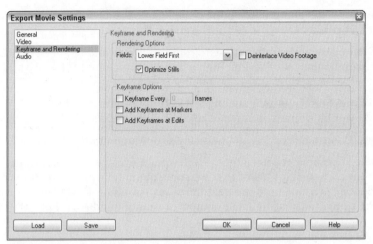

Figure 19-4: The Keyframe and Rendering section of the Export Movie Settings dialog box.

A good starting point is to enter the number of keyframes per second that match the number of frames per second. So, if your frame rate is 30 frames per second, set the keyframe rate to 30. This creates one keyframe for every 30 frames of video. Enter 60 to create one keyframe every two seconds. If you want more keyframes, lower the number in the keyframe field. When setting keyframes, it is often recommended that the number of keyframes should evenly divide into the frame rate. Also, images displaying motion generally require more keyframes than images without a lot of motion.

To help ensure smooth transitions, you may want to force Premiere Pro to create a keyframe at transitions and edits. To set keyframes at Edit points, select the Add Keyframes at Edits option in the Export Movie Settings dialog box. To set keyframes at specific points in your production, set Markers at points where you want Premiere Pro to create a keyframe and then select the Add Keyframe at Markers option in the Export Movie Settings dialog box.

Tip   To see a visual representation of the keyframes in a clip, select it in the Project window, then choose Clip ➪ Properties. Next click Data Rate. The Red Bars in the graph represent keyframes.

Changing Audio Settings

When you export your final project, you may want to change the audio settings. To access the audio options, choose Audio from the Export Movie Settings dialog box. The settings in the Audio section of the Export Movie Settings dialog box, shown in Figure 19-5, are as follows:

✦ **Compressor.** In the compressor pop-up menu, choose a compressor if desired. (The audio CODECs are reviewed at the end of this section.)

✦ **Sample Rate.** Lower the rate setting to reduce file size and to speed up the rendering of the final production. Higher rates produce better quality and increase processing time. (CD-ROM quality is 44 kHz.)

✦ **Sample Type.** Stereo 16-bit is the highest setting; 8-bit mono is the lowest setting. Lower bit depths produce smaller files and reduce rendering times.

✦ **Channels.** Choose either Stereo (2 channels) or Mono (1 channel).

✦ **Interleave.** This option determines how frequently audio is inserted into the video frames. Choosing 1 frame in the pop-up menu tells Premiere Pro to load the audio for the frame until the next frame is processed. However, this can cause the sound to break up if the computer cannot handle a lot of audio data quickly.

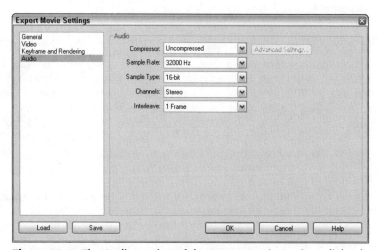

Figure 19-5: The Audio section of the Export Movie Settings dialog box.

Choosing QuickTime audio CODECs

Following is a brief review of several QuickTime audio CODECs. You must specify a CODEC only if you want to add compression to sound. For each CODEC, the compression ratio appears next to its name:

✦ **ULaw 2:1.** Used as a common audio format on Unix platforms. ULaw is used for digital telephony in both North America and Japan.

✦ **16-bit Endian and 16-bit Little Endian.** Not used for video editing. Used by hardware engineers and software developers.

✦ **24-bit integer and 32-bit integer soft.** Not used for video editing. Used by hardware engineers and software developers.

✦ **IMA Designed by the Interactive Multimedia Association.** This cross-platform format can be used to compress audio for multimedia.

✦ **32-bit floating point and 64-bit floating point.** Not used for video editing. Used by hardware engineers and software developers.

✦ **ALaw.** Used for European digital telephony.

✦ **Qdesign Music CODEC.** Can be used for high-quality Web output. Can provide CD-ROM quality over a modem.

✦ **Qualcomm Pure Voice.** A speech format. Shouldn't be used at an audio rate higher than 8 kHz.

✦ **MACE 3:1 and MACE 6:1.** Macintosh audio CODEC that can be used for QuickTime movies for PCs and Macs. MACE 3:1 provides better quality because it uses less compression.

Choosing Video for Windows audio CODECs

Premiere Pro offers the following audio compression options when exporting a project as a Video for Windows file:

✦ **Indeo audio software.** Good for Web output of music and speech. Created for use with Indeo video CODECs.

✦ **Truespeech.** Used for speech over the Internet. Works best at low data rates.

✦ **Microsoft GSM 6.10.** Used for speech only. Used for telephony compression in Europe.

✦ **MS-ADPCM.** Microsoft's version of an Adaptive Differential Pulse Code Modulation compressor. Can be used for CD-ROM quality sound.

✦ **Microsoft IMA ADPCM.** Used for cross-platform multimedia. Developed by the Interactive Multimedia Association.

✦ **Voxware CODECs.** Can be used for speech output on the Web. Best at low data rates.

Exporting MPEG Files

If you want to export your movie in MPEG format, you must use the Adobe Media Encoder rather than Premiere Pro's Export Movie command. The MPEG export module enables you to export MPEG files specifically set for playback on different formats that can be played on a DVD player. To create an MPEG file, you need do little more than click a few buttons and name your file.

Note   The Adobe Media Encoder is also used to create Windows Media Files and QuickTime Streaming and RealMedia files. Using these options is covered in Chapter 21.

If you don't want to export your Premiere Pro project to DVD but want to create an MPEG file, you can also choose to create a generic MPEG1 or MPEG2 file. You might want to use a generic MPEG file for Web use, or for importing into a multimedia application.

Using the Adobe Media Encoder

Adobe's Media Encoder provides an efficient means of creating quality MPEG files for a variety of DVD formats that can be viewed on DVD players. The different DVD formats described in this section are options available in software that burns DVDs. The different formats allow for different screen sizes and different data rates. Some enable subtitles, links, and menus to be integrated into the DVD production.

Using the Adobe Encoder is quite simple: To create an MPEG file from the Timeline, first click the Timeline that you want to export and then choose File ➪ Export ➪ Adobe Media Encoder. This opens the Transcode Settings dialog box, shown in Figure 19-6.

The Transcode Settings dialog box enables you to choose these options from the Format drop-down menu:

✦ **MPEG1.** This option creates a generic MPEG1 file at 720×480 pixels with a frame rate of 29.97 frames per second. The default bit rate is 1.7MB per second. If you want to edit these defaults, select the Video check box in the Summary column of the Transcode Settings dialog box.

✦ **MPEG1-VCD.** This format uses MPEG1 encoding and provides a frame size of 352×240 (NTSC). VCD disks can be played in standard CD-ROM drives, yet can play as much as 74 minutes of audio and video.

✦ **MPEG2.** This option creates a generic MPEG2 file. The default bit rate for the generic MPEG2 file is 4.2MB per second — over twice the rate of an MPEG1 file. By clicking the Video section (click the word Video, not the checkbox) in the Transcode Settings dialog box, you can change a variety of settings for the generic file.

✦ **MPEG2-DVD.** This option is the Hollywood standard, which can provide over two hours of entertainment. This format utilizes a full frame of 720×480 pixels. When the file is exported, audio and video are separated into two MPEG2 files. The video file extension is m2v; the audio file extension is a .wav (NTSC) or .mpa (for PAL systems) file.

✦ **MPEG2-SVCD.** Uses MPEG2 encoding. Provides a frame size of 480 × 480. This format can provide titles, manuals, and links. It's a fairly new format supported by major electronics companies such as Sony, Philips, Matsushita, and JVC.

For each choice you can view settings by clicking in the Summary column. These settings can be changed to tweak the export. Although most users will not change the defaults, as mentioned earlier, clicking the Video check box in the Summary column allows you to change output bit rate and aspect ratio. The video section also allows you to change from NTSC to PAL format. Figure 19-7 shows the video options for the MPEG2-DVD setting.

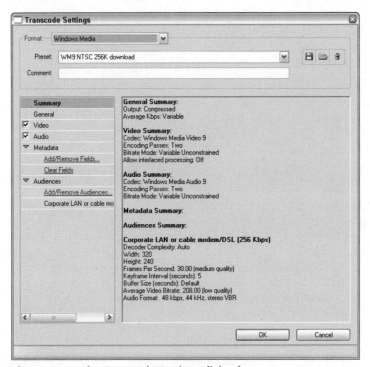

Figure 19-6: The Transcode Settings dialog box.

Completing the MPEG export

After you've chosen a format in the Transcode Settings dialog box, you can simply click OK to start the process of creating an MPEG stream of your work. If you've made changes to any of the video or audio defaults, you may want to save your settings

by clicking the disk icon in the dialog box. (To load settings, click the folder icon.)
After clicking OK, name your file in the Save File dialog box. At this point, you can
click in the Export Range drop-down menu to choose whether to save the Entire
Sequence or the current work area. You can also check settings by clicking the
Settings button. This reopens the Transcode Settings dialog box where you can edit
your MPEG specifications. When you're ready to export the file, click Save.

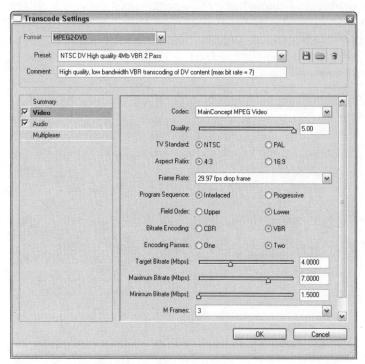

Figure 19-7: MPEG2-DVD export settings.

Burning a DVD

If you want to export your Premiere Pro project to DVD, you can burn the DVD
directly from Adobe Premiere Pro. If you burn a DVD directly from Premiere Pro,
you won't be able to create menus or add any navigational graphics. However, you
can create chapters that correspond to Timeline markers on the Timeline.

Cross-Reference Adobe Encore provides tools for creating DVDs with menus and navigational buttons. Encore is covered in Chapters 24 and 25.

Here are the steps for burning a DVD from Premiere Pro:

1. **To begin the export process, choose Export ⇨ Export to DVD.** This opens the Export to DVD dialog box, shown in Figure 19-8. Four options are available: General, Encoding, DVD Burner, and Summary.

2. **To name your disc, select General in the left pane and then choose Custom from the Disc Name drop-down menu.** This opens the Disc Name dialog box where you can enter a name for the DVD. Note also that this dialog box allows you to set Chapters at marker points. If desired, you can also choose to make the DVD *loop*, or play again and again — a feature that might be handy if you are creating a presentation that you want to be viewed again and again at a public setting.

3. **Click Encoding in the left pane to choose whether to export as NTSC or Pal and to designate what portion of the Timeline you want to export.**

4. **Finally, to burn your DVD, select DVD Burner from the left pane.** In this section, shown in Figure 19-9, you can select the DVD burner and how many copies to create. This section also shows whether your DVD is online. To start burning the DVD, click the Record button.

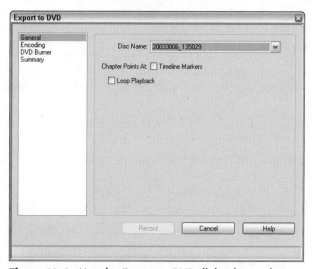

Figure 19-8: Use the Export to DVD dialog box to burn a DVD directly from Premiere Pro.

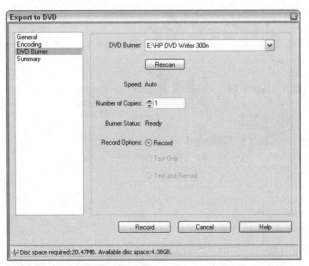

Figure 19-9: Use the DVD Burner section of the Export to DVD dialog box to record a DVD.

Summary

To view a Premiere Pro movie on a CD-ROM or the Web or to view it on a computer system that does not have Premiere Pro installed, you must export the Premiere Pro file in QuickTime, AVI, or MPEG format. If you want to create a DVD from your Premiere Pro project, you must export the project to an MGEG2 file.

✦ To change export settings, click the Settings button in the Export Movie dialog box.

✦ When exporting, you can change Video, Keyframe and Rendering, and Audio settings.

✦ Choosing the correct CODEC and reducing frame rates and frame size reduces file size of the exported production.

✦ To export your movie as an MPEG files, choose File ➪ Export ➪ Movie ➪ Adobe Media Encoder.

✦ To burn a CD directly from Premiere Pro, choose File ➪ Export to DVD.

✦   ✦   ✦

Outputting to the Web and Intranets

If you're a video producer or Web designer, at some point,
you'll undoubtedly want to show one of your Premiere Pro
video productions on your Web page, on a client's Web page,
or on a company intranet. Before you start creating digital
movies for the Web or intranet pages, however, having an idea
of exactly how a browser loads a digital movie onto a Web
page and what options are available to you is helpful. For
example, when a QuickTime movie is displayed on a Web
page, you can have it play immediately, or you can add controls to have the user start and stop the movie. This chapter
provides an overview of the movie file formats for the Web
and discusses how to add a digital movie to the Web and the
QuickTime HTML options available.

Web Delivery Options

You don't need to be a Webmaster or Java programmer to play
a Premiere movie on a Web or intranet page. To get started, all
you need to know is a little HTML. As you'll find out from reading this chapter, movies can be displayed by using a simple
HTML *embed* tag, as illustrated in the following example:

```
<EMBED SRC="mypremiere.mov", WIDTH=320,
HEIGHT=240>
```

In this case, the name of the movie is my mypremiere.mov. Its
frame size is 320 × 240 pixels. The embed command tells the
browser to load the movie from a Web server and use a plug-in
to play the movie. Although this technique works, it can lead
to poor playback. Unless the movie is saved so that it can
stream or use progressive playback, the viewer needs to wait
until the entire movie is downloaded to his or her hard drive
before he or she can view it. It's almost like having to wait for

a VCR to play the program once before you can view it. If you want to display digital movies on a Web or intranet page, you should investigate two delivery choices designed to enhance playback quality: *streaming* and *progressive download*.

Streaming video

If you can afford it, streaming is the best vehicle for delivering digital video over the Web or an intranet. In many ways, streaming is similar to cable TV. You see the program as it arrives at your home or office. No portion of the file is downloaded before or during playback. Instead, it is *buffered* to memory first and then displayed onscreen. Typically, the video is streamed at different data rates: a data rate for modems (narrow band connections) as well as data rates for faster connections (broadband).

Note
Streaming video does not use the Web standard HTTP (Hypertext Transfer Protocol). HTTP determines exactly the formatting, transmittal method, and responses Web servers and browsers use when responding to commands issued over the Internet. Instead of HTTP, streaming media uses Real Time Streaming Protocol (RTSP), which not only allows streaming media, but also provides users with the power to interact with the streaming server. For example, RTSP allows viewers to rewind video and jump to different chapters in QuickTime movies.

Often the viewers click an onscreen button to request a data stream based upon whether they have a slow or fast connection. This "on-demand" Web broadcasting comes at a price. To handle the streams of video and audio, a high-speed connection, such as a DSL, cable modem, or T1, is required.

Furthermore, special server software is needed to stream the video. Often, the server software and video content are on a separate computer that just handles video streaming.

The three primary producers of streaming media software are Apple, Microsoft, and Real Networks. Apple's QuickTime streaming software (www.quicktime.com) is part of its OS X server package. Apple also provides QuickTime streaming software for Linux and Windows NT. Microsoft provides Windows Media server software (www.microsoft.com/windows/windowsmedia/default.asp) with its Windows 2000 server package. Real Networks server software must be purchased from RealMedia (www.realnetworks.com).

Progressive download

For short video clips, progressive download often can provide a suitable alternative to streaming media. Although progressive download doesn't provide video and audio quality as high as that in streaming media, it allows the beginning of the video clip to be played before it is downloaded. For most producers, this is the key to preventing viewers from surfing away while the video downloads. However, unlike streaming media, the video is actually downloaded to the viewer's hard drive, which allows the viewer to keep a copy of the production. A further drawback is that playback can become distorted if the data rate of the Web connection slows. In contrast, streaming media removes portions of the video to keep the playback consistent (often the viewer doesn't notice).

Note For an in-depth discussion of streaming media, see www.adobe.com/smprimer. For the latest on streaming media as well as a few streaming media tutorials, check out www.streamingmedia.com. If you're looking for a job in the streaming media industry, click the careers link on the aforementioned Web page.

Web File Formats

Before you begin planning to output your digital movies to the Web or an intranet, you should be familiar with the different movie file formats that can be viewed in a browser connected to the Web or an intranet. The file formats listed here all require that some form of plug-in be installed in the browser software. Saving QuickTime Windows Media and RealVideo files for the Web is covered in Chapter 21.

✦ **QuickTime.** Apple's QuickTime format is one of the most popular Web video file formats. It is cross-platform and provides good quality. QuickTime provides numerous HTML options that can change how the movie appears on the Web. Different QuickTime tracks (discussed later in this chapter) can also be added to Web-based movies.

Although not a requirement for Web playback, for the best results, QuickTime movies should be streamed by Apple's QuickTime streaming software. This software is included with Apple's Mac OS X server package. As mentioned earlier, Apple Computer has created QuickTime Streaming Server versions for Windows NT and Linux. Premiere Pro users can quickly create QuickTime streaming-ready movies by exporting their movies using Adobe's Media Encoder (File ⇨ Export ⇨ Adobe Media Encoder).

✦ **Windows Media format.** Video created in Windows Media format is loaded on a Web page into Microsoft's Window's Media Player. In Premiere, you can output projects in Windows Media format by choosing File ⇨ Export ⇨ Adobe Media Encoder. The current version, Windows Media 9, provides compression improvements from 15 to 50 percent over Windows Media 8. Microsoft's Web page claims that it provides the "highest fidelity audio and best quality video at any bit rate from dial-up to broadband."

✦ **RealVideo.** RealNetworks' streaming video format is probably the most popular format available. For true high-quality video, the RealVideo encoded movies must be created with RealNetworks streaming software CODEC. Premiere's Export Timeline ⇨ Advanced RealMedia Export enables you to export Premiere movies in RealVideo format.

✦ **Audio Video Interleave (AVI).** All Windows computers are equipped to read Microsoft AVI files; however, because AVI is not cross-platform, it is not often used on the Web. For Web use, Microsoft has dropped the format and replaced it with the more sophisticated Windows Media Format.

Understanding HTML

If you plan to output digital video to the Web, you should have an understanding of how digital movies are loaded onto a Web page. With this knowledge, you'll be able to control how your movie is displayed and when it begins to play. Your first step is to understand how Hypertext Markup Language (HTML) can be used to load text and images on a Web page.

How a movie is loaded onto a Web page

When you see a QuickTime movie on a Web page, it appears because the HTML code instructs the browser to load the movie from a Web server. HTML is a series of text codes or tags that tell the browser what to do. Although numerous programs exist that can write HTML code for you, you could construct an entire Web page using a simple text editor. For example, this HTML code snippet `<b>Web Movies</b>` tells the Web browser to put the words **Web Movies** on a page in bold type.

As an example, we created a simple Web page with a QuickTime movie on it (see Figure 20-1). To create the page, we used Adobe GoLive, which automatically created the following HTML instructions. (Loading a QuickTime movie into GoLive is covered later in this chapter.)

```
<html>

<head>
<meta http-equiv="content-type" content="text/html;charset=iso-
8859-1">
<meta name="generator" content="Adobe GoLive 6">
<title>Web Movie Center</title>
</head>

<body bgcolor="#ffffff">
<div align="center">
<h1>WEB MOVIES</h1>
<h1><embed src="mymovie.mov" width="310" height="348"
type="video/QuickTime" controller="false" autoplay="true"></h1>
</div>
</body>
</html>
```

To those unfamiliar with HTML, the code may look complicated. However, after you become familiar with the syntax, you will find HTML coding quite easy. If you scan through the code, you'll see several HTML *tags*, such as `<head>` and `<body>`. Each tag designates a specific area or formatting section in the page. Most tags begin with a word, such as `<title>`. At the end of the section, the tag is repeated with a / (forward slash) in front of it. For example, the end tag of `<title>` is `</title>`.

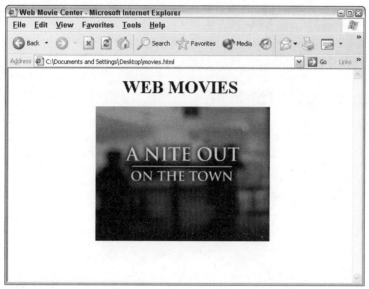

Figure 20-1: A sample Web page that contains a QuickTime movie.

Here's a review of the some of the more important elements in the HTML code, shown previously:

✦ <html> — This tag simply tells the browser that the HTML coding system will be used.

✦ <head> — The "head" area of the page provides the browser with information concerning the character set used (within the meta tag). If scripting languages such as JavaScript will be used, this information normally appears in the "head" area as well.

✦ <title> — The window title of the browser page appears within the title tag.

✦ <body> — The main elements of a Web page are found within the body area. Notice that the body tag ends just above the ending </html> tag. Within the body is the information that loads the QuickTime movie.

✦ <embed> — The embed tag loads the digital movie plug-in. The src section provides the name of the digital movie that will be loaded from the Web server. The height and width sections show the width and height of the movie on the page.

The type section tells the browser that a QuickTime movie is being loaded. controller="false" tells the browser not to place the QuickTime controller. autoplay="true" tells the browser to start playing the movie as soon as the page loads.

To enable the movie to be seen on the Web, the page must be named. If we name the page Index.htm, most Web servers will load this as the home page for a Web site. For the page and movie to appear, both must be copied to the Web server that hosts the Web site.

QuickTime settings for Web pages

Because QuickTime is one of the most popular digital video Web formats, we've provided a list of HTML tags that enable you to customize how a QuickTime movie appears on a Web page. Many of the tags are simple true/false statements, such as Loop=True or Loop=False. These tags, described next, are easily inserted using a word processor that saves files in standard text format. However, using a Web-page layout program to insert these tags, such as Adobe GoLive, is easiest.

✦ Bg color—Background color for the movie. Example: bg color="#FF0000". (Colors are created in hexadecimal code when assigned in HTML. FF0000 displays red.)

✦ Cache=True/False—Caches the movie. (Netscape browsers read the cache setting; Internet Explorer does not.) This allows the movie to be loaded faster if the user returns to the page.

✦ Controller=True/False—Adds the QuickTime controller, which enables the user to start and stop the movie.

✦ Hidden=True/False—Hides the QuickTime movie but plays the audio.

✦ HREF—Enables you to enter a clickable link. When the user clicks the QuickTime movie, the browser jumps to the specified Universal Resource Locator (URL), or Web address. (Example: HREF=http//:myhomepage.com/Page-3.com)

✦ Target=—This option is related to the HREF tag. When the movie jumps to a URL, it tells the movie which frame to play in. (Note that frame is an HTML frame, not a digital video frame.) You can include a frame name or common frame tags, such as _self, _parent, _top, or _blank. (Example: target = _ top)

✦ Loop=True/False—Plays the movie nonstop. You can also choose Loop=Palindrome, which plays the move from beginning to end, then from end to beginning.

✦ Play every frame=True/False—Forces every frame to be played. If this option is activated, every frame of the movie is played. This option is usually not turned on, primarily because it could slow movie playback and it could throw the soundtrack out of sync or turn it off entirely.

✦ Scale—Enables you to resize the movie. (Example: Scale=2 doubles the movie size.)

✦ Volume—Enables you to control the volume. Uses values from 0 to 256. By default, the value is set to 256. To turn off the sound, use Volume=0.

Loading Streaming Video on a Web Page

Setting up video to be streamed over a Web page is slightly more involved than setting up a digital movie to progressively download from a Web page. Although differences exist between setting up files for Windows Media Server, RealNetworks' Helix Server and Apple's QuickTime Streaming Server require the creation of a pointer or *metafile*. Typically, the pointer or metafile is a small file saved on a Web server. When a user clicks a link on a Web page, the metafile causes the streaming media plug-in to load, and provides instructions as to which movie to load off the streaming media server.

The following sections provide brief, general summaries of the steps involved for setting up streaming files for Windows Media Server, RealMedia Helix Server, and QuickTime Media Server. For specific instructions, consult user documentation.

In all cases, you save your clip to a directory on your streaming media server. The Web server will contain HTML code that points to the Web server.

Windows Media

Windows Media Server requires you to set up a metafile on your Web server. This is a file that the browser uses to load the Windows Media plug-in, which in turn instructs the streaming media server to play the movie. General steps for setting up the process are described next. For more information, see `www.microsoft.com/windows/windowsmedia/default.aspx`.

1. **Export your Premiere project as a Windows Media file using Adobe Media Encoder (File ➪ Export ➪ Adobe Media Encoder).** Assume that the name of this movie is MyWindowsMovie.asm.

2. **Upload the exported movie to the correct directory on your media server.**

3. **Create a metafile in a text editor. The metafile includes instructions as to the location of the actual movie file.** The text of the metafile could be as simple as this:

```
<ASX version="3.0"
<Entry>
<Title>My Movie Title</Title>
<ref HREF=" mms://ServerName/Path/MyWindowsMovie.wmv
</Entry>
</ASX
```

4. **Name the file MyWindowsMovie.asx. Note that the filename of the movie is the same as the actual exported Windows media file, but uses an .asx file extension.** Save the file on your Web server.

5. **On your Web page, write HTML that creates a link to the .asx file.** The HTML might look something like this:

```
<A HREF="myWindowsmove.asx">Click to play movie</A>
```

RealVideo streaming

The process of loading a streaming movie for a RealNetworks streaming media server requires setting up a metafile or *ram* file on your Web server that includes the path to the digital movie. When a user clicks on a link, the browser instructs the RealMedia plug-in to load and sends the URL of the movie to the plug-in. Here's an overview of the steps involved. For more information about RealNetworks streaming products, see www.realnetworks.com.

1. **Export your Premiere project as a RealMedia file using the Adobe Media Encoder (File ➪ Export ➪ Adobe Media Encoder).** Assume that the name of this movie is MyRealMovie.rm.

2. **Upload the exported movie to the correct directory on your media server.**

3. **Create a metafile in a text editor.** The metafile includes instructions as to the location and name of the actual media file. The text of the metafile could be as simple as this:

   ```
   Rtsp: //servername/path/MyRealmovie.rm
   ```

4. **Name the file MyRealMovie.ram. Note that the filename includes the name of the exported RealMedia file, but uses an .ram file extension.** Save the file on your Web server.

5. **On your Web page, write HTML that creates a link to the .ram file.** The HTML might look something like this:

   ```
   <A HREF ="myRealMovie.ram">My movie is here/A>
   ```

QuickTime streaming

When setting up a movie for QuickTime streaming, you must create a "reference movie" on your Web server. The reference movie is a small file that contains reference information about the movie or movies to be loaded from the QuickTime Streaming Media Server. Within the reference movie is the URL of the QuickTime movie that must be loaded. If the media stream contains alternate files for different connection speeds, the URLs of those movies are also included in the reference movie. For detailed information, see Apple's QuickTime Web site, which provides detailed step-by-step information: www.apple.com/quicktime/products/qtss/.

1. **Export a QuickTime streaming movie file using the Adobe Media Encoder (File ➪ Export ➪ Adobe Media Encoder).** By default, this movie will seek a "hinted" track. The hinted track contains information about the server, packet size, and the protocol needed for streaming. If you are not using the Adobe Media Encoder, but QuickTime Pro, make sure you create the movie as a hinted movie. Assume the name of your movie is MyQTmovie.mov.

2. **Create a reference movie for the clip and its alternatives.** A reference movie is a movie on the Web server that points to the actual movie. The easiest way to create a reference movie is to use Apple's MakeRef movie, which you can download from its QuickTime Web site. When creating the reference movie, you name the URLs of the Web server. You must also do this for all alternate movies that might be loaded at different connection speeds. The URL in the movie might be something like this:

```
rtsp://qtmedia.mywebsite.com/MyQTmovie.mov
```

3. **Save the movie using a filename such as refMyQTMovie.mov.**

4. **Create a link for your movie, such as the following:**

```
<A HREF="refMoviemypremieremovie.mov">my movie</A>
```

You could also embed the movie with a command such as this:

```
<EMBED SRC="ref.mov" WIDTH="pixels" HEIGHT="pixels"
AUTOPLAY="true" CONTROLLER="true" LOOP="false"
PLUGINSPAGE="http://www.apple.com/quicktime/download/">
```

Placing a QuickTime Movie in a Web Page with Adobe GoLive

Adobe GoLive is one of the best Web-page layout programs for QuickTime movie producers. GoLive even features a QuickTime tab, which enables you to edit the tracks of a QuickTime movie and add special effects. GoLive's palettes allow you to quickly and easily place a QuickTime movie on a page.

On the DVD-ROM

A trial version of Adobe GoLive is included on the DVD that accompanies this book.

Following are the steps for adding a QuickTime movie to a Web page and for editing its attributes with Adobe GoLive:

1. **Create a new window in GoLive for the Web page by choosing File ➪ New.**

2. **If the Objects palette is not opened, open it by choosing Window ➪ Objects.** Click the QuickTime icon in the basic palette, shown in Figure 20-2, and drag it to the page. GoLive provides a placeholder for the QuickTime movie. The position of the placeholder determines where the movie appears on the page.

Figure 20-2: Adobe GoLive's Objects palette includes a QuickTime icon.

3. **To specify the filename and attributes, open the Inspector palette by choosing Window ⇨ Inspector.**

4. **In the Inspector palette, click the Basic tab, shown in Figure 20-3.**

Figure 20-3: The Inspector palette's QuickTime movie Basic tab.

5. **To select the QuickTime movie you want to load, click the folder icon in the Basic tab section.** Doing this opens a dialog box in which you can choose the QuickTime movie from your hard disk. (Alternatively, if you have a Web site already designed, you can drag the Point-and-Shoot icon directly to the file in your Adobe GoLive site window on your computer's desktop.)

After the movie is placed in a Web page, the width and height attributes are set automatically.

6. **Click the More tab in the Inspector palette, shown in Figure 20-4.**

Figure 20-4: The Inspector palette's QuickTime movie More tab.

7. **If you want to enter a name for your movie (for HTML coding use only), type a name in the Name field.** The Page section enables you to designate a page from which to download the QuickTime plug-in. If you want to add padding between the movie and surrounding text, enter a value in pixels in HSpace, for horizontal space, and/or VSpace, for vertical space. To hide the movie and only play back audio, select the Is Hidden check box.

8. **To specify more HTML controls specific to QuickTime, click the QuickTime tab, shown in Figure 20-5.** Clicking check boxes and entering data into fields automatically creates the HTML codes for the options described. For example, clicking the Link check box and then typing **myhomepage.com/page 2** tells the browser to switch to page 2 on the Web site if the user clicks the movie.

9. **If you want to preview the movie while in GoLive, click the Open Movie button at the bottom of the QuickTime tab.** When the movie appears, the Basic tab provides track, size, and data rate formation about the movie, as shown in Figure 20-6.

Figure 20-5: The Inspector palette's QuickTime movie QuickTime tab.

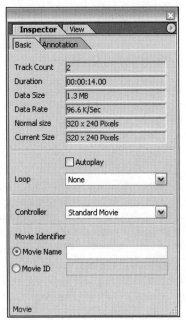

Figure 20-6: The Basic tab provides track, size, and data rate information.

Using QuickTime Tracks for the Web

QuickTime provides several hidden movie tracks that can add to the versatility of the Web and intranet movies. For example, QuickTime enables you to create an *HREF track* that can make the browser jump to another Web page at a specific point in the movie. QuickTime also provides a *chapter track*, which enables a user to click a chapter name and jump to that section of the movie. Perhaps the most unusual QuickTime track is the *sprite track*. The sprite track enables you to add graphics and provide interactivity to the QuickTime movie. For example, by using a sprite track, you can add a button that is assigned an action to your QuickTime movie. When the user clicks the button, the action occurs, such as restarting the movie, going to another Web page, or turning up the volume.

The following sections show you how to add tracks to a QuickTime movie. The first section shows how to add an HREF track with Adobe Premiere Pro. The sections that follow show you how to create chapter and sprite tracks with Adobe GoLive.

Creating a Web link in Premiere Pro

Adobe Premiere enables you to add an HREF track in a QuickTime movie. Using the HREF track, you can make the users' browsers jump to another Web location while the QuickTime movie plays. In Premiere Pro, this QuickTime feature is called a *Web link*.

You set up a Web link within Premiere Pro using Markers. Your first step is to add a Marker to either a clip or a Timeline.

Before you can add a Web link to a Premiere QuickTime movie, you must add a Marker to the Timeline. A Marker adds a visual clue on the Timeline for specific important points in a movie. Following are the steps for adding a Marker to the Timeline. (Before following these steps, you should have at least one clip in the Timeline.)

1. **Activate the Timeline window by clicking it.**

2. **If a clip is selected in the Timeline, deselect it.**

3. **Click and drag the current-time indicator in the Timeline window to move to the frame where you want to set the Web link.**

4. **Choose Marker ⇨ Set Sequence Marker ⇨ Unnumbered.** The marker appears on the Timeline.

Note　You can also create a Marker by clicking and dragging a Marker icon in the Timeline window to a specific frame in the current sequence.

5. **Now that you've created a Marker, double-click it in the Timeline window to open the Marker dialog box, shown in Figure 20-7, to specify the URL you want to jump to.**

6. **In the Marker dialog box, enter a URL, such as** `http://myhomepage.com/page_2.htm`. You can enter a frame in the Frame Target field if you are using HTML framesets. Frames are handy tools if you want to create an effect in which the QuickTime movie begins in one section of the Web page and then jumps to and plays in another section. To create this effect, you need to enter the name of the URL and the filename for the frame in the Frame Target area.

Note   Web links can only be created from Timeline Markers. You cannot create a Web link from a clip marker.

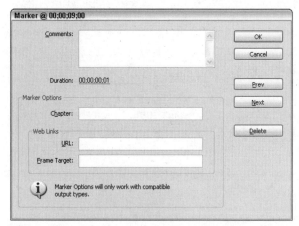

Figure 20-7: Premiere Pro's Marker dialog box allows the movie to open a Web page at a specific point in the movie.

Using Adobe GoLive to edit and create QuickTime tracks

Adobe GoLive provides extensive support for QuickTime tracks for use on the Web. Using GoLive, you can add HREF links as well as chapter tracks and sprite tracks.

The following sections show you how to create and edit QuickTime video tracks in Adobe GoLive. Before you begin, here are the basic steps for loading a QuickTime movie and viewing its tracks so that you can edit them. (For a complete explanation of GoLive's QuickTime editing options, see the online help manual or the GoLive users' guide.)

Note   GoLive also enables you to create QuickTime movies and to add effect tracks to them.

1. **To open a QuickTime movie in GoLive to edit tracks, choose File ⇨ Open.** In the Open dialog box, use the mouse to navigate to the QuickTime movie you want to open and then click OK. The movie opens in GoLive's Preview tab.

   To edit or add tracks to use on the Web, you must view the QuickTime movie in a Timeline. (Figure 20-8 shows a Timeline with HREF, chapter, and sprite tracks.) To view the Timeline for the QuickTime movie, choose Movie ⇨ Show Timeline Editor.

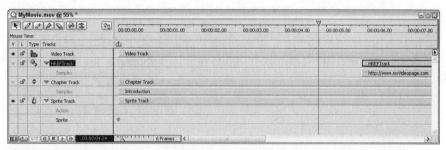

Figure 20-8: The QuickTime Timeline with HREF, chapter, and sprite tracks.

2. **Select the QuickTime tab in the Objects palette (Window ⇨ Objects).** The different icons that appear enable you to edit and add tracks (see Figure 20-9).

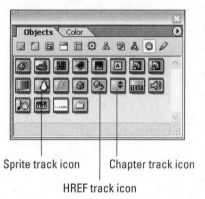

Figure 20-9: The QuickTime Objects palette with track icons.

Sprite track icon   Chapter track icon

HREF track icon

Adding an HREF track

You can use QuickTime's HREF track to create Web links. Unlike Premiere Pro, GoLive enables you to create both clickable and nonclickable Web links.

You can use this feature in a page with HTML frames. When the movie plays, you can send it to the URL of the frame and specify that it play in the top part of a frame or in a new window.

Here's how to add a QuickTime HREF track and to specify a Web link with Adobe GoLive:

1. **To create a new HREF track, click and drag the HREF icon from the QuickTime section of GoLive's Object palette to the Tracks section of the Timeline.**

2. **Activate the New Sample tool (Pencil icon) and click the triangle next to the HREF track to open the samples track.**

3. **Create a new samples track by clicking and dragging with the New Sample tool in the blank sample HREF area of the Movie Timeline (which is beneath the background track).**

4. **Position the HREF track in the area where you want to have the Web link occur.** To shorten or lengthen the track, click and drag the edge of the track.

5. **Open the Inspector palette, shown in Figure 20-10, by choosing Window ⇨ Inspector.** The time readout in the Inspector palette shows the start and stop times for the Web link action.

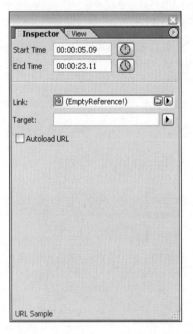

Figure 20-10: The Inspector palette.

6. **If desired, use the Divide Sample tool to divide the track into the specific number of HREF segments you want.** (Do this only if you want to create multiple clickable links.)

7. **Select the sample area of the track that you want to assign to the URL. In the Inspector palette, enter the linking HREF.** You can use the GoLive Point-and-Shoot icon to link to a Web site. If you are using frame sets, enter the frame that you want to use in the target box. You can click the Target pop-up menu to open a list of standard frame set locations, such as _top, _parent, _self, and _blank. For example, _top loads the movie into a full browser window and replaces any framesets, and _blank opens the movie into a blank browser window.

8. **If you want to have the URL load automatically so that the user does not have to click the QuickTime movie, select Autoload URL.**

Creating a chapter track

QuickTime chapter tracks enable Web page visitors to jump to different areas of a QuickTime movie. When a chapter track is created, QuickTime adds a pop-up menu with the different chapters in it. All the Web page visitor needs to do is click the pop-up menu to move to that segment of the movie.

Here's how to add a chapter track to your QuickTime movie:

1. **To create a new chapter track, click and drag the Chapter icon from the QuickTime section of the Objects palette (choose Window ⇨ Objects to open the Objects palette) to the Tracks section of the Timeline.**

2. **Activate the New Sample tool (Pencil icon) and click the triangle next to chapter track to open the samples track.**

3. **Create a new samples track by clicking and dragging with the New Sample tool in the blank samples area of the movie Timeline (which is beneath the background track).**

4. **Open the sample area of the chapter track and then click and drag in the Timeline area in the sample track to create the new sample.**

5. **To create multiple chapters, activate the Divide Sample tool and click along the sample track to divide it into different segments.**

6. **Choose Window ⇨ Inspector to open the Inspector palette.**

7. **Activate the Arrow Selection tool and then select each chapter.** After you select the chapter, enter a name in the Chapter Title field in the Inspector palette, as shown in Figure 20-11. Do this for each segment in the chapter samples track.

8. **To edit the time for each track, use the Arrow tool to click and drag the position of the sample or edit the track length by clicking the edge.** As you click and drag, the time readout in the Inspector palette changes.

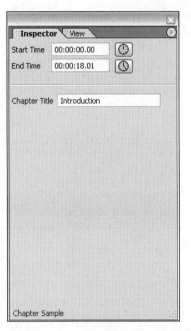

Figure 20-11: Entering a chapter name in the Inspector palette.

Creating interactivity with sprite tracks

Interactive sprites are the most sophisticated effect that you can add to a QuickTime movie in Adobe GoLive. (The term *sprite* is often used to represent a graphic or object that can be used repeatedly.) After you add a sprite track to a QuickTime movie, you can import graphics and use the graphics for added visual effect, or even as interactive buttons.

There are countless ways to use sprites and interactive behaviors. Following is a short example to give you an idea of the possibilities. This example shows you how to import a graphic into a QuickTime movie and have the image change when the user moves the mouse over it. We also show you how to assign an action to the graphic. Because creating and using sprites can be a time-consuming process, we've broken the project into three short sections.

Adding sprite tracks

The following simple steps show you how to create a Sprite track that can be used to add graphics and interactivity to a QuickTime move:

1. **To create a new sprite track, click and drag the Sprite icon from the QuickTime section of the Object palette (choose Window ⇨ Objects to open the Objects palette) to the Tracks section of the Timeline.**

2. If you want to rename the track, double-click it and enter a new name.

Importing graphics

You can import graphics to use as sprites in the sprite track of a QuickTime movie. For example, you can create tiny buttons or characters that appear and disappear while the QuickTime movie plays. After the graphics are imported, you can load them into the sprite track and create interactivity. In this example, you'll import two graphics into the sprite track. However, after the graphics are added to the sprite track, they do not appear until you place them into a sprite subtrack. (Creating sprite subtracks is discussed later in this section.)

Note   You can load the following graphic formats into sprite tracks: JPEG, GIF, PICT, BMP, and PSD (Photoshop native format).

1. Select the sprite track in the Tracks section of the Timeline.

2. If the Inspector palette is not opened, open it by choosing Window ➪ Inspector palette.

3. Click the Images tab in the Inspector palette, as shown in Figure 20-12.

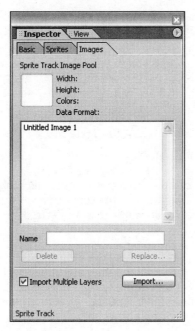

Figure 20-12: The Images tab in the Inspector palette.

4. **Before importing graphics, deselect multiple layers (otherwise, you might import layers with nothing in them).** To import graphics, click the Import button in the Images tab. When the Open dialog box appears, select the graphics you want to add and then click Add for each graphic. Click Done when finished.

5. **Importing graphics opens the Compression Settings dialog box, shown in Figure 20-13. If desired, change the Quality settings and the Compressor.**

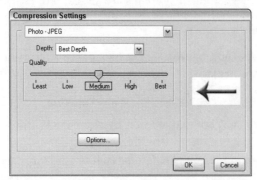

Figure 20-13: You can change compression settings in the Compression Settings dialog box.

Creating sprite subtracks

Importing sprites adds them to the Tracks sprite pool. Now they can be used as many times as desired in sprite subtracks. In a sprite subtrack, you can control sprite positioning and switch from one sprite to another.

1. **Select the sprite track in the Tracks section of the Timeline.**

2. **Click the Sprites tab in the Inspector palette.**

Note   You can change the background color of the sprite track by clicking the background color check box in the Sprites tab and then clicking the color swatch. (By default, the sprite track is black.) You can also set a blending mode for the track by clicking the Basic tab in the Inspector palette.

3. **Click in the Add New Sprites field, as shown in Figure 20-14.** Enter the number of sprite subtracks that you want to add and then press the Tab key. If you want to create a simple rollover effect or a simple action, type **1**. Doing this adds a sprite subtrack to the Timeline and creates a keyframe for the sprite. (A diamond in the subtrack area of the Timeline represents the keyframe.)

Figure 20-14: Type the number of subtracks that you want to add in the Add New Sprites field.

Changing location and creating simple behaviors

If you want the sprites to switch sprite images or sprite positions in the subtrack as the movie plays, you must create more keyframes and then use the Inspector to switch images or locations. Here's how:

1. **In the Timeline, select the keyframe for the subtrack.**

2. **If you want to change the positions of the sprite, enter the new coordinates in the position section of the Basic tab in the Inspector palette.**

You can also make a sprite invisible at a keyframe by deselecting the Visible check box in the Basic tab of the Inspector palette.

3. **If you want to switch graphic images, select the image from the Image pop-up menu in the Basic tab of the Inspector palette.**

4. **To create a new keyframe, press Option/Alt, click and drag the keyframe in the Timeline track to the right, and then release the mouse button.**

After creating a keyframe, you can change images or image positions.

5. **If you want to create interactivity or a rollover effect, click in the Over swatch (for a rollover) or in the Click Inside or Click Outside boxes in the Basic tab of the Inspector palette.** Then choose the image that you want to switch to when the mouse rolls over or clicks inside or outside of the image. A Click Inside effect is shown in Figure 20-15.

Figure 20-15: Switching images with a mouse click in the Basic tab.

Assigning actions to a sprite

GoLive enables you to assign an action when the user clicks or moves the mouse over a sprite. For example, when the user clicks a sprite, you can have the movie increase volume, return to its beginning, or jump to another Web page. While assigning actions, remember that actions only occur at keyframes. Therefore, you may need to create many keyframes to give the user enough time to click the sprite.

Here's how to assign actions to a sprite:

1. **Select the keyframe where you want the action to occur.**

2. **Click the Action tab in the Inspector palette.**

3. **Choose an event in the event list, such as Mouse Down, Mouse Click, or Mouse Enter.**

4. Click the New Action icon (dog-eared page icon).

5. In the pop-up menu at the bottom of the screen, choose an action, such as Movie Set Volume, Movie GoTo Time, or Movie GoTo Beginning, as shown in Figure 20-16.

6. Click the Apply button.

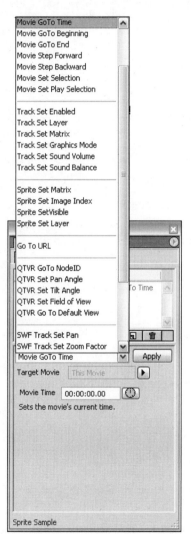

Figure 20-16: Assigning an action to a sprite.

Previewing and saving your work

When you are finished creating sprites and assigning actions to them, you can pre-view your work by clicking the Play icon (triangle) at the bottom of the Timeline. You can also slowly preview your sprite work by clicking and dragging the Edit line Marker over the Timeline.

At this point, you can save your movie by choosing File ➪ Save. Then choose Movie ➪ Export Movie. In GoLive's Save Exported File dialog box, click the Options button to review or change the QuickTime video settings and then click OK to save the movie.

Summary

If you will be exporting a movie to the Web or to an intranet, knowing the HTML options available to you can help you add features to your movies. A program such as Adobe GoLive can simplify the task of loading a digital movie onto a Web page and the task of writing the HTML code. QuickTime movies enable you to add many features that can be utilized on the Web, including the following:

✦ You can add a clickable HREF track to a QuickTime movie.

✦ You can add a chapter pull-down menu that appears on a Web page. When a user clicks the chapter name, the movie jumps to that section.

✦ You can add sprite graphics to a QuickTime movie and add interactivity.

✦   ✦   ✦

Exporting Video to the Web

Now that more and more Internet users log on to the Web using speedy broadband connections, video producers will undoubtedly be exporting their Web files with streaming media in mind.

Streaming media enables users to watch a video program as it downloads. Before the advent of streaming media, Web users had to wait for an entire clip to download before the video actually started to play. When media is streamed, information packets are sent by special streaming server software such as RealNetworks RealVideo Server, Microsoft's Windows Media Server, or Apple's QuickTime Streaming Media Server.

Fortunately, Premiere Pro users can easily export video for streaming media projects or for slower modem connections. Adobe Media Encoder provides a simple and straightforward means for outputting video files in streaming and non-streaming formats. This exporting module, installed within Premiere Pro, takes the guesswork out of choosing the appropriate output settings for Web viewing. You can export your Premiere Pro projects in RealVideo, Windows Media, or QuickTime formats. Furthermore, presets built into the Encoder enable you to easily export one clip optimized for multiple bandwidths. In other words, you can export a high-quality file to the Web or an intranet and have the Encoder create versions for users with either high- or low-bandwidth connections. Thus, when you output to an intranet or the Web, the Adobe Media Encoder presets can save you time and help ensure quality playback for users who view your videos.

Encoding Terms

This chapter provides an overview of different Web encoding formats, particularly those used for streaming media. As you choose different formats, you'll see a variety of arcane encoding terms such as two-pass encoding, variable bit rate, and constant bit rate; some encoding terms will frequently surface in different dialog boxes. These terms appear regardless of whether you are exporting to Windows Media, RealMedia, or QuickTime format. Before continuing, you might want to review some non-technical definitions:

✦ **Two-pass encoding.** Two-pass encoding increases the digital quality of exported video. When two-pass encoding is used, the video that is processed is actually processed twice. The first time, the encoder analyzes the video to determine the best manner to encode it. On the second pass, it uses the information gathered in the first pass to encode it. As you might guess, two-pass encoding takes longer than single pass, but increases the quality of the encoded video.

✦ **Variable bit rate.** Variable bit rate varies the bit rate of a clip as it plays back. When a high-action scene needs more bits or bandwidth, the encoding process delivers the extra bits; in areas that don't require high-bandwidth, it lowers the bit rate. Thus, for clips that vary in action, VBR can provide better quality than constant bit rate, (CBR), which does not vary the bit rate of the clip as it plays back.

✦ **Keyframe.** When some CODECs compress video, they can compare each frame with subsequent frames and can save only the information that changes. When the information changes, the CODEC saves a full frame of video only when it needs to. This frame is often called a *keyframe*. So CODECs that use keyframes can reduce the file size of exported video. Typically, a keyframe setting is divisible by the frame rate. Therefore, at 30 frames per second, you might see a keyframe of 30, meaning one keyframe is created every second (30 frames). A keyframe of 60 would create one keyframe every two seconds.

✦ **Metadata.** Metadata for Web video clips is text data about the clip that can be searched for on the World Wide Web. Often metadata information includes information such as title, date, and creator. Windows Media, RealMedia, and QuickTime all allow the inclusion of metadata categories within their files. Depending on the file format and the Web formatting, metadata about movie clips can sometimes be viewed by right-clicking in the movie and then choosing Properties.

Windows Media Format

Premiere Pro's Adobe Media Encoder allows you to export movies in Windows Media format, Microsoft's newest audio and video format. Windows Media movies can play back in Internet Explorer and can be streamed from Microsoft's Streaming Media server. Windows media files are recognizable by their .wmv file extension. WMV files can be read by Windows Media Player version 7 and higher.

Exporting to Windows Media format

To export in Windows Media format, start by selecting the sequence in the Project window that you want to export in the Project window. If you want to create a Windows Media file from only the current work area, click and drag the Work area bar borders so that they encompass the sequence area that you want to export. If you want to export a clip, select the clip in the Project window (later you can choose to export the entire clip or from the clip's in to out points). When you're ready to start the export process, choose Export ➪ Movie ➪ Adobe Media Encoder. In the Transcode Settings dialog box, choose Windows Media in the Format menu. In the Preset drop-down menu, choose the best preset for your intended audience. The presets are descriptions of the type of Web connection that you expect your audience to be using. Figure 21-1 shows many of the preset choices.

For example, if your target audience is using a 56 Kbps modem, you can choose the preset WM9 NTSC 32K download. You can see a summary of the video and audio settings in Figure 21-2. Notice that this choice uses variable bit rate encoding, with two passes. The frame width is 320 by 240, and the frame rate is 30 frames per second. If you need to choose slower dial-up choice, pick one of the Windows Media 8 dial-up modem choices.

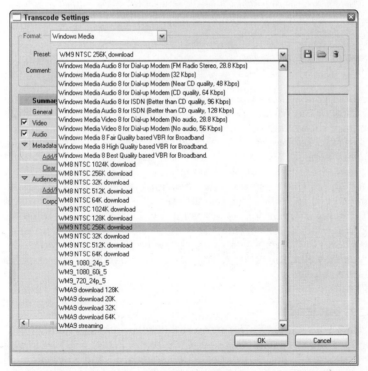

Figure 21-1: The Windows Media formats.

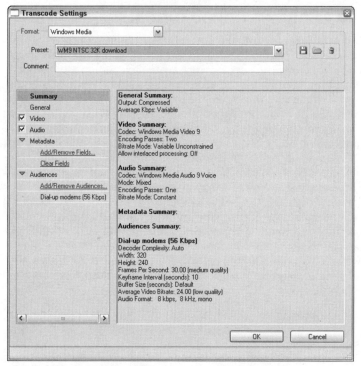

Figure 21-2: Windows Media preset for 56 Kbps modem.

If you want to export your video for broadband connections, you might choose either the WM9 256K or the WM9 512K download. When you pick the WM9 512K option, the Summary shows that this choice should be targeted for Broadband, Cable Modem, and DSL. To view how the data will be encoded, click the Video section in the Summary area.

The Video section shows that this preset uses two encoding passes and variable bit rate mode. Now, you can see other encoding information by clicking on the word Broadband in the Summary area. This changes the window to show the frame width, height, frames per second, and keyframe intervals, as well as the video bit rate and audio format, as shown in Figure 21-3. Although there is generally no need to change these settings, you may edit any of them. For instance, you might want a smaller frame size in your Web page.

Changing target audiences
If you want to target your export file for more audiences, click Add/Remove audiences under the Audience heading. This opens the Select Target window, as shown in Figure 21-4, where you can add other connection speeds. To add a target audience, simply click in a check box next to the target connection; to remove a connection, click in a box that was already selected.

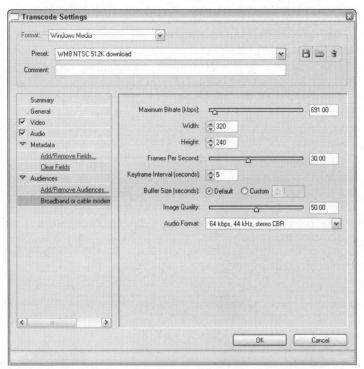

Figure 21-3: Encoding format for broadband, cable modem, and DSL audiences.

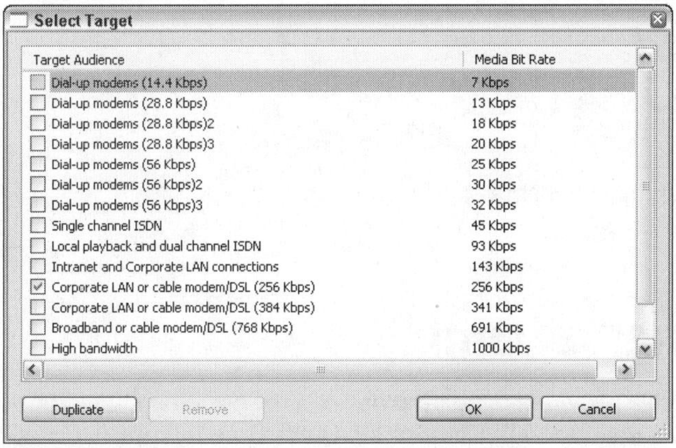

Figure 21-4: Add or Remove Target audiences in the Select Target window.

Adding metadata

If you want to add searchable metadata to the export file, click the Add/Remove Fields under the Metadata Summary section. If you don't see the words Add/Remove Fields, click the triangle next to Metadata to open this section. In the Select Metadata window, shown in Figure 21-5, click the fields that you want to include with your video. After you click OK, a dialog box opens allowing you to enter information into the fields.

Creating the export file

After you've selected a profile and entered the metadata text desired, you're ready to create the Windows Media export file. To start the process, click OK in the Transcode Settings dialog box. If you've changed any of the default presets, the Choose Name dialog box appears allowing you to name your custom preset. Next, the Save dialog box opens. Here you can choose to export the entire sequence or the work area only. If you selected a clip rather than a sequence, the Export Range dialog box allows you to export the clip or from the clip's in to out point. Next, click the Save button to export the file, or you can quickly change settings by clicking the Settings button.

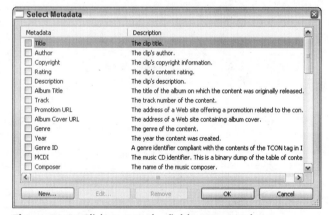

Figure 21-5: Click next to the field names to choose metadata fields.

Using QuickTime Streaming

The Adobe Media Encoder provides exporting options for creating QuickTime streaming media files. As discussed in Chapter 20, QuickTime is Apple's cross-platform digital media format. QuickTime streaming files can be used on Apple's Streaming Media Server as well as the RealNetworks RealMedia Streaming Server. Not only are QuickTime files cross platform, but also Apple's Streaming Media Server is available for Windows NT and UNIX platforms.

Note   You can also prepare a QuickTime movie for streaming by exporting a Premiere Pro movie by choosing File ⇨ Export ⇨ Movie and choosing QuickTime as a setting. You can then use Apple's QuickTime Pro to export the file for Apple's QuickTime Media server.

Choosing a QuickTime media format

If you want to export your movie in a streaming QuickTime format, start by selecting the sequence in the Project menu. If you want to export only the work area, change the work area boundaries so that they encompass only the sequence area you want to export. If you want to export a clip, select it in the Project window. After you've selected the sequencer clip, choose File ⇨ Export ⇨ Adobe Media Encoder. To start the process of creating a QuickTime streaming file, choose QuickTime in the format drop-down menu in the Transcode Settings dialog box. Next choose one of the QuickTime streaming presets in the Preset drop-down menu. The preset choices are shown in Figure 21-6.

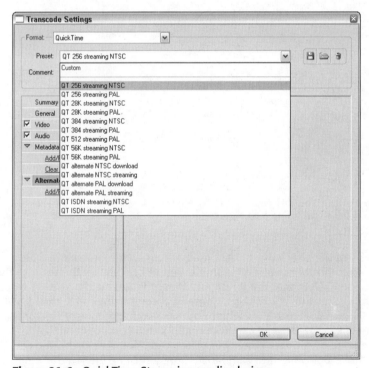

Figure 21-6: QuickTime Streaming media choices.

The QuickTime format provides a variety of different choices. If you want to export your file for a variety of different connection settings, including broadband, choose QT alternate NTSC download. Figure 21-7 shows the list of different connection alternatives. When you select the Alternates heading, the Transcode dialog box allows you to create a prefix for the different alternate connection files and set a target path for saving all the files.

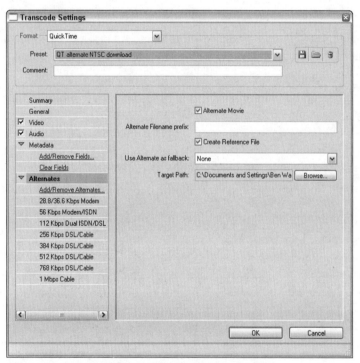

Figure 21-7: QuickTime streaming alternate settings.

If you click on any of the alternates in the Summary area, the Transcode dialog box reveals the encoding settings. For example, Figure 21-8 shows the settings for 1 Mbps Cable modem. Note that the Width and Height is 320 by 240 at 29.97 frames per second, with a data rate of 750 Kbps. Contrast these settings with the 28.8 modem option, shown in Figure 21-9, which exports at a frame size of 160 by 120 and a frame rate of 6.0. All settings use a Sorenson Video compression CODEC, which is frequently used for exporting QuickTime Web files. If desired, you can also use the Add/Remove button to add or remove more alternate files to the list.

Figure 21-8: Settings for a 1 Mbps Cable modem.

If you are working with QuickTime, it's a good idea to take a look at the General settings for exporting. To access them, click General in the Summary area. In the General summary area, set your QuickTime movie to Autoplay, to play as soon as it appears on the Web page; and/or you can have it loop or keep repeating. Leave the Hinted Movie option selected. The QuickTime server uses the hinted track to stream media.

Using metadata

Like the Windows Media and RealMedia formats, the QuickTime export allows you to create metadata fields. To choose the fields, click Add/Remove Fields in the Transcode Settings dialog box and then select the fields you want to add. After you choose the fields, click the word Metadata in the Summary area. The right side of the dialog box changes to fields in which you can enter the metadata text (see Figure 21-10).

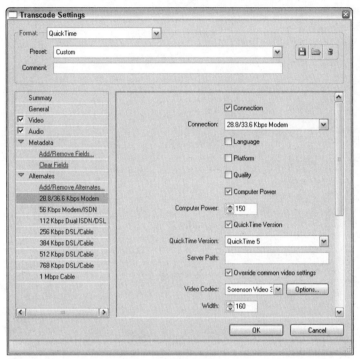

Figure 21-9: Settings for a 28 Kbps modem.

Creating the QuickTime export file

After you've selected a profile and entered any metadata for the file to be exported, you're ready to create the QuickTime export file. To start the process, click OK in the Transcode Settings dialog box. If you've changed any of the default presets, a dialog box appears allowing you to name your custom preset. Next, the Save dialog box opens. Here you can choose to export the entire sequence or the work area only. If you selected a clip rather than a sequence, the Export Range dialog box allows you to export the entire clip or from the clip's in to out points. Next, click the Save button to export the file, or you can quickly change settings by clicking the Settings button.

Figure 21-10: QuickTime Metadata field entry.

Exporting to RealMedia Format

The Adobe Media Encoder's RealMedia export formats enable you to create digital movies in RealMedia format, one of the most popular streaming video formats used on the Web. RealMedia became popular because it was one of the first true streaming video formats. As the data streams, the RealPlayer (or newer RealOne Player) software and the RealMedia server communicate to ensure that the data is sent at the best data rate. The RealMedia options in the Transcode Settings dialog box enable you to create one video clip for multiple audiences. Like the Windows Media and QuickTime formats, you can export an entire sequence, the current work area, or a clip for viewers using different connection speeds. When the clip is downloaded, RealMedia switches to either the faster stream for faster connection users or the slower stream for slower dial-up modem users.

After you've finished your production work, you can start the export process by selecting the sequence that you want to export and choosing File ➪ Export ➪ Adobe Media Encoder. If you want to export a clip instead, select the clip in the Project window. If you want to export only the work area, change the work area boundaries so that they encompass only the area that you want to export. When the Adobe Media Encoder opens, choose RealMedia from the Format drop-down list.

Start by picking a preset. As mentioned earlier, a preset is a description of the type of Web connection that you expect your audience to be using. When you choose a RealMedia preset, the General section of the Transcode Settings dialog box shows whether two-pass encoding is used and may also have the following options:

✦ **Allow Recording.** Select this option to enable users to save the clip on their computers by clicking a Record button that appears in the browser. If you don't select this option, the Record button is grayed.

✦ **Allow Download.** Select this option to enable users who don't have the RealPlayer plug-in to save the clip directly to their hard drives.

If you're outputting to the Web using a streaming media server, pick a streaming media choice such as RM9 Streaming broadband. If the video is not going to be streamed, pick a download choice. To see or change the frame size, click Video in the Summary area. The video settings for Streaming broadband are shown in Figure 21-11. The Video content drop-down list will often include the following choices:

✦ **Normal Motion.** Use this option for clips that include some motion and stills.

✦ **Smoothest Motion.** Select this option for clips that feature limited motion.

✦ **Sharpest Motion.** Use this option for sporting events and other action clips.

✦ **Slide Show.** This makes your video appear as a series of still frames.

Like the Windows Media and QuickTime formats, RealMedia also allows you to add or subtract target audiences by clicking Add/Remove Audience in the Summary section. If desired, you can edit the target audience settings by clicking any of the target audiences listed in the Summary area. RealMedia also allows you to add metadata, in much the same way that you add metadata to Windows Media and QuickTime streaming files: Click Add/Remove Fields in the Summary area and then click Metadata to enter the data.

Creating the RealMedia export file

After you've selected a profile and entered any metadata for the file to be exported, you're ready to create the RealMedia export file. To start the process, click OK in the Transcode settings dialog box. If you've changed any of the default presets, a dialog box appears allowing you to name your custom preset. Next, the Save dialog box opens. Here you can choose to export the entire sequence or the work area only.

If you selected a clip rather than a sequence, the Export Range dialog box only allows you to export the entire clip or from the clip's in to out point. Next, click the Save button to export the file, or you can quickly change settings by clicking the Settings button.

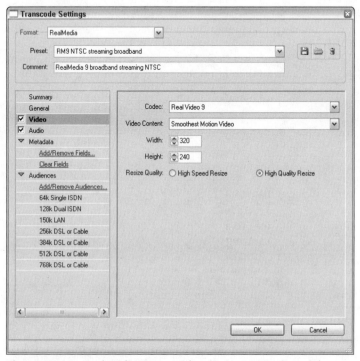

Figure 21-11: RealMedia Preset Video Summary section of the Transcode Settings dialog box.

Summary

Slow Web connection speeds can make downloading digital video a time-consuming task. Premiere Pro's Adobe Media Encoder takes advantage of video streaming and helps optimize download times.

✦ Use the Windows Media Format to export files for different target audiences in Windows media format.

✦ Use the QuickTime format to export files for Apple's Streaming Media server.

✦ Use the RealMedia format to export files for RealNetwork's RealMedia Media Server.

✦   ✦   ✦

Exporting to Videotape

Despite the excitement generated by outputting video to the World Wide Web, videotape still remains one of the most popular mediums for distributing and showing high-quality video productions. Provided you have the right hardware, Adobe Premiere Pro enables you to export clips and complete projects to videotape.

Professionals who demand high-quality output can also have Premiere Pro export their projects to an Advanced Authoring Format (AAF) file. An AAF file is a multimedia file format that allows Premiere Pro users to send data to other digital video editing systems.

This chapter discusses the steps you need to take to output your Premiere Pro files to videotape or to an AAF file.

Preparing to Export Video

In order to export your Premiere Pro Project to videotape, your system must support device control, which enables you to start and stop a videotape recorder or camcorder directly from Premiere Pro. If you have a DV camcorder and your computer has an IEEE 1394 port, chances are you'll be able to use device control. However, before you get started, you may want to add black video or bars and tones to the beginning of your project.

Adding black video, color bars, and tone

If you are sending your Premiere Pro Project to a video production facility, you may want to add black video to the beginning of your project. The extra black video will provide the production facility more time to get its equipment rolling before your project begins. Here's how to create black video:

1. **Click the New Item button at the bottom of the Project window.**

2. **In the pop-up menu, shown in Figure 22-1, choose Black Video.** This adds five seconds of black video to the Project window.

3. **To add the black to the Monitor window, double-click the Black Video in the Project window.** You can then click the Insert button in the Monitor window to insert it into your project. (You can also simply drag it into the Timeline window to place it into a sequence.)

In order to calibrate color and audio, production facilities set their electronic equipment to color bars and a 1 kHz tone. If you are working with a video production facility, you can easily add bars and tone to your Premiere Pro Project. Here's how:

1. **Click the New Item button at the bottom of the Project window.**

2. **In the pop-up menu, shown in Figure 22-1, choose Bars and Tone.** This adds five seconds of color bars and a tone to the Project window.

3. **To increase the duration of the bars and tone, select Bars and Tone in the Project window (or right-click the bars and tone in the Project window) and then choose Speed/Duration in the drop-down menu.** In the Clip Speed/Duration dialog box, add the desired time in frames.

4. **To add the bars and tone to the Monitor window, double-click the bars and tone in the Project window.** You can then click the Insert button in the Monitor window to insert into your project. (You can also simply drag it into the Timeline window to place it into a sequence.)

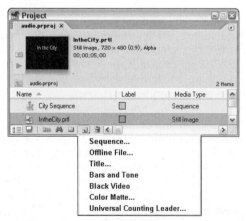

Figure 22-1: Click the New Item button to add black video and bars and tone.

Checking project settings

Before exporting to videotape, review your production's project settings by choosing Project ⇨ Project Settings ⇨ General. Review the Video, Audio, and Keyframe and Rendering sections. As you view the settings in these dialog boxes, make sure that they are set to the highest-quality output, because Premiere Pro uses these settings when exporting to videotape.

Note   The video settings in Premiere Pro are explained in several chapters in this book, so we do not repeat them here. You may, however, want to review the Fields setting in the General options, of the Project Settings dialog box, as shown in Figure 22-2.

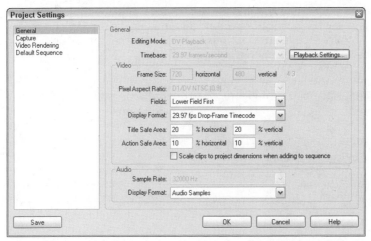

Figure 22-2: The General options in the Project Settings dialog box.

Fields are only relevant when exporting to videotape. The NTSC, PAL, and Secam standards divide each frame into two fields. In NTSC video, where the frame rate is approximately 29.97 frames per second, approximately 30 video frame appear each second. Each frame is divided into two fields that appear for a 60th of a second. PAL and Secam display a video frame every 25 frames, and each field is displayed each 50th of a second.

When the field is displayed, it displays alternating scan lines. Thus, the first frame may scan lines 1, 3, 5, 7, and so on. After the first field is scanned, the frame then scans lines 2, 4, 6, 8, and so on. So, in some respects you might conceptualize a video frame to be like a child's puzzle with the video fields being two zigzagging, interlocking pieces. If you view only one of the pieces, you don't get a sharp picture. In fact, if you could freeze a field onscreen, you would see an image with blurry lines.

When setting export settings, you can choose Upper Field First or Lower Field First, depending on which field your system expects to receive first. If this setting is incorrect, jerky and jumpy video may be the result.

Note   If you don't know in what order your equipment expects fields, run a quick export of a project that includes motion. Export the project set to Upper Field First and then export it set to Lower Field First. The correct field setting should provide the best playback. Use this setting when you export your video project.

Checking device control settings

Before you begin exporting your project to videotape, check to be sure that your device control options are properly installed. These settings appear in the Premiere Program's Preferences dialog box. To open the Preferences dialog box and access the Device Control section directly, choose Edit ➪ Preferences ➪ Device Control.

Click the Device pop-up menu and choose the Device Control option for your equipment. (If you have digital video [DV] equipment, you may be able to choose DV Device Control 2.0.) Next, click the Options button. Doing so opens the DV Device Control Options dialog box, as shown in Figure 22-3.

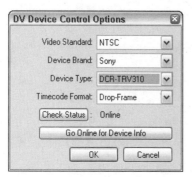

Figure 22-3: Choose your camcorder in the Device Type drop-down menu.

In the DV Device Control Options dialog box, choose the correct video standard (NTSC or PAL). Choose a Device Brand and a Device Type. Next, pick the timecode format you want to use in the Timecode Format menu. If your camcorder is off, turn it on and click the Check Status button. If all connections are properly set, the Offline readout should change to Online. If you are connected to the Internet, to check the compatibility of your camcorder with Premiere Pro, click Go Online for Device info. This command will bring you to a Web page that lists camcorders and their compatibility with Premiere Pro.

Setting digital video playback options

After you've checked your video and device control settings, your next step is to establish playback options. The choices are different, depending upon the hardware you are using.

If you are using digital video equipment, start by connecting the IEEE 1394 cable from your camcorder or tape deck to your computer.

Now, set the playback to your camcorder by following these steps:

1. **Turn on your camcorder or recording device.** If you are using a camcorder, make sure it is set to the VCR or VTR setting.

2. **To set the playback to a digital video recording device, choose Project ⇨ Project Settings.** In the General options panel, choose DV Playback in the Editing Mode pop-up menu.

3. **Click the Playback Settings button.**

If you choose DV Playback in the Editing Mode field, the DV Playback Options dialog box, as shown in Figure 22-4, appears.

Figure 22-4: Setting playback options to a DV camcorder or VCR.

Following is a list of the options in the DV Playback Settings dialog box:

✦ In the Video Playback section:

• **Play Video on DV Hardware.** Select this option to play back on your camcorder or VCR.

✦ In the Audio Playback section:

• **Play Audio on DV Hardware.** Select this option to play back audio on your camcorder or VCR.

• **Play Audio on Audio Hardware.**

♦ In the Real-Time Effects section:

- **Playback on DV Hardware and Desktop.** Select this option to play back effects on both DV hardware and your desktop.

- **Playback on Desktop Only.**

♦ In the Export to Tape section:

- **Play Audio on DV Hardware.** Select this option to play the Audio on DV Hardware when you export.

- **Play Audio on Audio Hardware.** If you want to export to Audio Hardware, choose this option instead.

Exporting with Device Control

The following section describes how to export to videotape with device control for DV hardware.

Before starting the export session, make sure that you have set the DV control options in the DV Playback Settings dialog box and that you have reviewed your video settings.

Exporting using DV device control

To export to videotape using DV device control, follow these steps:

1. **Turn on your videotape deck and load the tape on which you are recording into your tape deck.** To record using DV device control, you must insert a tape pre-striped with timecode into your tape deck; then write down the timecode location at which you want to begin recording.

2. **Select the Sequence that you want to export by clicking it in the Project window.**

3. **Choose File ⇨ Export ⇨ Export to Tape.**

4. **In the Export to Tape dialog box, as shown in Figure 22-5, select Activate Recording Device.** This tells Premiere Pro to take control of the recording device.

5. **If you don't want the recoding to begin at the current location, choose Assemble at timecode; then enter the timecode where you want recording to begin.**

6. **In the Delay Movie Start field, enter a delay in quarter-frames.** (Some devices need this delay to sync the recording device with the movie after starting the recording process.)

7. **In the Preroll field, enter the number of frames you want to back up before the specified timecode.** This enables the tape to attain the proper speed before recording. Five seconds (150 frames) is usually sufficient.

8. **Click Record.**

Figure 22-5: The Export to Tape dialog box instructs Premiere Pro to take control of the recording device.

Exporting without Device Control

If your hardware setup does not allow device control, you can still record to videotape by manually controlling your video recording device. Here are the steps:

1. **Make sure your camcorder or recording device is connected properly.**

2. **Turn on your videotape deck and load the tape onto which you are recording into your tape deck.**

3. **Select the sequence that you want to export by clicking it in the Project window.** You should be able to see the sequence on your video display.

4. **Cue the tape recorder to the position where you want to begin recording.**

5. **Move the current-time indicator to the start of your Premiere Pro movie.**

6. **Press the Record button on your recording device.**

7. **Press the Play button in the Monitor window.**

8. **After you are done recording, click the Stop button in the Monitor window and then press the Stop button on your recording device.**

Exporting to AAF Format

In your day-to-day work as a digital video editor or producer, you may find the need to re-create your Premiere Pro Project on another video system, perhaps a high-end system. Re-creating your project from scratch on another system could prove to be costly and time consuming. Fortunately, you can export your Premiere Pro Project as in Advanced Authoring Format (AAF). This standard industry format, which was created in the late 1990s, has been embraced by a variety of high-end video systems. Theoretically, you should be able to export your Premiere Pro Project in AAF format and later import the file into another system. After the import, you should be able to work with all of your files and footage. But, realistically, how accurately the high-end system reads the AAF file may vary from system to system.

Exporting to AAF is quite easy. Simply select the Project window and choose Project ➪ Export Project as AAF. In the Save dialog box that appears, enter a name for the AAF file.

Note   For details about which Adobe Premiere Pro effects are supported when exporting to AAF format, open the AAF plug-in.doc file found in the Adobe Premiere Pro folder.

Summary

Premiere Pro allows you to output your movies directly to videotape. You can output with or without device control.

✦ Premiere Pro uses File ➪ Export ➪ Export to Tape to export to videotape.

✦ Premiere Pro uses the settings in the Project Settings dialog box when outputting to videotape.

✦ If you want to create an AAF file, choose Project ➪ Export Project as AAF.

✦   ✦   ✦

Outputting to CD-ROM, Macromedia Director, and Macromedia Flash

CHAPTER

23

Although the number of digital movies appearing on the World Wide Web seems to grow each day, the most widely used medium for distributing digital movies is CD-ROM. Virtually every computer sold today includes a CD-ROM drive, and many sold today are at least 12 times faster than those sold just five years ago. A standard CD-ROM holds 650MB of data, usually enough space for at least 30 minutes of compressed digital video. CD-ROMs also are among the cheapest and most durable digital media available.

Many multimedia producers who distribute their work on CD-ROM find that to truly take advantage of the medium, they need to add interactivity to their Adobe Premiere Pro presentations. A popular interactive multimedia program is Macromedia Director. If you import a Premiere Pro movie into Director, you can create buttons that start, stop, and rewind your Premiere Pro movie. You can also put several Premiere Pro movies into different Director frames and create buttons that enable the viewer to move from one movie to another.

This chapter guides you through the steps for exporting your Premiere Pro movie to CD-ROM. The chapter begins with the steps for choosing compression settings for Premiere Pro movies that will be exported to CD-ROM. It includes an overview of how to use Macromedia Director to create interactive behaviors to control digital movies. Because many multimedia producers will soon be moving their interactive productions to the Web, we've included a section on Macromedia Flash — undoubtedly the most popular application for creating interactive productions on the Web.

Exporting Premiere Pro Movies to CD-ROM

Outputting Premiere Pro movies to CD-ROM often presents the multimedia producer with a dilemma: The higher quality settings that are necessary when exporting a Premiere Pro movie can result in poor quality playback. This problem is especially true if you export your Premiere Pro project for viewing on older computer systems that have slow CD-ROM drives. When you export, you may need to make small compromises in quality to ensure that your Premiere Pro movie plays back well on older systems.

Before you begin the process of exporting a movie for CD-ROM output, understanding what is involved in the process is a good idea. Here is an overview of the process:

1. **Create a project with either a DV or non-DV setting.**

2. **Complete all editing in Premiere Pro.** Decide whether you want to export the entire Timeline to one movie or export it to several movies that you might want to integrate into a Macromedia Director project.

3. **To export for QuickTime or AVI, first select the sequence you want to export and then choose File ➪ Export ➪ Movie. Click the Settings button to choose AVI or QuickTime.** If you want to export using an MPEG format (MPEG1 is suitable for CD-ROM), choose File ➪ Export ➪ Adobe Media Encoder.

4. **Specify Premiere Pro export settings, including the frame size, frame rate, and compressor.**

5. **If you are importing your Premiere Pro movie into Director or another multimedia program, such as Macromedia Authorware, import the Premiere Pro movie into the program.** Then complete the final production in Director or Authorware.

6. **Record the final production to a CD-ROM using a CD-ROM recorder.** Most Mac CD-ROM recording software enables you to partition the CD-ROM to create a Mac version and a Windows version.

Output settings for CD-ROM

Before Premiere Pro turned "pro," earlier versions of the program provided the following multimedia project presets for both QuickTime and AVI movies.

Note   Many non-DV analog boards allow video to be captured at different frame sizes and frame rates.

✦ **Compressor.** Cinepak

✦ **Frame Size.** 320 × 240

✦ **Frame Rate.** 15.00

✦ **Color Depth.** Millions

The audio presets are as follows:

✦ **Rate.** 22050

✦ **Format.** 16-bit mono

These presets were primarily designed for square pixel footage captured on analog to digital boards. If you're creating Premiere Pro projects that will appear in CD-ROM productions (particularly in older computers), consider the preceding presets as minimum output settings. If you are working with DV footage, you can change Compressor settings, frame size, and frame rate when you export your movie.

If you want to export your files for CD-ROM productions, the steps are virtually identical to exporting your production as a digital movie, as described in Chapter 19.

Here's a summary of the steps:

1. **Complete your editing.**

2. **Select the Sequence that you want to export and choose File ⇨ Export ⇨ Movie.** If you want to change settings, click the Settings button in the Export Movie dialog box.

3. **Change settings as desired in the General, Video, Audio, Keyframe and Rendering, and Special Processing sections.** If you're exporting QuickTime movies, you may want to choose Sorenson Video, rather than Cinepak, as your compressor. Sorenson can provide higher-quality movies in smaller file sizes. (However, Cinepak is still considered the best compressor for older computers. Cinepak also allows color reduction to 256 colors, whereas Sorenson does not.) Figure 23-1 shows the Sorenson Video settings in the Export Movie Settings dialog box. One of the most import options in this dialog box is the Data Rate. The value entered in this dialog box limits the flow of data so that the video doesn't pour out at a rate the CD-ROM can't handle. Typical data rates for double-speed CD-ROM are between 200K and 250K per second. If you know that your project will be played on a 12-speed (12X) CD-ROM drive, Adobe recommends using 1.8MB per second for a 24X CD-ROM, 3–3.6MB.

Note   To view a tech note on limiting data rates in Premiere Pro from Adobe's support knowledgebase, point your browser to www.adobe.com/support/techdocs/a60a.htm.

Tip   If you reduce the number of frames per second in the Frame Rate menu, you can usually increase the data rate.

4. **After editing settings in the Export Movie Settings dialog box, click OK.**

5. **In the Export Movie dialog box, name your file.**

6. **Click Save.** If you are using Cinepak compression and are exporting a long movie, the compression process may take quite some time.

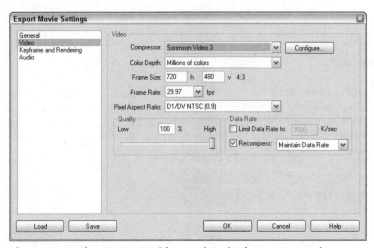

Figure 23-1: The Sorenson Video settings in the Export Movie Settings dialog box.

Using Macromedia Director

Macromedia Director is a powerful and widely used multimedia-authoring program. Like Premiere Pro, Director enables you to import graphics files from such programs as Adobe Photoshop and Adobe ImageReady. It also enables you to import source images from Macromedia FireWorks and Macromedia Flash.

Although Director is often used for creating animated sequences, to Premiere Pro users it offers the power of adding interactivity to digital movies. Unlike Premiere Pro, Director features a powerful programming language called Lingo. By using Lingo, you can create scripts or behaviors that enable the user to jump from frame to frame or to start and stop Premiere Pro movies imported into Director. For instance, using both Premiere Pro and Director, you can create educational productions that enable users to choose what areas they want to learn and what video segments they want to see.

Director overview

To understand how Premiere Pro movies can be integrated into a Director presentation, you should become familiar with the various elements of the Director interface. Director makes use of three primary screen areas: the Stage, the Score, and the Cast windows (see Figure 23-2). The *stage* is where all animation and activity take place. In Figure 23-2, you can see a Premiere Pro movie created from the Chapter 1 tutorial files on the Premiere Pro DVD (the scene is from clip 705008f.mov from Digital Vision's Night Moves CD). You might view this as equivalent to Premiere Pro's Monitor window. The *score* is somewhat similar to Premiere Pro's Timeline. In the Director score, each frame is represented by a tiny rectangle. Each track in Director is called a *channel.* All program elements imported or created in Director are automatically added to its *cast.* To start the process of creating a production, cast members are dragged from the cast window to the stage. Cast members can include graphics such as buttons, digital movies, text, audio, and behaviors.

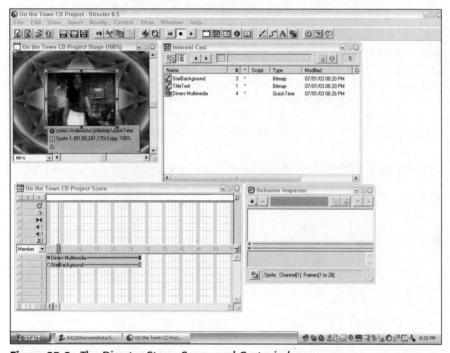

Figure 23-2: The Director Stage, Score, and Cast windows.

Importing Premiere Pro movies into Director

For Premiere Pro users, one of Director's most valuable features is that it enables you to import and control QuickTime and AVI movies. Before you can use a Premiere Pro movie in Director, you must first import it into the program.

To import a QuickTime or AVI movie into Director, follow these steps:

1. **If you have multiple casts in Director, start by selecting the cast you want to import the digital movie into and then choose File ➪ Import.**

2. **In the Import Files dialog box, select the digital movie that you want to import.**

3. **If you are importing only one file, click the Import button.** Otherwise, select another digital movie and then click Add.

4. **When you are done adding movies, click Import.** After the movie is imported, it is loaded as a cast member in the Cast window.

Changing movie properties

Although you most likely will control digital movies in Director using Lingo, you can easily change settings that affect playback in the Cast Member Properties windows. To open the Property Inspector window shown in Figure 23-3, select the digital movie in the Cast tab and then click the Info button. The digital movie's properties window (in the Property Inspector) enables you to choose to play back both video and sound, or one or the other. Perhaps the most important choice in the dialog box is the Paused check box. This enables you to prevent the movie from playing as soon as the viewer enters the frame that contains the video. If you select the Paused button, you can use Lingo to have the user start and stop the movie. If you select Loop, the digital video movie plays continuously.

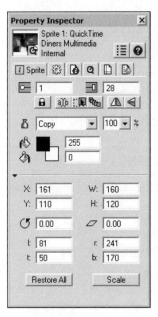

Figure 23-3: The Property Inspector window.

QuickTime movies enable the QuickTime controller to appear onscreen as a device for starting and stopping QuickTime movies. Many multimedia producers choose not to show the controller, preferring to create their own interface and controlling it with Lingo.

Usually, the Sync to Soundtrack option is selected. The other choice in the pop-up menu—Play Every Frame—can result in video playing without audio. If the Director to Stage option is selected, you can place other cast members over QuickTime movies.

Placing the movie onstage

For a digital movie to be viewed in Director, it must be positioned in Director's Stage window. Before dragging the movie from the Cast window to the Stage window, most Director users select the frame that the QuickTime or AVI movie will reside in. Typically, a background and buttons are created in Director or Adobe Photoshop. After the frame in the Score window is selected, clicking and dragging the movie from the Cast window to the Score window puts the movie on that frame.

At this point, the Director producer must decide whether he or she wants the movie to play in one Director frame or whether the movie should play over multiple Director frames. Projects are often easier to manage if the movie plays in one Director frame. When movies play in one frame, Director must stop its own playback head and turn the processing over to the QuickTime or AVI movie.

Pausing the playback head with the Tempo channel

If you set up Director to play a movie in one frame, you must tell Director to halt and wait for the end of the QuickTime movie or wait for a button to tell it to move off the frame. The easiest way to tell Director to wait for the end of a movie is to specify this in Director's Tempo channel.

To access the Tempo channel controls for the movie, simply double-click the Tempo channel frame directly above the movie frame. In the Tempo channel dialog box, shown in Figure 23-4, select Wait for Cue Point and then click {End} in the Cue Point pop-up menu.

Figure 23-4: Director's Tempo channel dialog box enables you to pause the playback head while a digital video movie plays.

Pausing the playback with a behavior

Although the Tempo channel provides a quick way of stopping Director's playback head, most experienced Director users don't use it because it does not provide as much power as does Lingo. To pause the playback head while a digital movie plays, you can use a Lingo behavior instead of the Tempo channel. Fortunately, for non-programmers, Director comes packaged with prewritten behaviors. You can use a prewritten behavior to pause the playback head by dragging the Hold on Current Frame behavior from Director's Behavior Library (in the Navigation section) into the Score channel frame that appears directly above the digital movie frame. (The Score channel appears above channel 1.)

Using Lingo

Although playing QuickTime and AVI windows from within Director is quite easy, learning a few Lingo commands to control navigation and start and stop QuickTime movies is helpful. Director provides a simple interface to get you started creating Lingo scripts. The following section shows you how to create a simple navigational script using Director's Behavior Inspector. After you learn how to use the Behavior Inspector, you can create scripts that control QuickTime and AVI moves.

Creating behaviors

Director *behaviors* are Lingo scripts that can be used to control navigation and to control QuickTime movies. After you create a behavior, you can click and drag it over an onscreen object such as a button. If the behavior includes commands for mouse events, you can program the behavior to execute when the user clicks the mouse on the object that contains the behavior.

The following are steps for creating a simple navigational behavior:

1. **Choose Window ⇨ Inspectors ⇨ Behavior.**

2. **To create a new behavior, click the + button and then choose New Behavior.**

3. **In the New Behavior dialog box, enter a name for your behavior and then click OK.**

4. **To utilize the Behavior Inspector window's automatic scripting features, click the arrow in the middle of the dialog box to expand it.** The dialog box is shown in Figure 23-5.

5. **In the Events section in the Behavior Inspector dialog box, click the + sign and choose an event to trigger your behavior.** For most button-triggered programs, choose Mouse Up or Mouse Enter. Choose Mouse Up instead of Mouse Down to enable the user to release the mouse. If a Mouse Down triggers the event, the user cannot cancel after clicking the mouse. If you use a Mouse Up event, the user can cancel the event by moving the mouse off the button before releasing the mouse.

6. **In the Actions section, select an Action category.** For example, if you are creating a navigational button, choose Navigation.

7. **In the menu that appears, pick a specific action such as Go To Frame.** If you choose Go To Frame, enter the frame number you want to go to.

8. Click OK.

9. If you want to see the Lingo script that was created, click the Script window icon.

10. Close the Behavior Inspector window by clicking the Close icon.

11. To use your behavior, drag it from the Cast window and release it over an object such as a button graphic in the Stage window.

Figure 23-5: Create behaviors in the Behavior Inspector dialog box.

Creating your own Lingo

When you know the basics of creating behaviors, you can begin using Lingo to control QuickTime and AVI movies. Most of the Lingo that controls QuickTime and AVI movies refers to the movie by the channel the movie is in or its cast member name or number. When you drag a movie from the Cast window to the stage, the movie becomes known as a *sprite*. Lingo addresses different sprites according to the channel the sprite is in. Thus, if you dragged a digital video movie into channel 1, you refer to it as *Sprite 1*.

To create your own behaviors that control QuickTime movies, you can use the Behavior Inspector dialog box to get you started and then enter the Lingo commands that control digital video movies by opening the Script Window dialog box and entering them there. The following sections review some commonly used Lingo commands that control digital video movies.

Playing movies with Lingo

If you want to create Lingo buttons that start, stop, and reverse QuickTime movies, you can set and change the sprite's Movie Rate property and the Movie Rate function. The following are common movie rate values:

Play   1

Stop   0

Reverse   −1

 Note   You can slow down the movie by setting the movie rate to .5.

Here's a simple script that starts a QuickTime movie in channel 3 when the user clicks the mouse on an object containing the following behavior:

```
On mouseUp
Set the movieRate of Sdprite 3 to 1
End MouseUp
```

Or, in Director 7 and later versions, you can use "dot syntax":

```
On mouseUp
sprite(3).movieRate=1
End mouseUp
```

Checking movie duration

Director's MovieTime and Duration commands are more helpful Lingo utilities. Use MovieTime to check how much of a QuickTime movie has played. Duration measures the length of a QuickTime movie. Both Duration and MovieTime are measured in *ticks* (one tick equals one-sixtieth of a second), not frames. By constantly comparing the MovieTime property of a QuickTime movie to its duration, you can tell when the movie actually stops playing. When the movie stops playing, you can then send Director's playback head to another frame. The following Lingo is an example. A movie script that is executed when the production starts puts the duration of a QuickTime movie into a *variable* called gmovduration. In this example, the QuickTime movie is in Director's third channel (like a video track). In Lingo, this is designated as Sprite 3.

```
Global gmovduration
Put the Duration of Sprite 3 into gmovduration
```

Another script, executed when the playback head exits a frame, compares the current MovieTime of the QuickTime movie to its duration. If the MovieTime is less than the duration, then the movie hasn't ended yet. Thus, the Lingo script keeps Director playback on the current Director frame. The Lingo command "go to the frame" keeps the playback head in the current frame. When the QuickTime movie finishes, its MovieTime is no longer less than its duration. At this point, the "go to the frame" section of the code is not executed, so Director's playback moves on to the next frame in the Director production.

```
Global gmovduration
On Exit Frame
Put the MovieTime of Sprite 3 into myMovieTime
If myMovieTime < gmovduration then go to the frame
End
```

You can also change the `MovieTime` of a digital movie with a script like this:

```
Set the Movietime of Sprite 3 to 360
```

The dot syntax version would be as follows:

```
sprite(3).Movietime=360
```

The preceding Lingo code results in the playback of the QuickTime movie jumping to the new time position you have assigned.

Changing digital movie settings

The movie settings in the Cast Properties window that controls looping and whether the movie pauses when the playback head enters the frame are easily controlled with Lingo commands.

For example, at the beginning of a movie or at a certain point in a movie, you can turn off looping with the following line of Lingo code:

```
Set the loop of member "Mymovie" =True
```

Or you can stop the movie from playing when the playback head enters the frame with this Lingo:

```
Set the PauseAtStart of Member "Mymovie"=TRUE
```

Playing a portion of a digital movie

Director also enables you to start and stop a digital video movie from any point in the movie using its `StartTime` and `StopTime` commands. Using these Lingo commands, you can create a button labeled Show intro or Show interview. When the user clicks the button, only the specified segment is played. `StartTime` and `StopTime` are measured in ticks. For example, this Lingo snippet tells Director to start the digital movie one minute into the digital movie:

```
Set the startTime of sprite 1=360
```

or

```
sprite(1).startTime=360
```

To set the stop point of the movie you could use this Lingo snippet:

```
Set the StopTime of sprite 10=720
```

or

```
Sprite(10).stoptime=720
```

Other Lingo commands

Director includes numerous Lingo commands that work with QuickTime movies. For example, Lingo includes commands that can turn QuickTime soundtracks on and off. Lingo can determine whether QuickTime or Video for Windows is installed on a computer, and it can tell the video producer when keyframes occur. Lingo commands are well documented in Director's Lingo dictionary. However, if you are a Director beginner, be forewarned: You won't become a Lingo expert overnight.

Using Macromedia Flash with Premiere Pro Movies

Macromedia Flash is undoubtedly responsible for livening up more Web pages with animation and music than any other computer application. It doesn't take many mouse clicks in a Web browser to land in a Flash-centric site. In fact, throughout the world, Flash movies appear on thousands of Web sites. Flash is used for virtually everything that moves on animated logos, full-featured cartoons, and interactive games. Many sites even use Flash to create interactive forms that post data to databases and display the results as animation. Fortunately, Premiere Pro users can take advantage of all that Flash has to offer. The current version of Flash can import QuickTime, AVI, MPEG, and Windows Media files.

The Flash production process

Like Director, Flash is an animation program that features a powerful authoring language designed to provide interactivity that goes well beyond the simple links provided by HTML. Unlike Director and Premiere Pro, graphics created in Flash are not based on pixels; they are based on vectors. *Vector images* are based on mathematical coordinates, not pixels. Vector images are the foundation of programs like Adobe Illustrator and Macromedia Freehand. In Illustrator and Freehand, you can click and drag the mouse to create an image and move it and bend it with ease. The image transformations are quickly processed by mathematical computations. To display the image on a computer screen, Flash renders the vector-based data to a screen image. When a Flash movie is viewed in a Web browser, the vector graphics scale to fit the user's window.

In Director and Premiere Pro, on the other hand, a grid of pixels comprises every frame. When you change the color of a pixel-based image, you change individual pixels in the image. When you tilt or transform the image, the pixels need to be mathematically rearranged in the pixel grid. This grid-like foundation means that pixel-based image files are larger than vector-based image files and take longer to download.

To create its vector-based images, Flash features a rich set of drawing and color tools. However, if the developer needs graphics created in other programs, such as

Photoshop or Illustrator, he or she can easily import them. Images are animated in a timeline interface, somewhat similar to Premiere Pro's. Instead of video tracks, however, Flash supports a multitude of superimposition effects using layers.

When the developer is finished creating graphics and animation and has added interactive buttons or forms, he or she "publishes" a Flash movie. Publishing creates an SWF file that can be saved to a Web server. During the publishing process, Flash can write an HTML file containing the scripting code that loads flash onto a Web page. The movie appears in a Web browser courtesy of a Flash plug-in that must be installed in the user's browser. Fortunately for Flash developers, the Flash plug-in is one of the most popular in the world. According to Macromedia, it is installed in more than 400,000,000 browsers.

Integrating Premiere Pro movies into Flash

Although an in-depth discussion of working with Flash is beyond the scope of this book, this section shows how you can easily import a Premiere Pro movie into Flash and create a simple script attached to a frame that sends the movie's playback head to another frame.

To load a Premiere Pro movie into Flash, choose File ➪ Import. After you select the movie from your hard drive, Flash enables you to choose whether to embed the movie into Flash or simply link to it (see Figure 23-6). If you want to use Flash to create another QuickTime movie, you can choose the link option; otherwise, you want to embed the movie into the Flash file for use on the Web.

After you choose to embed the movie in Flash, the Import Video Settings dialog box appears (see Figure 23-7). This dialog box enables you to specify quality settings and to synchronize the imported movie's frame rate to the Flash frame rate.

After the video is imported, it appears in the Flash Timeline. You can access each of the movie's frames by clicking a frame in the Timeline. As the movie plays, you can use Flash's graphic creation and text tools to embellish your production. For example, you can add a new layer by clicking an icon in the Timeline. To keep yourself organized, name your layers. Figure 23-8 shows a QuickTime movie in a layer beneath a Text layer. (You can add text to Flash without creating a new layer.) To tilt the text, we simply clicked and dragged a text handle. Changing text styles is simply a matter of selecting the text and choosing an option from Flash's text menu. You can create simple animation just by creating a keyframe (Insert ➪ Keyframe) and moving objects that appear on stage.

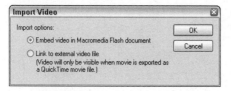

Figure 23-6: Flash enables you to embed a Premiere Pro movie into a Flash project.

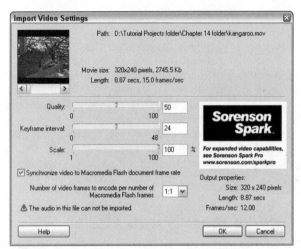

Figure 23-7: Embedding a Premiere Pro movie into an animated project.

Figure 23-8: Text and QuickTime movie layer in Flash.

Creating an ActionScript

Flash's ActionScript language is the key to producing sophisticated Web interactivity. If you know JavaScript, you won't have too much trouble wading into the enticing waters of ActionScript. Like Director's Lingo scripting language, Flash's ActionScript can create interactive buttons and objects onscreen. ActionScript can also control how a movie plays. For example, at a specific point in your movie, you can attach a script that tells the movie to jump to a specific frame and stop. At the stopping point, you can start up another movie or wait for the user to click a button to proceed.

Attaching an ActionScript to a frame is quite simple. Start by clicking the frame where you want to trigger the ActionScript. Next, open the Action window by choosing Windows ➪ Actions. To create a script that controls a movie, click the Actions icon and then click the Movie control icon. Flash displays a list of choices for your ActionScript. Figure 23-9 shows the Go to and Play option chosen. You can use this script command to go to a specific frame and stop to wait for more commands.

After you've completed your Flash work, you can choose File ➪ Publish Preview to preview your work in Flash, viewing your work locally in your default Web browser.

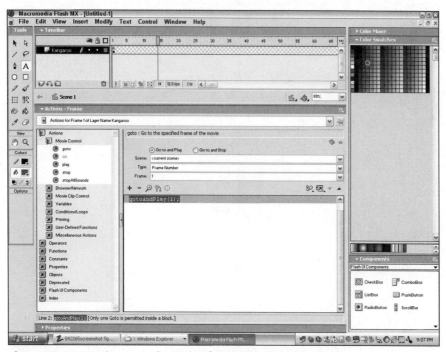

Figure 23-9: Creating an ActionScript that goes to a frame and stops.

To learn more about Flash, visit the Macromedia Web site, `www.macromedia.com`. Premiere Pro users who want to fully explore integrating interactivity with digital video will certainly want to investigate all that Flash has to offer.

Summary

The most widely used medium for distributing digital movies is CD-ROM. Many Premiere Pro movies are imported into interactive multimedia programs such as Macromedia Director before the project is saved to CD-ROM. When exporting a movie that will play on CD-ROM, your export settings should be based on the system that will be playing your movie. This chapter covered the following:

✦ Lower quality settings must often be used to play back digital video movies on slower systems.

✦ The most common compressor used for exporting digital video for CD-ROM has been Cinepak. Sorenson Video is now commonly used for exporting movies that will be played on mid- to high-end machines.

✦ If you want to add interactivity to a Premiere Pro movie, you can export your movie into Macromedia Director or Macromedia Flash.

✦ Macromedia Director's programming language, Lingo, features many commands that enable onscreen clickable buttons that can start and stop digital video movies.

✦ Macromedia Flash enables you to integrate Premiere Pro movies into Web multimedia projects.

✦　✦　✦

Premiere Pro and Beyond

Using Adobe Encore to Create DVDs

Adobe Encore DVD is a high-end DVD authoring program that allows you to create interactive DVDs. Using Encore DVD, you can import MPEG and AVI files that you've edited in Premiere Pro and turn them into professional DVDs. With Encore DVD, you can create menus and navigational buttons that add sophisticated interactivity to your Premiere Pro projects. Since many of Encore's navigational links are automatically created by dragging and dropping graphics onscreen, it probably will not take Premiere Pro users long to get up and running in Encore. Although the interface is different from Premiere Pro's, most users will probably find themselves right at home in Encore's Project and Timeline windows. This chapter provides an overview of the basics of DVD authoring. So follow along, and you'll see how to integrate Premiere Pro footage into a DVD project that includes interactive buttons.

Note The chapter leads you through the steps of creating and burning a DVD. If you don't have a DVD burner but have a CD burner, you can still follow along. Encore can save shorter DVD projects to CDs. But these must be played in a DVD player.

Note A downloadable version of Adobe Encore is available at www.adobe.com. If you want to create a DVD project using this chapter as a guide, you can use a Premiere Pro project for your video source footage. However, in order to import it into Encore DVD, you must export the project in either MPEG-2 or AVI format. Exporting in MPEG-2 and AVI formats is covered in Chapter 19.

Touring Encore DVD

The following sections provide a brief overview of Encore DVD's Project window and palettes. Encore DVD's palettes can be accessed even if a project is not onscreen. However, in order to see Encore's Project window, you first need to create a new project. Here are the steps:

1. **Choose File ▷ New Project.** The New Project Settings dialog box appears (see Figure 24-1).

2. **Choose whether you want to use the NTSC (US Standard) or the PAL (European) video standard and click OK.**

Figure 24-1: Choose a video standard in the New Project Settings dialog box.

The Project window and its tabs

After the new project is created, you'll see a Project tab, which is one of four tabs that are part of Encore DVD's Project window (yes, the Project tab is in a window referred to as the Project window). The four tabs: Project, Menu, Timelines, and Disc allow you to perform all major tasks related to a project. To access any of the tabs, click on the tab or choose a tab name from Encore DVD's Window menu. Like Premiere Pro's Project window, Encore DVD's Project tab allows you to view project assets (video, audio, and graphics) that comprise your project. The Menu tab allows you create and manage menus and where you'll place navigational buttons. Encore DVD's Timeline tab provides a bird's eye overview of your project and allows you to set chapter markers. The Disc tab is used for burning DVDs.

Once you have a project open onscreen, Encore DVD's windows become useful tools for DVD creation. Like Premiere Pro's windows, Encore DVD's can be dragged apart and reunited in different combinations. The windows always rest above the Project window tabs and can be opened by choosing a window's name from the Window menu.

The Properties palette

Encore's Properties palette is a multipurpose info palette that provides details about what is selected in different windows. Figure 24-2 shows the Properties palette displaying information about an Encore menu page. The information in the window changes to reflect different items that you click in the Project window. For example, if you click a video clip in the Project window's Project tab, the Properties palette displays information about the clip's location, and duration.

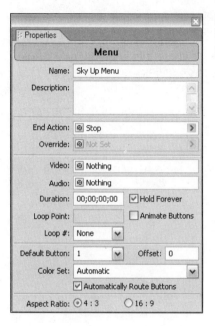

Figure 24-2: The Properties palette provides information about different Encore DVD production elements.

The Layers palette

The Layers palette allows you to manipulate layers used in menus. You can show, hide, and change the stacking order of objects on menu screens. The Layers palette is shown in Figure 24-3.

Figure 24-3: The Layers palette displays information about graphic elements on a menu page.

The Character palette

Use the Character palette to specify type options for characters created for buttons and menus. Use the character drop-down menus to change typefaces, type size, and style. The Character palette is shown in Figure 24-4.

Figure 24-4: Use the Character palette to change type settings.

The Library palette

The Library palette is stocked with templates for menus, buttons, and various backgrounds. Use the window to quickly create interactive graphics screens. In the section "Using menu templates," later in this chapter, you use a menu screen from the Library palette as the foundation for a menu screen that you can edit for your own use. The icons at the bottom of the window allow you to change views so that you can see Only Menus, Only Buttons, or Only Backgrounds. The New Menu button creates a copy of the selected menu screen so it can be customized.

The Timeline window and Menu Editor window

As you work through the tutorial in this chapter, you'll take a look at the Timeline window, and you'll work in the Menu Editor window. Here's a brief description of these windows:

✦ **Timeline window.** The Timeline window provides a bird's-eye view of your DVD media sources in sequential order. Unlike Premiere's Timeline, Encore DVDs display only one video and one audio clip. You can also use Encore DVD's Timeline window to create subtitle tracks and choose the language for subtitles.

✦ **Menu Editor.** Use the Menu Editor window to create and edit DVD menus. Here you can place or edit buttons in menus and add text and images to menu screens.

Importing source video and audio

Encore DVD allows you to import AVI files, WAV files, and most common graphics formats. In Encore DVD, source material such as video clips, graphics, and sound files are called *assets*. Photoshop users will be happy to learn that Encore DVDs are fully compatible with Photoshop, and you can load Photoshop layers in as separate buttons in a menu. To load an asset into Encore, choose File ⇨ Import as Asset. In the Import as Asset dialog box, select the file you want to import and click Open.

If you export one of your Premiere projects as an AVI movie (choose File ⇨ Export ⇨ Movie), you can import it directly into Encore DVD by choosing File ⇨ Import asset. Encore also can import MPEG video files, but it will not import QuickTime files. Like Premiere, all imported source material appears in the Project window (in the Project tab), as shown in Figure 24-5. (The image seen in the Project tab in Figure 24-5 is from the Tutorial Project in Chapter 1, file 705027f from Digital Vision's NightMoves CD.)

> **Note**   Encore DVD can import MPEG-2 files, which are considered DVD-compliant (meaning that they meet DVD recording standards). Encore DVD can also import some non-DVD-compliant files, such as NTSC AVI files — which must have a frame size of 720 x 480, 720 x 486, or 404 x 480 with a frame rate of 24 frames per second or 29.97 frames per second. PAL files must have a frame size of 720 x 576 or 704 x 576 with a frame rate of 25 frames per second. Files that are not DVD-compliant are transcoded by Encore to make them DVD-compliant. Working with DVD-compliant files saves times, because Encore DVD does not need to transcode them when you burn a DVD or import files. DVD-compliant file types include .wav files (48 kHz, 16 or 24 bit) and .aif files (though not .aif-c). Also note that when you import AVI files, Encore DVD automatically imports audio. If you import MPEG files, you will need to import the audio separately.

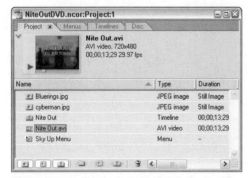

Figure 24-5: Encore's Project window with video and graphics files.

Using menu templates

To most computer users, the term *menu* refers to a drop-down list of choices that appear at the top of a computer application. In the world of DVD development, a menu is a screen with interactive buttons. Typically, the first screen you see when viewing a DVD production is a menu screen. Clicking a button on the menu might bring you to another menu or start the production playing. In this section, you'll choose a menu from a list of predesigned templates to use for your project.

You use Encore's Library palette to load a background and preset buttons to get you started creating your opening DVD screen.

1. **Click the Library palette to access it.** (If it isn't onscreen, choose Window ➪ Library.) Figure 24-6 shows the menu window with a list of templates.

2. **Note the three buttons at the bottom of the window. From left to right these are the Show Menus, Show Buttons, and Show Images buttons. Click the Show Menus button to display the menus.**

3. **Choose a menu from the list by clicking it.** (Note that the submenus in the list are simply alternate versions of other menus.)

4. **Now create a new menu based upon the template by clicking the New Menu button at the bottom of the window.** The new menu appears onscreen in the Menu Editor, as shown in Figure 24-7. The menu is now listed in the Project and Menu tabs.

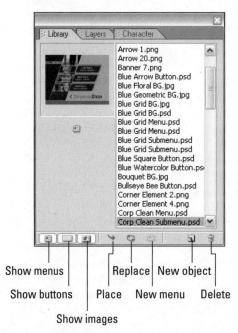

Figure 24-6: The Library palette with predesigned templates.

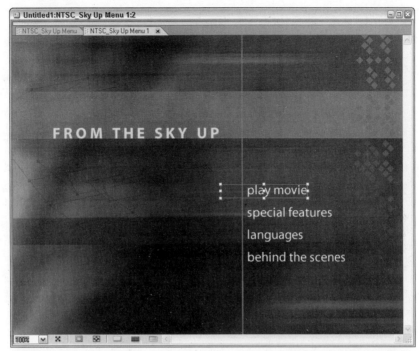

Figure 24-7: Use the Menu Editor screen to edit text and buttons on the menu.

Editing the menu

Now you can customize the menu by changing the text and placement of buttons. You can edit the menu using the menu-editing tools shown in Figure 24-8.

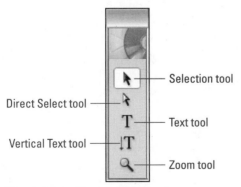

Figure 24-8: Menu-editing tools.

Here's a review of the tools:

✦ **Selection tool.** Use to select all buttons in a button set. Buttons that look alike in a template menu are usually part of a button set.

✦ **Direct Select tool.** Use to select, move, and resize individual objects, such as buttons.

✦ **Text tool.** Use the Text tool to create and edit text.

✦ **Vertical Text tool.** Use the Vertical Text tool to create and edit vertical text.

✦ **Zoom tool.** Use the Zoom tool to zoom in and out.

Use the Direct Select tool to move objects onscreen. Use the Text tools to edit the text in the buttons. You can also use the Arrange, Align, and Distribute commands found in the Object menu. These commands allow you to quickly move and align objects onscreen. Figure 24-9 shows an expanded view of this menu.

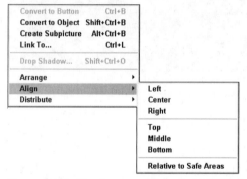

Figure 24-9: Use Arrange, Align, and Distribute as you edit the menu.

Creating button links

In this section, you link the buttons on your menu page to the video. This link triggers the video to play when the user clicks a button. Set up the screen windows so that you can see the Project tab and the Menu Editor. To create a link to a button, follow these steps:

1. **Click on the video file in the Project tab that you want to link and drag it over the button to which you want to link.** When the video is positioned over the button, release the mouse.

Caution   If you don't release the mouse over a button, Encore creates new button on the menu page.

2. **With the Selection tool activated, click the linked button.** Observe the Properties palette. Note that the Link field displays the link to the button, as shown in Figure 24-10.

3. **Observe the Timeline.** Click the Timeline tab and note that Encore DVD created a Timeline for the video file.

4. **Repeat Steps 1 and 2 to create more links to buttons, as needed.**

Figure 24-10: A linked button listed in the Properties palette.

Examining the Timeline

Encore's Timeline tab provides a graphic display of the video and audio in your project. The Timeline can display a track for video as well as for audio and subtitles. Figure 24-11 shows a Timeline with an AVI video file and its audio file.

Note   If you import an AVI with audio, the audio file is imported automatically with it. If you import MPEG-2 files rather than AVI files, you will need to import the audio separately.

Click the Timeline in the Project tab. Look at the Properties palette. The End Action field in the Properties palette displays the name of the linked video, which indicates that, after the video is over, the original menu will be displayed.

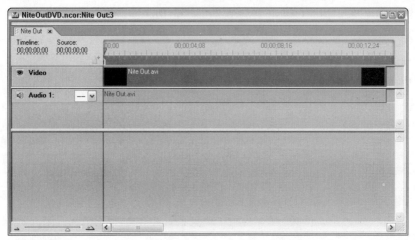

Figure 24-11: Encore's Timeline provides a graphical representation of linked audio and video files.

Previewing the DVD

After you've created your menus and button links, you're ready to preview your DVD project. When you run the preview, Encore DVD creates a simulation mode where you can test the button links:

1. **To preview your DVD project, choose File ⇨ Preview.**

2. **When the project switches to Preview mode, click the menu screen buttons to check that all the links work properly.**

3. **If you need to fix a link, click the button in the Project tab and correct the link in the Properties palette.**

Burning the DVD

After you've previewed your work and tested the button links, you're ready to burn a DVD. You'll find burning options for the DVD on the Disc tab. Here are the steps:

1. **In the Project window, select the Disc tab, shown in Figure 24-12.**

2. **In the first field, name the DVD.**

3. **In the drop-down menu, specify the DVD size that you are using.**

4. **Insert a blank DVD into your DVD burner.**

5. **Click the Build Project button.**

6. **Save the project when the Save alert appears.**

7. **At this point, you should see your DVD recorder listed in the Make DVD dialog box.**

8. **Click the Build button.** The progress indicator will display an alert when the DVD is complete.

9. **Play the DVD in your DVD player.**

Figure 24-12: The burning options for the DVD are on the Disc tab.

As you work with Encore DVD, you'll see that it provides other options for creating DVDs. You can access all the following options by choosing File ➪ Build DVD.

✦ **Make DVD Folder.** This option creates a directory on your hard drive of the DVD structure. You can play back the DVD from the stored disk structure for testing purposes.

✦ **Make DVD Image.** Creates an image of the DVD on your hard drive that can be used to master the DVD with a third-party mastering program.

✦ **Make DVD Master.** Creates a DVD on digital linear tape (DLT). DLTs are used for mass duplication of DVDs.

Summary

Encore DVD is a DVD production application. Using Encore DVD, you can design DVD menus with interactive buttons and preview and burn DVDs.

✦ Use File ➪ Import as Asset to load source material into Encore DVD.

✦ The Library palette provides numerous predesigned buttons and menus.

✦ You can create linked buttons by dragging a video file from the Project tab into the Menu Editor.

✦ Preview your DVD by choosing File ➪ Preview.

✦   ✦   ✦

Customizing DVD Screens and Navigation in Adobe Encore DVD

This chapter takes you into the world of DVD creation. In the previous chapter, you see how to quickly create a DVD project with a menu screen and interactive buttons. This chapter focuses on customization. It covers how to create menus and buttons using your own graphic images and how to customize links from buttons to menus, from buttons to DVD chapters, and from buttons to the Timeline.

This chapter provides a step-by-step look at how to create a custom DVD presentation in Encore DVD (see the sidebar "Custom DVD presentation" later in this chapter). After you read through this chapter, you'll be ready to go into DVD production.

On the DVD-ROM A sample video, graphic button, and background are included in the Chapter 25 folder in the Adobe Premiere Pro DVD folder.

Creating Menus and Buttons from Still Images

Although Encore's menu templates provide a quick means for making menus and buttons, multimedia and design professionals will undoubtedly want to create their own based upon digitized images or backgrounds. This section shows you how to create menus from scratch. Before you begin, it's a good idea to plan your entire menu structure. Design your menu on paper, and use flow charts to plan navigation. After you've created all your source material or assets, you're ready to start.

Creating menus from scratch

Encore DVD works hand-in-hand with Adobe Photoshop. Although Encore DVD can read TIF, JPEG, and BMP graphics, your best is to create images in Photoshop and import them directly into Encore DVD, particularly because Encore DVD can interpret a Photoshop layer as a button.

Note   In order for Encore DVD to correctly interpret Photoshop layers as DVD elements, layer-naming prefixes are required in Photoshop. For instance, a layer set with buttons requires a "+" prefix, and subpicture (button highlight images) layer sets require a "=" prefix.

Custom DVD presentation

The general steps for creating a custom DVD presentation are as follows (we cover many of these steps in this chapter):

1. **Create the video and audio in Premiere Pro.** (Note that Markers in Premiere Pro can be used as chapters in Encore DVD.)

2. **Plan the navigation for the DVD production.**

3. **Create the buttons and background screen for the menus in Photoshop or another graphics application.**

4. **Import audio, graphics, and other assets into Encore.**

5. **Create a custom menu in Encore.**

6. **Place the background screen and buttons into Encore.**

7. **Create a Timeline or Timelines.**

8. **Create chapters in Timelines.**

9. **Link buttons to chapters.**

10. **Create disc navigation.**

11. **Preview the DVD project and burn a disc.**

If you want to create a menu from scratch, the steps are quite simple. Make sure that the frame size of your image matches the size of your project. The default aspect ratio in Encore DVD is 4:3. (You can change this to the DVD Widescreen format of 16:9.)

1. **If you haven't created a new project, create the project by choosing File ⇨ New Project. Click the NTSC or PAL choice and click OK**

2. **Import the background screen that you want to use for your menu by choosing File ⇨ Import as Asset. In the Import as Asset dialog box, select your file and click Open.**

3. **Choose Menu ⇨ New Menu (you can also click the New Menu button at the bottom of the Project palette).** The menu appears in the Project window.

4. **To rename the menu window, right-click on the New Menu listing in the Project palette and enter a new name in the Rename Menu dialog box.** Alternatively, you can rename the menu in the Name field of the Properties window.

5. **Drag the background image from the Project window into the Menu Editor (see Figure 25-1).**

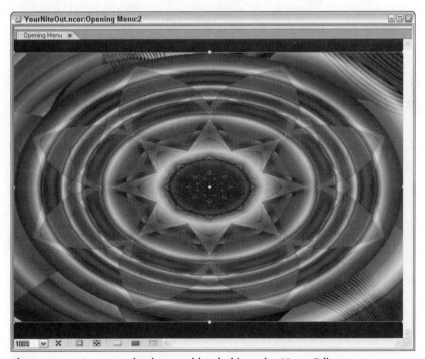

Figure 25-1: A custom background loaded into the Menu Editor.

Adding buttons to the menu

After you've created your custom menu, you may want to add buttons you've created in Photoshop or another graphic application to your DVD screen. To add buttons, follow these steps:

1. **Import graphic elements into your project by choosing File ➪ Import as Asset.**

2. **Drag the button graphic or button graphics to the Menu screen.**

3. **With the button graphic selected, choose Object ➪ Convert to Button.**

4. **If you want all the buttons on the menu to be similar, drag the same button object to the menu screen as many times as you want; then repeat Step 3 so that Encore recognizes them as different buttons.** Figure 25-2 shows four buttons created in Photoshop added to a menu.

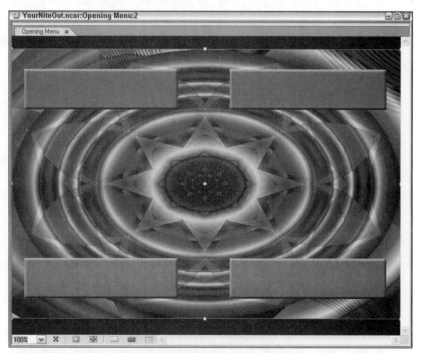

Figure 25-2: Buttons created in Photoshop used in Encore.

Menu Editor controls

When working in the Menu Editor, use the Object menu to align and distribute your buttons. You can also press the arrow directional keys to move selected objects right, left, up, and down. In the Menu Editor, the buttons at the bottom of the screen provide the following utilities:

✦ **Show Safe Area.** Displays the title and action-safe zones — zones that help ensure that text and graphics are not cut off from the TV monitor. If your production will be viewed on a television monitor, don't place text beyond the inner title safety zone and don't place crucial visual objects outside of the outer action safety zone.

✦ **Show Button Routing.** Routing buttons are menu buttons that can be used as DVD remote control buttons. If you turn off the Automatically Route button option in the Menu palette, remote control routing for buttons will be displayed in the menus.

✦ **Show Normal Subpicture Highlight.** Subpictures allow you to create different color button states for activated buttons. This option displays the unselected state for buttons.

Note

To use subpictures for buttons, choose Object ➪ Convert to Subpicture. Setting highlight colors for subpictures is discussed in the next section.

✦ **Show Selected Subpicture Highlight.** This option displays the selected or highlighted state for buttons.

✦ **Show Activated Subpicture Highlight.** This option displays the activated state for buttons. (Activation requires selecting a button with the remote control and pressing Enter. However, buttons can be set to Auto Activate when simply clicked by the mouse. To set a button to Auto Activate, select the button and choose Auto Activate from the Properties palette.)

Using Color Sets for Menus and Buttons

When you click a button or move the mouse over a button, it typically changes colors, or when you click text, it also changes colors. The different colored pictures that appear when you activate buttons are referred to as subpictures. Encore assigns colors to subpictures using color sets. Fifteen colors comprise each color set, and each menu can use only one specific color set. Because you can have many different menus in a DVD production, you can use multiple color sets. However, to help ensure a consistent look throughout a project, utilizing only one color set for your project is a good idea.

By default, Encore DVD uses one predefined color set. If you don't want to use this default color set, you can change its colors, or you can create your own. Once defined, you can save color sets and use them in other projects. To view the color sets, choose Edit ➪ Color Sets ➪ Menu. This opens the Menu Color Set dialog box, shown in Figure 25-3.

At first, the layout of the Menu Color Set dialog box may look confusing. The grouping in the dialog box shows three different colors for normal states, three different colors for selected states, and three different colors for activated states. Each set of three colors is called a *highlight group*. Thus, you could use one highlight group for buttons labeled part 1, part 2, and so on, and another highlight group for buttons labeled "next chapter" or "previous chapter." As mentioned earlier, only one color set is allowed for each menu. If you want to change colors for any color set, simply click the color swatch and adjust the colors in the color picker dialog box that appears, or change the percentage field. If you want to create a new color set, click the New Color Set button (the page icon to the left of the disc icon).

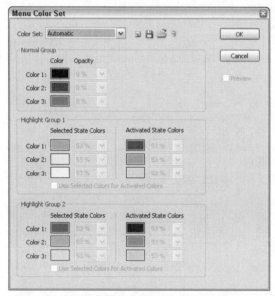

Figure 25-3: The Menu Color Set dialog box controls the highlight color for buttons.

Changing menu color sets

You can easily change color sets using the Menus tab and Properties palette. Here are the steps:

1. **Select the Menus tab in the Project window.**

2. **Select the menu whose color set you want to set or change.** You can Shift+click to add to other menus to the selection.

3. **If the Properties palette isn't open, choose Window ⇨ Properties to open it.**

4. **Click the Color Set pop-up menu and select a color set.** If you haven't created your own custom color set, choose Menu Default.

Choosing highlight groups for subpictures

You can also easily change highlight groups using the Menus tab and Properties palette. Here are the steps:

1. Select the button or buttons for which you want to create a subpicture; then choose Object ⇨ Convert to Subpicture.

2. Select the Menus tab of the Project window.

3. Select the menu to whose subpictures you want to assign colors.

4. In the button section of the tab, select the button or buttons whose colors you want to set (press Shift+click to select more buttons).

5. If the Properties palette isn't open, choose Window ⇨ Properties to open it.

6. Activate the Properties palette by clicking it.

7. To assign a highlight group to the subpicture of the selected button(s), select a color group from the Highlight pop-up menu in the Properties palette.

Creating and Using Timelines

After you've planned your navigation and created your menus and buttons, you'll need to create a Timeline for your DVD production. Like Premiere Pro's Timeline, Encore's provides a visual representation of source footage and sound. However, in Encore, the Timeline displays only one video track and one audio track. Figure 25-4 shows a Timeline with the current-time indicator and a chapter Marker. For NTSC productions, the Timeline frame rate is 29.97 frames per second; for PAL, the frame rate is 25 frames per second.

 Note   The default length in the Timeline for still images is 6 seconds. To change the default length, choose Edit ⇨ Preferences ⇨ Timeline.

Figure 25-4: The Encore Timeline with video and audio tracks and chapter points.

Here's how to create a Timeline in Encore DVD and add video or still images to it:

1. **Create a new Timeline by choosing Timeline ⇨ New Timeline.**

2. **Drag the video or still image from the Project window into the Timeline.** Video clips are automatically positioned at the start of the Timeline and assigned to be Chapter 1. If you place still images on the Timeline instead, chapter entries are created at the beginning of each still image.

3. **Right-click a Timeline in the Project tab and then choose Rename in the pop-up menu to assign a name to the Timeline.** The Rename Timeline dialog box opens, where you can enter a name for the Timeline. You can also rename the Timeline by editing the name in the Properties palette.

4. **Select the video or still image in the Project window, and choose Timeline ⇨ New Timeline.** Adobe Encore DVD opens the Timeline window and creates a new Timeline with the video or still image already placed on the video track.

Tip

You can create a Timeline automatically and place images on it by selecting the video in the Project window and choosing Timeline ⇨ New Timeline.

Adding a chapter point to the Timeline

In DVD movie productions, chapter points typically are used as a means for jumping to specific scenes. In Encore DVD, you can mark a frame on the Timeline as a chapter point and then link menus, buttons, or other Timelines to it. To keep organized, you can assign names to chapter points and even write notes about specific chapter points. (You can write descriptive notes in the Properties palette when creating chapter points.)

Here's how to create chapter points on the Timeline:

1. **If the Timeline window is not onscreen, open it by Choosing Window ⇨ Timeline.**

2. **If you want to preview the video as you add chapter points, open the Monitor window by choosing Window ⇨ Monitor.**

3. **Click and drag the current-timeline indicator to the frame where you want to create the chapter point.**

Note

If you have placed an MPEG-2 video in the Timeline, you can click the Skip Forward or Skip Backward button to move to a GOP header (a *GOP* is a continuous Groups of Pictures and is usually 13 frames long), which is indicated by the white vertical lines at the bottom of the ruler. Chapter points for MPEG-2 files must start at the nearest prior GOP header. If you are working with AVI videos, Adobe recommends that chapter points be at least 15 frames apart to ensure best quality.

4. **To create a chapter point, choose Timeline ⇨ Add Chapter Point or click the Add Chapter button beneath the ruler in the Timeline window.**

Naming chapter points

After you've created a chapter point, you can assign it a descriptive name and provide a description of the chapter point in the chapter points' Properties palette. Here's how to create chapter point names and chapter point descriptions:

1. **If the Timeline window isn't open, open it by choosing Window ➪ Timeline.**

2. **Click the Timelines tab in the Project window and select the desired Timeline.** At the bottom of the frame, Encore displays the chapter points, as shown in Figure 25-5.

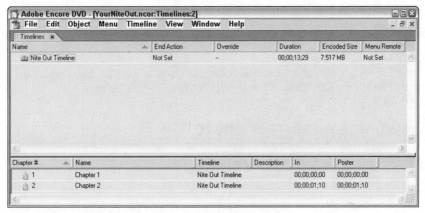

Figure 25-5: Chapter points appear in the Timeline tab.

3. **Select the desired chapter point in the Timeline window.**

4. **If the Properties palette is not open, choose Window ➪ Properties.** The Properties palette displays the chapter point's attributes.

5. **In the Properties palette, change the name of the chapter.**

6. **To add a description, click in the Description box and type a description of the chapter point.**

Customizing Navigation

After you've assembled your buttons in the Menu Editor, picked your subpicture colors, and added chapters, your next step is to ensure that the buttons lead your viewers in the right direction. The following sections provide details about looping menu buttons, menu navigation, first-play options, the duration the menu stays onscreen, and button navigation.

Setting First Play disc links

By default, your completed DVD begins to play when it displays the first menu you create. From this menu, you can direct navigation to go to any menu or chapter. Here's how to set First Play options for the disc:

1. **Choose Window ⇨ Disc to load the Disc tab in the Project window, or activate the Disc tab by clicking it.**

2. **Choose Window ⇨ Properties to load the Properties palette, or click the Properties palette tab to activate it.**

3. **Activate the First Play pop-up menu by clicking the Arrow icon.** Choices for First Play appear in the submenus, as shown in Figure 25-6. Choose the chapter or the menu you want to use as your First Play location. You can also click and drag the Pick Wick icon (the curlicue icon in the pop-up menu) to the chapter or menu.

Note

Only 20 menus and Timelines are displayed in the First Play pop-up menu. To see other choices, choose Specify Other from the pop-up menu.

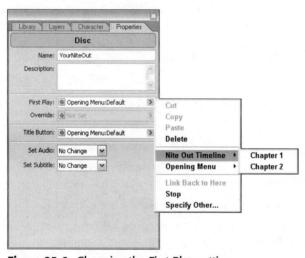

Figure 25-6: Changing the First Play setting.

4. **If you want to use the Pick Wick icon, make sure that the Project tab is visible onscreen and then drag the First Play Pick Wick icon to any of the following destinations:**

   • To a menu or Timeline in the Project tab

   • To the chapter in the Timeline

   • To the menu or button in the Menus tab

Note The optional Override options specify the end action for the first-play link, overriding the default end action of the menu or Timeline. In the Override field, you can designate a menu and the button to highlight or a Timeline and starting chapter point.

Setting menu display time and looping

If you're planning to have your DVD displayed at a kiosk or at a public locale such as a museum, you may want to use Encore's menu display settings to control navigation if no one clicks a button. Menu-timing choices are controlled in the menu's Properties palette. Activate the palette for a menu by first clicking the menu in the Project palette and then clicking the Menu tab. The timing choices are as follows:

✦ **Hold Forever.** The menu is displayed until an action is taken. This is the default setting.

✦ **Duration.** Set the duration in time. For a motion menu, the Duration should be the time multiplied by the Loop settings.

✦ **Loop #.** Use the Loop setting to choose how many times the menu repeats itself.

✦ **Loop Point.** Use the Loop Point setting for animated buttons. Click the Animate Button check box and enter the time in the Loop Point field.

Setting button navigation

Without question, the most common interactive navigational tool in DVD productions is the button. When linking buttons in Encore DVD, you must link to another menu or to a chapter point in a Timeline. When linking a button, the most versatile means is to use the button's Property palette.

Here are the steps to create a link from a menu button to a menu or chapter point. When creating the link, you can link directly from the button in the Menu Editor, or you can create a link from the button via the Menus tab.

1. **If the Menus tab isn't activated, choose Window ➪ Menus.**

2. **In the Menus tab, click the menu that contains the buttons that you want to link or double-click the menu, which opens the menu in the Menu Editor window.**

3. **Select the button from which you want to create a link.** If you are working in the Menu Editor, select a button with the Selection tool, which selects the button set.

4. **If the Properties window isn't open, choose Window ➪ Properties.**

5. **Click the Link pop-up menu and choose the button or chapter point from the submenu, as shown in Figure 25-7 or click the Pick Whip icon and drag it to a Timeline or menu in the Project palette.** Note that if you are linking to a Timeline, you link to a chapter point within the Timeline, setting a specific point as to where the video should begin to play.

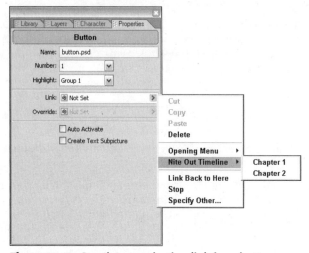

Figure 25-7: Creating a navigation link for a button.

Setting Timeline Navigation

When you activate the Timeline tab in the Project window, Encore DVD provides two navigation choices. You can set an end action for the Timeline, or you can set a menu remote link. An end action specifies where the navigation heads when the Timeline finishes playing. The menu remote choice creates a destination for the DVD navigation when the user clicks the remote control. Normally, when the viewer clicks the remote control, navigation returns to the last menu used. Here are the steps for setting these Timeline navigation choices:

1. **Select a Timeline in the Project tab.**

2. **If the Properties palette isn't open, open it by choosing Window ⇨ Property. If the Properties palette's tab is open onscreen, click it.** The Property tab will now show properties for the selected Timeline.

3. **In the Properties palette, select a destination for End Action by clicking the pop-up menu down arrow and choosing an option from the submenu, as shown in Figure 25-8.** Notice that Figure 25-8 shows another Timeline as a possible navigational link. If doing so is more convenient, you could also create the link by clicking and dragging the Pick Whip icon to an asset in the Project window.

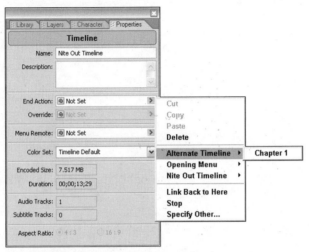

Figure 25-8: Setting end action navigation.

4. **In the Properties palette, select a destination for Menu Remote by clicking the pop-up menu down arrow and choosing an option from the submenu.** If doing so is more convenient, you could also create the link by clicking and dragging the Pick Whip icon to an asset in the Project window.

Summary

Encore enables you to import custom-made graphics and buttons to use for a DVD production. You can also customize button links.

✦ Use Object ➪ Convert to Button to designate a graphic object as a button.

✦ Use Object ➪ Convert to Subpicture to use a graphic as a highlighted object when activated.

✦ Change color settings for activated buttons by setting the highlight group in the Properties palette.

✦ Create new chapters in the Timeline tab of the Project window.

✦ Use the Properties palette to set links for button.

✦   ✦   ✦

Trimming Clips in After Effects

CHAPTER

26

Adobe Premiere Pro features a complete set of video-editing tools. However, from time to time, you may need to make a few quick edits in Adobe After Effects 6.0. Adobe After Effects is another digital video editing application created by Adobe Systems. It provides certain functionality that Premiere Pro does not, such as creating Bézier masks in the Composition window (see Chapter 29), creating motion paths, and composite projects (see Chapter 30). We've included a trial version of After Effects 6.0 on the DVD that accompanies this book. You can go to www.adobe.com for details on purchasing the product. If you import a video clip into After Effects to create masks or special effects, you may find it more convenient to change the clips' in and out points while you work in After Effects.

Cross-Reference   See Chapter 30 to learn how to create special effects in After Effects; Chapter 29 covers creating masks in After Effects.

After you trim clips in After Effects, you can save your work as either an AVI movie or a QuickTime movie. Later, you can import the AVI movie or the QuickTime movie into Adobe Premiere Pro for more video editing and compositing. You can also export your After Effects work as a sequence of separate graphic files. Later, you can import the sequence folder into Premiere Pro.

Many digital video producers use both Premiere Pro and After Effects 6.0 to create a project. This chapter introduces you to trimming a video clip in After Effects using the Layer window, as well as trimming in the Timeline window. The chapter also shows you how to export clips from After Effects as AVI movies, QuickTime movies, and graphic sequences.

Cross-Reference   For information on editing video clips using Adobe Premiere Pro, refer to Chapters 7 and 13.

In This Chapter

Trimming using the Timeline window

Trimming using the Layer window

Exporting your After Effects work

Importing After Effects files to Premiere Pro

Trimming in After Effects: What's It All About?

In Adobe After Effects, you can use either the Layer window or the Timeline window to trim a video clip from a Premiere Pro project. You can trim a clip at the beginning or at the end of a video clip. When you trim at the beginning, you change the clip's *in point*. When you trim at the end of the video clip, you change the clip's *out point*. As in Premiere Pro, even though the in and out points change after editing, the original in and out points are always accessible. You can reedit the clip at any time.

> **Note**   When you trim the in point in the Layer window, the clip is edited in the Timeline window, but its starting time in the composition doesn't change. Also, when you trim a still image, only the duration of the still image changes, not the actual still image.

Creating an After Effects project

Trimming video clips in After Effects' Timeline window is easy. To trim a video clip using After Effect's Timeline window, you need to have an After Effects project onscreen with at least one video clip in the Timeline window. You can also import a Premiere project into After Effects and trim the Premiere Pro project using After Effects' Timeline window.

Here's how to create an After Effects project and import video clips and Premiere projects:

1. **Choose File ➪ New Project to create a new project.** You can also choose to load an existing After Effects project, or you can load a Premiere project. (If you want to import a Premiere project into After Effects, skip Steps 2, 3, 4, 5, and 6 and jump to Step 7.)

2. **Choose Composition ➪ New Composition to create a new composition.** The Composition Settings dialog box appears (see Figure 26-1).

3. **Set the Frame Size to the same size as that of the project.** Choose a preset and notice that the Width and Height values automatically change. If you want, you can change the Frame Rate and Resolution settings. If you are working with a Premiere Pro project that uses a Non-DV preset, select the appropriate Non-DV preset from the Preset pop-up menu in the Composition Settings dialog box. For DVD output, choose a DV preset.

4. **Click OK to close the dialog box.**

5. **Choose File ➪ Import ➪ File or Multiple Files. Locate a video clip to use and click Open.** Continue selecting clips and clicking Open. When you have imported all the video clips and still images you are going to use in the project, click the Done button.

> **On the DVD-ROM**   If you want, you can follow along using the video clips found in the Chapter 26 folder on the DVD that accompanies this book. The video clips are Digital Vision's 800052f.mov and 800063f.mov from the Flux CD-ROM.

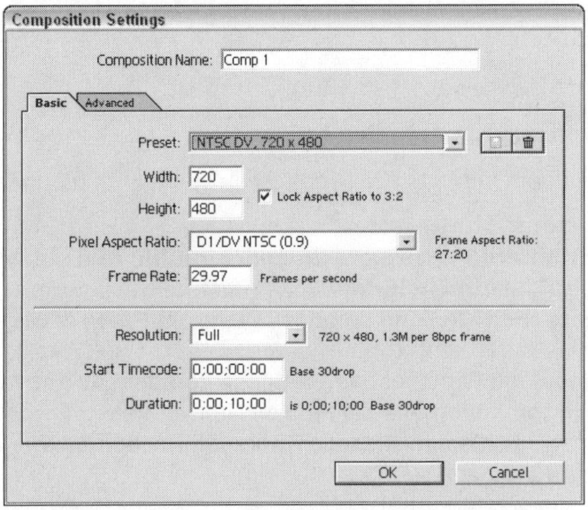

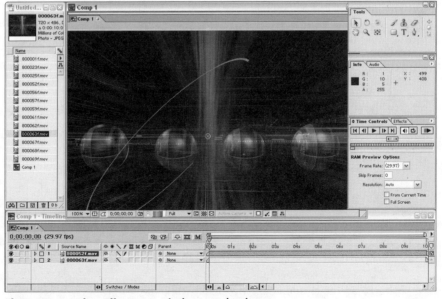

Figure 26-1: The Composition Settings dialog box enables you to set the frame size of your project.

6. **Drag the clips from the Project window to the Composition window.** The items will appear in layers in the Timeline window. To change the order of the clips, just drag one layer above another. Figure 26-2 shows the After Effects 6.5 windows and palettes.

Figure 26-2: After Effects 6.5 windows and palettes.

7. **To load a Premiere Pro project into After Effects, choose File ⇨ Import ⇨ File.**

8. **Locate the Premiere Pro project you want to import.**

9. **Set the Import As pop-up menu to Project.**

10. **Click Open.** After Effects imports the Premiere project, which appears in the After Effects Project window.

11. **Double-click the Premiere Pro project Composition file to display the Premiere files in the Timeline window.** The Timeline window appears with layers. The layers are the video and sound tracks from the Premiere project.

Note   You can also load an Adobe Photoshop layered file into After Effects by choosing File ⇨ Import ⇨ File. In the Import File dialog box, choose a file and then set the Import As pop-up menu to Composition. For more information on working with Adobe Photoshop, turn to Chapter 27.

Trimming Using the Timeline Window

When you have an After Effects project with the items you need in the Timeline window, you can trim them using the Timeline window. Trimming using the Timeline window is easy. You can trim using the Timeline window by either dragging the in and out points in the layer duration bar or by using the current-time indicator.

Trimming with the layer duration bar

A video clip's duration in the Timeline window is displayed as a layer duration bar. Figure 26-3 shows the layer duration bar before trimming. Figure 26-4 shows the layer duration bar after trimming. Here's how to trim using the layer duration bar:

✦ **To trim the in point.** Click at the beginning of a clip and drag to the right to change the in point and to trim the video clip.

✦ **To trim the out point.** Click at the end of a clip and drag to the left to change the out point and to trim the video clip.

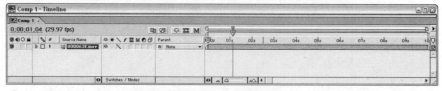

Figure 26-3: The layer duration bar before trimming.

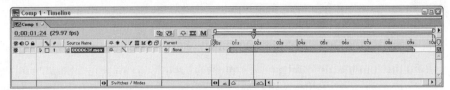

Figure 26-4: Trimming the in point and out point with the Timeline window.

Trimming with the current-time indicator

Follow these steps to trim a clip at the current-time indicator:

1. **Click the layer in which your video clip resides.**

2. **Move the current-time indicator to the point you want to trim.**

3. **Trim the in or out point:**
   - To trim the in point, press Alt+[.
   - To trim the out point, press Alt+].

Trimming Using the Layer Window

Trimming in the After Effects 6.0 Layer window is similar to trimming in Premiere Pro's Monitor window except that trimming a clip's in point in the After Effect's Layer window doesn't affect the clip's relative starting position in the Timeline window. In other words, no gap appears in front of it when you remove frames from the clip's in point.

Here's how to trim using the Layer window:

1. **Choose File ➪ New Project to create a new project. You can also choose to load a project.** If you want to import a Premiere project into After Effects, skip Steps 2, 3, and 4 and jump to Step 5.

2. **Choose Composition ➪ New Composition to create a new composition.** The Composition Settings dialog box appears.

3. **Set the Frame Size to be the same size as the size of the project.** Choose a preset; notice that the Width and Height values automatically change. If you want, you can change the Frame Rate and Resolution values.

4. **Choose File ➪ Import ➪ Multiple Files.** When the Import File dialog box appears, select a file.

5. **Set the Import As menu to Footage.**

6. **Click Open to import the selected file.** Continue selecting files and choosing Open until you've imported all the files you need. To close the dialog box, click Done.

7. **Drag the items from the Project window to the Composition window.** The items will appear in the Timeline window.

8. **To load a Premiere Pro project into After Effects, choose File ⇨ Import ⇨ File.**

9. **In the Import File dialog box, choose a Premiere Pro project and set the Import As pop-up menu to Project.**

10. **Click Open to import the Premiere Pro project into After Effects.** The Premiere project then appears in After Effects' Project window.

11. **Double-click the Composition file to display the Composition files in the Timeline window.** The Timeline window appears with layers representing the video and sound tracks from the Premiere project.

12. **To display the Layer window (shown in Figure 26-5), either double-click the layer you want to use or click the layer and choose Layer ⇨ Open Layer Window.** The Layer window opens.

13. **Click the In and Out buttons, shown in Figure 26-5, to trim the clip.** Just move the current-time indicator to where you want to set either the in or out point and then click the In or Out button in the Layer window.

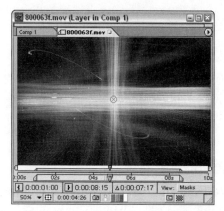

Figure 26-5: Trimming a clip using the In and Out buttons in the Layer window in After Effects 6.0.

The trimmed portion of your video footage appears in the Timeline window as outlines, as shown in Figure 26-6.

Figure 26-6: A trimmed clip appears in the Timeline window as outlines.

Exporting Your Adobe After Effects Files

To export your After Effects projects, you can choose either the File ➪ Export command or the Composition ➪ Make Movie command. If you want to export your After Effects work so that you can import it into Adobe Premiere Pro, you must save the After Effects file as either an AVI movie or a QuickTime movie or as an *image sequence,* a series of separate graphic files, rather than a stream of video frames.

Note   You can choose to export either the entire After Effects project, or you can just export a section of the After Effects project. To export a portion of your After Effects work, click the Timeline window and move the work area bar (this bar appears where the current-time indicator is located) over the area you want to save.

Exporting a QuickTime movie from After Effects

Almost any machine can read QuickTime and AVI movies. To quickly save your After Effects project as either a QuickTime or AVI movie, follow these steps:

1. **Make sure the Timeline window is the active window.** Click the Timeline window to activate it.

2. **Choose File ➪ Export ➪ AVI or File ➪ Export ➪ QuickTime Movie.** The Save As dialog box appears.

3. **Name your movie, then click Save.** When exporting an AVI movie, the AVI Settings dialog box appears. When exporting a QuickTime movie, the Movie Settings dialog box appears (see Figure 26-7).

4. **Click the Settings button in the Video section.** The Compression Settings dialog box appears.

5. **Click the top pop-up menu to choose a type of compression.**

6. **Click OK to set the compression and close the Compression dialog box.**

7. **Set any desired options in the Movie Settings dialog box that appears when exporting a QuickTime movie.**
   - Click the Filter button to apply a filter (video effect) to your work.
   - Click the Size button to apply a custom size to your work.
   - Click the Sound Settings button to change the sound settings.

8. **In the Movie Settings dialog box, click OK to save your work as a QuickTime movie. In the AVI Settings dialog box, click OK to save your work as an AVI movie.**

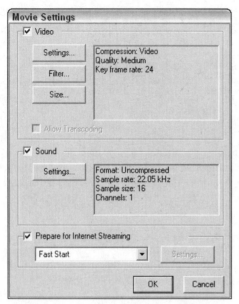

Figure 26-7: The Movie Settings dialog box.

Exporting an image sequence from After Effects

A quick way to save your After Effects work in a sequence format is to use the File ⇨ Export command. You can save your sequence file in Photoshop format. A Photoshop sequence file can be imported into Premiere Pro or Adobe Photoshop for more editing.

Here's how to save your work as an image sequence using the File ⇨ Export command:

Note Before you begin, create a new folder on your hard disk and name it. You will use this folder to save your sequence files.

1. **Make sure that the Timeline window is the active window.** Click the Timeline window to activate it.

2. **Choose File ⇨ Export ⇨ Image Sequence.** The Save As dialog box appears.

3. **Save your sequence image in the new folder you created.** All the sequence files will be saved in the folder.

4. **Click Save.** The Export Image Sequence Settings dialog box appears (see Figure 26-8).

5. **Select a format option type (BMP, JPEG MacPaint, Photoshop, PICT, PNG, QuickTime Image, SGI, TGA, or TIFF).** You can also set the frames per second. By default, the Frames per second option is set to Best. If you want to use a different option, click the menu.

Tip   For best results, save your image sequence in Photoshop format if you will be importing it into Adobe Premiere Pro.

6. **Click the Options button in the Export Image Sequence Settings dialog box to view and set the compression and color options.** Click OK to exit compression and color options and return to the Export Image Sequence Settings dialog box.

7. **In the Export Image Sequence Settings dialog box, click OK to create a sequence.** The Export dialog box displays how long the sequence will take and how many frames will be created in the sequence.

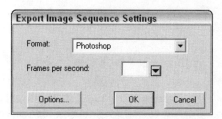

Figure 26-8: The Export Image Sequence Settings dialog box.

Note   Turn to the end of this chapter to learn how to import the sequence into Adobe Premiere Pro.

The Make Movie command

The Composition ➪ Make Movie command offers precise control of your rendering options. For better quality files, use this command to save your After Effects project as either a QuickTime movie or an image sequence.

Follow these steps to save your work using the Composition ➪ Make Movie command.

Note   You can choose to export either the entire After Effects project or just a section of the After Effects project. To export a portion of your After Effects work, click the Timeline window and move the work area bar (this bar appears where the current-time indicator is located) over the area you want to save.

1. **Click the Timeline window to activate it.**

2. **Choose Composition ➪ Make Movie.**

3. **In the dialog box that appears, name the movie.**

4. **Click Save.** If you are outputting to a sequence, create a new folder in which to save your sequence frames before naming and saving your file. The Render Queue dialog box appears (see Figure 26-9), enabling you to change the Render Settings and the Output Module.

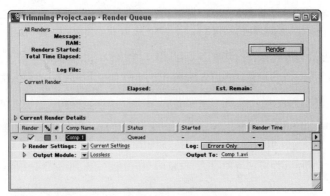

Figure 26-9: The Render Queue dialog box.

5. **To view and change the Render Settings, click the Current Settings to display the Render Settings dialog box.**

6. **Choose the resolution with which you want your work to be saved by clicking the Resolution menu.** Be careful not to use a resolution higher than what you are working with, because your work will appear blurry. You can choose a resolution lower than what you are working with. You may want to reduce the resolution of your work if you want to reduce the file size of the final movie, which may be an issue if you are outputting to the Web or e-mailing your movie to someone.

7. **Click the Time Span menu to specify whether you want to output a designated work area or an entire composition.**

8. **To view and change the Output Module, click Lossless.** The Output Module Settings dialog box appears.

9. **Click the Format menu to save your work as either a QuickTime movie or a sequence.**

10. **Click the Channels and Depth menus to select how many colors you want your movie to be saved with.**

11. **In the Output Module Settings dialog box, click the Audio Output section to select the audio output you want.**

12. **When you are ready to output your After Effects work, click the Render button in the Render Queue dialog box.**

Importing After Effects Files into Premiere Pro

You may want to load the AVI file or QuickTime movie or Photoshop sequence file you exported from After Effects into Premiere Pro. Here's how to import a file:

1. **In Adobe Premiere Pro, choose File ➪ New Project to create a new Premiere project.**

2. **Choose File ➪ Import.**

3. **Locate either the AVI file or QuickTime file.**

4. **Click Open.** The file appears in the Project window, ready for you to drag it to a video track in the Timeline window.

Follow these steps to import a Photoshop sequence file (that was created in After Effects) into Premiere Pro:

1. **In Adobe Premiere Pro, choose File ➪ New Project to create a new Premiere project.**

2. **Choose File ➪ Import.**

3. **In the Import dialog box, locate the sequence folder.**

4. **Click the Import Folder button**. The Sequence folder appears in the Project window. You can now drag it to a video track in the Timeline window.

Summary

If you import clips into After Effects 6.0 to create special effects, you may want to also edit the in and out points of the clips while you are in After Effects. Later, you can import the clips into Adobe Premiere Pro as AVI, QuickTime movies, or as a sequence of separate graphic files.

✦ In After Effects, you can trim clips in the Timeline window or Layer window.

✦ Clips can be trimmed by clicking the edge of a clip and dragging or by pressing a keyboard command. To trim the in point, press Alt+[. To trim the out point, press Alt+].

✦ To import a sequence of graphics created in After Effects into Premiere Pro, choose File ➪ Import. In the Import dialog box, locate the file and click the Import Folder button.

✦   ✦   ✦

The Photoshop Connection

During video production, you may want to export still frames from your Adobe Premiere Pro project for use on a Web page or in a print document, such as a brochure. If you export the still frames to Adobe Photoshop, you can prepare them for print and optimize them for the Web. You can even export an entire Premiere project with all of its video tracks into After Effects. Once in After Effects, each track appears as a separate layer. A frame exported from After Effects to Photoshop retains its layers. A frame exported from Premiere Pro to Photoshop does not.

Photoshop can also be used as an image data source. You can use Photoshop to create backgrounds, titles, or images with alpha channels. These images can then be integrated into a Premiere Pro project.

Exporting a Premiere Pro Frame to Photoshop

Although Premiere Pro is primarily used for creating desktop video projects, you can easily export a video frame from your project to use as a still image. The frame can be any individual frame from a clip, or it can display a frame from a transition or video effect.

In addition to using the still frame for print purposes, you can use the still frame to create or enhance a Web site or to create a background scene in an interactive presentation. After the frame is in Photoshop, you can edit the clip's colors, convert the clip to grayscale or black and white, and even add or delete items or people from a clip.

Cross-Reference   To learn how to export an entire video clip as a QuickTime or AVI movie, see Chapter 19. To learn how to export a Premiere Pro video clip to Photoshop as a Filmstrip file, see Chapter 18.

Here's how to export a frame from Adobe Premiere Pro:

1. **Open or create a Premiere** Pro **project.**

2. **After you have a Premiere** Pro **project onscreen, locate the frame you want to export.** Start by opening the Monitor window. To display the Monitor window, choose Window ➪ Show Monitor.

3. **Use the Frame Forward and Frame Back buttons in the Monitor window to locate the frame you want to export.** Figure 27-1 shows the frame that we want to export in the Monitor window.

Figure 27-1: The still frame that will be exported.

4. **After you have chosen the frame you want to export, choose File ➪ Export ➪ Frame.**

5. **In the Export Frame dialog box, you can name your frame.** Also notice that below the File name field, the frame's make and video size appear. Click the Settings button if you need to change the file format and image size.

6. **In the Export Frame Settings dialog box, shown in Figure 27-2, General should be selected.** To choose a file format, click the File Type pop-up menu. You can choose TIFF, Targa, Windows Bitmap, or CompuServe GIF. If you are going to use the still frame for print, you'll probably want to save your file in TIFF format. Use the Targa format if you are going to import this frame into a 3D program. If you are going to use this frame for multimedia purposes, choose Windows Bitmap.

Figure 27-2: The Export Frame Settings dialog box's General settings enable you to export a still frame as a TIFF, Targa, BMP, or GIF file.

If you are going to use the frame for the Web and want to reduce the number of colors in the image to 256, use the GIF format. When you pick the GIF format, a Compile Settings button appears. You can click this button and choose whether you want your GIF file to be dithered and whether you want the image to contain a transparent background.

The Export Frame Settings dialog box Video settings enable you to change the color depth and choose a compressor and frame size for the exported still frame.

Note   If you are going to use this frame for multimedia purposes, you may want to import the still frame into Macromedia Director. To learn more about using Premiere Pro and Macromedia Director, turn to Chapter 23.

7. **When you finish adjusting the General and Video settings, click OK to return to the Export Frame dialog box.**

8. **In the Export Frame dialog box, click Save to save the frame in the format chosen.** The frame just saved appears onscreen. If this is the right frame, you can close the file and export another frame or quit Premiere Pro and load Photoshop to import the frame.

Importing a still frame from Premiere Pro into Photoshop

After you've exported a still frame from Premiere Pro, you'll probably want to import it into Photoshop to either color-correct it or incorporate it into a collage or other project.

Here's how to import a still frame from Premiere Pro into Photoshop:

1. **Load Adobe Photoshop.**

2. **Choose File ⇨ Open.**

3. **In the Open dialog box, locate and select the Premiere Pro file you saved as a still image. Then click the Open button to import the Premiere Pro file into Photoshop.**

4. **When the Premiere still image file opens in Photoshop, you see all the tracks flattened in one layer.**

If you want to load a Premiere Pro frame into Photoshop and have the tracks appear as separate layers, you must export the frame to Adobe After Effects first, which is discussed in the following section.

Exporting an After Effects Frame to Photoshop

You can use After Effects to export a frame from a Premiere Pro project to Photoshop. If you import a Premiere Pro project into After Effects, then you can export a frame from the Premiere Pro project that is in After Effects to Photoshop. In After Effects, the video tracks from a Premiere Pro project appear as separate layers. Following are the steps to import a Premiere Pro project into After Effects and then export a frame from the Premiere Pro project that is in After Effects to Photoshop:

1. **Load Adobe After Effects.**

2. **Choose File ⇨ New ⇨ Project. In the New Project dialog box, pick a preset and type a name for your project. Then click OK.**

3. **Choose File ⇨ Import ⇨ File.** In the Import File dialog box that appears, locate the Premiere Pro project you want to import. Then set the Import As pop-up menu to Composition. Click Import to import the Premiere project into the After Effects project.

4. **Double-click the Composition file in the Project window to display the Timeline window and Composition window.** In the Timeline window, all Premiere Pro tracks appear as layers. In the Composition window, you see the layers as a composite.

5. **Move the current-time indicator in the Timeline window to the frame you want to export.**

6. **Choose Composition ⇨ Save Frame As ⇨ Photoshop Layers to save the still frame with all of its layers.** To save a still frame as a composite without the layers, choose Composition ⇨ Save Frame As ⇨ File.

7. **To open the file in Photoshop, load Adobe Photoshop and choose File ⇨ Open to open the file.** When the file opens, the video tracks from Premiere appear in different Photoshop layers.

Creating and Importing a Photoshop Sequence File into Premiere Pro

In this section, you learn how to create a presentation by first exporting four frames from Adobe Premiere Pro into Adobe Photoshop to create a sequence file. In the Photoshop sequence file, each frame becomes a layer. Text is added to each of the layers (frames). Afterwards, the Photoshop layer file is imported into Premiere Pro as a sequence file where sound is added to create a presentation. Figure 27-3 shows four frames of a Premiere Pro project created using a Photoshop sequence file.

Figure 27-3: Frames from a Premiere Pro presentation (FashionShow) created using an photoshop Adobe sequence file.

To create a Photoshop sequence file by exporting frames from a Premiere Pro video clip, follow these steps:

1. **Open a Premiere Pro project with a video clip that you want to use to create a presentation.** If you want to use the video clip that was used to create the presentation shown in Figure 27-3, create a new Premiere Pro project and then choose File ➪ Import. Locate the file (Digital Vision's 567026f.mov CityMix video clip) and click Open.

2. **Drag the video clip from the Project window to Video track 1 in the Timeline window.**

Digital Vision's 567026f.mov CityMix video clip (used to create the frames in Figure 27-3), is found in the Chapter 27 folder (which is in the Tutorial Projects folder) on the DVD that accompanies this book.

3. **Export four frames.** To export each frame, move the Timeline Marker to the frame you want to export. Then choose File ➪ Export ➪ Frame. Click the Settings button. In the Export Frame Settings dialog box, click the File Type pop-up menu and choose TIFF. Click OK. In the Export Frame dialog box, name your frame and then click Save to export the frame.

The first frame we exported was at 00:00 on the Timeline, the second frame was at 01:07 on the Timeline, the third frame was at 12:26 on the Timeline, and the fourth frame was at 21:16 on the Timeline.

4. **Create a new Photoshop file with the same dimensions as the Premiere Pro video clip and name it Fashion.**

5. **Use Photoshop to open all the exported frame files.**

6. **Drag and drop each exported frame file into the Fashion file.** Each frame should now be a layer in the Photoshop Fashion file.

The bottom layer should be the frame that you want to appear first and the top layer should the frame you want to appear last.

7. **To rearrange the layers, click and drag them up or down in the Layers palette.**

8. **Close all the files except the Fashion file.**

9. **Click on the eye icon to hide all the layers except the bottom layer.**

10. **Use the Horizontal Type tool to create type in the bottom layer.**

In Adobe Photoshop CS, you can create text on a path.

11. **Move the mouse to the place on the image where you want the text to appear and click the mouse once.** Begin typing.

12. **With the text selected, select a font and size.** You can also add tracking (spacing between the letters). To do so, use the Character palette. Choose Window ➪ Character to display the Character palette.

13. **To add interesting effects to your text, choose Layer ➪ Layer Style, then choose an effect.** To create the text effect shown earlier in Figure 27-3, we used the Drop Shadow, Inner Shadow, Outer Shadow, Color Overlay, and Pattern Overlay Layer Style options. After you apply the effects, the effects appear in the Layers palette. We also used the Warp Text option on the text. This option is found just the below the menu bar.

14. **To move the text onscreen, drag it with the Move tool.**

Note You may be wondering why we didn't just use Premiere Pro to create the text. We used Photoshop to create the text, and not Premiere Pro, because Photoshop has powerful layer style features that enable you to create 3D text effects.

15. **Now that you've created some text and stylized it, you can duplicate it and then edit it to use on another layer.** To do so, follow these steps:

   a. **To duplicate the text layer, click and drag the text layer over the Create a New Layer icon in the Layers palette.**

   b. **Click the eye icon above the bottom layer to display the next layer.**

   c. **Drag the duplicated text layer above the displayed layer.**

   d. **Now, use the Move tool to move the text into the desired location.**

   e. **Use the Horizontal Type tool to edit the text.**

16. **To add text to the third layer from the bottom, first display the layer by clicking on the eye icon in the Layers palette.** Next, you need to duplicate, move, and edit the text as you did in the preceding step. After you've done that, repeat this process to add text to the fourth layer from the bottom.

17. **Merge the text down to the frame below it by selecting the text layer and choosing Merge Down from the Layers palette pop-up menu.** Do this for each text layer. This way, you have only four layers, rather than eight.

18. **Choose File ⇨ Save to save your work.** Be sure to save your work in Photoshop format with all of its layers.

Now you are ready to import the Photoshop sequence file into Premiere Pro to create a presentation:

1. **Choose File ⇨ New ⇨ Project to create a new project. In the New Project dialog box, pick a DV-NTSC (Standard 32 KHz) preset that matches the dimensions of the Photoshop file.**

2. **Choose File ⇨ Import and locate the Photoshop file and click Open.** When the Import Layered File dialog box appears, click the Import As pop-up menu and choose Sequence, as shown in Figure 27-4. Click OK to import the Photoshop file as a sequence.

Figure 27-4: Premiere Pro's Import Layered File dialog box allows you to import sequence files.

The Photoshop sequence file will appear in the Project window as a folder with the layers within the folder, as shown in Figure 27-5.

Figure 27-5: When you import a Photoshop sequence file into Premiere Pro, the contents of the file appear in a folder in the Project window.

3. **Open the sequence folder if it is not already open; in the folder, double-click FashionSequence.** Notice that all the layers of the sequence appear in a separate video track in the Timeline window, shown in Figure 27-6. The Photoshop files appear in Project window and Timeline window in the same order as they did in the Layers palette in Photoshop. The file FashionSequence is in the Chapter 27 folder, which is in the Tutorial Projects folder that is on the DVD that accompanies the book.

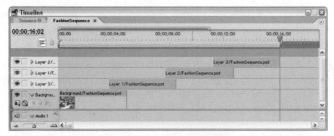

Figure 27-6: Double-click the sequence file in the Project window to have the sequence appear in the Timeline window.

Note   If you create a graphic at 720 × 480 (or 720 × 486) in a square pixel program such as Adobe Photoshop 7 and import it into a Premiere Pro NTSC DV project, the graphic may appear distorted in Premiere Pro. The graphic is distorted because Premiere Pro automatically converts it to a non-square 0.9 pixel aspect ratio. You can convert the imported Photoshop graphic file back to square pixels. First, select the graphic image in the Project window. Then choose File ⇨ Interpret Footage. In the Pixel Aspect Ratio section of the Interpret Footage dialog box, click Conform to and choose Square Pixels (1.0) in the pop-up menu and click OK. Although this technique works, it may result in a reduction in graphic quality. If you are using Photoshop 7, your best bet is to create full-screen graphics for DV projects at 720 × 534 or 720 × 540 (768 × 576, PAL). After creating your graphics, import them into Premiere Pro with the General Project Settings option "Scale clip to project dimensions when adding to sequence" selected. This will squeeze the graphic to fit into your DV project without distortion.

If you are creating full-screen graphic files in Photoshop CS for a Premiere Pro DV project, create them in Photoshop CS using the 720 × 480 DV preset. If you use this preset (which sets the Photoshop pixel aspect ratio to .9), you should be able to import Photoshop files seamlessly into a Premiere Pro DV project without any distortion.

4. **Use the Selection tool to move the clips in the Timeline window so that they appear as seen in Figure 27-6.** The end of the first clip should overlap the beginning of the second clip. The end of the second clip should overlap the beginning of the third clip, and the third clip should overlap the beginning of the fourth clip.

5. **Now add transitions to the overlapping areas between the clips.** We added the Dither Dissolve transition to the overlapping areas of the first and second clips. To the overlapping areas of the second and third clips, we used the Roll Away transition. To the overlapping areas between the third and fourth clips, we used the Page Peel Transition.

6. **To complete your presentation, add some sound to it by choosing File ⇨ Import.** Locate and select a sound file. Then click Open to import the file. We used Digital Vision's 730005aw.wav Acoustic Chillout clip.

You can find Digital Vision's 730005aw.wav Acoustic Chillout clip in the Chapter 27 folder (which is on the Tutorial Projects folder) on the DVD that accompanies this book.

7. **To preview the presentation, click the Play button in the Monitor window.** Be sure to save your work when you are finished.

Creating a Photoshop File with an Alpha Channel

To have the bird.psd file (shown in Figure 27-7) appear in Premiere Pro without its background, you must select the bird and then save the selection to an alpha channel. When you load the file into Premiere Pro, the alpha channel enables you to use the Motion Settings to animate the bird, without its background appearing.

Figure 27-7: Photoshop file of a bird before creating an alpha channel.

After you load Photoshop, follow these steps to select an image and save the selection to an alpha channel:

1. **Open the file with the image you want to isolate.**

On the DVD-ROM

To use the bird image (shown in Figure 27-7), load the bird.psd file found in the Chapter 27 folder (which is on the Tutorial Projects folder) on the DVD that accompanies this book.

2. **Use a Photoshop Selection tool (the Pen tool, the Magic Wand, or the Lasso tool) to select the image you want to isolate from the background.** We used the Polygonal Lasso tool to select the bird. For a soft-edged selection, we set the Lasso tool to have a feather radius of 1.

3. **With the selection onscreen, choose Select ⇨ Save Selection.** In the Save Selection dialog box, shown in Figure 27-8, we clicked the Channel pop-up menu and set it to New and left the Operation radio button set to New Channel. Then we clicked Save to save the selection to an alpha channel.

Note

To load a saved selection, choose Select ⇨ Load Selection.

Figure 27-8: The Save Selection dialog box enables you to save a selection to an alpha channel.

4. **To see the alpha channel, choose Window ⇨ Channels.** In the Channels palette, you see a Red, a Green, a Blue, and an Alpha channel, as shown in Figure 27-9. Click Alpha 1 in the Channels palette to display the alpha channel. The alpha channel shown in Figure 27-10 displays the white area as the selected area. The white area is the only area that Premiere Pro reads. The black area represents the area that Premiere Pro won't read. (This happens only if the Color Indicates option, in the Channel Options dialog box, is set to Masked Areas — the default setting. To display the Channel Options dialog box, double-click Alpha 1 in the Channels palette.)

5. **To import this file into Premiere Pro with the alpha channel, save the alpha channel with the file by choosing File ⇨ Save As.** In the Save As dialog box, click the Format pop-up menu and choose Photoshop format. In the Save section, only the Alpha Channel option should be selected. Click Save to save the file.

Figure 27-9: The Channels palette with its channels.

Figure 27-10: The Photoshop file with the alpha channel displayed.

Placing a Photoshop alpha channel file into a Premiere Pro project

Now that you've created a Photoshop file with an alpha channel, you are ready to import it into Premiere Pro. After it's in Premiere Pro, you'll use the bird image to create a project called Freebird. Figure 27-11 shows a few frames from the Freebird Premiere Pro project.

Figure 27-11: Frames from the Freebird project.

To create the Freebird project, we used two Photoshop files — a background file (3dwindow.psd) and an alpha channel file (bird.psd) — and created some text using Premiere's Adobe Title Designer. Here's how to import a Photoshop file with an alpha channel into a Premiere project:

1. **Load Adobe Premiere Pro. Then choose File ➪ New ➪ Project to create a new project.** In the New Project dialog box, pick the Square-Pixel 640 x 480 Non-DV preset, name your project, and click OK.

2. **In a new Premiere project, choose File ➪ Import.**

3. **In the Import dialog box, locate the Photoshop file with an alpha channel (bird.psd) and click Open.** Premiere stores the file in the Project window.

4. **Choose File ➪ Import to import a background video clip or image.** We used the file 3dwindow.psd for the background.

On the DVD-ROM

The bird image (bird.psd), and the background image (3dwindow.psd) are located in the Chapter 27 folder (which is on the Tutorial Projects folder) on the DVD that accompanies this book.

5. **Drag the bird file from the Project window to Video track 2 in the Timeline window.**

6. **Drag the background file (3dwindow.psd) from the Project window to Video track 1 in the Timeline window.** In Video track 3, you'll place some text created using the Adobe Title Designer. Figure 27-12 shows the Timeline window for the Freebird project.

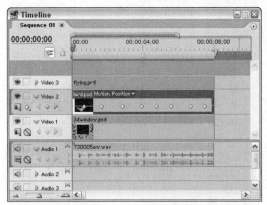

Figure 27-12: The Timeline window used to create the Freebird project.

7. **Choose File ➪ New ➪ Title.** In the Adobe Title Designer window, shown in Figure 27-13, make sure the Show Video option is selected so that you can see the background image. Select the Type tool, move the cursor to the black area of the background, and type the text **Freebird**. Choose a font. We used Alba Super Regular.

   To animate the bird image, we used Premiere Pro's Motion settings, shown in Figure 27-14. The Motion settings are found in the Effect Controls window. The bird in the Freebird project moves from the top-right corner down to the bottom-left side.

8. **To start the animation, move the Edit line to the beginning of the clip, and click the word Motion in the Effect Controls window. Move the bird to the top-left corner. Click on the Position Toggle Animation icon to create a keyframe. Now keep moving the Edit line and the bird to create more keyframes.**

9. **To preview the Freebird project, click the Play button in the Monitor window.** By creating an alpha channel for the bird file, you can have the bird image move without having the background move with it. In order to create the alpha channel, we had to create and save a selection around the bird (refer to the previous section to learn how). When you save a selection, Photoshop saves the selection as a mask in an alpha channel. Because the bird image is in Video track 2, between the text that is in Video track 3 and the background image that is in Video track 1, when you add motion to the bird, the bird will move from behind the text to in front of the text.

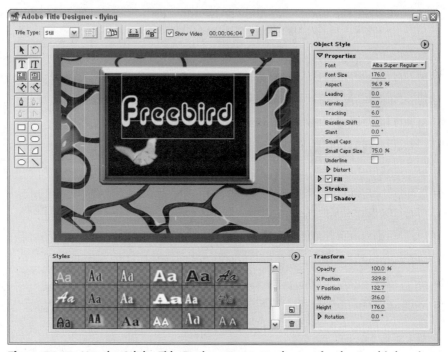

Figure 27-13: Use the Adobe Title Designer to create the text for the Freebird project.

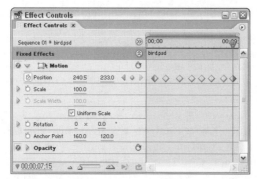

Figure 27-14: The Effect Controls window shows the keyframes used to animate the bird in the Freebird project.

10. Choose File ➪ Import to import a sound clip. We used Digital Vision's 730005aw.wav Acoustic Chillout clip.

On the DVD-ROM

Digital Vision's 730005aw.wav Acoustic Chillout clip is found in the Chapter 27 folder (which is on the Tutorial Projects folder) on the DVD that accompanies this book.

11. Choose File ➪ Save to save your work.

Summary

You can easily export a frame from Premiere Pro to Photoshop or export Photoshop files into Premiere Pro.

✦ If you want to load a Premiere Pro frame into Photoshop and have a Premiere Pro frame appear as a layer, export the Premiere project to After Effects first.

✦ Premiere Pro automatically reads the background transparency of Photoshop layers. It does not convert Photoshop transparency into a white background.

✦ Premiere Pro can use Photoshop alpha channels to create transparency effects.

✦   ✦   ✦

Using Adobe Premiere Pro and Adobe Illustrator

Adobe Illustrator is one of the most powerful desktop illustration programs available for personal computers. Using Adobe Illustrator, graphic designers can place text on a curve or bend and reshape the letters in a word. Illustrator, which is a *vector-based* program, provides designers with the power they need to create virtually any shape that can be drawn. In vector-based programs, shapes are defined mathematically and can easily be moved and reshaped. In Adobe Illustrator, shapes appear as *paths* filled or outlined with color. Onscreen, a path resembles a wireframe outline with tiny squares called *anchor points*. Editing the anchor points edits the path.

For Adobe Premiere Pro users, Adobe Illustrator opens up a new world of possibilities. Adobe Illustrator type and shapes can be imported directly into Adobe Premiere Pro. When Premiere Pro opens an Illustrator file, it automatically converts it from Illustrator's vector format to Premiere Pro's *raster* format and appears with transparent backgrounds. This conversion enables you not only to use the Illustrator text but also to use shapes created in Illustrator as masks.

Working with Illustrator Type

You can create type effects in Adobe Illustrator 10 and then import them into Adobe Premiere Pro for use as title effects, logos, credits, and more. You can also import Illustrator type into Premiere Pro and use the type as a mask and have a video clip run through the shape of the text, as described later in this chapter.

Note For creating title effects and logos, you may want to use Adobe Illustrator CS's new 3D shapes and type tool features. Adobe Illustrator CS also allows you to wrap artwork around shapes.

Adobe Illustrator features six tools with which to create type.

The Type tool enables you to create text that reads horizontally, from left to right.

The Area Type tool is used to create type inside a shape. You can select the Ellipse, Polygon, Star, or Rectangle tools to create a shape. To create more elaborate shapes, you can apply one of Illustrator's Effect commands to a shape, such as the Punk & Bloat command (Effect ➪ Distort & Transform ➪ Punk & Bloat). With a shape onscreen, click inside the shape with the Area Type tool and then start typing. Your text appears onscreen in the shape of the path shape and reads from left to right.

The Path Type tool creates text on a path. To use the Path Type tool, you first need to create a path. You can create a path using the Pen, Pencil, Paintbrush, or Ellipse tool. You can also use the Spiral tool to create a spiral path on which the text can appear (see Figure 28-1).

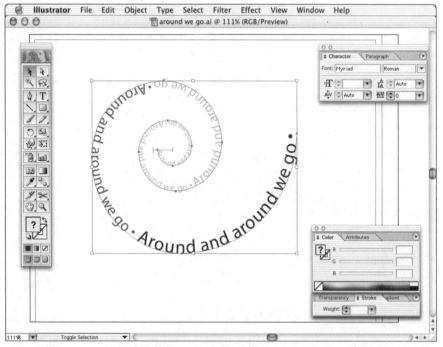

Figure 28-1: A spiral path with text.

After you've created a path, click it with the Path Type tool and start typing. The text appears on the path as you type (as shown in Figure 28-1). In some cases, the font size may be too big to appear on the path. In this case, you may need to scale down the font size. To do so, click and drag over the text with the Path Type tool to select it. Then choose Type ➪ Size and pick a size or click the Font Size pop-up menu in the Character palette. To display the Character palette, choose Type ➪ Window ➪ Type ➪ Character.

The Vertical Type tool flows text from top to bottom (vertically), rather than from left to right (horizontally) as the Type tool does. To create vertical text, click the Vertical Type tool in the Toolbox, click in the document where you want the type to appear, and then start typing.

The Vertical Area Type tool works like the Area Type tool. Both type tools create type within a path. When type appears while using the Vertical Area Type tool, it appears from top to bottom (vertically) inside the path rather than from left to right (horizontally) as it does when using the Path Area Type tool.

The Vertical Path Type tool works similarly to the Path Type tool. Both type tools create type on a path. However, instead of the type appearing left to right (horizontally) as it does when using the Path Type tool, it appears top to bottom (vertically).

Follow these steps to learn how to use Illustrator's type tools:

1. **Load Adobe Illustrator, if it is not already loaded.**

2. **Choose File ➪ New to create a new document.** The New Document dialog box appears (see Figure 28-2).

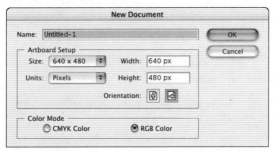

Figure 28-2: Adobe Illustrator's New Document dialog box.

3. **Set the Artboard Size to 640 × 480pixels (or the frame size that you will be using in Premiere), set Color Mode to RGB Color, and click OK.** A new document appears.

4. **Set the Fill color to the desired type color.** Double-click either the Fill swatch in the Tools palette (the top, overlapping square toward the bottom of the Tools palette) or the Fill swatch in the Color palette (the top, overlapping square at the top-left side of the Color palette). The Color Picker dialog box appears.

Tip   By default, Illustrator uses the Fill color as the type color. If you set the Fill color to the color you want the text to be, you won't have to worry about changing it later.

5. **Click a color in the Select Color area or on the color slider next to it.** If you are creating a project for the Web, be sure to select the Only Web Colors option.

6. **Click OK.** The Fill color changes to the newly selected color. If you decide to change the Fill color, the easiest way to pick a new color is to use the color bar in the Color palette. To display the Color palette, choose Window ➪ Color. In the Color palette, click a color in the color bar at the bottom of the palette to change the fill color. To create a new color, move the sliders in the middle of the palette.

7. **To apply a stroke to the text, click the Stroke swatch (which is below the Fill swatch) and pick a color.** Select a color either by using the Color Picker dialog box — accessed by double-clicking the Stroke swatch in the Tools or Color palette — or by dragging the sliders and/or color bar in the Color palette. To set the size of the stroke, click the Weight menu in the Stroke palette and pick a size. To display the Stroke palette, choose Window ➪ Stroke.

8. **Set the Fill color to black.** Click the Default Fill and Stroke Color icon, which is below the overlapping Fill and Stroke swatch in the Tools palette. This sets the Stroke swatch to black and the Fill color to white. Next, click the Swap Fill and Stroke icon (the curved arrow next to the Fill and Stroke swatch) to set the Fill to black and the Stroke to white. To use the Illustrator text as a mask with a video clip run through the shape of the text, you must set the Fill color to black. Now you are ready to use a Type tool to start creating some type.

9. **Select one of the Type tools in Illustrator.**

10. **Move the cursor to the middle of the document.**

11. **Click the document and type a word or two.**

12. **Choose Window ➪ Type ➪ Character and Window ➪ Type ➪ Paragraph to display either the Character or Paragraph palette.**

13. **Click and drag over the area you want to stylize.** You can stylize either an entire word or a letter or two in the word.

For a more interesting text effect, you can use one of the Effect commands to alter the text path. Figure 28-3 shows the Effect ➪ Distort & Transform ➪ Free Distort command when applied to text.

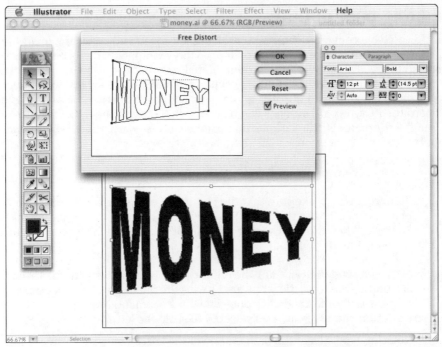

Figure 28-3: The Free Distort dialog box can be used to distort text.

Converting Illustrator type to path outlines

You may want to convert your Illustrator type into outline paths so that you can manipulate it further as shown earlier in Figure 28-1. To manipulate path outlines, click the type path's anchor points using the Direct Selection tool (the white arrow) and move the anchor points to alter the type path and the type itself. Essentially, this enables you to create your own type designs.

Note   When you convert text to outline format, it is no longer considered a font. The outline paths now appear as art, not text. So, if you send an Illustrator file to another person, that person won't need to have the font on their machine.

Here's how to convert your type into outline type paths:

1. **Create text with one of Illustrator's type tools.**

2. **Use the Selection tool to select the type.**

3. **Choose Type ⇨ Create Outlines to convert the text from type to art.**

Editing path outlines

After you have converted your text into outlines, Illustrator views the text as art (a path that is in the shape of text). You'll probably manipulate, distort, or enlarge the text so that when you import it into Premiere Pro, you can run a video clip through the text, as shown later in Figure 28-6. Type path outlines are enlarged with the Scale tool, rotated with the Rotate tool, and moved with the Selection tool. With Adobe Illustrator 10, type path outlines can be manipulated using the Reflect, Shear, and Free Transform tools. They can be distorted using the Warp, Reshape, and Twist tools.

Here's how to scale, rotate, and move path outlines:

✦ **Enlarging text.** Make sure that the text is selected (use the Selection tool, the black arrow). To use the Scale dialog box, double-click the Scale tool in the Toolbox. When the Scale dialog box appears, as shown in Figure 28-4, make the adjustments you want and click OK to scale the text.

✦ **Scaling a single letter.** Click the outline path of the letter with the Group Selection Type tool (the white arrow with the plus sign). Next, select the Scale tool in the Toolbox and click once on your document. Now click and drag on the letter with the Scale tool selected to scale the letter.

✦ **Rotating type.** Select the path outline of the letter you want to select. Next, click the Rotate tool in the Toolbox (next to the Scale tool in the Toolbox) and click in your document. Next, click and drag on the letter to rotate it. If you want to display the Rotate dialog box, press and hold the Option/Alt key while you click the text with the Rotate tool.

✦ **Moving type.** Click inside the letter using the Group Selection tool and drag the letter to where you want to move it. You can also use the arrow keys on your keyboard to move the letter onscreen. By default, the arrow keys are set to move in 1-pixel increments. You can change the increments in the Keyboard Increment section of the Preferences General dialog box. To access this dialog box, choose Edit ➪ Preferences ➪ General.

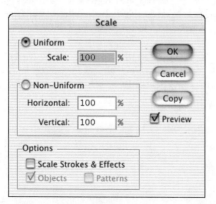

Figure 28-4: The Scale dialog box enables you to scale paths.

Editing with anchor points

Type outlines can be manipulated so that you can create new typefaces. You manipulate type path outlines by moving either anchor points or directional lines. Figure 28-5 shows a type path outline before and after manipulation.

Figure 28-5: Path type outline before and after manipulating.

To move an anchor point, click it with the Direct Selection tool (the white arrow) and then drag. Illustrator also enables you to move multiple anchor points at one time. To select more than one anchor point, press and hold the Shift key as you select anchor points. You can also click and drag over the anchor points you want to select.

Tip   You can also press the arrow keys on your keyboard to move a selected anchor point. Anchor points move keyboard increments that are set in the General Preferences dialog box. To display the General Preferences dialog box, choose Edit ⇨ Preferences ⇨ General.

Editing with directional lines

Curves on a path are created from a *curve anchor point*. Curve anchor points have *directional lines*, which determine the size and arc of your curve. Clicking and dragging a directional line changes the form of the curve.

Other ways to adjust the type path outline include using the Pen + tool, Pen – tool, and the Convert tool. Use the Pen + tool to click the path to add an anchor point. This anchor point can then be manipulated. Clicking an anchor point with the Pen – tool deletes it. Use the Convert tool to click on a corner anchor point to convert the corner anchor point to a curve anchor point, and vice versa.

Adobe Illustrator 10 enables you to create some interesting distortions with the Warp tool. You can convert plain path outlines into interesting and unusual ones.

Using an Illustrator Text Shape in a Premiere Pro Project

Earlier in this chapter, you learn how to use Illustrator to create type and then convert the type into type shapes. This section shows you how to use Illustrator's Type tool to create text, convert it into a type shape, and then import it into a Premiere Pro project that uses the text shape as a mask. The Premiere Pro project in this chapter's examples features a video clip playing through and behind the Illustrator text shape. Figure 28-6 shows frames from a Premiere Pro project that has a video clip running inside and behind an Illustrator text shape.

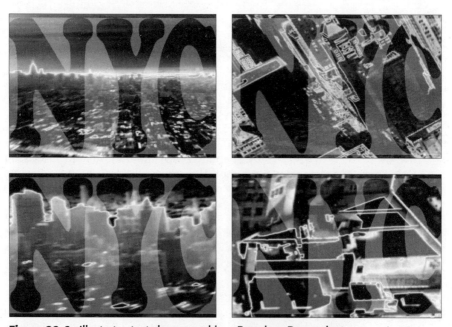

Figure 28-6: Illustrator text shape used in a Premiere Pro project.

The following steps show how to create an Illustrator text shape and then import it into a Premiere Pro project and use it as a mask.

On the DVD-ROM

The images shown in Figure 28-6 are on the DVD that accompanies this book. The images are an "NYC" text shape created in Illustrator, a black-and-white video clip of New York City from Digital Vision's CityMix collection (567005f.mov), and a sound clip from Digital Vision's City Life/Urban Moods collection (576002s.aif).

1. **Load Adobe Illustrator and create a new document.** The document should be the same size as your Premiere Pro project. If you don't have access to Adobe Illustrator, skip Steps 1–4.

2. **Select one of Illustrator's type tools.**

3. **Choose a font and type size.**

4. **Set the foreground color to black so that the text you create is black.** The black text is used later as a mask in Premiere Pro.

5. **Create some text.**

Cross-Reference

To learn about using the different Illustrator type tools, see the section "Working with Illustrator Type" earlier in this chapter.

6. **Manipulate the text in Illustrator.** Either choose Effect ⇨ Distort & Transform or convert the type into outlines using the Direct Selection tool. To convert the type into outlines, select it with the Selection tool and choose Type ⇨ Create Outlines. Figure 28-7 shows the Illustrator text shape we created for the project shown in Figure 28-6. We converted the NYC text into outlines and then manipulated the text by using the Direct Selection tool.

7. **After you've created an Illustrator text shape, save your file in Illustrator format.** Premiere Pro can then read the file information. If you want, you can quit Adobe Illustrator.

8. **Load Premiere Pro and create a new project.**

9. **Import an Illustrator text shape, a video clip, and a sound clip.** Choose File ⇨ Import to import the files needed for this project. If you want, you can import the files we used to create the frames shown in Figure 28-6. You can find them in the Chapter 28 folder (which is in Tutorial Projects folder) on the DVD that accompanies this book. They are NYC.ai and Digital Vision's video clip 567005f.mov (from CityMix CD-ROM) and the sound clip 576002s.aif from Digital Vision's City Life/Urban Moods collection.

10. **Drag the video clip to Video track 1, the Illustrator text shape to Video track 2, and if you want, a sound clip to Audio track 1.** If the text shape is not as long as the video clip, you can click the end of the text shape in the Timeline window and drag to the right until it's the same duration as the video clip. (For more information on basic editing, refer to Chapter 7.) If the sound clip is longer than the video clip, you can use the Razor tool to cut it. (For more information on editing sound clips, turn to Chapter 8.)

Figure 28-7: An Illustrator text shape created in Illustrator.

11. **Select the text shape in Video track 2.**

12. **Choose Window ⇨ Workspace ⇨ Effects.** In the Effects palette, open the Video Effects folder.

13. **Open the Keying folder and drag the Screen Key effect over the text shape in Video track 2.**

14. **In the Effect Controls window, use the Screen Key settings to create transparency with the dark areas of the clip in Video track 1.** Use the Screen Key settings to reduce the Opacity so that you can see more of the video clip in Video track 2. Drag the Cutoff values to the left to make the clip in Video track 1 more transparent and see more of the background. Drag the Cutoff values to the right to have the video clip in Video track 1 more opaque.

Note Choosing the Multiply Key Type option results in the opposite effect of the Screen Key Type option. Using the Key Type option enables you to run the video clip inside or behind the text shape. For more information on using Key Type effects, refer to Chapter 15.

15. **To soften the edges of the text shape, blur it by using the Gaussian Blur video effect.** To do so, select the text shape in Video track 2. In the Effects palette, open the Blur & Sharpen folder and drag the Gaussian Blur video effect over the text shape in Video track 2. The Effect Controls window will appear onscreen if it is not there already. Drag the Blurriness slider a little to the right. Figure 28-8 shows all the windows and palettes used to create the frames for the NYC project.

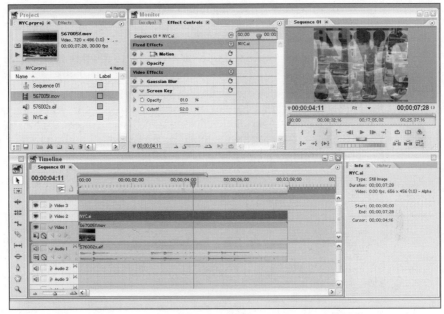

Figure 28-8: The Premiere Pro windows used to create the project in Figure 28-6.

16. **Choose File ➪ Save to save your project.**

17. **Click the Play button in the Monitor window to preview the project.** If you want, you can make a movie by choosing File ➪ Export ➪ Movie. Click the Settings button if you want to change the settings of your movie. For more information on outputting your Premiere Pro projects to movies, turn to Chapter 19.

Creating Masks in Illustrator

The Illustrator drawing capabilities make it the perfect place to create intricate masks for Premiere Pro. This example shows you how to create a simple shape in Illustrator that can be used as a mask in Premiere Pro.

Here's how to create a simple mask:

1. **Load Adobe Illustrator, if it isn't running already.**

2. **Choose File ➪ New to create a new document.** In the New Document dialog box, set the Artboard Size and choose RGB Color for the Color Mode.

3. **Select the Rectangle, Ellipse, Polygon, or Star tools (shown in Figure 28-9) from the Toolbox.**

Figure 28-9: Illustrator's Rectangle, Ellipse, Polygon, and Star tools.

4. **Click and drag to create a shape or Alt+click to display the tool's dialog box.** In the dialog box that appears, make your adjustments.

5. **Click OK to create the shape.** The shapes you create are filled with whatever the Fill and Stroke colors are in the Toolbox. If you want, you can change the Fill and Stroke color by double-clicking the Fill or Stroke swatch in the Toolbox. When the Color Picker appears, make your adjustment and click OK. Figure 28-10 shows the Star dialog box and a star it created.

Experiment with using different fill shades. Filling with black, white, and different shades of gray and colors will result in different effects in Premiere.

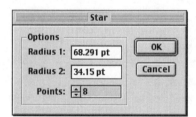

Figure 28-10: The Star dialog box and the star it created.

6. **When you have a shape onscreen, experiment with creating a few different shapes using one of the Effect commands.**

Figure 28-11 shows how we transformed a star shape into a blob shape using the Effect ⇨ Distort ⇨ Roughen dialog box.

Figure 28-12 shows the star transformed into a snowflake using the Effect ⇨ Distort & Transform ⇨ Zig Zag.

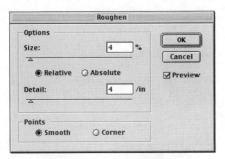

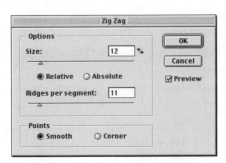

Figure 28-11: A star before and after applying the Roughen command.

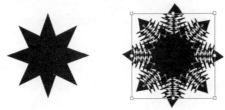

Figure 28-12: The Zig Zag command transformed a star into a snowflake.

An interesting effect was created when we used the Effect ⇨ Distort ⇨ Photocopy command, which is shown in Figure 28-13. To use this command, you must first rasterize the shape by using the Effect ⇨ Rasterize command.

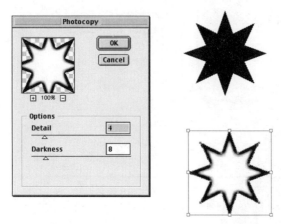

Figure 28-13: The Photocopy command copied and altered the star.

The following figures (Figures 28-14 through 28-18) show the things that can be done with Adobe Illustrator's Effect commands.

- The star shape was twirled using the Twirl command, shown in Figure 28-14.

- Figure 28-15 shows how a star is transformed into a sun shape using the Effect ➪ Distort & Transform ➪ Punk & Bloat command.

- Figure 28-16 shows how a black star is transformed into a grayscale star using the Effect ➪ Sketch ➪ Note Paper command.

Figure 28-14: The Twirl command twirled the star.

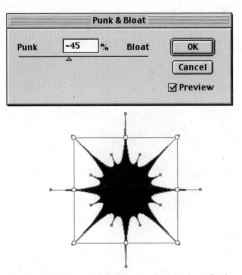

Figure 28-15: A star is transformed with the Punk & Bloat command.

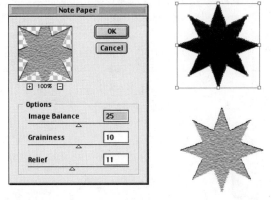

Figure 28-16: A black-and-white star is transformed with the Note Paper command.

- Figure 28-17 shows how a star shape is converted to an ellipse using the Effect ➪ Convert to Shape ➪ Ellipse command.

- Figure 28-18 shows the Blur ➪ Gaussian Blur command applied to the ellipse shape we created from a star shape.

Note   You can also transform simple shapes created in Adobe Illustrator 10 into more elaborate shapes using the Reshape, Twist Warp, Twirl, Pucker, Bloat, Scallop, Crystallize, and Wrinkle tools.

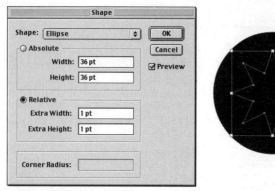

Figure 28-17: A star shape is converted to an ellipse with the Ellipse command.

Figure 28-18: The Gaussian Blur command applied to an ellipse shape.

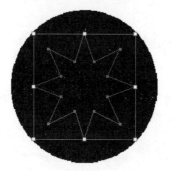

Importing an Illustrator File as a Mask

After you know how to use Illustrator to create type and manipulate it into type shapes, you can import the shapes into Premiere Pro and use them as masks. Here's how:

1. **Choose File ⇨ New ⇨ Project.**

2. **Choose File ⇨ Import, locate a video clip, and then click Open.** We used Digital Vision's Ambient Space 434023f.mov video clip.

On the DVD-ROM

Digital Vision's Ambient Space 434023f.mov clip is located in the Chapter 28 folder on the DVD that accompanies this book.

3. **Drag the video clip from the Project window to Video track 2 in the Timeline window.**

4. **Click the video clip in Video track 2.**

5. **Choose Window ⇨ Workspace ⇨ Effects to display the Effects window and Effect Controls window.**

6. **Drag the Image Matte Key effect from the Effects window to the video clip in Video track 2.** The Image Matte Key Type option is a good choice to use when you would like a video clip to be seen through an Illustrator image. If you want, you can reverse the effect by clicking the Reverse check box or by changing the Composite Using option.

7. **Click the Setup button in the Effect Controls window.** When the Select a Matte Image dialog box appears, choose an Illustrator shape file. We used the Startwirl.ai file located in the Chapter 28 folder located in the DVD that accompanies this book. Click Open to view the star in the Monitor window. Notice that the white areas on the outside of the star don't show up in the preview. Only the black areas show through. The video clip shows through the black areas.

On the DVD-ROM

You can find the Startwirl.ai file in the Chapter 28 folder on the DVD that accompanies this book.

8. **Choose File ⇨ Import to import a clip to appear in the background.** Either import a video clip or a Photoshop or Illustrator file. We imported an Illustrator file that we created by using the Raindrop RGB Style. This file (surplus.ai) is on the DVD that accompanies this book. Figure 28-19 shows the surplus background with the twirl star image matte applied to a video clip.

Figure 28-19: A frame of a video clip through an Illustrator twirled star shape with an Illustrator background.

Creating a Mask Using Photoshop and Illustrator

Combining the strengths of Adobe Photoshop and Adobe Illustrator, you can create elaborate masks. Start by using Photoshop to save a scanned photograph, an image captured with a digital camera, or a stock image. Then load the file into Illustrator and use one of the path-creating tools to create a path around the area in the photo you want to import into Adobe Premiere Pro. In Figure 28-20, we used Illustrator's Paintbrush tool to create a path. After the path is in Premiere Pro, you can have a video clip running in the background, as shown in Figure 28-21.

Here's how to create a complex mask using both Adobe Photoshop and Adobe Illustrator:

1. **Scan or capture an image into Adobe Photoshop with a scanner, digital camera, or a digital camcorder.**

2. **Save the file in either Photoshop or TIFF format.** Many photo-finishing labs can develop your film as well as archive the pictures on a DVD, CD-ROM, or floppy disk.

On the DVD-ROM

Figure 28-20 shows the sample image (girl.psd) we used in this section. If you want, you can load this image from the Chapter 28 folder on this book's DVD.

Figure 28-20: Sample photo used to create a mask in Photoshop and Illustrator.

3. **Load Adobe Illustrator.**

4. **Chose File ⇨ Open.** Locate the digitized Photoshop image and open it.

5. **Choose Window ⇨ Show Layers.**

6. **In the Layers palette, double-click the layer.** The Layer Options dialog box appears (see Figure 28-21).

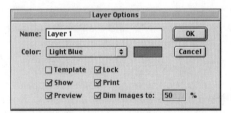

Figure 28-21: The Layer Options dialog box enables you to lock and dim a layer.

7. **Click both the Lock and Dim image options to lock and dim the layer.** Make sure that the Dim option is set to 50%.

8. **Click OK for the effects to take place.**

9. **Click the New Layer menu in the Layers palette to create a new layer.** In the Layer Options dialog box that appears, name the layer and then click OK.

10. **Select the Pen, Pencil, or Paintbrush tool.**

11. **Trace the dimmed image's outline.** If you use the Pen tool, a small circle appears next to the tool when the starting and finishing points meet. When this happens, click to close the path, if you want to create a closed path. Figure 28-22 shows the sample image dimmed in a layer and a few path strokes created with the Paintbrush in another layer.

Figure 28-22: The dimmed image is in one layer, and the Paintbrush paths are in another layer.

When you are drawing, it's easier to see the image you are tracing if you trace with a stroke and no fill, as shown in Figure 28-23. If you draw with a fill, you won't see the image in the layer below. To set the Fill to none, click the Fill swatch (the top overlapping square) in the Toolbox and then click the third small square (the one with the dialog line) below the Fill swatch. Click the Stroke swatch (behind the Fill swatch) and then click the first small square to set the stroke color to black. Choose Window ➪ Stroke to display the Stroke palette. The Stroke palette enables you to choose the width of your stroke.

12. **After you've created a few paths, you may want to hide the bottom layer with the image in it to see how your path strokes are appearing.** Click the eye icon next to the layer you want to hide.

13. **After you have a path, fill it with black if you want to use it as a solid mask in Premiere Pro.** You may want to fill the path with a shade of gray to create a translucent mask.

14. **When you finish tracing over the dimmed image, you can delete it.** You may, however, first want to use the File ➪ Save As command to duplicate the file.

15. **Save your final file in Illustrator format.**

16. **Load Adobe Premiere Pro and then create a new project.**

Figure 28-23: The traced image created in Illustrator.

17. **Choose File ➪ Import.** Locate the Illustrator file you want to import and then click Open.

The screen shots in this section feature the traced image created in the preceding section. If you want, you can load the girl.ai file from the Chapter 28 folder on this book's DVD. Or, if you prefer, you can import an Illustrator file that has text.

18. **Drag the Illustrator file from the Project window to Video track 2 in the Timeline window.**

19. **Choose File ➪ Import.** Locate a video clip and then click Open. We used an Illustrator file (placemat.ai) that we created using the Scribble &Tweak command (Effect ➪ Distort & Transform ➪ Scribble & Tweak).

You can find the placemat.ai file in the Chapter 28 folder on the DVD that accompanies this book.

20. **Drag the Illustrator file or video clip from the Project window to Video track 1 in the Timeline window.** You should now have a video clip in Video track 1 and an Illustrator file in the Video track 2. To make the background more interesting, we applied the Color Balance (HLS) effect and animated the effect over time by changing the Hue.

21. Click the Play button in the Monitor window to preview the project.
Figure 28-24 shows a frame of the project.

Figure 28-24: An Illustrator mask over a background.

Summary

You can use Adobe Illustrator to create text and masks for Premiere Pro projects.

✦ Illustrator features six type tools: the Type tool, Area Type tool, Path Type tool, Vertical Type tool, Vertical Area Type tool, and the Vertical Path Type tool.

✦ You can create shapes in Illustrator using the Rectangle, Ellipse, Polygon, and Star tools.

✦ When creating masks using Illustrator, the Alpha Channel, Screen, or Multiply keys are best used when you only want the black or colored areas of the mask to appear.

✦ The Image Matte Key Type option is the best option when you want a video clip to be seen through an Illustrator image.

✦ You can create complex masks by using both Adobe Photoshop and Adobe Premiere Pro.

✦   ✦   ✦

Working with Masks in Adobe After Effects 6.0

Matte effects are undoubtedly one of the more interesting special effects provided by Adobe Premiere Pro. In Chapters 15 and 16, you learned how mattes can be used to hide portions of one video clip in a track behind the masked area of a shape in another video track.

If you want to create a matte effect in Premiere Pro, one technique is to create a shape in another program to use as a mask and import it into Premiere Pro. Although this is a rather straightforward and simple process, it does not enable you to create the mask at the same time as previewing the clip with which it will be used. Nor does it enable you to change the matte's shape as the clip runs.

If you need to create sophisticated matte effects, you can turn to Adobe After Effects. In After Effects 6.0, you can create masks using the After Effects Pen tool, edit them, and animate them over time. You can also import Adobe Illustrator and Adobe Photoshop files into After Effects to be used as masks. After Effects also enables you to import Illustrator and Photoshop paths or Photoshop alpha channels to be used as masks.

This chapter looks at Adobe After Effects' masking options. It also discusses the features that Premiere Pro lacks but which you still may want to use to add interesting and unusual matte effects to Premiere Pro. To do this, you can import a Premiere Pro project into After Effects and use After Effects' masking capabilities to add pizzazz to your clips.

After Effects Masks: An Overview

In Adobe After Effects 6.0, you can load a video clip or an entire Premiere Pro project into After Effects and isolate an area by using a mask so that the viewer only sees a portion of the video clip or project. In After Effects 6.0, masks can be created using *paths*. A path is similar to a wireframe line onscreen that can be used to create anything from shapes with sharp corners to flowing waves created from perfect curves. After Effects 6.0 allows you to create four types of masks: Rectangular, Elliptical, and RotoBézier. To create a rectangular-shaped mask, use the Rectangular Mask tool in the Tools palette. To create an elliptical-shaped mask, use the Elliptical Mask tool in the Tools palette. If you are creating any other shaped mask, you work with either a Bézier or RotoBézier mask. To create a Bézier mask, you can use the Pen tool, which is found in the Tools palette. Note that when you use the Pen tool in After Effect's 6.0, you can also click the RotoBézier option. The RotoBézier option enables you to more easily create curves.

The Pen tool in After Effects is quite similar to the Pen tool in Adobe Illustrator and Adobe Photoshop. You can edit the path using the Pen +, Pen –, and Convert tools. All of these tools reside in the same location in the Toolbox as the Pen tool. You can use the Selection tool (arrow tool) in the Tools palette to edit a point on the path by clicking the point and dragging it to the position you want. If you double-click the path with the Selection tool, you can move, scale, or rotate the path as a whole. The effects of a mask are displayed in the Composition window. Masks are edited in either the Composition or the Layer window. Masks can be altered over time by using the Timeline window.

Creating Oval and Rectangle Masks

You can have a lot of fun creating interesting effects with masks. Figure 29-1 shows a frame with a video clip before applying a rectangular mask. Figure 29-2 shows the same frame after an oval mask was used on the video clip's perimeter. We then placed a still image in the background. For an added effect, we applied the Twirl command (Effect ⇨ Distort ⇨ Twirl) to the background still image.

Figure 29-1: An After Effects frame before using a mask.

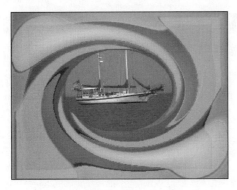

Figure 29-2: An After Effects frame created using an oval mask.

Here's how to create an oval or rectangle mask in After Effects:

1. **Load After Effects.**

2. **Choose File ➪ New ➪ New Project to create a new project.**

3. **Choose Composition ➪ New Composition to create a new composition.**

4. **In the New Composition dialog box, set the frame size.** To create the frame shown in Figure 29-1, we set the width and height frame to NTSC, 640 × 480 pixels, and imported a video clip that was 160 × 120. That way, we had plenty of room to see the background beneath the video clip.

5. **Choose File ➪ Import ➪ File.**

6. **In the Import File dialog box, select a file that you want to mask and then set the Import As menu to Footage.** You can use one of the video clips found on the DVD that accompanies this book. The video clip used in Figure 29-1 is called sailboat.mov and is found in the Chapter 29 folder on the DVD that accompanies the book. Also in the Chapter 29 folder is a video clip from Digital Vision that you can use. The Digital Vision clip is from the CityMix CD-ROM (576004p.mov).

7. **Click Import to import a video clip you want to mask.** The imported video clip appears in the Project window.

8. **Choose File ➪ Import ➪ File to import another video clip to use in the background or import a still image to use as the background.** You'll be better able to view the effect of the mask. Locate the still image or video clip that you want to import.

On the DVD-ROM

When creating a mask in After Effects 6.0 for the first time, you may want to use just a simple video clip for the mask and a still image as the background. If you want, you can use the video clip of the sailboat.mov and the shapes.psd we used in this section. The sailboat.mov video clip and the shapes.psd still image are found in the Chapter 29 folder on the DVD that accompanies this book.

Note If desired, you can create your own background using the After Effects 6.0's new Brush tool. To use the Brush tool, start by choosing Layer ➪ New ➪ Solid. In the Solid Footage Settings dialog box, name the solid and set the presets. Then click OK. When the solid appears in the Timeline window, double-click it to display the solid in the Layer window. Then select the Brush from the Tools palette and begin painting. Use the Paint palette to change the painting color and brush size.

9. **To apply an effect to the background, choose a command from the Effect menu.** In Figure 29-2, we applied the Effect ➪ Distort ➪ Twirl command. Next to the triangle in front of the background clip is the lock column. Click it so that the background clip will not be affected when you begin to work with the video clip you will be masking.

10. **Click and drag the imported video clip that you will mask to the middle of the Composition window.** Not only does the video clip appear in the Composition window, but it also appears in the Timeline window.

11. **Click and drag the imported background clip from the Project window to the Timeline window.** Make sure that you place the image or clip beneath the video clip that has the mask. If it isn't, click and drag it in the Timeline window and place it below the video clip that you will mask.

12. **Select the video clip in the Timeline window.**

13. **Click the triangle in front of the name of the video clip to display its options.** Notice that presently there is not a Mask option available.

14. **To add a mask the shape of the selected video clip, choose Layer ➪ Mask ➪ New Mask.**

Note You can use the Rectangular Mask tool in the Tools palette to create a rectangular-shaped mask. To create an elliptical-shaped mask, use the Elliptical Mask tool in the Tools palette.

Notice that in the Timeline window, the selected video clip now has a Masks option.

15. **Click the triangle in front of the word Masks in the Timeline window. Then click the triangle in front of the word Mask 1 to reveal the Mask 1 options.** The options are Mask Shape, Mask Feather, Mask Opacity, and Mask Expansion.

16. **To change the shape of the mask, either click Shape, which is next to Mask Shape in the Timeline window, or choose Layer ➪ Mask ➪ Mask Shape.** The Mask Shape dialog box appears (see Figure 29-3).

17. **To convert the mask to an ellipse, click Ellipse, in the Mask Shape dialog box.** Don't change the Bounding box values and leave the Units menu set to pixels. Click OK to see the effects of the mask in the Composition window.

18. **To preview the effect of the mask over time, move the current-time indicator along the Timeline.**

19. Save your file by choosing File ➪ Save.

If you want, you can continue editing the mask. The mask can be edited by using the Mask 1 options. For more information on editing a mask, proceed to the next section.

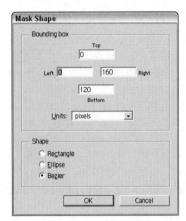

Figure 29-3: The Mask Shape dialog box enables you to pick a shape for your mask.

Editing a Mask with the Layer Window, Layer Menu, and Timeline Window

After you've created a mask, you can use the Layer menu and the Layer window, along with the Selection tool in the Tools palette, to edit the mask. You can also edit a mask by using the Mask options in the Timeline window. Here are a few mask-editing tips:

✦ **To edit the mask, the mask must be selected.** If the mask isn't selected, you can select it by double-clicking the name of the clip you are working on in the Timeline window. In the Layer window that appears, click the path to select it. You can also select a mask by clicking it in the Timeline window.

✦ **The mask can be edited in the Layer window or the Composition window.** If you change the path in the Layer window, you'll be able to see the effect of the mask on the video clip in the Composition window. Figure 29-4 shows the path and the mask in the Layer window.

✦ **A mask can be edited by using the Mask options in the Timeline window.** In the Timeline window, click the triangle in front of the clip with the mask that you want to edit. When the masks for that clip appear, click the triangle in front of the Mask that you want to edit. The mask options allow you to invert the mask, edit the shape, change the opacity, or expand the mask. It also allows you to soften the edges of the mask.

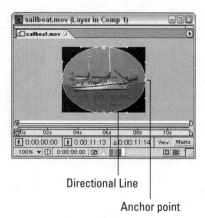

Figure 29-4: The Layer window shows the mask as a path.

Directional Line

Anchor point

Here's how to edit a mask:

1. **Start by selecting the Mask in the Timeline window that you want to edit.** The mask should be displayed in the Composition window.

2. **With the mask selected in the Timeline window, you can choose Layer ⇨ Mask ⇨ Free Transform Points to transform the mask.** Notice that in the Composition window, the mask appears with a bounding box with handles around it. In the Composition window, click and drag on one of the handles to increase or decrease the size of the mask. Move the mouse over one of the handles and wait for the cursor to change to a curved line with arrows at either end. Then drag in the direction you want to rotate the mask. To activate the changes, double-click inside the mask shape in the Composition window.

Tip

If you want to cancel the changes you made to your mask, choose Layer ⇨ Mask ⇨ Reset Mask to reset the mask to its original state. If desired, you can remove the mask by choosing Layer ⇨ Mask ⇨ Remove Mask and then choosing Layer ⇨ Mask ⇨ New Mask to create a new mask and start over again.

3. **To resize a mask using the Selection tool, choose the Selection tool from the Tools palette. Then click and drag one of the four corners of the mask in either the Composition or Layer window.** To display the mask in the Layer window, double-click the clip in the Timeline window. To keep the proportions of the mask as you change the size of the mask, press and hold the Shift key as you drag.

4. **To increase or decrease the expansion of a mask, click and drag the Mask Expansion values.** The Mask Expansion values are found in the Timeline window in the Mask section of the selected video clip.

5. **To change the shape of a mask, use the Layer ⇨ Mask ⇨ Mask Shape command or the Mask Shape option in the Timeline window.**

6. **To display the mask's path in the Layer window, double-click the video clip's name in the Timeline window or double-click inside the mask.** The mask appears as a path in the Layer window. To display the anchor points, you may need to click the path with the Selection tool found in the Tools palette.

7. **To edit the path, click an anchor point (shown in Figure 29-5) using the Selection tool. Then press an arrow key on your keyboard to move the anchor point up, down, or to the right or left.** As you edit the path, the mask in the Composition window is affected. Clicking and moving the directional line in the oval path changes the shape of the curve.

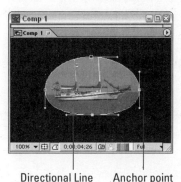

Directional Line   Anchor point

Figure 29-5: You can edit an oval path by moving anchor points and directional lines.

8. **To display the mask's path in the Composition window, double-click Comp 1 in the Project window.** Click on the mask with the Selection tool to select it.

9. **Click and drag inside the mask with the Selection tool to move the mask.** Click the edge of the mask to display the path of the mask.

10. **With the Selection tool, click either an anchor point or directional line to edit the path.**

11. **With the mask in the Timeline window, change the opacity of the mask by choosing Layer ⇨ Mask ⇨ Opacity.** In the Opacity dialog box, set the opacity you want. Click OK and notice the change in the Composition window. You can also change the opacity of a mask by using the Mask Opacity option in the Timeline window.

12. **To soften your mask's edges, you can apply a feather by choosing Layer ⇨ Mask ⇨ Mask Feather. In the Feather Mask dialog box, type a small value to create a small feather.** A large value results in a large feather. You can also feather a mask by using the Mask Feather option in the Timeline window.

13. **To adjust the colors of the clip, you can use any of the Effect ⇨ Adjust commands or the Effect ⇨ Image Control commands.** Once you apply a command, use the Effect Controls window to adjust the controls for that command.

14. **To stroke the mask, choose Effect ⇨ Render ⇨ Stroke. Use the Effect Controls window to set the stroke color, width, and opacity.** You can also set a fill color by choosing Effect ⇨ Render ⇨ Fill. Again, use the Effect Controls window to set the fill color and opacity and to use a fill mask.

15. **Choose Effect ⇨ Perspective ⇨ Basic 3D to swivel and tilt the mask in 360 degrees. To apply a shadow to the mask, choose Effect ⇨ Perspective ⇨ Drop Shadow or Radial Shadow. To apply a bevel to the mask, choose Effect ⇨ Perspective ⇨ Bevel Alpha or Bevel Edges.** The controls for the Perspective commands can be adjusted using the Effect Controls window.

16. **Use the Effect ⇨ Distort ⇨ Bezier Warp command to warp the mask using Beziers. Use the Beziers and the controls in the Effect Controls window to adjust the warp.**

17. **To invert the mask (reverse the effect of the mask), choose Layer ⇨ Mask ⇨ Inverse. To bring the mask back to the state it was before you inverted it, choose Layer ⇨ Mask ⇨ Inverse.**

18. **To change how the mask is displayed over the background, choose Layer ⇨ Mask ⇨ Mode and then choose a mode.** By default, the mode is set to Add.

Creating a Bézier Mask

The Pen tools used in programs such as Illustrator, Photoshop, Macromedia Freehand, and CorelDRAW provide digital artists with the power to draw virtually any shape imaginable. The After Effects Pen tool provides similar power — except instead of using the Pen tool to create works of art, After Effects users can use the Pen tool to create masks.

Figure 29-6 shows the first frame of a video clip without a Bézier mask. Figure 29-7 shows the same frame with a Bézier mask applied to the chipmunk in the clip. In order to isolate the chipmunk from the background, we used a Bézier mask — because using an oval or rectangle obviously wouldn't provide the desired effect. After we isolated the chipmunk from its background by applying the mask, we added a background still image. To make the background image more interesting, we applied the Effect ⇨ Stylize ⇨ Mosaic command. Finally, we added type on a path by using the After Effects Effect ⇨ Text ⇨ Path Text command.

Cross-Reference To use the After Effects Path Text command, you first need to create a New Solid (Layer ⇨ New Solid). For more information on creating and animating text in After Effects, turn to Chapter 30.

Figure 29-6: A frame from a video clip without a Bézier mask.

Figure 29-7: A frame from a video clip with a Bézier mask.

Here's how to create a simple Bézier mask using the After Effects Pen tool:

1. **In After Effects, create a new project by choosing File ⇨ New ⇨ New Project.**

2. **Choose Composition ⇨ New Composition to create a new composition.**

3. **In the New Composition dialog box, specify a frame size.** To create the frame shown in Figure 29-6, we set the width and height frame size to NTSC, 640 × 480 pixels.

4. **Choose File ⇨ Import ⇨ File to import a video clip you want to mask.** In the Import File Import dialog box, choose a file and then set the Import As menu to Footage. Choose Open to import the selected video clip. The imported video clip appears in the Project window.

On the DVD-ROM

If you want to use the video clip of the chipmunk.mov shown in Figure 29-6, you can find it in the Chapter 29 folder on the DVD that accompanies this book.

5. **Drag the video clip to the middle of the Composition window.** The video clip not only appears in the Composition window, but it also appears in the Timeline window. Notice that the current-time indicator is at the beginning of the clip. Any changes you make to the clip will affect only where the current-time indicator is positioned.

6. **Double-click the video clip's name in the Timeline window to display the video clip in the Layer window.**

7. **Select the Pen tool in the Tools palette. After you have selected the Pen tool, you can click RotoBézier option in the Tools palette. The RotoBézier option facilitates making Bézier paths that contain many curves.**

8. **Create a path around the image.** Click in the image you want to isolate. Keep clicking the perimeter of the image with the Pen tool to create a path around the image. When the first and last points meet, a tiny circle appears next to the Pen icon. Click the mouse to close the path. As you create a Bézier path in the Layer window, the effect of the mask appears in the Composition window. Figure 29-8 shows the chipmunk without a mask. Figure 29-9 shows the mask path in the Layer window and the effect of the mask.

Figure 29-8: The chipmunk before the mask.

Figure 29-9: The mask path in the Layer window and the mask effect.

Note   If you find the Pen tool difficult to use, you can start by using the Elliptical Mask tool or Rectangular Mask tool to create a path and then use the Pen and Selection tools to edit the path.

9. **To see the effects of the mask over a background, choose File ⇨ Import ⇨ File to import a file. Import either a still image or video clip to use as the background.** In the Import File dialog box, locate a file and click Open. In Figure 29-9, we used the file 12squares.psd as the background. This file is located in the Chapter 29 folder in the DVD that accompanies the *Adobe Premiere Pro Bible*.

10. **When the background clip appears in the Project window, drag it below the clip in the Timeline window.** To make the background image more interesting, we applied the Effect ⇨ Stylize ⇨ Mosaic command. To lock the background so that it doesn't move, click the Lock column (next to the triangle icon) in the Timeline window.

11. **To see a preview of your work, choose Composition ⇨ Preview ⇨ RAM Preview.**

12. **To add text on a path, choose Layer ⇨ New ⇨ Text and then choose Effect ⇨ Text ⇨ Path Text. In the Path Text dialog box that appears, type** Chipmunk Software.

    Use the Font pop-up menu to choose a font. Click OK to apply the text to your project. Use the Effect Controls window to edit the path text. To have the text appear around a circle, click the Shape Type pop-up menu in the Effect Controls window and choose Circle. Notice that when you work with text in After Effects, a new layer is created in the Timeline window.

Note   To add horizontal text to your project, click the Horizontal Type tool in the Tools palette. Next move the cursor to the Composition window and then click the mouse button and begin typing. Use the Character palette to change the font and font size. To convert horizontal type into a path outline, select the type with the Selection tool. Then choose Layer ⇨ Create Outlines. The path outline of the text can be edited with the Selection tool. The path outline can also be used as a mask.

13. **Save your file by choosing File ⇨ Save.**

Editing paths with the Pen tool

You can edit a path in After Effects 6.0 by using the Selection tool to select an anchor point and move it, or you can click on a directional line with the Selection tool to change the shape of a curve. You can use the Convert tool, which is found in the same location as the Pen tool, to convert a curve to a corner point, or vice versa. If you need more anchor points, select the Pen + tool and click the path to add a point at that location. To omit a point, click it with the Pen tool.

Animating a Mask with the Timeline Window

You can edit a mask's shape, location, feather, and opacity over various time intervals using After Effects Timeline window, Composition window, and Layer window. Figure 29-10 shows the effects of animating a mask at different points in time. Notice that the mask shape changes as the video progresses.

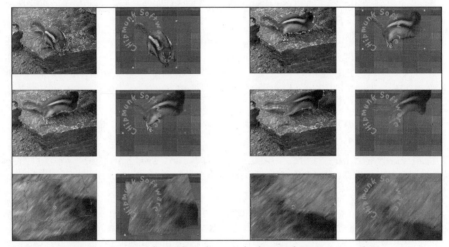

Figure 29-10: The frames show that the mask shape changes over time.

To use the Timeline window to edit a mask over time, follow these steps.

 Note   Before you begin, you should have a clip in the Timeline window. That clip should also have a mask.

1. **Click the triangle next to the video clip's name in the Timeline window.**

2. **Click the triangle in front of the word Masks to display the mask.**

3. **Click the triangle in front of the mask you want to edit to show the mask options.** The Mask options are as follows:

   • **Mask Shape.** Allows you to set the shape to either Rectangle, Oval, or Bézier.

   • **Mask Feather.** Allows you to apply a horizontal or vertical feather to the edges of a mask.

   • **Mask Opacity.** Allows you to change the opacity. To make the mask translucent, set the Opacity to less than 100%.

- **Mask Expansion.** Allows you to expand the mask using pixels values.

- **Mask mode.** By default the mode is set to Add. (Next to the modes, After Effects provides an area that you can click if you want to invert the mask.)

4. **Move the current-time indicator to the beginning of the clip in the Timeline window.**

5. **Click the stopwatch next to the mask option that you want to animate.** In Figure 29-10, we changed the mask's shape so that it would follow the chipmunk as it moved over time. To animate the mask shape, click the stopwatch in front of Mask Shape. Notice that a keyframe is created in the Timeline window. To animate a mask, you need to create keyframes.

6. **To create another keyframe, move the current-time indicator over to the right just a bit. Then edit the mask shape.** To follow an image the way we did in Figure 29-10, you need to move and edit the mask path in either the Composition or Layer window using either the Selection or Pen tool.

7. **When you've finished editing the mask path in the current-time location, move the current-time indicator again to the right.**

8. **Again edit the mask shape.** As you edit the mask shape, notice that another keyframe is created. Continue moving the current-time indicator and editing the mask until you've reached the end of the clip in the Timeline window. You can also edit a mask option from a point other than the beginning. For Figure 29-10, we started editing the opacity at the middle of the Timeline.

Follow these steps to edit the opacity of a mask:

1. **Move the current-time indicator to the beginning of the clip in the Timeline window.**

2. **Click the stopwatch in front of the Opacity option.** Notice that a keyframe is created. A keyframe is created with the Opacity's default settings, 100%.

3. **Move the current-time indicator to the middle of the clip in the Timeline window.**

4. **Change the mask opacity option by clicking and dragging on the Mask Opacity value in the Timeline window.** Note that you can also use the Mask Opacity command (Layer ➪ Mask ➪ Mask Opacity). When the Mask Opacity dialog box appears, type a number and click OK. In Figure 29-10, we changed the Opacity setting to 50%.

5. **Preview the project by choosing Composition ➪ Preview ➪ RAM Preview.** When the current-time indicator reaches the keyframe in the middle of the Timeline, the opacity changes to the value you entered in Step 4.

6. **Make the opacity (mask option) gradually change from the middle of the clip to the end of the clip.** Move the current-time indicator to the end of the clip. Next, set the desired opacity option.

Importing Masks from Illustrator or Photoshop

You can import a black-and-white Illustrator or Photoshop file into After Effects to use as a mask. The Illustrator or Photoshop file can be used to isolate areas in a video clip, as shown in Figure 29-11. Figure 29-12 shows the black-and-white Illustrator file used as a mask.

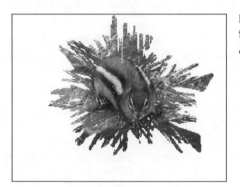

Figure 29-11: The effect of an Illustrator file used as a mask on a video clip in After Effects.

Figure 29-12: The black-and-white Illustrator file used as a mask.

Here's how to use Adobe Illustrator and Adobe Photoshop to create a mask in After Effects:

1. **In Adobe Illustrator 10, create a shape using the Rectangle, Oval, Star, or Polygon tool. Fill the shape with black. To distort the shape, use the Warp tool. Apply a filter or effect to the shape to create a more interesting shape.** Do not rasterize the shape. When you are done creating the shape, choose File ⇨ Save. In the Save dialog box, set the Save as type pop-up menu to Illustrator, and click Save.

2. **In Adobe Photoshop 7.0, Choose File ⇨ New to create a new file. In the New dialog box, choose a preset, set the Mode to RGB Color, and make the background transparent.** Click OK to create a new file.

   In Photoshop, you can use various tools to create a shape. Try using the Brush tool or the Custom Shape tool. Before using one of these tools, set the Foreground color in the Toolbox to black. Then pick a brush size and shape. You can also use the Lasso tool to create a selection.

   After you've created the selection, fill it with black by choosing Edit ⇨ Fill. In the Fill dialog box, set Use pop-up menu to Black, the Mode to Normal, and the Opacity to 100%. The Preserve Transparency option should not be selected. Click OK. To deselect the selection, choose Select ⇨ Deselect.

   To create a more unusual shape, you can apply one of Photoshop's filters. After you've created a shape, choose File ⇨ Save. In the Save dialog box, set the Format pop-up menu to Photoshop and click Save.

3. **After you have created a black shape in Adobe Illustrator or Adobe Photoshop, load After Effects and create a new project by choosing File ⇨ New ⇨ Project and a new composition by choosing Composition ⇨ New Composition.** When importing the Adobe Photoshop file, make sure to choose a shape or layer from the Choose Layer pop-up menu that appears.

4. **Import the Photoshop or Illustrator file, as well as a video clip, into the project by choosing File ⇨ Import ⇨ Multiple Files.**

On the DVD-ROM

In the Chapter 29 folder on the DVD that accompanies this book, you will find Photoshop shape files (puzzle.psd and balloon.psd) and Illustrator shape files (starfish.ai and roughen.ai). In the Digital Vision folder in the Chapter 29 folder is a video clip from Digital Vision that you can use. The Digital Vision clip is from Digital Vision's CityMix CD-ROM (567004f.mov).

5. **Drag the video clip from the Project window to the middle of the Composition window.**

6. **Drag the Photoshop or Illustrator black-and-white file below the video clip in the Timeline window.**

7. **Click the Mode column that appears next to the file's name in the Timeline window.** Click either the Lighten or Darken mode. (In Figure 29-11 the Lighten mode was used to lighten the dark areas.) The light (white) areas are not affected; only the dark areas (black areas) are. If you use the Darken mode, the dark area (black) in the image is not affected, but the light (white) area is affected.

   Experiment with the other modes, such as Overlay, Difference, and Saturation. If you have various layers in your project, you may want to set a Track Matte. The Track Matte column is next to the Mode column in the Timeline window.

Using Illustrator Paths as Masks

Hardcore Adobe Illustrator users will most likely prefer to create their masks in Illustrator, which provides more path-editing commands than does After Effects. Fortunately, importing an Illustrator file into After Effects is a simple copy-and-paste operation. Here are the steps:

1. **In Illustrator, select the path and all of its anchor points and then choose Edit ⇨ Copy.**

2. **Switch to After Effects, open the Layer window for the target layer, and then choose Edit ⇨ Paste.**

Summary

Although Adobe Premiere Pro provides numerous matting effects, it does not enable you to create sophisticated masks or edit masks over time as you can in Adobe After Effects.

✦ After Effects 6.0 enables you to create oval, rectangle, and Bézier masks.

✦ In After Effects 6.0, you can edit masks in both the Layer and Composition window using the Pen tool and the Selection tool and by using the commands in the Layer menu.

✦ After Effects masks can be edited over time using the Timeline window.

✦   ✦   ✦

Adding Special Effects in Adobe After Effects

Although Adobe Premiere Pro is packed with powerful video effects, at times you may want to create composite motion or text effects that may not be possible within the confines of Premiere Pro's menus and windows. If your project requires a bit more pizzazz than Premiere Pro seems able to produce, consider using Adobe After Effects 6.0.

After Effects 6.0 can create dozens of effects that aren't possible in Premiere Pro. For example, you can fine-tune a motion path's shape as you would a curve in Adobe Illustrator or Photoshop. You can also rotate text 360 degrees along a curve over time. After Effects enables you to run multiple clips simultaneously in the video frame — creating a three-ring circus of video effects.

This chapter's goal is not to persuade you to use After Effects over Premiere Pro, but to show you how the two can work together to create the ultimate video production. Both programs have their strengths, and you can use this to your advantage.

How After Effects Works

After Effects 6.0 combines some of the features of Photoshop 7.0 and Premiere Pro. To start a project in After Effects, first create a new *composition*. A composition determines the type of movie you will be creating. In the Composition Settings dialog box, you pick your settings for width, height, and frame rate. Then you import all the images, sounds, titles, and video clips you need to create your video production. Like Premiere Pro, After Effects stores all of these imported items in a Project window. As you need footage items, you drag them from the Project window into the Timeline window. Unlike Premiere Pro, the items in the Timeline window are not stored in video or sound tracks. Video and sound clips don't appear in different tracks; instead, they are organized as layers. In this way, Adobe After Effects works like Adobe Photoshop. In both programs, you also can apply transformations (scale, rotate, and so on), effects, and masks to the layers. Adobe After Effects, however, enables you to animate the transformation, effects, and masks over time; in Adobe Photoshop, each layer's properties remain static.

Cross-Reference

If you import a Photoshop file into Adobe ImageReady, you can make animation frames from your layers and output the file as a QuickTime movie. See Chapter 12 for an example of how to do this.

Importing Premiere Pro Projects

You can import an entire Premiere Pro project along with its transitions and effects directly into After Effects to take advantage of the program's powerful features, such as animating transformations and masks over time.

Follow these steps to import a Premiere Pro project into After Effects 6.0:

1. **In After Effects, choose File ⇨ Import ⇨ File.** The Import File dialog box appears.

2. **Select the Premiere Pro project you want to import and set the Import As menu to Composition.**

3. **Click Import.** After Effects 6.0 imports the Premiere Pro project. The video and sound tracks now appear as layers in the Timeline window. The first layer in the Timeline window is the first video or sound track that appears in the Premiere Pro Timeline window.

4. **If needed, you can now click a layer and animate it over time, using either one of the Effect commands, one of the Layer ⇨ Mask commands, and/or one of the Transform options in the Timeline window.** These options can be animated over time using keyframes — similar to the way Premiere Pro uses keyframes with video effects.

Note

Not only can you import a Premiere Pro project into After Effects, but also you can output your Premiere Pro project as a QuickTime movie and then import the QuickTime movie into After Effects by choosing File ⇨ Import ⇨ File (for older versions of Premiere, choose Footage File). In the Import File dialog box, select a QuickTime movie to import. Set the Import As pop-up menu to Footage. Then choose Import to import the movie into After Effects.

Importing and Animating Photoshop Files

To animate a Photoshop file in After Effects, you can either create a folder and place all the Photoshop files in it and import it as a Photoshop Sequence or import a Photoshop file with layers like the one shown in Figure 30-1. When you import a Photoshop file with layers as a composition, a folder is created in the Project window with the layers inside the folder.

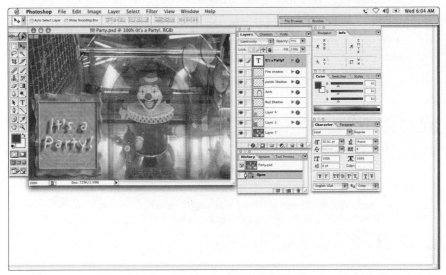

Figure 30-1: "It's a Party" file in Photoshop with its layers.

Here's how to import a Photoshop file with layers into an After Effects project:

1. **Create a Photoshop file that has layers, as the image in Figure 30-1 does, and save it in Photoshop format.** Follow these steps to create layers in Photoshop:

   a. **Load Photoshop.**

   b. **Choose File ➪ New to create a new file.**

   c. **In the New dialog box, set the width and height to the size you want your After Effects movie to be.**

   d. **Set the Mode to RGB Color and the Contents to Transparent.**

   e. **Create a background with the painting tools and filters.** You can also scan or digitize one with a digital camcorder.

   f. **Click the Create New Layer icon in the Layers palette or choose New Layer from the Layers palette pop-up menu.** To open the Layers palette, choose Window ➪ Show Layers.

g. **Create an image in the new layer.** You could also copy and paste a digital image into a new layer. If you want, you can copy the Clown.psd file that is in the Chapter 30 folder in the DVD that accompanies the book.

h. **Create another new layer.** Keep creating layers until you have all the layers needed. If you want, you can also use Photoshop's Horizontal Type tool to create text in a layer.

i. **Save the file in Photoshop format.**

2. **Quit Photoshop and load After Effects.**

3. **In After Effects, choose File ➪ New ➪ New Project.** The Project window appears.

4. **Choose File ➪ Import ➪ File.** The Import File dialog box appears.

5. **Locate the Photoshop file you want to import.** Set the Import As pop-up menu to Composition.

6. **Click Open.** In the Project window, folder and composition icons appear in the Project window (see Figure 30-2). You can find the Photoshop file (Party.psd) shown in Figure 30-2 on the DVD that accompanies the book.

   • **To see the Photoshop layers, either double-click the folder or click the triangle.**

   • **To view the layers in the Composition window and Timeline window, double-click the composition icon, which is in the Comp folder that is in the Project window.** Notice that the layers appear in the Composition window and the Timeline window. The layers also appear in the Timeline window in the same order as they did in Photoshop's Layers palette. You don't have to drag each layer to the Timeline window. After Effects automatically places them there.

   • **To decrease or increase the view of the Composition window, choose Zoom out or Zoom in from the View menu.**

Note   To import various Photoshop files as a sequence, create a folder and place the Photoshop files in the folder. Then, in After Effects, choose File ➪ Import ➪ Multiple Files. When the Import Multiple Files dialog box appears, click the first Photoshop file of the sequence; then click the Photoshop Sequence option and click Open. Continue to select files, select the Photoshop Sequence option, and click Open until you have selected all the files. When you are finished, click Done.

After importing a Photoshop file, you can *animate* its layers. When you animate a layer, you either transform it (scale, rotate, or change opacity and/or position), apply an effect (such as distortion), or apply a mask to the entire layer or just a portion.

Note   In Adobe Photoshop, you can use the Modes menu to create composite effects between layers. To display the modes, click the Switches/Modes option at the bottom of the palette until you see the word Mode next to the Source Name column.

Click triangle to expand folder

Folder icon

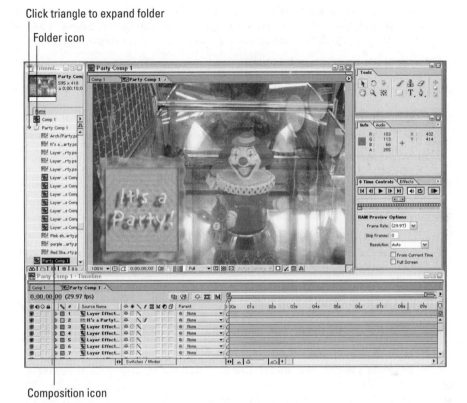

Composition icon

Figure 30-2: "It's a Party" layers shown in After Effects.

Follow these steps to animate Photoshop layers in After Effects:

1. **Click the triangle beside one of the layers in the Timeline window.** When you expand the layer, the Transform option appears.

Note   In order to edit text from Photoshop in After Effects 6.0, you need to first select the Photoshop text layer in the Timeline window in After Effects. Then choose Layer ➪ Convert to Editable Text.

2. **Click the triangle next to Transform.** Notice that the Anchor Point, Position, Scale, Rotation, and Opacity options are visible. You can animate the layer's anchor point, position, scale, rotation, or opacity.

3. **To animate the layer's position, first move the current-time indicator to the beginning of the clip and click the stopwatch icon in front of the word Position.** A keyframe is created.

4. **Move the current-time indicator to the right.**

5. **Change the position of the layer either by adjusting the Position values in the Timeline window or by moving the layer in the Composition window.** After changing the layer position, a new keyframe is created.

6. **To continue animating the position of the layer over time, continue moving the current-time indicator to the right and then move the layer in the Composition window.** Another keyframe is created.

7. **When you are done, click the Transform triangle.**

8. **To animate a layer using an effect, choose a layer in the Timeline window.**

9. **Move the current-time indicator to the beginning of the clip.**

10. **Click the Effect menu and choose an effect.**

11. **Click the Effects triangle in the Timeline window.** The name of the effect you choose appears onscreen. In front of the effect name is a stopwatch icon. Click the stopwatch icon to create a keyframe.

12. **Move the current-time indicator to the right. Then alter the effect in the Effect Controls window.** Notice that another keyframe is created.

13. **Again, move the current-time indicator and alter the effect. Another keyframe is created.**

14. **When you are done, click the Effects triangle.**

15. **Choose File ➪ Save to save your work as an After Effects project.**

16. **To preview your work, choose Composition ➪ Preview ➪ RAM Preview.**

To export your work as a QuickTime movie, choose File ➪ Export ➪ QuickTime Movie. In the Save As dialog box that appears, name the file. In the Movie Settings dialog box, make the necessary adjustments and click OK to save the file. After you've saved your work as a QuickTime movie, if you want, you can import it into a Premiere Pro project as you would any other file.

Importing and Animating Illustrator Files

In this section, you learn how to import an Illustrator file with layers into After Effects and animate it. We used this technique to create a project filled with butterflies.

Here's how to import an Illustrator file with layers into After Effects:

1. **Using Illustrator, create a file with layers, like the one shown in Figure 30-3, and save it in Illustrator format.** Here is a summary of the steps:

   a. **Load Illustrator.**

   b. **Choose File ➪ New to create a new file.** In the New dialog box, name the file and then set the Color mode to RGB Color.

c. **Set the artboard width and height to your After Effects project size pixel dimensions.**

d. **To create the Butterfly project, click the Paintbrush tool in the toolbox.**

e. **Choose Window ⇨ Brush Libraries ⇨ Animal Shapes.**

f. **Click the butterfly shape.**

g. **Click in the artboard area to create a butterfly.** Click again and again.

h. **Choose Window ⇨ Layers to open the Layers palette.**

i. **To create a new layer, click the Create New Layer icon in the Layers palette or choose New Layer from the Layers palette pop-up menu.**

j. **In the new layer, click the artboard to create a butterfly in the new layer.** Then create another new layer and create another butterfly. Repeat the process until you have nine layers with butterflies, as shown in Figure 30-3.

k. **Create another new layer.** This should be your tenth layer. In this layer use the Pencil tool to create a curve.

l. **Create some type using the Path Type tool.** We typed "Summer time brings butterflies" for the image in Figure 30-3.

m. **Save your file in Illustrator format.**

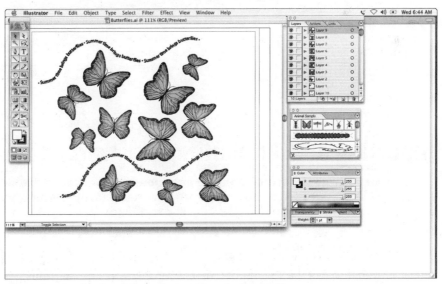

Figure 30-3: The Butterfly project as seen in Adobe Illustrator.

2. **To import the Illustrator file, choose File ⇨ Import ⇨ File. In the Import File dialog box, set the Import As pop-up menu to Composition. Locate the Illustrator file you want to import and choose Import.**

The Adobe Illustrator file (butterflies.ai) seen in Figure 30-3 can be found in the Chapter 30 folder that is on the DVD that accompanies the book.

Notice that a folder icon and composition icon appear in the Project window as shown in Figure 30-4.

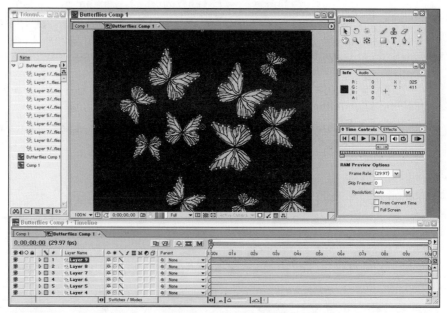

Figure 30-4: The Butterfly project as seen in Adobe After Effects.

3. **To see the Illustrator layers, either double-click the folder or click the triangle. To view the layers in the Composition and Timeline windows, double-click the preview in the Project window.** Notice that the layers appear in the Composition window and the Timeline window.

4. **To decrease or increase the view of the Composition window, choose Zoom out or Zoom in.** The layers also appear in the Timeline window in the same order as they appeared in Illustrator's Layers palette. You don't have to drag each layer to the Timeline window — After Effects automatically places them there.

5. **To animate the Illustrator layers, click the triangle of one of the Timeline window's layers.** You can choose to animate that layer's masks or effects or to transform the layer itself.

6. **Try animating the butterflies by rotating, moving, and scaling them and applying effects over time.**

7. **Choose File ⇨ Save to save your work.**

Creating and Animating Type Using After Effects

In After Effects 6.0, you create type either by directly using the Horizontal Type tool in the Composition window or by choosing Layer ⇨ New ⇨ Text. After Effects recognizes three different types of text: Basic Text, Numbers, and Path Text. When you select the Basic Text option, you can create horizontal or vertical text. You can also use the Basic Text option to animate one letter of a word at a time. The Numbers option enables you to create numbers. Path Text creates text on a path.

Because you cannot create type on a path or around a circle in Premiere Pro, the following example covers creating path type. Figure 30-5 shows a frame from the Path Type project along with the Composition window. We used the Rotate option, found in the Timeline window, to animate text around the curve to create the text in this example.

Following the Path Type project example, there is an example on how to animate horizontal text using After Effects 6.0's new Animate Text command.

Figure 30-5: A frame from the Path Type project shown in the Composition window.

Follow these steps to create and animate path text in After Effects:

1. **Choose File ⇨ New ⇨ New Project.** Instantly, the Project window appears.

2. **Choose Composition ⇨ New Composition.** The Composition Settings dialog box appears (see Figure 30-6).

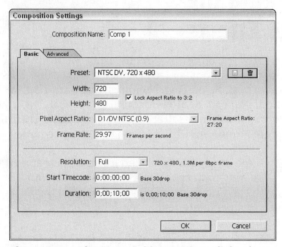

Figure 30-6: The Composition Settings dialog box.

3. **Name your composition and then choose the width and height that you'll be using.**

4. **Click OK to create a new composition and to display the Timeline window.**

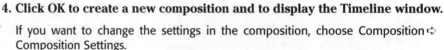

Note   If you want to change the settings in the composition, choose Composition ⇨ Composition Settings.

5. **To import a background clip, choose File ⇨ Import ⇨ File to import a file that will work as a background for the path text.**

   To create your own background, you need to create a new solid layer.

6. **Choose Layer ⇨ New ⇨ Solid. When the Solid Footage Settings dialog box appears (see Figure 30-7), type a name for your layer in the Solid Footage Settings dialog box. Leave the width and height alone and click OK to create a new solid.** (Usually the width and height are the same as the composition.)

   Notice that a new solid layer appears in the Timeline window. The new solid layer also takes up the entire size of the Composition window. After creating a new solid layer, you can apply different effects. We applied the Effect ⇨ PS Tiles command and the Effect ⇨ Stylize ⇨ Mosaic command to create a background for our project.

Figure 30-7: The Solid Footage Settings dialog box.

7. **If you imported a background file, drag the background file from the Project window to the Timeline window.** The background file immediately turns into a layer.

8. **Move the current-time indicator to the position in the Timeline in which you want to apply path text.**

9. **Choose Layer ➪ New ➪ Text to create new text layer.**

10. **Choose Effect ➪ Text ➪ Path Text to create text on a path.**

11. **In the Path Text dialog box, shown in Figure 30-8, enter some text in the text field and pick a font.**

12. **Click OK to close the dialog box and view your text on a curve in the Composition window.** The Effect Controls window appears at the same time as the text on the curve appears in the Composition window (see Figure 30-9).

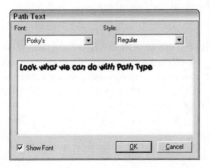

Figure 30-8: Type some text in the Path Text dialog box.

Note   If you can't see the text, you may need to click the background file and drag it below the text icon in the Timeline window.

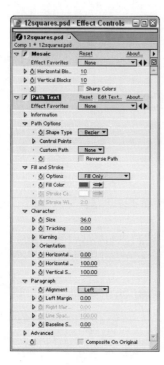

Figure 30-9: You can use the Effect Controls window to adjust the text in the composition.

13. **Use the Effect Controls window to change the size, tracking (letter spacing), fill, and stroke color or to edit the text you just wrote.**

- **To change the size of the text, click and drag the Size slider in the Effect Controls window.**

- **To edit the text on the curve, click the word Edit Text at the top of the Effect Controls window.** When the Path Type dialog box appears, you can edit the text. Click and drag over the letters you want to change.

- **To choose whether you want your text to be filled, stroked, or be filled with a stroke surrounding it, click the Options pop-up menu in the Fill and Stroke section.** To change the fill or stroke color, click the color swatch next to the word Fill Color or Stroke Color. When the Color dialog box appears, pick a color and then click OK. You can also use the Eyedropper tool to change a color. To change the fill or stroke color to the color you've selected with the Eyedropper, click the Eyedropper next to either the word Fill Color or Stroke Color and then click a color from the background file. To change the stroke color's width, click the Stroke Width option and then type a number.

- **Clicking the Shape Type pop-up menu lets you choose whether you want the shape of the text to be on a Bézier, Circle, Loop, or Line.** Click the circles to adjust the type path shape.

Note If the Effect Controls window is not onscreen, you can display it by first clicking a layer you want and then choosing Effect ⇨ Effect Controls.

14. **Choose Circle from the Shape Type pop-up menu in the Effect Controls window to have the text appear on a circle.**

15. **To rotate text around a curve and animate it, you can click the triangle in front of the Path Text layer in the Timeline window to display its features and click the Transform triangle to display the Rotation option.** Then follow these steps:

    Move the current-time indicator to the Timeline's beginning and click the stopwatch icon next to the Rotation option to create your first keyframe. Then move the current-time indicator over on the Timeline and click the degree amount next to the Rotation option. When the Rotation dialog box appears, type a degree amount and click OK to create another keyframe. Continue moving the current-time indicator on the Timeline and changing the Rotation degree to create keyframes. Continue until you have a number of keyframes or until you've created a complete rotation.

16. **Choose File ⇨ Save to save your work. To preview your work, choose Composition ⇨ Preview ⇨ RAM Preview.**

17. **To import this project into Premiere Pro, create a QuickTime movie and choose File ⇨ Export ⇨ QuickTime Movie.** In the Save dialog box that appears, name the file. In the Movie Settings dialog box, make the necessary adjustments and click OK to save the file.

Follow these steps to create horizontal text and animate it using After Effects 6.0's new Animate Text command:

1. **Move the current-time indicator to the position in the Timeline in which you want to apply horizontal text.**

2. **Select the Horizontal Type Tool from the Tools palette and start typing in the Composition window.** As soon as you add text to the Composition window, a text layer appears in the Timeline window. Use the Character palette to change the font and font size.

3. **Move the current-time indicator to the position in the Timeline in which you want animate the horizontal text.**

4. **Choose Animation ⇨ Animate Text. Then choose the option you want to animate.** You can animate the text's position, you can scale the text, and you can rotate it or change its color. Once you've chosen an animation option, the Animator option appears in the Timeline window. Click the stopwatch next to the Animator option to create a keyframe.

5. **Move the current-time indicator to the right and adjust the Animator option.** Another keyframe is created. Continue this step as many times as you need to.

Working with Motion Paths

After Effects provides more control of motion effects than does Premiere Pro. In After Effects, you can create motion along a path by moving an object along the object's anchor point. When moving an object along its anchor point, you are essentially using a path similar to Illustrator and Photoshop paths. Figure 30-10 shows a butterfly that's been animated in After Effects using its anchor point. Notice that the path is visible in the Layer window.

Cross-Reference For more information on using the Motion controls in Premiere Pro, refer to Chapter 17.

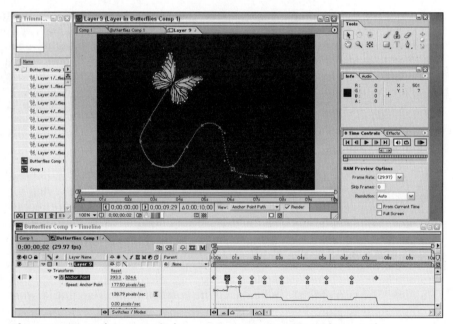

Figure 30-10: In the Layer window, you can see a motion path created.

Animating with anchor points

Here's how to animate an object in After Effects using its anchor point:

1. **Load or create a new project in After Effects.**

2. **Import a Photoshop or Illustrator object.** If you want, use the butterflies.ai file from the companion DVD's Chapter 30 folder. When importing the file, be sure to select Composition from the Import As pop-up menu in the Import File dialog box. That way, all the layers from the file will be imported.

3. **Double-click the Comp file in the Project window to display the file's layers in the Timeline window. Then select a layer from the Timeline window.**

4. **Expand the layer by clicking the triangle next to the layer in the Timeline window.** The Transform options are displayed.

5. **Click the Transform triangle to display the Transform options.**

6. **Move the current-time indicator to the Timeline's beginning, or to where you want to start animating your object.**

7. **Click the stopwatch icon next to the words Anchor Point.**

8. **Double-click the layer in the Timeline window to display the Layer window.**

9. **In the Layer window, choose Anchor Point Path from the View pop-up menu.**

10. **In the Layer window, click the circle and move it to where you want the path to begin.**

11. **Move the current-time indicator to a new position in the Timeline and then move the circle again to start creating the motion path.** Continue moving the current-time indicator and move the circle in succession until you've finished creating your motion path. To edit the motion path, you can move the layer keyframe, direction handles, or direction lines.

    Depending upon the path you've created, you may want to use the Layer ➪ Transform ➪ Auto-Orient Rotation command. The Auto-Orient Rotation command enables you to rotate an object along a path so that the object is facing a different direction.

12. **Preview the motion you just created.** You can choose one of three commands:

    • Composition ➪ Preview ➪ Motion with Trails (fastest)

    • Composition ➪ Preview ➪ Wireframe Preview

    • Composition ➪ Preview ➪ RAM Preview (slowest)

13. **If you want to keep your work, save it.**

Animating with Sketch a Motion

The Sketch a Motion option enables you to draw your path freehand.

Here's how to animate using Sketch a Motion:

1. **Load or create a new project in After Effects.**

2. **Import a Photoshop or Illustrator object.** If you want, use the butterfies.ai file from the companion DVD's Chapter 30 folder. When importing the file, make sure to select Composition from the Import As pop-up menu that is in the Import File dialog box. That way, all the layers from the file will be imported.

3. **Double-click on the Comp file in the Project window to display the file's layers in the Timeline window. Select a layer from the Timeline window.**

4. **Choose Window ➪ Motion Sketch to display the Motion Sketch window.**

5. **Click the Start Capture button in the Motion Sketch window.**

6. **Move the cursor to the Composition window.**

7. **Press and hold the mouse button while you draw your motion path.** As soon as you let go of the mouse button, After Effects stops creating the motion sketch. The motion sketch is displayed in Figure 30-11.

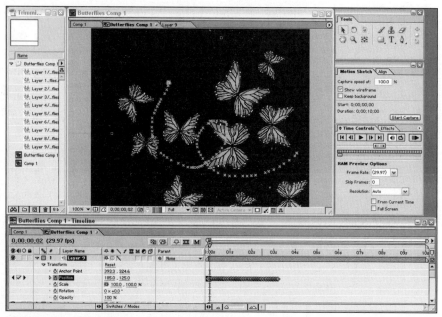

Figure 30-11: The motion sketch appears in the Composition window. The motion sketch is created with the Motion Sketch palette.

8. **Click the triangle in front of the layer you have selected in the Timeline window.**

9. **Click the triangle in front of the word Transform.** Notice that the Motion Sketch command has created keyframes in front of the Position section of the Timeline window.

10. **Preview the motion.** Choose the Composition ➪ Preview ➪ Motion with Trails command, the Composition ➪ Preview ➪ Wireframe Preview command, or the Composition ➪ Preview ➪ RAM Preview command.

Creating a Composite Video Clip

You can use After Effects to create a *composite video clip*. A composite video clip consists of a few video clips displayed side by side on the screen at the same time, as shown in Figure 30-12. To create the Venice project illustrated in Figure 30-12, we placed two video clips side by side and then added some text below the two clips. If your project called for it, you could have three or four video clips. The video clips that you use to create a composite clip can be Premiere Pro projects, video captured from your digital camcorder, or even stock video clips.

Figure 30-12: The first frame from the Venice project is an example of a composite clip.

Here's how to create a composite video clip in After Effects:

1. **Choose File ➪ New ➪ New Project.**

2. **Choose Composition ➪ New Composition.** The Composition Settings dialog box appears.

3. **In the Composition Settings dialog box, name your composition.** Pick the correct frame size for your project's width and height.

4. **Click OK to create a new composition.**

5. **Choose File ➪ Import ➪ Multiple Files.** The Import Multiple File dialog box appears.

6. **In the Import File dialog box, set Import As option to Footage.**

7. **Select the video clips and then click Import.** If you want, you can use the clips shown in Figure 30-12 (gondola.mov and cruising.mov), which are found in the Chapter 30 folder on the DVD that accompanies this book.

8. **Drag the video clips you imported from the Project window to the Composite window.** If you want your composite to appear as it does in Figure 30-12, place the video clips so that they are diagonally across from each other. You can also place two clips side by side or on top of each other on the left side of the Composition window and place text to the right of the video clips. You can also fill the Composite window with video clips and have no text.

9. **If you want your composite to include text, as shown in Figure 30-12, first create a new text layer.** To create a text layer, first click the Composite window to activate the layer. Choose Layer ⇨ New ⇨ Text.

10. **With the new text layer onscreen, type the text and pick a font.** As you type, notice that in the Timelinewindow, the Type layer is selected.

11. **Use the Character window to edit your text.**

12. **To bevel and add a drop shadow to your text, choose Effect ⇨ Perspective ⇨ Bevel Alpha, and Effect ⇨ Perspective ⇨ Drop Shadow.**

13. **To create the background that appears behind the text, as shown in Figure 30-12, you first need to create another solid layer.** Choose Layer ⇨ New ⇨ Solid. In the Solid Footage Settings dialog box, click the Eyedropper tool and pick a color from one of the video clips. This is the color that appears in the solid. Leave the other settings as they are. If you want, name the solid. Click OK to create the new solid. When the new solid appears in the Timeline window, it appears in front of the text you just created. If you want to create a special effect for the background, use one of the commands found in the Effect menu. We used the Effect ⇨ Noise ⇨ Fractal Noise command.

14. **To see the text, click the new solid layer in the Timeline window and drag it below the text.** Figure 30-13 shows the Timeline windows for the Venice composite project.

15. **Choose File ⇨ Save to save your work.**

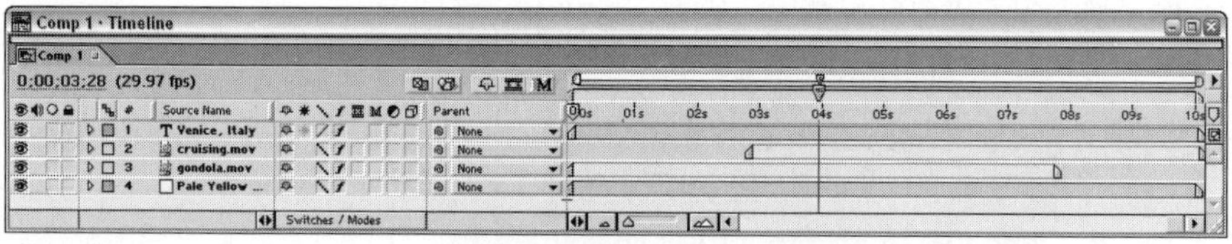

Figure 30-13: The Timeline window for the Venice composite project.

Tip You can save a frame of your After Effects project as a Photoshop file, either with or without layers. To do so, choose Composition ➪ Save Frame As ➪ Photoshop Layers or Composition ➪ Save Frame As ➪ File.

16. **To preview your work in RAM, choose Composition ➪ Preview ➪ RAM Preview.**

17. **To export your work as a QuickTime movie, choose File ➪ Export ➪ QuickTime Movie.** When the Save As dialog box appears, name your movie and click Save. When the Movie Settings dialog box appears, click the Video Settings button to set the compression, color depth, and frames per second. Click the Filter button if you want to apply a filter to your clip. Beware of changing the Size button. Either leave the size as is, or change your movie's size. You can also adjust sound settings and choose whether you want to stream for the Web. Make the necessary adjustments and click OK to create a QuickTime movie.

Note To export your movie in a different format, choose Composition ➪ Make Movie. In the Render Queue dialog box, click the triangle in front of the Composition being rendered. Next, click Lossless, which is next to the Output Module option. In the Output Module Settings dialog box, click the Format pop-up menu and choose a format. Available format options include Animated GIF, BMP Sequence, Cineon Sequence, ElectricImage IMAGE, FLC/FLI, Filmstrip, IFF Sequence, JPEG Sequence, MPS, PCX Sequence, PICT Sequence, PNG Sequence, Photoshop Sequence, Pixar Sequence, QuickTime Movie, SGI Sequence, TIFF Sequence, and TARGA Sequence.

After you've created a QuickTime movie, you can import the QuickTime movie into a Premiere Pro project for further editing.

Summary

Although Adobe Premiere Pro features many video effects, Adobe After Effects 6.0 provides more motion and compositing effects.

✦ You can import a Premiere Pro movie directly into After Effects 6.0.

✦ You can animate text over time in After Effects.

✦ You can open multiple QuickTime movies into After Effects.

✦   ✦   ✦

Appendixes

What's on the DVD

This appendix provides you with information on the contents of the DVD that accompanies this book. For the latest and greatest information, please refer to the ReadMe file located at the root of the DVD. Here is what you will find:

✦ System requirements

✦ Using the DVD with Windows XP

✦ What's on the DVD

✦ Troubleshooting

System Requirements

Make sure that your computer meets Adobe Premiere Pro's minimum system requirements listed in this section. If your computer doesn't match up to most of these requirements, you may have a problem using the contents of the DVD.

For Windows XP:

✦ PC with Intel Pentium III 800 Mhz processor or faster (Pentium 4, 3 GHz is recommended).

✦ At least 256MB of RAM installed on your computer; for best performance, 1GB or more is recommended.

✦ Microsoft Windows XP Professional or XP Home Edition with Service Pack 1 installed.

✦ 800MB of available hard-disk space for installation. Additional hard-disk space is required for project files.

✦ A DVD drive is required for installation. (A DVD recordable drive [DVD-R/RW+R/RW] is required to use Premiere Pro's Export to DVD function.)

Using the DVD with Windows XP

To install the items from the DVD to your hard drive, follow these steps:

1. **Insert the DVD into your computer's DVD drive.**

   A window will appear with the following options: Install, Explore, PDFs, Links, and Exit.

   - **Install:** Gives you the option to install the supplied software and/or the author-created samples on the DVD.

   - **Explore:** Allows you to view the contents of the DVD in its directory structure.

   - **PDFs:** Lets you access the electronic version of this book.

   - **Links:** Opens a hyperlinked page of Web sites.

   - **Exit:** Closes the autorun window.

If you do not have autorun enabled or if the autorun window does not appear, follow these steps to access the DVD:

1. **Click Start ⇨ Run.**

2. **In the dialog box that appears, type *d*:\setup\setup.exe, where *d* is the letter of your DVD drive.** This will bring up the autorun window previously described.

3. **Choose the Install, Explore, PDFs, Links, or Exit option from the menu (see preceding list for description of these options).**

What's on the DVD

The following sections provide a summary of the software and other materials you'll find on the DVD.

Tutorial files

In the Tutorial Projects folder are still images, video, and sound clips for following along with the exercises in the book. You can click Explore from within the DVD interface to browse these images on the DVD. The still images are in Photoshop, Illustrator, JPEG, and PICT file formats. The digital video clips are in either AVI or QuickTime file format. Many of the files used are from Digital Vision, providers of royalty-free still and moving images. The sound files are in either AIFF or Wav format. The files are divided into chapter folders that are associated with the chapters in the book. Please note that the images in the Tutorial Projects folder are for instructional purposes only. They are not for commercial use.

Software trials

On the DVD are various software tryouts from Adobe Systems. They are Adobe Encore DVD, Adobe After Effects, Adobe Photoshop, Adobe Illustrator, Adobe GoLive, and Adobe Acrobat Reader. Note that Adobe does not provide technical support for the software tryouts. Also included on the DVD are Discreet cleaner XL, Macromedia Director MX, and Macromedia Flash MX 2004.

For more information on these software trials, go to these Web sites: www.adobe.com, www.discreet.com, and www.macromedia.com.

Note We have included the tryout version of Premiere Pro (Adobe Systems, Inc.). Use Adobe Premiere Pro to edit and manipulate your video clips.

✦ **Adobe After Effects (Adobe Systems, Inc.).** The tryout version of Adobe After Effects is a 30-day tryout version. Use Adobe After Effects to create digital video special effects.

✦ **Adobe Encore DVD (Adobe Systems, Inc.).** The tryout version of Adobe Encore DVD is a 30-day tryout version. Use Adobe Encore DVD to for DVD authoring.

✦ **Adobe GoLive (Adobe Systems, Inc.).** The tryout version of Adobe GoLive is a 30-day tryout version. Use Adobe GoLive to create content for the Web.

✦ **Adobe Illustrator (Adobe Systems, Inc.).** The tryout version does not allow you to save, print, or export your work. Use Adobe Illustrator to create vector graphics.

✦ **Adobe Photoshop (Adobe Systems, Inc.).** We have included the tryout version of Adobe Photoshop. Use Adobe Photoshop to edit digital images.

✦ **Discreet cleaner XL (Discreet, Inc.).** The trial version of Discreet cleaner is a 30-day trial version. Use Discreet cleaner to optimize your digital video.

✦ **Macromedia Director MX (Macromedia, Inc.).** The trial version of Macromedia Director is a 30-day trial version. Use Macromedia Director to author your presentations.

✦ **Macromedia Flash MX 2004 (Macromedia, Inc.).** The trial version of Macromedia Flash is a 30-day trial version. Use Macromedia Flash to create interactive Web experiences.

Shareware programs are fully functional, trial versions of copyrighted programs. If you like particular programs, register with their authors for a nominal fee and receive licenses, enhanced versions, and technical support. *Freeware programs* are copyrighted games, applications, and utilities that are free for personal use. Unlike shareware, these programs do not require a fee or provide technical support. *GNU software* is governed by its own license, which is included inside the folder of the GNU product. See the GNU license for more details.

Trial, demo, or evaluation versions are usually limited either by time or functionality (such as being unable to save projects). Some trial versions are very sensitive to system date changes. If you alter your computer's date, the programs will "time out" and will no longer be functional.

PDF files

Each chapter in the book has been converted to a PDF file. You can load the files onto your computer and search for specific topics as you work with Premiere Pro. You will need to install a copy of Adobe's *Acrobat Reader* (also included on this DVD) to view these files.

Troubleshooting

If you have difficulty installing or using any of the materials on the companion DVD, try the following solutions:

✦ **Turn off any antivirus software that you may have running.** Installers sometimes mimic virus activity and can make your computer incorrectly believe that it is being infected by a virus. (Be sure to turn the antivirus software back on later.)

✦ **Close all running programs.** The more programs you're running, the less memory is available to other programs. Installers also typically update files and programs; if you keep other programs running, installation may not work properly.

✦ **Reference the ReadMe file:** Please refer to the ReadMe file located at the root of the DVD for the latest product information at the time of publication.

If you still have trouble with the DVD, please call the Customer Care phone number: (800) 762-2974. Outside the United States, call (317) 572-3994. You can also contact Customer Service by e-mail at techsupdum@wiley.com. Wiley Publishing, Inc., will provide technical support only for installation and other general quality control items; for technical support on the applications themselves, consult the program's vendor or author.

✦   ✦   ✦

Places to Visit on the Web

Y ou can use the following list of Web resources as a guide to digital video software and hardware manufacturers and distributors. Also included are a variety of resources that should prove valuable to digital video producers.

Software

www.apple.com

This site offers access to Apple's QuickTime site as well as useful information about MPEG-4 (`www.apple.com/mpeg4`).

www.abobe.com

Check Adobe's site for Premiere upgrades and tech support. The site also includes Premiere tutorials, as well as samples from professionals in the digital video field. Be sure to sign up for an e-mail newsletter that provides updates and important Premiere technical information.

www.corel.com

Go to this Web site to find out more about Corel Painter, discussed in Chapter 16.

www.discreet.com

Find out more about Discreet Cleaner (a tryout version is included on the *Adobe Premiere Pro Bible* DVD) as well as other Discreet programs for editing and creating special effects and animation.

www.macromedia.com

This site is maintained by Macromedia, the makers of Director, Authorware, and Flash. Many Premiere digital movies wind up in Director and Authorware projects. Download free trial software at this site, which includes lots of tech notes for Macromedia projects.

www.microsoft.com/windows/windowsmedia

Get updates on the latest Microsoft Windows Media and streaming video products.

www.quicktime.com

Download the latest version of QuickTime or upgrade to QuickTime pro. The site includes developer and licensing information as well as links to many sites using QuickTime.

www.realnetworks.com

Find out about RealNetworks audio and video streaming products. Download the latest plug-ins.

General Resources

www.adobe.com/support/forums/main.html

A users group forum for Adobe products. You can ask questions or scroll through other users' questions and answers.

www.aftra.com

This is the American Federation of Television and Radio Artists. Here you can find out about using union talent, contacts, and industry news.

www.dmnforums.com

DMN Forums has forums for various products, including Adobe Premiere Pro. On this site, you can also find newsletters that contain the information about digital media.

www.dv.com

This is the digital video Web magazine, an excellent source of hardware and software information, as well as technical articles. It features news, tutorials, and a buyer's guide. The site enables you to search back issues for product information and technical articles.

www.dvpa.com

This is the Web site for the Digital Video Producers Association. Membership enables access to thousands of stock clips available online for instant download.

www.digitalmedia.net

This site is a hub for accessing multiple sites about digital media hardware, software, and production.

www.ieee.com

This is the Web site for the Institute of Electricians and Electronics Engineers. It contains information on products and services for engineers.

www.videomaker.com

Web site for Videomaker magazine. You'll find articles on video as well as online workshops.

Hardware

www.adstech.com

Check out this site for info on the ADS Pyro video card. Here you can purchase products and download drivers.

www.apple.com

Virtually all new Macs include FireWire ports for transferring digital video directly to desktop or laptop. Purchase a Mac here or find out the latest from Apple's tech support library.

www.canon.com

At this site, you can find out about Canon DV cameras and other products.

www.dell.com

Several Dell computers include digital video cards. Purchase a computer or video board for your computer.

www.digitalvoodoo.net

Find out more about the Iridium HD video board, which was designed for high-end compositing.

www.hewlett-packard.com

Find out more about Hewlett-Packard's products, from desktops and workstations to monitors and from projectors to printers.

www.epson.com

Learn more about Epson's color printers.

www.guitarcenter.com

This Web site has information on music hardware and software.

www.harman-multimedia.com

Learn more about powered satellite speakers and subwoofers for your computer.

www.hp.com

At this site, you can learn more about Hewlett-Packard's color printers.

www.jvc.com

Details about JVC professional and consumer video equipment are available at this site.

www.matrox.com

Matrox is the creator of video boards and video capture boards (Millennium, Marvel, and so on). Obtain prices and compatibility information.

www.olympus.com/digital

At this site, you can learn more about Olympus's digital cameras.

www.pinnaclesys.com

Find out about tech specs for Pinnacle's PC video boards and editing systems, and also broadcast-quality equipment.

www.shure.com

This site includes information on Shure's audio products as well as downloadable technical guides.

www.sony.com

Most Sony laptops include i.LINK digital video ports that conform to the IEEE 1394 standard. Find out about the latest Sony computers, monitors, digital camcorders, and professional video equipment.

www.wacom.com

At this site, you can learn more about Wacom's pen tablets and Wacom's Cintiq interactive pen.

Stock Image, Sound, and Video Clips

www.digitalvisiononline.com

Many of the video and sound clips in this book are from Digital Vision. At its site, you can learn more about its products.

www.smartsound.com

Visit this site to learn more about stock sound clips.

✦　　✦　　✦

Licensing QuickTime

If you plan to distribute a Premiere Pro movie on a CD-ROM as a QuickTime movie, you probably want to include QuickTime along with your production on the CD. Because QuickTime is available at no charge from Apple's Web site, you may be tempted to just copy the QuickTime installers to your CD. However, to legally distribute QuickTime, you must obtain a software license from Apple.

Obtaining a license is easy and usually free of charge. To obtain a license, start by visiting the QuickTime Web site, www.quicktime.com. On the main QuickTime page, click the Developer link. Under ADC resources, click the Software Licensing link.

Doing this opens up a page describing why you need to license Apple's software products. Next, click the Agreements On Line link and then click the QuickTime choice. This brings you to http://developer.apple.com/mkt/swl/quicktime.html.

Next, you need to download a PDF file that includes the licensing contract and licensing information. Most multimedia producers need to click the QuickTime Software SDA Agreement link. If you need to license QuickTime within your business or organization, click the QuickTime Site License link.

Print the PDF forms, fill them out, and then send them to Apple at the following address:

Apple Computer, Inc.
Software Licensing M/S 198-SWL
2420 Ridgepoint Drive
Austin, TX 78754

◆   ◆   ◆

The Digital Video Recording Studio

Setting up a small studio to create desktop digital video movies often involves the purchase of computer, video, and sound equipment. For digital video producers, editors, and graphic designers without a technical background, evaluating hardware can be a frustrating and confusing undertaking.

This appendix provides a hardware overview, describing some of the hardware you may consider purchasing. The sections here are meant to provide you with a general idea of the hardware components that you may need to purchase or rent when shooting a video production. For a thorough analysis of using digital video hardware, you might check several resources: Web sites of hardware manufacturers (such as www.sel.sony.com, www.canon.com, or www.apple.com), magazine Web sites (www.DV.com), or publishers of books specializing in DV and file production (www.focalpress.com). Another good resource is your local library. Many video books written over the past 20 years include video shooting, sound, and lighting chapters that are still relevant today. Finally, you may want to investigate television production workshops and classes provided by local colleges and universities.

Computers

For most Premiere Pro users, the most important element in their digital studio is their computer. The general rule for running Premiere Pro is to get the fastest system you can afford.

The minimum system requirements for Premiere Pro include the following. Please remember that these are the minimum specifications. They may not be adequate for your needs if you are outputting professional video productions.

Note that digital video typically consumes 13GB per hour of footage.

Windows requirements

✦ 800 MHz Pentium-III processor (Pentium 4 3.02 GHz recommended)

✦ Microsoft Windows XP Pro or XP Home Edition with Service Pack 1

✦ 256MB RAM or more recommended

✦ 256-color video display adapter

✦ 800MB of available hard disk space for installation

✦ For DV: 1394 interface and dedicated large-capacity 7200 RPM UDMA 66 IDE or SCSI hard disk or disk array

✦ CD-ROM drive (DVD-R/RW+R/RW required to export to DVD)

✦ For third-party capture cards: Adobe Premiere-certified capture card

✦ 1024 x 768 32-bit color display adapter

✦ Optional: ASIO audio hardware device: surround speaker system for 5.1 audio playback

Processing speed

A computer system's central processing unit (CPU) and the speed of its hard drive (or disks) determine its overall speed when working with multimedia projects.

Many consider the computer's CPU to be the brains of the system. Modern processors, such as the Pentium 4, are faster and more sophisticated than the Pentium III chips. Chip speed is measured in *megahertz* (MHz) — a million clock cycles per second — where a higher number indicates a faster chip. Thus, a 900 MHz chip is faster than an 800 MHz chip. As this book goes to press, 3-gigahertz (GHz) processors and higher are the state of the art in processors.

Coprocessors

Two CPUs are better than one. Premiere Pro, unlike many computer programs, takes full advantage of computer systems with two or more processors. Preview rendering speeds should be dramatically increased with multiple processors.

Hard drive speed

Hard drive speed is generally evaluated by the revolutions per minute, seek speed, and data transfer rate. Most of the faster hard drives provide a rotational speed of at least 7200 RPM (revolutions per minute). Some high-capacity drives have a rotation speed of 10,000 RPM.

Seek speed essentially measures the time it takes to seek out the section of the hard drive that it needs to read to or write to. Seek time is measured in milliseconds. Thus, a seek time of 8.5 ms is faster than 9.5 ms. A hard drive's transfer rate determines how fast the drive can transfer data. A High Capacity UltraSCSI (Small Computer Systems Interface) drive may be able to support a transfer rate of 320MB per second. The actual sustained transfer rate of the hard drive (how long it takes a hard drive to save data to its platters) will be slower. For instance, the sustained data rate of Maxtor's Atlas 19K III Ultra 320 is 55MB/sec — certainly fast enough for video capture (to capture video, Adobe recommends a minimum sustained transfer rate of 3MB per second, preferably a sustained transfer rate of 6 MB per second). Note that the actual video transfer rates are probably about half the maximum transfer rates of a hard drive.

If you are capturing video, it's also recommended that you maintain a separate hard disk just for video capture, and keep the disk defragmented. If you're interested in finding more about hard drive storage and hard drive storage rates go to www.storagereview.com.

IEEE boards

Most high-end PCs are now sold with built-in IEEE 1394 cards. The IEEE standard has been pioneered by Apple computer, which calls the IEEE 1394 standard FireWire (Sony calls it i.LINK). IEEE 1394 ports enable you to copy digitized audio and video from a DV camcorder or DV tape recorder directly to your computer. The actual digitization process takes place in the camera. The IEEE 1394 port enables the transfer of data at high speeds from the camcorder to the computer, or from computer to hard disk. The top transfer rate for the IEEE 1394/FireWire standard is a blistering 400MB per second. FireWire supports up to 63 connected devices and cables up to 14 feet long.

If your computer does not have an IEEE port, you may be able to purchase an add-in IEEE card for $50, and sometimes even less. The IEEE 1394 port can also be used to attach a hard disk or CD-ROM recorder. Prices of IEEE 1394/FireWire peripherals have been dropping steadily. You should be able to purchase a 30GB drive for less than $500. (Drives for portables are more expensive.)

Companies such as Pinnacle Systems and Miro sell high-end IEEE 1394 video boards, which can cost over $1,000. High-end DV cards usually enable you to export files in MPEG-2 format. MPEG-2 is a high-compression video format that provides extremely high-quality output. Most MPEG-2 boards enable you to export your files to DVD-ROM format. A further benefit of high-end cards is that most processing chips are built into the cards and, therefore, can create and/or render digital effects at high speeds.

Video cards

A third-party video card can speed the display of video effects in real time and often improve image quality. While you're taking a break from your video production work, these cards also speed the processing of 3D games. Newer, faster boards are AGP, Accelerated Graphics Port, which can deliver high-performance graphics to Pentium-based motherboards. One of the chief advantages of the AGP bus is that it delivers four times the bandwidth of the PCI bus. (The PCI, peripheral component interconnect, is a high-performance system that handles the transfer of data from the CPU to expansion slots. It is standard on most computers.) Furthermore, the AGP bus reduces bottlenecks between the computer's CPU and RAM, providing very high transfer of graphics data.

If you're interested in AGP boards, check out Radeon9700 Pro AGP, which retails for under $400. On its manufacturer's Web site (www.ati.com), the card is championed as the "world's fastest and most advanced graphics board." According to the manufacturer (ATI), the 9700 Pro can process eight pixels simultaneously, twice as many as competing products. If you are looking for a lower-priced card, take a look at PNY's Verto GeForce4 Ti4600 AGP card, which retails for about $300 or less. (See www.pny.com for more details.)

Go to www.intel.com/technology/agp for a technical review of AGP technology.

RAID arrays

To help attain extremely high transfer rates, many multimedia producers have installed RAID array systems, in which data is shared among several hard drives. RAID systems (Redundant Array of Independent Disks) can split the data transfer over two or more hard disks in a procedure known as *striping*. Because the computer can read and write from multiple drives, transfer rates are increased. Many RAID systems use Ultra-SCSI connections (IDE-RAID systems are also available), which provide faster transfer than standard Mac and PC ATA connections or standard SCSI connections.

Peripheral Storage Devices

As you work with digitized video and sound, you are consuming large amounts of storage space. Where do you store clips and sounds that you no longer need to access directly from your hard disks? One of the most common storage solutions is to use a DLT (Digital Linear Tape) or Super DLT drive. DLT tape drives can store several gigabytes of data to over a 100GB. For instance, Quantum's DLT1 stores 40GB at 3MB per second. Quantum's SDLT 220 can store 110GB at a transfer rate of 11MB per second (if compression is used, it can store approximately twice is much data). Apart from using DLT tapes as backup drives, they can also be used to master DVDs. Quantum, IBM, Hewlett-Packard, and Dell all sell DLT drives. Many companies that sell DLTs use Quantum drives. You can find more information about DLTs at www.quantum.com/AM/products/dlt.

For long-term storage, yet slower recording and slower loading, you can use a CD/DVD recorder to record directly onto a CD-ROM or a DVD drive. Most high-end computer models include a DVD drive that allows you to record on DVD rewritable DVD-ROMs, which can store about 4.7GB on a single drive. CD-ROMs store about 650MB.

Analog Capture Boards

Analog capture boards accept an analog video signal and digitize video to a computer's hard disk or other storage device. On the PC, most analog boards are add-in boards that must be purchased separately from the computer system. If you are not shooting video using a DV system, you may consider purchasing an analog board. The three formats used by analog boards are *composite video*, *S-video,* and *component* video.

+ **Composite video.** Provides fair to good quality capture. In this system, the video brightness and color components are combined into one signal. Most composite boards have three cables: one video and two sound cables. Many of the older DV camcorders that are still on the market enable you to place analog tape in them and transfer data using composite signals. Many VHS tape recorders allow input from composite video.

+ **S-video.** Provides a higher quality video signal than composite video because luminance and color are separated into two different signals. Most analog boards that provide S-video also allow composite output. S-video is considered better quality than VHS. Most VHS tape recorders allow input from S-video. (Many DV cameras provide an S-video port to enable you to transfer DV footage to VHS tape decks.)

+ **Component.** Component video provides broadcast quality video. In component video, two channels handle color and one channel handles luminance. Although composite and S-video boards enable connections to camcorder and consumer tape decks, component boards enable a connection to broadcast quality Beta SP tape decks.

Digital Video Cameras

Every few months, a new crop of digital video camcorders hits the market with more features than the last group. If you are considering purchasing a camcorder, you have many options to consider. If you already have a camcorder, should you upgrade to a DV camcorder? If your budget allows, the answer should be yes, definitely.

DV camcorders, especially the newer ones that use mini-cartridges, provide higher quality video and sound output than Hi-8 and 8mm format camcorders. DV cameras provide more lines of horizontal resolution images than older cameras, thus color is better and images are sharper.

DV cameras digitize and compress the signal directly in the camera. The DV compression uses a data rate of 25 megabits (Mb) per second; thus, the compression standard is often known as DV 25. As mentioned earlier, one chief advantage of a DV camera is that you can connect it directly to a computer with an IEEE 1394 port.

Your best bet is to survey the Web pages of camcorder manufacturers, such as Sony, Canon, and JVC. Look at the features listed and compare prices. (Canon's Web page currently allows you to download user manuals, which can help you understand all the features in the camera.) The more you pay, the better the camera and the more features offered.

Better DV camcorders usually create pictures with more pixels. For example, the Canon Elura has a ¼-inch CCD (charge coupler device, responsible for converting the image into a signal that can be digitized) that provides 380,000 pixels; however, some cameras — such as the Canon XLS, Canon GL1, Sony TVR900, and Sony DCR-VX2000 — provide three CCDs with 27,000 pixels per CCD, which provide a sharper image. (More expensive cameras boast over 500 lines of horizontal resolution.)

Another consideration is accessories. Some cameras enable you to change lenses and have more control for changing exposure and shutter speed. If audio is important, you might check whether your camera can connect to a wireless microphone or to an audio mixer. Another feature to consider is whether you want to be able to use older analog tape formats. Some models can take a Hi-8 or 8mm tape and digitize the video right in the camera, so it can be transferred to the computer's IEEE 1394 port (rather than to an analog capture board). Most models feature an S-video port so that the digital video data can be transferred to a consumer VHS tape recorder.

Lenses

Most casual users of video equipment simply purchase a camera and use whatever lens is mounted on the camera. If you keep working with video equipment, you should learn a bit about lenses. Virtually all camcorders sold today include zoom lenses. For example, Canon's XL1S, one of the more expensive pro-consumer cameras on the market, features a *16x* zoom. The modifier *16x* indicates that the camera can zoom in to make the focal length 16 times greater. This enables you to alter the built-in focal length of the XL1S from 5.5mm to 88mm (this lens is interchangeable with other lenses).

The focal length is the middle of the lens to the point where an image begins to appear, usually measured in millimeters. The focal length indicates exactly what image areas can appear in the lens. If the focal length is low, the viewing area is large; if the focal length is large, the viewing area is correspondingly smaller. Thus, if you focus on a subject with a smaller focal length, such as 10mm (a wide angle lens), you see more of the subject than at 50mm (telephoto). At 10mm you might see an image of a person from head to toe; at 50mm only the person's face is seen in a closeup.

Many cameras provide digital zooms of up to 50x. Although this provides further zooming capabilities, the picture quality usually isn't as good as optical zooming. When viewing the specs of high-range cameras, you frequently see the f-stop range. The f-stops control the iris opening of the camera. The lower the f-stop, the greater the amount of light allowed in. Higher f-stops allow less light in. Canon's XL1 provides a range of 1.6–16 (you can adjust the shutter speed on this camera as well). This enables you to set manual exposure and provides greater control over depth-of-field.

Depth-of-field is typically defined as the area from the nearest point in focus to the furthest point in focus. Having sufficient depth-of-field is especially important if a subject you are shooting is moving. You don't want the subject moving in and out of focus. The focal length of the lens, the distance of the subject from the camera, and the f-stop setting all determine depth-of-field.

Microphones

Although most camcorders feature a built-in microphone, you may want to purchase an external microphone to capture better quality audio. For sophisticated audio recording, you may want to purchase a mixer that enables you to accept multiple sound inputs and enables you to monitor and set recording levels.

If you are purchasing a microphone, you want to become familiar with several common audio terms. The first one is *frequency response*, which describes the pick up or sensitivity range of sound for the microphone, from low to high sounds. Sound waves are measured in cycles per second (Hz). The human ear is sensitive to a range from 20Hz to 16,000Hz. A microphone frequency response determines the range of sounds it can record. An expensive studio microphone could have a range from 20 to 20,000Hz.

Microphones are divided into different categories, according to the inner electronics that control the capture of sound. The primary categories are *condenser*, *dynamic*, and *crystal*.

Condenser mics are generally used as studio mics. They are usually expensive. But you get what you pay for. They are sensitive and provide a broad frequency response. Electret condensers are a subcategory of condenser microphones, which can be powered with a small battery provider. They are good for reproduction of narration. Because these microphones are especially sensitive to heat and humidity, care must be taken when using and storing them.

Dynamic microphones are often used as external mics for camcorders. They are inexpensive and usually quite durable. Although the sound quality recorded from dynamic microphones is not excellent, it is generally good enough for most DV taping sessions.

Crystal mics are the least expensive. They do not record a large frequency range and should generally be avoided.

Another basic audio concept to understand about microphones is that they utilize different pick-up patterns. Mics can be omnidirectional or unidirectional.

✦ **Omnidirectional.** These mics pick up sounds from all directions. If you are not recording in a noisy area and want to capture all sounds from the recording site, you probably want to use an omnidirectional microphone.

✦ **Unidirectional.** These microphones pick up sound primarily from one direction. If you are recording in a noisy room and want to record someone speaking, a unidirectional can help eliminate background sounds.

To further specify how microphones pick up sounds, microphone manufacturers provide polar graphs showing the response of a microphone. A polar graph is plotted over 360 degrees with the center of the graph depicting the center of the microphone. The round curves depict the area from which the microphone picks up sound. The graph patterns are described as cardioid, super-cardioid, and bidirectional.

✦ **Cardioid.** Picks up sounds primarily from the front of the mic. They eliminate sounds from the back of the mic and can pick up some sounds from the side. If you stand in front of the mic, most cardioids accept a 30-angle range.

✦ **Bidirectional.** Picks up sounds primarily from the front and back of the microphone.

On a more technical level, mics are considered either high or low *impedance*. Measured in ohms, impedance is an electrical term indicating resistance in the circuit. Most professional (and thus high quality) audio/video equipment and studio equipment is low impedance. Low impedance equipment is often called Low-Z. Less expensive equipment is generally high impedance (called Hi-Z). Generally short-cabled microphones are Hi-Z; long cable microphones are Low-Z (15 feet or longer).

As you work with audio, you also see the terms *balanced* and *unbalanced* to describe audio cabling. Short cables with high impedance equipment using RCA mini-plugs are using unbalanced lines. Most nonbroadcast camcorders provide unbalanced lines. Balanced lines feature XLR and cannon plugs (shielded cables), which eliminate buzzing sounds and other electronic noise. Expensive pro-consumer camcorders, such as the Cannon l XL1, provide a connection to a CLR plug for hookup to an audio mixer.

Tip   You may also want to visit audio equipment manufacturer Shure's Web site, which includes technical publications such as "Guide to Audio Systems for Video Production" by Shure engineer Christopher Lyons. This publication—which reviews microphones, mixers, and covers topics such as "Connecting a Mixer to a Camcorder" and "How to Handle Some Common Miking Situations"—can be downloaded from Shure's Web site at www.shure.com.

Lighting

Lighting is one of the crucial factors determining video quality. If you are shooting indoors, you should investigate lighting equipment and learn the basics of setting up lights. If you're new to video, you might take a basic studio production course, or read a book on television lighting (the Focal press offers a variety of books on this subject).

If you are primarily going to be shooting interior scenes and want to produce high-quality video, you should investigate purchasing a lighting kit, along with lighting utilities, such as scrims and barn doors (these can limit and control lights).

Although this appendix is not designed to serve as a lighting guide, to properly light a scene, you typically include a key light and a fill light, with a backlight added to provide more depth. The key light is the main source of illumination. Often the key light is set at a 45-degree angle between the camera and the subject. The fill light, often placed on the opposite side of the camera from the key, helps lighten shadow areas produced by the key.

If you are setting up lights on-location, be wary of blowing out a fuse. A typical U.S. consumer circuit is a 15-amp line and does not handle more than 1,800 watts (multiply total amps times voltage to obtain the total watts used, $120 \times 15 = 1800$). It's a good idea to add up all the watts you are using, including any camera equipment, before you start plugging in electrical equipment. Also remember that other electrical equipment may be using the circuit as well.

✦   ✦   ✦

Index

Continued

Continued

Continued

Continued

Continued

Continued

Continued

Continued

Continued

Continued

Wiley Publishing, Inc.
End-User License Agreement

READ THIS. You should carefully read these terms and conditions before opening the software packet(s) included with this book "Book". This is a license agreement "Agreement" between you and Wiley Publishing, Inc. "WPI". By opening the accompanying software packet(s), you acknowledge that you have read and accept the following terms and conditions. If you do not agree and do not want to be bound by such terms and conditions, promptly return the Book and the unopened software packet(s) to the place you obtained them for a full refund.

1. **License Grant.** WPI grants to you (either an individual or entity) a nonexclusive license to use one copy of the enclosed software program(s) (collectively, the "Software") solely for your own personal or business purposes on a single computer (whether a standard computer or a workstation component of a multi-user network). The Software is in use on a computer when it is loaded into temporary memory (RAM) or installed into permanent memory (hard disk, CD-ROM, or other storage device). WPI reserves all rights not expressly granted herein.

2. **Ownership.** WPI is the owner of all right, title, and interest, including copyright, in and to the compilation of the Software recorded on the disk(s), CD-ROM or DVD "Software Media". Copyright to the individual programs recorded on the Software Media is owned by the author or other authorized copyright owner of each program. Ownership of the Software and all proprietary rights relating thereto remain with WPI and its licensers.

3. **Restrictions on Use and Transfer.**

    (a) You may only (i) make one copy of the Software for backup or archival purposes, or (ii) transfer the Software to a single hard disk, provided that you keep the original for backup or archival purposes. You may not (i) rent or lease the Software, (ii) copy or reproduce the Software through a LAN or other network system or through any computer subscriber system or bulletin-board system, or (iii) modify, adapt, or create derivative works based on the Software.

    (b) You may not reverse engineer, decompile, or disassemble the Software. You may transfer the Software and user documentation on a permanent basis, provided that the transferee agrees to accept the terms and conditions of this Agreement and you retain no copies. If the Software is an update or has been updated, any transfer must include the most recent update and all prior versions.

4. **Restrictions on Use of Individual Programs.** You must follow the individual requirements and restrictions detailed for each individual program in the About the DVD appendix of this Book. These limitations are also contained in the individual license agreements recorded on the Software Media. These limitations may include a requirement that after using the program for a specified period of time, the user must pay a registration fee or discontinue use. By opening the Software packet(s), you will be agreeing to abide by the licenses and restrictions for these individual programs that are detailed in the About the DVD appendix and on the Software Media. None of the material on this Software Media or listed in this Book may ever be redistributed, in original or modified form, for commercial purposes.

5. Limited Warranty.

  (a) WPI warrants that the Software and Software Media are free from defects in materials and workmanship under normal use for a period of sixty (60) days from the date of purchase of this Book. If WPI receives notification within the warranty period of defects in materials or workmanship, WPI will replace the defective Software Media.

  (b) WPI AND THE AUTHOR(S) OF THE BOOK DISCLAIM ALL OTHER WARRANTIES, EXPRESS OR IMPLIED, INCLUDING WITHOUT LIMITATION IMPLIED WARRANTIES OF MERCHANTABILITY AND FITNESS FOR A PARTICULAR PURPOSE, WITH RESPECT TO THE SOFTWARE, THE PROGRAMS, THE SOURCE CODE CONTAINED THEREIN, AND/OR THE TECHNIQUES DESCRIBED IN THIS BOOK. WPI DOES NOT WARRANT THAT THE FUNCTIONS CONTAINED IN THE SOFTWARE WILL MEET YOUR REQUIREMENTS OR THAT THE OPERATION OF THE SOFTWARE WILL BE ERROR FREE.

  (c) This limited warranty gives you specific legal rights, and you may have other rights that vary from jurisdiction to jurisdiction.

6. Remedies.

  (a) WPI's entire liability and your exclusive remedy for defects in materials and workmanship shall be limited to replacement of the Software Media, which may be returned to WPI with a copy of your receipt at the following address: Software Media Fulfillment Department, Attn.: Adobe Premiere Pro Bible, Wiley Publishing, Inc., 10475 Crosspoint Blvd., Indianapolis, IN 46256, or call 1-800-762-2974. Please allow four to six weeks for delivery. This Limited Warranty is void if failure of the Software Media has resulted from accident, abuse, or misapplication. Any replacement Software Media will be warranted for the remainder of the original warranty period or thirty (30) days, whichever is longer.

  (b) In no event shall WPI or the author be liable for any damages whatsoever (including without limitation damages for loss of business profits, business interruption, loss of business information, or any other pecuniary loss) arising from the use of or inability to use the Book or the Software, even if WPI has been advised of the possibility of such damages.

  (c) Because some jurisdictions do not allow the exclusion or limitation of liability for consequential or incidental damages, the above limitation or exclusion may not apply to you.

7. U.S. Government Restricted Rights. Use, duplication, or disclosure of the Software for or on behalf of the United States of America, its agencies and/or instrumentalities "U.S. Government" is subject to restrictions as stated in paragraph (c)(1)(ii) of the Rights in Technical Data and Computer Software clause of DFARS 252.227-7013, or subparagraphs (c) (1) and (2) of the Commercial Computer Software-Restricted Rights clause at FAR 52.227-19, and in similar clauses in the NASA FAR supplement, as applicable.

8. General. This Agreement constitutes the entire understanding of the parties and revokes and supersedes all prior agreements, oral or written, between them and may not be modified or amended except in a writing signed by both parties hereto that specifically refers to this Agreement. This Agreement shall take precedence over any other documents that may be in conflict herewith. If any one or more provisions contained in this Agreement are held by any court or tribunal to be invalid, illegal, or otherwise unenforceable, each and every other provision shall remain in full force and effect.